NP 49

MEDITERRANEAN PILOT
VOLUME V

Coasts of Libya, Egypt, Israel,
Lebanon and Syria, South coasts of Greek islands
from Kríti to Ródos and Turkey with the island of Cyprus.

TENTH EDITION
2008

PUBLISHED BY THE UNITED KINGDOM HYDROGRAPHIC OFFICE

Area formerly covered by *Mediterranean Pilot Volume II:*

First published	1877
2nd Edition	1885
3rd Edition	1895
4th Edition	1905

Mediterranean Pilot Volume V:

First published	1915
2nd Edition	1925
3rd Edition	1937
4th Edition	1950
5th Edition	1961
6th Edition	1976
6th Edition (*Revised*)	1988
7th Edition	1999
8th Edition	2002
9th Edition	2005

PREFACE

The Tenth Edition of *Mediterranean Pilot Volume V* has been prepared by T.C. Harrison, Master Mariner. The United Kingdom Hydrographic Office has used all reasonable endeavours to ensure that this Pilot contains all the appropriate information obtained and assessed by it at the date shown below. Information received or assessed after that date will be included in *Admiralty Notices to Mariners* where appropriate. For details of *Admiralty Notices to Mariners* and guidance on their use, see *The Mariner's Handbook.*

This edition supersedes the Ninth Edition (2005), which is cancelled.

Information on currents and climate has been based on data provided by Met Office, Exeter.

The following sources of information, other than United Kingdom Hydrographic Office Publications and Ministry of Defence papers, have been consulted:

Greece

Charts
Sailing Directions for Greek Coasts, Hellenic Navy Hydrographic Service
Volume B (2004) with Supplement 3/2008
Volume D (2007)

Turkey

Charts
Turkish Harbour Regulations

Other publications

Local Port Authorities
Port Handbooks produced by Port Authorities
Lloyds List
Lloyd's List Ports of the World 2008
Lloyd's Register Fairplay Ports and Terminals Guide 2007-2008
The Statesman's Yearbook 2008
Whitaker's Almanack 2008
France Instructions Nautiques Volume D6 (2008)
Greek Waters Pilot (tenth edition 2007 with supplement), Rod Heikell (Imray, Laurie, Norie and Wilson Limited)
Turkish Waters and Cyprus Pilot (seventh edition 2006 with supplements), Rod Heikell (Imray, Laurie, Norie and Wilson Limited)

Mr M. S. Robinson
Chief Executive of the United Kingdom Hydrographic Office

United Kingdom Hydrographic Office
Admiralty Way
Taunton
Somerset TA1 2DN
England
11th December 2008

CONTENTS

CHAPTER 7

DISTANCES TABLE

INDEX

EXPLANATORY NOTES

Admiralty Sailing Directions are intended for use by vessels of 150 gt or more. They amplify charted detail and contain information needed for safe navigation which is not available from Admiralty charts, or other hydrographic publications. They are intended to be read in conjunction with the charts quoted in the text.

This volume of Sailing Directions will be kept up-to-date by the issue of a new edition at intervals of approximately 3 years, without the use of supplements. In addition important amendments which cannot await the new edition are published in Section IV of the weekly editions of *Admiralty Notices to Mariners*. A list of such amendments and notices in force is published quarterly. Those still in force at the end of the year are reprinted in the *Annual Summary of Admiralty Notices to Mariners*.

This volume should not be used without reference to Section IV of the weekly editions of Admiralty Notices to Mariners.

References to United Kingdom Hydrographic Office publications and *The International Code of Signals*:

The Mariner's Handbook gives general information affecting navigation and is complementary to this volume of Sailing Directions.

Ocean Passages for the World and *Routeing Charts* contain ocean routeing information and should be consulted for other than coastal passages.

Admiralty List of Lights or *Admiralty Digital List of Lights* should be consulted for details of lights, lanbys and fog signals, as these are not fully described in this volume of Sailing Directions.

Admiralty List of Radio Signals should be consulted for information relating to coast radio stations, pilotage services, vessel traffic services, port operations, radar beacons and radio direction finding stations, meteorological services, radio aids to navigation, Global Maritime Distress and Safety System (GMDSS) and Differential Global Positioning System (DGPS) stations, as these are only briefly referred to in this volume of Sailing Directions.

Admiralty Digital Radio Signals Volume 6 may also be consulted for information relating to pilotage services, vessel traffic services, port operations and ship reporting systems.

Annual Summary of Admiralty Notices to Mariners contains, in addition to the temporary and preliminary notices, and amendments and notices affecting Sailing Directions, a number of notices giving information of a permanent nature covering radio messages and navigational warnings, distress and rescue at sea and exercise areas.

The International Code of Signals should be consulted for details of distress and life-saving signals, international ice-breaker signals as well as international flag signals.

Remarks on subject matter:

Buoys are generally described in detail only when they have special navigational significance, or where the scale of the chart is too small to show all the details clearly.

Chapter index diagrams in this volume show only those Admiralty charts of a suitable scale to give good coverage of the area. Mariners should consult NP 131 *Catalogue of Admiralty Charts and Publications* for details of larger scale charts.

Chart references in the text normally refer to the largest scale Admiralty chart but occasionally a smaller scale chart may be quoted where its use is more appropriate.

Firing, practice and exercise areas. Submarine exercise areas are mentioned in Sailing Directions. Other firing, practice and exercise areas may be mentioned with limited details. Signals and buoys used in connection with these areas may be mentioned if significant for navigation. Attention is invited to the Annual Notice to Mariners on this subject.

Names have been taken from the most authoritative source. When an obsolete name still appears on the chart, it is given in brackets following the proper name at the principal description of the feature in the text and where the name is first mentioned.

Port plans in this book are intended to assist the mariner in orientation and they are not to be used for navigation. The appropriate scale of chart should always be used.

Tidal information relating the daily vertical movements of the water is not given. For this information *Admiralty Tide Tables* or *Admiralty Total Tide* should be consulted. Changes in water level of an abnormal nature are mentioned.

Time difference used in the text when applied to the time of High Water found from the *Admiralty Tide Tables*, gives the time of the event being described in the Standard Time kept in the area of that event. Due allowance must be made for any seasonal daylight saving time which may be kept.

Wreck information is included where drying or below-water wrecks are relatively permanent features having significance for navigation or anchoring.

Units and terminology used in this volume:

Bands is the word used to indicate horizontal marking.

Bearings and directions are referred to the true compass and when given in degrees are reckoned clockwise from 000° (North) to 359°
Bearings used for positioning are given from the reference object.
Bearings of objects, alignments and light sectors are given as seen from the vessel.
Courses always refer to the course to be made good over the ground.

Conspicuous objects are natural and artificial marks which are outstanding, easily identifiable and clearly visible to the mariner over a large area of sea in varying conditions of light. If the scale is large enough they will normally be shown on the chart in bold capitals and may be marked "conspic".

Depths are given below chart datum, except where otherwise stated.

Distances are expressed in sea miles of 60 to a degree of latitude and sub-divided into cables of one tenth of a sea mile.

Elevations, as distinct from heights, are given above Mean High Water Springs or Mean Higher High Water whichever is quoted in *Admiralty Tide Tables*, and expressed as, "an elevation of ... m". However the elevation of natural features such as hills may alternatively be expressed as "... m high" since in this case there can be no confusion between elevation and height.

Heights of objects refer to the height of the object above the ground and are invariably expressed as "... m in height".

Latitude and Longitude given in brackets are approximate and are taken from the chart quoted.

Metric units are used for all measurements of depths, heights and short distances, but where feet/fathoms charts are referred to, these latter units are given in brackets after the metric values for depths and heights shown on the chart.

Principal marks are marks which qualify for inclusion and are outstanding and clearly visible throughout most of the waterway (or 15 to 20 miles of the waterway for particularly long waterways) as marks by day or lights by night; thereby being associated with the waterway as a whole, rather than being confined to any single set of Directions with it. In particular:

Landmarks comprise buildings and structures (including lighthouses, whether major lights or not), daymarks and natural features. They may be on the coast or farther inland, provided they are distinctly visible from seaward.
Major lights is used in Sailing Directions to refer to all lights with a range of 15 miles or over.
Offshore marks include light vessels, light floats, LANBY's, buoyant beacons, and oil production platforms.

Prominent objects are those which are easily identifiable, but do not justify being classified as conspicuous.

Stripes is the word used to indicate markings which are vertical, unless stated to be diagonal.

Tidal streams and currents are described by the direction towards which they flow.

Time is expressed in the four-figure notation beginning at midnight and is given in local time unless otherwise stated. Details of local time kept will be found in *Admiralty List of Radio Signals Volume 2*.

Winds are described by the direction from which they blow.

ABBREVIATIONS

The following abbreviations are used in the text:

AIS	Automatic Identification System
ALC	Articulated loading column
ALP	Articulated loading platform
AMVER	Automated Mutual Assistance Vessel Rescue System
ARCS	Admiralty Raster Chart Service
ASL	Archipelagic Sea Lane
ATBA	Area To Be Avoided
ATLAS	autonomous temperature line acquisition system
AVCS	Admiralty Vector Chart Service
°C	degrees Celsius
CALM	Catenary anchor leg mooring
CBM	Conventional buoy mooring
CDC	Certain Dangerous Cargo
CHA	Competent Harbour Authority
cm	centimetre(s)
COTP	Captain of the Port
CVTS	Co-operative Vessel Traffic System
DART	Deep-ocean Assessment and Reporting Tsunamis
DF	direction finding
DG	degaussing
DGPS	Differential Global Positioning System
DPG	Dangerous and Polluting Goods
DSC	Digital Selective Calling
DW	Deep Water
dwt	deadweight tonnage
DZ	danger zone
E	east (easterly, eastward, eastern, easternmost)
ECDIS	Electronic Chart Display and Information System
EEZ	exclusive economic zone
ELSBM	Exposed location single buoy mooring
ENC	Electronic Navigational Chart
ENE	east-north-east
EPIRB	Emergency Position Indicating Radio Beacon
ESE	east-south-east
ETA	estimated time of arrival
ETD	estimated time of departure
EU	European Union
FAD	fish aggregating device
feu	forty foot equivalent unit
fm	fathom(s)
FPSO	Floating production storage and offloading vessel
FPU	Floating production unit
FSO	Floating storage and offloading vessel
ft	foot (feet)
g/cm^3	gram per cubic centimetre
GMDSS	Global Maritime Distress and Safety System
GPS	Global Positioning System
GRP	glass reinforced plastic
grt	gross register tonnage (obsolete)
gt	gross tonnage
HAT	Highest Astronomical Tide
HF	high frequency
hm	hectometre
HMS	Her (His) Majesty's Ship
hp	horse power
hPa	hectopascal
HSC	High Speed Craft
HW	High Water
IALA	International Association of Lighthouse Authorities
IHO	International Hydrographic Organization
IMDG	International Maritime Dangerous Goods
IMO	International Maritime Organization
ISPS	International Ship and Port Facility Security Code
ITCZ	Intertropical Convergence Zone
ITZ	Inshore traffic zone
JRCC	Joint Rescue Co-ordination Centre
kHz	kilohertz
km	kilometre(s)
kn	knot(s)
kW	kilowatt(s)
LANBY	Large Automatic Navigation Buoy
LASH	Lighter Aboard Ship
LAT	Lowest Astronomical Tide
LF	low frequency
LHG	Liquefied Hazardous Gas
LMT	Local Mean Time
LNG	Liquefied Natural Gas
LOA	Length overall
LPG	Liquefied Petroleum Gas
LW	Low Water
m	metre(s)
m^3	cubic metre(s)
mb	millibar(s)
MCTS	Marine Communications and Traffic Services Centres
MF	medium frequency
MHz	megahertz
MHHW	Mean Higher High Water
MHLW	Mean Higher Low Water
MHW	Mean High Water
MHWN	Mean High Water Neaps
MHWS	Mean High Water Springs
MLHW	Mean Lower High Water
MLLW	Mean Lower Low Water
MLW	Mean Low Water
MLWN	Mean Low Water Neaps
MLWS	Mean Low Water Springs
mm	millimetre(s)
MMSI	Maritime Mobile Service Identity
MRCC	Maritime Rescue Co-ordination Centre
MRSC	Maritime Rescue Sub-Centre
MSI	Marine Safety Information
MSL	Mean Sea Level
MV	Motor Vessel
MW	megawatt(s)
MY	Motor Yacht
N	north (northerly, northward, northern, northernmost)
NATO	North Atlantic Treaty Organization

Navtex	Navigational Telex System
NE	north-east
NNE	north-north-east
NNW	north-north-west
No	number
nrt	net register tonnage (obsolete)
nt	net tonnage
NW	north-west
ODAS	Ocean Data Acquisition System
PEC	Pilotage Exemption Certificate
PEL	Port Entry Light
PLEM	Pipe line end manifold
PMSC	Port Marine Safety Code
POL	Petrol, Oil & Lubricants
PSSA	Particularly Sensitive Sea Areas
PWC	Personal watercraft
RCC	Rescue Co-ordination Centre
RMS	Royal Mail Ship
RN	Royal Navy
RoRo	Roll-on, Roll-off
RT	radio telephony
S	south (southerly, southward, southern, southernmost)
SALM	Single anchor leg mooring system
SALS	Single anchored leg storage system
SAR	Search and Rescue
Satnav	Satellite navigation
SBM	Single buoy mooring
SE	south-east
SHA	Statutory Harbour Authority
SPM	Single point mooring
sq	square
SRR	Search and Rescue Region
SS	Steamship
SSCC	Ship Sanitation Control Certificate
SSE	south-south-east
SSCEC	Ship Sanitation Control Exemption Certificate
SSW	south-south-west
STL	Submerged turret loading
STS	ship to ship
SW	south-west
SWATH	small waterplane area twin hull ship
teu	twenty foot equivalent unit
TRITON	Triangle Trans-Ocean Buoy Network
TSS	Traffic Separation Scheme
UHF	ultra high frequency
UKC	under-keel clearance
UKHO	United Kingdom Hydrographic Office
ULCC	Ultra Large Crude Carrier
UN	United Nations
UT	Universal Time
UTC	Co-ordinated Universal Time
VDR	Voyage Data Recorder
VHF	very high frequency
VLCC	Very Large Crude Carrier
VMRS	Vessel Movement Reporting System
VTC	Vessel Traffic Centre
VTMS	Vessel Traffic Management System
VTS	Vessel Traffic Services
W	west (westerly, westward, western, westernmost)
WGS	World Geodetic System
WMO	World Meteorological Organization
WNW	west-north-west
WSW	west-south-west
WT	radio (wireless) telegraphy

GLOSSARY

Arabic (A), Greek (G), Hebrew (H), Italian (I) and Turkish (T) terms and words found on charts and in the Sailing Directions.

NB - Greek (G) words in italics are obsolete or obsolete transliterations; see xxi and 1.11

Foreign word	*Language*	*English meaning*
abiad, abyad, abyadh	A	white
ada	T	island
adalar	T	islands
adası	T	peninsula
agam	H	lake
ágios, agía, ágioi, ágiou	G	saint, (m, f, n), saints, holy
ağiz	T	mouth
ahmar	A	red (masculine)
ain, ‘ain	A	spring
ak	T	white
ákra	G	cape, point
akropolis	G	citadel
akrotírio (*akrotírion*)	G	promontory, cape
aktí	G	shore, coastline
al	A	the
alikí	G	saltpans
alamet	T	beacon
ammos	G	sand
anatolikós, -i, -ón	G	east, eastern
angáli	G	bight, open bay
angirovóli,-on	G	anchorage
aswad	A	black
anak, a’naq	A	cliff
apováthra	G	landing place, wharf
arish, arisha	A	dune
avathés	G	shoal
áyios, ayía, áyioi, áyiou	G	saint, (m, f, n), saints, holy
aziz	T	saint
bab	A	narrow strait, gate
bahr, bahra	A	river, lake
baia	I	bay
baidā, bādiya	A	desert
balad	A	town, village, land
balçrk	T	clay, mud, silt
banchina	I	quay
banco, banchi	I	banks
bati	T	west, west wind
batak	T	swamp, marshland
bataklik	T	swamp, marshland, uicksand
behira	A	lake
be’er	H	well
bet	H	house
biār, bir	A	wells, well
bizza	H	marsh
boğaz	T	strait, channel, estuary
boghaz, būghāz	A	entrance channel
bu (abbrev. abū)	A	father, chief
bucak	T	creek
buḩeiret, buhireh	A	lake, marsh
bük	T	creek
burj	A	tower
burnu (abbr. -br)	T	point, cape, headland, promontory
burun	T	point, cape, headland, promontory
büyük	T	great
calata	I	wharf, unloading quay
çamur	T	mud
capo	I	cape, headland
casa	I	house
casino	I	country house, club
castel, castello	I	castle
cattedrale	I	cathedral
çay	T	river, stream
chersónisos	G	peninsula
chorío	G	village
collina	I	hill
collinette	I	small hill
çorak	T	marsh (salt)
dağ	T	mountain
dahl	A	bank
daram	H	south
daram-ma’arava	H	south-west
daram-mizrah	H	south-east
demir yeri	T	anchorage
deniz	T	sea
dere	T	stream, valley
dhíavlos	G	strait
dhiékplous	G	passage
dhióriga	G	canal, channel
dhiórix	G	canal
díavlos	G	channel, strait
dióryga	G	canal, channel
döküntü	T	reef
dytikós	G	west, western
el	A	the
‘emeq	H	valley, plain, basin
even	H	stone
’ez	H	tree
fanale	I	light
fanâr	A	lighthouse
fanós	G	light
fáros	G	lighthouse
forte	I	fort
fortino	I	small fort
froúrio, (*froúrion*)	G	fort, stronghold
gadol	H	great
gâmi‘	A	mosque
garb, garp	T	west
gasr	A	castle
gebel	A	hill
gera	A	lake

Foreign word	*Language*	*English meaning*
geziret, gezira	A	island
gharb	A	west
ghubbet	A	bay
giv'at	H	hill
glóssa	G	tongue, language
göl	T	lake
golfo	I	gulf, bay
gremnós	G	cliff, precipice
gurup	T	sunset
hajar	A	stone, rock
halat	A	drying sandbank
hamrā	A	red (feminine)
har	H	mountain
hashafet	A	rocks in water
hassar, hissar	A	rock
hazaz	H	gravel
hisar	T	castle, fort
hof	H	coast
hol	H	sand
hursha	H	wood (trees)
I	H	island
iç	T	inner
ichthyotrofeío, (*ikhthiotropío*)	G	fishery, fishing stakes
ífalos, -i	G	below-water reef, -s
íformos	G	roadstead
ípsome	G	height (elevated ground)
'ir	H	town, city
irmak	T	river
isola	I	island
isolotto	I	islet
ísplous	G	entrance (for vessels)
isthmós	G	isthmus
jam, jāme	A	mosque
jabal	A	mountain, hill, island
janub	A	south
jazirat	A	island
jebel	A	mountain, hill, island
jūn	A	bay
kaba çakıl	T	gravel
kabir	A	big
kafr	A	village
kalat	A	castle
kale	T	fortress, castle
kapi	T	gate, pass
kara	T	black, land, mainland
kasba	A	citadel
kástro, (*kástron*)	G	castle, fortress
katafanís, -es	G	conspicuous
kávos	G	cape, headland, promontory
kefalí	G	head
kefar	H	village
kefr	A	village
kelat	A	castle
kenesiyya	H	church
khalîg	A	gulf, bay
khánia	G	village
khashm	A	spur
khersínisos, (*khersónisos*)	G	peninsula
khorío, khoríon	G	village
kible	T	south
kibli	A	south
kilise	T	church
kimatothrávstis	G	breakwater
kırmızı, kızıl	T	red
klímax	G	scale (of chart)
kólpos	G	gulf
kôm	A	mound, hillock
koryfí, (*korifí*)	G	peak, summit
kothon	A	port, anchorage
köprü	T	bridge
körfez	T	gulf
koy	T	bight, cove, creek
köy	T	village
koyu	T	deep
krímnos	G	cliff, precipice
kücük	T	small
kulat	A	castle
kum	T	gravel
kule	T	tower, spire, peak
kymatothrávstis	G	breakwater
lefkós, -í, -on	G	white
levkós, -í, -on	G	white
liman	T	bay, harbour, port
liménas	G	harbour, port
limenískos	G	small harbour, cove
limín	G	harbour, port
límni	G	lake, marsh,
limnothálassa	G	lagoon
lodos	T	south-west wind
lófos, -i	G	hill, -s, low ridge
ma'arava	H	west
ma'gana	H	anchorage
maghreb, maghrub	A	west
mallâḥet	A	salt marsh, flat or lake
márabút, marabout	A	monument, tomb
marina	I	beach, landing place
marsa	A	bay, cove, harbour, anchorage
maşabb	A	river mouth
masjid	A	mosque
matla	A	east
mávros, -i, -on	G	black
ma'yanot	H	springs (of water)
médene, manāra, manār	A	minaret
megálos, -i, -on	G	big
mendirek	T	mole
mercan	T	coral
mers, mersa	A	bay, cove, harbour, anchorage
mezah	H	jetty, mole
mezuda	H	fort
mifraz	H	bay
migdal	H	tower
migdallor	H	lighthouse
mikrós, -í, -ón	G	small
mîna, mīnā', minat	A	harbour, bay
minare	T	minaret

Foreign word	*Language*	*English meaning*
minqar	A	point
mirjan	A	coral
misgad	H	mosque
mishor	H	plain, plateau
mizrah	H	east
molo	I	breakwater, mole
mólos	G	mole
monastírio, (*monastírion*)	G	small monastery, church
moní	G	monastery, abbey
montagna	I	mountain
monte	I	mount
naḥl	H	river, stream, watercourse
nahr	A	river
namal	H	harbour, port
natur	A	tower
nabi, nebi	A	tomb
nehir, nehri	T	river
nişan	T	beacon
nisí, -á	G	island, -s
nisída, -ídes	G	islet, -s
nisídha, nisídhes	G	islet, -s
nisís	G	islet
nísos, -oi	G	island, -s
nord	I	north
nótios	G	southern
nótos	G	south
nuovo	I	new
oasi	I	oasis
ormískos	G	cove, small bay, inlet, creek
orman	T	forest
órmos, -i	G	bay, -s
óros, -oi	G	mountain, -s
ova	T	plain
pediás (*pedhiás*)	G	plain
pétra	G	rock, stone
pólis	G	city, town
póros	G	passage, sound
porthmeío	G	ferry
porthmós	G	narrows of a strait
potamós	G	river
poúnda	G	point
poyraz	T	north-east
prokymáia (*prokimáia*)	G	quay
provlíta (*provlís*)	G	jetty, pier, wharf
punta	I	point, summit
pýrgos (pírgos)	G	tower
pýrsos (*pirsós*)	G	beacon
qalaat	A	castle
qanât	A	canal
qasr	A	castle
qatan	H	small
qornet	A	peak
rada	I	road
ra's, ras	A	cape, point
raṣīf	A	mole
révma	G	current, stream
ryáki, (*ríax*)	G	brook
ridotto	I	redoubt
rocca	I	rock
rosh	H	cape, headland
ruzgar	T	wind
sabakat, sabkhat,	A	salt lake, lagoon, or marsh
sabbia	I	sand
saghira	A	small, little
saiyid	A	lord, master (title of descendants of the Prophet and Saints)
sakije	A	canal
samandira	T	buoy, float
sancak	T	flag, district
saray	T	palace, court
sarây	A	palace
sarı	T	yellow
sark	T	east
sarki	T	eastern
sarp	T	cliff, steep, rough, rocky, stony
scogliera	I	ridge of rocks awash
scoglio	I	rock, reef
sébcha, sebkha	A	salt lake, lagoon, or marsh
sebchet	I	salt marsh
secca	I	reef, sandbank, shoal
secche	I	group of shoals, reef
seghir	A	small, little
segnale	I	signal, mark
şehir	T	city, town
sela‘	H	rock in water
set, sed	T	mole
shab, sha'b	A	rock, reef, rocky shoal
shamāl	A	north
shark	A	east
shatt	A	bank, beach
sherm, sharm	A	cove, creek, inlet
shi'b	A	rock, reef, rocky shoal
shimāl, shmal	A	north
sidi	A	lord, master (title of descendants of the Prophet and Saints)
sığlık	T	bank, shoal, shallow
şımal	T	north
simantír (*simandír*)	G	buoy
sirocco	I	south-east
siyah	T	black
skála	G	small port, berth, landing
skópelos, -oi	G	reef, -s, drying rock, -s
stavrós	G	cross
stená	G	straits
stenó, (*stenón*)	G	strait
su	T	stream
sud	I	south
ṣukhûr	A	reefs
ţâbiyet	A	fort
tabya	T	battery, earth-work, bastion
tall, tālia	A	hill
tallet	A	mountain

Foreign word	*Language*	*English meaning*
taraf, tarf	A	cape
tel	H	hill
télma	G	swamp
teloneío (*teloníon*)	G	custom house
tell	A	hill
tepe	T	hill, tumulus, peak
thálassa	G	sea
topuk	T	bar of a river, sandspit
torre	I	tower
tranós	G	large
uad	A	valley, river bed, river
uadi	I	valley, river bed, river
umm	A	mother
vathís, -ía, -í	G	deep
vecchio	I	old, ancient
vilayet	T	province, district
vóreios	G	northern
vorrás	G	north
vounó, -á	G	hill, -s, mountain, -s
vrachonisída, (*vrakhonisídha*)	G	rocky islet
vrachónisis, (*vrakhónisis*)	G	rocky island
vráchos, -oi, (*vrákhos, -oi*)	G	rock, -s (above and below water)
wād, wadi, wed	A	valley, river bed, river
xéra	G	reef
ya'ar	H	forest
yam	H	sea
yar	T	cliff, precipice
yol	T	channel, road
ýfalos, -oi	G	reef, -s, shoal, -s
ýpsilós	G	high
ýpsoma	G	height (elevated ground)
zafon	H	north
zafon-ma'arava	H	north-west
zafon-mizrah	H	north-east
zuq	H	cliff

ROMANIZATION SYSTEM FOR ARABIC BGN/PCGN 1956 System

This system was adopted by the BGN in 1946 and by the PCGN in 1956 and has been applied in the systematic romanization of geographical names in Bahrain, Egypt, Iraq, Jordan, Kuwait, Lebanon, Libya, Oman, Qatar, Saudi Arabia, Sudan, Syria, Tunisia, the United Arab Emirates and Yemen, all of which have been covered by published BGN gazetteers.

Uniform results in the romanization of Arabic are difficult to obtain, since vowel points and diacritical marks are generally omitted from both manual and machine writing. It follows that correct identification of the words which appear in any particular name, knowledge of its standard Arabic-script spelling including proper pointing, and recognition of dialectal and idiosyncratic deviations are essential.

In order to bring about uniformity in the Roman-script spelling of geographical names in Arabic-language areas, the system is based insofar as possible on fully pointed modern standard Arabic.

CONSONANT CHARACTERS

	Arabic				Romanization	Examples and Remarks	
	Final	Medial	Initial	Independent			
1				ء	not romanized in word-initial position	ابو كمال	Abū Kamāl
					' in all other positions	بئر زيت	Bi'r Zayt [2]
						صنعاء	Şan'ā'
2	ـا			ا	not romanized in word-initial position	ام العمد	Umm al 'Amad [3]
3	ـب	ـبـ	بـ	ب	b	البحرين	Al Baḩrayn
4	ـت	ـتـ	تـ	ت	t	الكوت	Al Kūt [4, 5]

	Arabic				Romanization	Examples and Remarks	
	Final	Medial	Initial	Independent			
5	ـث	ـثـ	ثـ	ث	th	الثليثوات	Ath Thulaythuwāt [5]
6	ـج	ـجـ	جـ	ج	j	الجزيرة	Al Jazīrah
7	ـح	ـحـ	حـ	ح	ḩ	المحمودية	Al Maḩmūdīyah [6]
8	ـخ	ـخـ	خـ	خ	kh	خيبر	Khaybar [5]
9	ـد			د	d	دمنهور	Damanhūr [5]
10	ـذ			ذ	dh	ذهب	Dhahab [5]
11	ـر			ر	r	الروضة	Ar Rawḑah
12	ـز			ز	z	الزاوية	Az Zāwīyah
13	ـس	ـسـ	سـ	س	s	سليمانية	Sulaymānīyah [5]
14	ـش	ـشـ	شـ	ش	sh	الشام	Ash Shām [5]
15	ـص	ـصـ	صـ	ص	ş	قيصومة	Qayşūmah [6]
16	ـض	ـضـ	ضـ	ض	ḑ	ضور	Ḑawr [6]
17	ـط	ـطـ	طـ	ط	ţ	القنيطرة	Al Qunayţirah [6]
18	ـظ	ـظـ	ظـ	ظ	z̧	ابو ظبي	Abū Z̧aby [6]
19	ـع	ـعـ	عـ	ع	ʻ	ابو عريش	Abū ʻArīsh
20	ـغ	ـغـ	غـ	غ	gh	بغداد	Baghdād
21	ـف	ـفـ	فـ	ف	f	الفرات	Al Furāt
22	ـق	ـقـ	قـ	ق	q	قطر	Qaţar
23	ـك	ـكـ	كـ	ك	k	الكويت	Al Kuwayt [5]
24	ـل	ـلـ	لـ	ل	l	حلب	Ḩalab
25	ـم	ـمـ	مـ	م	m	مكة	Makkah
26	ـن	ـنـ	نـ	ن	n	نخل	Nakhl
27	ـه	ـهـ	هـ	ه	h	جبل هارون	Jabal Hārūn [4, 5]
28	ـو			و	w	وادي غضا	Wādī Ghaḑā
29	ـي	ـيـ	يـ	ي	y	اليمن	Al Yaman [2, 7]

VOWEL CHARACTERS AND DIACRITICAL MARKS

	Arabic	Romanization	Examples and Remarks	
1	□َ	a	البصرة	Al Başrah
2	□ِ	i	الرياض	Ar Riyāḑ
3	□ُ	u	القدس	Al Quds
4	□َا	ā	باب المندب	Bāb al Mandab [3]
5	□ِي	ī	المدينة	Al Madīnah
6	□ُو	ū	صور	Şūr
7	□َى	á	مرسى مطروح	Marsá Maţrūḩ
8	□ْ	not romanized		
9	□َيْ	ay	صيدا	Şaydā
10	□َوْ	aw	الدوحة	Ad Dawḩah
11	□ً	a^n		See note 8.
12	□ٍ	i^n		See note 8.
13	□ٌ	u^n		See note 8.
14	□ّ	doubling of consonant letter		See note 9.
15	أ	’		See note 10.
16	آ	ā in word-initial position	آلبو معيط	Ālbū Mu‘ayţ [11]
		’ā in word-medial position	قرآن	Qur’ān

NUMERALS

٠	١	٢	٣	٤	٥	٦	٧	٨	٩
0	1	2	3	4	5	6	7	8	9

Although Perso-Arabic script is written from right to left, numerical expressions, e.g., ١٩٥٦ → **1956**, are written from left to right.

NOTES

1. The symbol □ represents any Arabic consonant character.

2. *Hamzah* (ء) is written in Arabic over all initial *alifs* except those which belong to the definite article **al** or bear a *maddah.* (See note 10.) When the purpose is to indicate the presence of a glottal stop, *hamzah* is written over medial and final *alif* (ا), *wāw* (و), and *yā'* without dots (ى). *Hamzah* following *kasrah* (□) is written ئ. Almost always the *yā'* is in the initial or medial form and the dots are omitted. Example: بئر . *Hamzah* following *ḍammah* (□) is written ؤ . *Hamzah* following a long vowel is written without a bearer and is positioned on the line of print like a regular character. The romanization of *hamzah* (') should always be carefully distinguished from that of *'ayn* (').

3. *Alif* as such is not romanized when it is a bearer of *hamzah,* but see *fatḥah alif* (ا□) and *alif maddah* (آ) in the vowel table. See also note 1 above and note 10.

4. In certain endings, an original *tā'* (ت) is written (ة), i.e., like *hā'* with two dots, and is known as *tā' marbūṭah.* It is romanized **h**, except in the construct form of feminine nouns, where it is romanized **t**, instead. Example: *hamzah, hamzat al qat'* . The ending *fatḥah hā'* (ه□) may be romanized **a·h** when the character *hā'* (ه) is not silent. Example: **Muntaza·h**. See also note 4.

5. Occasionally, the character sequences تـه , كـه , دهـ , and سـه occur. They may be romanized **t·h**, **k·h**, **d·h**, and **s·h** in order to differentiate those romanizations from the digraphs **th**, **kh**, **dh**, and **sh**. See also note 3.

6. Where special considerations are paramount, the sub-dot (□̣) may be used in place of the cedilla.

7. The character *yā'* (ي) is also used in writing *alif maqṣūrah,* in which the dots are omitted. See *alif maqṣūrah* (ى□) in the vowel table.

8. The classical Arabic grammatical endings written with the nunation symbols (*tanwīn*) may be romanized, when necessary, by **a**^{n}, **i**^{n}, **u**^{n}. In modern Arabic, these endings have become silent and should not be romanized: classical *alifu*^{n}, modern *alif.*

9. Doubled consonant sounds are represented in Arabic script by placing a *shaddah* (□ّ) over a consonant character. In romanization the letter should be doubled. When the definite article **al** precedes a word beginning with one of the "sun letters" — **t, th, d, dh, r, z, s, sh, ş, ḍ, ṭ, ẓ, l**, or **n** — the **l** is assimilated in the pronunciation, thus yielding **tt, thth,** etc., in romanization. Example: **An Nīl**, not **Al Nīl.**

10. *Hamzat al waşl* (ا), which is utilized only in the pointing of classical Arabic, is romanized ', as illustrated in the classical form of its name *hamzatu 'l waşli.*

11. Since *maddah* (ٓ), which is placed over *alif* (ا), nearly always occurs in word-initial position, no confusion results from the use of ā for *alif maddah* (آ) as well as for *fatḥah alif* (اَ) .

ROMANIZATION SYSTEM FOR GREEK ELOT 743 System BGN/PCGN 1996 System

This romanization system supersedes the one which was approved by the BGN and the PCGN in 1962. It corresponds to the system devised by the Greek Organization for Standardization and approved for international use at the Fifth United Nations Conference on the Standardization of Geographical Names in 1987.

	Greek					Romanization	Examples	
1	Α	α	*Α*	*α*		a	Άρτα	Árta
		αι		*αι*		ai	Ακταίο	Aktaío
		αϊ		*αϊ*		aï	Νεράϊδα	Neráïda
		αυ		*αυ*	before β, γ, δ, ζ, λ, μ, ν, ρ, and all vowels	av	Μαυροβούνι	Mavrovoúni
		αυ		*αυ*	before θ, κ, ξ, π, σ, τ, φ, χ, ψ and word final	af	Ναύπλιο	Náfplio
		αυ		*αυ*	when α is stressed or when υ occurs with dieresis	ay	Ταΰγετος	Taÿgetos
2	Β	β	*Β*	*β*		v	Βόλος	Vólos
3	Γ	γ	*Γ*	*γ*	before all vowels, and consonants other than γ, ξ, and χ	g	Γαράζο Γουριά Άγναντα Γλυφάδα	Garázo Gouriá Ágnanta Glyfáda
					before ξ and χ	n	Αγχίαλος	Anchíalos
		γγ		*γγ*		ng	Λόγγος	Lóngos
		γκ		*γκ*		gk	Λαγκάδα	Lagkáda
4	Δ	δ	*Δ*	*δ*		d	Δένδρα	Déndra

	Greek					Romanization	Examples	
5	Ε	ε	*Ε*	*ε*		e	Ερέτρια	Erétria
		ει		*ει*		ei	Ηράκλειο	Irákleio
		εϊ		*εϊ*		eï	Μαρινέϊκα	Marinéïka
		ευ		*ευ*	before β, γ, δ, ζ, λ, μ, ν, ρ, and all vowels	ev	Ρεύματα	Révmata
		ευ		*ευ*	before θ, κ, ξ, π, σ, τ, φ, χ, ψ and word final	ef	Λευκάδα	Lefkáda
		ευ		*ευ*	when ε is stressed or when υ occurs with dieresis	ey	rare	
6	Ζ	ζ	*Ζ*	*ζ*		z	Ζεμενό	Zemenó
7	Η	η	*Η*	*η*		i	Ηράκλειο	Irákleio
		ηυ		*ηυ*	before β, γ, δ, ζ, λ, μ, ν, ρ, and all vowels	iv	rare	
		ηυ		*ηυ*	before θ, κ, ξ, π, σ, τ, φ, χ, ψ and word final	if	rare	
		ηυ		*ηυ*	when η is stressed or when υ occurs with dieresis	iy	rare	
8	Θ	θ	*Θ*	*θ*		th	Θεσπιές	Thespiés
9	Ι	ι	*Ι*	*ι*		i	Ίρια	Íria
10	Κ	κ	*Κ*	*κ*		k	Καλαμάκι	Kalamáki
11	Λ	λ	*Λ*	*λ*		l	Λίμνη	Límni
12	Μ	μ	*Μ*	*μ*		m	Μαραθώνας	Marathónas
		μπ		*μπ*	initially and word final	b	Μπέχρος	Béchros
					medially	mp	Τέμπη	Témpi
13	Ν	ν	*Ν*	*ν*		n	Νεστάνη	Nestáni
		ντ		*ντ*		nt	Ντία	Ntía
14	Ξ	ξ	*Ξ*	*ξ*		x	Ξάνθη	Xánthi

	Greek					Romanization	Examples	
15	Ο	ο	*Ο*	*ο*		o	Όθος	Óthos
		οι		*οι*		oi	Δελφοί	Delfoí
		οϊ		*οϊ*		oï	Δοϊράνι	Doïráni
		ου		*ου*		ou	Βούναργο	Voúnargo
		ου		*ου*	when stressed or when υ occurs with dieresis	oy	rare	
16	Π	π	*Π*	*π*		p	Παύλος	Pávlos
		μπ		*μπ*	initially and word final	b	Μπέχρος	Béchros
					medially	mp	Τέμπη	Témpi
17	Ρ	ρ	*Ρ*	*ρ*		r	Μερόπι	Merópi
18	Σ	σ	*Σ*	*σ*		s	Άσσος	Ássos
		ς		*ς*	(word final)	s	Σάμος	Sámos
19	Τ	τ	*Τ*	*τ*		t	Τίρυνθα	Tíryntha
		ντ		*ντ*		nt	Πέντε Βρύσες	Pénte Vrýses
20	Υ	υ	*Υ*	*υ*		y	Υλίκη	Ylíki
21	Φ	φ	*Φ*	*φ*		f	Φιλοθέη	Filothéi
22	Χ	χ	*Χ*	*χ*		ch	Χαραυγή	Charavgí
23	Ψ	ψ	*Ψ*	*ψ*		ps	Ψαρά	Psará
24	Ω	ω	*Ω*	*ω*		o	Ωρωπός	Oropós

NOTES

1. Stress is shown in Greek by the use of the acute accent. This mark will be represented in romanization by an acute accent, e.g., Αθήνα → **Athína**, Ντία → **Ntía**. If the stressed vowel is written as a sequence of two vowel characters in Greek, the second vowel character would usually carry the accent. In romanization the acute accent would in these cases similarly be placed over the second vowel letter, e.g., Οινούσσες → **Oinoússes**, Οίτι → **Oíti**.

When a syllable containing one of the combinations αυ, ευ, or ηυ carries the stress, this is usually marked in Greek on the character υ. When these character combinations are romanized av, af, ev, ef, iv or if, the stress should be placed on the preceding vowel letter, e.g., Αύρα → **Ávra**, Γαύριο → **Gávrio**, Καλλιπεύκα → **Kallipéfka**. When the character combinations αυ, ευ, ηυ or ου are romanized ay, ey, iy or oy, and the stress is found in Greek on the character υ, then in romanization the stress would be marked on the letter y.

Stress accents are sometimes omitted in Greek, for example, in words and names printed wholly in uppercase characters, but in romanization the stress should always be determined and marked with an acute accent. Usually there is no stress above the vowel character of monosyllabic words, e.g., Κως → **Kos**. In Greek abbreviations, any accent which may be found should not be romanized.

2. The dieresis should be shown in romanization where it occurs in Greek, e.g., Μαρινέϊκα → **Marinéïka**, Αχαΐα → **Achaïa**.

3. In some older maps and publications employing an older form of the Greek language, certain accents and non-alphabetical characters may be encountered. These should be treated as follows:

Greek accent	Representaion in romanization
´ (acute accent)	´ (acute accent)
` (grave accent)	´ (acute accent)
˜ (tilde)	´ (acute accent)

Any other marks and accents not previously mentioned should be ignored.

Notes on pronunciation of transliterated Greek geographical names

An acute accent indicates the syllable to be stressed.

A diaeresis over the second of two vowels indicates that both vowels are sounded, as in the English word 'co-operate'.

Letters are pronounced as in English with the following exceptions:

Transliterated Greek	*Pronunciation*
av	Before voiced sounds as written ie 'av' otherwise 'af'.
ev	Before voiced sounds as written ie 'ev' otherwise 'ef'.
g	As in 'go'.
gh	As for 'g' but softer.
i, oi	As 'i' in 'machine'.
ch	As 'ch' in Scottish 'loch'.

Notes on Turkish geographical names

Ottoman Turkish was originally written in Arabic script, but was converted to Roman letters in 1928.

There are eight vowels, four back (a, ı, o, u) and four front (e, i, ö, ü). If the vowel of the first syllable of a word is a back vowel succeeding vowels will normally also be back vowels; similarly front vowels follow front vowels. Exceptions to this rule are mainly in words of foreign origin and then, in general, suffixes follow the vowel in the last syllable. This is known as the rule of vowel harmony.

Suffixes are used when words are declined to indicate their case, and to give additional meanings. These normally follow the rule of vowel harmony. Those most commonly used in this book are:

Possessive -ı, -i, -u, -ü.	Samsun Körfezi = Samsun Bay, from körfez = bay.
Possessive -sı, -si, -su, -sü. (after a final vowel)	Marmara Adası = Island of Marmara, from ada = island.
Plural -lar, -ler.	Adalar = Islands.
Adjective -lık, -lik	Kayalık = Rocky, from kaya = rock.

For place names which are composed of two nouns the possessive case is used for the second noun. However when they are made up of an adjective and a noun the nominative case is used, eg:

Ada = Island	Deniz = Sea
Büyük Ada = Large Island	Kara Deniz = Black Sea
Zeytin Adası = Zeytin Island	Ege Denezi = Aegean Sea
İskele = Jetty	Liman = Harbour
İc İskele = Inner Jetty	Dış Liman = Outer Harbour
Gümrük İskelesi = Customs Jetty	Bandırma Limanı = Bandirma Harbour

Pronunciation

Generally stress is laid equally on all syllables of a word. Letters are pronounced as in English with the following exceptions:

c	As 'j' in jealous.
ç	As 'ch' in 'chop'.
ğ	Between two front vowels—as 'y' in 'yet'.
ğ	Between two back vowels—not sounded, but preceding vowel is lengthened.
ı	As something between 'i' in 'big' and 'u' in 'bug'.
j	As 'su' in 'pleasure'.
ö	As 'u' in 'urn' or 'ea' in 'earth'.
ş	As 'sh' in 'shop'.
ü	As 'e' in 'yew'.
er	As 'air' in 'fair'.
ey	As 'ai' in 'pain'.
ay	As 'i' in 'mine'.

Transliteration Table for Hebrew

BGN/PCGN 1962 SYSTEM*

Hebrew letter	*Name of letter*	*Transliteration*	*Remarks*
א	alef	ʾ	See note 1
בּ	bet	b	See note 2
ב	vet	v	
גּ and ג	gimmel	g	See note 2
דּ and ד	dalet	d	See note 2
ה	he	h	Omit when final unless written with a dot (mappiq) i.e. הּ
ו	waw	w	
ז	zayin	z	
ח	ẖet	ẖ	
ט	tet	t	
י	yod	y	
כּ (final ךּ)	kaf	k	See note 2
כ (final ך or ךְ)	khaf	kh	
ל	lamed	l	
מ (final ם)	mem	m	
נ (final ן)	nun	n	
ס	samekh	s	
ע	ʾayin	ʿ	This is a turned comma
פּ	pe	p	See note 2
פ (final ף)	fe	f	
צ (final ץ)	ẕade	ẕ	
ק	qof	q	
ר	resh	r	
שׁ	shin	sh	
שׂ	sin	s	
תּ and ת	taw	t	See note 2
ג׳		(ğ)	These three letters, and certain other modified letters not included in this system, are used on Hebrew maps to render Arabic and other non-Hebrew names. (Modifications involve dots and circumflexes as well as ticks). Names on which these letters occur will not be transliterated but should be treated in accordance with notes 6 and 7.
ז׳		(ž)	
צ׳		(č)	
	Vowels		
◌ַ	pattaẖ	a	
◌ֲ	ẖatef pattaẖ	a	
◌ָ	{ qameẕ	a	
	{ qameẕ qatan	o	
◌ֶ	segol	e	
◌ֱ	ẖatef segol	e	
◌ֵ	ẕere	e	
◌ֵי	'long'' ẕere	e	
◌ְ	{ shewa naʾ	e	See Note note 3
	{ shewa naẖ	omit	
◌ִ	ẖireq	i	
◌ִי	'long' hireq	i	
◌ֳ	ẖatef qameẕ qatan	o	
◌ֹ	ẖolem	o	
וֹ	'long' ẖolem	o	
◌ֻ	qibbuẕ	u	
וּ	shureq	u	

* Based on the Hebrew Academy system as used by the Survey of Israel.

EXPLANATORY NOTES

1. Every medial alef bearing bearing a vowel or shewa is transliterated, e.g. גַּלְאוֹן (Gal'on), בְּאֵר שֶׁבַע (Be'er Sheva'), נֶאְדָּר (Ne'dar). Alef is not transliterated when initial or used as matter lectionis, e.g. אֵלָה (Ela), סָאסָא (Sasa).

2. The dot placed within the body of the consonants בּ, גּ, דּ, כּ, פּ and תּ when they occur at the beginning of a name or after an unvowelled consonant in the middle of a name is known as the 'weak' dagesh. It alters the sound of בּ, כּ and פּ to b, k and p. The phonetic distinction between ג and גּ, ד and דּ, and ת and תּ has now been lost and these pairs of letters are transliterated identically.
The same dot may also be placed within the body of any consonant (including the six above mentioned but excluding א, ה, ח, ע and ר) to indicate the 'strong' dagesh. This is rendered in transliteration by doubling the letter; the digraph sh is not doubled.. The 'strong' dagesh can be distinguished from the 'weak' dagesh since the former is always preceded by a vowel, e.g., עַכּוֹ ('Akko) but טוּלְכַּרְם (Tulkarm). But see note 4.

3. Shewa nah ('quiescent' shewa) marks the end of a closed syllable and is not pronounced. Shewa na' is a short neutral vowel.

4. The definite article ה is capitalized in transliteration and run together with the following word whose initial letter bearing the dagesh is also capitalized but not doubled, e.g., HaYogev. If the initial letter is 'ayin the following vowel is capitalized, e.g., Ha'Ogen.

5. 'Furtive' pattah, which is written under final he mappiq, het and 'ayin, but pronounced before and not after these three consonants, is transliterated before the letter under which it is written, e.g., רוֹקֵחַ (Roqeaẖ).

6. The non-Hebrew elements of commemorative names derived from roman-alphabet languages should be spelled as in the original, e.g., Kefar Masaryk (not Masariq), Balfouriyya (not Balfuriyya), Kefar Szold (not Sold).

7. Arabic names written in the Hebrew alphabet should be transliterated according to the following special rules:
(*a*) Hebrew consonants will be transliterated according to the table above with the following amendments and additions:

א	omit	זּ	dh
ג	j	ח'	kh
ד'	dh	ט	t
דּ	ḍ (dot below d)	ע'	gh
ח	ḥ	צ'	ṣ
הַ, הֶ	(final) a	ת'	th

(*b*) Hebrew vowel points will be transliterated as follows:

◌ְ	no vowel	וּ	ū (see also (*c*) below)
◌ַ	a	◌ֵי	ei
◌ִ	i	◌ַיּ	aiy
◌ֻ	u	◌ִיּ	īy
◌ָ	ā	וֹ	au
◌ִי	ī		

(*c*) Dagesh is rendered by doubling the letter or digraph, except in the case of בּ and כּ . וּ should be rendered u unless it it vowelled, when it will be rendered ww, e.g., חֻוָּרַה (Huwwara).
(*d*) An unassimilated Arabic article is written אל or אֶל and should be transliterated el (not al).
An assimilated Arabic article is written אַ־ or אֶ־ followed by a dagesh in the initial consonant of the succeeding word. This will be given effect to by transliterating the letter or digraph affected once as part of the article and once as part of the following word, e.g., אֶ־שַּׁהְלַה (Es Sahla).
(*e*) A hyphen should be used in transliteration to separate h or ḥ from preceding d, ḍ, dh, gh, k, s, ṣ, sh, t, ṭ and th.
(*f*) The circumflex accent which is sometimes used to indicate stress should be ignored in transliteration.

NOTES

Chapter Index Diagram

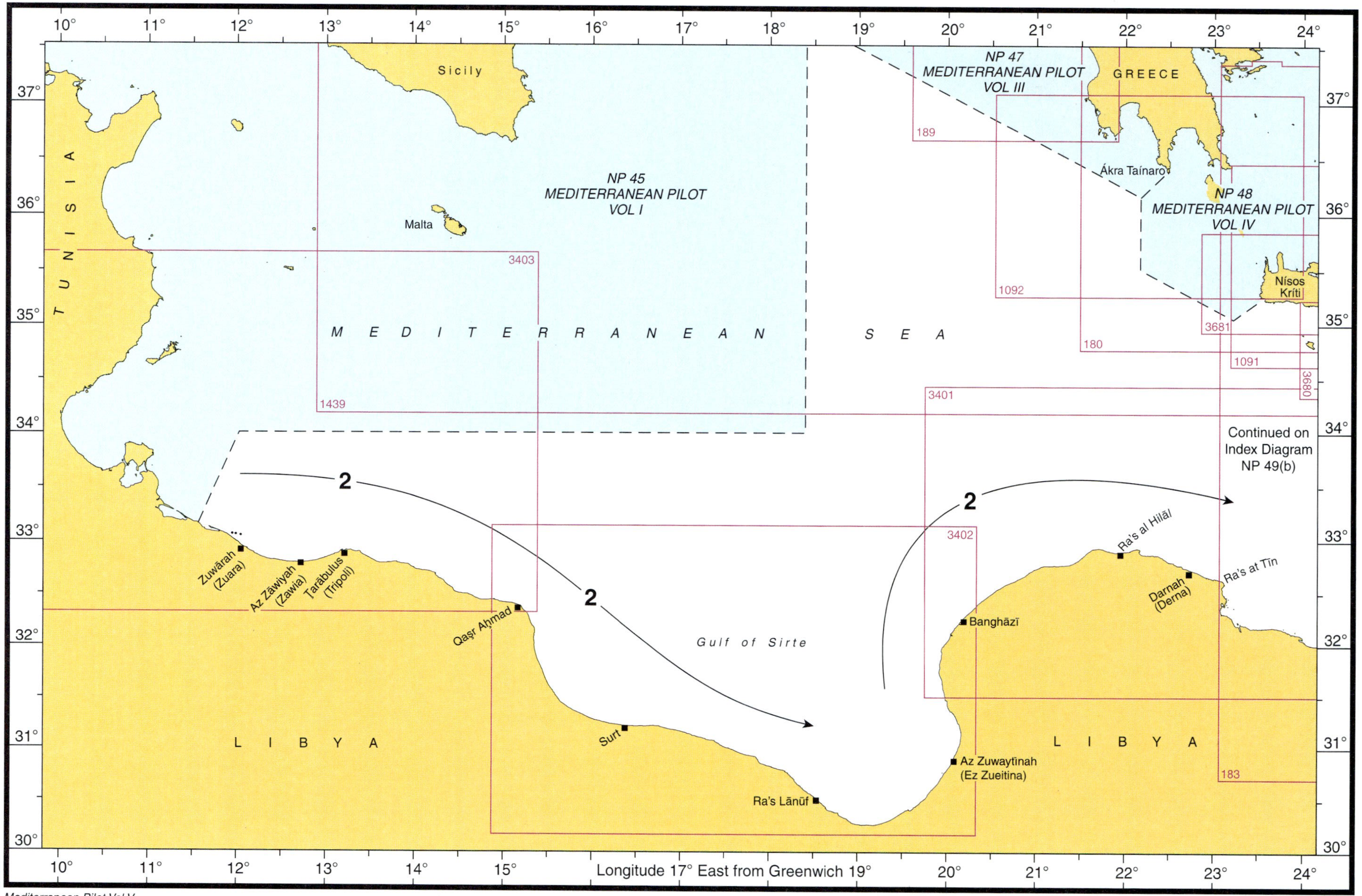

Mediterranean Pilot Vol V

NP 49(a)

Chapter Index Diagram

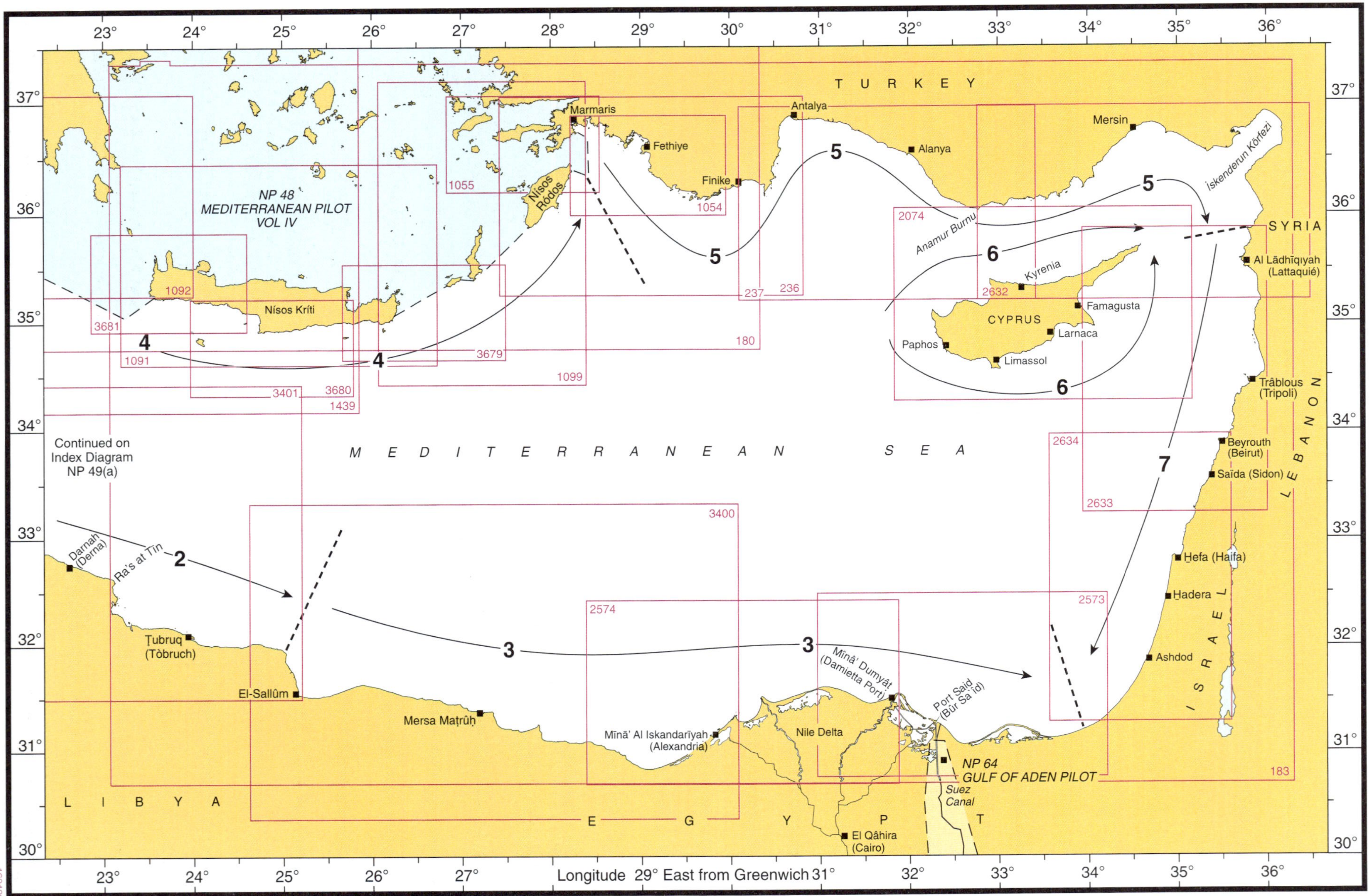

LAWS AND REGULATIONS APPERTAINING TO NAVIGATION

While, in the interests of safety of shipping, the United Kingdom Hydrographic Office makes every endeavour to include in its hydrographic publications details of the laws and regulations of all countries appertaining to navigation, it must be clearly understood:-

(a) that no liability whatever can be accepted for failure to publish details of any particular law or regulation, and

(b) that publication of details of a law or regulation is solely for the safety and convenience of shipping and implies no recognition of the international validity of the law or regulation.

MEDITERRANEAN PILOT

VOLUME V

CHAPTER 1

NAVIGATION AND REGULATIONS
COUNTRIES AND PORTS
NATURAL CONDITIONS

NAVIGATION AND REGULATIONS

LIMITS OF THE BOOK

Chart 4302

Area covered

1.1

1 This volume contains Sailing Directions for the E part of the Mediterranean Sea within the following limits:

	Lat N	Long E
From Ra's Ajdir	33°10′	11°34′
NNE to	34°00′	12°00′
Thence E to	34°00′	18°22′
Thence N to	37°45′	18°22′
Thence ESE to	36°10′	22°15′
Thence S to	35°30′	22°15′
Thence ESE to	35°05′	23°20′
Thence NE to Ákra Kriós	35°14′	23°35′
Thence E along the spine of Nísos Kríti to Ákra Tráchilas, the SE point of Nísos Kríti	35°02′	26°14′
Thence ENE to Ákra Chélathros, the S point of Nísos Kásos, excluding Stenó Kásou	35°20′	26°53′
Thence NE along the spine of Nísos Kásos to Ákra Aktís, the NE point of Nísos Kásos	35°26′	27°01′
Thence ESE to Ákra Kastéllos, the S point of Nísos Kárpathos, excluding the passage between Nísos Kásos and Nísos Kárpathos	35°24′	27°08′
Thence NE through Nísos Kárpathos to Ákra Vólakas	35°28′	27°14′
Thence NE to Ákra Prásson, the SW point of Nísos Ródos, excluding Stenó Karpáthou	35°53′	27°45′
Thence NE along the spine of Nísos Ródos to Ákra Voúdi, the E point of Nísos Ródos	36°23′	28°15′
Thence ESE to	36°20′	28°23′
Thence N to	36°43′	28°23′
Thence WNW to Kadırga Burnu, excluding Rhodes Channel and approaches	36°44′	28°18′
Thence E and S within the coast of Turkey, S within the coast of Syria, SSW within the coasts of Lebanon and Israel, and W within the coast of Egypt to Port Said (Bûr Sa'îd), excluding Suez Canal	31°16′	32°19′
Thence W within the coasts of Egypt and Libya to Ra's Ajdir	33°10′	11°34′

TRAFFIC AND OPERATIONS

Ship movement reporting systems

Egypt

1.2

1 There are Vessel Traffic Management Systems in operation at Mīnā' Al Iskandarīyah (Alexandria) (31°10′N

29°50′E) (3.83), Mînâ’ Dumyâṭ (Damietta Port) (31°29′N 31°45′E) (3.181) and Port Said (Bûr Sa‘îd) (31°16′N 32°19′E) (3.205).

Fishing

1.3

1 During certain seasons of the year large fishing nets, known as madragues or tonnara, are moored in places off the coast of Libya for the purpose of catching tunny fish. The nets, which should be avoided, may be found as many as 5 miles or more offshore.

2 Tunny fisheries are marked by the shapes and lights (diagram 1.3) shown from boats or floats moored seaward of the central outer portion of the main nets or the return, whichever extends further, at a height of at least 5 m above the sea.

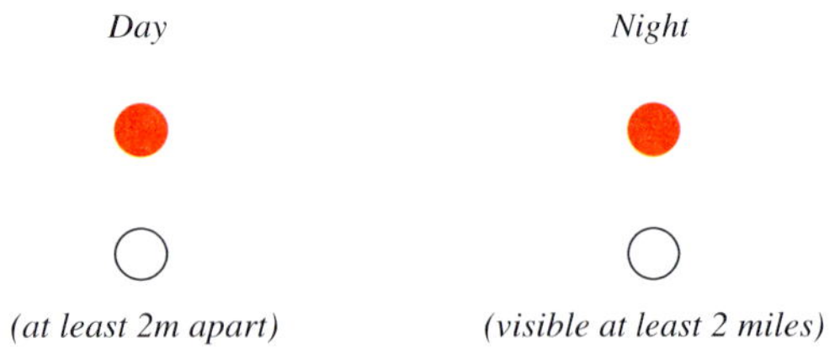

Tunny fisheries - signals (1.3)

3 Tunny nets which do not extend more than 1½ cables from the coast, and which are not placed in a position traversed or frequently anchored in by shipping, are exempt from showing the prescribed night signals.

4 Off the coast of Tripolitania (1.74) practical difficulties may temporarily prevent the proper marking of tunny fisheries and may affect their dimensions and position. Generally, such fisheries are allotted an extent of water measuring about 3 miles on its front, 5½ miles on its W side and 5 cables on its E side. When these nets are laid out, in order to avoid the possibility of fouling them, vessels should keep at least 6 miles from the coast and exercise great caution when entering or leaving a port.

Marine farms

1.4

1 Marine farming equipment may be encountered in many of the bays and inlets in the area covered by this volume. The approximate position of known farms is shown on the charts; however, development has been rapid and marine farms can be quickly established or moved without any warning. Marine farms, which may be fixed or floating structures, are usually fixed to the seabed by a spread of anchors which can be extensive. The position of anchors, where used, may be marked by buoys.

2 **Caution.** Mariners are cautioned to avoid areas of marine farms, and to note that their presence has rendered many hitherto accepted anchorages either unsuitable or limited in swinging space.

Exercise areas

Firing practice and exercise areas

1.5

1 Naval exercises and firing practices take place from time to time in certain areas. The areas are mentioned in the relevant geographical chapters. Warnings of firing practices and exercises are promulgated either by local notices to mariners, coast radio stations, or both.

For general information on such areas see *Annual Notice to Mariners No 5*.

Submarine exercise areas

1.6

1 Submarines may exercise in the area covered by this volume. Notice of exercises is given only in exceptional circumstances and therefore all vessels should keep a good lookout for submarines.

The Mariner’s Handbook and *Annual Notice to Mariners No 8* give general information on the characteristics of submarines and visual signals used to denote their presence.

Marine exploitation

Oil and gas fields

1.7

1 Oil rigs and platforms may be encountered off the coasts of Libya, Egypt and Israel. Production platforms and associated structures including tanker moorings, storage tankers and platforms on pipelines, generally exhibit morse (U) lights, aircraft obstruction lights and sound fog signals. These installations are usually protected by safety zones which may extend up to 500 m from their outer edges.

2 Vessels must be navigated with caution when passing close to offshore installations and structures.

Pipelines

1.8

1 Mariners are advised not to anchor or trawl in the vicinity of pipelines. Gas from a damaged oil or gas pipeline could cause an explosion, loss of a vessel’s buoyancy or other serious hazard. Pipelines are not always buried and may effectively reduce the charted depth by up to 2 m. They may also span seabed undulations and cause fishing gear to become irrecoverably snagged, putting a vessel in severe danger. See *Annual Notice to Mariners No 24* and *The Mariner’s Handbook*.

CHARTS

Admiralty charts

1.9

1 British Admiralty charts covering the area of this volume are adequate for use on passage and for entering the principal ports and harbours.

Charts of Greek and Turkish coastal waters have been compiled mainly from Greek and Turkish government charts and from earlier British surveys. In other areas the charted information has been derived from British surveys, French, Italian, United States, Israeli and Egyptian government charts, and other sources.

Foreign charts

1.10

1 Charts of Greek and Turkish coastal waters and ports are published by the Greek and Turkish Hydrographic Services respectively. The charts may be obtained from the publishing authorities listed below and in the *Catalogue of Admiralty Charts and Publications*; they are not issued by the United Kingdom Hydrographic Office nor are they corrected by *Admiralty Notices to Mariners*.

Publishing authorities:

2 *Egyptian charts*:
Egyptian Navy Hydrographic Department,
Shobat Al Misaha Al Baharia
Ras el Tin, ALEXANDRIA.

3 *Greek charts*:
Hellenic Navy Hydrographic Service,
TGN 1040,
ATHÍNAI.
E-mail: info@hnhs.gr
Website: www.hnhs.gr

4 *Israeli charts*:
Israel Navy, Hydrographic Branch
MPOB 01068 IDF.

5 *Turkish charts*:
Seyir, Hidrografi ve Oşinografi Dairesi Başkanliği,
34805 Çubuklu Bekoz,
İSTANBUL.
E-mail: info@shodb.gov.tr
Website: www.shodb.gov.tr

Greek orthography

1.11

1 The names on Greek charts published prior to 1985 were given in Katharévousa, but on Greek charts dated after 1985 names may be found in either Katharévousa or Demotikí (see Languages at 1.96). Where names in Demotikí are available they have been transliterated into Roman letters and used in this volume, and, as opportunity offers, will be included on Admiralty charts.

2 A further complication is introduced by the fact that in accordance with international agreement a revised system of transliteration (ELOT 743) has been adopted for use with Greek geographical names, and British Admiralty charts and publications are incorporating the resulting changes as opportunity provides.

3 As a result of these ongoing changes, there may be discrepancies between some names on the charts and those in this volume; for example, the Greek word for 'islet' may appear as Nisís, Nisídha or Nisída.

Datums

1.12

1 **Vertical.** The datum mainly used on charts is that of the country whose waters the chart covers.

Horizontal. The datum mainly used is that of the country whose waters the chart covers. Older charts are based on local datums. Some modern Admiralty series charts of the area are now based on the World Geodetic System (1984) Datum.

2 Most charts carry a note referring to the shift to be applied to satellite derived positions before they are plotted. In the absence of such a note it should not be assumed that such a shift is negligible.

Differences in graduation may be apparent when transferring positions from one chart to another. When in doubt it is advisable to transfer positions relative to common charted features rather than to geographical co-ordinates.

AIDS TO NAVIGATION

Lights

1.13

1 Navigational lights are the responsibility of the appropriate national authorities.

Major lights are those with a nominal range of 15 miles or greater.

Light-structures only are described in the body of this book. For further details of the lights, see *Admiralty List of Lights Volume E.*

Landmarks

1.14

1 Caution is necessary when evaluating the descriptions given in this volume concerning landmarks, such as trees, and the colour and shape of buildings etc. New buildings may have been erected and old trees or houses destroyed, so that marks, which may at one time have been conspicuous on account of their isolation, shape or colour, may no longer exist or may now be difficult to identify.

Buoyage

1.15

1 IALA Maritime Buoyage System Region A (red to port) applies throughout the area covered by this volume. However, mariners are advised that some buoys and beacons may not conform to the IALA system. For details of the system see *IALA Maritime Buoyage System* and *The Mariner's Handbook.*

RADIO FACILITIES

General

1.16

1 For full details of radio stations, broadcasts, navigation systems and facilities see the relevant volumes of *Admiralty List of Radio Signals.*

Satellite navigation systems

1.17

1 **Global positioning system.** The Navstar Global Positioning System (GPS), a joint military and civil satellite navigation system owned and operated by the United States Department of Defense, provides world wide position fixing.

The system is referenced to the datum of the World Geodetic System 1984 (WGS84) and therefore positions obtained must be adjusted, if necessary, to the datum of the chart being used.

2 **Global Navigation Satellite System.** The Russian Global Navigation Satellite System (GLONASS) is similar to GPS in that it is a space-based navigation system which provides world wide position fixing.

The system is referenced to the Soviet Geocentric Co-ordinate System 1990 (SGS90) and as for GPS positions must be adjusted, if necessary, to the datum of the chart being used.

3 **DGPS.** Differential GPS compares the position of a fixed point, referred to as the reference station, with positions obtained from a GPS receiver at that point. The resulting differences are then broadcast as corrections to suitable receivers to overcome the inherent and imposed limitations of GPS.

4 **Caution.** Satellite navigation systems are under the control of the owning nation which can impose selective availability or downgrade the accuracy to levels less than that available from terrestrial radio navigational systems. Therefore satellite based systems should only be utilised at the user's risk.

For full details of these systems see *Admiralty List of Radio Signals Volume 2.*

Other radio aids to navigation

1.18

1 Racons are to be encountered throughout the area covered by this volume.

Radio navigational warnings

NAVAREA III warnings

1.19

1 The area covered by this volume lies within the limits of NAVAREA III. Details of warnings and a list of those in force are issued by the Co-ordinator NAVAREA III,

Instituto Hidrografica de la Marina, Cadiz, Spain. NAVAREA III warnings are broadcast through:

a) National coast radio stations.
b) SafetyNET (Enhanced Group Calling International SafetyNET).

Coastal navigation warnings

1.20

1 Warnings are broadcast in English and national languages through national coast radio stations.

Local warnings

1.21

1 Local warnings cover the area within the limits of jurisdiction of a harbour or port authority and may be issued by those authorities. They may be issued in the national language only and supplement the coastal navigational warnings by giving information which the ocean-going ship may normally not require.

Radio weather services

METAREA III warnings/bulletins

1.22

1 The World Meteorological Organization (WMO) has established a global service for the broadcast of high seas weather warnings and routine weather bulletins, through the Enhanced Group Calling International SafetyNET Service. METeorological service AREAS (METAREAS) are identical to the 16 NAVAREAS within the World-Wide Navigational Warning Service (WWNWS).

2 Each METAREA has a designated National Meteorological Service responsible for issuing high seas weather warnings and bulletins. The designated authorities are not necessarily in the same country as the NAVAREA co-ordinators. Weather Warnings and routine bulletins are broadcast through:

3 a) National coast radio stations.
b) SafetyNET (Enhanced Group Calling International SafetyNET).

Meteorological broadcasts by radio-facsimile

1.23

1 The area covered by this volume lies within the radio-facsimile broadcast coverage area of national coast radio-facsimile stations.

National weather services

1.24

1 National weather warnings and weather bulletins are issued through national coast radio stations.

Radio medical advice

1.25

1 Mariners may obtain medical advice by radio through the International Radio-Medical Centre (CIRM) in Rome.

REGULATIONS

International regulations

Submarine cables and pipelines

1.26

1 Mariners are warned that every care should be taken to avoid anchoring or trawling in the vicinity of submarine cables or pipelines.

See *The Mariner's Handbook* for information on the *International Convention for the Protection of Submarine Cables*, together with advice on the action to be taken in the event of fouling a cable or pipeline.

Pollution

1.27

1 **General information.** *The International Convention for the Prevention of Pollution from Ships 1973* was adopted by the International Conference on Marine Pollution convened by IMO in 1973. It was modified by the Protocol of 1978 relating thereto and adopted by the International Conference on Tanker Safety and Pollution Prevention convened by IMO in 1978. The convention, as modified by the protocol, is known as *MARPOL 73/78*.

2 The Mediterranean Sea is defined as a Special Area for the purpose of the Convention. *MARPOL 73/78* and Annexes are described in detail in *The Mariner's Handbook.*

European Community regulations

Directive 2002/59/EC

1.28

1 **General information.** This Directive establishes a common vessel traffic monitoring and information system throughout European Community (EC) waters. The principal provisions are described below. They apply in general to all commercial vessels over 300 gt but the rules concerning the notification of carriage of dangerous and polluting goods apply to all vessels regardless of size.

2 **Caution.** These extracts are for reference purposes only and are not to be regarded as a statement of the applicable law. The full text of the regulations is the sole authoritative statement of the applicable law and it is recommended that it is consulted. The regulations to which the following refer is *Directive 2002/59/EC* or the appropriate enabling legislation drafted by individual member states.

1.29

1 **Ship reports.** All vessels bound for a port within the EC must report to the port authority at least 24 hours prior to arrival, or, if the voyage is less than 24 hours, no later than the time of departure from the previous port. The report shall include the following information:

Name, call sign, IMO or MMSI number.
Port of destination.
ETA and ETD at port of destination.
Total number of persons onboard.

2 Upon receipt of a ship's report, the port authority will notify the national coastguard authority by the quickest means possible. This information will then be pooled in the European-wide telematic network called SafeSeaNet.

Any amendments to the initial ship report must be notified immediately.

1.30

1 **VTS.** All vessels are to participate in and comply with VTS systems operated by EC member states and also those systems operated by member states in conjunction with co-operating non-member states. This includes those systems operated by member states outside their territorial waters but which are operated in accordance with IMO guidelines.

Routeing Schemes. All vessels must comply with IMO-adopted TSS and Deep Water route regulations. (See IMO publication *Ships' Routeing Guide*).

1.31

1 **AIS and VDR**. All vessels are to be equipped with AIS and VDR. The systems shall be in operation at all times.

By 2008 individual coastguard stations throughout the EC are required to be able to receive AIS information and to relay it to all other coastguard stations within the EC.

1.32

1 **Notification of dangerous and polluting goods.** All vessels leaving an EC port are to report dangerous and polluting goods as specified within the Directive to the harbour authority. Vessels arriving from outside EC waters must transmit a report to their first EC port or anchorage upon departure from their port of loading. If, at the time of departure, the port of destination in the EC is not known, the report must be forwarded immediately such information becomes known. Where practical, this report is to be made electronically and must include the information described in Annex 1 (3) of the Directive.

2 When a harbour authority receives a dangerous or polluting cargo report, it shall retain the report for use in the event of an incident or accident at sea, forwarding it whenever requested by the national coastguard authority.

1.33

1 **Reporting of Incidents and Accidents**. Whenever a vessel is involved with one of the following, the coastguard authority of the EC coastal state is to be informed immediately;

(a) any incident or accident affecting the safety of the ship;

(b) any incident or accident which compromises shipping safety, such as a failure likely to affect a ship's manoeuverability or seaworthiness;

(c) any event liable to pollute the waters or shores of the coastal state;

(d) the sighting of a slick of polluting material or drifting containers and packages.

The owner of a vessel, who has been informed by the master that one of the above has occurred, must inform the coastguard and render any assistance that may be required.

1.34

1 **Measures to be taken in the event of exceptionally bad weather or sea conditions.** If, on the advice of the national meteorological office, the coastguard authority deems a threat of pollution or a risk to human life exists due to impending severe weather, the coastguard authority will attempt to inform the master of every vessel about to enter or leave port as to the nature of the weather and the dangers it may cause.

2 Without prejudice to measures taken to give assistance to vessels in distress, the coastguard may take such measures as it considers appropriate to avoid a threat of pollution or a risk to human life. The measures may include:

(a) a recommendation or a prohibition on entry or departure from a port;

(b) a recommendation limiting, or, if necessary, prohibiting the bunkering of ships in territorial waters.

3 The master is to inform his owners of any measures or recommendations initiated by the coastguard. If, as a result of his professional judgement, the master decides not to act in accordance with measures taken by the coastguard, he shall inform the coastguard of his reasons for not doing so.

1.35

1 **Measures relating to incidents or accidents at sea.** The coastguard authority will take measures to ensure the safety of shipping and of persons and to protect the marine and coastal environment. Measures available to EC states include;

(a) a restriction on the movement of a ship or an instruction to follow a specific course.

(b) a notification to put an end to the threat to the environment or maritime safety;

2 (c) sending an evaluation team aboard a ship to assess the degree of risk and to help the master remedy the situation;

(d) instructing the master to put in at a place of refuge in the event of imminent peril, or, causing the ship to be piloted or towed.

The owner of the ship and the owner of the dangerous or polluting goods onboard must cooperate with the coastguard authority when requested to do so.

1.36

1 **Places of refuge.** EC states are required to designate places of refuge where a vessel which has undergone an accident or is in distress can receive rapid and effective assistance to avoid environmental pollution.

Regulation (EC) No 417/2002

1.37

1 This regulation establishes a timetable for the phasing out of all single-hull petroleum tankers of more than 5000 dwt in European waters. Ultimately only double-hull tankers or tankers of equivalent design will be permitted to visit European ports and offshore terminals.

The timetable is based upon a vessel's date of build, its design and the type of petroleum carried. The schedule for Category 1 and 2 tankers is already complete and completion for Category 3 tankers will occur in 2015. Categories are as defined in the regulation.

Border controls

1.38

1 The Schengen Convention is an association of European Union countries established to increase freedom of movement between participating states, while strengthening border controls with other nations. Within the area covered by this volume, Greece is a member of the Convention.

Vessels intending to enter a port of a member country are required to give advance notification to the appropriate Coast Guard command centre no later than 24 hours before arrival at the port using the form *Notification in Advance* (6 hours notice is required for fishing vessels).

Regulations — Libya

Caution

1.39

1 Vessels not complying with Libyan regulations when within Libyan territorial waters will be subject to punitive penalties. For limits claimed see 1.75.

Advance information

1.40

1 Vessels bound for any Libyan port must inform the appropriate port authority or agent in Libya, after leaving the last port of call, giving the following information:

Vessel's name, call sign and nationality.
Name and address of the owner.
Name and nationality of the master.
Number of crew and any passengers.
Gross tonnage.
Cargo type and quantity.
Destination port.
Expected duration of stay in the port.
Date of arrival (ETA).

2 Vessels must then contact the nearest Libyan coast radio station 24 hours before arriving at one of the Approach Reporting Points (1.41), confirming the above, and in addition supply the following information:

Position, speed and course at that moment.
Approach Reporting Point to be used.
Sea state.
Vessel's condition.

3 **Flags.** When in Libyan waters vessels must display their national flag, and at the foremast the Libyan flag.

Approach Reporting Points

1.41

1 The Libyan authorities have stated that all vessels making for Libyan ports must pass through one of the following designated Approach Reporting Points:

Destination	*Approach point(s)*
Zuwārah (Zuara) (2.34)	33°03′N 12°15′E
Ţarābulus (Tripoli) (2.59)	33°00′N 12°58′E
	33°05′N 13°04′E
	33°07′N 13°10′E
	33°05′N 13°19′E
Qaşr Aḩmad (2.120)	32°34′N 15°16′E
Ra's Lānūf (2.174) & Gulf of Sirte	32°43′N 19°06′E
Marsá al Burayqah (El-Bréga) Oil Terminal (2.206)	32°43′N 19°06′E
Az Zuwaytīnah (Ez Zueitina) Oil Terminal (2.236)	32°43′N 19°06′E
Banghāzī (2.272)	32°03′N 19°50′E
	32°09′N 19°49′E
	32°17′N 19°53′E
	32°20′N 20°06′E
Darnah (Derna) (2.323)	32°58′N 22°42′E
Ţubruq (Tòbruch) (2.343)	32°10′N 24°02′E
Al Khums (Homs, Khoms) (2.102)	Range of 12 miles
Az Zāwiyah Oil Terminal (2.49)	Range of 12 miles

2 On arrival at an approach point vessels must report their position, course and speed to the appropriate port authority.

Radio communication

1.42

1 Within Libyan territorial waters all vessels must maintain communication with Libyan coast radio stations and keep continuous watch on VHF. For the correct VHF channel on which to call individual ports see *Admiralty List of Radio Signals Volume 6 (3).*

Anchoring

1.43

1 Ships may anchor only in the anchorage areas shown on the charts. All vessels must anchor as instructed by the port authority, and must not shift berth except on the instruction of the port authority.

Pollution

1.44

1 Refuse and contaminated water must not be dumped. See also information at 1.27.

Movement between ports

1.45

1 Permission must be obtained before proceeding from one Libyan port to another.

Regulations — Egypt

1.46

1 **Permission** to enter Egyptian waters must be requested from the Egyptian authorities 48 hours prior to arrival.

ETA should be confirmed at least 24 hours in advance, giving last port of call, position, course and speed.

2 **Radio communication** must be established with Port Authorities when within 24 miles of the coast in order to receive entry instructions.

On passage vessels should keep at least 12 miles off the Egyptian coast by day, and at least 24 miles off at night.

Regulations — Greece

Fortified areas

1.47

1 Severe penalties may be imposed on persons found taking photographs or collecting hydrographic information within 10 km of a Greek naval or military fortified area. Where these regulations apply in the vicinity of prohibited areas, they may be applicable outside those areas or within channels passing through the areas.

Regulations — Turkey

Diving restrictions

1.48

1 In order to protect underwater cultural and natural conditions, Turkish authorities have prohibited diving in certain areas. The areas concerned are described in local orders and official advice must be sought before any diving takes place.

Regulations — Syria

Advance information

1.49

1 Vessels bound for Syrian ports are required to communicate the following information, through a Syrian coast radio station, when within 50 miles of the Syrian coast:

Ship's name, and former name, if any.
Nationality.
2 Type of vessel.
Position and time.
Route and speed.
Port of destination.

Arrival information

1.50

1 **Entry.** When entering Syrian territorial waters vessels should pass the following information to the appropriate pilot-station or signal tower:

Ship's name.
Nationality.
Nature of cargo.
ETA at the waiting area.

2 **Flags.** When in Syrian waters vessels must display their national flag and the Syrian flag.

Use of radio. Unauthorised use of radio in Syrian ports or anchorages is prohibited.

Regulations — Lebanon

Approved ports

1.51

1 Only certain ports within Lebanon are approved for use by ships commercially. Ships attempting to enter other ports will be formally banned and severely penalised. The approved ports are:

Trâblous (Tripoli) (7.97).
Joûnié (Juniye) (7.143).
Beyrouth (Beirut) (7.154).
Saïda (Sidon) (7.189) and Zahrānī (Sidon) Terminal (7.196).
Sour (Tyr) (7.211).

2 In addition certain private and specialised ports such as Chekka (7.129) and Sel'ata (7.135) are also approved.

Ports are open to traffic during the following periods:

Beyrouth — 24 hours.
Trâblous, Saïda and Sour — between 0500 and 2000 hours.

Passage between the above ports is limited between 0500 and 2000 hours.

Entry

1.52

1 All vessels entering Lebanese territorial waters should obtain permission to enter from the Maritime Chamber 24 hours in advance, through the agent.

Also, all vessels should call Beyrouth Port Control during the daytime only, on VHF, to request permission to enter Lebanese territorial waters.

For details of reports to be made and information required see *Admiralty List of Radio Signals Volume 6 (3).*

Navigation

1.53

1 United Nations Interim Force In Lebanon (UNIFIL) Maritime Task Force (MTF) is monitoring merchant traffic sailing towards Lebanese ports or transiting Lebanese Territorial Waters. The UNIFIL MTF is acting in accordance with United Nations Security Council Resolution (UNSCR) 1701.

2 Vessels must approach approved ports by the recognised sea lanes where they will be subject to regulation by the maritime and customs authorities before continuing to legal ports of destination. The sea lanes for the ports of Trâblous, Beyrouth and Saïda are established as follows:

3 Entry should be carried out by navigating on a course of 090° from a distance of at least 3 miles from opposite the relevant port.

Exit should be carried out by navigating on a course of 270° from a distance of at least 3 miles from opposite the relevant port.

Passage between these ports should be carried out within Lebanese territorial waters at a distance of 3 miles off the coast.

Regulations — Israel

Chart 2634

Routes

1.54

1 The Israeli authorities advise vessels approaching the Israeli coast to do so only through the approach routes shown on the chart. Coasting traffic must follow within the coastal route shown on the chart.

Vessels navigating in Israeli territorial waters are advised not to exceed a speed of 15 kt.

Advance information

1.55

1 All vessels (including small craft) bound for Israeli ports are required to transmit an IMOT report (Israeli Ministry of Transport) when 100 miles from the Israeli coast (or 25 miles for small craft). The report must be sent to the Israeli Navy by fax or e-mail. The Israeli Navy will confirm receipt by Inmarsat C.

For details of the information required in the report see *Admiralty List of Radio Signals Volume 6 (3).*

Winter restrictions

1.56

1 Any vessel bound for an Israeli port shall not be permitted to enter Israeli Territorial Waters from 1 November to 30 April if by certification she is constrained by sea state, wind force, maximum distance from land, port of refuge or length of voyage.

Prohibited areas

1.57

1 Certain areas off the Israeli coast are closed to navigation. These areas are described in the body of the book.

Pollution reporting

1.58

1 All vessels navigating in Israeli waters must report any dangerous occurrences, strandings, and possible incidents of pollution, to the Maritime and Coastal Anti-pollution Division, via Ḫefa (Haifa) coast radio station.

Ballast water

1.59

1 In order to prevent the import of non-native aquatic organisms into the waters of the ports of Israel from ships' ballast water discharges, all ships destined for Israeli ports must exchange any ballast water that has not been taken from an open ocean.

2 The best method of protecting harbour waters from foreign organisms that may exist in the ballast water collected in foreign harbours and near shore areas is for the ballast water to be exchanged in open ocean, beyond any continental shelf or fresh water current effect.

3 For vessels calling at Israeli Mediterranean ports, ballast exchange must be carried out in the Atlantic Ocean when practicable. Vessels failing to comply with this procedure will not be permitted to pump out their ballast water during their stay in the port or while navigating along the coast of Israel.

4 A record of the location, date and time of the ballast water exchange should be entered in the ship's log book, or in other suitable documentation, such as an official ballast water record book. Masters of vessels will be requested to provide ship inspectors (pilots) with a completed ballast water exchange report.

SIGNALS

National

Greece and Turkey

1.60

1 Greek and Turkish warships, submarines and aircraft use signals and instructions similar to those described in *Annual Notices to Mariners Nos 5 & 8.*

Syria

1.61

1 The following signals are used in Syrian ports:

Sound signal	*Light signal*	*Meaning*
Six short blasts	Six flashes (from foremast)	Attacked by thieves
Six long blasts	Six long flashes	Fire on board or alongside
Two long blasts	Two long flashes	Serious injury
Four long blasts	Four long flashes	Stranding

DISTRESS AND RESCUE

General information

Global Maritime Distress and Safety System

1.62

1 The Global Maritime Distress System (GMDSS) enables Search and Rescue authorities on shore, in addition to shipping in the immediate vicinity of a vessel in distress, to be rapidly alerted to an incident so that assistance can be provided with the minimum of delay. The sea area covered by this volume lies within the Search and Rescue Regions of Libya, Egypt, Greece, Turkey, Cyprus, Syria, Lebanon and Israel.

2 Details of the GMDSS and the associated coast radio stations are given in *Admiralty List of Radio Signals Volume 5* and *Volume 1 (1)*.

Automated Mutual-assistance Vessel Rescue system

1.63

1 The Automated Mutual-assistance Vessel Rescue (AMVER) system, operated by the United States Coast Guard, is an international maritime mutual assistance organization which provides important aid to the development and co-ordination of search and rescue efforts in many offshore areas of the world. Participation in the system is voluntary.

2 Details are given in *Admiralty List of Radio Signals Volume 1 (1)*.

Rescue services

General

1.64

1 For information on Rescue Services see *Admiralty List of Radio Signals Volume 5*.

Libya

1.65

1 Coast radio stations at Ţubruq (Tòbruch) and Banghāzī maintain a continuous listening watch on international distress frequencies.

Egypt

1.66

1 The Ministry of Defence Cairo is responsible for search and rescue in Egyptian waters. The rescue service consists of a Joint Rescue Co-ordination Centre at Cairo and a Maritime Rescue Co-ordination Centre, for the Mediterranean coast of Egypt, at Mīnā' Al Iskandarīyah (Alexandria). A network of coast radio stations maintains a continuous listening watch on international distress frequencies.

Greece

1.67

1 The overall authority for search and rescue in Greek waters is the Safety of Navigation Division, Ministry of Mercantile Marine, Aegean and Island Policy, Hellenic Coastguard, Piraeus. Search and rescue within the area covered by this book is delegated to the following two Maritime Rescue Co-ordination Sub-Centres of the Maritime Search and Rescue Region of Greece:

2 Rescue Co-ordination Sub-Centre Chaniá covering the coast of Crete.

Rescue Co-ordination Sub-Centre Ródos covering the coasts of Kásos, Kárpathos and Ródos.

A network of coast radio stations maintains a continuous listening watch on international distress frequencies.

Turkey

1.68

1 Search and rescue, for the area which lies within the Maritime Search and Rescue Region of Turkey, is the responsibility of the Maritime Rescue Co-ordination Centre Mersin. Three Maritime Rescue Co-ordination Sub-Centres are established at Marmaris, Antalya and İskenderun. A network of coast radio stations maintains a continuous listening watch on international distress frequencies.

Cyprus

1.69

1 Search and rescue in Cypriot waters is the responsibility of RCC Larnaca. Cyprus operates a maritime radio service which maintains a continuous listening watch on international distress frequencies.

Syria

1.70

1 For Syrian waters the General Director of Ports in Al Lādhiqīyah (Lattaquié) is responsible for co-ordinating search and rescue operations. A network of coast radio stations maintains a continuous listening watch on international distress frequencies.

Lebanon

1.71

1 The Lebanese Navy, with a Rescue Co-ordination Centre at Beyrouth (Beirut), is responsible for search and rescue in Lebanese waters. Lebanese Naval Bases and the coast radio station at Beyrouth maintain continuous listening watch on international distress frequencies.

Israel

1.72

1 The Israeli Navy and Air Force are responsible for search and rescue in Israeli waters. The Rescue Co-ordination Centre is based at the Israeli Navy and Air Force Headquarters and is reached through Ḫefa (Haifa) Radio, which is one of a network of radio stations on the Mediterranean coast of Israel maintaining a continuous listening watch on international distress frequencies.

COUNTRIES AND PORTS

General

1.73

1 For details of claimed territorial and fishing limits see *Annual Notice to Mariners No 12.*

LIBYA

General description

1.74

1 Libya or Lībiyā, officially known as Socialist Peoples' Libyan Arab Jamahiriya or SPLAJ, lies between Tunisia and Egypt. The country has an estimated area of 1 759 540 sq km, and a coast about 1100 miles in length between its W and E boundaries.

2 The country is divided into the provinces of Tripolitania, in the NW, Cyrenaica, in the NE, Fezzan, in the SW, and Kufra Oasis, in the SE.

Ţarābulus (Tripoli) (32°54′N 13°11′E) (2.59) is the capital of the country, and Banghāzī (32°07′N 20°03′E) is the second city.

National limits

1.75

1 Libya claims territorial waters of 12 miles. In addition, all waters S of 32°30′N in Gulf of Sirte are claimed as Libyan internal waters.

History

1.76

1 In ancient times the Phoenicians, Carthaginians, Greeks, Romans, Vandals and Byzantines ruled all or parts of Libya.

In the seventh century the Arabs conquered Libya, and in succeeding centuries most of the people adopted Islam and the Arabic language and culture.

In the sixteenth century the Turks conquered the country, which remained a part of the Ottoman empire until invaded by Italy in 1911 after which it became an Italian colony.

2 In 1943, during the course of the Second World War, the Italians were expelled from Libya. Tripolitania and Cyrenaica were then placed under British, and Fezzan under French, administration.

In 1951 Libya became an independent, sovereign, federal kingdom which lasted until 1969 when the king was deposed by a group of army officers.

Government

1.77

1 Libya is an Islamic Arabic Socialist 'Mass State'.

Government is effected by popular assemblies (Basic Peoples' Congresses). There are about 2000 of these assemblies. From these assemblies Peoples' Committees are appointed to carry out policy and to deal with provincial and urban affairs, being responsible to 26 municipality Peoples' Congresses. All these Congresses and Committees provide delegates for a General Peoples' Congress, which is the highest policy making body in the country. The heads of the government departments which carry out national policy are chosen by the General Peoples' Congress.

2 For administrative purposes the country is divided into 13 regions.

Population

1.78

1 In 2007 the population of Libya was approaching 6 million.

Languages

1.79

1 Arabic is the official language.

Physical features

1.80

1 Hilly areas with elevations of 900 m lie in the N of the country, S of Ţarābulus and E of Banghāzī, and another hilly area lies in the S and SW of the country; between these lie barren rock-strewn plains and vast sand seas. Except for scattered oases, only the narrow coastal strip and the slopes of the N hill areas are suitable for cultivation.

Industry and trade

1.81

1 The principal industries are the production of crude oil and natural gas, food processing and textiles.

Agricultural products include tomatoes, watermelons, potatoes, olives, onions, wheat, dates, barley and oranges. Livestock production includes sheep, goats, cattle, camels and chickens.

The principal export is crude oil, which accounts for 30% of GDP. Natural gas output is growing at a faster rate than that of any other producer, with a 79·5% increase in 2005 over the 2004 total. Iron ore deposits have been found in the south.

EGYPT

General description

1.82

1 Egypt, officially called Arab Republic of Egypt and known to the Egyptians as Mişr, lies between Libya and Israel and extends S to the parallel of 22°N. The total area of the country is 997 739 sq km, but the cultivated and settled area comprising the Nile valley, delta and oases covers only 35 189 sq km.

2 El Qâhira (Cairo) (30°00′N 31°20′E) is the capital city.

National limits

1.83

1 Egypt claims territorial waters of 12 miles and an exclusive economic zone of 200 miles. For further details see *Annual Notice to Mariners No 12.*

History

1.84

1 After the collapse of the last pharaonic dynasty in 525 BC, Egypt suffered a succession of foreign invaders. A vassal of the Persian empire at the time of Alexander's invasion in 332 BC, the country was linked thereafter with the Hellenistic civilizations of the Mediterranean for thirteen centuries.

In 1798 the French under Napoleon invaded Egypt, but were forced to withdraw by the British, in alliance with the Ottoman Turks, after only three years. In the wake of the French departure, Mohammed Ali, an Albanian officer in the Turkish army, emerged as ruler of the country.

2 Following the Arabi Revolt of 1879–1882, the British occupied the country and remained de facto rulers for the

next 40 years. In 1922 Egypt became an independent kingdom. In 1952 King Farouk was deposed and the country became a republic.

In 1956 Egypt nationalized the Suez Canal. This resulted in Britain, France and Israel joining forces to attack Egypt until forced by the United Nations and the USA to withdraw.

3 A United Arab Republic, consisting of Egypt and Syria, was formed in 1958. This lasted until Syria left in 1961. Egypt kept the name United Arab Republic until 11th September 1971 when a new consitution renamed the country the Arab Republic of Egypt.

In March 1979 President Muhammad Anwar Sadat signed a peace treaty with Israel, bringing to an end several years of sporadic conflict.

Government

1.85

1 Egypt has a democratic, socialist system of government. It consists of the People's Assembly with 444 members directly elected from 222 constituencies for a five year term, and 10 members appointed by the President. The President of the Republic is nominated by the People's Assembly and confirmed by plebiscite for a term of six years. The President appoints the Prime Minister and a Council of Ministers, and may appoint one or more vice presidents.

Population

1.86

1 In 2005 the population of Egypt was estimated to be 74 million. In 2003 57·8% of the population were rural.

Languages

1.87

1 Arabic is the official language of the country. English and, to a lesser extent, French are spoken.

Physical features

1.88

1 Except in the valley of River Nile, the only river in Egypt, the country is chiefly desert.

River Nile, the longest river in the world, is estimated to be 4160 miles in length from its source to the Mediterranean Sea. The river has a regular yearly rise and fall, attaining its maximum level in about mid-September and its minimum about the end of May. The Aswân High Dam (24°05′N 32°52′E) controls the flow of water down-stream of it throughout the year. A few miles N of El Qâhira the river divides into two main streams which enter the Mediterranean by Maṣabb Rashîd (Rosetta Mouth) (31°30′N 30°20′E) and Maṣabb Dumyâṭ (Damietta Mouth) (31°32′N 31°51′E) respectively. The area enclosed between the two branches is the present delta of the River Nile.

2 The Suez Canal, which connects the Mediterranean with Gulf of Suez, is described in *Red Sea and Gulf of Aden Pilot.*

Industry and trade

1.89

1 In 2002 agriculture accounted for 16·5% of GDP, industry 34·8% and services 48·7%. Egypt is Africa's largest producer of a number of crops, including wheat, rice, tomatoes, potatoes and oranges. Other products include crude oil, cement, petroleum and phosphates.

2 Suez Canal earns considerable revenues. Tankers too large for Suez Canal discharge crude oil at Ain Sukhna Oil Terminal (29°35′N 32°20′E) on the W side of Gulf of Suez. The oil is then carried by SUMED (Suez-Mediterranean) pipeline to Sidi Kerir Oil Terminal (31°03′N 29°40′E) on the Mediterranean coast. The pipeline has an annual capacity of 124 million tonnes.

3 The principal exports are petroleum and petroleum products, cotton yarn and fabrics, clothing, foodstuffs, chemicals and aluminium. Main imports are machinery and transport equipment, foodstuffs, manufactured goods, chemical products and mineral fuels.

GREECE

General description

1.90

1 Greece, known to the Greeks as Ellás, is bounded on the N by Albania, Republic of Macedonia and Bulgaria; on the E by Turkey and the Aegean Sea; on the S by the E part of the Mediterranean Sea; and on the W by the Ionian Sea.

Athínai (Athens) (38°00′N 23°45′E) is the capital of the country.

The Greek mainland comprises the following regions:

Pelopónnisos, formerly known as Morea, a large peninsula connected to the rest of the mainland by an isthmus 4 miles in width.

2 Central Greece, which extends from the Ionian Sea to the Aegean Sea and includes Nísos Évvoia.

Ípiros, formerly Epirus, in the W and extending to the Albanian border.

Thessalía, formerly Thessaly, in the E.

Makedonía, formerly Macedonia, in the N and extending to the Albanian, Macedonian and Bulgarian borders.

Thráki, formerly Western Thrace, bordered on the N by Bulgaria and on the E by Turkey.

3 About one fifth of the total area of Greece consists of more than 1400 islands, of which about 170 are inhabited, lying in the Ionian and Aegean Seas. The principal islands and island groups are as follows:

Iónioi Nísoi, which lie in the Ionian Sea off the W coast of Greece.

Nísos Kríti (4.3), generally referred to as Kríti and formerly known as Crete, the largest of the islands, which forms the S limit of the Aegean Sea. Due to its position, fertility and population, Kríti is one of the most important islands in the E Mediterranean. Iráklion (35°22′N 25°09′E) is the administrative and commercial centre of the island.

4 Kikládes Nísoi, commonly called The Cyclades, which lie in the central part of the S Aegean.

Dodekánisos, commonly called The Dodecanese and sometimes known as the Southern Sporadhes, which mostly lie in the E part of the S Aegean. The group includes Nísos Kásos (4.86), Nísos Kárpathos (4.86), Nísos Ródos (4.92) and Nísos Meyísti (Kastellorízon) (5.83).

Nísoi Vórioi Sporádes, commonly known as the Northern Sporadhes, a group lying NE of Nísos Évvoia.

Eastern Sporadhes, which lie in the E part of the N Aegean.

National limits

1.91

1 Greece claims a limit of 6 miles for both its territorial waters and fisheries jurisdictions. For further details see *Annual Notice to Mariners No 12.*

History

1.92

1 From the end of the political independence of the city states of ancient Greece to the early years of the nineteenth century Greece was ruled successively by the Roman, Byzantine and Ottoman Empires.

2 The Greek War of Independence began in 1821 and continued until 1829 when, by the Treaty of Adrianople, Turkey finally recognized the independence of Greece. At that time the country comprised Pelopónnisos, Central Greece, Kikládes Nísoi and Nísoi Vórioi Sporádes.

3 The Greek vision was to bring all Greeks of the declining Ottoman Empire into the new state. The realisation of this idea took many years, and its pursuit created tensions between Greece and its neighbours, particularly Turkey, which have persisted to the present time. The principal secessions of territory to Greece after independence were as follows:

4 1864 Iónioi Nísoi, by Britain.
1881 Thessalía and Ípiros, by Turkey.
1913 Makedonía, Kríti and Eastern Sporadhes, by Turkey.
1918 Thráki, by Bulgaria.
1947 Dodekánisos, by Italy.

In 1920 Eastern Thrace and Smyrna, now known as İzmir, were ceded to Greece by the Treaty of Sèvres.

5 In 1921–22 the Greeks took the offensive against the Turks in pursuit of their claims in Anatolia. From Smyrna the Greek army advanced to within 60 miles of Ankara before being repulsed.

In 1923 the Treaty of Lausanne returned Eastern Thrace and Smyrna to Turkey and provided for the exchange of Greek and Turkish minorities. During World War II (1939-1945) Greece was occupied by the Italians and Germans.

In 1981 Greece became a full member of the European Community.

Government

1.93

1 On gaining independence a monarchy was established which lasted until 1924 when a republic was proclaimed. The monarchy was restored in 1935, but after various vicissitudes it was finally terminated by referendum on 8th December 1974. Since then Greece has been a presidential parliamentary republic with a governmental structure similar to those in most European countries. The president, who is head of state, is elected by parliament for a term of five years. The president appoints a prime minister and, on the latter's advice, the remaining members of government. The president is advised by the Council of the Republic.

Population

1.94

1 In 2005 the population of Greece was estimated to be 11·12 million.

Religion

1.95

1 The Greek Orthodox Church is the established religion of the country.

Languages

1.96

1 Greek is the official language of the country. The modern language contains many features of classical Greek which has existed for 3000 years.

2 In the nineteenth century a form of Greek known as *Katharévousa* was devised to purify the language and return it to a form nearer to that of the ancient dialect from which it developed. However, *Katharévousa* never became widely established and in 1976 it was abolished as a language of university instruction and government. The form of present day spoken Greek, which has become the language of modern literature, is generally termed *Demotikí.*

3 Apart from Greek, the languages most commonly understood are English, French and Italian.

Physical features

1.97

1 The Greek mainland is mountainous. Much of the country is dry and rocky, and little more than a quarter of the land is arable. In some of the mountainous regions, especially Pelopónnisos, there are extensive tablelands. In its general aspect the country presents a series of striking and interesting contrasts; fertile tracts covered with vineyards, olive groves, cornfields or forests lie close to rugged heights and rocky precipices.

2 Rivers are few in Greece. All are obstructed at their entrances by shoals, and few can be entered even by boats.

The islands of the Aegean archipelago are all high. Many are of volcanic origin, and others are composed of white marble. Some of the islands are fertile and picturesque; others, mostly the smaller ones, are masses of rock and devoid of vegetation.

Industry and trade

1.98

1 Agriculture employs about 17% of the working population of Greece, and its products make up about a third of the country's exports. The principal products are cotton, sugar beet, olives and olive oil, fruits and vegetables, cereals, tobacco and wines. Fishing, mainly from the sea, accounted for a total catch of 94 388 tonnes in 2001.

2 Manufacturing industry employs about 15% of the labour force and its products make up nearly a half of exports. The principal industries are textiles, clothing and shoes, cement, mining and metals, chemicals, petrochemicals, processing agricultural products, and steel. Oil is produced from a small oilfield off the W coast of Nísos Thásos.

TURKEY

General description

1.99

1 Turkey, known to the Turks as Türkiye, is bounded on the W by the Aegean Sea, on the NW by Greece and Bulgaria, on the N by the Black Sea, on the NE by Georgia and Armenia, on the E by Azerbaijan and Iran, and on the S by Iraq, Syria and the E part of the Mediterranean Sea. The country lies partly in Asia and partly in Europe, the two parts being separated by the straits connecting the Aegean and Black Seas. The Asian part is called Anadolu, formerly Anatolia or Asia Minor; the European part, which comprises only 3% of the land area of the country, is called Trakya, formerly Eastern Thrace.

2 Ankara (39°57′N 32°54′E) is the capital of the country, and İstanbul (41°01′N 28°58′E), formerly Constantinople, is the largest city.

National limits

1.100

1 Turkey claims a limit of 12 miles for both its territorial waters and fisheries jurisdiction, except in the Aegean Sea where the limit claimed is 6 miles. For further details see *Annual Notice to Mariners No 12.*

History

1.101

1 At the end of the thirteenth century the Turks, who had been dominant in central Asia and the E part of Asia Minor for the previous two centuries, took control of the Asiatic territories of the Byzantine Empire and the Ottoman Empire came into being. During succeeding centuries the Ottomans gradually acquired more of the Byzantine Empire, absorbing the whole of it after their capture of Constantinople in 1453. In subsequent conquests the Ottoman Empire advanced into Syria, Mesopotamia and Egypt, and reached its W limit before Vienna in 1529 and again in 1532.

2 In the nineteenth century Russia and the European powers, and internal troubles, combined to weaken the Ottoman Empire. In 1827 a combined Russian, French and British fleet destroyed the Turkish fleet at Navarino.

During the Crimean War (1854–56), fought to frustrate Russian aspirations for the control of Constantinople, France and Britain supported Turkey.

3 Continual unrest in the Balkans for the remainder of the nineteenth century led to two Balkan Wars in 1912–13 which further reduced the Ottoman Empire. Finally, as a result of the First World War (1914–18) in which Turkey allied itself to Germany, the boundaries of the Ottoman Empire were reduced to Anatolia and a small area around Constantinople.

4 In 1923, after a bitter war in which the invading Greeks were expelled from Anatolia, the Ottoman Empire came to an end and modern Turkey came into being under the leadership of Mustafa Kemal, subsequently known as Kemal Atatürk.

Government

1.102

1 Turkey is a democratic, secular republic with a parliamentary form of government and an independent judiciary. The legislative body, with 550 elected members, is known as the Grand National Assembly.

2 Under the latest constitution, adopted by referendum in 1982, the president of the republic is chosen by the assembly for a term of seven years. The president appoints a Council of Ministers who are responsible to the Grand National Assembly. Executive powers are shared between the president and the prime minister.

Population

1.103

1 In 2005 the population of Turkey was estimated to be 73·2 million.

Religions

1.104

1 The Constitution guarantees freedom of religion but forbids its political exploitation or any impairment of the secular character of the republic. In 1992 there were 58·2 million Moslems, two-thirds Sunni and one-third Shi'ite.

2 The Greek Orthodox, Gregorian, Armenian, Armenian Apostolic and Roman Catholic churches are represented in Istanbul, and there are small Uniate, Protestant and Jewish communities.

Languages

1.105

1 Turkish is the official language of the country. English, which is taught extensively, is mostly used commercially. German or French are known by many technicians and professional people.

Physical features

1.106

1 The main physical feature of Turkey is a belt of young mountain ranges with a mean elevation of about 1100 m, dominating the N and S and encircling the Central Anatolian Plateau. North of the plateau are the Pontic Mountains, and to its S rise the Taurus Mountains.

2 Western Anatolia has elongated mountain ridges separated by depressed floors. The W side of W Anatolia is broken by broad valleys, and the deeply indented coastline throws out long rocky promontories into the Aegean Sea. Central Anatolia is a semi-arid plateau divided into several basins. Eastern Anatolia comprises lofty ranges and recent volcanic cones, such as Ağri Daği (Mount Ararat), the highest peak in Turkey at 5128 m.

3 Earthquakes are frequent all over Turkey, especially in the SE and W, and the region is remarkable for the number of its thermal and mineral springs.

There are several lakes in Turkey the largest being that of Van Gölü. It is a salt lake, variable in size, and without an outlet. The rivers of Turkey are of no great importance. A few are navigable by boats for short distances from their mouths.

Industry and trade

1.107

1 Agriculture accounts for 45% of the workforce but only 11·5% of GDP. Principal crops include: wheat, sugar beet, tomatoes, barley, melons and watermelons, maize, potatoes, grapes, cottonseed, oranges, apricots, olives, hazelnuts and mandarins. Turkey is the largest producer of apricots and hazelnuts. Fishing accounted for a catch of 463 074 tonnes in 2003.

2 Manufacturing industry accounts for about a third of the gross national product. Products include cement, crude steel, iron and steel bars, fuel oils, coke, sugar, fertilizers, paper and paperboard, cotton yarn, olive oil, woven fabrics, TV sets, refrigerators, vehicles and cigarettes.

3 In 2002 the principal exports were machinery and automotive industry products, ready-made garments, textiles, food products, iron and steel.

CYPRUS

General description

1.108

1 Cyprus, situated in the NE part of the E basin of the Mediterranean, is an island with an area of about 3572 square miles. Nicosia (35°10′N 33°21′E) is the capital of the island.

National limits

1.109

1 Cyprus claims territorial waters of 12 miles. For further details, see *Annual Notice to Mariners No 12.*

History

1.110

1 Greek colonies were established in Cyprus in about the middle of the second millennium BC, and later the island formed part of the Persian, Roman and Byzantine empires. In 1193 the island became a Frankish kingdom, in 1489 a Venetian dependency, and in 1571 it was conquered by the Turks.

2 In 1878 the Turks ceded Cyprus to Great Britain for administrative purposes. In 1914 the island was annexed by Great Britain, and in 1925 it was given the status of a crown colony.

In 1960 Cyprus became an independent republic within the British Commonwealth of Nations, Britain retaining sovereignty over military bases at Akrotiri and Dekelia.

3 In 1974 Turkey invaded and occupied the N part of the island, roughly the area N of a line from Stavromeni Point (35°11′N 32°37′E), through Lefka and Nicosia, to Famagusta (35°07′N 33°56′E). In 1983 Turkish-Cypriots declared the area an independent state, to be known as the Turkish Republic of Northern Cyprus (TRNC), but it has not been recognized by any country other than Turkey.

4 In 2002 the United Nations (UN) presented a peace plan to the Greek and Turkish Cypriot leaders for a common state with two component states, along the lines of Switzerland and its cantons; but in 2003 the talks collapsed. However, as a goodwill measure the TRNC opened the Green Line separating the island's two sections in April 2003.

5 In a referendum in April 2004, the Greek Cypriots rejected a UN plan to reunite the island while Turkish Cypriots voted in favour. As a result, in the short term, European Union (EU) benefits and laws will apply only to the Greek Cypriot community. Cyprus became a member of the EU in May 2004.

Government

1.111

1 Cyprus is governed by a President and a Vice-President, together with a Council of Ministers and a House of Representatives, containing 80 members. The House of Representatives, which serves for five year periods, consists of 56 Greek Cypriots and 24 Turkish Cypriots. To elect members a proportional representation system is used, in which voting is compulsory.

Population

1.112

1 In 2005 the population of Cyprus was estimated to be 835 000, made up of 85% Greek origin and 11% of Turkish origin.

Languages

1.113

1 Greek and Turkish are the official languages. English is widely understood, especially in commercial circles.

Religions

1.114

1 The Greek Orthodox Church is the predominant religious body in Cyprus. Members of the Turkish community are mostly Moslems. Protestant and Roman Catholic churches exist in the main towns.

Physical features

1.115

1 Two mountain ranges run generally E and W through the island. The S range, which is the more extensive and lofty, occupies most of the S part of the island and culminates in Mount Troodos (6.188). The N range extends along the coast from Cape Kormakiti to Cape Andreas, a distance of 90 miles, with Kyrenia Mountains forming the W half and Karpas Mountains the E half. Buffavento (6.211), in Kyrenia Mountains, is the highest point of the N range.

2 Mesaoria, the agricultural heart of Cyprus, is a treeless plain from 8 to 18 miles in width extending across the island from Morphou Bay to Famagusta Bay. The streams traversing it are winter torrents which descend N from the S mountain range but scarcely reach the sea; of these Pedieo and Yialias flow into a reservoir which is used for irrigation. However, although the island is subject to drought, water is plentiful below the surface in the valleys and plains.

Industry and trade

1.116

1 The main industry is tourism but business services catering to international companies accounted for 14% of GDP in 2003 and financial intermediation contributed about 5%. There is an active insurance market and a developing securities market. The chief agricultural products are milk, potatoes, cereals, citrus fruit, meat, grapes, olives, almonds and other vegetables.

2 The only heavy industries are petroleum refining, electricity generation, and cement production. Light manufacturing industries include the production of textiles and clothing, food, chemicals and furniture. Mining is carried on, the principal products being gypsum, bentonite, umber and other ochres, and copper.

3 The most important exports are medicinal and pharmaceutical products, clothing, cigarettes, citrus fruit, potatoes, cement, wine and footwear.

SYRIA

General description

1.117

1 Syria, known to the Syrians as Sūriyah, has a total area of 71 500 square miles. It is bounded on the N by Turkey, on the E by Iraq, on the S by Jordan and Israel, and on the W by Lebanon and Mediterranean Sea. The coastline extends from Kassab Bay (35°56′N 35°55′E) to the mouth of Nahr al Kabīr, 78 miles S.

2 Damascus (33°30′N 36°18′E), one of the oldest continuously inhabited cities in the world, is the capital of the country.

National limits

1.118

1 Syria claims territorial waters of 12 miles. For further details see *Annual Notice to Mariners No 12.*

History

1.119

1 Ancient Syria, the fertile strip between the Mediterranean coast and the desert of N Arabia, formed part of all the great empires of the E Mediterranean and SW Asia: Egyptian, Hittite, Babylonian, Assyrian, Persian, Hellenistic, Roman, Arab and Ottoman.

After the First World War (1914–1918), as part of the Levant States, Syria was included in the French mandate from the League of Nations. Its present largely artificial boundaries were demarcated by 1925.

2 In 1941, during the course of the Second World War, Syria was occupied by the British and Free French.

In 1946 the French granted independence, and the Syrian Republic became a founder member of the Arab League.

In 1958 Syria merged with Egypt to form the United Arab Republic, but in 1961 seceded to become independent as the Syrian Arab Republic.

Government

1.120

1 Syria is a republic governed by a President assisted by a Cabinet of ministers. The President is elected for seven years by universal suffrage and has wide powers, including the right to appoint ministers.

Population

1.121

1 In 2005 the population of Syria was estimated to be 19 million. Arabs form about 90% of the population, Kurds, Armenians, Circassians and Turks the remainder.

Languages

1.122

1 Arabic is the official language of the country, spoken by 80% of the population, while 6% speak Kurdish, 3% Armenian and 2% other languages. English is widely understood, and French is spoken by some.

Religions

1.123

1 Muslims form about 86% of the population, and Christians about 13%.

Physical features

1.124

1 Physically Syria consists of three areas from W to E: the coast, the mountains, and the Syrian Desert.

The coastal area stretches N to S for only about 110 miles between Turkey and Lebanon and varies in width from about 2 miles in the N to 12 miles in the S. The coastal area's numerous springs and underground water supplies make intense cultivation possible year-round and this region is the most densely settled part of the country.

2 The mountain area comprises two ranges running parallel to the coast: the Jabal al Nuşayrīyah, average elevation 600 to 900 m, in the N, and the Jebel esh Sharqi, or Anti-Lebanon Range, average elevation 1800 to 2100 m, in the S. Mount Hermon, in the S with an elevation of 2814 m, is Syria's highest point.

Asi Nehri (5.324), or Orontes River, the principal river of the mountainous region, flows in a N direction through the Ghāb Depression, a 40 mile wide rift valley between the two mountain ranges. The undulating plains of the Syrian Desert occupy the rest of the country.

3 The Euphrates River, traversing E Syria from NW to SE, is the country's most important water source and its only navigable river.

Industry and trade

1.125

1 The agricultural sector generates 30% of gross domestic product but over half of Syria's export earnings come from crude petroleum. Sodium chloride and bitumen deposits are worked, and there is an abundance of good calcareous building stone and basalt. Phosphate and gypsum are also produced. There are indications of lead, copper, antimony, nickel, chrome and other minerals being widely distributed.

The more important industries include cement, fuel oils, fertilizers, cotton yarn, vegetable oil, textiles, electrical goods, carpets and cigarettes.

2 Agriculture, formerly the main industry, has been replaced by manufacturing and mining. The principal crops are wheat, sugar beet, fruits, maize and barley. Sheep, goats, cattle, asses and chickens are reared.

The principal exports are petroleum and petroleum products, vegetables, fruit and cotton. Considerable revenue is received from oil pipelines which cross Syrian territory.

The main imports are machinery and transport equipment, foodstuffs, iron and steel, chemicals, and textile yarn.

LEBANON

General description

1.126

1 Lebanon, known to the Lebanese as Loubane, has an area of about 4036 square miles. It is bounded N and E by Syria, S by Israel, and W by Mediterranean Sea.

Beyrouth (Beirut) (33°54′N 35°31′E) (7.154) is the capital of the country.

National limits

1.127

1 Lebanon claims territorial waters of 12 miles. For further details, see *Annual Notice to Mariners No 12.*

History

1.128

1 In ancient geography much of Lebanon was Phoenicia. The ports of Arvad, now known as Jazīrat Arwād (7.96), Jebaïl, previously known as Byblus (7.128), Saïda (Sidon) (7.189) and Tyr, or Sour (7.211), were centres of trade and culture; at times they were independent city states, at other times they were absorbed into the Egyptian, Assyrian, Persian, Macedonian, and Roman empires. After the Romans the country was ruled in turn by Arabs, Crusaders, Mameluks, and Turks.

2 At the end of the First World War (1914–1918) Lebanon was occupied by Allied forces, and in 1923 it came under French mandate from the League of Nations.

In 1941, during the course of the Second World War (1939–1945), the country was occupied by British and Free French forces and proclaimed an independent state.

Since independence Lebanon's history has been defined largely by its presidents. The terms of the first two presidents ended in political turmoil, and in 1958, during the last months of President Chamoun's term, an insurrection broke out. In response to an appeal by the Lebanese Government, US forces were sent in to restore peace.

3 In 1975 a full scale civil conflict broke out partly because of the large number of Palestinian refugees in the country and the presence of Palestinian commandos. Frequent clashes between the Israelis and the commandos endangered civilians in the S of Lebanon and unsettled the country. In 1976 an Arab Deterrent Force, composed largely of Syrian troops moved in at the Lebanese Governments request and most fighting ended soon after.

4 In 1978, after a series of clashes between Israeli forces and Palestinian guerillas in Lebanon, Israeli forces crossed into Lebanon. Under pressure from the United Nations Israel withdrew, but in June 1982 Israel again invaded

Lebanon to engage the forces of the Palestine Liberation Organisation. In August 1982 the Palestine Liberation Organisation withdrew its forces from Lebanon. In 1985 Israel withdrew most of its forces from Lebanon, apart from a small residual force and an Israeli supported militia, stationed in a buffer zone in S Lebanon. This residual force was withdrawn in 2000.

Government

1.129

1 Lebanon is a parlimentary republic, consisting of a President at its head and an elected National Assembly. The president serves for nine years. The National Assembly has 128 deputies evenly divided between Christians and Moslems.

Population

1.130

1 In 2005 the population of Lebanon was estimated to be 3·58 million. The majority are Arabs, with some Moslems and Christians.

Languages

1.131

1 Arabic is the official language. English and French are widely spoken in official and commercial circles.

Physical features

1.132

1 Lebanon is a mountainous country, about half lying at elevations of more than 900 m. Bekaa, a fertile valley, lies between two mountain ranges paralleling the coast: Jebel Liban (7.124), or Lebanon Range, on the W and Jebel esh Sharqi, or Anti-Lebanon Range, on the E. The W slopes of Jebel Liban are not generally steep, and form the most productive part of the country.

Industry and trade

1.133

1 Lebanon is essentially an agricultural country. The forests of the past have been denuded by exploitation and the unrestricted grazing of goats. The main crops are tomatoes, sugar beet, potatoes, grapes, citrus fruits, apples, olives and bananas. Goats, sheep, cattle, pigs, and poultry are raised.

Manufacturing industry is small but growing. It includes food and drink, textiles, tobacco, foundries, cement, bricks, petroleum and chemicals. Oil refineries are situated at Trâblous (Tripoli) and Saïda (Sidon).

2 The main exports are agricultural products, chemicals, machinery and transport equipment, precious metal jewellery and gold. The main imports are machinery and transport equipment, manufactured goods, foodstuffs, chemicals and petroleum.

ISRAEL

General description

1.134

1 Israel, known to the Israelis as Yisra'el, is bounded N by Lebanon, NE by Syria, E by Jordan, SW by Egypt, and W by Mediterranean Sea. In 1998 the area of the country, including the Golan Heights and E Jerusalem, had an area of 21 946 sq km.

2 Jerusalem (31°46′N 35°13′E) was proclaimed capital of the country in 1950, but it is not recognized as such by most countries which maintain their embassies in Tel Aviv (32°05′N 34°46′E).

National limits

1.135

1 Israel claims territorial waters of 12 miles, reducing to 3 miles off Gaza. For further details see *Annual Notice to Mariners No 12.*

History

1.136

1 Palestine, the name given by the Romans to the area now known as Israel, has a long history of occupation by foreign powers. Egyptians, Babylonians, Persians, Greeks, Romans, Arabs, Crusaders and Turks all, through the centuries, conquered the country and were, in turn, defeated by their successors. In 1922 the country became a British mandate under the League of Nations.

2 The centuries-old desire of the Jews to return to what they regard as their homeland led to the formation of the Zionist movement at the end of the nineteenth century. Jewish immigration grew between the First and Second World Wars, and greatly increased after the end of the Second World War in 1945.

3 On 14th May, 1948 the state of Israel came into being with the declaration of independence of a Jewish National Assembly. The Arab states, not recognizing the declaration, invaded the country the following day and the Israeli War of Independence ensued. Following armistice negotiations in the first half of 1949, boundary lines were established but these were not acknowledged by the Arab states.

In 1967, and again in 1973, further fighting broke out between Israel and the neighbouring Arab states. At the conclusion of the fighting and subsequent disengagements Israel remained in occupation of the West Bank and the Gaza Strip.

4 In 1978, after a series of clashes between Israeli forces and Palestinian guerillas in Lebanon, Israeli forces crossed into Lebanon. Under pressure from the United Nations Israel withdrew, but in June 1982 Israel again invaded Lebanon to engage the forces of the Palestine Liberation Organisation. In August 1982 the Palestine Liberation Organisation withdrew its forces from Lebanon. In 1985 Israel withdrew most of its forces from Lebanon.

In 1979 Egypt signed a peace treaty with Israel and in 1993 an Israeli-Palestine agreement was signed providing for limited Palestinian self-rule in the Gaza Strip and Jericho. In 2005 Israel withdrew from the Gaza Strip (Occupied Palestinian Territory).

Government

1.137

1 Israel is a parliamentary democracy with a President as head of state and a Prime Minister as head of government. The parliament, known as the Knesset, has a single chamber of 120 members elected by universal suffrage.

Population

1.138

1 In 2005 the population of Israel was estimated to be 6·99 million.

Languages

1.139

1 The official languages of the country are Hebrew and Arabic.

Physical features

1.140

1 Israel consists of a coastal plain backed by ranges of mountains which on their E sides descend to the rift valley of River Jordan and Dead Sea, and Negev Desert in the S. The mountains attain elevations of more than 1000 m. Dead Sea, 396 m below sea level, is the lowest point on Earth.

Industry and trade

1.141

1 Services account for about 82% of GDP, industry 16% and agriculture 2%. In addition to mixed farming, poultry raising, citriculture and vineyards are the main agricultural activities.

A wide range of products is manufactured, processed or finished, including chemicals, metal products, textiles, tyres, diamonds, paper, plastics, leather goods, glass and ceramics, building materials, precision instruments, tobacco, foodstuffs and electrical goods.

2 Potash, bromine and other salt deposits, as well as natural gas, are exploited in the Dead Sea area. A number of oil wells are in operation.

The main exportable commodities are: citrus fruit and by-products, fruit juices, flowers, wines and liquor, sweets, polished diamonds, chemicals, tyres, textiles, metal products, machinery, electronic and transportation equipment.

3 The chief imports were machinery and apparatus, diamonds, chemicals and related products, petroleum and road vehicles.

PRINCIPAL PORTS, HARBOURS AND ANCHORAGES

1.142

Place and position	*Remarks*
Libya	
Az Zāwiyah Oil (Zawia) Terminal (2.49) (32°48′N 12°42′E)	Oil terminal
Ţarābulus (Tripoli) (2.59) (32°54′N 13°11′E)	Commercial port and naval base
Al Khums (Homs, Khoms) (2.102) (32°41′N 14°15′E)	Commercial port
Qaşr Aḩmad (2.120) (32°22′N 15°13′E)	Commercial port
As Sidrah (Es Sider) Oil Terminal (2.156) (30°38′N 18°21′E)	Oil terminal
Ra's Lānūf (2.174) (30°31′N 18°35′E)	Oil terminal
Marsá al Burayqah (El Bréga) (2.206) (30°25′N 19°35′E)	Oil terminal
Az Zuwaytīnah (Ez Zueitina) Oil Terminal (2.236) (30°51′N 20°03′E)	Oil terminal
Banghāzī (2.272) (32°07′N 20°03′E)	Commercial port
Ţubruq (Tòbruch, Tobruk) (2.343) (32°04′N 24°00′E)	Commercial port and oil terminal
Egypt	
Mersa Maţrûḩ (3.30) (31°22′N 27°14′E)	Small commercial port
El ‘Alamein Oil Terminal (3.63) (30°56′N 28°50′E)	Oil terminal
Sidi Kerir Oil Terminal (3.70) (31°03′N 29°40′E)	Oil terminal
Mīnā’ Al Iskandarīyah (Alexandria) (3.83) (31°09′N 29°47′E)	Large commercial port and naval base
El Ma‘dîya (3.152) (31°16′N 30°09′E)	Ammonia port
Idku LNG Port (3.156) (31°21′N 30°19′E)	LNG port
Mînâ’ Dumyâţ (Damietta Port) (3.181) (31°29′N 31°45′E)	Commercial port
Port Said (Bûr Sa‘îd) (3.205) (31°16′N 32°19′E)	Commercial port
Greece	
Nísos Kríti	
Órmos Kaloí Liménes (4.51) (34°56′N 24°48′E)	Bunkering station
Nísos Ródos	
Ródos (36°27′N 28°14′E) (See *Mediterranean Pilot Volume IV*)	Small commercial port
Turkey	
South coast	
Marmaris (5.19) (36°51′N 28°16′E)	Small harbour with secure anchorage
Karaağaç Limanı (5.29) (36°50′N 28°25′E)	Sheltered anchorage
Fethiye Limanı (5.61) (36°38′N 29°06′E)	Small commercial port
Antalya (5.130) (36°53′N 30°42′E)	Commercial port
Mersin (5.197) (36°48′N 34°38′E)	Commercial port
İskenderun Körfezi - N terminals (5.246) (36°52′N 36°02′E)	Oil and gas terminals and fertilizer factory pier
İsdemir (5.272) (36°44′N 36°11′E)	Commercial port
İskenderun (5.293) (36°36′N 36°11′E)	Commercial port
Cyprus	
South coast	
Limassol (6.40) (34°40′N 33°02′E)	Commercial port
Larnaca (6.90) (34°55′N 33°38′E)	Commercial port
East coast	
Famagusta (6.132) (35°07′N 33°56′E)	Commercial port

Place and position	*Remarks*
North coast	
Kyrenia (6.200) (35°20′N 33°19′E)	Ferry port
Syria	
Al Lādhiqīyah (Lattaquié) (7.14) (35°31′N 35°46′E)	Commercial port
Bāniyās (Banias) Oil Terminal (7.43) (35°13′N 35°57′E)	Oil terminal
Ţarţūs (Tartous) (7.67) (34°54′N 35°53′E)	Commercial port and oil terminal
Jazīrat Arwād (7.96) (34°51′N 35°51′E)	Sheltered anchorage with depths from 9 to 11 m
Lebanon	
Trâblous (Tripoli) (7.97) (34°26′N 35°51′E)	Commercial port and oil terminal
Joûnié (Juniye) (7.143) (33°59′N 35°38′E)	Small commercial and fishing port
Beyrouth (Beirut) (7.154) (33°54′N 35°31′E)	Commercial port
Zahrānī (Sidon) Terminal (7.196) (33°30′N 35°20′E)	Oil terminal
Sour (Tyr) (7.211) (33°16′N 35°12′E)	Small harbour and secure anchorage for small vessels
Israel	
Ḫefa (Haifa) (7.223) (32°50′N 34°59′E)	Commercial port with oil terminal and shipyard
Ḫadera (7.263) (32°28′N 34°53′E)	Coal and oil terminal for power station
Ashdod (7.282) (31°50′N 34°38′E)	Commercial port and oil terminal
Ashqelon Oil Terminal (7.315) (31°40′N 34°33′E)	Oil terminal

PORT SERVICES — SUMMARY

Docking facilities

1.143

1 Ports with docking facilities, and where available the size of the largest vessel that can be accommodated, are as follows:

2 **Libya**

Ţarābulus. (Tripoli) One floating dock; maximum capacity 5000 tons (2.83).

Banghāzī. Floating dock; details unknown (2.294).

3 **Egypt**

Mīnā' Al Iskandarīyah. (Alexandria) Two drydocks, one floating dock and shiplifts; maximum capacity 85 000 dwt (3.121).

Port Said (Bûr Sa'îd). Three floating docks; maximum capacity 25 000 tonnes (3.247).

4 **Cyprus**

Limassol. One floating dock; maximum capacity 1360 tonnes (6.67).

Famagusta. Two slipways; maximum capacity 2500 dwt; one small floating dock (6.155).

5 **Lebanon**

Trâblous (Tripoli). Slipway; maximum capacity 1000 tonnes (7.118).

Beyrouth (Beirut). Slipway; maximum capacity 1000 tons (7.175).

6 **Israel**

Ḫefa. (Haifa) Floating dock; maximum capacity 21 075 tonnes (7.248).

Other facilities

Compass adjustment

1.144

1 Limassol (6.67).
Famagusta (6.155).
Beyrouth (Beirut) (7.175).

Ship Sanitation Certificates

1.145

1 Ship Sanitation Control and Exemption Certificates:

Mīnā' Al Iskandarīyah (Alexandria) (3.122).
Ad Dukhaylah (El Dikheila) (3.122).
Mînâ' Dumyâţ (Damietta Port) (3.202).
Port Said (Bûr Sa'îd) (3.248).
Marmaris (5.23).
Fethiye (5.66).
Alanya (5.166).
Antalya (5.151).
Mersin (5.222).
İskenderun (5.316).

1.146

1 Ship Sanitation Control Exemption Certificates only:

Ţarţūs (Tartous) (7.88).

NATURAL CONDITIONS

MARITIME TOPOGRAPHY

Seabed

1.147

1 Over most of the area covered by this volume the continental shelf is narrow, being less than 5 miles in width in many parts, and generally up to about 40 miles elsewhere; beyond it the bottom falls away more or less steeply to depths of over 1000 m. In these deeper parts the seabed is by no means featureless, but over most of the area its composition does not appear to vary greatly. The predominant constituents are muds of various colours, black, grey, blue and yellow, and globigerina ooze; volcanic ash, from eruptions N of the area, also occurs.

2 On the continental shelf, and on the island shelf around Cyprus, sand and rock are the most common constituents. The N African coast generally shows a progression from inshore sand and rock, through sand, to the deep water mud; in the vicinity of River Nile delta, mud and muddy sand occur extensively. Gravelly sand also occurs locally off the coasts.

Certain major structural features, or physiographic provinces of the seabed, are worthy of mention.

3 Mediterranean Ridge is the largest feature. It extends W from Cyprus, then passes midway between Kríti and the coast of Libya before trending NW towards the peninsula of Italy, thus being about 1000 miles in length but only between 40 and 100 miles in width. It varies in depth between approximately 1300 m and 2500 m, and exhibits rugged topography, the seabed materials apparently being comparatively hard. There are several knolls on the ridge, particularly in its central part.

4 Apart from Mediterranean Ridge, the following smaller features of positive relief are worthy of mention: Eratosthenes Tablemount, about 50 miles S of the S extremity of Cyprus; Anaximander Ridge, about 40 miles S of the coast of Turkey in longitude 30°E; and a seamount (33°40′N 19°50′E) at the SE end of Sicilia Basin. On all these upstanding features, rock may outcrop on the seabed.

5 Mediterranean Ridge is flanked on its S side by a narrow elongated basin. To the E of longitude 26°E, this basin has a central depth of over 3000 m, and is known as Herodotus Basin; however, the basin also extends W, parallel with Mediterranean Ridge, to merge into Sicilia Basin, a broader depression of similar depth, SE of Sicily.

6 Between Sicilia Basin and the head of Gulf of Sirte is a generally unremarkable continental rise. However, between the latter and the extensive continental shelf off Tunisia, there is a distinctive province consisting of a continental borderland, on which lie a number of banks, some of which probably remain to be discovered.

7 Nile Fan, a major feature between Herodotus Basin and the coast of Egypt, is a sloping depositional area which extends seaward for many miles off River Nile delta.

Volcanic activity

1.148

1 No active volcanoes exist within the area covered by this volume.

Seismic activity

1.149

1 The area is seismically active, and moderately liable to earthquake shocks.

CURRENTS AND TIDAL STREAMS

Currents

General information

1.150

1 The Mediterranean receives, from the rivers that flow into it, only about a third of the amount of water that it loses by evaporation. Still greater losses of water result from a sub-surface outflow through Strait of Gibraltar which removes from Mediterranean Sea to Atlantic Ocean the highly saline and dense water resulting from evaporation. These losses are compensated by a strong surface inflow from the Atlantic to the Mediterranean. A similar, though much less pronounced, pattern prevails between Mediterranean Sea and Black Sea; water flows out of the Mediterranean through Çanakkale Boğazı (40°01′N 26°10′E) at depth, and into it at the surface.

Currents diagrams

1.151

1 In the current diagrams 1.151.1 and 1.151.2, arrows indicating the Predominate Direction, Average Rate and Constancy are shown, which are defined as follows:

Predominant Direction. The mean direction within a continuous 90° sector containing the highest proportion of observations from all sectors.

2 **Average Rate** as indicated by the figures in the diagrams. It is emphasised that rates above and below those shown may be experienced.

Constancy, as indicated by the thickness of the arrows, is a measure of persistence; eg low constancy implies marked variability in rate and, particularly, the direction of the current.

Currents in the central southern and eastern parts of the Mediterranean

1.152

1 From the Sicilian Channel the current sets ESE towards the Nile Delta but with two clockwise flows off the coast of NW Libya in the Gulfs of Gabès and Sirte.

The ESE flow off the coast of NE Libya is joined by a S flow to the W and E of Kríti and with a clockwise flow centred near Cyprus. The data in the NE Mediterranean is relatively sparse but to the S of Cyprus the current is predominately E with great variability.

2 To the S of Kríti the currents are very variable but with a slightly higher frequency of W setting currents, particularly in spring, and with a rate rarely exceeding 1 kn. Further S, the currents turn to the S then ESE near 34°N in summer.

Effects of strong winds

1.153

1 After prolonged periods of strong winds from a constant direction, a wind-drift current may be generated, the rate of which varies according to the wind speed and direction. These wind-drift currents may reduce or enhance the main underlying current.

Tidal streams

1.154

1 Tidal streams in the area covered by this volume are, for the most part, weak and inappreciable.

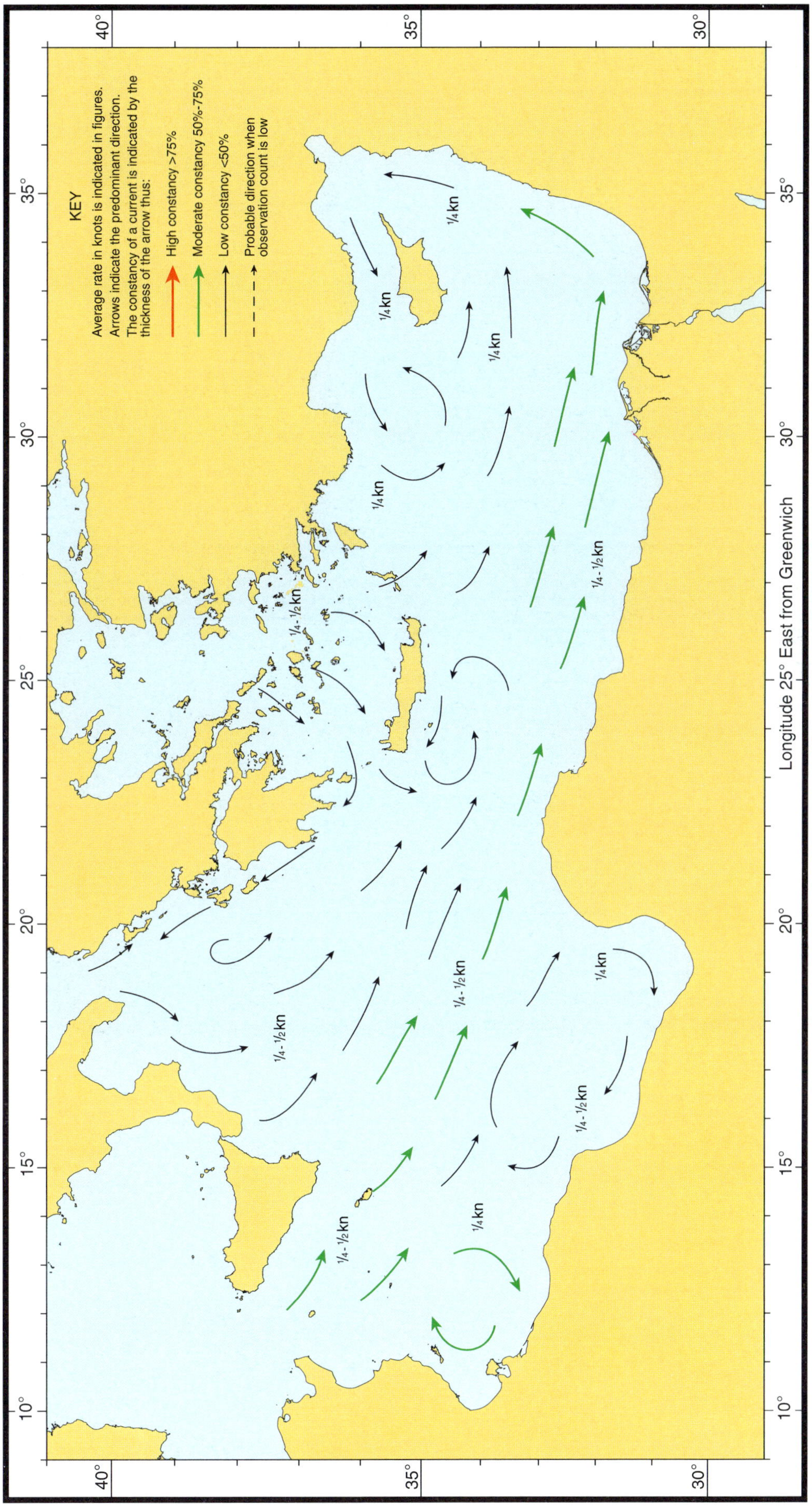

Predominant surface currents DECEMBER to FEBRUARY (1.151.1)

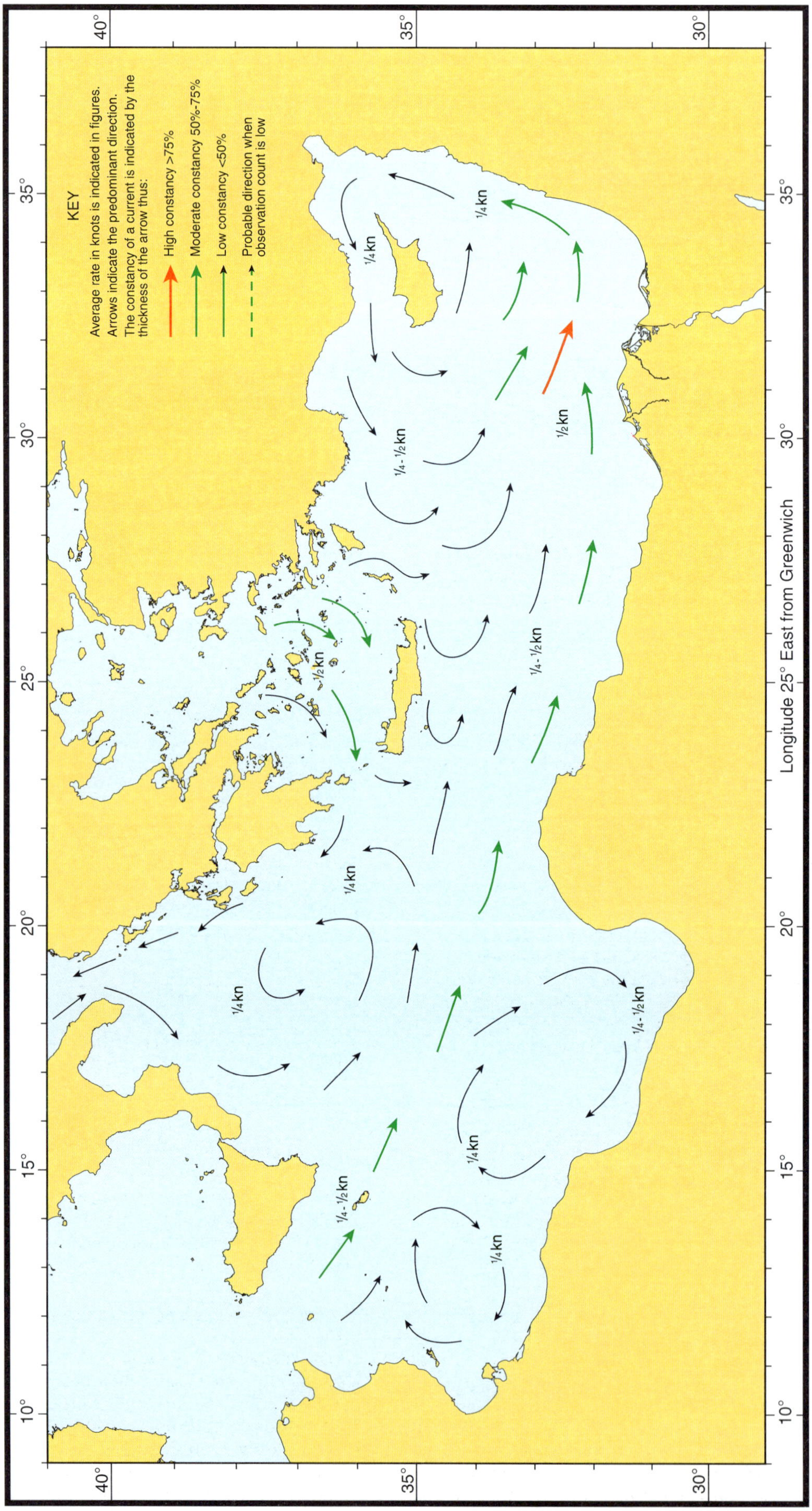

Predominant surface currents JUNE to AUGUST (1.151.2)

SEA LEVEL AND TIDES

Sea level

1.155

1 In the central Mediterranean, during February, March and April, the mean sea level may fall as much as 0·4 m below normal.

2 Marrobbio, consisting of waves or surges either isolated or in series, may raise the sea level by 0·6 or 0·9 m, during undisturbed weather. The period of the waves varies from 10 to 26 minutes. They are most marked on the SW coast of Sicily, but they occur all along the W, S and E coasts and round the islands between Sicily and the coast of Africa, and also on the latter coast in the vicinity of Ţarābulus (Tripoli). They are known as Marrobbio, Marrubbio and Carrobbio in different localities of Sicily. Their origin is probably associated with fairly abrupt changes in the meteorological conditions prevailing in the Mediterranean as a whole, and not necessarily with changes in local conditions.

Tides

1.156

1 Tides in the area are mainly semi-diurnal. The range is very small, in most places 0·3 m or less and nowhere exceeding 0·5 m. Consequently, meteorological conditions may often have more effect on sea level than the tide.

SEA AND SWELL

General information

1.157

1 For definitions of sea and swell, and the terminology used in describing their characteristics, see *The Mariner's Handbook*.

Sea conditions

1.158

1 Sea waves are generated locally by the wind and can be very variable in direction. Strong winds often give rise to short, steep and very rough seas and are a well known feature in the N of the region. Within the area covered by this volume, moderate to rough seas are encountered, in winter, on about 35% to 40% of occasions in the W and N of the area and 25% to 30% in the SE. In the summer the percentage decreases to around 20% to 25% of occasions around Kríti and about 10% to 15% elsewhere.

Swell conditions

1.159

1 Diagrams 1.159.1 and 1.159.2 give swell roses for January and July. Swells of over 4 m are relatively rare although the frequency of moderate to heavy swells, in winter, is relatively high along the N African coast in association with strong to gale force NW winds. Moderate swells over the Mediterranean are usually associated with prolonged spells of W winds, and SW winds along the coasts of Cyprus and Turkey.

SEA WATER CHARACTERISTICS

Salinity and density

Salinity

1.160

1 For an explanation of salinity as applied to seawater, and units used, see *The Mariner's Handbook*. Salinity in Mediterranean Sea remains fairly stable throughout the year, with isohalines running N to S across the area covered by this volume. The values do, however, vary across the area. Values vary between 37·50 and 37·75 in the W up to 39·00 and 39·25 in the E. In the E the isohalines curve under Cyprus and run E to W with small areas of slightly lower salinity off the coasts of Turkey in the extreme NE and Egypt in the extreme SE.

Density

1.161

1 For an explanation of density as applied to seawater, and units used, see *The Mariner's Handbook*. The density of seawater in the area covered by this volume varies both seasonally and across the area. In winter in the S Aegean the density value is 1·02900 g/cm^3. The isopicnals curve around this and values decrease to 1·02800 g/cm^3 in the S and W of the area. In summer when density tends to be at its lowest, values decrease to 1·02675 g/cm^3 in the NE, 1·02525 g/cm^3 in the SE, and 1·02550 g/cm^3 in the W. The isopicnals curve around these extremes running E to W in the centre of the area.

Sea surface temperature

General information

1.162

1 Diagrams 1.162.1 and 1.162.2 show the mean sea surface temperature for February and August. The sea surface temperature usually falls to a minimum in February with a mean of around 14°C in the W and about 17°C in the E. Maximum sea temperatures are normally reached in August with a mean of around 26°C in the W and 29°C in the NE.

Variability

1.163

1 Between May and December the sea surface temperatures may differ by around 2° to 3°C, and from January to April by about 1° to 2°C. In shallow coastal waters and inlets the variations can be higher. The difference between the mean air temperature and the mean sea surface temperature seldom varies by more than 1°C.

CLIMATE AND WEATHER

General information

1.164

1 The following information on climate and weather should be read in conjunction with the information contained in *The Mariner's Handbook* which explains in more detail many aspects of meteorology and climatology of importance to the mariner.

2 Weather reports and forecasts covering the area are regularly broadcast in the various languages of the region and also in English; for details see *Admiralty List of Radio Signals Volume 3 (1)*.

General conditions

1.165

1 The summers are prolonged, hot and dry, with very little cloud. Winters are usually short and mild and with most of the rain, which is low along the African coast, falling during this period. Even in winter, bad weather is usually of a relatively short duration, with clear or sunny spells between any periods of unsettled weather. Gales are most frequent between December and March, particularly in the N and extreme SW of the area.

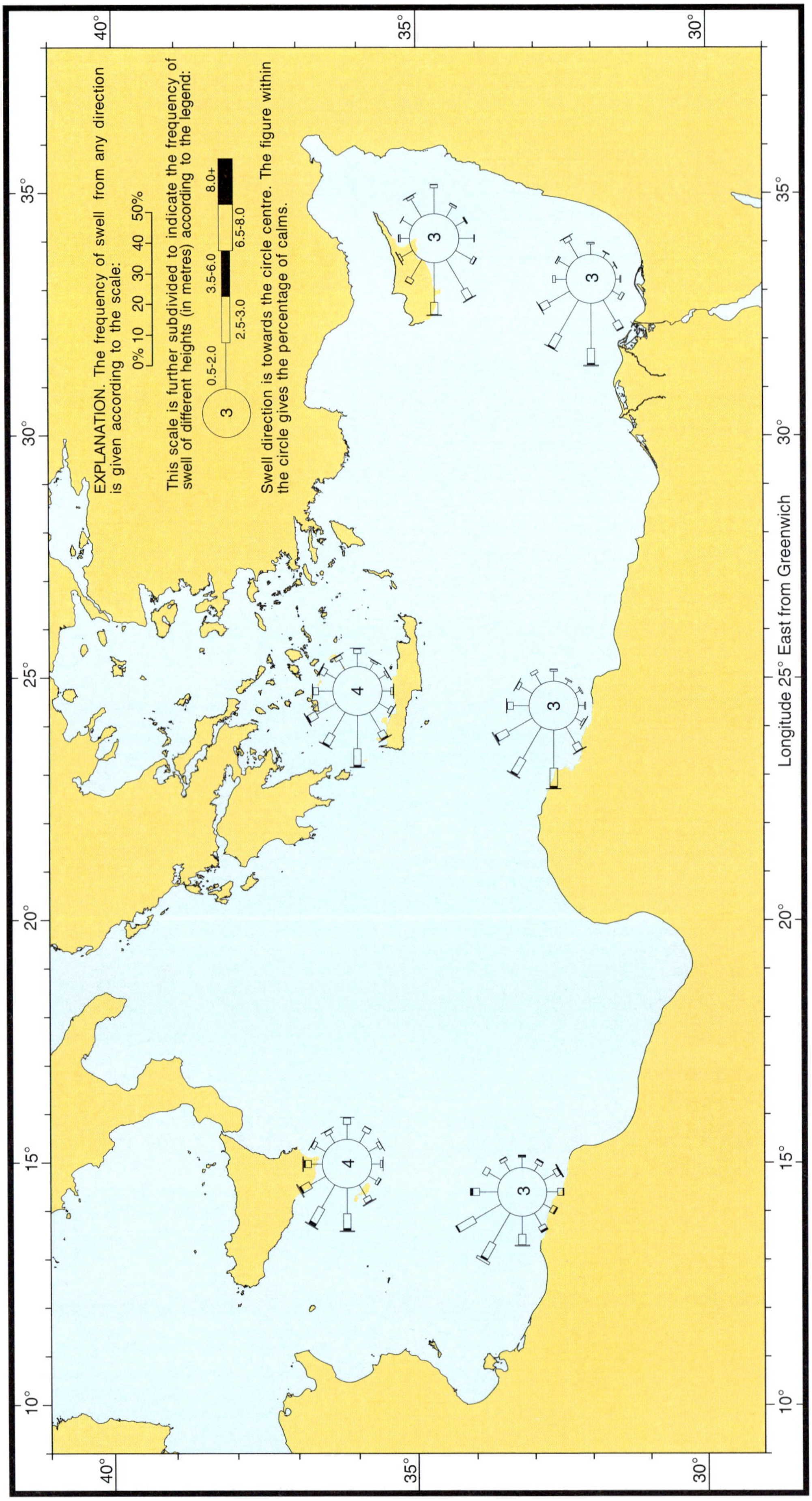

Swell distribution JANUARY (1.159.1)

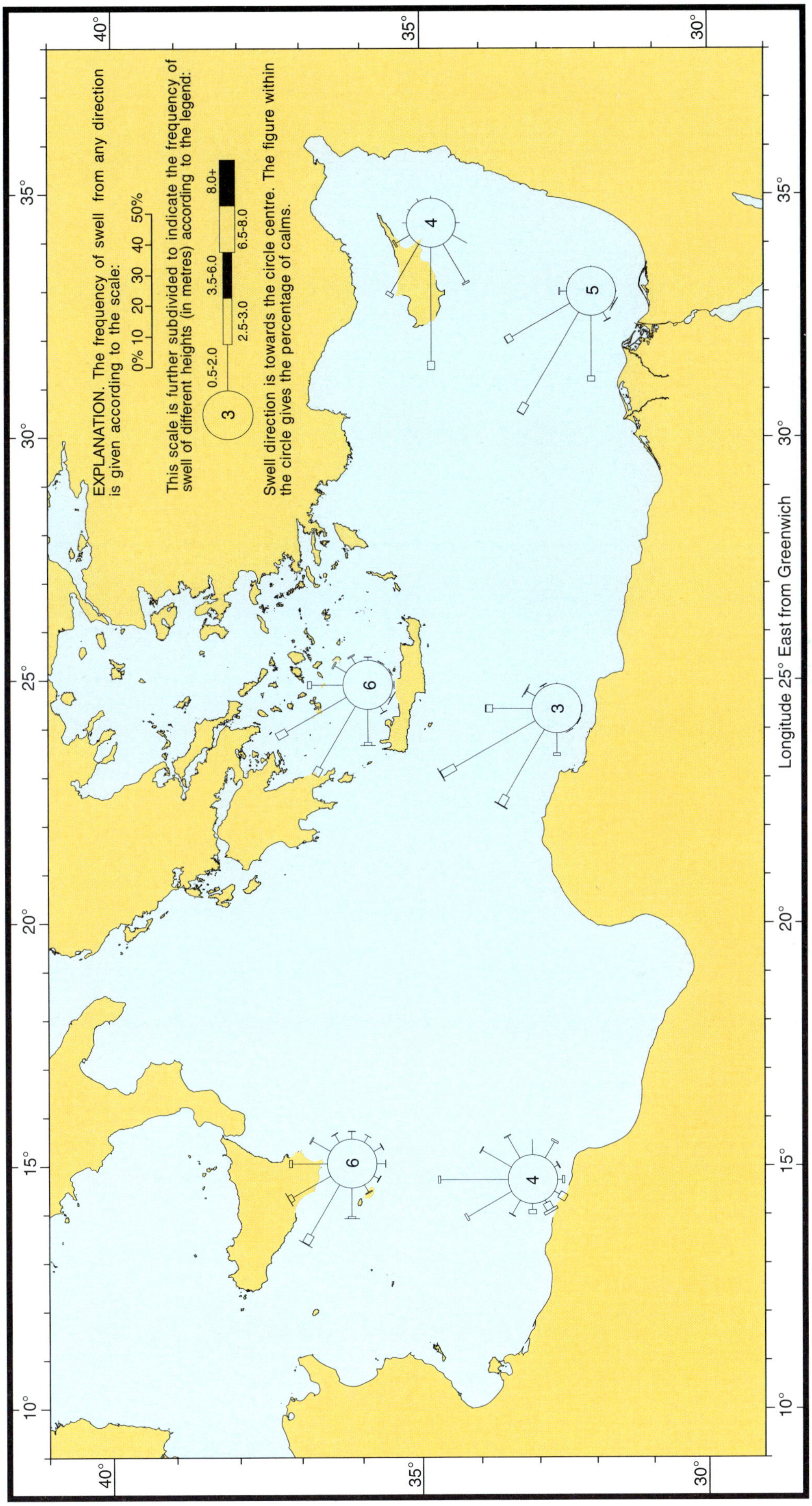

Swell distribution JULY (1.159.2)

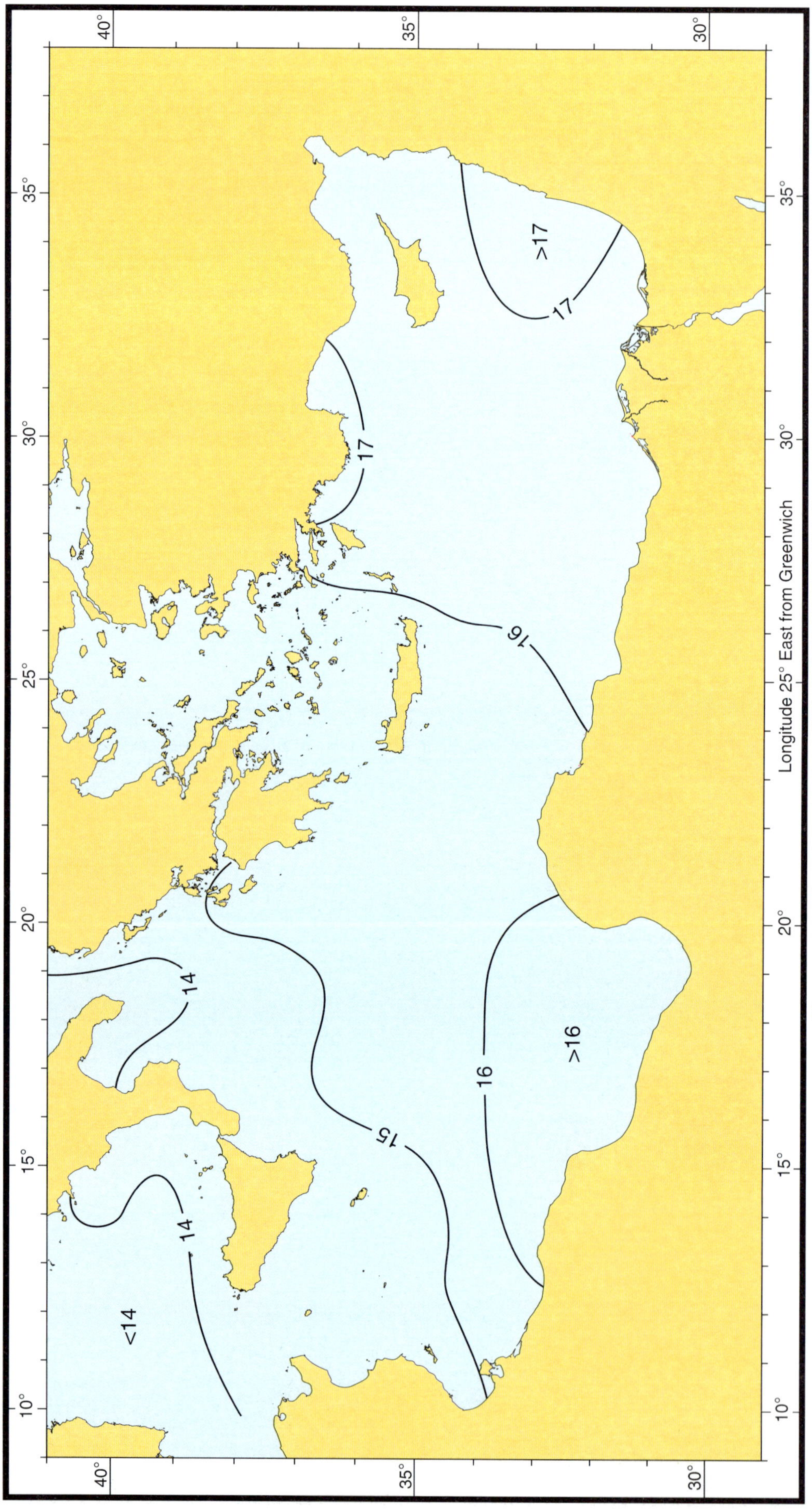

Mean sea surface temperature (°C) FEBRUARY (1.162.1)

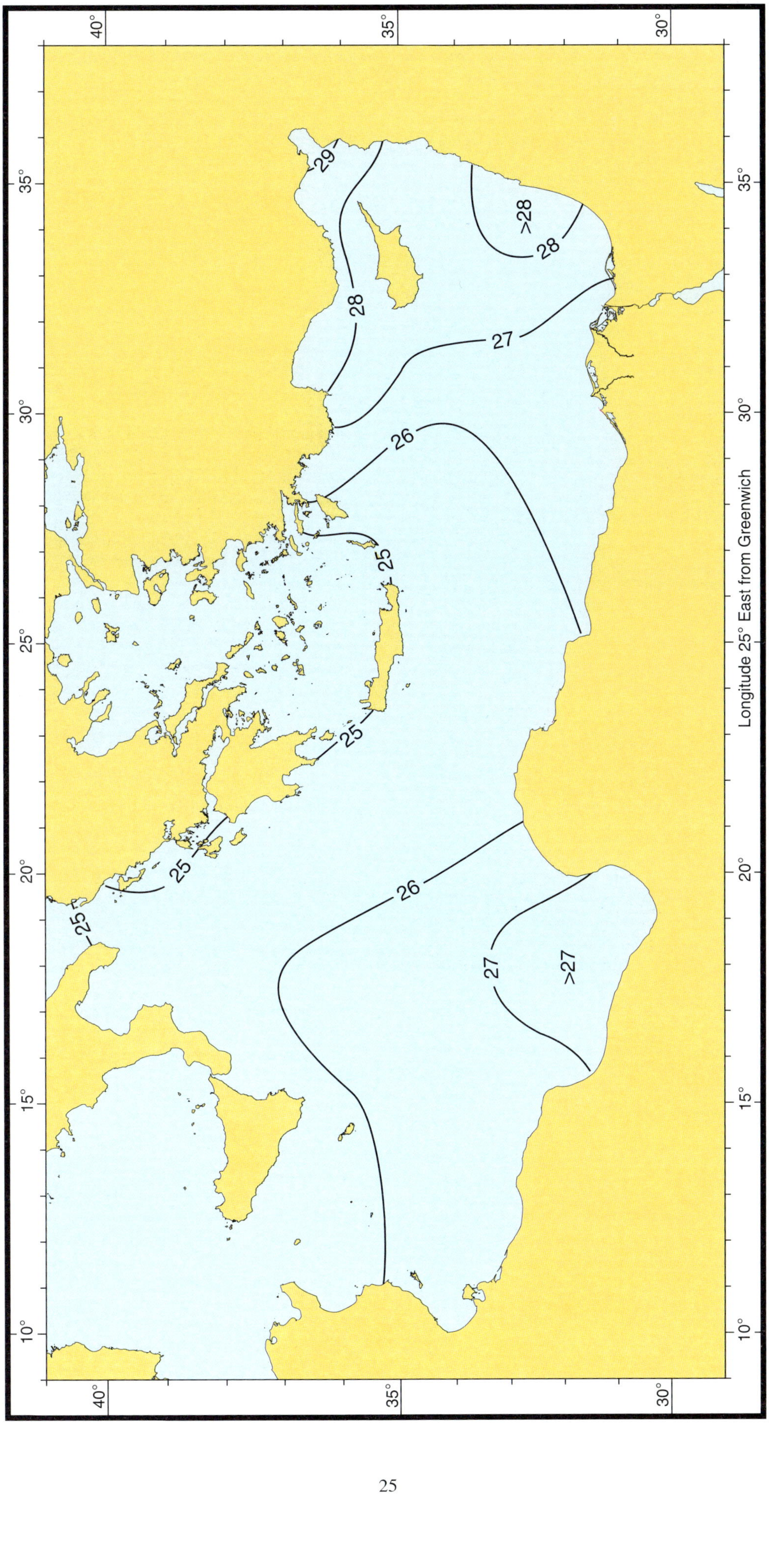

Mean sea surface temperature (°C) AUGUST (1.162.2)

2 Visibility is generally good but thick haze can be a problem at times near coasts, particularly in the S of the area. Radiation fog may sometimes occur in coastal areas on calm clear nights in winter but generally clears by mid-morning.

3 Outbreaks of cold N to NW winds are most frequent in winter and often give rise to squally thunderstorms, strong to gale force winds and rough seas.

Pressure

Average distribution

1.166

1 The average pressure distribution at mean sea level in January and July is shown on the accompanying diagrams 1.166.1 and 1.166.2 and illustrate the typical mean pressure fields for winter and summer.

2 From November to March pressure is usually lower over Mediterranean Sea than over the surrounding land masses. By June the W extension of the Asian anticyclone to Europe has normally collapsed and, together with an E extension of the Azores anticyclone and low pressure over Syria, results in a N to NW airflow over the central and E parts of the Mediterranean.

Variability

1.167

1 It is emphasised that the diagrams 1.166.1 and 1.166.2 depict average pressure distributions of very variable pressure patterns and which may change markedly from day to day. This is particularly so in the cool season when mobile depressions, troughs and ridges of high pressure cross the region.

2 There is a small diurnal variation of pressure of about 0·5 hPa (mb). Maxima occur at about 1000 and 2200 local time and minima at around 0400 and 1600. Mobile depressions or ridges of high pressure often obscure the diurnal variation.

Anticyclones

1.168

1 The Azores anticyclone, the sub-tropical high-pressure belt centred over the Atlantic, has a major controlling influence on the climate of the Mediterranean. In the cool season, when the anticyclone is centred at its most S latitude, a ridge often extends E to Spain or NW Africa. Atlantic depressions moving E along the N flank of the anticyclone often move into the Mediterranean from NW to bring disturbed weather to the region.

2 In late spring and summer the Azores anticyclone usually intensifies, with a ridge frequently extending ENE towards the Alps. This ridge effectively forces Atlantic depressions further N, away from the Mediterranean, and normally results in settled summer conditions.

3 In winter a W extension of the Asian anticyclone to central Europe is common and may be the source of very cold air, which often invades the Mediterranean during this period. When a ridge of high pressure extends to the Balkans or central Europe, it can induce strong N to NE winds over the Aegean.

Depressions

1.169

1 Diagram 1.169 shows the tracks of typical depressions affecting the Mediterranean. Most of them move E or SE whilst those that form over Algeria tend to move between E and NE. Depressions are most frequent in winter with many of them forming over the NW part of the Mediterranean and over Algeria. They tend to be slow moving, taking around three days to transit the area between Sicily and Cyprus, and frequently become almost stationary near Cyprus for a few days.

2 In spring, E-moving depressions become less frequent and less intense, and follow tracks slightly more to the S as the season advances. Depressions originating over Algeria and Tunisia are most frequent in spring and autumn. Those that track just S of the N coasts of Libya and Egypt can give rise to the worst Sciroccos (1.173). Depressions are relatively rare in summer; however, a tropical cyclone was reported for the first time in summer to the SW of Greece in the mid–1990s.

Fronts

1.170

1 Most depressions have associated frontal systems; see *The Mariner's Handbook* for a full description of warm fronts, cold fronts, and occlusions. Warm fronts are mostly weak in the E Mediterranean and rarely accompanied by prolonged periods of precipitation. Cold fronts in contrast are often very active with a sudden veer of wind, usually to the N or NW. They often give rise to violent conditions with severe squalls and thunderstorms, and along the N African coast may result in sand-storms.

2 Secondary cold fronts or troughs of low pressure may follow behind the main cold front as further outbreaks of cold air arrive, and with the original front dissipating. The secondary cold fronts may have little cloud or precipitation associated with them because of the dryness of the continental air, but bring with them a sudden increase in wind strength. Thus the mariner should be particularly wary, as there may be little warning of the approach of a secondary front other than a small preliminary fall of the barometer and a temporary decrease in wind.

Winds

Average distribution

1.171

1 Wind roses showing the frequency of wind distribution for several areas in January and July are given in diagrams 1.171.1 and 1.171.2.

Open sea

1.172

1 In winter winds are very variable particularly in the NE of the area, but with W to NW winds being most frequent, and in spring NW winds become increasingly predominant. During the summer months the winds are predominantly between N and WNW but mainly W in the extreme NE of the area.

Special regional winds

1.173

1 Diagram 1.173 shows the names of the main regional winds of the Mediterranean which are described as follows:

Etesian (Greece) or **Meltemi** (Turkey) are the predominant N to NW winds affecting the Aegean and SW Turkey in summer. The mean strength of these winds is force 3 to 4, occasionally increasing to force 5 or 6.

2 **Scirocco**, or **Siroco**, is the name given to the hot, dry wind from N Africa. It is called **Ghibli** in Libya and **Khamsin** between Cyrenaica and Lebanon. The word Khamsin is the Arabic word for fifty as these winds are said to be most frequent in the fifty days following the Coptic Easter. Scirocco winds from the S may result in temperatures of 40°C or more and with a humidity as low as 3% along the N African coast. Winds may reach force 6

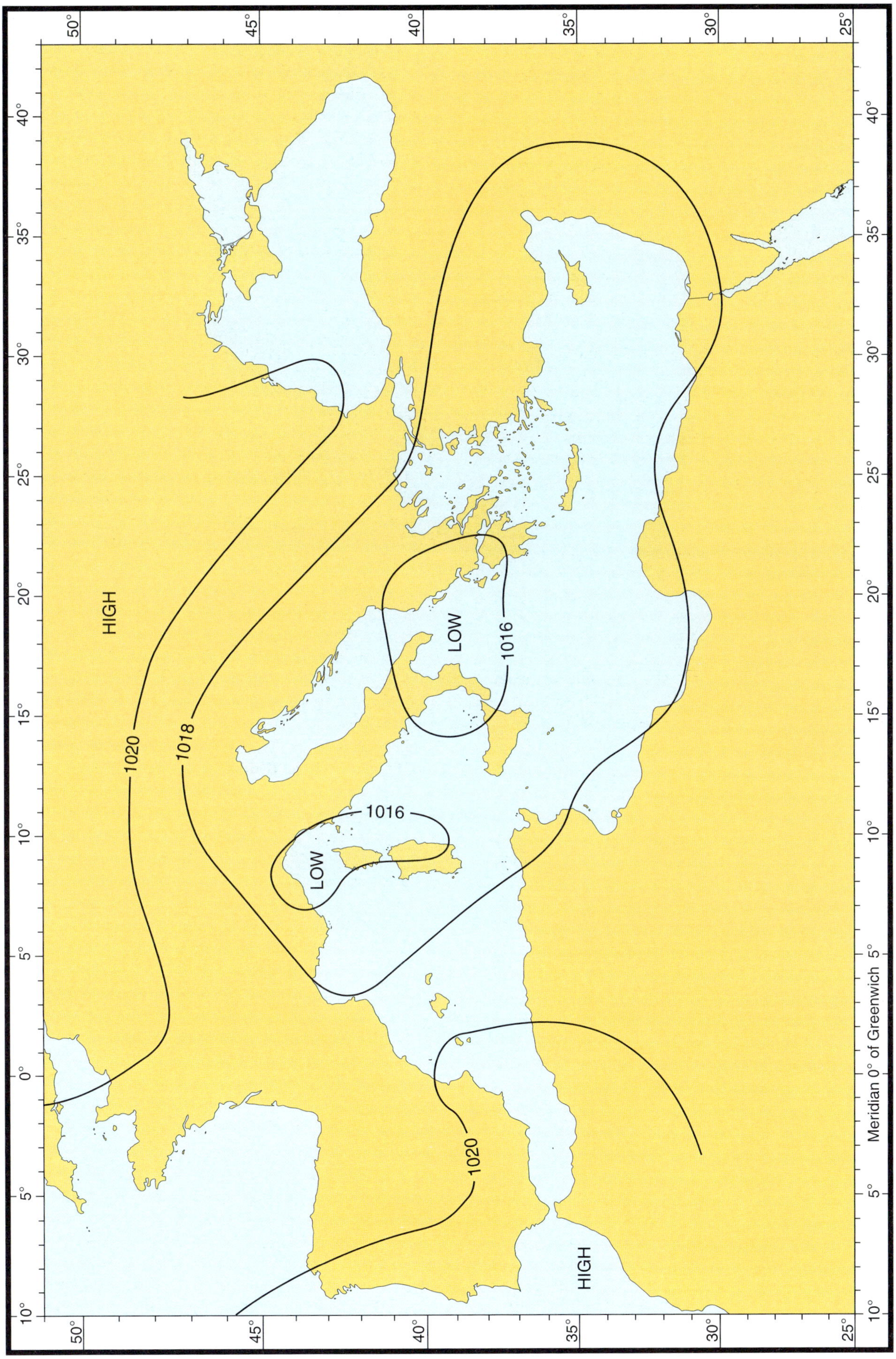

Mean barometric pressure (hPa) JANUARY (1.166.1)

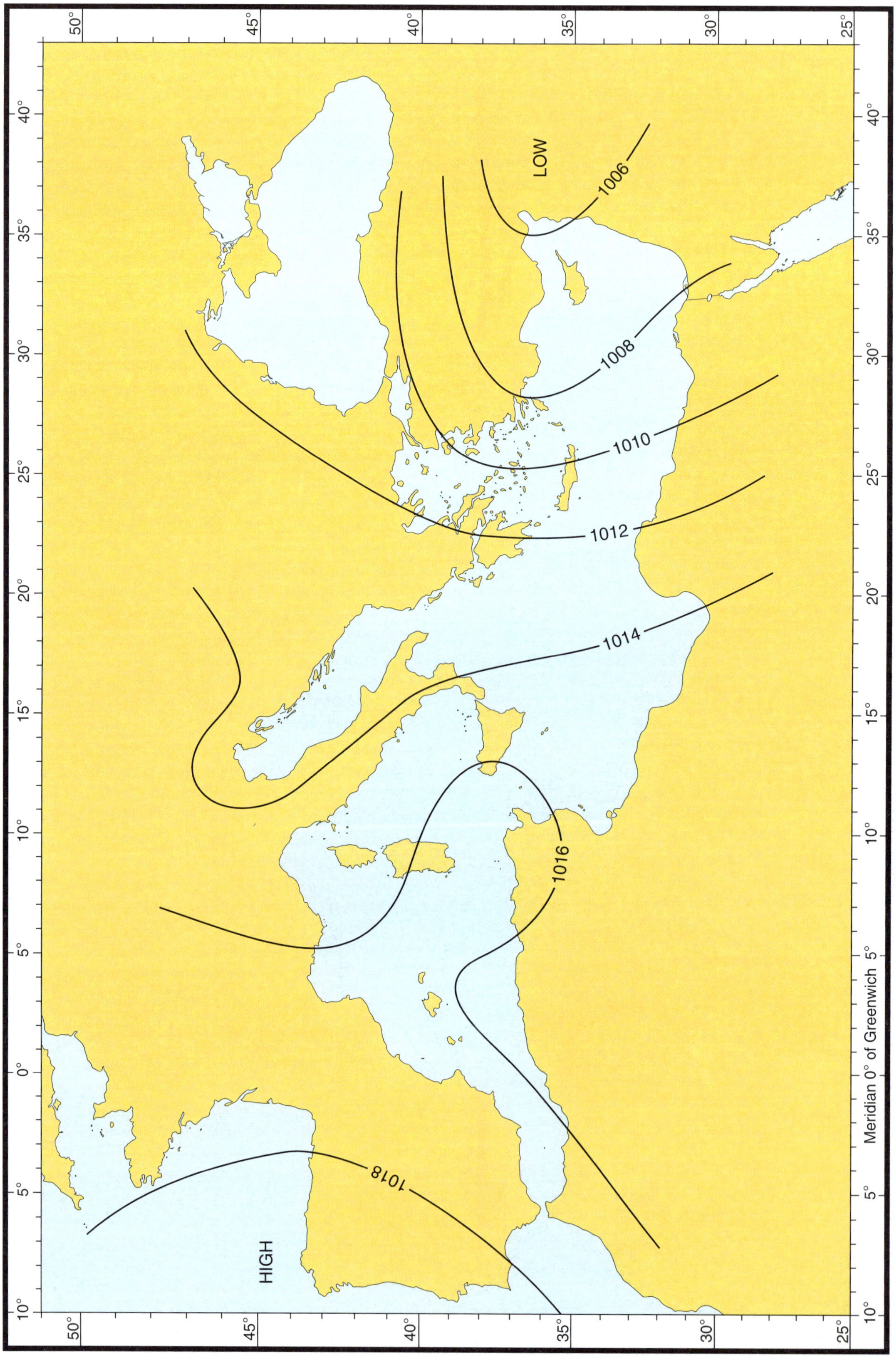

Mean barometric pressure (hPa) JULY (1.166.2)

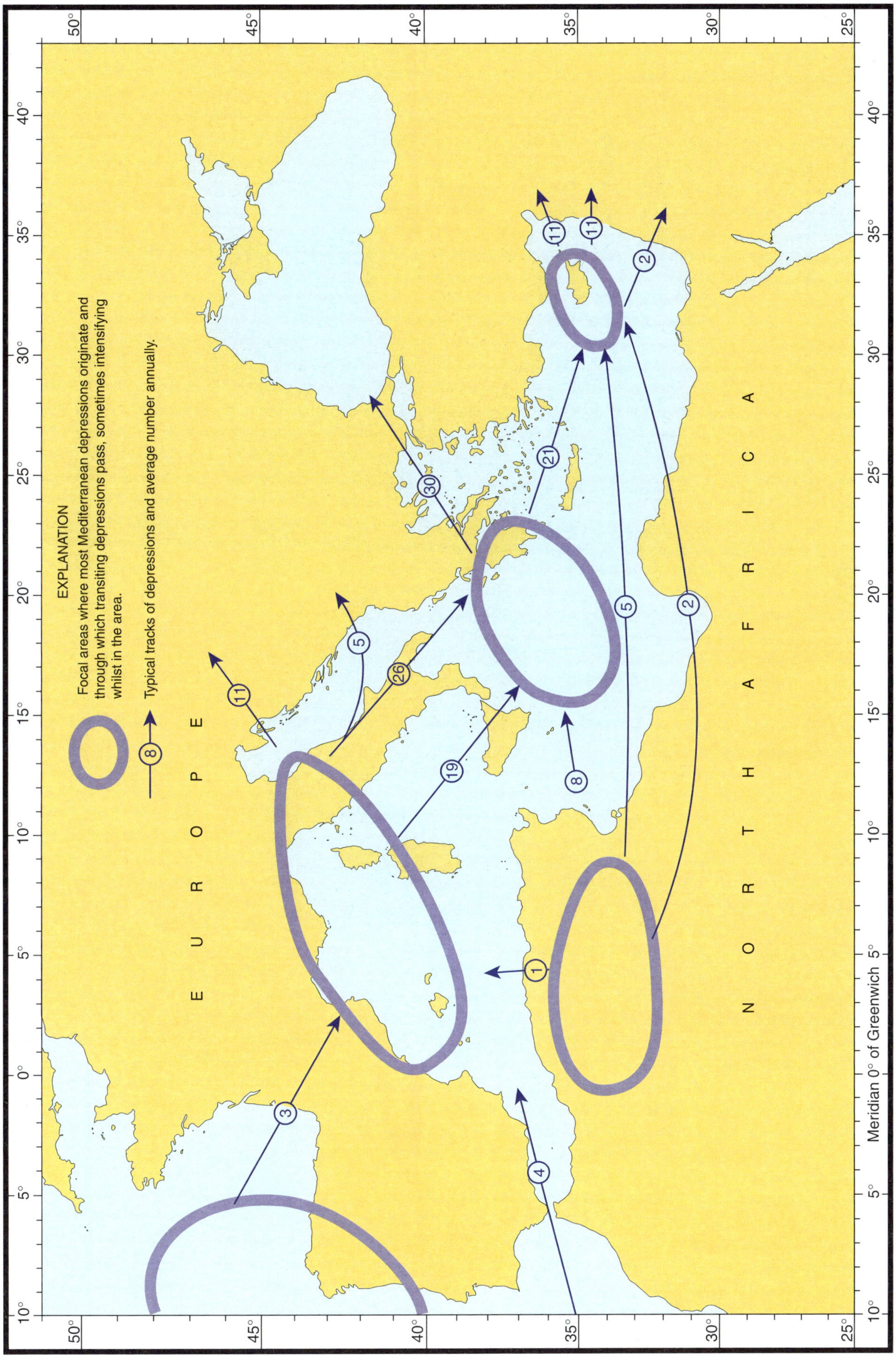

Mediterranean Sea - Typical tracks of depressions (1.169)

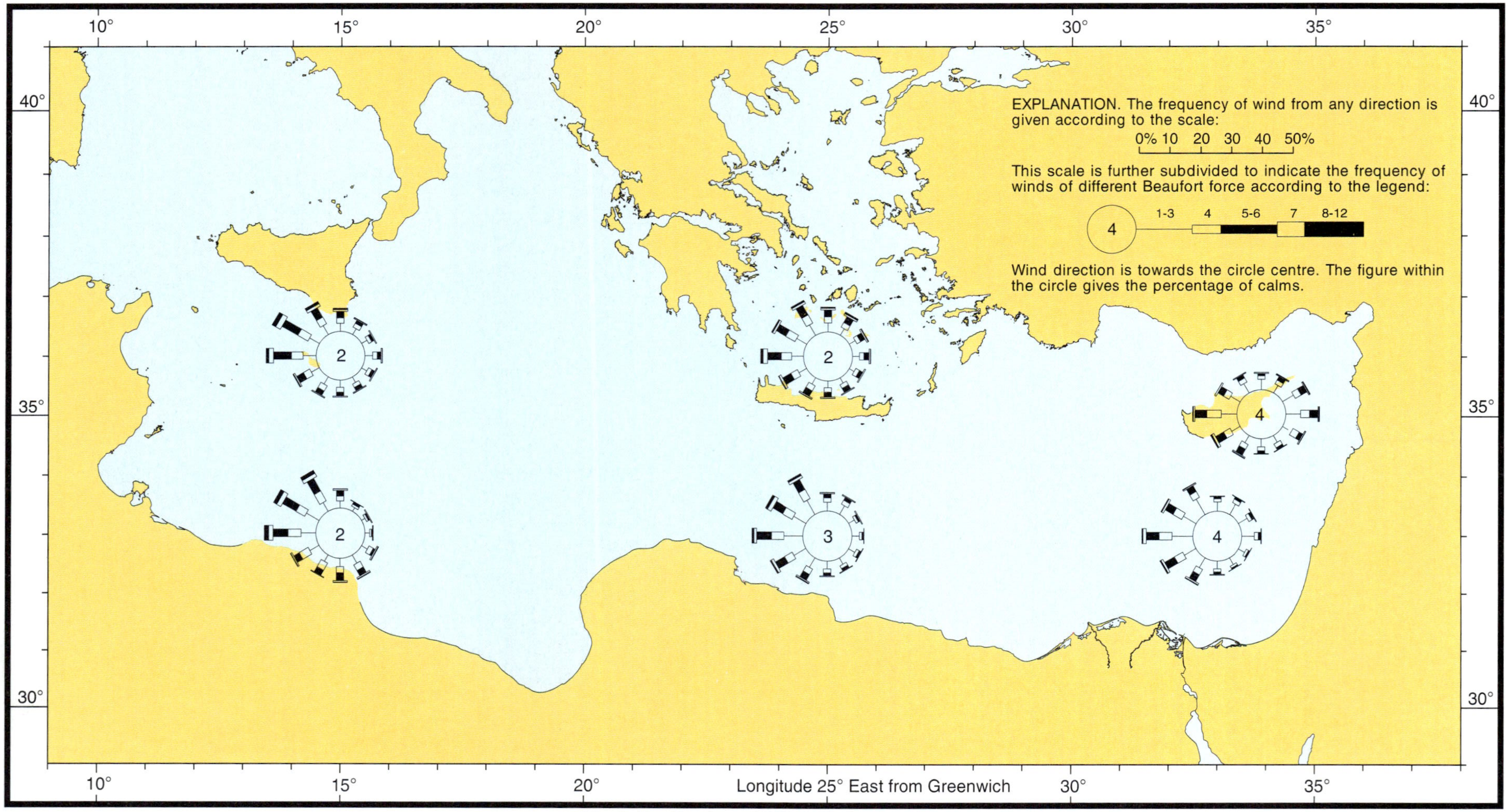

Wind distribution JANUARY (1.171.1)

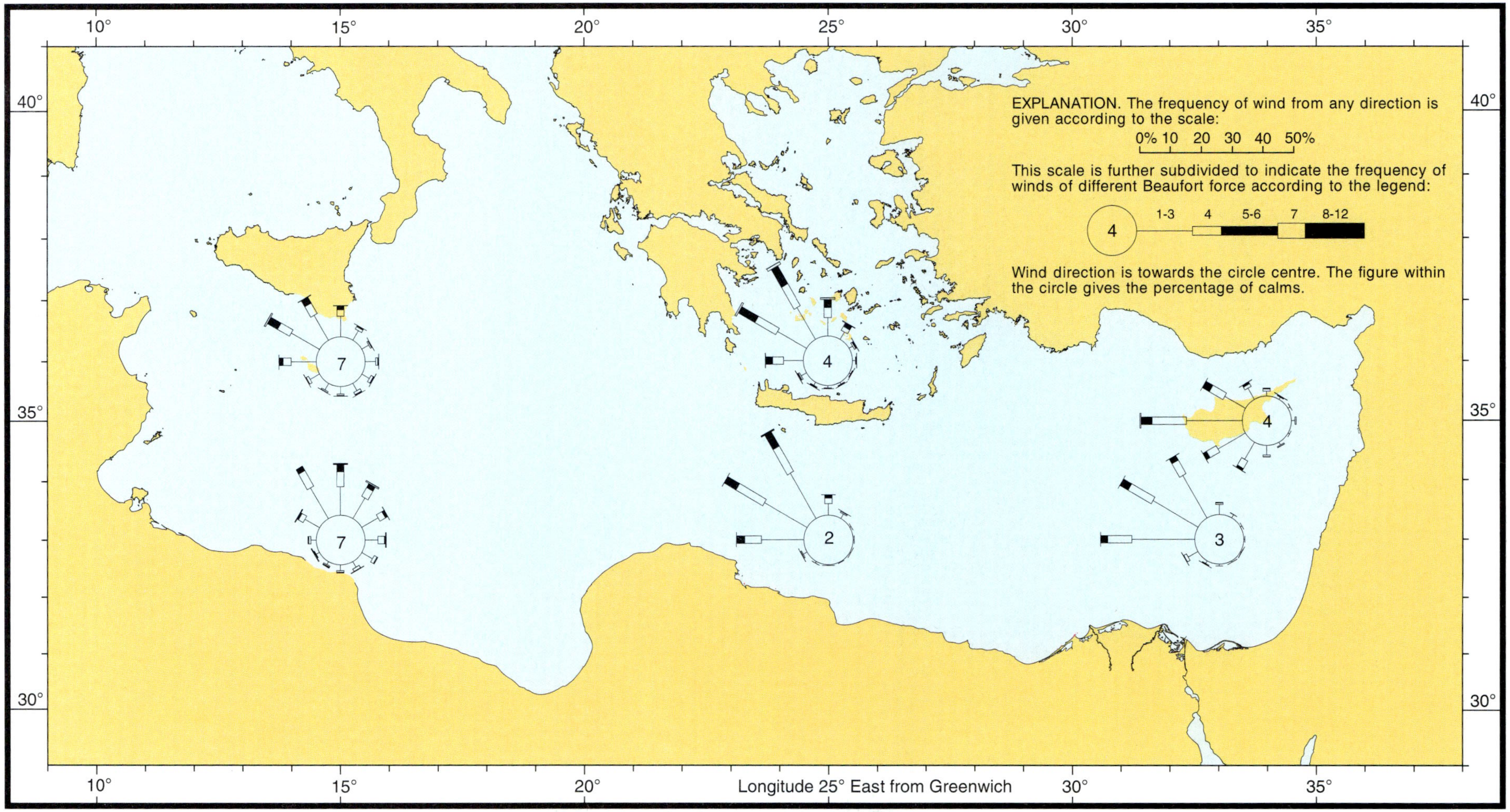

Wind distribution JULY (1.171.2)

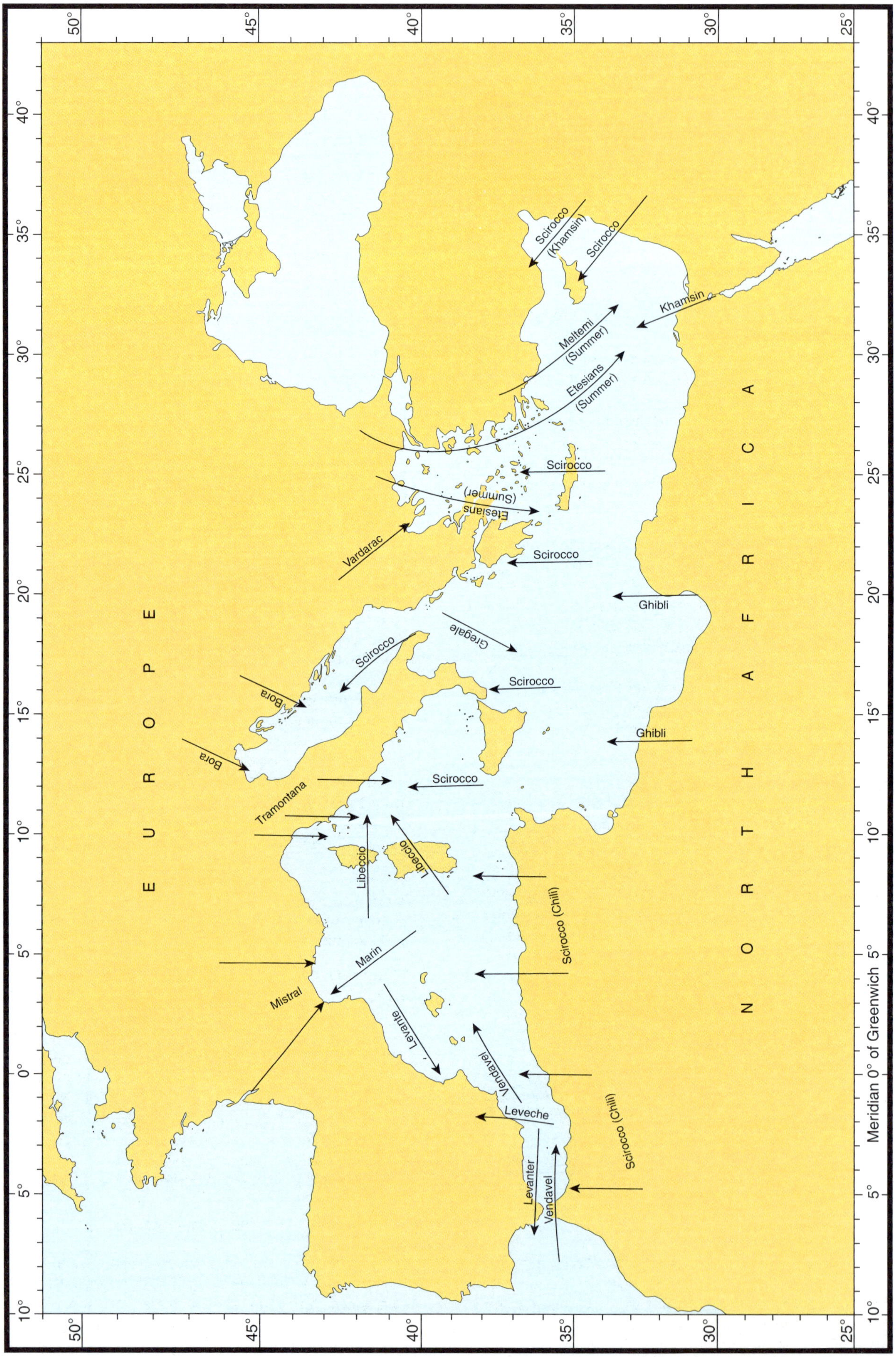

Mediterranean Sea - Main regional winds (1.173)

to 8 and with the associated sand-storms reduce the visibility to below fog limits. These winds may extend several hundred miles to the N, but become increasingly humid as they move N, and can give rise to coastal fog with high temperatures along the S coasts in the N. The most severe Scirocco/Khamsin usually occur in late spring and autumn but seldom in summer, but the frequency varies greatly from year to year. On average they occur on around two to three occasions in April and May but infrequently at other times, and may last from between 1-2 hours and three days. The conditions most likely to give rise to the S winds of the Khamsin are high pressure to the E of Nile Delta and an E-moving depression crossing the E Mediterranean or Cyrenaica. As the depression moves E of Egypt, the wind veers to the NW, the dust soon clears, the temperatures rapidly fall and the humidity rises sharply.

3 **Gharra** is a line of squally thunderstorms moving in from the NE to affect Gulf of Sirte, usually between January and March.

Cold Scirocco is a dry E wind occurring in winter over Israel, which may give rise to abnormally low temperatures.

Coastal winds

1.174

1 Winds in coastal areas are largely controlled by the general pressure distribution of the area but, within about 20 miles of the coast, topography and land or sea breezes often produce significant local modifications to both the wind strength and direction. Straits, headlands and steep sided valleys may cause local increases in wind strength due to funnelling.

2 For further information see the wind summaries in the climate information (1.184) for a number of coastal stations within the area covered by this volume.

Land and sea breezes

1.175

1 Land and sea breezes are very pronounced in all parts of the area in summer. Even in the cool season they are sometimes apparent in fine settled weather, particularly in the S. In summer the sea breeze usually commences around 1000 on the N African coast and gradually freshens until mid-afternoon when it commonly reaches force 4 in many places. Elsewhere the sea breeze sets in a little later and reaches a maximum of about force 3 to 4. Thereafter it weakens and eventually ceases shortly after sunset. The direction is usually onshore in the morning but will often slowly veer during the day to blow almost parallel to the coastline.

2 The land breeze often begins to set-in in the late evening and reaches maximum strength in the early hours of the morning, fading around sunrise; it is normally lighter than the sea breeze. At other times the sea and land breezes may strengthen or weaken the prevailing wind.

Gales

1.176

1 Over the open waters, gales (force 7 and above) are rare in summer with a frequency of occurence of 1% or less, but around 3% along the coast of S Turkey. In January the frequency of occurrence of winds of force 7 and over is about 10% in the W and around Kríti, 7% in the NE, and 5% in the SE.

Cloud

1.177

1 In summer, prolonged spells of fine weather prevail over the whole of the open water with an average of about 1 okta of cloud. In general there is usually slightly more cloud on the coasts in E areas than over the open seas. See the climate information (1.184) for mean cloud amounts.

2 In winter months the average cloud amount is around 5 oktas in the N and 4 oktas in the S. Long periods of cloudy or overcast skies are uncommon, and there are good spells of fine weather, especially in the S.

3 In E coastal areas there is a tendency for the cloud to decrease in the afternoon in summer and marginally increase in all coastal areas in winter.

Precipitation

Rain

1.178

1 Rainfall is seasonal with nearly all of it falling between October and April, except for the NE where the wet season is slightly longer. On the N African coast most of the rain is associated with W or NW winds, but from the coast of Israel to the S coast of Turkey it is more usually associated with SW winds. Much of the rainfall is the result of cold fronts crossing the area; they are often accompanied by thunderstorms in winter. Rainfall is generally of short duration except for the NE of the area where depressions may become slow moving or stationary.

2 Along the N African coast the average rainfall varies between 50 and 300 mm, with some of the lowest values in the extreme SE of the area. The amount of rainfall at any one location is dependent upon its exposure to the prevailing winds and its elevation. Between June and the middle of September rain is rare along this coast.

3 Rainfall amounts are significantly higher along the coasts in the N and E of the area. Along the S coast of Turkey rainfall amounts vary from around 1000 mm in the W to 700 mm in the E; and in the E of the area from around 890 mm at Al Lādhiqīyah (Lattaquié), to 530 mm at Tel Aviv.

See climate information (1.184) for average rainfall.

Snow

1.179

1 Snow usually falls in winter in coastal areas above about 1200 m but rarely at sea level, even in the N of the area.

Thunderstorms

1.180

1 Thunderstorms occur throughout the region and are most frequent in the N in winter and rare across the whole of the area in summer. The annual frequency is between 2 and 10 along the N African coast, with the highest frequency in those areas exposed to the prevailing winds.

2 In the N and NE of the area thunderstorms may be accompanied by hail. The annual frequency of thunderstorms is around 30 to 35 and with nearly all of those occurring between October and early May.

Fog and visibility

1.181

1 Visibility over the open sea is usually good but with a few days of fog between April and August. Radiation fog sometimes forms in coastal areas towards sunrise but generally clears soon afterwards. Such fogs are more common in winter than in summer but are not particularly frequent.

2 During strong Scirocco conditions the visibility may be reduced by dust and sand-storms to fog limits in coastal areas in the S, and may be significantly reduced over the open sea to the N. Reduced visibility may be caused by industrial smoke and haze in some coastal areas in summer which may be carried out to sea overnight with offshore land breezes.

3 Mirages are a fairly frequent occurence in summer in coastal areas in the S and near Cyprus on calm summer mornings.

Air temperature

1.182

1 Over the open sea in January the mean air temperature is around 14°C in the N, 15°C in the SW, and 16°C in the extreme SE. In July the mean air temperature is around 25°C in the NW, 25° to 26°C in the S, and 27°C in the NE. The difference between the mean sea surface temperature and that of the overlying air is seldom more than 1° to 2°C. However, the air temperature may temporarily become 4°C lower than the sea surface temperature following the passage of a cold front in winter. Similarly, air temperature over open waters may become more than 5°C warmer than sea temperature when a Scirocco/Khamsin spreads N, and this difference may be maintained for two to three days.

2 In coastal areas the seasonal and diurnal variations of temperature are greater than over the open sea, although sea breezes have an important moderating influence which inhibit excessive afternoon temperatures in summer. The average daily maximum temperature in February is around 15°C in the N of the area and 18° to 19°C in the S; the average daily minimum is 6°C in the N and 9° to 10°C in the S. Frost is rare in the S but does occur on a few occasions in winter in Cyprus, Lebanon, Syria, and the coastal areas of Turkey.

3 In August the average daily maximum is around 32°C in the N and S; the average daily minimum is about 22°C, although slightly lower in the coastal areas in the E. In the S coastal areas the temperatures may reach 40°C or more on some occasions and 50°C slightly further inland, mainly in association with the S winds of a Scirocco.

For the mean and extreme temperatures for a number of coastal stations in the area see climate information (1.184).

Humidity

1.183

1 Humidity is inversely related to air temperature; thus high humidity is associated with low temperatures and vice versa. Maximum humidity normally occurs around dawn and the minimum in the early afternoon. Over the open sea the mean value of the humidity in January is around 71% near Malta and 67% in the E near Cyprus. In July the mean humidity is around 77% to 79% in the S 76% in the NW and NE, and 74% near the W coast of Kríti.

2 Very low humidity occurs along the coast from Libya to Syria with Scirocco and Khamsin winds. Over the sea the dry Scirocco winds are rapidly modified and the humidity increases with the distance from the coast. Hence very high humidity is associated with these Scirocco winds in the N and NW which have long sea tracks.

CLIMATE INFORMATION

1.184

1 The tables which follow give data for several coastal stations (diagram 1.184) that regularly undertake weather observations. Some of these stations have been resited and so the position given is relevant to the data provided.

These data are average conditions and refer to the specific location of the observing station, they may not be representative of the conditions elsewhere.

2 The following notes indicate ways in which conditions over the open sea may differ from those at the nearest reporting station for which a table is published:

Wind speed is nearly always greater over the sea than over the land, although funnelling in narrow inlets can result in an increase in wind strength.

Precipitation figures are usually fairly applicable to coastal waters, but become less applicable with increasing distance from the coast. Where there are high cliffs, or where a range of hills rises sharply behind the reporting station, then, with onshore winds, the station may record considerably more precipitation than would be experienced a few miles out to sea.

3 Temperatures over the sea are less variable than over the land. In winter, the temperature is usually higher over the sea, especially during the night. In summer, it is usually lower than over the land, especially in the day time.

Topography has a marked effect on local conditions. For further details see *The Mariner's Handbook.*

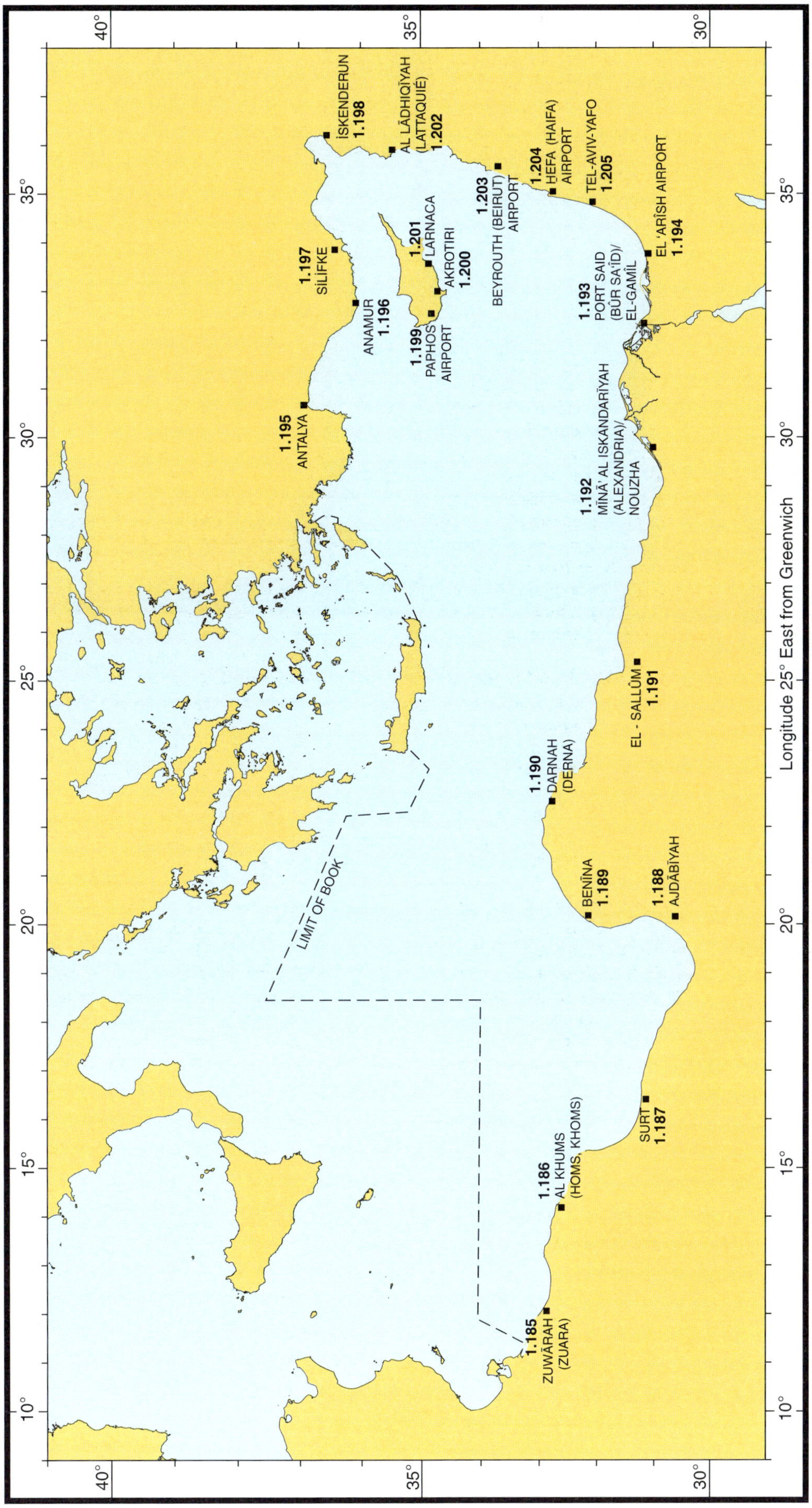

Location of climate stations (1.184)

1.185

WMO No 62007

ZUWĀRAH (ZUARA) (32° 55′ N, 12° 07′ E) Height above MSL - 3 m

Climatic Table compiled from 16 to 28 years observations, 1960 to 1998

Month	Average pressure at MSL	Temperatures				Average humidity		Average cloud cover		Precipitation		Wind distribution - Percentage of observations from																		Mean wind speed		Number of days with		
												0800									1400													
		Mean daily max.	Mean daily min.	Mean highest in each month	Mean lowest in each month	0500	1400	0500	1400	Average fall	No. of days with 2·5 mm or more	N	NE	E	SE	S	SW	W	NW	Calm	N	NE	E	SE	S	SW	W	NW	Calm	0800	1400	Gale	Fog	Thunder
	hPa	°C	°C	°C	°C	%	%	Oktas		mm																				Knots				
January	1021	18	9	24	4	78	64	3	4	26	4	4	2	6	4	9	37	33	3	3	14	8	6	3	5	14	32	14	5	8	10	1	1	1
February	1022	19	9	26	5	76	59	2	3	18	2	10	5	5	7	9	28	25	5	6	24	10	10	3	5	12	20	14	2	8	10	⊕	1	⊕
March	1017	20	11	30	6	80	65	2	3	12	1	15	9	11	6	9	20	19	5	7	29	23	11	3	4	5	12	12	2	9	11	1	1	⊕
April	1014	22	14	35	9	80	65	2	3	10	2	11	11	20	8	10	10	16	3	12	27	31	19	2	2	6	5	8	0	8	12	1	1	0
May	1014	24	17	39	13	82	70	2	3	6	1	15	13	26	5	10	8	8	3	12	27	34	25	2	2	3	3	4	⊕	8	11	1	1	⊕
June	1014	28	21	39	16	84	73	2	2	1	⊕	14	21	27	6	5	5	3	4	15	19	45	24	1	⊕	2	2	5	1	8	11	⊕	1	⊕
July	1015	30	23	39	20	86	72	1	1	⊕	0	10	17	22	6	5	9	7	2	23	20	48	24	1	1	1	2	3	⊕	6	10	⊕	⊕	0
August	1014	32	24	41	20	83	70	1	1	0	0	8	18	20	7	8	8	6	1	24	21	46	24	1	1	2	1	3	1	6	9	⊕	⊕	⊕
September	1015	31	23	40	18	80	66	1	2	6	1	9	13	16	12	12	13	8	1	16	21	35	31	2	2	3	3	3	0	7	10	⊕	⊕	1
October	1017	28	19	35	13	76	62	2	3	28	2	6	11	10	9	14	22	15	2	10	20	29	17	2	5	8	8	9	3	7	9	1	1	1
November	1017	24	13	31	7	74	58	2	4	43	3	8	6	3	4	10	37	22	5	5	18	7	8	3	7	17	25	10	4	8	9	⊕	1	1
December	1020	19	10	25	4	79	64	3	4	58	4	7	5	2	2	9	38	30	3	4	15	3	4	2	6	19	34	12	6	8	9	1	1	1
Means	1017	25	16	44*	2§	80	66	2	3	–	–	10	11	14	6	9	20	16	3	11	21	27	17	2	3	8	12	8	2	8	10	–	–	–
Totals	–	–	–	–	–	–	–	–	–	208	20	–	–	–	–	–	–	–	–	–	–	–	–	–	–	–	–	–	–	–	–	6	9	5
Extreme values	–	–	–	47†	-1‡	–	–	–	–	–	–	–	–	–	–	–	–	–	–	–	–	–	–	–	–	–	–	–	–	–	–	–	–	–
No. of years observations	16	16				16		16		28		16									16									16		16	16	16

* Mean of highest each year
§ Mean of lowest each year

† Highest recorded temperature
‡ Lowest recorded temperature

⊕ Rare
⊖ All observations

1.186

WMO No 62012

AL KHUMS (HOMS, KHOMS) (32° 39′ N, 14° 16′ E) Height above MSL - 22 m

Climatic Table compiled from 4 years observations, 1995 to 1998

Month	Average pressure at MSL	Temperatures				Average humidity		Average cloud cover		Precipitation		Wind distribution - Percentage of observations from																		Mean wind speed		Number of days with		
												0800									1400													
		Mean daily max.	Mean daily min.	Mean highest in each month	Mean lowest in each month	0300	1400	0300	1400	Average fall	No. of days with mm or more	N	NE	E	SE	S	SW	W	NW	Calm	N	NE	E	SE	S	SW	W	NW	Calm	0800	1400	Gale	Fog	Thunder
	hPa	°C	°C	°C	°C	%	%	Oktas		mm																				Knots				
January	1019	19	10	24	7	83	58	3	4			2	2	4	⊕	15	32	7	6	33	15	4	4	4	24	9	14	18	8	4	8	⊕	0	⊕
February	1022	19	9	25	5	85	60	2	3			10	2	2	2	7	22	12	5	36	23	16	⊕	2	3	8	15	30	3	5	10	1	⊕	2
March	1018	19	10	26	7	86	68	2	3			21	⊕	4	1	6	17	8	8	35	32	7	7	1	7	5	4	36	⊕	6	12	1	0	⊕
April	1015	22	13	31	8	85	59	2	3			13	5	10	5	10	11	2	7	37	24	16	24	5	8	4	1	19	⊕	5	12	1	⊕	⊕
May	1015	26	17	38	12	82	61	2	2			9	6	3	3	17	15	4	6	38	19	26	26	8	10	3	⊕	7	2	4	12	⊕	0	1
June	1015	30	21	42	15	77	57	2	2			11	5	2	7	9	15	3	11	36	31	9	29	8	8	4	1	9	⊕	5	11	0	0	⊕
July	1015	31	22	42	17	82	60	1	1			9	2	6	4	12	15	⊕	7	46	21	28	30	4	5	5	2	5	0	3	12	⊕	0	0
August	1015	32	23	40	20	84	58	1	1			6	5	6	1	14	10	2	5	53	21	22	36	10	6	2	⊕	2	0	2	11	⊕	0	0
September	1014	31	23	42	19	80	60	2	3			9	4	4	⊕	13	15	8	4	43	27	25	25	9	7	1	⊕	7	⊕	3	12	0	0	⊕
October	1017	27	19	34	14	79	54	2	4			4	⊕	5	2	10	27	14	2	36	22	25	13	8	3	8	3	16	2	4	10	0	⊕	2
November	1018	24	14	31	9	74	50	2	4			8	⊕	⊕	⊕	17	41	13	3	20	19	10	2	5	9	15	14	19	7	5	9	⊕	0	1
December	1018	20	11	26	6	74	52	3	4			2	⊕	⊕	1	6	46	14	5	27	11	4	3	6	9	19	25	21	4	4	9	⊕	0	1
Means	1017	25	16	_*	_§	81	58	2	3	–	–	9	2	4	2	11	22	7	6	37	22	16	17	6	8	7	7	15	2	4	11	–	–	–
Totals	–	–	–	–	–	–	–	–	–			–	–	–	–	–	–	–	–	–	–	–	–	–	–	–	–	–	–	–	–	3	⊕	7
Extreme values	–	–	–	_†	_‡	–	–	–	–	–	–	–	–	–	–	–	–	–	–	–	–	–	–	–	–	–	–	–	–	–	–	–	–	–
No. of years observations	4	4				4		4				4									4									4		4	4	4

* Mean of highest each year
§ Mean of lowest each year

† Highest recorded temperature
‡ Lowest recorded temperature

⊕ Rare
⊖ All observations

1.187

WMO No 62019

SURT (31° 13′ N, 16° 35′ E) Height above MSL - 14 m
Climatic Table compiled from 16 to 30 years observations, 1960 to 1998

Month	Average pressure at MSL	Temperatures				Average humidity		Average cloud cover		Precipitation		Wind distribution - Percentage of observations from																		Mean wind speed		Number of days with		
		Mean daily max.	Mean daily min.	Mean highest in each month	Mean lowest in each month	0500	1400	0500	1400	Average fall	No. of days with 0·1 mm or more	0800 N	0800 NE	0800 E	0800 SE	0800 S	0800 SW	0800 W	0800 NW	0800 Calm	1400 N	1400 NE	1400 E	1400 SE	1400 S	1400 SW	1400 W	1400 NW	1400 Calm	0800	1400	Gale	Fog	Thunder
	hPa	°C	°C	°C	°C	%	%	Oktas		mm																				Knots				
January	1021	18	10	24	6	75	59	3	4	46	7	10	5	1	5	22	32	17	3	5	13	6	1	5	11	12	22	29	1	9	12	1	1	1
February	1019	19	10	28	6	73	55	2	4	29	3	9	4	1	4	27	26	18	5	6	20	12	2	4	10	10	11	30	2	9	12	1	1	⊕
March	1017	21	12	32	7	73	58	3	4	11	3	14	6	4	9	23	20	11	6	7	26	18	6	3	10	5	6	26	0	9	12	1	1	1
April	1014	23	14	36	9	73	58	2	3	9	2	16	8	7	15	23	11	8	4	9	28	31	8	5	9	3	2	14	1	9	12	1	2	⊕
May	1014	26	17	40	11	75	64	2	3	4	1	15	12	8	16	19	6	6	5	13	27	40	10	4	7	2	⊕	10	⊕	8	12	1	1	1
June	1014	29	21	42	15	78	67	2	2	1	<1	18	10	6	15	19	5	5	7	15	30	44	12	2	3	3	1	6	⊕	8	11	1	1	⊕
July	1014	30	22	38	16	84	69	1	1	0	0	18	11	4	8	13	10	5	7	24	44	39	5	1	1	1	⊕	9	0	6	11	⊕	1	⊕
August	1014	31	23	36	19	83	66	1	1	0	0	15	11	3	9	15	13	4	3	26	40	45	5	1	1	1	1	7	⊕	5	10	1	1	0
September	1015	30	22	40	19	78	64	2	2	4	0	11	10	5	15	23	12	5	3	17	30	43	9	1	4	2	1	9	1	7	10	1	1	1
October	1018	29	19	37	15	74	58	2	3	29	5	8	5	4	15	30	21	6	2	10	28	26	6	4	12	7	4	13	1	8	11	⊕	1	1
November	1018	24	15	32	10	75	55	2	4	21	3	7	4	⊕	5	31	30	15	3	6	17	8	1	5	14	14	14	26	1	9	11	⊕	1	1
December	1020	20	11	26	6	71	55	3	4	55	7	6	3	⊕	4	23	37	20	2	6	11	6	⊕	2	12	16	24	27	3	9	11	1	1	1
Means	1016	25	16	44*	4§	76	61	2	3	–	–	12	7	4	10	22	19	10	4	12	26	27	5	3	8	6	7	17	1	8	11	–	–	–
Totals	–	–	–	–	–	–	–	–	–	209	29	–	–	–	–	–	–	–	–	–	–	–	–	–	–	–	–	–	–	–	–	9	13	7
Extreme values	–	–	–	47†	2‡	–	–	–	–	–	–	–	–	–	–	–	–	–	–	–	–	–	–	–	–	–	–	–	–	–	–	–	–	–
No. of years observations	16	16				16		16		30		16									16									16		16	16	16

* Mean of highest each year
§ Mean of lowest each year
† Highest recorded temperature
‡ Lowest recorded temperature
⊕ Rare
⊖ All observations

1.188

WMO No 62055

AJDĀBĪYAH (30° 43′ N, 20° 10′ E) Height above MSL - 7 m

Climatic Table compiled from observations 1984 to 2005

Month	Average pressure at MSL	Temperatures				Average humidity		Average cloud cover		Precipitation		Wind distribution - Percentage of observations from																		Mean wind speed		Number of days with		
												0800									1400													
		Mean daily max.	Mean daily min.	Mean highest in each month	Mean lowest in each month	0800	1400	0800	1400	Average fall	No. of days with 0·1 mm or more	N	NE	E	SE	S	SW	W	NW	Calm	N	NE	E	SE	S	SW	W	NW	Calm	0800	1400	Gale or above	Fog	Thunder
	hPa	°C	°C	°C	°C	%	%	Oktas		mm																				Knots				
January	1022	18	8	23	5	68	55	4	4	27	5	5	5	7	7	23	10	5	4	34	21	4	4	5	11	5	12	28	10	5	8	0	0	0
February	1020	19	8	25	4	61	49	3	3	25	4	11	6	7	9	21	8	6	9	23	26	3	4	3	12	5	8	32	7	7	9	0	0	1
March	1018	22	11	31	6	52	43	3	3	14	3	15	10	11	9	19	5	7	12	12	27	5	4	5	11	2	4	34	8	9	10	0	0	0
April	1015	27	14	37	7	43	38	3	3	2	1	18	10	10	11	23	3	4	11	10	35	3	4	6	14	2	3	29	4	9	11	0	0	0
May	1015	31	18	40	12	42	39	2	2	2	0	16	8	14	13	17	3	3	13	13	35	3	5	4	9	3	3	34	4	9	11	0	0	0
June	1015	34	20	42	14	41	39	1	1	0	0	24	10	11	12	15	2	2	12	12	40	3	3	3	5	1	2	40	3	8	12	0	0	0
July	1014	33	21	41	17	48	46	1	0	6	0	33	14	5	4	4	2	3	20	15	45	4	1	1	1	0	1	46	1	6	13	0	1	0
August	1014	34	22	39	18	51	47	1	0	1	0	34	11	5	5	5	2	1	14	23	49	4	0	0	1	1	2	42	1	5	13	0	1	0
September	1016	34	20	40	17	48	43	1	1	3	0	18	11	10	11	15	5	3	9	18	35	3	1	1	7	3	3	44	3	6	11	0	1	0
October	1018	30	17	36	13	51	44	2	2	9	1	9	8	9	12	28	6	2	3	23	32	3	3	4	11	4	2	34	7	7	8	0	0	0
November	1019	25	13	30	8	57	48	3	3	13	3	6	4	11	10	27	9	4	4	25	19	3	3	7	16	4	6	31	11	6	7	0	0	0
December	1021	20	9	25	5	64	55	3	4	43	6	6	4	4	11	27	10	5	5	28	19	3	3	4	18	7	12	23	11	6	7	0	0	1
Means	1017	27	15	43*	3§	52	46	2	2	–	–	16	8	9	9	19	5	4	10	20	32	3	3	3	10	3	5	35	6	7	10	–	–	–
Totals	–	–	–	–	–	–	–	–	–	145	23	–	–	–	–	–	–	–	–	–	–	–	–	–	–	–	–	–	–	–	–	2	5	3
Extreme values	–	–	–	49†	-2‡	–	–	–	–	–	–	–	–	–	–	–	–	–	–	–	–	–	–	–	–	–	–	–	–	–	–	–	–	–
No. of years observations	22	22				22		22		21		22									22									22		22	22	22

* Mean of highest each year
§ Mean of lowest each year

† Highest recorded temperature
‡ Lowest recorded temperature

⊕ Rare
⊖ All observations

1.189

WMO No 62053

BENĪNA (32° 06′ N, 20° 16′ E) Height above MSL - 132 m

Climatic Table compiled from observations 1974 to 2005

Month	Average pressure at MSL	Temperatures				Average humidity		Average cloud cover		Precipitation		Wind distribution - Percentage of observations from																		Mean wind speed		Number of days with		
		Mean daily max.	Mean daily min.	Mean highest in each month	Mean lowest in each month	0800	1400	0800	1400	Average fall	No. of days with 0·1 mm or more	0800 N	0800 NE	0800 E	0800 SE	0800 S	0800 SW	0800 W	0800 NW	0800 Calm	1400 N	1400 NE	1400 E	1400 SE	1400 S	1400 SW	1400 W	1400 NW	1400 Calm	0800	1400	Gale or above	Fog	Thunder
	hPa	°C	°C	°C	°C	%	%	Oktas		mm																				Knots				
January	1020	16	10	20	6	71	66	5	5	57	9	8	7	7	22	15	5	9	11	16	18	2	3	10	11	9	19	23	5	11	12	1	0	1
February	1019	17	9	23	6	67	61	5	5	37	7	12	4	8	20	14	6	10	17	9	19	2	1	8	11	11	19	27	2	13	13	1	0	1
March	1017	20	11	28	6	58	55	4	5	27	5	14	4	7	18	14	5	14	18	6	23	2	3	7	10	9	15	30	1	14	15	1	0	1
April	1015	24	14	34	8	49	47	4	4	4	2	17	4	8	18	11	5	12	18	7	27	2	2	8	8	5	12	35	1	14	16	2	0	0
May	1015	28	17	38	11	42	44	3	3	31	1	23	3	5	16	11	5	8	23	6	35	3	1	6	4	6	10	35	0	13	16	1	0	0
June	1015	31	21	39	14	44	43	2	2	14	0	30	4	3	9	9	5	9	27	4	44	3	1	1	4	2	6	39	0	12	16	1	1	0
July	1014	31	22	38	18	52	51	2	1	0	0	39	3	1	1	3	2	7	41	3	46	1	0	0	0	1	4	48	0	12	17	1	1	0
August	1014	31	22	37	20	54	52	2	2	0	0	37	2	1	1	3	4	8	39	5	43	1	1	0	0	1	5	49	0	11	16	0	0	0
September	1016	31	21	37	17	51	51	2	2	4	1	24	6	3	9	11	7	7	23	10	42	1	0	1	3	6	8	39	0	11	15	1	0	0
October	1017	28	19	34	14	54	54	3	4	14	3	17	4	5	21	18	6	7	14	8	31	2	1	3	10	9	9	34	1	11	13	0	0	1
November	1018	23	15	28	9	61	58	4	5	43	7	9	5	9	21	22	5	8	13	8	18	2	3	10	16	9	15	25	2	13	12	0	0	1
December	1020	18	11	22	7	68	64	5	5	77	10	8	3	6	29	19	4	6	13	12	14	3	3	11	16	13	14	20	6	11	11	1	0	1
Means	1017	25	16	40*	4§	56	54	3	4	–	–	20	4	5	15	13	5	9	21	8	30	2	2	5	8	7	11	34	1	12	14	–	–	–
Totals	–	–	–	–	–	–	–	–	–	308	45	–	–	–	–	–	–	–	–	–	–	–	–	–	–	–	–	–	–	–	–	9	4	6
Extreme values	–	–	–	44†	-3‡	–	–	–	–	–	–	–	–	–	–	–	–	–	–	–	–	–	–	–	–	–	–	–	–	–	–	–	–	–
No. of years observations	32	32				32		32		21		32									32									32		32	32	32

* Mean of highest each year
§ Mean of lowest each year

† Highest recorded temperature
‡ Lowest recorded temperature

⊕ Rare
⊖ All observations

1.190

WMO No 62059

DARNAH (DERNA) (32° 46′ N, 22° 39′ E) Height above MSL - 26 m

Climatic Table compiled from 16 to 30 years observations, 1960 to 1998

Month	Average pressure at MSL	Temperatures				Average humidity		Average cloud cover		Precipitation		Wind distribution - Percentage of observations from																		Mean wind speed		Number of days with		
		Mean daily max.	Mean daily min.	Mean highest in each month	Mean lowest in each month	0500	1400	0500	1400	Average fall	No. of days with 0·1 mm or more	0800									1400									0800	1400	Gale	Fog	Thunder
												N	NE	E	SE	S	SW	W	NW	Calm	N	NE	E	SE	S	SW	W	NW	Calm					
	hPa	°C	°C	°C	°C	%	%	Oktas		mm																				Knots				
January	1020	17	11	19	9	71	64	4	5	64	11	14	2	1	⊕	19	33	8	16	6	15	5	3	3	9	16	10	34	6	15	13	2	⊕	1
February	1019	17	11	23	9	73	62	3	5	45	8	11	2	⊕	1	23	32	8	18	5	15	5	3	2	11	12	9	40	5	16	16	3	⊕	⊕
March	1017	18	12	28	9	75	61	3	5	26	6	11	3	2	4	15	29	10	18	9	18	7	5	3	7	7	5	41	5	13	14	2	⊕	⊕
April	1015	21	14	32	10	71	58	3	4	10	3	8	1	3	3	12	24	8	26	16	17	10	11	3	7	5	5	39	3	12	14	2	⊕	⊕
May	1015	23	17	34	13	74	63	2	3	5	2	5	2	2	4	9	12	9	39	19	17	14	7	1	5	4	7	41	3	10	13	2	0	1
June	1015	27	21	38	18	71	64	1	2	<1	<1	6	2	2	1	5	8	11	49	17	13	9	7	⊕	2	2	10	55	3	11	13	1	0	⊕
July	1013	28	23	35	20	79	67	1	1	0	0	8	⊕	⊕	⊕	1	4	12	66	9	15	1	⊕	0	1	1	10	72	1	12	16	1	0	0
August	1014	29	24	32	22	78	68	2	2	0	0	13	⊕	⊕	0	2	7	10	62	7	14	2	⊕	0	⊕	1	6	78	⊕	12	15	1	⊕	0
September	1016	28	22	34	19	76	64	2	2	8	1	16	⊕	⊕	⊕	6	19	11	35	11	22	7	6	0	2	2	4	55	3	10	12	1	⊕	⊕
October	1018	27	19	33	15	75	60	2	3	51	5	10	2	1	2	14	37	4	19	11	24	14	5	1	4	6	5	38	3	11	10	1	⊕	⊕
November	1018	23	16	28	11	76	57	3	5	24	5	7	3	⊕	2	23	39	7	12	7	15	9	4	1	13	17	7	29	5	14	13	2	0	1
December	1019	19	12	22	9	73	60	4	5	57	9	7	3	⊕	3	20	42	7	13	5	13	7	3	2	13	24	9	26	4	15	14	2	⊕	1
Means	1017	23	17	41*	7§	74	62	2	3	–	–	9	2	1	2	12	23	9	32	10	17	8	5	1	6	8	7	45	3	13	14	–	–	–
Totals	–	–	–	–	–	–	–	–	–	290	50	–	–	–	–	–	–	–	–	–	–	–	–	–	–	–	–	–	–	–	–	20	⊕	4
Extreme values	–	–	–	46†	1‡	–	–	–	–	–	–	–	–	–	–	–	–	–	–	–	–	–	–	–	–	–	–	–	–	–	–	–	–	–
No. of years observations	16	16				16		16		30		16									16									16		16	16	16

* Mean of highest each year
§ Mean of lowest each year

† Highest recorded temperature
‡ Lowest recorded temperature

⊕ Rare
⊖ All observations

1.191

WMO No 62300

EL - SALLÛM (31° 34′ N, 25° 10′ E) Height above MSL - 4 m

Climatic Table compiled from 13 to 30 years observations, 1960 to 1995

Month	Average pressure at MSL	Temperatures				Average humidity		Average cloud cover		Precipitation		Wind distribution - Percentage of observations from																		Mean wind speed		Number of days with		
		Mean daily max.	Mean daily min.	Mean highest in each month	Mean lowest in each month	0500	1400	0500	1400	Average fall	No. of days with 1 mm or more	0800									1400									0800	1400	Gale	Fog	Thunder
												N	NE	E	SE	S	SW	W	NW	Calm	N	NE	E	SE	S	SW	W	NW	Calm					
	hPa	°C	°C	°C	°C	%	%	Oktas		mm																				Knots				
January	1020	19	10	24	7	80	52	3	4	21	3	2	4	3	3	5	15	34	30	5	8	9	6	4	5	13	26	26	3	7	7	⊕	1	⊕
February	1018	19	10	25	6	79	47	3	4	15	3	4	4	4	4	8	16	30	23	6	10	14	10	7	5	16	19	19	0	7	7	⊕	⊕	0
March	1017	21	11	29	7	72	46	2	3	7	1	5	10	5	5	6	14	23	21	12	12	24	12	3	7	10	14	17	1	5	7	⊕	⊕	0
April	1015	24	14	34	10	69	46	1	2	6	1	10	11	9	5	3	6	19	20	17	17	30	14	8	4	5	11	11	1	4	6	⊕	1	0
May	1014	26	17	39	13	70	48	1	2	2	0	15	7	11	6	6	3	11	20	22	18	35	20	9	4	3	3	6	2	4	6	⊕	⊕	0
June	1013	30	20	40	17	73	46	<1	1	1	0	11	7	8	4	4	4	13	32	18	25	37	13	4	2	3	2	12	1	4	6	0	⊕	0
July	1011	31	22	37	20	80	48	<1	<1	0	0	16	5	8	1	1	3	17	43	6	31	42	8	1	1	1	4	13	⊕	4	6	⊕	⊕	⊕
August	1011	32	22	36	20	82	52	<1	1	0	0	8	7	9	2	1	4	16	47	6	29	46	11	2	⊕	⊕	2	10	1	4	6	⊕	⊕	⊕
September	1015	30	21	36	18	77	52	<1	1	0	0	14	8	3	1	2	8	22	36	6	25	45	9	2	2	2	4	12	⊕	4	6	0	0	0
October	1017	27	18	34	15	74	51	1	2	13	1	8	11	2	2	4	8	27	28	11	22	42	11	2	2	6	4	11	1	4	5	⊕	⊕	0
November	1018	24	15	29	11	67	48	1	3	10	1	6	6	2	3	4	16	36	17	11	12	20	13	4	6	13	20	11	1	5	5	0	⊕	⊕
December	1019	20	11	25	7	67	51	1	3	17	1	5	2	2	2	3	17	34	26	9	10	14	4	2	3	16	26	20	3	6	6	⊕	⊕	0
Means	1016	25	16	43*	5§	74	49	1	2	–	–	9	7	5	3	4	9	23	29	11	19	30	11	4	3	7	11	14	1	5	6	–	–	–
Totals	–	–	–	–	–	–	–	–	–	92	11	–	–	–	–	–	–	–	–	–	–	–	–	–	–	–	–	–	–	–	–	⊕	2	⊕
Extreme values	–	–	–	48†	4‡	–	–	–	–	–	–	–	–	–	–	–	–	–	–	–	–	–	–	–	–	–	–	–	–	–	–	–	–	–
No. of years observations	13	13				13		13		30		13									13									13		13	13	13

* Mean of highest each year
§ Mean of lowest each year

† Highest recorded temperature
‡ Lowest recorded temperature

⊕ Rare
⊖ All observations

WMO No 62318

MĪNĀ' AL ISKANDARĪYAH (ALEXANDRIA) / NOUZHA (31° 12′ N, 29° 57′ E) Height above MSL - 7 m

Climatic Table compiled from 16 to 30 years observations, 1960 to 1998

Month	Average pressure at MSL	Temperatures: Mean daily max.	Temperatures: Mean daily min.	Temperatures: Mean highest in each month	Temperatures: Mean lowest in each month	Average humidity: 0500	Average humidity: 1400	Average cloud cover: 0500	Average cloud cover: 1400	Precipitation: Average fall	Precipitation: No. of days with 1 mm or more
	hPa	°C	°C	°C	°C	%	%	Oktas	Oktas	mm	
January	1020	18	10	22	5	79	58	4	5	51	1
February	1018	18	10	25	5	78	56	3	6	27	3
March	1016	20	11	28	6	79	56	3	4	13	1
April	1014	24	14	36	8	79	51	2	3	4	1
May	1014	26	17	37	12	81	55	2	3	1	0
June	1012	28	21	37	15	82	57	2	1	0	0
July	1009	29	23	33	19	81	61	2	2	0	0
August	1010	30	24	33	20	81	61	2	2	0	0
September	1013	29	22	33	17	81	56	2	2	1	0
October	1016	27	18	32	14	80	55	2	3	11	1
November	1017	23	14	28	9	80	56	3	4	29	2
December	1019	20	11	24	5	81	57	3	5	52	1
Means	1015	24	16	39*	4§	80	57	2	3	–	–
Totals	–	–	–	–	–	–	–	–	–	189	10
Extreme values	–	–	–	45†	1‡	–	–	–	–	–	–
No. of years observations	16	16				16		16		30	

Month	Wind 0800: N	NE	E	SE	S	SW	W	NW	Calm	Wind 1400: N	NE	E	SE	S	SW	W	NW	Calm	Mean wind speed: 0800	Mean wind speed: 1400	Days with Gale	Days with Fog	Days with Thunder
																			Knots	Knots			
January	9	10	9	7	22	18	7	14	3	14	9	7	5	5	15	20	25	⊕	6	11	1	2	1
February	13	5	10	11	18	16	9	16	3	14	6	4	5	4	13	26	28	0	7	12	1	2	2
March	12	9	12	12	17	8	12	17	2	21	8	7	2	3	5	24	31	0	7	12	⊕	2	1
April	15	13	13	16	9	5	10	20	1	28	9	5	5	2	3	13	36	0	7	11	⊕	1	⊕
May	17	9	15	11	3	5	14	25	⊕	32	6	4	2	2	2	10	42	0	7	11	⊕	1	⊕
June	21	4	7	5	3	4	18	38	⊕	23	3	2	⊕	⊕	⊕	10	61	0	7	11	⊕	1	0
July	12	2	1	1	3	4	20	58	⊕	13	⊕	⊕	0	0	0	15	71	⊕	8	12	⊕	⊕	0
August	21	2	1	3	3	3	16	52	⊕	18	1	0	⊕	0	0	10	71	0	7	12	⊕	1	0
September	30	5	4	8	9	5	4	34	1	33	5	⊕	0	0	1	8	54	0	6	11	⊕	1	0
October	26	13	8	11	15	9	2	14	2	36	8	2	0	1	2	12	39	0	5	11	⊕	1	⊕
November	15	13	11	9	21	11	5	12	4	27	13	4	2	4	9	16	27	0	5	10	⊕	2	1
December	10	7	6	9	25	21	5	14	3	17	7	6	5	4	20	20	21	0	6	10	⊕	3	1
Means	17	7	8	9	12	9	10	26	2	23	6	3	2	2	6	16	42	⊕	6	11	–	–	–
Totals	–	–	–	–	–	–	–	–	–	–	–	–	–	–	–	–	–	–	–	–	2	17	6
Extreme values	–	–	–	–	–	–	–	–	–	–	–	–	–	–	–	–	–	–	–	–	–	–	–
No. of years observations	16									16									16		16	16	16

* Mean of highest each year
§ Mean of lowest each year

† Highest recorded temperature
‡ Lowest recorded temperature

⊕ Rare
⊖ All observations

1.193

WMO No 62332

PORT SAID (BÛR SA'ÎD) / EL - GAMÎL (31° 17′ N, 32° 14′ E) Height above MSL - 6 m

Climatic Table compiled from 12 to 30 years observations, 1960 to 1998

Month	Average pressure at MSL	Temperatures				Average humidity		Average cloud cover		Precipitation		Wind distribution - Percentage of observations from																		Mean wind speed		Number of days with		
		Mean daily max.	Mean daily min.	Mean highest in each month	Mean lowest in each month	0500	1400	0500	1400	Average fall	No. of days with 1 mm or more	0800									1400									0800	1400	Gale	Fog	Thunder
												N	NE	E	SE	S	SW	W	NW	Calm	N	NE	E	SE	S	SW	W	NW	Calm					
	hPa	°C	°C	°C	°C	%	%	Oktas		mm																				Knots				
January	1019	18	12	22	8	78	63	2	4	18	2	11	14	6	4	10	41	11	4	1	16	13	6	2	3	22	15	23	1	12	11	1	1	1
February	1018	18	12	25	8	76	60	2	4	12	2	7	11	7	6	14	35	12	7	2	15	17	5	1	4	21	12	26	0	11	12	1	⊕	1
March	1016	19	13	26	10	75	60	2	4	10	1	9	14	7	7	7	31	13	10	1	25	23	4	⊕	2	12	11	24	0	12	14	⊕	⊕	1
April	1013	22	16	32	12	76	63	2	3	5	1	17	24	12	5	8	14	9	10	⊕	38	30	3	⊕	2	5	3	20	0	11	13	1	⊕	⊕
May	1013	25	19	32	13	76	64	2	2	4	0	22	22	6	5	5	14	10	16	1	62	14	4	0	1	2	1	17	0	10	14	1	⊕	1
June	1010	28	22	35	17	77	64	1	<1	0	0	20	10	4	2	3	23	16	21	2	52	9	1	⊕	0	⊕	2	36	0	8	13	⊕	⊕	0
July	1008	30	24	34	22	79	64	2	<1	0	0	11	4	1	1	3	41	28	12	1	41	2	⊕	0	0	2	3	52	0	8	13	1	0	0
August	1009	30	25	33	23	79	64	2	<1	0	0	15	4	1	1	1	39	26	13	2	47	2	0	0	0	1	2	47	0	8	12	⊕	⊕	0
September	1012	29	24	32	20	76	63	1	1	3	0	26	13	2	1	5	25	16	12	⊕	54	8	0	0	0	1	1	37	0	9	12	1	⊕	⊕
October	1014	27	22	31	18	76	63	1	2	8	1	26	21	3	4	7	18	15	6	⊕	50	18	⊕	0	⊕	3	3	25	1	9	11	1	⊕	⊕
November	1016	23	18	27	13	76	61	2	3	7	1	13	20	4	5	11	27	12	7	1	26	19	3	⊕	4	11	13	25	0	11	12	1	1	1
December	1018	19	14	23	10	79	63	2	4	16	2	9	12	2	6	16	39	11	4	2	15	12	4	1	3	30	17	19	⊕	10	11	1	1	⊕
Means	1014	24	18	37*	5§	77	63	2	2	–	–	15	14	5	4	7	29	15	10	1	37	14	3	⊕	1	9	7	29	⊕	10	12	–	–	–
Totals	–	–	–	–	–	–	–	–	–	83	10	–	–	–	–	–	–	–	–	–	–	–	–	–	–	–	–	–	–	–	–	9	3	5
Extreme values	–	–	–	45†	2‡	–	–	–	–	–	–	–	–	–	–	–	–	–	–	–	–	–	–	–	–	–	–	–	–	–	–	–	–	–
No. of years observations	12	12				12		12		30		12									12									12		12	12	12

* Mean of highest each year
§ Mean of lowest each year

† Highest recorded temperature
‡ Lowest recorded temperature

⊕ Rare
⊖ All observations

1.194

WMO No 62337

EL 'ARÎSH AIRPORT (31° 05′ N, 33° 49′ E) Height above MSL - 32 m
Climatic Table compiled from 14 to 30 years observations, 1960 to 1998

Month	Average pressure at MSL	Temperatures				Average humidity		Average cloud cover		Precipitation		Wind distribution - Percentage of observations from 0800									Wind distribution - Percentage of observations from 1400									Mean wind speed		Number of days with		
		Mean daily max.	Mean daily min.	Mean highest in each month	Mean lowest in each month	0500	1400	0500	1400	Average fall	No. of days with 1 mm or more	N	NE	E	SE	S	SW	W	NW	Calm	N	NE	E	SE	S	SW	W	NW	Calm	0800	1400	Gale	Fog	Thunder
	hPa	°C	°C	°C	°C	%	%	Oktas		mm																				Knots				
January	1019	19	8	25	4	83	53	2	4	28	2	1	1	2	12	44	21	13	⊕	5	16	11	5	4	6	7	24	27	⊕	5	6	⊕	⊕	1
February	1017	19	8	28	4	81	51	2	4	16	1	2	1	1	16	38	22	16	3	3	17	11	2	3	3	9	21	34	⊕	5	8	⊕	⊕	1
March	1015	21	10	30	6	81	52	2	3	13	1	3	1	5	14	30	18	24	3	2	30	15	2	1	1	2	11	38	0	5	9	⊕	1	⊕
April	1013	26	12	39	7	79	49	2	3	11	0	7	4	7	15	26	11	19	6	4	39	19	3	1	1	1	3	33	0	5	9	0	⊕	⊕
May	1013	28	15	40	10	83	51	2	2	1	0	7	6	9	13	22	8	21	12	2	57	11	1	⊕	⊕	1	1	29	0	4	9	⊕	⊕	⊕
June	1010	30	18	38	14	83	51	1	<1	0	0	6	2	5	8	19	12	33	15	1	52	4	1	⊕	0	⊕	1	42	⊕	3	8	⊕	⊕	0
July	1008	32	21	36	17	86	54	2	<1	0	0	3	1	1	5	16	19	44	11	3	50	3	1	0	0	⊕	1	46	0	3	8	⊕	⊕	0
August	1008	32	21	35	19	88	56	1	<1	0	0	3	1	1	4	18	27	38	5	4	50	⊕	0	⊕	⊕	0	1	48	0	3	7	⊕	⊕	0
September	1012	31	20	35	16	86	56	2	1	0	0	4	2	2	8	25	20	28	5	7	51	4	⊕	1	0	⊕	2	42	0	3	8	0	⊕	0
October	1015	28	17	35	13	85	55	1	2	6	0	1	1	2	13	43	15	15	2	9	50	8	0	1	1	1	3	37	⊕	3	7	⊕	⊕	⊕
November	1017	25	12	30	8	84	53	1	3	9	1	1	⊕	2	13	47	18	11	2	6	32	13	2	2	3	5	11	31	⊕	4	6	⊕	⊕	⊕
December	1018	21	9	26	4	81	53	2	4	22	1	1	⊕	2	8	51	19	16	1	2	15	14	4	2	5	9	22	28	1	4	6	⊕	⊕	⊕
Means	1014	26	14	41*	3§	83	53	2	2	–	–	3	2	3	11	31	18	23	5	4	39	9	2	1	2	3	8	36	⊕	4	8	–	–	–
Totals	–	–	–	–	–	–	–	–	–	106	6	–	–	–	–	–	–	–	–	–	–	–	–	–	–	–	–	–	–	–	–	⊕	1	2
Extreme values	–	–	–	45†	1‡	–	–	–	–	–	–	–	–	–	–	–	–	–	–	–	–	–	–	–	–	–	–	–	–	–	–	–	–	–
No. of years observations	14	14				14		14		30		14									14									14		14	14	14

* Mean of highest each year
§ Mean of lowest each year

† Highest recorded temperature
‡ Lowest recorded temperature

⊕ Rare
⊖ All observations

1.195

WMO No 17300

ANTALYA (36° 53′ N, 30° 42′ E) Height above MSL - 54 m

Climatic Table compiled from 16 to 30 years observations, 1960 to 1998

Month	Average pressure at MSL	Temperatures				Average humidity		Average cloud cover		Precipitation		Wind distribution - Percentage of observations from																			Mean wind speed		Number of days with		
		Mean daily max.	Mean daily min.	Mean highest in each month	Mean lowest in each month	0500	1400	0500	1400	Average fall	No. of days with 1 mm or more	0800									1400									0800	1400	Gale	Fog	Thunder
												N	NE	E	SE	S	SW	W	NW	Calm	N	NE	E	SE	S	SW	W	NW	Calm					
	hPa	°C	°C	°C	°C	%	%	Oktas		mm																				Knots				
January	1018	15	5	19	0	76	55	3	4	238	10	40	4	1	3	1	1	3	46	1	21	11	9	15	16	8	2	14	3	7	7	⊕	⊕	4
February	1017	15	6	20	0	75	54	3	4	191	10	38	6	1	2	2	1	2	47	1	19	7	8	17	25	7	2	13	1	7	9	⊕	⊕	4
March	1015	17	7	23	2	77	54	3	4	102	7	37	7	1	2	2	1	2	42	6	10	6	5	17	41	9	2	10	1	6	8	⊕	⊕	3
April	1013	21	10	27	6	79	56	2	4	48	5	38	8	3	1	2	⊕	1	39	7	5	2	3	21	52	9	2	5	1	5	8	⊕	⊕	4
May	1012	26	15	33	9	78	57	2	3	28	3	30	12	7	4	2	2	3	27	13	4	2	3	22	55	9	2	3	0	4	8	0	⊕	3
June	1009	31	19	38	15	71	51	1	2	9	1	29	8	6	7	2	2	2	34	9	5	2	2	21	58	8	⊕	4	0	7	9	0	1	2
July	1006	34	22	41	18	65	47	1	1	5	1	22	9	8	7	3	2	2	38	10	9	6	1	19	55	4	2	5	0	6	8	⊕	⊕	1
August	1007	34	22	40	19	68	49	<1	1	2	0	25	10	5	2	1	1	2	40	14	6	2	1	20	63	7	0	2	⊕	5	8	⊕	1	1
September	1011	31	19	37	15	67	47	<1	1	13	1	35	9	1	⊕	1	1	2	42	9	4	1	2	24	61	4	⊕	4	0	5	8	⊕	⊕	1
October	1015	27	14	33	10	68	46	1	3	70	4	44	7	⊕	⊕	1	⊕	1	42	4	11	6	2	14	50	9	1	6	1	6	7	0	⊕	4
November	1017	20	10	26	5	76	54	2	4	150	6	42	6	2	1	3	⊕	2	43	2	13	9	9	15	30	9	1	10	3	6	6	⊕	1	4
December	1018	16	7	21	1	78	58	3	4	223	10	40	8	1	3	3	1	2	41	1	22	13	10	10	15	8	2	15	5	7	6	0	1	5
Means	1013	24	13	42*	-1§	73	52	2	3	–	–	35	8	3	3	2	1	2	40	6	11	6	5	18	44	7	1	7	1	6	8	–	–	–
Totals	–	–	–	–	–	–	–	–	–	1079	58	–	–	–	–	–	–	–	–	–	–	–	–	–	–	–	–	–	–	–	–	⊕	4	36
Extreme values	–	–	–	45†	-3‡	–	–	–	–	–	–	–	–	–	–	–	–	–	–	–	–	–	–	–	–	–	–	–	–	–	–	–	–	–
No. of years observations	16	16				16		16		30		16									16									16		16	16	16

* Mean of highest each year
§ Mean of lowest each year

† Highest recorded temperature
‡ Lowest recorded temperature

⊕ Rare
⊖ All observations

1.196

WMO No 17320

ANAMUR (36° 05′ N, 32° 50′ E) Height above MSL - 4 m
Climatic Table compiled from observations 2002 to 2005

Month	Average pressure at MSL	Temperatures: Mean daily max.	Temperatures: Mean daily min.	Temperatures: Mean highest in each month	Temperatures: Mean lowest in each month	Average humidity: 0800	Average humidity: 1400	Average cloud cover: 0800	Average cloud cover: 1400	Precipitation: Average fall	Precipitation: No. of days with 0·1 mm or more	Wind 0800: N	Wind 0800: NE	Wind 0800: E	Wind 0800: SE	Wind 0800: S	Wind 0800: SW	Wind 0800: W	Wind 0800: NW	Wind 0800: Calm	Wind 1400: N	Wind 1400: NE	Wind 1400: E	Wind 1400: SE	Wind 1400: S	Wind 1400: SW	Wind 1400: W	Wind 1400: NW	Wind 1400: Calm	Mean wind speed: 0800	Mean wind speed: 1400	Number of days with: Gale or above	Number of days with: Fog	Number of days with: Thunder
	hPa	°C	°C	°C	°C	%	%	Oktas		mm																				Knots				
January	1015	16	9	19	4	71	76	5	5	216	14	31	8	23	1	6	5	5	0	21	18	7	25	6	8	7	16	2	11	4	4	0	0	2
February	1015	15	7	19	2	64	63	4	4	106	10	24	2	13	11	22	6	6	6	10	13	3	24	6	9	8	24	5	8	3	4	0	0	2
March	1015	18	10	22	5	65	68	3	3	54	8	15	1	9	9	52	3	4	1	6	10	2	10	6	19	24	20	1	8	4	4	0	0	1
April	1013	21	13	26	8	74	70	3	3	48	6	5	0	9	16	49	5	8	0	8	4	0	13	6	34	16	13	1	13	5	5	0	0	1
May	1010	26	17	31	13	83	72	2	2	14	2	0	0	8	12	74	3	0	0	3	2	2	9	7	37	22	12	0	9	5	5	0	0	0
June	1009	30	21	35	17	88	74	1	1	4	3	2	0	2	12	80	0	0	0	4	3	2	19	2	47	15	9	0	3	5	5	0	0	2
July	1005	34	24	39	22	83	60	0	0	0	0	3	0	0	10	85	1	1	0	0	1	0	11	3	42	30	10	0	3	6	5	0	0	0
August	1006	33	24	37	22	80	63	1	1	5	0	1	0	1	4	92	2	0	0	0	0	1	7	0	46	34	10	0	2	7	5	0	0	0
September	1011	31	21	33	18	70	68	1	1	1	0	3	0	1	7	76	9	1	0	3	1	0	8	1	28	38	19	0	5	6	5	0	0	0
October	1014	28	18	32	11	67	68	2	2	15	3	6	1	4	7	74	4	1	0	3	7	0	4	4	24	22	12	1	26	5	3	0	0	1
November	1016	23	14	27	9	59	68	3	3	143	9	21	0	17	9	29	1	3	0	20	15	1	21	7	10	1	13	1	31	3	3	0	0	5
December	1018	16	9	20	5	66	71	4	4	171	10	46	1	23	1	7	1	0	2	19	24	2	25	7	8	2	15	1	16	3	4	0	0	3
Means	1013	24	15	36*	2§	72	68	3	2	–	–	13	1	9	8	54	3	3	1	8	8	2	15	5	26	18	14	1	11	5	4	–	–	–
Totals	–	–	–	–	–	–	–	–	–	777	65	–	–	–	–	–	–	–	–	–	–	–	–	–	–	–	–	–	–	–	–	0	0	17
Extreme values	–	–	–	42†	0‡	–	–	–	–	–	–	–	–	–	–	–	–	–	–	–	–	–	–	–	–	–	–	–	–	–	–	–	–	–
No. of years observations	4	4				4		4		4		4									4									4		4	4	4

* Mean of highest each year
§ Mean of lowest each year

† Highest recorded temperature
‡ Lowest recorded temperature

⊕ Rare
⊖ All observations

1.197

WMO No 17330

SİLİFKE (36° 23′ N, 33° 56′ E) Height above MSL - 15 m
Climatic Table compiled from observations 1984 to 2005

Month	Average pressure at MSL	Temperatures				Average humidity		Average cloud cover		Precipitation		Wind distribution - Percentage of observations from																		Mean wind speed		Number of days with		
		Mean daily max.	Mean daily min.	Mean highest in each month	Mean lowest in each month	0800	1400	0800	1400	Average fall	No. of days with 0·1 mm or more	0800									1400									0800	1400	Gale or above	Fog	Thunder
												N	NE	E	SE	S	SW	W	NW	Calm	N	NE	E	SE	S	SW	W	NW	Calm					
	hPa	°C	°C	°C	°C	%	%	Oktas		mm																				Knots				
January	1019	15	7	19	2	56	59	4	4	93	8	15	3	11	1	3	1	28	34	4	8	4	18	7	10	2	22	18	11	6	4	0	0	2
February	1017	16	7	21	2	53	56	4	4	67	8	10	4	16	5	5	1	28	28	3	9	2	18	10	16	5	16	19	5	6	5	1	0	2
March	1015	18	10	24	5	52	56	3	4	47	6	6	2	20	12	20	3	20	16	1	6	1	15	7	38	9	14	7	3	5	4	0	0	2
April	1013	23	13	29	9	56	56	4	3	29	5	2	1	23	21	30	7	9	6	1	3	1	12	10	45	15	10	2	2	6	4	0	0	2
May	1011	27	17	33	11	58	56	3	3	21	3	2	1	19	23	37	7	6	5	0	2	1	10	11	54	11	6	3	2	5	4	0	0	2
June	1009	30	20	35	15	60	57	2	1	3	1	1	1	20	20	47	4	5	2	0	1	1	7	12	66	7	4	1	1	5	4	0	0	2
July	1006	33	23	37	19	60	59	2	1	1	0	1	1	13	20	49	3	8	5	0	0	1	11	10	66	8	3	0	1	5	4	0	0	1
August	1007	33	24	37	19	59	60	2	1	2	0	3	0	12	19	51	3	6	6	0	1	0	11	9	66	9	2	1	1	5	4	0	0	0
September	1011	32	21	36	17	52	57	2	1	3	1	2	1	15	16	39	4	12	11	0	1	0	7	6	65	9	6	3	3	5	4	0	0	1
October	1015	28	18	34	12	46	57	2	2	38	4	4	1	15	12	18	2	27	20	1	4	0	11	8	41	7	11	8	10	5	3	0	0	3
November	1018	21	13	27	7	52	60	3	3	93	7	10	2	10	3	7	1	38	27	2	8	3	11	7	12	4	17	17	21	5	3	0	0	3
December	1019	16	9	21	4	57	60	4	4	110	9	12	3	11	2	5	1	28	35	3	9	3	15	5	6	2	21	23	16	6	4	0	0	2
Means	1013	24	15	38*	1§	55	58	3	3	–	–	6	2	15	13	26	3	18	16	1	4	2	12	9	40	7	11	9	6	5	4	–	–	–
Totals	–	–	–	–	–	–	–	–	–	507	52	–	–	–	–	–	–	–	–	–	–	–	–	–	–	–	–	–	–	–	–	2	0	22
Extreme values	–	–	–	40†	-3‡	–	–	–	–	–	–	–	–	–	–	–	–	–	–	–	–	–	–	–	–	–	–	–	–	–	–	–	–	–
No. of years observations	22	22				22		22		22		22									22									22		22	22	22

* Mean of highest each year
§ Mean of lowest each year

† Highest recorded temperature
‡ Lowest recorded temperature

⊕ Rare
⊖ All observations

1.198

WMO No 17370

İSKENDERUN (36° 36′ N, 36° 11′ E) Height above MSL - 4 m

Climatic Table compiled from 16 to 28 years observations, 1960 to 1998

Month	Average pressure at MSL	Temperatures				Average humidity		Average cloud cover		Precipitation		Wind distribution - Percentage of observations from																		Mean wind speed		Number of days with		
		Mean daily max.	Mean daily min.	Mean highest in each month	Mean lowest in each month	0500	1400	0500	1400	Average fall	No. of days with 1 mm or more	0800									1400									0800	1400	Gale	Fog	Thunder
												N	NE	E	SE	S	SW	W	NW	Calm	N	NE	E	SE	S	SW	W	NW	Calm					
	hPa	°C	°C	°C	°C	%	%	Oktas		mm																				Knots				
January	1019	15	8	19	3	69	58	3	4	90	11	4	3	3	20	46	14	7	3	2	18	14	5	10	22	6	13	12	1	4	5	⊕	⊕	2
February	1017	16	9	21	3	69	58	3	4	107	10	7	4	3	22	42	12	5	3	2	24	13	8	9	13	5	11	16	1	4	5	⊕	⊕	3
March	1015	18	11	25	6	73	61	3	4	93	10	7	7	11	18	25	14	8	3	7	22	11	6	4	7	5	20	24	1	3	5	⊕	⊕	5
April	1013	22	15	31	10	77	63	4	4	80	6	12	16	15	7	12	10	14	9	5	18	9	4	2	4	6	35	24	0	3	6	⊕	⊕	3
May	1012	25	18	32	11	78	68	4	3	70	5	31	13	7	4	5	5	20	13	2	15	7	2	1	2	5	41	27	⊕	3	6	⊕	⊕	3
June	1009	28	22	32	18	79	69	3	2	13	2	24	15	5	2	2	5	27	20	2	7	2	0	⊕	1	9	55	26	0	4	7	0	0	2
July	1006	30	25	34	22	80	70	4	2	3	1	25	14	4	3	2	5	30	16	1	10	1	⊕	0	⊕	7	63	19	0	4	8	0	⊕	⊕
August	1007	31	25	34	22	77	68	3	1	11	2	19	13	8	5	5	8	28	12	2	10	⊕	0	0	⊕	5	63	23	0	3	7	0	0	⊕
September	1011	30	23	34	19	73	61	2	2	30	4	10	8	9	7	20	14	13	6	14	18	5	0	0	1	3	45	28	1	2	5	⊕	⊕	2
October	1015	27	19	33	14	73	57	2	3	73	7	3	2	3	22	42	12	5	1	9	26	12	3	4	4	2	24	24	1	2	4	⊕	⊕	6
November	1017	21	14	26	9	68	57	2	4	71	7	3	3	4	26	47	8	3	3	2	27	16	7	7	16	3	11	13	⊕	3	5	⊕	⊕	4
December	1019	17	10	22	5	69	57	3	4	98	9	3	3	3	19	51	11	6	2	1	18	11	4	11	31	6	12	8	1	4	5	⊕	⊕	3
Means	1010	23	17	36*	1§	74	62	3	3	–	–	12	8	6	13	25	10	14	8	4	18	8	3	4	8	5	33	20	1	3	6	–	–	–
Totals	–	–	–	–	–	–	–	–	–	739	74	–	–	–	–	–	–	–	–	–	–	–	–	–	–	–	–	–	–	–	–	⊕	⊕	33
Extreme values	–	–	–	40†	-3‡	–	–	–	–	–	–	–	–	–	–	–	–	–	–	–	–	–	–	–	–	–	–	–	–	–	–	–	–	–
No. of years observations	16	16				16		16		28		16									16									16		16	16	16

* Mean of highest each year
§ Mean of lowest each year

† Highest recorded temperature
‡ Lowest recorded temperature

⊕ Rare
⊖ All observations

1.199

WMO No 17600

PAPHOS AIRPORT (34° 43′ N, 32° 29′ E) Height above MSL - 8 m

Climatic Table compiled from observations 1984 to 2005

Month	Average pressure at MSL	Temperatures				Average humidity		Average cloud cover		Precipitation		Wind distribution - Percentage of observations from																		Mean wind speed		Number of days with		
												0800									1400													
		Mean daily max.	Mean daily min.	Mean highest in each month	Mean lowest in each month	0800	1400	0800	1400	Average fall	No. of days with 0·1 mm or more	N	NE	E	SE	S	SW	W	NW	Calm	N	NE	E	SE	S	SW	W	NW	Calm	0800	1400	Gale or above	Fog	Thunder
	hPa	°C	°C	°C	°C	%	%	Oktas		mm																				Knots				
January	1018	17	8	20	3	61	67	4	4	79	12	3	7	18	15	12	12	24	8	1	5	7	14	7	6	7	24	27	3	8	8	1	0	6
February	1017	17	8	21	3	60	64	4	4	61	10	2	4	10	18	14	12	30	9	1	4	5	12	7	7	9	34	21	1	9	10	1	0	5
March	1015	18	9	23	4	63	65	4	4	39	7	1	0	7	13	16	18	39	5	1	2	2	7	7	5	8	49	19	1	9	10	0	0	4
April	1013	21	11	28	7	64	67	4	4	17	5	1	1	5	15	12	14	48	3	1	1	1	5	8	4	8	59	13	1	10	10	0	0	2
May	1012	24	14	30	10	69	71	3	3	7	2	0	0	2	9	13	18	56	2	0	1	0	1	5	4	4	72	12	1	8	10	0	1	1
June	1010	28	18	31	14	73	73	1	1	1	0	0	0	0	7	13	23	56	1	0	0	0	1	1	1	6	83	8	0	8	10	0	1	0
July	1007	30	20	33	17	73	73	1	1	0	0	0	0	0	4	15	26	54	1	0	0	0	0	0	2	9	86	3	0	7	9	0	0	0
August	1008	30	21	33	18	72	74	1	1	0	0	0	0	0	5	14	25	56	0	0	0	0	0	1	2	8	87	2	0	7	9	0	0	0
September	1012	29	19	32	16	67	69	1	2	3	1	0	0	0	5	13	22	59	1	0	0	0	1	1	2	3	77	15	1	8	10	0	0	1
October	1015	26	16	30	13	60	66	3	3	22	4	1	1	2	10	14	23	47	2	0	2	1	3	4	3	4	46	35	2	8	8	0	0	5
November	1017	22	13	26	7	58	66	4	4	52	7	1	3	7	15	18	13	37	4	2	5	5	9	6	5	5	23	37	5	8	7	1	0	6
December	1018	19	10	22	4	60	69	5	5	96	11	2	5	14	22	14	11	21	9	2	10	6	17	6	6	7	16	25	7	8	7	1	0	7
Means	1014	23	14	35*	2§	65	69	3	3	–	–	1	2	5	11	14	18	44	4	1	2	2	6	4	4	7	55	18	2	8	9	–	–	–
Totals	–	–	–	–	–	–	–	–	–	377	59	–	–	–	–	–	–	–	–	–	–	–	–	–	–	–	–	–	–	–	–	4	2	37
Extreme values	–	–	–	38†	-4‡	–	–	–	–	–	–	–	–	–	–	–	–	–	–	–	–	–	–	–	–	–	–	–	–	–	–	–	–	–
No. of years observations	22	22				22		22		22		22									22									22		22	22	22

* Mean of highest each year
§ Mean of lowest each year

† Highest recorded temperature
‡ Lowest recorded temperature

⊕ Rare
⊖ All observations

1.200

WMO No 17601

AKROTIRI (34° 35′ N, 32° 59′ E) Height above MSL - 23 m

Climatic Table compiled from observations 1995 to 2005

Month	Average pressure at MSL	Temperatures				Average humidity		Average cloud cover		Precipitation		Wind distribution - Percentage of observations from																		Mean wind speed		Number of days with		
		Mean daily max.	Mean daily min.	Mean highest in each month	Mean lowest in each month	0800	1400	0800	1400	Average fall	No. of days with 0·1 mm or more	0800									1400									0800	1400	Gale or above	Fog	Thunder
												N	NE	E	SE	S	SW	W	NW	Calm	N	NE	E	SE	S	SW	W	NW	Calm					
	hPa	°C	°C	°C	°C	%	%	Oktas		mm																				Knots				
January	1017	17	9	20	4	74	57	4	4	78	12	26	21	8	0	2	2	12	18	11	1	6	32	4	9	13	31	2	2	6	10	1	0	11
February	1017	17	9	21	4	71	55	4	4	60	9	19	15	7	0	0	1	18	26	14	1	3	26	5	10	19	34	2	0	6	11	1	0	8
March	1015	19	10	23	5	68	54	4	4	30	7	15	13	8	1	0	2	26	20	15	1	3	14	4	13	24	39	2	0	5	11	1	0	5
April	1013	22	13	27	8	65	56	4	4	19	5	4	13	20	1	3	3	33	10	13	1	2	15	2	9	22	47	1	1	7	12	0	1	5
May	1012	26	17	31	13	61	55	2	2	3	2	3	9	29	2	5	7	30	6	9	0	0	9	3	7	27	54	0	0	6	11	0	2	3
June	1009	29	21	33	18	61	58	1	1	0	0	3	17	31	2	6	7	25	3	6	0	0	3	1	7	39	49	1	0	5	11	0	3	1
July	1006	30	23	33	21	64	61	1	1	0	0	2	14	24	3	6	12	29	3	7	0	0	0	1	6	42	51	0	0	5	12	0	4	0
August	1007	31	23	34	21	67	62	1	1	0	0	5	14	17	3	4	6	33	8	10	0	0	0	0	4	34	62	0	0	5	12	0	1	1
September	1011	29	21	33	18	60	56	1	1	3	1	11	16	6	1	2	3	27	21	13	0	0	1	1	9	30	59	0	0	4	12	0	0	1
October	1015	27	17	31	13	58	53	2	3	14	3	18	11	3	0	1	1	15	33	18	0	1	7	3	11	33	43	1	1	3	10	0	0	7
November	1017	23	13	26	9	64	54	3	4	40	6	22	15	6	0	1	2	9	27	18	1	4	28	9	13	18	24	3	0	5	10	0	0	9
December	1018	19	11	22	6	75	59	4	5	86	11	26	20	6	1	1	3	9	19	15	2	5	31	5	11	17	26	3	0	6	10	1	0	10
Means	1013	23	15	34*	2§	66	57	3	3	–	–	13	15	14	1	3	4	22	16	12	1	2	14	3	9	27	43	1	0	5	11	–	–	–
Totals	–	–	–	–	–	–	–	–	–	333	56	–	–	–	–	–	–	–	–	–	–	–	–	–	–	–	–	–	–	–	–	4	12	59
Extreme values	–	–	–	39†	-1‡	–	–	–	–	–	–	–	–	–	–	–	–	–	–	–	–	–	–	–	–	–	–	–	–	–	–	–	–	–
No. of years observations	11	11				11		11		11		11									11									11		11	11	11

* Mean of highest each year
§ Mean of lowest each year

† Highest recorded temperature
‡ Lowest recorded temperature

⊕ Rare
⊖ All observations

1.201

WMO No 17609

LARNACA (34° 53′ N, 33° 38′ E) Height above MSL - 2 m

Climatic Table compiled from observations 1976 to 2005

Month	Average pressure at MSL	Temperatures: Mean daily max.	Temperatures: Mean daily min.	Temperatures: Mean highest in each month	Temperatures: Mean lowest in each month	Average humidity: 0800	Average humidity: 1400	Average cloud cover: 0800	Average cloud cover: 1400	Precipitation: Average fall	Precipitation: No. of days with 0·1 mm or more
	hPa	°C	°C	°C	°C	%	%	Oktas		mm	
January	1018	17	8	19	3	79	57	4	5	68	10
February	1017	17	7	21	2	78	55	4	4	40	8
March	1015	19	9	24	4	73	55	4	4	40	7
April	1013	23	12	29	7	63	53	3	4	16	4
May	1012	26	16	33	11	59	52	3	3	13	2
June	1009	30	19	35	16	62	52	1	2	2	1
July	1006	32	22	37	19	65	53	1	1	0	1
August	1007	33	22	36	19	64	52	1	1	0	0
September	1011	31	20	35	16	60	50	1	1	5	1
October	1015	28	17	32	12	60	50	2	3	16	3
November	1017	23	13	27	7	70	52	3	4	45	6
December	1018	18	9	22	4	79	57	4	5	83	9
Means	1013	25	14	38*	1§	68	53	3	3	–	–
Totals	–	–	–	–	–	–	–	–	–	328	52
Extreme values	–	–	–	41†	-1‡	–	–	–	–	–	–
No. of years observations	30	30				30		30		23	

Month	Wind 0800: N	NE	E	SE	S	SW	W	NW	Calm	Wind 1400: N	NE	E	SE	S	SW	W	NW	Calm	Mean wind speed: 0800	Mean wind speed: 1400	Number of days with: Gale or above	Fog	Thunder
																			Knots				
January	18	3	1	1	2	7	9	53	6	12	19	15	10	19	16	3	5	1	7	10	1	0	7
February	19	3	1	1	2	10	12	45	7	11	15	16	8	21	19	3	7	0	6	11	1	0	6
March	21	4	1	1	3	10	9	40	11	6	11	12	11	26	27	2	4	1	6	12	0	1	5
April	22	15	10	3	7	17	6	13	7	2	5	14	9	36	31	1	2	0	6	13	0	1	3
May	10	16	23	9	19	12	3	5	3	1	2	8	8	43	37	0	1	0	6	14	0	1	2
June	7	12	31	15	24	7	1	2	1	0	0	3	5	56	34	1	1	0	6	14	0	3	1
July	7	11	26	12	28	10	1	3	2	0	0	2	4	56	38	0	0	0	6	15	0	4	0
August	9	14	22	10	19	12	2	6	6	0	0	2	3	57	38	0	0	0	5	15	0	1	0
September	21	9	8	3	12	13	7	15	12	0	2	5	6	55	32	0	0	0	5	13	0	0	1
October	23	2	1	1	2	6	9	46	10	3	8	12	12	40	21	2	2	0	5	11	0	0	6
November	20	3	0	1	2	5	7	56	6	9	17	21	12	21	13	2	4	1	6	10	0	0	7
December	17	2	2	1	3	6	7	55	7	11	18	19	8	18	16	3	5	2	6	10	1	0	8
Means	16	8	11	5	10	10	6	28	6	5	8	11	8	37	27	1	3	0	6	12	–	–	–
Totals	–	–	–	–	–	–	–	–	–	–	–	–	–	–	–	–	–	–	–	–	4	11	46
Extreme values	–	–	–	–	–	–	–	–	–	–	–	–	–	–	–	–	–	–	–	–	–	–	–
No. of years observations	30									30									30		30	30	30

* Mean of highest each year
§ Mean of lowest each year

† Highest recorded temperature
‡ Lowest recorded temperature

⊕ Rare
⊖ All observations

1.202

WMO No 40022

AL LĀDHIQĪYAH (LATTAQUIÉ) (35° 31′ N, 35° 46′ E) Height above MSL - 7 m

Climatic Table compiled from 16 to 26 years observations, 1960 to 1998

Month	Average pressure at MSL	Temperatures				Average humidity		Average cloud cover		Precipitation		Wind distribution - Percentage of observations from																		Mean wind speed		Number of days with		
												0800									1400													
		Mean daily max.	Mean daily min.	Mean highest in each month	Mean lowest in each month	0500	1400	0500	1400	Average fall	No. of days with 1 mm or more	N	NE	E	SE	S	SW	W	NW	Calm	N	NE	E	SE	S	SW	W	NW	Calm	0800	1400	Gale	Fog	Thunder
	hPa	°C	°C	°C	°C	%	%	Oktas		mm																				Knots				
January	1019	16	9	19	4	68	57	4	5	134	12	⊕	20	46	14	3	8	5	1	3	3	9	18	19	4	6	17	15	3	8	8	⊕	⊕	4
February	1018	16	9	21	3	65	56	3	5	151	13	3	18	38	15	4	9	8	2	5	2	10	11	13	4	9	19	19	2	8	9	⊕	⊕	3
March	1016	18	11	24	7	67	57	4	5	93	9	3	18	25	20	6	10	7	2	8	2	11	7	5	2	8	30	21	2	7	9	1	⊕	5
April	1014	21	14	30	10	73	61	4	4	32	7	7	14	13	16	18	13	7	4	8	2	12	2	3	1	10	34	23	2	7	10	1	⊕	3
May	1013	24	17	32	13	78	67	4	3	29	3	9	7	7	9	24	23	10	4	7	1	8	1	2	1	13	38	22	1	7	10	⊕	⊕	2
June	1010	27	21	32	17	78	71	3	2	5	2	3	1	⊕	9	41	33	8	2	3	0	3	0	1	1	19	50	20	0	7	10	⊕	⊕	⊕
July	1007	28	24	32	21	78	72	3	3	1	⊕	1	⊕	1	9	52	28	5	1	3	⊕	3	1	⊕	1	22	60	12	⊕	8	10	0	⊕	0
August	1008	29	24	32	22	76	70	3	2	8	1	1	⊕	4	22	38	27	2	1	5	0	1	0	0	1	15	59	21	0	7	9	⊕	⊕	⊕
September	1012	29	22	34	18	72	63	2	2	22	2	5	4	12	36	14	13	2	2	14	⊕	8	0	⊕	2	5	44	28	⊕	5	9	⊕	⊕	1
October	1015	27	18	30	14	66	54	2	3	57	3	5	14	32	23	3	4	5	1	15	3	17	4	3	2	4	25	27	3	5	7	⊕	⊕	4
November	1017	22	14	27	9	66	52	3	4	111	7	3	22	46	12	2	4	4	2	4	6	16	10	13	4	5	15	18	6	6	7	⊕	⊕	5
December	1019	17	10	21	4	68	55	3	5	244	10	2	24	45	11	2	6	5	1	3	5	8	16	23	4	4	11	17	5	7	8	1	⊕	5
Means	1014	23	16	36*	2§	71	61	3	4	–	–	3	12	22	16	18	15	6	2	6	9	6	7	2	10	34	20	10	2	7	9	–	–	–
Totals	–	–	–	–	–	–	–	–	–	887	69	–	–	–	–	–	–	–	–	–	–	–	–	–	–	–	–	–	–	–	–	3	⊕	32
Extreme values	–	–	–	40†	-3‡	–	–	–	–	–	–	–	–	–	–	–	–	–	–	–	–	–	–	–	–	–	–	–	–	–	–	–	–	–
No. of years observations	16	16				16		16		26		16									16									16		16	16	16

* Mean of highest each year
§ Mean of lowest each year

† Highest recorded temperature
‡ Lowest recorded temperature

⊕ Rare
⊖ All observations

WMO No 40100

BEYROUTH (BEIRUT) AIRPORT (33° 49′ N, 35° 29′ E) Height above MSL - 19 m

Climatic Table compiled from 25 to 30 years observations, 1960 to 1998

Month	Average pressure at MSL	Temperatures				Average humidity		Average cloud cover		Precipitation		Wind distribution - Percentage of observations from																		Mean wind speed		Number of days with		
		Mean daily max.	Mean daily min.	Mean highest in each month	Mean lowest in each month	0500	1400	0500	1400	Average fall	No. of days with 2·5 mm or more	0800									1400									0800	1400	Gale	Fog	Thunder
												N	NE	E	SE	S	SW	W	NW	Calm	N	NE	E	SE	S	SW	W	NW	Calm					
	hPa	°C	°C	°C	°C	%	%	Oktas		mm																				Knots				
January	1018	18	11	21	7	72	61	4	5	191	10	2	11	32	17	19	3	2	1	13	10	6	2	3	19	25	15	17	4	6	8	⊕	1	5
February	1017	17	11	22	7	72	61	4	5	133	9	2	9	27	14	18	7	3	1	17	8	5	2	2	11	32	18	20	3	5	9	1	1	5
March	1015	19	12	26	8	72	61	4	4	111	6	2	8	12	14	20	11	3	1	29	9	4	2	2	10	30	21	20	2	5	9	⊕	1	5
April	1013	22	15	30	11	70	60	3	4	46	4	5	7	4	4	21	27	8	4	20	9	6	1	1	8	40	18	17	1	6	9	⊕	⊕	2
May	1012	25	18	33	15	75	65	3	3	15	2	4	3	1	1	12	46	16	7	10	9	4	⊕	⊕	5	39	21	20	1	7	9	⊕	1	1
June	1010	28	21	34	19	71	67	1	2	2	⊕	1	1	0	0	10	69	15	3	2	2	1	0	0	2	54	30	12	0	8	10	0	⊕	⊕
July	1007	29	23	34	22	69	67	1	1	<1	⊕	⊕	1	0	⊕	24	67	6	1	2	1	1	0	0	2	70	20	6	0	10	11	⊕	⊕	⊕
August	1008	30	24	34	24	70	65	1	2	<1	⊕	1	1	⊕	⊕	27	54	10	3	4	⊕	⊕	0	0	2	59	30	10	0	7	10	⊕	1	0
September	1012	29	23	33	21	69	61	2	2	2	⊕	4	10	7	3	25	27	7	2	15	7	2	0	0	1	35	28	26	1	5	9	⊕	⊕	⊕
October	1015	27	21	31	17	67	58	2	3	60	4	1	14	21	11	18	7	1	1	27	13	5	1	1	5	24	22	30	2	3	8	⊕	1	2
November	1017	23	16	27	12	64	57	3	4	101	7	3	11	37	11	13	2	2	1	19	14	5	1	2	9	25	16	25	3	4	7	⊕	⊕	4
December	1018	19	12	23	9	71	60	4	5	164	10	1	14	34	16	14	4	2	1	13	12	6	2	4	16	24	15	18	4	5	7	⊕	1	5
Means	1013	24	17	36*	5§	70	62	3	3	–	–	2	7	14	8	19	28	6	2	14	8	4	1	1	7	38	21	18	2	6	9	–	–	–
Totals	–	–	–	–	–	–	–	–	–	825	52	–	–	–	–	–	–	–	–	–	–	–	–	–	–	–	–	–	–	–	–	1	7	29
Extreme values	–	–	–	43†	0‡	–	–	–	–	–	–	–	–	–	–	–	–	–	–	–	–	–	–	–	–	–	–	–	–	–	–	–	–	–
No. of years observations	25	25				25		25		30		25									25									25		25	25	25

* Mean of highest each year
§ Mean of lowest each year

† Highest recorded temperature
‡ Lowest recorded temperature

⊕ Rare
⊖ All observations

1.204

WMO No 40155

ḪEFA (HAIFA) AIRPORT (32° 49′ N, 35° 03′ E) Height above MSL - 8 m

Climatic Table compiled from 10 to 28 years observations, 1960 to 1998

Month	Average pressure at MSL	Temperatures				Average humidity		Average cloud cover		Precipitation		Wind distribution - Percentage of observations from																		Mean wind speed		Number of days with		
		Mean daily max.	Mean daily min.	Mean highest in each month	Mean lowest in each month	0500	1400	0500	1400	Average fall	No. of days with 1 mm or more	0800									1400									0800	1400	Gale	Fog	Thunder
												N	NE	E	SE	S	SW	W	NW	Calm	N	NE	E	SE	S	SW	W	NW	Calm					
	hPa	°C	°C	°C	°C	%	%	Oktas		mm																				Knots				
January	1019	17	9	21	4	74	54	3	4	175	11	1	1	10	56	15	4	2	2	8	10	1	19	15	9	13	12	16	4	7	9	0	⊕	4
February	1018	17	9	23	3	75	54	3	4	109	8	0	1	7	50	16	7	5	5	10	9	1	6	15	7	24	12	25	1	7	9	⊕	1	4
March	1016	19	10	27	6	76	53	3	4	41	6	2	3	7	41	18	8	6	6	9	15	3	7	5	3	19	14	32	1	6	9	0	1	2
April	1014	23	13	33	7	73	53	3	3	25	3	6	3	9	31	11	10	7	15	8	14	1	4	4	4	14	16	42	2	6	9	0	1	1
May	1013	25	17	34	11	81	59	3	2	5	1	14	6	6	12	6	12	10	24	10	16	1	⊕	2	0	11	16	54	⊕	6	9	0	⊕	⊕
June	1010	29	20	35	15	83	56	2	1	1	⊕	14	4	2	7	6	22	16	19	11	8	1	0	0	0	15	26	50	0	5	9	0	1	0
July	1007	31	23	34	18	81	55	2	2	1	⊕	6	2	1	4	11	37	18	13	9	4	0	0	0	1	21	35	39	0	6	9	0	0	0
August	1008	31	23	34	19	82	57	2	1	1	⊕	6	2	4	8	11	31	16	18	5	8	0	⊕	0	⊕	16	32	42	0	5	9	0	⊕	0
September	1012	29	21	33	15	79	57	2	2	3	1	15	6	6	16	10	15	12	17	4	20	1	⊕	0	⊕	8	21	50	0	4	9	⊕	⊕	0
October	1015	28	18	34	13	77	55	1	2	25	2	3	5	14	39	19	3	3	7	8	22	1	3	4	2	5	14	48	⊕	5	9	⊕	⊕	2
November	1017	24	15	30	10	70	49	2	3	94	7	1	1	12	50	24	4	3	3	3	14	6	14	14	10	9	10	24	⊕	8	9	0	⊕	3
December	1018	19	11	24	6	74	53	2	4	185	11	2	1	9	53	20	4	5	3	4	9	5	13	19	13	11	10	17	4	8	8	0	⊕	5
Means	1014	24	16	38*	4§	77	55	2	3	–	–	6	3	7	30	14	13	9	11	7	12	2	6	6	4	14	18	37	1	6	9	–	–	–
Totals	–	–	–	–	–	–	–	–	–	665	50	–	–	–	–	–	–	–	–	–	–	–	–	–	–	–	–	–	–	–	–	⊕	4	21
Extreme values	–	–	–	44†	-2‡	–	–	–	–	–	–	–	–	–	–	–	–	–	–	–	–	–	–	–	–	–	–	–	–	–	–	–	–	–
No. of years observations	10	10				10		10		28		10									10									10		10	10	10

* Mean of highest each year
§ Mean of lowest each year

† Highest recorded temperature
‡ Lowest recorded temperature

⊕ Rare
⊖ All observations

1.205

WMO No 40176

TEL AVIV – YAFO (32° 05′ N, 34° 46′ E) Height above MSL - 4 m

Climatic Table compiled from 11 to 27 years observations, 1995

Month	Average pressure at MSL	Temperatures				Average humidity		Average cloud cover		Precipitation		Wind distribution - Percentage of observations from																		Mean wind speed		Number of days with		
		Mean daily max.	Mean daily min.	Mean highest in each month	Mean lowest in each month	0500	1400	0500	1400	Average fall	No. of days with 1 mm or more	0800									1400									0800	1400	Gale	Fog	Thunder
												N	NE	E	SE	S	SW	W	NW	Calm	N	NE	E	SE	S	SW	W	NW	Calm					
	hPa	°C	°C	°C	°C	%	%	Oktas		mm																				Knots				
January	1019	17	9	22	5	78	59	3	4	131	10	3	3	24	37	15	4	4	2	8	11	3	5	5	4	28	24	17	3	7	10	0	1	1
February	1017	17	9	24	6	79	58	3	4	93	9	1	3	19	32	17	5	7	3	12	5	2	2	3	5	32	25	25	1	8	11	⊕	1	3
March	1015	19	11	27	7	78	59	3	3	58	8	3	5	14	31	14	12	9	4	8	8	1	4	2	⊕	25	24	36	1	7	11	⊕	⊕	⊕
April	1013	23	14	30	9	77	59	2	2	15	3	7	2	6	12	14	21	13	9	15	17	1	⊕	⊕	1	12	26	42	⊕	6	11	⊕	⊕	0
May	1013	25	17	32	12	80	62	3	2	4	1	9	2	3	4	8	34	17	13	11	16	0	⊕	⊕	⊕	6	31	46	⊕	7	11	⊕	1	⊕
June	1010	27	20	32	16	79	63	3	1	0	0	4	⊕	⊕	1	11	56	14	9	5	5	⊕	0	1	0	11	47	37	0	7	11	0	⊕	⊕
July	1007	29	23	33	19	82	63	2	1	0	0	⊕	0	⊕	3	17	68	7	3	3	⊕	⊕	0	0	0	11	55	23	0	7	10	0	⊕	0
August	1008	30	23	33	20	82	63	2	1	0	0	⊕	0	1	11	25	52	6	2	4	0	0	0	0	⊕	7	63	30	0	6	10	⊕	⊕	0
September	1011	29	22	32	18	79	59	2	1	2	⊕	3	3	4	30	23	17	5	3	11	5	0	0	0	⊕	1	35	58	0	5	11	0	0	0
October	1014	27	19	32	14	79	56	2	2	18	2	2	3	21	43	12	6	⊕	3	11	14	⊕	1	1	1	9	25	49	0	5	11	0	⊕	1
November	1016	23	15	30	9	75	55	2	3	79	6	3	4	27	41	8	2	4	3	8	10	3	5	5	3	16	23	35	0	6	10	⊕	1	3
December	1018	19	11	25	5	77	59	3	4	129	9	2	2	21	44	15	3	4	3	7	9	3	3	4	6	30	20	24	2	7	10	1	⊕	3
Means	1013	24	16	37*	4§	79	60	2	2	–	–	3	2	11	24	15	24	8	5	8	8	1	2	2	2	15	34	35	1	6	11	–	–	–
Totals	–	–	–	–	–	–	–	–	–	529	48	–	–	–	–	–	–	–	–	–	–	–	–	–	–	–	–	–	–	–	–	1	4	11
Extreme values	–	–	–	43†	1‡	–	–	–	–	–	–	–	–	–	–	–	–	–	–	–	–	–	–	–	–	–	–	–	–	–	–	–	–	–
No. of years observations	11	11				11		11		27		11									11									11		11	11	11

* Mean of highest each year
§ Mean of lowest each year

† Highest recorded temperature
‡ Lowest recorded temperature

⊕ Rare
⊖ All observations

1.206

METEOROLOGICAL CONVERSION TABLE AND SCALES

Fahrenheit to Celsius

°Fahrenheit

°F	0	1	2	3	4	5	6	7	8	9
					Degrees Celsius					
-100	-73·3	-73·9	-74·4	-75·0	-75·6	-76·1	-76·7	-77·2	-77·8	-78·3
-90	-67·8	-68·3	-68·9	-69·4	-70·0	-70·6	-71·1	-71·7	-72·2	-72·8
-80	-62·2	-62·8	-63·3	-63·9	-64·4	-65·0	-65·6	-66·1	-66·7	-67·2
-70	-56·7	-57·2	-57·8	-58·3	-58·9	-59·4	-60·0	-60·6	-61·1	-61·7
-60	-51·1	-51·7	-52·2	-52·8	-53·3	-53·9	-54·4	-55·0	-55·6	-56·1
-50	-45·6	-46·1	-46·7	-47·2	-47·8	-48·3	-48·9	-49·4	-50·0	-50·6
-40	-40·0	-40·6	-41·1	-41·7	-42·2	-42·8	-43·3	-43·9	-44·4	-45·0
-30	-34·4	-35·0	-35·6	-36·1	-36·7	-37·2	-37·8	-38·3	-38·9	-39·4
-20	-28·9	-29·4	-30·0	-30·6	-31·1	-31·7	-32·2	-32·8	-33·3	-33·9
-10	-23·3	-23·9	-24·4	-25·0	-25·6	-26·1	-26·7	-27·2	-27·8	-28·3
-0	-17·8	-18·3	-18·9	-19·4	-20·0	-20·6	-21·1	-21·7	-22·2	-22·8
+0	-17·8	-17·2	-16·7	-16·1	-15·6	-15·0	-14·4	-13·9	-13·3	-12·8
10	-12·2	-11·7	-11·1	-10·6	-10·0	-9·4	-8·9	-8·3	-7·8	-7·2
20	-6·7	-6·1	-5·6	-5·0	-4·4	-3·9	-3·3	-2·8	-2·2	-1·7
30	-1·1	-0·6	0	+0·6	+1·1	+1·7	+2·2	+2·8	+3·3	+3·9
40	+4·4	+5·0	+5·6	6·1	6·7	7·2	7·8	8·3	8·9	9·4
50	10·0	10·6	11·1	11·7	12·2	12·8	13·3	13·9	14·4	15·0
60	15·6	16·1	16·7	17·2	17·8	18·3	18·9	19·4	20·0	20·6
70	21·1	21·7	22·2	22·8	23·3	23·9	24·4	25·0	25·6	26·1
80	26·7	27·2	27·8	28·3	28·9	29·4	30·0	30·6	31·1	31·7
90	32·2	32·8	33·3	33·9	34·4	35·0	35·6	36·1	36·7	37·2
100	37·8	38·3	38·9	39·4	40·0	40·6	41·1	41·7	42·2	42·8
110	43·3	43·9	44·4	45·0	45·6	46·1	46·7	47·2	47·8	48·3
120	48·9	49·4	50·0	50·6	51·1	51·7	52·2	52·8	53·3	53·9

Celsius to Fahrenheit

°Celsius

°C	0	1	2	3	4	5	6	7	8	9
					Degrees Fahrenheit					
-70	-94·0	-95·8	-97·6	-99·4	-101·2	-103·0	-104·8	-106·6	-108·4	-110·2
-60	-76·0	-77·8	-79·6	-81·4	-83·2	-85·0	-86·8	-88·6	-90·4	-92·2
-50	-58·0	-59·8	-61·6	-63·4	-65·2	-67·0	-68·8	-70·6	-72·4	-74·2
-40	-40·0	-41·8	-43·6	-45·4	-47·2	-49·0	-50·8	-52·6	-54·4	-56·2
-30	-22·0	-23·8	-25·6	-27·4	-29·2	-31·0	-32·8	-34·6	-36·4	-38·2
-20	-4·0	-5·8	-7·6	-9·4	-11·2	-13·0	-14·8	-16·6	18·4	-20·2
-10	+14·0	+12·2	+10·4	+8·6	+6·8	+5·0	+3·2	+1·4	-0·4	-2·2
-0	32·0	30·2	28·4	26·6	24·8	23·0	21·2	19·4	+17·6	+15·8
+0	32·0	33·8	35·6	37·4	39·2	41·0	42·8	44·6	46·4	48·2
10	50·0	51·8	53·6	55·4	57·2	59·0	60·8	62·6	64·4	66·2
20	68·0	69·8	71·6	73·4	75·2	77·0	78·8	80·6	82·4	84·2
30	86·0	87·8	89·6	91·4	93·2	95·0	96·8	98·6	100·4	102·2
40	104·0	105·8	107·6	109·4	111·2	113·0	114·8	116·6	118·4	120·2
50	122·0	123·8	125·6	127·4	129·2	131·0	132·8	134·6	136·4	138·2

HECTOPASCALS (hPa) TO INCHES

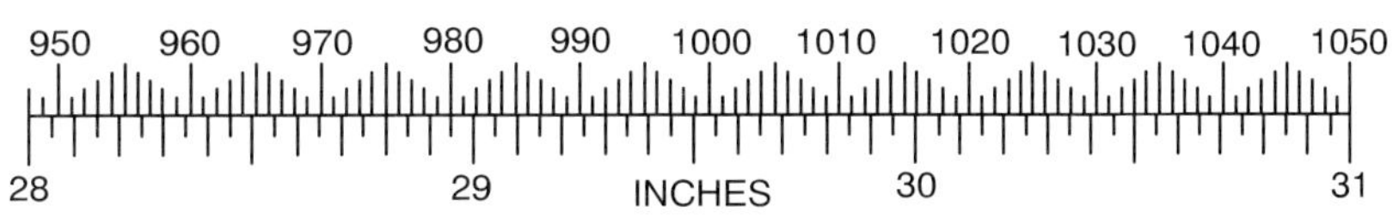

MILLIMETRES TO INCHES

(1) (for small values)

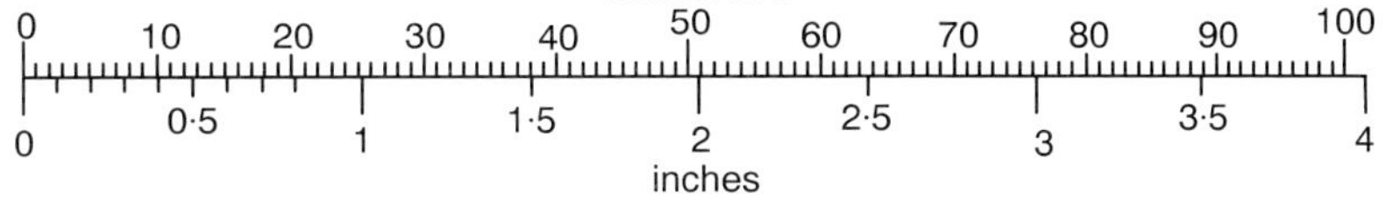

(2) (for large values)

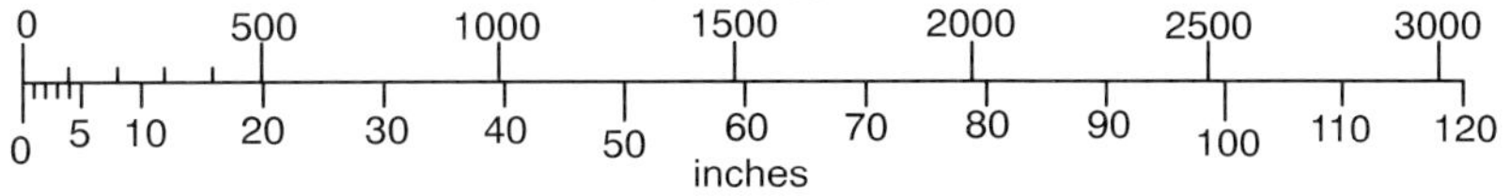

Chapter 2 - Ra's Ajdir to Ra's Al Muraysah

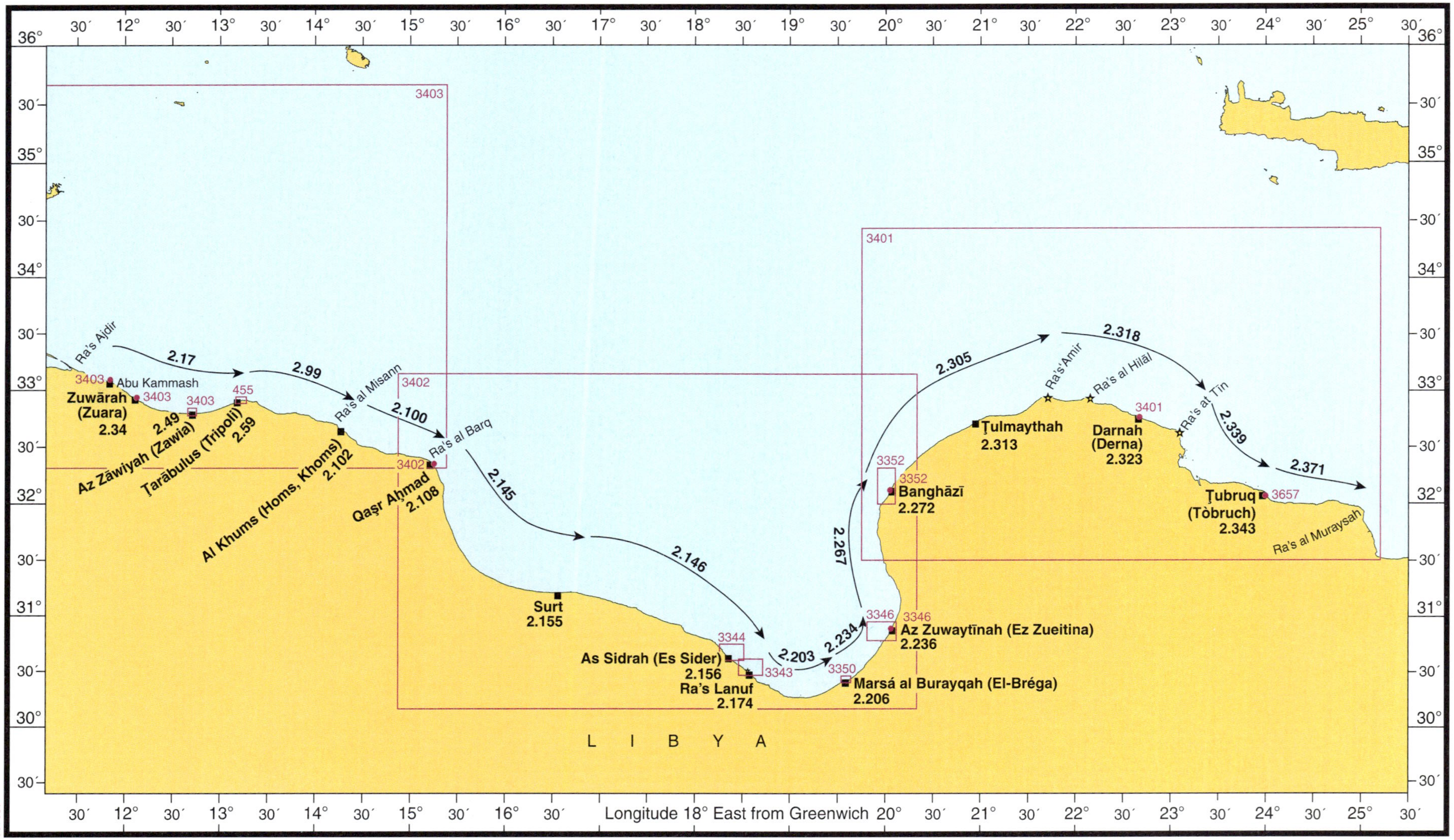

CHAPTER 2

COAST OF LIBYA — RA'S AJDIR TO RA'S AL MURAYSAH

GENERAL INFORMATION

Charts 176, 183

Scope of the chapter

2.1

1 The area covered by this chapter comprises the coastal waters of Libya from Ra's Ajdir (33°10′N 11°34′E) to Ra's al Muraysah (31°55′N 25°02′E), about 680 miles E.

The description includes the principal ports of Ţarābulus (Tripoli) (2.59), Qaşr Aḩmad (2.120), Banghāzī (2.272) and Ţubruq (Tòbruch) 2.343), and the oil terminals at Az Zāwiyah (2.49), As Sidrah (Es Sider) (2.156), Ra's Lānūf (2.174), Marsá al Burayqah (El-Brega) (2.206) and Az Zuwaytīnah (Ez Zueitina) (2.236).

2 The chapter is divided into the following sections:

Ra's Ajdir to Ra's al Barq (2.7).
Gulf of Sirte (2.113).
Banghāzī to Ra's al Muraysah (2.298).

Topography

2.2

1 From Ra's Ajdir (33°10′N 11°34′E) to Banghāzī (32°07′N 20°03′E) the coast is generally low and sandy, with rocky reefs extending some distance seaward. Between Banghāzī and Darnah (32°46′N 22°38′E) the coast is high. Farther E it becomes generally lower with sandhills. The coast W of Ra's Ajdir is described in *Mediterranean Pilot Volume 1*.

Fishing

2.3

1 Tunny nets may be laid out at certain seasons every year from various points on the coast of Libya, and may extend 5 miles offshore. For further details see 1.3.

Regulations

2.4

1 **Territorial sea.** All vessels must comply with standard marine regulations issued on 10th October 1990 by the Libyan Authorities when in Libyan waters, which are limited by 12 nautical miles from the coastline and in the Gulf of Sirte by the latitude of 32°30′N.

2 **Radio reporting.** All vessels arriving, departing or on passage between Libyan ports must maintain regular radio contact with the authorities, and pass through the designated Approach Reporting Point when approaching port. For details of reports and information required see *Admiralty List of Radio Signals Volume 6 (3)*. For further information on regulations see 1.39.

3 **Submarine cables.** Mariners are advised that the Libyan authorities have established cable protection zones around many submarine cable runs and that damage to a submarine cable is likely to incur heavy penalties (see 1.26 and 1.43).

Weather

2.5

1 Vessels anchoring in the roadsteads of Libya during the winter season are recommended, with the harbour authority's permission (see also 1.43), to leave the anchorage used by day for working cargo and to anchor farther out for the night, as at times there are strong winds, and occasionally gales, from the NW.

Rescue

2.6

1 For information on rescue see 1.65 and *Admiralty List of Radio Signals Volume 5*.

RA'S AJDIR TO RA'S AL BARQ

GENERAL INFORMATION

Charts 3403, 3402, 3401, 176

Area covered

2.7

1 The area covered by this section comprises:

Ra's Ajdir to Ţarābulus (2.9).
Ţarābulus (2.59).
Ţarābulus to Ra's al Barq (2.92).

Coastal shelter

2.8

1 Between Ra's Ajdir (33°10′N 11°34′E) and Ra's al Barq, 190 miles ESE, Ţarābulus (32°54′N 13°11′E) and Al Khums (32°41′N 14°15′E) (2.102) are the only harbours capable of accommodating sea-going vessels of any size.

2 Small vessels may obtain anchorage with some degree of shelter at Zuwārah (32°56′N 12°07′E) (2.34) and Marsá Şabrātah (32°49′N 12°27′E) (2.57).

RA'S AJDIR TO ŢARĀBULUS

General information

Chart 3403

Route

2.9

1 From a position N of Ra's Ajdir (33°10′N 11°34′E) the route leads ESE, for about 80 miles, to a position N of Ţarābulus (32°54′N 13°11′E).

Topography

2.10

1 The coast between Ra's Ajdir and Zuwārah, 30 miles ESE, is generally very low and sandy; for the first 16 miles it is bordered by lagoons. El Kousha, a hummock, stands 1½ miles W of Ra's Ajdir.

From Ra's Gioggig (32°56′N 12°07′E) (2.34) the coast is low with sandy dunes to Marsá Şabrātah, 17 miles ESE, near which it becomes rocky, high and steep.

2 The coast E of Marsá Şabrātah is comparatively steep to, with irregular patches of rock on and below the tide line. A coastal ridge of sandy rock, sparsely covered by grass, with occasional patches of low cliff, rises fairly

steeply from the shore to elevations of about 24 m near Şabrātah, and to about 38 m, 20 miles to the E. The main coastal road and railway lie behind this ridge, with a cultivated area farther inland.

3 Between Marsá Şurmān, a slight indentation, 3 miles E of Şabrātah, and Marsá Dīlah, 8 miles farther E, the coast is low.

The coast between Janzūr and Ra's al Aḩmar, 6 miles ENE, is rugged and uncultivated.

Submarine exercise area

2.11

1 A submarine exercise area exists seaward of the coast between Zuwārah (32°56′N 12°07′E) and Ţarābulus, 55 miles E, in the area indicated on the charts.

Prohibited area

2.12

1 An entry prohibited area (32°56′N 12°55′E), shown on the chart, lies within 10 miles of the coast between Marsá Dīlah (32°48′N 12°45′E) and Ra's al Aḩmar, 20 miles ENE.

International boundary

2.13

1 The boundary between Tunisia and Libya runs S from Ra's Ajdir (33°10′N 11°34′E).

Submarine cables

2.14

1 Submarine cables come ashore about 1 mile E of Ra's al Aḩmar (32°53′N 13°09′E). For information on submarine cables see 1.26.

Directions

(continued from Mediterranean Pilot Volume I)

Principal marks

2.15

1 **Landmarks:**

Tower (elevation 218 m) (32°59′N 11°50′E).

Radio mast (elevation 110 m) (32°54′N 12°03′E).

Radio mast (red lights) (32°45′N 12°44′E).

House (white) (32°47′N 12°48′E) with a turret and flagstaff at Bir Suria.

Two radio masts (elevation 168 m) (32°51′N 13°05′E), marked by obstruction lights.

2 Radio mast (elevation 103 m) (32°41′N 13°08′E), marked by obstruction lights.

Radio mast (elevation 122 m, red lights) (32°52′N 13°11′E).

Castle (32°53′N 13°11′E) (2.77).

Major light:

Aero light (32°54′N 13°16′E) (2.77) at Ţarābulus.

Other aids to navigation

2.16

1 **Racons:**

Bouri Oilfield West Platform (33°54′N 12°36′E).

Bouri Oilfield SPM (33°55′N 12°39′E).

Bouri Oilfield East Platform (33°55′N 12°41′E).

Mellitah Fairway Light Buoy (32°55′N 12°16′E).

Mellitah SPM (32°54′N 12°15′E).

Ra's Ajdir to Ţarābulus

2.17

1 From a position NNE from Ra's Ajdir (33°10′N 11°34′E), a low and inconspicuous point marked by a beacon (2.18), the track leads ESE, passing (with positions from Marsá Şabrātah Light (32°49′N 12°27′E) (2.57)):

2 NNE of Secca Ehdouz (42 miles NW), a rocky shoal which lies in the approaches to Marsá al Burayqah (2.56). In this area the water is very clear in the vicinity of shoals, and the bottom can be seen, in places, at a depth of over 18 m. Caution is necessary, however, when approaching the coast and frequent soundings should be taken. Thence:

SSW of a shoal (46 miles NW), with a depth of 16 m over it, thence:

NNE of Abu Kammash (34 miles NW) (2.27), thence:

3 NNE of a dangerous wreck (20 miles NW), which lies 4 miles offshore from Zuwārah (2.34), thence:

NNE of Marsá Şabrātah (2.57), thence:

Clear of an obstruction (16½ miles NE), thence:

NNE of Az Zāwiyah Oil Terminal (14 miles E) (2.49), thence:

NNE of an entry prohibited area (26 miles ENE) (2.12), thence:

To a position N of Ţarābulus (32°54′N 13°11′E) (2.59).

2.18

1 **Useful marks:**

Beacon (masonry pyramid, white globe topmark, 10 m in height) standing on Ra's Ajdir (33°10′N 11°34′E). The beacon is situated near a clump of bushes and is difficult at times to distinguish.

Tower (32°49′·2N 12°57′·5E).

2 Tunny factory at Janzūr (32°51′N 13°01′E); the white buildings and two black chimneys are visible from about 6 miles offshore.

Ţarābulus Lighthouse (32°54′·2N 13°10′·6E) (2.77).

(Directions continue for the coastal route at 2.98)

(Directions for Ţarābulus are given at 2.77)

Al Jurf Oilfield

2.19

1 **Description.** Al Jurf Oilfield (33°52′N 12°03′E) consists of a single lighted oil platform, BD1, connected to ten production wells and by a submarine pipeline to FPSO *Farwah,* lying to a SPM 1½ miles farther WSW.

Port Authority. Compagnie Des Petroles Total (CPTL): Dhat el Imad Tower 2 , PO Box 91171, Tripoli, Libya.

2 **SBM.** Didon SBM (33°47′N 11°53′E) is situated 8 miles SW of Al Jurf Oilfield.

Bahr Essalam Gasfield

General information

2.20

1 **Description.** Bahr Essalam Gasfield (33°36′N 12°46′E) consists of a single lighted gas platform, Sabratha, connected by a submarine pipeline to production wells and the shore at Mellitah (32°52′N 12°14′E) (2.42). The pipeline also continues seaward, NNE from the platform.

Bouri Oil Terminal

General information

2.21

1 **Position.** Bouri Oil Terminal (33°54′N 12°40′E) is situated in the Bouri Oilfield which contains a number of lighted production platforms and a SPM loading tower.

Function. The terminal, which consists of FSO *Sloug* moored to an SPM, is used for the export of crude oil.

2 **Traffic.** In 2007 there were 39 ship calls with a total of 2 629 177 dwt.

Port Authority. ENI Oil Ltd, PO Box 346, DahraBuilding, Ţarābulus, Libya.

Limiting conditions

2.22

1 **Maximum size of vessel handled.** Vessels of between 35 000 and 150 000 dwt are handled; maximum LOA 286 m; maximum beam 44 m; no draught restriction.

Arrival information

2.23

1 **Notice of ETA.** Vessels should send an ETA 72, 48 and 24 hours in advance to ENI Oil Ţarābulus.

Waiting area. There is a waiting area 2 miles S of the loading tower. Anchoring is strictly prohibited.

Pilots. Pilotage is provided by the Mooring Master who boards in the waiting area. For details see *Admiralty List of Radio Signals Volume 6 (3).*

2 **Tugs.** A tug is available.

Regulations. Bouri Oilfield is enclosed within an Entry Prohibited Area. Vessels should give the prohibited area a berth of at least 5 cables.

Berthing is carried out during daylight hours only.

Directions

2.24

1 From seaward to the waiting area the chart is sufficient guide.

Berth

2.25

1 Berthing is normally in tandem. When the berth is occupied one tug is secured aft.

Port services

2.26

1 **Facilities:** garbage and oily waste disposal not available; there are no facilities for receiving clean or dirty ballast.

Supplies. Fresh water and fuel available in cases of emergency only.

Abu Kammash

Chart 3403 plan of Abu Kammash

General information

2.27

1 **Position.** Abu Kammash (33°04′N 11°49′E) lies 70 miles WNW of Ţarābulus at the E end of Ra's al Mathbaz (2.30). It consists of a industrial factory complex, about 8 cables inland, which can be identified by two white tanks.

2 **Traffic.** In 2007 there were seven ship calls with a total of 46 104 dwt.

Port Authority. General Company for Chemical Industries (GCCI), PO Box 100/411, Zuwārah, Libya.

Limiting conditions

2.28

1 **Maximum size of vessel handled.** 149 m LOA, 7·5 m draught.

Arrival information

2.29

1 **Notice of ETA.** Vessels should request pilots and advise ETA via Zuwārah. For details of information required see *Admiralty List of Radio Signals Volume 6 (3).*

Pilotage is compulsory.

Tugs A small tug is available.

Directions

2.30

1 **Landmarks:**

Farwah Lighthouse (red tower on black and white building) (33°06′N 11°45′E) standing 2 miles ESE of Ra's al Tulayjah (33°07′N 11°41′E), the NW extremity of Ra's al Mathbaz, a narrow peninsula 8½ miles long.

Two white tanks (33°03′·8N 11°49′·2E), one larger than the other, standing in the factory complex.

2 Sīdī Sa'īd (33°03′·8N 11°50′·4E), a hill on the summit of which there are two marabouts. These small buildings, standing close together, form a very prominent mark when the sun shines on their white domes. A circular column, in ruins, stands on the summit of a nearby hill.

Sīdī 'Alī (3½ miles ESE of Sīdī Sa'īd), a hill with a square tower close to the ruins of a marabout on its summit.

Approach and entry

2.31

1 For details of Approach Reporting Points see 1.41, 2.4, and *Admiralty List of Radio Signals Volume 6 (3).*

From the fairway buoy (white conical) (33°06′·8N 11°51′·4E) the approach channel, which is reported to be dredged to a depth of 8 m over a width of about 150 m, leads SW for a distance of 1¾ miles to the pier. The channel is marked by four pairs of buoys (lateral), the positions of which are unreliable. It is reported that the channel is marked by leading lights, details of which should be obtained from the Port Authority. There is a turning area off the berth, about 300 m in diameter.

Berth

2.32

1 A **T**-jetty extends 6 cables NNE from the shore from a position 8 cables NNE of the factory. Lights are exhibited from the ends. Depth alongside the berth 8 m. There is a small jetty on the W side of the pier, close S of the head.

Cargoes handled: caustic soda and liquid, ethylene.

2 **Development.** A pipeline is to be constructed (2007) for direct importing of ethyl dichloride.

Port services

2.33

1 **Supplies.** In exceptional circumstances fresh water may be supplied by tanker; provisions are available.

Communications. International airport at Ţarābulus, 56 km distant.

Zuwārah

Chart 3403 plan of Zuwārah

General information

2.34

1 **Description.** Zuwārah (32°55′N 12°07′E), also known as Zuara, lies close S of a small peninsula which terminates in Ra's Gioggig. The town of Zuwārah may be identified by its palm trees, which extend along the coast for 5 miles to the W.

2 **Traffic.** Approximately 50 vessels visit the port annually.

Fishing. Tunny nets are laid off Ra's Gioggig. For details see 1.3.

Limiting conditions

2.35

1 **Controlling depths.** The outer part of the harbour has a charted depth of 5 m and the inner part a depth of 4 m.

Local weather. The harbour is unsafe in E and NE winds.

Arrival information

2.36

1 **Anchorages.** The anchorage area for vessels awaiting a berth is within 1 mile of 32°57′·0N 12°10′·5E. Anchorage may also be obtained in depths from 6·9 to 9·1 m, mud, with the N mole head bearing about 213°.

Pilot and tugs are available.

Harbour

2.37

1 **General layout.** The harbour is formed by N and S moles enclosing two small basins separated by a short jetty. The N mole extends about 4 cables ESE from Ra's Gioggig. Entrance is from E.

Climate information: see 1.184 and 1.185.

Directions

2.38

1 **Landmarks:**

Zuwārah Main Light (metal framework tower on white hut, black bands) (32°55′·5N 12°07′·2E).

House close WNW of the main light.

Tower (32°55′·2N 12°06′·5E) the position of which is approximate.

2 Two water towers, 1 cable WSW and 2 cables NW respectively of the tower.

Duna Horma (32°51′·2N 12°14′·5E), a conical sandy hillock about 14 m high.

Radio mast (elevation 110 m) (32°54′N 12°03′E).

Sīdī 'Abd ar Raḩman, a hill on which stands a marabout, close SW of the radio mast.

Approach and entry

2.39

1 **Approach Reporting Point.** Vessels approaching Zuwārah must pass through the Approach Reporting Point (33°03′N 12°15′E), as shown on the chart. For details of Approach Reporting Points see 1.41, 2.4 and *Admiralty List of Radio Signals Volume 6 (3).*

2 **Entry.** From the Approach Reporting Point the track leads SW for about 9½ miles, passing (with positions from Zuwārah Main Light (32°55′N 12°07′E)):

SE of a dangerous wreck (4 miles N), thence:

Clear of a light buoy (special, spherical) (2 miles NE), thence:

Clear of the fairway light buoy (safe water) (1 mile ENE).

3 Thence a buoyed channel leads SW for about 4½ cables and then WNW for a further 3½ cables to enter the harbour between the head of the N mole, from where a light (metal framework tower on white hut) is exhibited; and the elbow of the S mole from where a light is also exhibited.

Berths

2.40

1 **Outer harbour.** An angled jetty extends nearly 1 cable SE from 2 cables SE of Ra's Gioggig. The jetty can accommodate vessels drawing up to 4 m on its N side, and up to 5 m on its S side.

The S basin, with depths of 4 m, is fully quayed.

2 **Development** plans include construction of a new industrial harbour with facilities to handle general, container and liquid cargoes.

Port services

2.41

1 **Facilities.** Medical facilities in town.

Supplies: fresh water in limited quantities by road tanker; fresh provisions in small quantities.

Communications. International airport at Ţarābulus, 125 km distant.

Mellitah

General information

2.42

1 **Position and function.** The facility at Mellitah (32°52′N 12°14′E) consists of a gas and solid sulphur loading jetty, with a light at its head, which extends for about 1¼ miles NNE from the shore. Two SPM mooring buoys 1½ and 1¼ miles farther out are located in positions: 32°54′·5N 12°14′·1E, and 32°54′·3N 12°15′·1E. A fairway light buoy is laid in position 32°54′·9N 12°15′·6E.

2 A small harbour for tugs and workboats is located close E of the root of the jetty.

Port Authority. ENI Gas BV, Ţarābulus, Libya.

Limiting conditions

2.43

1 **Maximum size of vessel handled:** 160 000 dwt.

Arrival information

2.44

1 **Notice of ETA.** Initial ETA should be sent up to 7 days before arrival. If less than 7 days passage, ETA should be sent as soon as possible. Thereafter ETA should be confirmed 72, 48 and 24 hrs in advance.

Anchorage. An anchorage/waiting area is located about 1 mile NW of the fairway buoy.

Pilotage is compulsory.

2 **Tugs.** Two tugs are available and compulsory for berthing at the jetty. Their use is optional for the SPM's.

Regulations. Anchoring is not allowed E of a line joining the light on the jetty head with the fairway buoy, due to the presence of oil and gas submarine pipelines.

Transiting without the authorisation of the Mooring Master, and fishing, are not allowed within 1 km E and W of a line joining the jetty root to a position 1 km to seaward of the fairway buoy.

Aid to navigation

2.45

1 **Racon:**

Fairway light buoy (32°54′·9N 12°15′·6E).

Directions

2.46

1 From the fairway buoy the jetty berths, both E and W, are accessible through a channel 130 m long and 150 m wide. These lead to turning areas of 300 m diameter for the LPG berths, and 340 m for the solid sulphur berth. A minimum depth of 13 m is maintained in the turning areas.

2 The channels are marked by light buoys (cardinal), and sector lights, with a white light indicating the centre of the channel.

Berths

2.47

1 **Jetty:** Two loading berths for LPG (Propane and Butane), on E and W sides of the jetty; one berth for loading solid sulphur on the E side only. Minimum depth at all berths is 13 m. Vessels of 17 000 dwt and a maximum draught of 10 m can be accommodated.

2 **SPM No 1:** CALM buoy for loading oil and/or condensates is located in a depth of about 25 m. Vessels up to 113 000 dwt and a maximum draught of 15 m can be accommodated.

3 **SPM No 2:** CALM buoy for loading crude oil is located in a depth of about 30 m. Vessels up to 160 000 dwt and a maximum draught of 17·2 m can be accommodated.

Port services

2.48

1 No repair, fuel, fresh water or medical facilities are available. There are no shore facilities for the reception of dirty ballast.

Az Zāwiyah Oil Terminal

Chart 3403 plan of Az Zāwiyah

General information

2.49

1 **Position.** Az Zāwiyah Oil Terminal (32°48′N 12°42′E) and refinery, also known as Zawia Terminal.

Function. Offshore oil terminal.

Approach. Az Zāwiyah Oil Terminal does not have a designated Approach Reporting Point but vessels must report their position, course and speed when 12 miles away. For details of Approach Reporting Points see 1.41, 2.4, and *Admiralty List of Radio Signals Volume 6 (3).*

2 **Fishing.** Tunny nets are laid N from Marsá Dīlah (2.52); for further details see 1.3.

Port limits extend N from the shore to latitude 32°50′·5N between the meridians of 12°40′E and 12°44′E.

Traffic. In 2007 there were 141 ship calls with a total of 10 186 163 dwt.

Port Authority. Az Zāwiyah Refinery Co, PO Box 15715, Az Zāwiyah 6451, Ţarābulus, Libya.

Limiting conditions

2.50

1 **Maximum size of vessel handled.** Vessels up to 140 000 dwt and 19 m draught can be accommodated.

Local conditions. The berths are in the open sea, and main engines must be ready for immediate use at all times.

Arrival information

2.51

1 **Port operations.** Cargo operations, normally throughout 24 hours, may be interrupted by adverse weather, particularly during winter months.

Anchorage. On arrival vessels should anchor 1½ miles NW of No 1 Berth to await the pilot. The bottom is reported to be sand over rock.

2 **Pilotage,** available during daylight hours only, is compulsory from the anchorage and within the port limits. It is carried out by the Mooring Master who boards in the anchorage area, as shown on the chart. For details see *Admiralty List of Radio Signals Volume 6 (3).*

Tugs. Available from Ţarābulus if required.

Principal marks

2.52

1 **Landmarks** (positioned from the light at the jetty head (32°47′·6N 12°40′·8E)):

Building (3 cables SE).
Water tower (4¾ cables ESE).
Two flares (9½ cables E).
Chimneys (red obstruction lights) (9½ cables E).
Tanks (1¼ miles E).

2 Marsá Dīlah Lighthouse (red metal column on red and white chequered building) (3½ miles E) exhibited from Marsá Dīlah (32°48′N 12°45′E).
Radio mast (red lights) (32°45′N 12°44′E) (chart 3403).
House (6 miles E) (2.15) (chart 3403).

Berths

2.53

1 Offshore loading berths are as follows (positioned from head of jetty (32°47′·6N 12°40′·8E)):

No 1 Berth (1¼ miles NE) consists of a SBM for vessels of up to 100 000 dwt, maximum LOA 274 m and 17·0 m draught (8 cables NNE).

2 No 2 Berth (1½ miles ENE). Vessels berth using two anchors with the stern secured to three mooring buoys. For vessels of up to 25 000 dwt, maximum length 175 m and draught of 10·0 m.

No 3 Berth (8 cables NNE) consists of a SBM for vessels of up to 140 000 dwt and 19·0 m draught.

Lights are exhibited from each SBM.

Port services

2.54

1 **Facilities.** Hospital.

Supplies. No facilities available.

Communications. International airport at Ţarābulus, 56 km distant.

Anchorages and minor harbours

Ra’s Ajdir

2.55

1 A sheltered anchorage, suitable only for vessels drawing less than 3 m, is situated in a small deep 8 cables N of Ra’s Ajdir (33°10′N 11°34′E) (2.17). The approach, with the beacon (2.18) on Ra’s Ajdir bearing 191°, lies between two beacons (red iron framework, black topmarks) standing 6 cables N of Ra’s Ajdir. The tidal streams in this vicinity run NW and NE on the rising and falling tides respectively.

Local knowledge is required.

Marsá al Burayqah

2.56

1 **Description.** Marsá al Burayqah is entered between Ra’s al Tulayjah (33°07′N 11°41′E) (2.30) and a steep yellowish bluff, about 7 m high, on the mainland 4½ miles WSW. The bay extends 6 miles ESE between Ra’s al Mathbaz (2.30) and the mainland. Bu Kammāsh, on the mainland, 5 miles within Marsá al Burayqah, is a village with a fort, a grey barrack building with a flagstaff, now used as a frontier police post. There is a small mole suitable for fishing craft abreast the village; on the opposite side of the bay a pier extends S from Ra’s al Mathbaz.

2 **Local knowledge** is required.

Directions. The narrow entrance channel close W of Ra’s al Tulayjah has depths of about 1·5 m, with shoals on either side over which there is 0·3 to 0·6 m of water. The channel is difficult to distinguish at a distance, but in clear weather it is easy to follow between the lighter coloured shoals bordering it. A light buoy (can) is moored about 9 cables N of the entrance.

3 With W winds a strong current sets into the entrance channel and raises the water level in Marsá al Burayqah, with E winds the reverse is the case.

Useful mark:

Farwah Lighthouse (33°06′N 11°44′E) (2.30).

Marsá Şabrātah

2.57

1 **Description.** Marsá Şabrātah (32°49′N 12°27′E), a small cove, is sheltered by a line of rocks and shoals, some of which are above water, extending from it for 1¼ miles WNW, about 3 cables offshore.

Fishing. Tunny nets are laid NE and E from Marsá Şabrātah. For details see 1.3.

2 **Useful marks:**

Marsá Şabrātah Light-tower (red metal framework tower, white base, black band, 6 m in height) (32°49′N 12°26′E). A beacon (black and white stripes, square concrete, 3 m in height) stands 1 cable N of the light-tower.

Monument (32°48′·7N 12°22′·9E).

3 The white buildings of a tunny factory, with four thin iron chimneys, and the custom house, a small white building, stand prominently at the head of Marsá Şabrātah.

Anchorage is obtainable by small vessels in Marsá Şabrātah, in depths of about 6 m, rock. See caution at 2.5.

Şabrātah

2.58

1 **Description.** Şabrātah (32°49′N 12°28′E) is a village close inland of a small indentation 2 miles E of Marsá Şabrātah; close to the beach are the white buildings of a tunny factory. The village contains numerous ruins of the Roman town; the amphitheatre, now partially rebuilt, is situated on the slope of a hill and stands out on the skyline, particularly from E and W. A white marabout and some wind-motors stand W of the amphitheatre.

2 **Fishing.** Tunny nets are laid NW from Şabrātah. For details see 1.3.

Anchorage is obtainable about 2½ cables off Şabrātah; local knowledge is required. The bottom is rocky and uneven and the anchorage is exposed to winds N of W or E. See caution at 2.5.

Supplies. Provisions available.

ŢARĀBULUS

General information

Charts 455, 3403

Position

2.59

1 Ţarābulus (32°54′N 13°11′E), formerly known as Tripoli, is situated on low flat land. The old part of the town stands on Ra's az Zūr, a rocky promontory, and is surrounded by a wall flanked by bastions.

Function

2.60

1 Ţarābulus is the capital and principal port of Libya. In 1999 the city had an estimated population of 1·8 million.

The principal industries are tobacco growing, the dyeing and weaving of local wool and imported cotton yarn, and the production of olive oil. Matting, carpets, leather articles and fabrics embroidered with gold and silver are also manufactured.

2 Principal exports are tobacco, dates, figs, olives, grapes, almonds, salt, barley, esparto grass, ostrich feathers and sponges. Imports include foodstuffs, cotton and metal goods.

In 2003 the population was estimated to be 2 006 000.

Topography

2.61

1 Although the environs of Ţarābulus are low and flat, with arid sandy ground to the W, the appearance of the town from seaward is striking as the white buildings contrast with the palm trees, interspersed with gardens and villages, which thickly cover the surrounding countryside to the S and E.

Approach and entry

2.62

1 The port is approached through compulsory designated Approach Reporting Points, shown on the chart, and entered at Kaliyusha Bank, through dredged channels and between breakwaters, on the alignment of leading lights.

For details of Approach Reporting Points see 1.41, 2.4, and *Admiralty List of Radio Signals Volume 6 (3)*.

Mined areas

2.63

1 See 2.96.

Traffic

2.64

1 In 2007 there were 73 ship calls with a total of 995 896 dwt.

Port Authority

2.65

1 Socialist Ports Co., Tripoli.

Limiting conditions

Controlling depths

2.66

1 In 1978 the entrance channels were dredged to a depth of 11·7 m over a width of 150 m; in 1988 less water was reported.

The turning basin was dredged to a depth of 11·7 m in 1978, but less water was reported in 2005. Elsewhere, parts of the inner harbour are dredged to a depth of 9·7 m (1978).

Abnormal water levels

2.67

1 Northerly winds sometimes raise the level of the water by as much as 0·9 m. During February and March the mean level may fall 0·5 m below normal.

Density of water

2.68

1 Dock density 1·026 g/cm^3.

Maximum size of vessel handled

2.69

1 **Harbour:** 183 m LOA; 10 m draught.

Offshore tanker berth: 195 m LOA; 10·1 m draught.

Local weather and sea state

2.70

1 Mist or haze is common; haze is especially frequent with winds between E and S, and the coast should be approached with caution.

Strong NW winds raise a rough sea in the harbour entrance. The harbour should not be entered in these conditions.

Arrival information

Anchorage

2.71

1 The anchorage area lies about 1¾ miles N of Ţarābulus Lighthouse (32°54′·3N 13°10′·6E) (2.77), as shown on the chart. The holding ground is reported to be good.

Pilots

2.72

1 Pilotage is compulsory. Pilot boards 5 cables N of entrance to the approach channel; in bad weather the pilot boards inside the main breakwaters.

For details see *Admiralty List of Radio Signals Volume 6 (3)*.

Tugs

2.73

1 Tugs are available.

Harbour

General layout

2.74

1 The port fronts the NE side of the town and is comprised of an inner and outer harbour. The outer harbour is protected from NW by North East Breakwater, and from NE by North West Breakwater. The entrance, between the heads of the breakwaters, is 1 cable wide.

2 The inner harbour is protected from NW by Spanish Mole, which extends across Ra’s az Zūr Bank. It is protected from NE by a mole extending SE from the junction of Spanish Mole and North East Breakwater, and by Karamanli Mole.

3 A turning basin lies close within the entrance to the inner harbour.

Developments. An outer harbour with 4000 m of quayage and depth alongside 12 m (2007).

Traffic and port signals

2.75

1 The following signals (diagram 2.75) are displayed:

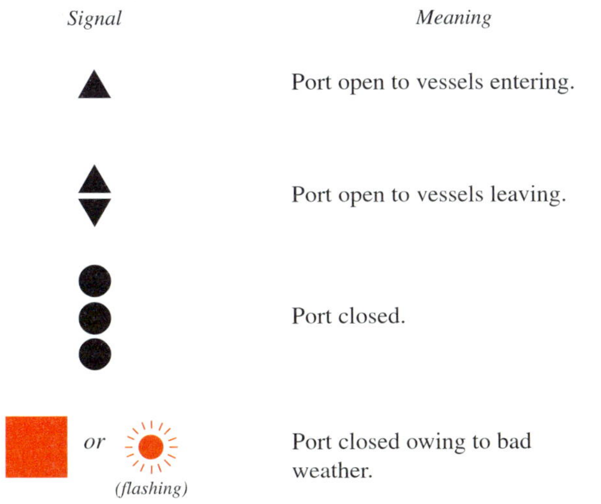

Ţarābulus - port entry signals (2.75)

2 The following signals, on whistle or siren, may be sounded by vessels at anchor or alongside:

Signal	*Meaning*
Succession of short blasts.	Fire alarm.
Short blast, two long blasts, short blast.	Police required.
Short blast, two long blasts.	Doctor required.
One long blast.	Lighters required.
Two long blasts.	Floating crane required.
Three long blasts.	Pilot required.
Four long blasts.	Tug required.

Ţarābulus (Tripoli) - Inner Harbour (2.74)

(Original dated 1999)

(Photograph - K Dixon)

Currents

2.76

1 Off the port the current is usually ESE-going at a rate of about ½ kn, but occasionally, during NE winds which predominate in summer, a WNW-going current is experienced. A surface current flowing across, or through, the harbour entrance is associated with the occurrence of the Marrobbio (1.155); this current may be very strong, rates of more than 3 kn having been observed, and it causes eddies and tide rips near the harbour entrance. It does not flow in one direction for more than 20 or 30 minutes, and then may flow strongly in the opposite direction. The oscillations in tidal level, and the associated tidal streams, gradually diminish.

Directions

(continued from 2.18)

Principal marks

2.77

1 **Landmarks** (with positions from Ţarābulus Light (32°54′·3N 13°10′·6E)):

Ţarābulus Lighthouse (white round tower, black bands, 27 m in height) standing on the root of Spanish Mole.

Water tower (light yellow, red obstruction light, elevation 46 m) (3 cables SSW).

Belfry of the church of Santa Maria degli Angeli, (elevation of 40 m) (3¾ cables SSW).

2 Castle (elevation 46 m) (5½ cables SSE) with two flagstaffs, situated at the SE corner of the wall surrounding the old town, of which it is the oldest building.

Cathedral with an octagonal dome (elevation 46 m) and belfry (elevation 60 m) (9½ cables SSE).

Dome (white) (1¼ miles SSE).

3 Radio mast (red obstruction lights, elevation 51 m) standing on the roof of the post office building (8¾ cables SSE).

Radio mast (red obstruction lights, elevation 122 m) (2 miles SSE) (chart 3403).

Major light:

Aero light (red and white chequered water tower) (occasionally exhibited) (32°54′·3N 13°16′·4E).

Outer approaches

2.78

1 Vessels approaching Ţarābulus must keep clear of the Entry Prohibited Areas, as shown on the chart, and pass through one of the Approach Reporting Points (2.62) before proceeding to the pilot boarding position (32°56′·3N 13°13′·4E).

Approach and entry

2.79

1 **Approach leading lights:**

Front light (red and white triangle point up) (32°54′·4N 13°13′·6E).

Rear light (red and white triangle point down) (130 m from front light).

From the vicinity of the pilot boarding position the alignment (175°) of these lights leads S for 1 mile through a channel, dredged (1978) to a depth of 11·7 m over a width of 150 m, across Kaliyusha Bank, passing (with positions from the front light):

2 E of No 1 Lighted Buoyant Beacon (starboard hand) (1¾ miles N), and:

W of No 2 Lighted Buoyant Beacon (port hand) (1¾ mile N), thence:

W of a dangerous wreck (1½ miles N) on the detached part of Kaliyusha Bank, thence:

E of E edge of Kaliyusha Bank (1¼ miles NNW), marked by No 3 Light Buoy (starboard hand). In strong N winds the sea breaks on the bank.

Thence from a position NW of No 4 Light Beacon (1 mile N) alter course onto the following leading line:

3 **Entry leading lights:**

Front light (column) (32°53′·8N 13°10′·9E).

Rear light (mast on building) (300 m from front light).

The alignment (233°) of these lights leads 1¾ miles SW through the channel to the inner harbour, passing between the heads of North East Breakwater and North West Breakwater, and between the heads of the inner moles.

Useful marks

2.80

1 North East Breakwater Head Light (black and white concrete column) (32°55′·2N 13°13′·0E).

North West Breakwater Head Light (red and white concrete column), 2 cables S of above light.

2 Light (black and white daymark on green concrete column, 10 m in height) (32°54′·5N 13°11′·8E) exhibited from the head of No 1 Pier.

Light (red and white daymark on red concrete column) (32°54′·3N 13°11′·9E) exhibited from the head of Karamanli Mole.

Berths

Inner harbour

2.81

1 With positions from the head (32°54′·3N 13°11′·9E) of Karamanli Mole:

Pier No 1 (2¼ cables NNW), the N inner mole, has 300 m of berthing space on its SW side with depths of 12 m; but see 2.66. Tanker berth.

2 **Pier No 2** (2¼ cables NW); about 860 m of berthing space; depths of 12 m alongside; but see 2.66. A floating dock (see 2.83) is permanently moored at its N root, close SW of Pier No 1.

Pier No 3 (3½ cables W); about 1000 m of berthing space; depths of 8 to 12 m alongside; but see 2.66.

3 **Spanish Quay** (8 cables W), at the inner end of Spanish Mole; about 530 m of berthing space; a RoRo berth lies close NE.

Karamanli Mole (2 cables SSE), the S inner mole, has an oil and gas berth on its inner face; least depth of 9 m alongside; but see 2.66. A Naval Base is located close S of the mole.

4 **South side** (7 cables SW). The S shore of the inner harbour, from close NW of the castle to Karamanli Mole, is fully quayed with various depths alongside.

Outer harbour

2.82

1 A Naval Base with a number of finger piers has been constructed in the SE corner of Outer Harbour. Depths alongside unknown.

Port services

Repairs

2.83

1 Medium repairs, including castings up to 50 kg, can be effected. There are two slipways, each 61 m long, with a combined lift of 500 tons.

A floating dock is moored in the inner harbour: length 136 m, breadth 23·4 m, depth over keel blocks at MHWS 6·4 m, lift 5000 tons.

Other facilities

2.84

1 There are hospitals in the town.

Supplies

2.85

1 Fuel alongside and by barge, fresh water by barge.

Communications

2.86

1 International airport at Ţarābulus.

Harbour regulations

2.87

1 Bilges must not be pumped out in the vicinity of the port, and every precaution must be taken to avoid fuel oil escaping into the harbour.

The use of radio by vessels in the harbour is prohibited.

Offshore tanker berth

Chart 3403

General information

2.88

1 **Description.** An offshore tanker berth, consisting of mooring buoys at the seaward end of a submarine pipeline serving an oil installation, lies about 6 miles E of Ţarābulus in position 32°55′·0N 13°20′·4E; depth alongside 16 m. It is enclosed by a restricted area, shown on the chart, the limits of which are marked by buoys. It lies between two mine danger areas (2.63) and within an extensive prohibited area (2.96).

2 **Topography.** The coast from the root of the NW Breakwater (32°54′N 13°13′E) to Ra's Tājūrā', 8 miles E, is sandy, and numerous rocks extend 5 cables offshore for the first 5 miles.

Directions

2.89

1 **Landmark:**

Tower (32°53′·7N 13°19′·8E), stands in an oil installation, from which a submarine pipeline extends 1 mile NNE to mooring buoys.

Major light:

Aero light (32°54′·3N 13°16′·4E) (2.77).

2.90

1 **Approach.** For regulations on approach see 2.78. In addition, as this berth lies within a prohibited area, no attempt should be made to enter without prior permission from the Port Authority.

Leading beacons:

Front beacon (32°53′·8N 13°21′·8E).

Rear beacon (900 m from front beacon).

2 From a position about 6½ miles NE of Ţarābulus Light (32°54′·2N 13°10′·6E), the alignment (135¼°) of these beacons leads about 4½ miles SE to the mooring buoys, passing NE of a patch, reported (1961) to have a depth of 8·2 m over it, 2½ miles NW of the front beacon.

An anchor target beacon stands about 1¼ miles W of the front beacon, to assist with positioning on berthing.

2.91

1 **Useful marks** (positioned from tower at 32°53′·7N 13°19′·8E):

A group of five small oil tanks (3¼ miles WNW), stands on the summit of a low brown cliff.

Control tower (3 miles W).

Water tower (2¼ miles WNW).

2 Sīdī al Andalusī (5¾ cables ESE), a marabout which stands on a hillock in the middle of a barren area and becomes prominent only when the sun shines on it.

Five radio masts (1½ miles SE); one of the masts is marked with red obstruction lights.

ŢARĀBULUS TO RA'S AL BARQ

General information

Chart 3403

Route

2.92

1 From a position N of Ţarābulus (32°54′N 13°11′E) the route leads ESE, for about 115 miles, to a position NNE of Ra's al Barq (32°22′N 15°12′E).

Topography

2.93

1 Between Ra's Tājūrā' (32°54′N 13°23′E) and Ra's Ḩallāb, 21 miles ESE, the coast is at first low and sandy, but later becomes high and rocky in places, with a line of reddish sand dunes. Jabal Tarhūnah, with elevations from 240 to 400 m extends parallel to the coast, at 12 to 18 miles inland, for about 30 miles E of the meridian of Ra's Tājūrā'.

2 Between Ra's Ḩallāb and Al Jazīrah, a dark-coloured rocky point 3 miles ESE, the low sandy coastline is broken by the mouths of streams. From Al Jazīrah to Ra's al Hamrā', 4¾ miles E, the coast continues low, with shifting sand dunes, fringed by rocks extending more than 5 cables offshore.

3 From Ra's al Hamrā' (32°46′N 13°57′E) to Sīdī 'Abd al 'Aţī (2.101), 6 miles SE, the coast becomes higher and is steep, interspersed with rocky points and small sandy bays, into which flow streams, which dry in summer, with groves of palms at their mouths. There are no off-lying dangers.

2.94

1 The coast E of Sīdī 'Abd al 'Aţī (32°43′N 14°03′E) (2.88) is hilly with a soft stone ridge, 18 to 49 m high, sloping to the sea; the shore is rocky, interspersed with small bays. The country is well cultivated, with many villages, and is well watered by several streams which dry in summer and have groves of palm trees at their mouths.

2 Between Sīdī Ramaḑān (32°43′N 14°08′E) and Ra's al Misann, 7 miles E, the coast can easily be identified from seaward by the line of yellow or red dunes which stand out clearly against the dark background of hills. Several reefs extend ½ cable offshore. From Ra's al Misann (32°41′N 14°14′E) to Ra's al Wazīf, 2¾ miles SE, the coast is barren.

3 The inland mountain range becomes very uniform in character E of Al Khums (32°41′N 14°15′E), with no prominent features. Ra's al Ḩammān (32°35′·4N 14°17′·8E), 117 m, is situated 4 miles SSE of Al Khums. Between Ra's al Wazīf (32°39′N 14°16′E) and Sīdī Barkū, 2½ miles SE, the coast is low and sandy. Punta Labdah, a black perpendicular cliff, was formerly the NW extremity of the Roman port of Leptis Magna, the ruins of which are now partly buried in the sand. Several ruined columns stand on Punta Labdah.

4 Between Sīdī Barkū (32°38′N 14°18′E) and Ra's Māqrū, 8 miles SE, the coast is low and sandy and densely covered with palm trees reaching nearly to the sea; near Ra's Māqrū it becomes higher with steep cliffs which appear red

when sunlit. Between Ra's Māqrū and Marsá Zlīţan, 8 miles ESE, the coast is bordered by sand dunes.

2.95

1 Between Marsá Zlīţan (32°30′N 14°34′E) (2.110) and Ra's Mu'ayrī, 4 miles E, the coast is fringed by rocky shoals extending up to 7 cables offshore. The land rises abruptly 1 mile W of Marsá Zlīţan, and continues high as far as Ra's Mu'ayrī. Ra's Mu'ayrī (32°29′N 14°39′E) can be identified from W, as it lies abreast the E of three small rounded summits which are red-coloured when sunlit. Ra's Mu'ayrī also marks the change from a belt of cultivated ground to a line of sand dunes.

2 The coast for 2 miles E of Ra's Mu'ayrī is sandy, backed by scattered dunes from 15 to 40 m high; thence it abruptly becomes rocky with a line of steep cliffs, from 20 to 30 m high, which have three remarkable clefts towards their W end. About 6 miles E of Ra's Mu'ayrī the coast again becomes low, but continues to be mainly rocky.

3 Between Ra's ar Rumaylah (32°26′N 14°51′E) and Sīdī al Hajj Aḩmad Marabout, 6 miles E, the coast is formed by sand dunes; the last 3½ miles of this stretch is mostly rocky, with dunes 50 to 70 m high, and shoals extending over 5 cables offshore. From Sīdī al Hajj Aḩmad Marabout to Ra's al Barq (2.100), 13½ miles ESE, the coast continues rocky varying in height from 24 to 30 m, becoming lower as Ra's al Barq is approached.

Prohibited and danger areas

2.96

1 An extensive area to which entry is prohibited, shown on the chart, extends about 12 miles offshore between Ţarābulus and Ra's al Ḩallāb (2.99), 29 miles ESE.

Within this area are two mine danger areas, shown on the chart and centred 3½ and 8 miles E of the harbour entrance, within which it was reported (1973) that mines had been laid.

2 In addition, also within the prohibited area and shown on the chart, there is an area where anchoring and fishing are prohibited, centred 6 miles E of Ra's Tājūrā (32°54′N 13°23′E). It encloses a landing for submarine cables. For information on cables see 1.26.

Dumping ground

2.97

1 A dumping ground (explosives) (32°55′N 15°10′E) lies about 30 miles offshore, as shown on the chart.

Directions

(continued from 2.18)

Principal marks

2.98

1 **Landmarks:**

Qaşr Khiyār Castle (32°41′N 13°50′E).

Gasr el Cussabat Castle (32°35′N 14°02′E). A radio mast (23 m in height), stands close E.

Gasr al Marqab (32°38′N 14°14′E), a massive isolated stone fort. A radio mast (elevation 162 m), stands close E.

2 Radio mast (elevation 90 m) (32°29′N 14°34′E), marked by obstruction lights.

Radio mast (elevation 114 m) (32°24′N 15°04′E), marked by obstruction lights.

Ţarābulus to Ra's al Misann

2.99

1 From a position N of Ţarābulus (32°54′N 13°11′E) (2.59), and clear of prohibited areas, the coastal route leads ESE, passing (with positions from Ra's al Wazīf Light (32°39′N 14°16′E)):

NNE of Ra's Tājūrā' Lighthouse (black and white chequered square masonry tower) (47 miles NW), thence:

2 NNE of Ra's al Ḩallāb (25 miles WNW), a dark-coloured rocky promontory 13 m high; shoal water extends about 3 cables offshore for 1 mile W, and a patch, with a least depth of 4·3 m over it, lies 5 cables NW. Ra's al Ḩallāb Light (metal framework tower on white round tower, 22 m in height) stands, with an adjoining house, on the promontory. Thence:

3 NNE of Ra's al Hamrā' (18 miles WNW). Bintal Rock lies close offshore 3 miles SE of Ra's al Hamrā'; the rock has a pointed top and is radar conspicuous.

The track then leads to a position NNE of Ra's al Misann (3 miles NW), a low rocky point.

Ra's al Misann to Ra's al Barq

2.100

1 From a position NNE of Ra's al Misann (32°41′N 14°14′E) the track continues ESE, passing (with positions from Ra's al Wazīf Light (32°39′N 14°16′E)):

NNE of Ra's al Wazīf. A light (white round tower, black bands, 19 m in height) is exhibited from Ra's al Wazīf. Thence:

2 NNE of Ra's Māqrū (10½ miles SE), thence:

NNE of Marsá Zlīţan Light (black metal framework tower on black square building, white stripes, 5 m in height) (17 miles ESE), exhibited ENE of Al Qalb, a prominent conical hill about 28 m high, thence:

3 NNE of Ra's Ḩammūd (30¼ miles ESE), a conical hill 49 m high. Ra's ar Rumaylah, 68 m high, lies 2 miles ESE of Ra's Ḩammūd, and may be identified by its black colouring between two yellowish belts and by three slight humps on its crest. To the E of Ra's Ḩammūd the bottom becomes more shelving, but is clear of dangers. Thence:

4 NNE of Ra's Mişrātah (45 miles ESE), an ancient Trierum promontory. Rocks extend for about 7 cables N of the point, but to the E the depths become more regular. Fnar el Cab, close S, is a dark-coloured hill, 59 m high, on which stands a pillar, which shows up well at a distance of 5 or 6 miles.

5 The track then leads to a position NNE of Ra's al Barq (50 miles ESE), a low rocky point close N of Qaşr Aḩmad (2.120); a light (2.134) is exhibited from the point. A large white house stands 2½ cables WNW of Ra's al Barq, and the remains of old Roman baths lie close W of the light-structure.

Useful marks

2.101

1 Fort Trig el-Gefàra (32°52′·3N 13°23′·8E), a prominent disused structure. A windmill, 3¾ miles SE of the fort, which is taller than the surrounding trees, shows up well on the skyline; a second, derelict, windmill stands 2½ miles SE.

Sīdī Abū an Nūr Marabout (32°47′·2N 13°36′·1E). It is almost obscured by dark bushes which show up well against the light sandy background. Nearby are some barracks; a white derelict fort, ¾ cable SE, is prominent.

2 Sīdī Subayh al Amān Marabout, (32°47′·4N 13°43′·6E) standing on the shore; a tunny factory stands close E.

Sīdī 'Abd al Ghanī Marabout (32°41′·0N 13°58′·2E) is prominent when the sun shines on it, appearing as a white building.

Sīdī 'Abd al 'Aṯī Marabout (32°43′·1N 14°02′·7E) is prominent, but is only visible seaward from NE.

Sīdī Ramaḏān Marabout (32°42′·5N 14°08′·2E) stands on a hillock near a small grove of palm trees, and with the sun on it is visible for about 10 miles.

3 Sīdī Miftāḥ Marabout (32°35′·2N 14°22′·0E), a large white domed building standing close to the beach. It shows up against the dark palm trees behind it, and is the only prominent object on this stretch of the coast.

Sīdī al Ḥājj Aḥmad Marabout (32°25′·5N 14°57′·0E).

Henscir el-Com (32°25′·0N 14°58′·8E), 1 mile SE of the above, a conical hill 23 m high, prominent from NW.

(Directions continue at 2.144)

Al Khums

39/10

General information

2.102

1 **Position.** The port of Al Khums (also known as Homs or Khoms) (32°41′N 14°15′E), an artificial harbour, is situated on the SE side of Ra's al Misann. The town of Al Khums lies 1½ miles SE, close within Ra's al Wazīf.

Function. The port handles motor vehicles, containers and other cargoes which do not require covered storage.

2 **Approach and entry.** The port is approached directly from seaward to the fairway light buoy (safe water) about 3 miles E of the harbour; the coastline is reported (1999) to give a good radar response at ranges of up to 18 miles. Al Khums does not have a designated Approach Reporting Point but vessels must report their position, course and speed when 12 miles distant. For details of Approach Reporting Points see 1.41, 2.4, and *Admiralty List of Radio Signals Volume 6 (3)*.

3 **Traffic.** In 2007 there were 65 ship calls with a total of 585 482 dwt.

Port Authority. Socialist Ports Co., Al Khums.

Limiting conditions

2.103

1 **Controlling depth** in the approach is reported (1999) to be 13 m.

Maximum size of vessel handled: 14 500 dwt, draught 12 m.

Climate information: see 1.184 and 1.186.

Arrival information

2.104

1 **Outer anchorage.** The designated anchorage is within 5 cables radius of 32°41′·7N 14°19′·3E, about 4 miles ENE from the harbour (see also 1.30).

Pilots. Pilotage, which is compulsory, is available during daylight hours only, and must be arranged in advance as the pilot is based in Ţarābulus. The pilot boards either at the anchorage, or 1 mile ESE of the breakwater head.

2 **Tugs.** Two tugs are available.

Regulations. Movement of vessels is restricted to daylight hours.

Harbour

2.105

1 **General layout.** The harbour consists of a basin enclosed on its NE side by a breakwater and on its SE side by a mole. The harbour entrance, between the mole and the breakwater, is reported (1999) to be about 90 m wide.

2 Three sides of the basin are quayed, and there is a **T**-shaped jetty in the S part.

Directions

2.106

1 From the pilot boarding position (2.104) the track leads WSW then NW towards the harbour entrance, passing:

SW of the breakwater head, and:

NE of two light buoys (special).

2 **Useful marks:**

Ra's al Wazīf Light (32°39′N 14°16′E) (2.100).

Minaret (2½ miles SE of the light).

Berths

2.107

1 There are 9 berths within the harbour, with alongside depths of between 8 and 12 m.

Port services

2.108

1 **Repairs.** Small repairs can be effected.

Supplies: fuel and fresh water are available with advance notice.

Al Khums Power Station

2.109

1 **General information.** Al Khums Power Station (32°37′·2N 14°20′·0E) may be identified by four chimneys (red with white bands, 100 m in height, red obstruction lights). A pier, which can be readily identified on radar, serves the power station. It projects 1500 m NNE from the shore about 3 cables N of the chimneys. There is a depth of 16 m at the head of the pier which is flanked by two berthing dolphins and fronted by two mooring buoys lying about 1½ cables NNE; the dolphins are marked by lights.

2 Vessels approaching the berth are required to contact Ţarābulus Port Control. It was reported (1989) that tankers with a maximum draught of 13 m use the pier. Vessels moor stern-to the head of the pier using both anchors to maintain position head out. Pilotage, which is compulsory, is available during daylight hours only, and must be arranged in advance as the pilot is based at Ţarābulus. Tugs are available from Al Khums.

Anchorages and harbour

Marsá Zlīţan

2.110

1 **Small vessels** may obtain shelter from E and NE winds inside a reef which lies parallel to the coast about 1 cable offshore, at Marsá Zlīţan (32°30′N 14°34′E); there is an opening at the W end of the reef, with a depth of 3·7 m and a second opening in the centre. A fishing port lies inside the reef with 430 m of quay for fishing vessels. Facilities: cold store; provisions and post office.

Local knowledge is required.

Qaryat az Zurayqī

2.111

1 Qaryat az Zurayqī (32°27′N 14°54′E) is a coastal oasis surrounded by high sandhills, in the centre of which is a

marabout. Between the oasis and Zreg Rocks, 4 cables offshore, there is an anchorage with depths of about 5·5 m, weed and sand, good holding ground, but practically no shelter. A large rock lies ½ cable offshore, 5 cables W of Zreg Rocks.

Local knowledge is required.

Marsá Dzeira

2.112

1 Marsá Dzeira (32°25′N 15°01′E) is a small anchorage lying inside a line of rocks. A tunny factory with a chimney, standing on the coast 2½ miles E of Henscir el-Com, provides a good mark for making the anchorage.

Local knowledge is required.

GULF OF SIRTE

GENERAL INFORMATION

Chart 3402

Area covered

2.113

1 The area covered by this section encompasses the Gulf of Sirte (32°00′N 18°00′E), ancient Syrtis Major and known to the Libyans as Khalīj Surt, which is entered between Ra's al Barq (32°22′N 15°12′E) and Banghāzī (32°07′N 15°13′E) (2.272), about 250 miles E. The section is arranged as follows:

2 Qaşr Aḥmad (2.120).
Ra's al Barq to Ra's Lānūf (2.140).
As Sidrah Oil Terminal (2.156).
Ra's Lānūf (2.174).
Ra's Lānūf to Marsá al Burayqah (2.199).
3 Marsá al Burayqah (2.206).
Marsá al Burayqah to Az Zuwaytīnah Oil Terminal (2.230).
Az Zuwaytīnah Oil Terminal (2.236).
Az Zuwaytīnah Oil Terminal to Banghāzī (2.261).
Banghāzī (2.272).

Movement reports

2.114

1 For details of reports to be made by vessels bound for a port in the Gulf of Sirte, see 1.40, 2.4, and *Admiralty List of Radio Signals Volume 6 (3)*.

Marine exploitation

2.115

1 Off this stretch of coast, oil rigs and vessels connected with oil-drilling operations may be encountered several miles offshore.

Prohibited area

2.116

1 Navigation is prohibited within a firing practice danger area, shown on the chart, centered on 31°33′N 19°30′E, on the E side of the Gulf of Sirte.

Currents

2.117

1 From Ra's Ţulmaythah (32°46′N 21°05′E) a branch of the main E-going current of the Mediterranean Sea turns S into the Gulf of Sirte, strengthening to between ½ and ¾ kn beyond Banghāzī. With strong N winds the rate is sometimes increased to 2 kn, whilst with S gales the current is greatly reduced or may cease altogether.

2 Along the S shore of the Gulf of Sirte the current generally runs NW, continuing to follow the coast for about 50 miles WNW of Ra's al Barq where it meets another branch of the main E-going current running ESE.

The combined current is thought to be deflected away from the coast to rejoin the main stream flowing towards N Cyrenaica, thus creating a clockwise circulation in the Gulf of Sirte.

Tides

2.118

1 Within the Gulf of Sirte the tidal rise is about 0·3 m.

Local weather

2.119

1 Between November and March rough seas at the SE head of the gulf may make boat work impracticable.

QAŞR AḤMAD

General information

Chart 3402, 3402 plan of Mişrātah (Qaşr Aḥmad)

Position and function

2.120

1 Qaşr Aḥmad (32°22′N 15°13′E) is a commercial port serving the town of Mişrātah, also known as Misurata, and the industrial area close S which includes a steelworks and a power station. It has facilities for handling dry bulk, petroleum, RoRo, container and general cargoes.

2 Principal imports and exports include iron ore, grain, construction materials, livestock, machinery and petroleum products. The population is about 200 000.

Topography

2.121

1 The coast S of Ra's al Barq (2.100) is low, with a line of dunes extending parallel to it, behind which lies Mişrātah Oasis.

Traffic

2.122

1 In 2007 there were 386 ship calls with a total of 6 682 089 dwt.

Approach and entry

2.123

1 The port is approached through the Approach Reporting Point (32°34′N 15°16′E) and entered through dredged channels on the alignment of leading lights. For details of Approach Reporting Points see 1.41, 2.4, and *Admiralty List of Radio Signals Volume 6 (3)*.

Port Authority

2.124

1 Socialist Ports Co., PO Box 2342, Qaşr Aḥmed, Libya.

Limiting conditions

Controlling depths

2.125

1 **Main harbour.** The approach channel was dredged to 13 m in 1978; for depths alongside berths see 2.137.

Steelworks harbour. Minimum depths within the dredged areas have been reported (1997) to be 19·5 m in the approach channel and 15 m within the harbour.

2 **Caution.** Dredged depths within the port are subject to siltation and liable to change. Mariners should consult the Port Authority for the latest information.

Maximum size of vessel handled

2.126

1 Tankers of up to 30 000 dwt and 11 m draught can be accommodated.

Density of water

2.127

1 Dock density 1·026 g/cm^3.

Arrival information

Notice of ETA

2.128

1 72, 48, 24 and 12 hours in advance.

Anchorage

2.129

1 A designated anchorage area for vessels, shown on the chart, is centred 5 miles ENE of Ra's al Barq Light (32°22′·3N 15°12′·7E) with charted depths of 25 to 37 m. Holding ground is poor and vessels are advised to vacate the anchorage if strong winds are imminent.

Prohibited anchorage

2.130

1 Anchorage is prohibited within 2 miles of the harbour.

Pilotage

2.131

1 Pilotage is compulsory and is available 24 hours. Pilot boards about 2 miles off the main harbour entrance; and, for the steelworks harbour, 1 mile from the fairway buoy. The pilot launch has a grey hull and white superstructure. For details see *Admiralty List of Radio Signals Volume 6 (3)*.

Tugs

2.132

1 Tugs are available.

Harbour

General layout

2.133

1 **Main harbour.** The main harbour is formed by two breakwaters enclosing the harbour area. The N breakwater extends 7 cables E from Ra's al Barq and the broad E mole extends 1 mile N from the shore, about 1¼ miles S, forming an E facing entrance about 180 m wide. Lights are exhibited from the head of each breakwater.

2 The harbour is divided by a broad central mole extending about 700 m N from the S end, forming two basins which contain the main cargo berthing areas. A short pier lies in the NW part of the harbour with a tanker berth at its head. It was reported (1991) that further development work was in progress.

3 **Steelworks harbour.** The steelworks harbour, situated 1 mile SE of the main harbour, is protected from N by an angled breakwater about 1 mile in length. A bulk handling berth lies on the inner side close E of the elbow, marked at its E limit by a light. A prominent gantry crane stands on the breakwater and a conveyor runs from the berth to the power station and steelworks.

Directions for entering harbours

Principal marks

2.134

1 **Landmarks** (positioned from Ra's al Barq Light):

Ra's al Barq Light (white metal framework tower on square tower, black stripes, 8 m in height) (32°22′·3N 15°12′·7E).

Water tower (1½ cables SSW).

2 Silos (7 cables ESE), standing on the E breakwater of the main harbour.

Water tower (9 cables SSE).

Dish aerial (1¼ miles SSE), standing near the root of the E breakwater.

Three chimneys (red lights) (2½ miles SSE).

Main harbour

2.135

1 **Approach.** Vessels must pass through the Approach Reporting Point (2.123), as shown on the chart.

Leading lights:

Front light (white triangle point up, red band) (32°22′·3N 15°12′·7E).

Rear light (white triangle point down, red band) (500 m from front light).

2 From a position about 1 mile E of the entrance the alignment (270°) of these lights leads to the harbour through the centre of the entrance channel, which was dredged (1978) to a depth of 13 m over a width of 150 m.

Steelworks harbour

2.136

1 **Approach.** Vessels must pass through the Approach Reporting Point (2.123), as shown on the chart.

Leading lights:

Front light (32°20′·6N 15°14′·4E).

Rear light (430 m from the front light).

2 From the vicinity of the fairway light buoy (safe water) (32°21′N 15°19′E) the alignment (263°) of these lights leads 3 miles W through the dredged channel, marked by pairs of buoys (lateral), passing (with positions from the N breakwater head light (32°20′·8N 15°15′·4E)):

3 N of an obstruction (1¼ miles E), thence:

N of obstructions (5 cables ESE).

The track then leads into the harbour. The dredged area within the harbour is marked by light buoys (lateral) and obstructions lie in the N part, close SSW of the berth.

Berths

Main harbour

2.137

1 In the NW corner of the harbour is a **T**-shaped pier, with a depth of 12 m alongside, for the use of tankers discharging oil products.

In the S part of the harbour there is about 3000 m of berth space, in two basins, with a least depth of 11 m alongside. There is a RoRo berth at the S end of the E basin, with a length of 200 m and a depth alongside of 11 m.

Steelworks harbour

2.138

1 There is a bulk handling berth on the inside of the N breakwater with a length of 350 m and a reported depth alongside of 19 m.

Port services

2.139

1 **Repairs.** Minor repairs undertaken.

Facilities. Hospital in Mişrātah.

Supplies. Fuel not available; fresh water by barge.

RA'S AL BARQ TO RA'S LĀNŪF

General information

Chart 3402

Route

2.140

1 From a position NNE of Ra's al Barq (32°22′N 15°12′E) the coastal route leads SE, for a distance of about 80 miles, to a position about 25 miles NW of Surt, thence ESE, for a distance of about 140 miles, to a position NNE of Ra's Lānūf (30°31′N 18°35′E).

Topography

2.141

1 Between Ra's al Barq (32°22′N 15°12′E) (2.100) and Ra's Ramlah, 23 miles SSE, the coast is bordered by sand dunes, almost devoid of vegetation, with a maximum elevation of 20 m, gradually becoming lower towards the S. The coast is rocky in places, and elsewhere there is a low sandy beach backed by salt lagoons.

Rās Tàtila, 4 miles SE of Ra's al Barq, is the termination of a prominent sandy hill 15 m high; the coast in this vicinity is rocky, and shoal water extends 5 cables offshore.

2 Between Qaşr al 'Ar'ar (32°12′N 15°19′E) and Ra's Ramlah, 11 miles S, the coast is mostly fringed with rocks awash, which extend up to 2½ cables offshore, over which the sea usually breaks.

Jabal al Malfá, a line of dunes with a maximum elevation of 22 m, extends between 3 and 16 miles S of Ra's Ramlah, from 1 to 1½ miles inland. Tual, near the N end, is a conical dune 17 m high, from a short distance N of which a white patch extends to the rocky coast. El-Taiara, on the coast abreast the S end of Jabal al Malfá, is a group of light-coloured sand dunes about 7 m high.

3 Maaten Giàber (31°32′N 15°33′E), 11 m high, 5 miles ESE of Gasr Giàber, is the N of a line of sand dunes lying parallel to the coast, from 1½ to 2 miles inland.

Between Bu'ayrāt al Ḩasūn (31°24′N 15°44′E) and Surt (2.155), 46 miles ESE, the coast is bordered by sand dunes of which the highest, Temed Hazzan, 14 miles ESE of Bu'ayrāt al Ḩasūn, is 16 m high and white coloured.

4 A line of dark coloured rocks, 6 miles ESE of Temed Hazzan, fringes the coast and is often visible at a considerable distance owing to refraction. The land E of these rocks rises to Saniet Mezauagh (31°09′N 16°19′E), 4 miles inland, identifiable by its slightly conical shape and dark colour, and by a white sand dune on the coast N of it.

5 Between Surt (31°13′N 16°35′E) and At Tāmah, 42 miles ESE, there are no off-lying dangers; the W end of this stretch of coast is rocky and reaches an elevation of 36 m. At Abyār al Qindīl, 3 miles farther ESE, the dunes show as three successive hummocks, the E of which is lighter in colour than the others.

6 Between Ra's al 'Uwayjā' (30°55′N 17°52′E) and Jābiyat al Yahūdīyah al Wasţīyah, 21 miles ESE, the coast continues low, although Jabal Bin Jawwād (30°48′N 18°00′E), 50 m high, has several rocky summits which can be easily identified from seaward. Between the summits several streams flow into the sea; farther inland is a higher ridge.

Current

2.142

1 The current off this stretch of coast is usually NW-going at a mean rate of ½ kn, but occasionally in winter with a strong NW wind it runs SE.

Marine exploitation

2.143

1 Between At Tāmah (31°05′N 17°24′E) and As Sidrah, 57 miles ESE, oil rigs and vessels connected with oil drilling operations may be met with, up to a distance of about 23 miles offshore.

Directions

(continued from 2.101)

Principal marks

2.144

1 **Landmarks:**

Gasr Giàber (31°33′N 15°28′E) a ruined fort standing on a hillock 16 m high.

El Garusk (31°05′·5N 16°59′·1E), 50 m in height, dark in colour with a flat summit, is the most prominent object on this coast. A radio tower stands 3 miles SW.

2 Red sand dune (30°57′·2N 17°41′·0E) with several black patches at its foot.

Jabal al Mudawwar (30°51′N 17°42′E), 121 m in height, which has a flat round summit.

Stranded wreck (30°48′N 18°06′E).

3 **Major lights:**

Surt Light (white water tower) (31°12′·5N 16°35′·6E).

Ra's Lānūf Light (30°30′·7N 18°32′·3E) (2.191).

Ra's al Barq to Surt

2.145

1 From a position NNE of Ra's al Barq the coastal passage leads SE, passing (with positions from Ra's Ramlah (32°00′N 15°21′E)):

NE of the approaches to Qaşr Aḩmad (22 miles NNW) (2.120), thence:

NE of a dangerous wreck (15 miles N) which lies 5 miles offshore from Qaşr al 'Ar'ar, the site of a ruined fort, thence:

2 NE of a shoal (10 miles N), with depths of 6·3 to 7·9 m over it, which extends 4 miles SSE, parallel to the coast, 2 miles offshore, thence:

NE of a stranded wreck (9 miles N); a spit with a depth of 2·4 m at its outer end extends 7½ cables offshore close SE of the wreck. Thence:

NE of a dangerous wreck (5 miles NNE), thence:

NE of Ra's Ramlah, thence:

3 NE of a stranded wreck (15 miles SSE) which lies 4 miles off the coast. Between this stranded wreck and Hissa Bank, 25 miles SSE, there are several dangerous wrecks as shown on the chart. Thence:

NE of Hissa Bank (40 miles SSE) which is composed of sand, weed and rocks and extends for 3 miles parallel to the coast, 2½ miles offshore, with a least depth of 4·3 m over it, thence:

4 NE of Zerid Rocks (45 miles SSE) which extend from a position 1 mile SE of Hissa Bank for 13 miles SE, with a least depth of 3·8 m. Both Hissa Bank and Zerid Rocks may be seen at a distance of about 4 cables, as the water over them is dark green, in contrast to the white and black patches elsewhere.

The track then leads to a position about 15 miles N of Surt (31°13′N 16°35′E) (2.155).

Surt to Ra's Lānūf

2.146

1 From a position about 15 miles N of Surt the route then leads ESE and SE, passing (with positions from At Tāmah (31°04′·8N 17°23′·1E)):

Clear of a shoal (38 miles NW) with a least known depth of 44 m over it, thence:

2 NNE of At Tāmah. A rocky submerged reef, with a least depth of 6·7 m over it, extends 1½ miles E of At Tāmah, with depths of 9 m between its outer end and the coast. A stranded wreck lies just E of the point and a radio tower stands 3 miles SW of the point. Thence:

3 NNE of Ra's al 'Uwayjā' (27 miles ESE) which terminates in a high dark rocky mass, prominent from seaward; a stranded wreck lies close SE of the point. A rocky reef, with a least depth of 2·7 m over it, extends 3¼ miles ESE from Ra's al 'Uwayjā'. Thence:

4 NNE of a dangerous wreck (34 miles ESE) which lies 5 miles off the coast. Between the wreck and the coast is a line of shoals with a least depth of 5·6 m over them. They extend from a position 7 miles ESE of Ra's al 'Uwayjā' for 9½ miles ESE. Thence:

5 NNE of Jābiyat al Yahūdīyah al Wasţīyah (46½ miles SE), the SE of three light-coloured sand dunes which increase in elevation from W to E and stand out clearly against a brown plain. It is readily distinguishable by its green bushes; a reef, with a least depth of 3·7 m over it, extends ESE from the point. Thence:

6 NNE of Rās al Yahūdīyah (51 miles SE) (Chart 3344). A shoal area, with a least depth of 3·5 m over it at its SE end, and marked by discoloured water, lies 7 cables SE. Thence:

NNE of As Sidrah Oil Terminal (56 miles SE) (2.156), thence:

To a position NNE of Ra's Lānūf Oil Terminal (69 miles SE) (2.174).

Useful marks

2.147

1 Radio tower (elevation 107 m) (31°23′N 15°38′E).

Three monuments (31°14′N 16°09′E).

Radio tower (elevation 107 m) (31°13′N 16°16′E).

As Sulţān (31°07′N 17°10′E), 15 m in height with a conical summit and several dark patches, is prominent, being part of a line of low reddish sand dunes.

2 Radio tower (elevation 146 m) (30°53′N 17°47′E).

Bir Nezla (30°54′N 17°53′E), a light coloured sand dune, surrounded by bushes, which is easily identifiable.

(Directions continue at 2.202)

Anchorages

Offshore

2.148

1 Between Ra's al Barq (32°22′·2N 15°12′·7E) and Ghìlman, a brown sand dune, 8½ miles SE, there are no dangers outside a distance of 1½ miles from the coast. The holding ground is good but there is no shelter.

Rās Cara

2.149

1 Rās Cara (32°08′N 15°22′E) provides shelter in NW winds for an anchorage S, with good holding ground. Bu Chedìa, 16 m high, bare and blackish, and Es Smaida, 14 m high, and brown, are two sand dunes situated 3¾ miles SSW and 6¼ miles S, respectively, of Rās Cara.

As Sulţān

2.150

1 A small cove close W of As Sulţān (31°07′N 17°10′E) (2.147), with a depth of 5·2 m in the middle, affords anchorage but no protection from strong winds. The village of As Sulţān, close by, consists of a few huts and is only visible from a short distance.

Local knowledge is required.

At Tāmah

2.151

1 Small vessels may obtain anchorage, sheltered from N and NW winds, S of the reef, off At Tāmah (31°05′N 17°24′E) (2.146).

Local knowledge is required.

Marsá al 'Uwayjā'

2.152

1 Marsá al 'Uwayjā' (30°54′N 17°53′E) affords shelter from N and NW winds. Anchorage may be obtained SE of the point in depths of about 7·3 to 12·0 m, sand and weed, good holding.

Local knowledge is required.

Jābiyat Yahūdīyah al Wasţīyah

2.153

1 Anchorage, sheltered from NW winds, may be obtained off Jābiyat Yahūdīyah al Wasţīyah (30°46′N 18°13′E) (2.146), S of the reef which extends ESE from Jābiyat Yahūdīyah al Wasţīyah. The anchorage has a bottom of sand with good holding ground.

Local knowledge is required.

Minor harbours

Bu'ayrāt al Ḩasūn

2.154

1 **Description.** Bu'ayrāt al Ḩasūn (31°24′N 15°44′E), a village which in 1950 was in ruins, may be identified by a white fort and a small white domed monument (not charted) which stand among the ruined buildings.

Approach. The approach to Bu'ayrāt al Ḩasūn should be made with the monument bearing 217° which leads between Hissa Bank and Zerid Rocks.

2 **Anchorage.** Sheltered anchorage may be obtained with the monument bearing 217°, 1¼ miles offshore in a depth of 5·7 m.

Berth. A wooden pier, 160 m long, extends NE from the village. Small powered vessels may berth on its SE side in depths of 1·8 to 3·0 m, but silting takes place and caution is necessary when proceeding alongside.

Surt

SURT GENERAL INFORMATION

2.155

41/10 1 **Description.** Surt (31°13′N 16°35′E) was probably the ancient port of Aspis, of which the remains of the moles are still above water.

Landmarks (positioned from Surt Light (31°12′·5N 16°35′·6E)):

Minaret (2¾ miles W).
El-Camusk (35 m in height) (2 miles SSW).
Radio tower (2¾ miles S).
Tuila (45 m in height) (2 miles SSE).

2 **Major light:**

Surt Light (31°12′·5N 16°35′·6E) (2.144).

Anchorage. A designated anchorage to serve a new port (see development below) is within 1 mile radius of 31°15′·8N 16°40′·9E (see also 1.41).

3 **Harbour.** The small harbour, now seldom used, is formed by ancient moles and has a sand bottom with patches of rock. Some protection is afforded to small vessels. Boats drawing less than 1·2 m can usually find complete shelter in a small pool with a soft sand bottom at the W end of the harbour.

4 **Development.** A new port is under construction (2007).

Climate information: see 1.184 and 1.187.

Entry. There are two entrance channels, the larger about 60 m wide. The alignment (180°) of the following pair of beacons leads through one of the entrances:

Front beacon (31°12′·7N 16°35′·2E).
Rear beacon (about 90 m from front beacon).

AS SIDRAH OIL TERMINAL

General information

Chart 3344

Position

2.156

1 As Sidrah (Es Sider) Oil Terminal (30°38′N 18°21′E) lies in the S part of the Gulf of Sirte, 14 miles NW of Ra's Lānūf (2.174).

Function

2.157

1 The terminal exports petroleum through offshore berths situated at the seaward end of submarine oil pipelines.

Topography

2.158

1 As Sidrah is a high white sand dune covered with bushes, which slopes steeply to the sea. Administrative buildings and a pumping station are situated on the shore.

Traffic

2.159

1 In 2007 there were 151 ship calls with a total of 18 115 305 dwt.

Port Authority

2.160

1 Waha Oil Company, PO Box 395, Ţarābulus, Libya.

Limiting conditions

Density of water

2.161

1 1·025 g/cm³.

Maximum size of vessel handled

2.162

1 305 000 dwt, LOA 355 m and 22·25 m draught.

Local weather

2.163

1 **Local weather.** The oil loading berths are untenable in winds of force 5 or more. Main engines must be kept at immediate readiness both in anchorage and at the berths.

Arrival information

Anchorage

2.164

1 The recommended anchorage for vessels awaiting a berth, as shown on the chart, lies between the parallels of 30°41′·5N and 30°43′·0N, and between the meridians of 18°22′E and 18°25′E. The depth is about 33 m over a bottom of sand, and the holding is reported to be very good. Arriving vessels must anchor in this designated area unless the terminal operator directs otherwise.

Prohibited anchorage

2.165

1 Anchorage is prohibited within an extensive area, the limits of which are shown on the chart, enclosing the whole of the offshore terminal.

Pilotage

2.166

1 Pilotage is compulsory and available 24 hours. The boarding area is in the vicinity of 30°40′·2N 18°23′·5E. The pilot boat is black with white upper works. The pilot and mooring party remain on board until the vessel leaves the terminal.

Tugs

2.167

1 Tugs are not available but there are launches to assist with mooring.

For details see *Admiralty List of Radio Signals Volume 6 (3)*.

Harbour

General layout

2.168

1 The terminal, in an open roadstead, consists of two buoyed berths, lying from 2 to 3½ miles offshore at the seaward end of submarine oil pipelines.

Directions

Principal marks

2.169

1 With positions from the water tower (30°38′N 18°21′E):

Water tower (elevation 55 m, red lights); radar conspicuous.
Radio mast (elevation 75 m, red lights) (1 cable W).
Oil tanks (3½ miles WSW); radar conspicuous.
Radio mast (50 m in height, red lights) stands 3 cables NW of the group of oil tanks; two dish aerials stand close to the mast.

Approach and entry

2.170

1 From the designated Approach Reporting Point (32°43′N 19°06′E) to the pilot boarding position at As Sidrah, the chart is sufficient guide. For details of Approach Reporting Points see 1.41, 2.4, and *Admiralty List of Radio Signals Volume 6 (3)*.

2 During the hours of darkness, leading lights and mooring buoy marker lights may be exhibited from time to time. The lights are for the use of pilots and mooring parties, and should generally be disregarded by vessels.

Berths

2.171

1 With positions from water tower (30°38′N 18°21′E):

No 4 Berth (2½ miles NNE) is a SBM for tankers up to 254 000 dwt, 350 m LOA and 17·7 m draught. The mooring buoy is marked by a light.

2 **No 5 Berth** (4 miles ENE) is a SBM for tankers up to 305 000 dwt, 355 m LOA and 22·2 m draught. The mooring buoy is marked by a light, and a light buoy (E cardinal) is laid 1 mile E of it. The alignment (223½°) of two beacons (topmarks black cross on white) situated on the shore, 1½ miles ESE of the water tower, leads to the buoy. At night a sector light is exhibited from the front beacon and both beacons are illuminated.

3 It is reported (2007) that berth No 1 is no longer in use but the buoys remain in position.

Boat harbour

2.172

1 A small artificial harbour for the use of port authority launches is situated 1 mile ENE of the water tower. Lights are exhibited from the heads of the N and S breakwaters, and a light buoy (starboard hand) is moored about 2½ cables ESE of the head. The approach to the harbour is marked by the alignment (215½°) of two beacons standing 5 cables S of the head of the N breakwater.

Port services

2.173

1 Medical assistance in cases of emergency; no other facilities.

RA'S LĀNŪF

General information

Chart 3343

Position

2.174

1 Ra's Lānūf (30°30′N 18°35′E) lies in the SW part of the Gulf of Sirte, about 120 miles SSW of Banghāzī (2.272).

Function

2.175

1 Ra's Lānūf is a commercial port consisting of an artificial harbour (Rasco) and a large offshore oil terminal (Sirtica). Its principal function is the export of crude oil, oil products and liquid gas. Imports are mainly general cargo and liquid chemicals. The harbour and terminal are run separately, only sharing the harbour for maintenance and service craft.

Topography

2.176

1 **Topography.** Ra's Lānūf is a low sandy point, and the coast in the vicinity is generally featureless.

Approach and entry

2.177

1 The port is approached through the Approach Reporting Point and the harbour is entered from E through a dredged channel. For details of Approach Reporting Points see 1.41, 2.4, and *Admiralty List of Radio Signals Volume 6 (3)*.

Traffic

2.178

1 In 2007 there were 368 ship calls at the oil terminal with a total of 20 805 842 dwt.

Port Authority

2.179

1 **Offshore oil terminal:** Veba Oil Operations BV, PO Box 690, Al Marharba Street, Ţarābulus, Libya.

Harbour: Ra's Lānūf Oil and Gas Processing Co Inc (Rasco), PO Box 1971, Banghāzī, Libya.

Caution

2.180

1 Owing to the existence in these waters of the fish commonly known as the Weaver fish, ships crew are warned to exercise extreme caution if fishing while lying off the port area. Their dorsal fins have spines containing poisonous venom which causes extreme pain and has toxic effects which may lead to other severe complications. Contact with these spines should be avoided at all costs.

Limiting conditions

Deepest berths

2.181

1 Offshore: No 3 and 4 SPM Berths (2.195).

Harbour: No 1 Pier (2.196).

Density of water

2.182

1 1·025 g/cm^3.

Maximum size of vessel handled

2.183

1 No 3 offshore berth: 300 000 dwt, 335 m LOA and 22 m draught.

Harbour: 50 000 dwt, LOA 250 m and 12·5 m draught.

Local weather

2.184

1 Winds in the area are generally unpredictable in direction and strength. Wind speeds up to 70 kn have been recorded.

Winds between SE and SW with speeds up to 45 kn are frequently experienced. Visibility is reduced by sand haze.

Arrival information

Anchorages

2.185

1 Designated recommended anchorage areas, shown on the chart, are centred as follows (positioned from Main Breakwater head (30°30′·6N 18°35′·7E)):

Offshore berths (2¾ miles N).

Harbour (2½ miles NE).

2 Depths in each anchorage area are about 31 m, sand, with reported good holding.

A secondary anchorage is available for the offshore berths, radius 1000 m, centered 30°34′·5N 18°37′·0E.

Pilotage

2.186

1 Pilotage is compulsory; for ETA and reporting requirements see *Admiralty List of Radio Signals Volume 6 (3)*.

Offshore berths. Pilot/Mooring Master boards in the waiting anchorage (30°30′·8N 18°38′·7E), as shown on the chart.

2 **Harbour.** Pilot boards close E of the Fairway Light Buoy (30°30′·7N 18°37′·7E), or in the waiting anchorage area 1 mile N, as shown on the chart.

Tugs

2.187

1 Tugs are available in the harbour. Launches assist with berthing and unberthing at the offshore berths.

Entry restricted area

2.188

1 Navigation and anchoring are prohibited, except for vessels using the oil loading berths, within an area, shown on the chart, extending W and SE from a light buoy (white spherical) (30°33′·9N 18°34′·5E).

Harbour

General layout

2.189

1 The artificial harbour is protected from N by Main Breakwater, extending 1¼ miles E from Ra's Lānūf, and from E by Lee Breakwater, about 1½ miles in length and angled NE and NW. A light is exhibited from the head of each breakwater which form the ESE-facing entrance.

2 The harbour contains a large dredged area, the limits of which are marked by light buoys (special). The main cargo handling area lies in the SE part and consists of three finger piers for oil and gas tankers, each with two berths on the NE side, and a quay for general cargo vessels. An enclosed jetty for small vessels lies in the NW part of the harbour outside the dredged area.

3 The offshore oil terminal lies close N of the harbour and consists of four berths, each lying at the seaward end of a submarine pipeline extending from the shore.

Currents

2.190

1 Currents, which appear to be mainly wind generated, vary from 1 to 3 kn and continue for 12 to 24 hours after the wind has ceased.

Directions

Principal marks

2.191

1 **Landmarks:**

Water tower (white, 52 m in height) (30°30′·6N 18°32′·3E). Ra's Lānūf Light is exhibited from the top of the tower.

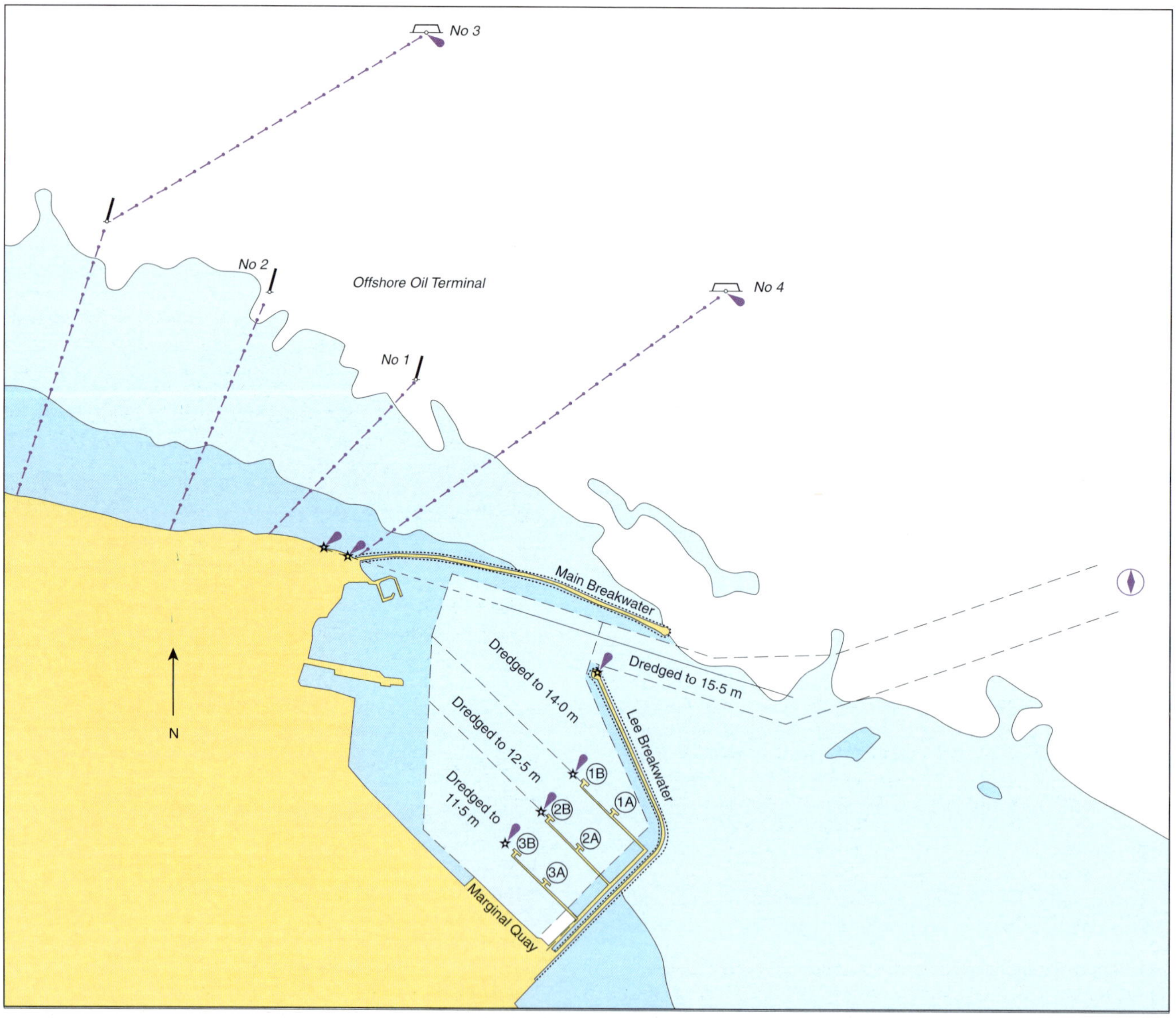

Ra's Lanuf (2.189)

Tanks (ten white, three black) (30°26′·9N 18°29′·9E) (chart 3402), standing near the summit of Gebel Aban Shah, a hill with a remarkable flat top.

2 **Major light:**

Ra's Lānūf Light, exhibited from the water tower above.

Approaches

2.192

1 From the designated Approach Reporting Point (32°43′N 19°06′E) (2.174) to the pilot boarding positions the chart is sufficient guide.

Harbour

2.193

1 From the vicinity of 30°30′·8N 18°37′·7E, the track leads WSW for about 1½ miles, passing (with positions from Main Breakwater Light (30°30′·6N 18°35′·7E)):

Clear of Fairway Light Buoy (safe water) (1¾ miles E), thence:

NNW of a shoal area (8 cables ESE), with a least depth of 6·1 m over it, thence:

To a position close N of a light buoy (port hand) (6 cables SE).

2 **Ra's Lānūf Leading Lights**:

Front light (white triangle point up, black stripe, on framework tower) (30°30′·8N 18°34′·3E).

Rear light (white triangle point down, black stripe, on framework tower) (220 m from front light).

The alignment (287½°) of these lights leads 8 cables through a channel, dredged to a depth of 15·5 m (1983), passing:

3 S of a light buoy (starboard hand) (2 cables ESE), thence:

Between the heads of Main Breakwater and Lee Breakwater into the harbour.

Useful marks

2.194

1 Main Breakwater Light (white and green structure) (30°30′·6N 18°35′·7E).

Lee Breakwater Light (white and red structure) (30°30′·5N 18°35′·4E).

Radio mast (red lights) (30°30′·9N 18°30′·4E).

Radio mast (red lights) (30°29′·9N 18°33′·2E).

Flare (30°29′·3N 18°34′·3E).

Flare (30°28′·3N 18°34′·9E).

Berths

Offshore berths

2.195

1 **General information.** Positions of the berths are as shown on the chart. At all berths the hose is embarked on the port side.

Berths 1 and 2 are each marked by a spar buoy and are in depths of about 23 m. Vessels berth bows seaward using two anchors with the stern secured to mooring buoys. Vessels up to 100 000 dwt can be accommodated.

2 **Berths 3 and 4** are SPMs in depths of about 29 m; the buoys are white and a light is exhibited from each.

Alongside berths

2.196

1 In the SE part of the harbour there are three parallel finger piers, with two berths on each of their NE sides, comprised of concrete caissons with adjacent berthing dolphins. Lights are exhibited from dolphins close off the head of each pier. Dredged depths (1983) and maximum size of vessels at the berths are as follows:

2 Nos 1A and 1B — 14·0 m. 50 000 dwt, 12·5 m draught; gas and fuel oil.

Nos 2A and 2B — 12·5 m. 30 000 dwt, 10·5 m draught; naptha and jet fuel.

Nos 3A and 3B — 11·5 m. 30 000 dwt, 9·5 m draught; liquefied gas cargoes.

Marginal Quay, the general cargo berth, lies close SW of the latter finger pier, and has a berthing face 675 m in length with a dredged depth (2007) of 11·0 m.

Port services

Facilities

2.197

1 Medical assistance may be available in case of emergency; no dirty ballast facilities.

Supplies

2.198

1 None available.

RA'S LĀNŪF TO MARSÁ AL BURAYQAH

General information

Chart 3402

Route

2.199

1 From a position NNE of Ra's Lānūf (30°31′N 18°35′E) the coastal route leads ESE, for 50 miles, to a position N of Marsá al Burayqah (30°25′N 19°35′E).

Topography

2.200

1 Between Ra's Lānūf and Ra's Umm al Gharānīq, 6 miles SE, the coast is sandy and fringed by rocks awash, which extend a short distance offshore. The inland ridge of hills SW of Ra's Lānūf assumes the shape of a tableland for a short distance, and includes Gebel Aban Shah (2.191).

2 Between Ra's al 'Alā' (30°23′N 18°48′E) and Al 'Uqaylah, 22 miles ESE, shoals lie up to 2½ miles offshore. A sandhill, 57 m high, lies 2 miles SW of Ra's al 'Alā'; SE of the point the coast continues low, barren and uniform in character. Extensive salt marshes lie behind the sand dunes on this section of the coast.

Marine exploitation

2.201

1 Between Ra's Lānūf and Marsá al Burayqah, oil rigs and vessels connected with oil-drilling operations may be encountered several miles offshore.

Directions

(continued from 2.147)

Principal marks

2.202

1 **Landmarks:**

Jubayl al 'Alā' (30°16′·8N 18°48′·0E) consists of two flat-topped ridges, 81 m high, separated by a remarkable cleft, and is the most remarkable part of the tableland which backs the coast.

2 Jabal Bū Khushaybah (30°15′·2N 19°08′·8E) is a remarkable conical hill, 37 m high.

Lim Resa (30°22′·8N 19°29′·6E), stands on the coast. It is a saddle-shaped hill which from a distance appears like an island.

3 **Major lights:**

Ra's Lānūf Light (30°30′·6N 18°32′·3E) (2.191).

Marsá al Burayqah West Breakwater Light (30°25′·1N 19°35′·4E) (2.220).

Marsá al Burayqah East Breakwater Light (30°25′·0N 19°35′·7E) (2.220).

Ra's Lānūf to Marsá al Burayqah

2.203

1 From a position NNE of Ra's Lānūf (30°31′N 18°35′E) the track leads ESE, passing (with positions from Jazīrat Bū Shu'ayfah (30°17′N 19°07′E)):

NNE of Ra's Umm al Gharānīq (26 miles WNW), a shoal spit, with a rock awash at its outer end, that extends 1 mile ESE, thence:

2 NNE of Ra's al 'Alā' (18 miles WNW), a low point from which shoal water extends E, with a depth of 3·2 m at its outer end. There are 4·9 m and 6·9 m patches 1 mile NE and 2¼ miles ESE, respectively, of the point. Thence:

NNE of Jazīrat Bū Shu'ayfah (2.205), a small island, to the pilot boarding position at Marsá al Burayqah.

3 **Useful marks:**

Jubayl al Khāsh (30°18′·5N 18°52′·8E), 49 m high, is situated 8 cables inland but is difficult to identify.

Sreghin (30°16′·2N 19°16′·0E), a dark hummock which shows up well against the sand dunes, a sand dune lies 3½ miles ENE.

Bishr (30°19′·2N 19°25′·3E), a flat-topped hill, 37 m high, covered in bushes.

(Directions continue at 2.233)

Anchorages

Ra's al 'Alā'

2.204

1 Anchorage for small vessels, sheltered from all winds except those between NE and SE, is obtainable SE of Ra's al 'Alā', in depths of from 6 to 9 m, sand and weed. A jetty, shown on the chart, about 150 m long, with a depth of 3·7 m alongside its head, lies close S of the point.

Local knowledge is required.

Al 'Uqaylah

2.205

1 **Description.** Al 'Uqaylah (30°16′N 19°12′E) may be identified by some red buildings, about 5 cables inland, 2¾ miles E of Jabal Bū Khushaybah, which have the appearance of forts. One building is surrounded by a wall on which there is a lookout station consisting of a dark-coloured framework tower, visible at a distance of 8 miles. A small isolated white fort with a turret at each corner stands N of these buildings on a hill 18 m high. Close to the coast is a small house painted in black and white chequers.

2 **Approaches.** Jazīrat Bū Shu'ayfah (30°17′N 19°07′E) is dark with a flat top, and can be readily distinguished against the yellow background of the beach.

Two lines of shoals lie parallel to the coast. The inner line, with a least depth of 2·6 m, extends from 1 mile W of Jazīrat Bū Shu'ayfah to a position 4 miles ENE of it. The outer line, with a least depth of 5·3 m, extends for 6¼ miles ENE from a position 7½ cables NW of Jazīrat Bū Shu'ayfah.

3 **Anchorage** may be obtained either N of Al 'Uqaylah or W between the inner line of shoals and the shore. Approach with the lookout station bearing 185°, and either anchor 1½ miles offshore on this bearing in a depth of 16 m, or, when Jabal Bū Khushaybah bears 230°, steer 260° and anchor in depths of from 10 to 20 m.

A good berth, with partial shelter from N and NW winds, is with Jazīrat Bū Shu'ayfah bearing 300°, distant 8 cables, in a depth of 14 m, sand and weed.

MARSÁ AL BURAYQAH

General information

Charts 3350, 3402

Position

2.206

1 Marsá al Burayqah (El-Bréga) (30°25′N 19°35′E) lies between Khashm Arīţū (Rās el-Magdàr) (30°26′N 19°38′E) and another point 3 miles SW, in an open bay situated in the SE corner of the Gulf of Sirte, about 100 miles SSW of Banghāzī.

Function

2.207

1 Marsá al Burayqah is a major commercial oil port which comprises an artificial harbour and several offshore oil loading berths. It has modern facilities for handling all types of tankers up to VLCC size, general cargo and RoRo vessels.

2 Principal exports include crude oil, liquefied gas, urea, methanol and other petroleum products. Imports include bulk liquid chemicals, building materials and general cargo.

Approach and entry

2.208

1 The port is approached through the Approach Reporting Point and the harbour is entered on the alignment of leading lights.

For details of Approach Reporting Points see 1.41, 2.4, and *Admiralty List of Radio Signals Volume 6 (3).*

Traffic

2.209

1 In 2007 there were 234 ship calls with a total of 8 344 383 dwt.

Port Authority

2.210

1 Sirte Oil Co., PO Box 385, Ţarābulus, Libya.

Limiting conditions

Density of water

2.211

1 Density of water in the dock is 1·025 g/cm^3.

Maximum size of vessel handled

2.212

1 **Offshore berths:** 300 000 dwt, length and draught unlimited.

Harbour: vessels up to a draught of 10 m (33 ft).

Local weather

2.213

1 Strong NW winds produce heavy swells which may lead to closure of the port.

Arrival information

Notice of ETA

2.214

1 72, 48 and 24 hours in advance.

Anchorage

2.215

1 The designated anchorage is a 3 mile diameter circle, as shown on the chart, located about 6½ miles N from the harbour entrance; depths are from 20 m to greater than 70 m (see also 1.43).

Pilotage

2.216

1 Pilotage is compulsory and available 24 hours. Pilot boards in the vicinity of Bréga Light Buoy, as indicated on the chart. Harbour radar is available to give assistance.

For details see *Admiralty List of Radio Signals Volume 6 (3).*

Tugs

2.217

1 Tugs are available in the harbour, and launches assist mooring at the offshore berths.

Restricted area

2.218

1 The offshore berths and the approach to the harbour are enclosed by a restricted area, as shown on the chart. Vessels are not permitted to enter this area without a pilot on board.

Harbour

General layout

2.219

1 The artificial harbour lies in the SW corner of a natural bay and is formed by two breakwaters which protect it from N. The W breakwater extends 3¾ cables E from the radar tower close to the W entrance point of the bay and the E breakwater extends about 4 cables W from the shore.

2 The W part of the harbour contains the liquefied gas berths on a detached jetty connected to the shore, a chemical jetty, a cargo pier and a petroleum product jetty on the S side of the W breakwater near its root.

3 The NE part of the harbour contains the methanol/ammonia berths on the S side of the E breakwater and the general cargo quays S of its root.

The offshore berths lie at the seaward end of submarine pipelines. There are six berths, of which, only Nos 2, 5 and 6 remain in use.

Directions

Principal marks

2.220

1 **Landmarks** (positioned from the radar tower (30°25′·0N 19°34′·9E)):

Radar tower (elevation 36 m (118 ft), red light).

Water tank (red) (6 cables SW). A ruined fort stands close NW.

Radio mast (red lights) (7 cables S).

Four flare towers (red lights) (1 mile SE). The flares, when burning, can be seen from a great distance.

2 **Major lights:**

Marsá al Burayqah West Breakwater Light (black structure) (30°25′·1N 19°35′·4E).

Marsá al Burayqah East Breakwater Light (30°25′·0N 19°35′·7E).

Caution

2.221

1 Marsá al Burayqah is fronted by many shoal banks which lie up to 2½ miles offshore, and depths generally are irregular.

Main approach

2.222

1 From the Approach Reporting Point (32°43′N 19°06′E) (2.206) the track leads SSE for 137 miles to the pilot boarding area near Bréga Light Buoy (30°27′·6N 19°35′·1E). The harbour is then entered on the following leading line.

Marsá al Burayqah Leading Lights:

Front light (black, white and red beacon) (30°24′·6N 19°35′·7E).

Rear light (similar structure) (770 m from front light).

2 The alignment (167½°) of these lights leads 2½ miles to the harbour entrance, passing (with positions from front light):

ENE of a patch (2¼ miles NNW), with a swept depth of 18·3 m (60 ft) over it, thence:

WSW of a 17·4 m (57 ft) patch (1¾ miles NNW); an isolated patch, with a depth of 18 m (59 ft) over it, lies close SSE. And:

3 ENE of the NE extremity of the coastal bank extending N for 1 mile from the point at El-Bréga. It has depths of less than 9 m (30 ft) over it and a least depth of 1·5 m (5 ft). The N extremity is marked by No 10 Light Buoy (starboard hand). Foul ground with numerous rocks awash extends 5 cables from the point. Thence:

4 ENE of a shoal (1½ miles NNW), marked by No 9 Light Buoy (starboard hand), and:

WSW of a shoal (1½ miles N), with a least depth of 6·7 m (22 ft) over it, marked by No 8 Light Buoy (port hand), thence:

5 WSW of No 3 Light Buoy (port hand) (1½ miles N), thence:

ENE of No 1 berth (disused) (1 mile NNW) and WSW of No 2 Berth (1 mile N), thence:

Between the breakwaters (5 cables NNW) into the harbour.

Alternative approach with lesser draught

2.223

1 **Leading lights:**

Front light (black, white and red beacon) (30°25′·2N 19°37′·4E).

Rear light (similar structure) (660 m from front light).

From the vicinity of the pilot boarding area near Bréga Light Buoy (30°27′·6N 19°36′·1E), the alignment (143¾°) of these lights leads SE for about 2 miles, passing (with positions from front light):

NE of a shoal area (1¾ miles NW), with a least depth of 9·8 m (32 ft) over it, marked by No 5 and No 6 Light Buoys (starboard hand), thence:

2 SW of El-Magdàr Reef (1½ miles N), an extensive rocky reef, on which there are two rocks awash; from the reef shoal patches extend 1 mile farther N. The reef lies 1 mile NW of Khashm Arīţū (Rās el-Magdàr), a point which is fringed by foul ground extending 2 cables NNW, and depths of less than 9 m (30 ft) extend 5 cables N.

The track then alters SW on to the following leading line.

3 **Inner Harbour Leading Lights:**

Front light (beacon) (30°24′·6N 19°35′·0E).

Rear light (beacon) (370 m from front light).

The alignment (224°) of these lights leads SW for about 1½ miles, passing (with positions from the front light):

SE of a shoal patch (1½ miles NE), with a least depth of 9·8 m (32 ft) over it, marked by No 4 Light Buoy (starboard hand), thence:

4 SE of No 2 offshore loading berth (1¼ miles NE), thence:

Between the breakwaters (6 cables NE) into the harbour.

Useful mark

2.224

1 Offshore Berth No 3 (30°26′·0N 19°33′·9E), a disused, steel artificial mooring island, 40 m in diameter. A light (metal tower, 21 m in height) is exhibited from the structure.

Berths

Offshore berths

2.225

1 **General information.** The offshore loading berths are only suitable for use in fair weather, and vessels will only be berthed when it is safe to do so. There may therefore be delays, particularly during the winter months. Operational berths are as follows (with positions from the radar tower (30°25′·0N 19°34′·9E)):

2 **Berth No 2** (9 cables NE), for loading crude and naphtha in a depth of 13·4 m (44 ft), and within an extensive area swept to a depth of 9·1 m (30 ft); consists of five numbered mooring buoys. Vessels berth heading NNW with both anchors down, stern and quarters secured to the buoys. Positioning is aided by the alignment of lights and beacons, as shown on the chart. Vessels of up to 55 000 dwt 244 m length and 12·8 m (42 ft) draught can be accommodated.

3 **Berth No 5** (2 miles NNW), consists of an SPM in a depth of 37 m (20 fm); a light is exhibited from the buoy. Vessels up to 300 000 dwt can be accommodated.

Berth No 6 (2 miles NW), consists of an SPM in a depth of about 42 m (23 fm); a light is exhibited from the buoy. Vessels of up to 300 000 dwt can be accommodated.

Harbour

2.226

1 **West side:**

Product Jetty, situated on the S side of the W breakwater, length 260 m. Vessels of up to 15 000 dwt 152·5 m length and 7·9 m (26 ft) draught can be accommodated. It is usable only in fair weather.

2 Dry cargo pier, extending S from the root of the W breakwater, length 192 m. Vessels of up to 15 000 dwt 152·5 m length and 7·9 m (26 ft) draught can be accommodated. A RoRo berth is available at the N end of this quay at the junction with the root of the W breakwater when the product jetty is not in use. Vessels may have to leave this pier in rough seas.

3 A basin for harbour craft, with depths of about 2 m, (7 ft) lies W of the gas berths on the W side of the harbour. It is enclosed by the acid jetty extending N and its entrance is between the end of the jetty and the dry cargo pier.

4 Liquid Gas Jetty, extending SE from the barge basin jetty. It has two berths, each consisting of a **T**-headed pier and breasting dolphins. Both (A) and (B) berths have 340 m mooring length and 80 m loading section. Dredged depth alongside 11·5 m (38 ft). Vessels up to 30 000 dwt 210 m length and 10 m (33 ft) draught can be accommodated.

5 **East side:**

Nos 1 and 2 chemical berths, situated on the S side of the E breakwater. Each berth consists of a **T**-headed pier with breasting dolphins. Both berths have 320 m mooring length and 84 m loading section. Dredged depth alongside 14 m (46 ft). Vessels up to 30 000 dwt 200 m length and 10·0 m (33 ft) draught can be accommodated.

6 General cargo quay, extending S from the root of the E breakwater, has a total of 394 m of berthing space. Vessels up to 15 000 dwt 152·5 m length and 9·2 m (30 ft) draught can be accommodated. RoRo vessels may also berth at this quay.

7 Urea berth, extending 200 m WSW from the S end of the general cargo quay has a depth alongside of 9.5 m. Vessels of up to 165 m length 22 or 26 m beam, (bagged or bulk) and 8·8 m (29 ft) draught can be accommodated.

8 An area S of the E breakwater, marked by light buoys (special), was dredged to a depth of 12·8 m (42 ft) in 1978. A salt water intake extends about 400 m NNE from the shore on the S side of the harbour in the central part. Its outer end is marked by light buoys.

Port services

Facilities

2.227

1 No facilities for repairs; medical assistance may be available in an emergency; no dirty ballast reception; no shore leave.

Supplies

2.228

1 None available.

Communications

2.229

1 Private airport nearby.

MARSÁ AL BURAYQAH TO AZ ZUWAYTĪNAH OIL TERMINAL

General information

Chart 3402

Route

2.230

1 From a position N of Marsá al Burayqah (30°25′N 19°35′E) the route leads NE, for a distance of about 36 miles, to a position NW of Az Zuwaytīnah (30°51′N 20°03′E).

Topography

2.231

1 A prominent black promontory, 4 miles NE of Khashm Arīţū (30°26′N 19°38′E) is surmounted by a ruined fort. Alizir, 4 miles farther NE, is a low hillock.

Depths

2.232

1 Attention is drawn to the coastal bank, with depths of less than 11 m, extending over 1 mile NW of Khashm Arīţū (30°26′N 19°38′E), thence 1½ miles NNE. Shoal areas continue along the coast from the N extremity of El-Magdàr Reef (2.223), and between Khashm Arīţū and Jabal Lamaresk, 14 miles NE, several shoals with depths less than 11 m lie up to 2½ miles offshore.

2 Between North Lamaresk Reef (30°40′N 19°47′E) and Jemmarisk Rock, 11 miles NE, the depths within 5 miles of the coast are irregular and navigation requires extreme caution, as uncharted dangers may exist. There is foul ground between Jemmarisk Rock and the shore.

Directions

(continued from 2.203)

Principal marks

2.233

1 **Landmarks:**

Jabal Lamaresk (30°35′N 19°51′E), 62 m high, a hillock with a truncated cone.

Radio mast (elevation 138 m) (30°50′·0N 20°03′·1E).

2 **Major lights:**

Light on radio mast (30°50′·0N 20°03′·1E) — as above.

Breakwater Head Light (30°54′·0N 20°04′·1E), exhibited from the head of the harbour breakwater at Az Zuwaytīnah.

Marsá al Burayqah to Az Zuwaytīnah

2.234

1 From a position N of Marsá al Burayqah the track leads NE, passing (with positions from Isheifa Rock (30°36′·2N 19°49′·8E)):

NW of South Lamaresk Reef (2¾ miles W), awash, thence:

NW of Isheifa Rock, above water, thence:

2 NW of North Lamaresk Reef (4½ miles NNW), awash, thence:

NW of Hericha Rock (11 miles NNE). Hericha Rock and Gharah Island lie on a line of shoals and above-water rocks which extends 14½ miles NE from North Lamaresk Reef, parallel to the coast. Thence:

3 NW of Gharah Island (12 miles NNE) (I Legaràh on chart 3346); the island is steep-to on its NE side, and two large above-water rocks lie close SW. Jemmarisk Rock (Scoglio Gemmàrisc) (chart 3346), fronts the shore 3¼ miles ESE of Gharah Island. Thence:

4 NW of a shoal patch (18 miles NNE), with a least depth of 7·3 m over it, marked by a light buoy (orange, pillar) on its SE side, and by a spar buoy (white) 2 cables off its SW side.

The track then leads to a position NW of the Fairway Light Buoy (21½ miles NNE) off Az Zuwaytīnah (30°51′N 20°03′E).

(Directions continue at 2.266)

Anchorage

Gharah Island

2.235

1 Anchorage is obtainable 2¾ cables S of Gharah Island (30°47′·5N 19°54′·2E), in a depth of about 15 m, well sheltered from N winds.

Local knowledge is required.

AZ ZUWAYTĪNAH OIL TERMINAL

General information

Charts 3346, 3402

Position

2.236

1 Az Zuwaytīnah (Ez Zueitina) Oil Terminal (30°51′N 20°03′E) lies in the SE part of the Gulf of Sirte, about 74 miles S of Banghāzī.

Function

2.237

1 Az Zuwaytīnah is a major offshore oil loading terminal with offshore berths at the seaward end of submarine pipelines. There is also an LPG terminal, with an alongside berth, at Az Zuwaytīnah.

Approach and entry

2.238

1 The port is approached through the designated Approach Reporting Point and entered from the Fairway Light Buoy.

For details of Approach Reporting Points see 1.41, 2.4, and *Admiralty List of Radio Signals Volume 6 (3).*

Traffic

2.239

1 In 2007 there were 118 ship calls with a total of 9 082 333 dwt.

Port Authority

2.240

1 Zueitina Oil Co., Sidi Issa Street, PO Box 2134, Ţarābulus, Libya.

Limiting conditions

Controlling depths

2.241

1 The least swept depth in the area of the offshore loading berths is 18·3 m, but charted depths are greater. The approaches are swept to a depth of 25·9 m.

Density of water

2.242

1 Density of water in the dock is 1·026 g/cm^3.

Maximum size of vessel handled

2.243

1 Offshore berths: up to 275 000 dwt and 20 m draught.

LPG Berth: LOA 214 m and a draught of 8·7 m.

Local weather

2.244

1 Squalls with wind speeds of 40 kn are reported to occur without warning. During the winter months NW gales may cause heavy seas and high swells. As the berths are in the open roadstead, engines should be kept at immediate readiness at all times.

Arrival information

Notice of ETA

2.245

1 Vessels should send ETA 72, 48 and 24 hours in advance. For details of information required see *Admiralty List of Radio Signals Volume 6 (3).*

Anchorage

2.246

1 The recommended anchorage for large vessels, shown on the chart, is centred 2¾ miles WNW of the harbour breakwater head (30°54′·0N 20°04′·1E). The holding ground is reported to be moderate.

The recommended anchorage for small vessels, shown on the chart and plan, is centred 8 cables SW of the breakwater head described above.

Prohibited anchorage

2.247

1 Anchorage is prohibited in the area fronting the offshore berths, as indicated on the chart.

Pilotage

2.248

1 Pilotage is compulsory and is carried out by the Mooring Master who remains on board for the duration of the loading operations. Pilot/Mooring Master boards close to the Fairway Light Buoy (safe water) (30°56′N 20°00′E) or in the anchorage, as indicated on the chart.

For details see *Admiralty List of Radio Signals Volume 6 (3).*

Tugs

2.249

1 Tugs and mooring launches are available.

Harbour

General layout

2.250

1 Az Zuwaytīnah Oil Terminal consists of five exposed offshore berths, and an LPG berth partially sheltered by Tre Scogli (2.254).

Climate information

2.251

1 There is a weather observing station at Ajdābīyah, 11 miles SSE of Az Zuwaytīnah Oil Terminal; for climate information see 1.184 and 1.188.

Directions

Principal marks

2.252

1 **Landmarks:**

Radio mast (elevation 138 m) (30°50′·0N 20°03′·1E), exhibiting red obstruction lights.

Oil tanks (white) (close S of the radio mast), reported to give a good radar response at a distance of 45 miles.

Sidi Alib (tomb) (7 cables NE of the radio mast).

2 Caserna Turea (30°54′N 30°05′E), ruined Turkish barracks.

Three white tanks (2 cables N of Caserna Turea) (not charted), reported conspicuous at a distance of 40 miles.

Three flares (7½ cables NE of Caserna Turea), from which rise columns of smoke.

3 **Major lights:**

Light on radio mast (30°50′·0N 20°03′·1E) — as above.

Breakwater Head Light (30°54′·0N 20°04′·1E), exhibited from the harbour breakwater.

Approach

2.253

1 From the Approach Reporting Point (32°43′N 19°06′E) (2.238) the direct track leads SSE for about 117 miles to the pilot boarding place near Fairway Light Buoy or the large vessel anchorage. However, vessels must keep clear of the Firing Danger Area, shown on the chart, centred 50 miles NW of Az Zuwaytīnah. The chart is sufficient guide.

Entry

2.254

1 **Offshore berths.** From the vicinity of the Fairway Light Buoy or the large vessel anchorage, these berths can be approached directly; the chart is sufficient guide.

LPG Berth. From the vicinity of the Fairway Light Buoy the approach to the LPG Berth is made on the following leading line.

2 Az Zuwaytīnah Leading Lights:

Front light (black and red rectangular topmark on mast, on tripod) (30°53′·3N 20°03′·7E).

Rear light (similar mark and structure) (750 m from the front light).

3 The alignment (135°) of these lights leads SE for about 3 miles, passing (with positions from the front light):

SW of Scoglio Nord (3 miles N), a group of rocks, the largest of which is 2 m high; a rock awash, 5 cables farther NNE, is nearly always marked by breakers. Between Tre Scogli and Scoglio Nord there are varying depths, and a 1·8 m patch. Thence:

Close NE of a light buoy (starboard hand) (1 mile NW), marking the line of track, thence:

4 NE of Trinity Shoal (7½ cables NW), a shoal patch with a rock awash. An extensive shoal area extends about 1 mile SSW with several rocks awash, including Airstrip Shoal. Farther SSW lie Bravo Shoal and Delta Shoal, both of which have rocks awash and lie shoreward of the offshore berths. And:

5 SW of Scoglio Sud (8 cables N), 4 m high and dark coloured, on the SW side of Tre Scogli, a remarkable group of rocks, which lie 1 mile offshore, and are joined to the coast by a narrow reef with depths of 2·1 to 4·0 m over it. Waffeya Light (white mast) is exhibited from Scoglio Sud.

6 Thence to a position about 5 cables from the front light near a light buoy (port hand) (4 cables NW) which marks the turning point for approaching the berth. The track then leads about 5 cables NE to the berth.

Berths

Offshore berths

2.255

1 With positions from the radio mast (30°50′·0N 20°03′·1E):

Alpha (4 miles NNW), an SPM in a depth of about 30 m. The berth is not in use and is marked by a light buoy.

2 Bravo (2¾ miles NNW) consists of a conventional group of mooring buoys in depths of about 20 m.

Vessels moor with at least 300 m (12 shackles) of cable on each anchor, with the stern secured to the mooring buoys. Light buoys are laid in the vicinity to assist in mooring. Maximum size of vessel 150 000 tonnes, 18·2 m draught.

3 Charlie (3¼ miles NW), an SPM exhibiting a light, in a depth of about 30 m. Maximum size of vessel 275 000 tonnes, 20 m draught.

Delta (2½ miles WNW) consists of a conventional group of mooring buoys in depths of about 20 m. Mooring arrangements are similar as Bravo. Light buoys are laid in the vicinity to assist in mooring. Maximum size of vessel 110 000 tonnes, 18·2 m draught.

4 Echo (3¼ miles W), an SPM in a depth of about 25 m. The berth is temporarily not in use (2007) and is marked by a light buoy.

All berths are connected by submarine pipelines to the shore. The delivery hose is embarked on the port side.

LPG Berth

2.256

1 The LPG Berth, 4 miles N of the radio mast, consists of an angled trestle bridge projecting from the elbow of the harbour breakwater, terminating in a loading platform with breasting dolphins and other dolphins off each end to assist in mooring. A light is exhibited from the W end of the berth. Vessels up to 214 m LOA can be accommodated; maximum draught 8·7 m.

Service craft harbour

2.257

1 The harbour is formed by a causeway extending about 3 cables WNW from the shore, 2½ cables N of Caserna Turea (30°54′N 30°05′E), at the end of which is a broad quay with an angled breakwater extending S from its outer end, enclosing the harbour which has a charted depth of 6·7 m. There is a total of about 460 m of berthing space on the N and W sides. A light (2.252) is exhibited from the head of the breakwater.

Port services

Facilities

2.258

1 Medical assistance in an emergency only; no shore leave.

Supplies

2.259

1 No fuel or fresh water; limited amount of fresh provisions.

Communications

2.260

1 There is an airfield at the terminal. The nearest international airport is at Banghāzī, 118 km distant.

AZ ZUWAYTĪNAH OIL TERMINAL TO BANGHĀZĪ

General information

Chart 3402

Route

2.261

1 From a position NW of Az Zuwaytīnah (30°51′N 20°03′E) the coastal route leads initially NNW then NNE, for a distance of about 78 miles, to a position NW of Banghāzī (32°07′N 20°03′E).

Topography

2.262

1 The coast between Az Zuwaytīnah Oil Terminal (30°51′N 20°03′E) and the village of Az Zuwaytīnah, 4 miles NNE, is sandy and backed by Collina Pessana, a reddish-coloured ridge, 24 m high. To the N of the village the coast has an arid and desert appearance of a reddish colour; there is a dark-coloured dune 2 miles N of the village.

2 East of Karkuretta (31°22′N 20°03′E), 27½ miles N of Az Zuwaytīnah, Jabal Ḩusayn, a chain of hills, runs parallel to the coast. Kurkūrah, extending between Karkuretta and Ra's Kurkūrah, 8 miles NW, is a belt of relatively fertile coastal dunes, backed by a large salt marsh behind which, 7 miles inland, lies a ridge of rocky hills on which stand some ruins.

3 Between Ra's Kurkūrah (31°29′N 20°00′E) and Sīdī Habīb, 7½ miles N, is a coastal tract of dunes and elevated ground. Between Sīdī Habīb and Ḩawsh Bū Sharbīyah (31°38′N 19°59′E) the coast becomes lower, of uniform appearance, and is covered with brushwood.

4 Qamīnis, a village 3 miles NE of Ḩawsh Bū Sharbīyah, contains a mosque with a white minaret visible between the palm trees. Two palm groves stand 2½ miles N of the village, and at their S end is a reddish-coloured hill, surmounted by an ancient fort with a small low tower on its S side.

Current

2.263

1 A strong current has been observed setting onshore between Az Zuwaytīnah (30°57′N 20°08′E) and Elfie Rock, 15 miles N.

Firing danger area

2.264

1 Navigation is prohibited in a firing practice area, shown on the chart, centred 25 miles W of Ra's Kurkūrah (31°29′N 20°00′E).

Stranded wrecks

2.265

1 A number of stranded wrecks lie along this section of coast, the positions of which are shown on the chart.

Directions

(continued from 2.234)

Principal marks

2.266

1 Gebbànet Sciahauán (31°02′·5N 20°11′·0E), a conical hill 30 m high, with a yellow building on its summit.

Sand dune (31°15′·6N 20°08′·1E), 28 m high.

Sidi el-Mscéiti (31°18′·0N 20°07′·6E), a marabout, lies at the S end of a stretch of white sand dunes 20 to 30 m high and covered with bushes.

2 Ḩawsh Bū Sharbīyah (31°38′·5N 19°58′·0E), a ruined fort.

Qaşr Mushaylī (31°43′·1N 19°57′·1E) in ruins. Sīdī Bū Fākhirah, a marabout 2 miles NNW, is partly in ruins.

Az Zuwaytīnah to Banghāzī

2.267

1 From a position NW of Az Zuwaytīnah, clear of the Fairway Light Buoy (30°56′N 20°00′E), the track leads

NNW for about 45 miles, passing (with positions from Ra's Kurkūrah (31°29′N 20°00′E)):

WSW of a number of shoal patches (33 miles S) that lie up to 2 miles offshore between Tre Scogli and the village of Az Zuwaytīnah, 4 miles NE. The depths up to 4 miles offshore are irregular and caution is required, as uncharted dangers may exist. Thence:

2 WSW of Elfie Rock (21½ miles SSE), awash. The rock marks the N extremity of a line of shoals which extend 11 miles S, with a least depth of 2·1 m over them. Between this line of shoals and the coast are depths of 11·0 to 14·6 m. Thence:

WSW of a shoal patch (17 miles SSE), with a depth of 8·2 m over it, thence:

WSW of Karkuretta (7½ miles SSE), thence:

WSW of a stranded wreck (2½ miles SSE), which is radar conspicuous, thence:

3 WSW of Ra's Kurkūrah, a low rocky point surmounted by the ruins of an old castle; the ruins are only 3 m high and not easy to distinguish. Between Ra's Kurkūrah and Ra's Tāwīnīs, 29 miles N, depths of 9 m and less extend up to 2½ miles offshore in places. Thence:

WSW of a dangerous wreck (7 miles NNW) to a position WSW of Ḩawsh Bū Sharbīyah (10 miles N).

2.268

1 Thence the track leads NNE for about 33 miles, passing (with positions from Ra's Tāwīnīs (31°57′·3N 19°56′·5E)):

WNW of a dangerous wreck (14 miles S), thence:

WNW of a dangerous wreck (7 miles SSW), thence:

WNW of two dangerous wrecks (3 miles SW), thence:

2 WNW of Ra's Tāwīnīs, a low sandy point that may be identified by a group of palm trees standing close inland of it. A spit with a least depth of 1·8 m extends 1¼ miles SSW from the point and a rock, with a depth of 3·4 m over it, lies 6 cables S of the point. Thence:

WNW of a dangerous wreck (2 miles WNW), thence:

3 WNW of Berenice Shoal (3 miles N) (Secca Berenice on chart 3352), a rock awash, that lies 1¼ miles offshore at the NW extremity of a rocky spit with depths of less than 5·5 m over it. A 3·7 m rocky patch lies 3¼ miles NE of Berenice Shoal and from a point on the coast 1¼ miles E of this patch a spit with depths of less than 3·7 m extends 1 mile N.

The track then leads to a position NW of Banghāzī (32°07′N 20°03′E) (2.272).

Useful marks

2.269

1 Sīdī Bū Rāwī (31°32′·0N 20°02′·1E), a white marabout prominent especially in afternoon sunlight.

Sīdī Habīb (31°35′·5N 19°59′·1E), a marabout. Talambu, a hill 1½ miles E of Sīdī Habīb, is also prominent.

2 Taribjah (31°52′·1N 19°57′·1E), a village containing a mosque with a minaret.

Sīdī Aḩmad Abū Fākhirah (31°56′·5N 19°58′·4E), a marabout, 19 m high; from S the dome appears yellow, but from N, especially when sunlit, it appears white.

Two palms (32°00′·8N 20°00′·3E) with a single prominent palm tree close N.

(Directions continue at 2.304)

Anchorages

Az Zuwaytīnah

2.270

1 **Description.** Az Zuwaytīnah (30°57′N 20°08′E), is a village 4 miles NE of the Az Zuwaytīnah Oil Terminal (2.236). It is situated near a large white masonry redoubt, in the centre of which is a wooden framework tower 20 m high. A reef lies parallel to the coast abreast the redoubt, ¾ cable offshore, with depths of 1·5 to 2·4 m between it and the coast. A passage through the reef, ¼ cable wide, should only be used with local knowledge.

2 **Anchorage** may be obtained 9 cables offshore, WNW of Az Zuwaytīnah village, in depths of about 14 m, sand, good holding ground, but depths in the approach to the anchorage are irregular, with a 7·3 m rocky patch. Small vessels may anchor 4½ cables offshore, over sand and weed bottom, abreast several prominent buildings which stand near the coast.

Kurkūrah Bay

2.271

1 Kurkūrah Bay lies SE of a reef and shoal patches which extend 1¾ cables S from Ra's Kurkūrah (31°29′N 19°59′E). The depths in the bay are regular, with a bottom of sand and weed. Anchorage may be obtained by vessels with Ra's Kurkūrah distant 6½ cables, in a depth of 6·4 m, sheltered from winds from NW through N to S.

Local knowledge is required.

BANGHĀZĪ

General information

Chart 3352

Position

2.272

1 Banghāzī (32°07′N 20°03′E), ancient Berenice, is the capital of Cyrenaica. It lies at the E entrance point of the Gulf of Sirte. The town, which contains many large, modern public buildings, stands on the extremity of a low point, and is backed by salt lakes and marshes, the latter being subject to inundation during N gales.

Function

2.273

1 It is a large commercial port serving the surrounding region, equipped to handle tankers, container, RoRo and general cargo vessels.

Principal exports include sheep, wool, hides, goat hair fabrics and woollen rugs. Imports include foodstuffs, tobacco, textiles, pottery, chemicals, petroleum products and construction materials.

In 2000 the population was estimated to be 912 000.

Approach and entry

2.274

1 The port is approached through one of the Approach Reporting Points and entered between the breakwater heads with the aid of a direction light.

For details of Approach Reporting Points see 1.41, 2.4, and *Admiralty List of Radio Signals Volume 6 (3).*

Traffic

2.275

1 In 2007 there were 343 ship calls with a total of 3 324 425 dwt.

Port Authority

2.276

1 Socialist Ports Co., Banghāzī, Libya.

Limiting conditions

Abnormal water levels

2.277

1 During February, March and April, especially during N and NE winds, the water level is very low, falling about 0·6 m below MSL. During June, July and August, especially with W and SW winds, the water level rises about 0·4 m above MSL.

Density of water

2.278

1 Density of water in the dock is 1·026 g/cm^3.

Maximum size of vessel handled

2.279

1 Up to 12 m draught. During the summer vessels of any size and draught can discharge into lighters at the anchorage, but heavy swell makes this impossible in winter.

Arrival information

Notice of ETA

2.280

1 Vessels should send ETA 48 and 24 hours in advance.

Anchorage

2.281

1 The anchorage area, shown on the chart, is centred 4 miles NW of the head of the N Breakwater (32°07′·0N 20°01′·8E).

Strong W winds cause a very heavy sea which renders the anchorage dangerous and during the winter it is seldom tenable.

Submarine cable area

2.282

1 Anchoring and fishing are prohibited within an area, shown on the chart, surrounding a submarine cable which comes ashore 3½ miles S of the N Breakwater head (32°07′·0N 20°01′·8E). For information on submarine cables see 1.26.

Pilotage

2.283

1 Pilotage is compulsory and available during daylight from 0700 to 2000. Pilots board about 5 cables off the harbour entrance, except in adverse conditions when the pilot boards inside the breakwater.

For details see *Admiralty List of Radio Signals Volume 6 (3).*

Tugs

2.284

1 Tugs are available and compulsory for vessels over 100 grt.

Harbour

General layout

2.285

1 The port of Banghāzī lies between Rās Bu Sceiba (32°05′·3N 20°02′·8E) and Ra's Sīdī Khuraybīsh (Ra's Khuraybīsh) 2½ miles NNE. The harbour is formed and enclosed by two breakwaters. The N Breakwater, extending about 1 mile WSW from its root close SW of Ra's Sīdī Khuraybīsh protects the N side. The W Breakwater extends about 1 mile SSE from a position close E of the N Breakwater head forming the main entrance about 180 m wide.

2 The main harbour area contains three basins, Inner Harbour on the E side, Old Harbour close inside the root of the N Breakwater, and Middle Harbour on the W side. The inner and middle parts are separated by a large irregular mole which is fully quayed.

3 The Outer Harbour lies close S of Middle Harbour and is enclosed by the S part of the W Breakwater and Outer Harbour Breakwater, close E. A partially submerged breakwater extends about 3¾ cables NNW from Rās Bu Sceiba.

Lights are exhibited from the head of each breakwater and at the entrance to each basin.

Traffic signals

2.286

1 The signals (diagram 2.286), for the information of vessels entering the port, are displayed on a mast at the Port Office (32°07′·1N 20°03′·1E).

Day *Night* *Meaning*

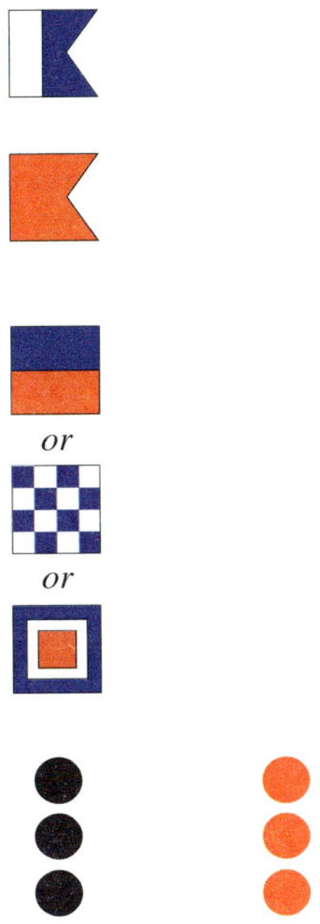

A vessel is at anchor in the roads.

A vessel is leaving the harbour.

or

or

A vessel has been sighted approaching the port from E, N or W respectively.

Port is closed.

Banghāzī - traffic signals (2.286)

Natural conditions

2.287

1 **Climate information.** There is a weather observing station at Benīna, 10 miles E of Banghāzī. See 1.184 and 1.189.

Current. Off Banghāzī the current is usually S-going.

Directions

Principal marks

2.288

1 **Landmarks** (positioned from Banghāzī Light (32°07′·5N 20°03′·8E)):

Banghāzī Light (brown water tower, 22 m in height), standing in a cemetery.

A disused lighthouse (white masonry tower, 33 m in height) (1 cable NW).

2 Minaret (33 m in height) (2 cables SSW).
Signal station (disused) (5½ cables SW), with a prominent mast (34 m in height).
Cathedral (7 cables SSW); a rectangular building surmounted by twin domes.
Dux Granary (1¼ miles SE).
3 Power station with chimneys (1¼ miles SSW).
Radio mast (elevation 82 m) (1¾ miles E).
Radio tower (red lights) (2½ miles SSW), standing on Rās Bu Scieba.
4 Radio mast (elevation 113 m) (3¼ miles SSE).
Radio mast (elevation 125 m) (3¼ miles S).

Major light:

Banghāzī Light — as above.

Approach and entry

2.289

1 From an Approach Reporting Point (2.274) proceed to a position WSW of the main entrance, within the white sector (064¾°–067¼°) of the entrance direction light (32°07′·1N 20°02′·5E), exhibited from the central part of North Breakwater. Thence, keeping within the white sector, proceed to the pilot boarding position 5 cables off the main entrance. The entrance channel has been dredged to a depth of 13·5 m (1988).

2 Attention is drawn to an obstruction (9 cables WNW) and a wreck with a depth of 6·7 m over it (4 cables S), of the North Breakwater Head Light.

For vessels proceeding to the Outer Harbour attention is drawn to a spit with a depth of 1·3 m at its outer end extending 7½ cables W from Rās Bu Sceiba (32°05′·3N 20°02′·8E).

Basins and berths

Middle Harbour

2.290

1 Middle Harbour lies between the E side of the W Breakwater and the large central mole. It contains 1150 m of berthing space on its E side, with charted depths of about 10·3 m. The W limit of the dredged area is marked by light buoys (special).

2 An oil berth, about 155 m long, lies close S of the N end of the W Breakwater. The berth and the approaches to it were dredged to 12·5 m (1988).

Inner Harbour

2.291

1 Inner Harbour lies between the town and the large central mole. On its W side there is a total of about 1200 m of general purpose berthing space with dredged depths (1988) of 6·5 to 12·5 m. A maintenance berth and floating dock lie in the SW corner.

2 The E side of the Inner Harbour contains the original older quays and moles with about 1120 m of berthing face with depths of about 5·9 m, and three pontoon berths on the central mole in the N part.

3 The bottom consists of sand, mud and weed, with occasional rocky patches. Silting is common during winter rains and periodic dredging is necessary to maintain depths. At its S end the Inner Harbour is crossed by Julyānah Bridge.

Old Harbour

2.292

1 Old Harbour is contained by the N Breakwater and Central Mole. It contains about 990 m of berthing space with dredged depths (1966) of 9·0 m. It has a RoRo terminal on its SE side.

Outer Harbour

2.293

1 The Outer Harbour is entered close E of the S end of the W Breakwater, passing N of the submerged breakwater head and W of the head of the Outer Harbour Breakwater. The NE side contains about 500 m of berthing face. The harbour was dredged to 5·5 m (1988).

Port services

Repairs

2.294

1 Minor repairs possible; floating dock.

Other facilities

2.295

1 Hospital, garbage disposal.

Supplies

2.296

1 Fuel; fresh water; provisions.

Communications

2.297

1 Airport at Benīna, 29 km E.

BANGHĀZĪ TO RA'S AL MURAYSAH

GENERAL INFORMATION

Chart 3401

Area covered

2.298

1 This section describes the waters of the coast of Libya from Banghāzī (32°07′N 20°03′E) to Ra's al Muraysah (31°55′N 25°02′E), about 250 miles E. It includes the major port of Ţubruq (32°04′N 24°00′E) and other minor harbours and anchorages along the coast. It is arranged as follows:

2 Banghāzī to Ra's 'Amir (2.299).
Ra's 'Amir to Ra's at Tīn (2.315).
Ra's at Tīn to Ţubruq including Khalīj al Bumbah (2.334).
Ţubruq (2.343).
Ţubruq to Ra's al Muraysah (2.367).

BANGHĀZĪ TO RA'S 'AMIR

General information

Chart 3401

Route

2.299

1 From a position NW of Banghāzī (32°07′N 20°03′E) the track leads NE, for about 100 miles, to a position N of Ra's 'Amir (32°56′N 21°42′E).

Topography

2.300

1 Between Ra's Sīdī Khuraybīsh (32°07′N 20°03′E) and Tūkrah, 36 miles NE, the coast consists of sand dunes about 10 m high, behind which lies a belt of land, parts of which are cultivated and fertile, the remainder being arid and stony. This coastal belt, interspersed with salt lagoons, rises gradually to a range of hills, about 250 to 330 m high, which extends in a NE direction to approach the coast. The hills are intersected by deep gullies.

2 Ar Rajmah, a village 15 miles E of Ra's Sīdī Khuraybīsh, stands at the S end of this range at an elevation of 321 m. A fort 1½ miles NW of the village stands at an elevation of 287 m.

3 Punta Driana (32°23′·6N 20°21′·0E) is a rocky but inconspicuous point which may be identified by numerous low, reddish-coloured ruins in the vicinity, and by Daryānah, a village 2¾ miles SW, consisting of white houses surrounded by palm trees. The grey ruins of Tanşulūkh, 1½ miles E of the point, show up well against the reddish background. Sabkhat al Kūz, a natural salt lake, extends from Punta Driana for 6 miles NE, close to the coast.

4 Between Tūkrah (32°32′N 20°34′E) and Ţulmaythah, 22 miles NE, the coast is rocky and bordered by a narrow sandy beach. The range of hills abreast this stretch of coast is rugged, with streams descending to the sea through deep gullies. The coast E of Ţulmaythah becomes more rugged and the ridges of hills approach nearer to the sea, rising steeply to about 300 m. A rocky bank on which there are some rocks awash and above water, extends 3 mile NE from Ţulmaythah, about 5 cables offshore.

5 Between Qaşr ad Dīsah (32°47′·3N 21°25′·1E) and Khashm al Kalb, 3 miles NE and 33 m high, there is a beach of sand and rocks, backed by a narrow strip of swampy ground with natural salt marshes. The coast is bordered with numerous rocks, some awash, but outside the distance of 1 mile there are no dangers.

Between Al Ḩanīyah (32°50′·9N 21°31′·5E) and Ra's al Ḩamāmah, 7 miles NE, there are a number of sandy coves indenting the low rocky coast, but they afford no shelter.

Wrecks

2.301

1 There are numerous stranded wrecks along this section of the coast, the positions of which are shown on the chart.

Currents

2.302

1 In the vicinity of the Cyrenaican coast between Ra's Ţulmaythah (32°46′N 21°05′E) and Ra's al Ḩamāmah, 30 miles ENE, the main E-going current of the Mediterranean Sea divides. The major part continues ESE towards the Gulf of Salûm at an average rate of about ½ kn, although during E gales the current E of Ra's al Ḩamāmah may be found running temporarily W.

2 The other branch of the E-going current turns S from Ra's Ţulmaythah into the Gulf of Sirte, as described at 2.117.

Water levels

2.303

1 The lowest water levels are experienced in February, March and April, especially with N and NE winds. The highest levels occur in June, July and August, especially with W and SW winds. During the remainder of the year there is practically no rise or fall. The tide range is about 0·4 m.

Directions

(continued from 2.269)

Principal marks

2.304

1 **Landmarks:**

Chimneys (32°12′N 20°08′E) (2.309).

Kawm al ‘Asal (32°20′N 20°31′E), 350 m high.

Fort (32°31′·5N 20°39′·0E). A radio mast (red obstruction lights, 61 m in height) stands close SW.

Water tower (ruined) (32°42′N 20°56′E).

2 Ţulmaythah Lighthouse (short black metal framework tower on white concrete structure with black bands, 16 m in height) (32°42′·9N 20°56′·5E), stands on a promontory on the W side of a bay.

Qaşr ad Dīsah (32°47′·3N 21°25′·1E) a prominent yellow dune, 33 m high.

3 Fort (32°50′·9N 21°32′·1E), which can be identified from Ra's Ţulmaythah, standing on sandhills. Al Ḩanīyah, a village, is situated amongst the sandhills.

Ra's ‘Amir Lighthouse (white concrete tower, black bands, 11 m in height) (32°56′N 21°42′E), exhibited from Ra's ‘Amir.

4 **Major light:**

Power Station Light (obstruction) (32°12′·2N 20°08′·2E), exhibited from chimneys, above.

Banghāzī to Ra's ‘Amir

2.305

1 From a position NW of Banghāzī the track leads generally NE, passing (with positions from Ţulmaythah Light (32°42′·9N 20°56′·7E)):

NW of a dangerous wreck (46 miles SW), thence:

NW of a 5 m patch (41 miles SW). A stranded wreck lies close W, otherwise the coast between Ra's Sīdī Khuraybīsh and Punta Driana is clear of dangers more than 1½ miles offshore. Thence:

2 NW of Secche di Driana (36 miles SW), a line of offshore shoals, with depths of 5 to 10 m over them, thence:

NW of a dangerous wreck (29 miles SW), thence:

3 NW of Tūkrah (22 miles SW), ancient Tauchira, which stands close to the coast. The village, surrounded by walls which are the best preserved Roman remains in the whole of Cyrenaica, has the appearance of a small fortified town with numerous buildings, dominated by one with a white tower, much higher than the others. A minaret is situated SW of the village. Thence:

4 NW of Zeyret Reef (12½ miles SW), thence:

NW of Batraba Reef (8 miles SW), thence:

NW of Ţulmaythah, a village standing on the shore of a small bay, from which a light is exhibited (2.304). The ancient port of Ptolemais lay within a breakwater, now destroyed, which extended parallel to the coast; the village is noted for its antiquarian remains. Behind the village the land rises to a range of high round-topped hills. Thence:

5 NW of Ra's Ţulmaythah (7½ miles ENE), a point that is steep-to and may be identified from the E and SW by a remarkable peak rising about midway up its seaward face, thence:

NW of Ra's al Ḩamāmah (37 miles ENE), ancient Phycus promontory, which may be identified by the ruins of a fort on it, and by the mouth of a large cave. 'Ilwat Mas'ūdah, 1¾ miles S, is 166 m high and a good landmark. Thence:

6 NW of a wreck (39 miles ENE). The wreck is that of a floating dock, stranded on the beach and conspicuous.

The track then leads to a position N of Ra's 'Amir, from where a light (2.304) is exhibited.

Useful marks

2.306

1 Monument (32°16′·9N 20°13′·7E).

Sīdī Suwaykir Light (white square tower, 15 m in height) (32°19′·8N 20°17′·5E). A marabout, small white square building without a dome, stands close E.

Sīdī 'Abd al Jawwād Marabout (32°27′·6N 20°29′·8E), Gasr et-Mtánneb, in ruins, and Sīdī 'Abd as Salām, stand on the coast 1½ miles N and 3 miles NNE respectively.

2 Sīdī al Mabrūk Marabout (32°35′·8N 20°42′·2E), is situated on the coast, with Sīdī Makhlūf Marabout, in ruins, 2 miles ENE.

Sīrat Sīdī Jamā'ah (32°38′·1N 20°48′·8E), a house with gable end facing seaward. A prominent building with a round tower stands 1¼ miles NE and 5 cables inland.

Sīdī 'Abd Allāh Marabout (32°41′·6N 20°54′·9E), is white with four domes, a battery adjoins it.

3 Water tower (white) (32°42′·0N 20°55′·9E). A ruin (close E of the water tower), comprises a large square tower, standing on a foundation of limestone rock.

Sīdī 'Abd ad Dā'im (32°53′·4N 21°35′·8E), a white marabout with a dome, which is hidden by a sand dune on a SE bearing.

(Directions continue at 2.317)

Banghāzī Oil Terminal

Charts 3352, 3401

General information

2.307

1 **Position.** Banghāzī Oil Terminal lies 3 cables SW of Al Minqār al Kabīr (32°10′·9N 20°06′·1E), 4½ miles NE of Banghāzī.

Function. The terminal handles petroleum products and LPG.

2 **Fishing.** Tunny nets are usually laid each year extending 2¼ miles W of Al Minqār al Kabīr (see also 1.3).

Port Authority. See Banghāzī (2.276).

Arrival information

2.308

1 **Pilotage and tugs** are compulsory and available from Banghāzī (2.283 and 2.284).

Harbour

2.309

1 **General layout.** The terminal consists of a single jetty extending 8 cables NW from the shore with berthing platforms at its head and close to the mid point. A mooring dolphin stands close off the head of the jetty from which a light is exhibited (32°11′·1N 20°05′·3E).

Directions

2.310

1 **Landmarks** (positioned from Al Minqār al Kabīr (32°10′·9N 20°06′·1E)):

Power station with three chimneys marked by red lights (2 miles NE). A light buoy (port hand) is moored close offshore at the end of the water intake.

Fort (1 mile S), reddish in colour and surmounted by a turret.

2 Sīdī Miftāh Marabout (6 miles SE), has a white dome and stands at an elevation of 66 m.

Al Kuwayfīyah (4 miles ENE), a penal colony, contains a battery and prominent white buildings.

Qaşr aţ Ţawīl (10½ miles ENE) is a Roman ruin, especially prominent from NW, standing at an elevation of 95 m.

2.311

1 **Approach and entry.** The terminal is approached through the Approach Reporting Point, the chart being sufficient guide.

For details of Approach Reporting Points see 1.41, 2.4, and *Admiralty List of Radio Signals Volume 6 (3).*

Berths

2.312

1 There are two platforms, each with a berthing face on both sides. The outer, at the head, has depths of about 15 m alongside and can accept vessels up to 50 000 dwt. A dolphin, close off its head, is used to assist in berthing. The inner platform, about 550 m from the shore, can accommodate vessels up to about 10 000 dwt with a maximum draught of 6·4 m.

Anchorages

Ţulmaythah

2.313

1 **Anchorage** is obtainable about 5½ cables NW of Ţulmaythah Light (32°42′·9N 20°56′·5E) (2.304), in a depth of 18 m, sand, good holding ground. Small vessels usually anchor with their sterns secured to the shore, but the anchorage is entirely exposed.

2 In summer, during fair weather, vessels drawing 2·4 m or less may approach to a distance of ¼ cable from piles situated 1 cable SE of the light structure. Boats may pass between the rocks, and land on the beach.

Offshore dangers. A submerged reef, well marked by breakers and discoloured water, extends about ¾ cable from a point 8 cables SW of Ţulmaythah Light.

3 An above-water rock, 1 cable NE of the light structure, lies near the outer end of a rocky reef extending NW from the shore; a larger above-water rock, and a rock awash, lie 1 cable and 4½ cables, respectively, farther NE.

Local knowledge is required.

Al Ḩanīyah

2.314

1 A small cove at Al Ḩanīyah (32°50′N 21°31′E) affords anchorage to small vessels. Larger vessels may anchor farther out over a sandy bottom, sheltered from S winds. A reddish coloured building, in ruins, stands close S of the cove.

Local knowledge is required.

RA'S 'AMIR TO RA'S AT TĪN

General information

Chart 3401

Route

2.315

1 From Ra's 'Amir (32°56′N 21°42′E) the route leads E, for about 23 miles, to Ra's al Hilāl, then ESE for about 53 miles to a position NNE of Ra's at Tīn (32°38′N 23°07′E).

Topography

2.316

1 Between Ra's al Ḩamāmah (32°55′N 21°38′E) and Ra's 'Amir, 4 miles NE, and thence to Sūsah, 14 miles farther E, there is a narrow rocky beach lying at the foot of some remarkable hills which rise steeply to elevations of more than 200 m, with a sea face like a wall, broken by deep ravines.

Shaḩḩāt (Cirene) a small town 11 miles SE of Ra's 'Amir, stands on two hills separated by a stream, and is of great archaeological interest.

2 The coast E of Sūsah (32°54′N 21°58′E) is less rugged than that to the W, and the slopes of the hills are less steep. A cave near the coast, 4½ miles E of Sūsah, is remarkable from N. Ru'ūs al Aşlāb, a group of sand dunes 45 m high, lies close to the coast, 7½ miles ENE of Sūsah; the S dune is marked by a cairn.

Between Ra's al Hilāl (32°55′N 22°11′E) and Ra's Bin Jabārah, 10½ miles ESE, the coast is steep and rugged. Wādī al Athrūn flows through a deep ravine midway between these points.

3 Zahrah, 6½ miles SE of Ra's al Hilāl, is a village with white buildings and a small minaret which show up well against a dark background.

Between Ra's Bin Jabārah (32°52′N 22°23′E), which may be approached to a distance of 5 cables, and Ra's Bū 'Azzah, 15 miles ESE, the coast is rocky and the range of hills, on which the remains of military works are visible, recedes inland.

4 The coast E of Darnah (32°46′N 22°39′E) is high, with bold cliffs backed by a high tableland, until near Ra's at Tīn, 25 miles E, where it becomes lower.

Directions

(continued from 2.306)

Principal marks

2.317

1 **Landmarks.**

Ra's 'Amir Lighthouse (32°56′N 21°42′E) (2.304).

Ra's al Hilāl Lighthouse (black and white chequered pyramid, 12 m in height) (32°55′·2N 22°10′·9E). A prominent watchtower stands 8 cables SW of the lighthouse; a white square building with a minaret prominent from the NE, stands 2½ miles S of the lighthouse.

2 Éluet Delfia (32°51′·2N 22°12′·5E), is a hilly spur.

Argub Malta (32°51′·8N 22°20′·7E) is a sharp-pointed conical hill, 301 m high. It is especially prominent when seen from the NW.

Radio mast (red lights) (32°44′·0N 22°39′·5E).

3 Sīdī Shu'ayb (32°35′·2N 22°58′·3E), a very prominent cylindrical tower standing on the tableland.

Major light:

Darnah Light (white tower, black stripes, 12 m in height) (32°44′·5N 22°40′·5E).

Ra's 'Amir to Ra's at Tīn

2.318

1 From a position N of Ra's 'Amir (32°56′N 21°42′E) the track leads E then ESE, passing (with positions from Ra's al Hilāl Light (32°55′·2N 21°10′·9E) (2.317)):

N of Sūsah (10½ miles W) (2.331), from which a light is exhibited, thence:

2 N and NNE of Ra's al Hilāl Light, which is obscured when bearing less than 100°. The point is moderately low, with foul ground extending 2 cables N from the NE part, and rocky patches extending over 1½ cables from its E extremity. Thence:

3 NNE of Jazīrat Kirissah (17 miles ESE), a group of rocky islets from which submerged rocks extend N. A stranded wreck lies on the E side of these islets. Thence:

Clear of, depending on draught, a shoal patch (19½ miles ESE), with a depth of 19·8 m over it, and:

4 Clear of a shoal patch (24½ miles E), reported (1964) to have a depth of 10·9 m over it, thence:

NNE of Ra's Bū 'Azzah (25 miles ESE). A monument and a disused lighthouse stand on the point.

5 The track then leads to a position NE of Ra's at Tīn (50 miles ESE), which projects as a low tongue of land; the high ground inland is a good landmark on all bearings. A light (2.338) is exhibited from the point. Foul ground, with a rock 2 m high, extends 1 mile offshore between Ra's at Tīn and Quşūr Arba', a rock lying 1¾ miles SSE. There is a conspicuous radio pylon on the point.

Useful mark:

Sīdī 'Awn Marabout (32°40′·2N 22°52′·2E).

(Directions continue at 2.338)

Darnah Power Station

Description

2.319

1 Darnah Power Station (32°47′N 22°35′E) is situated close SE of Wādī Bū Musāfir, 4 miles WNW of Darnah. The main building of the power station, with an elevation of 32 m, appears as a light-coloured rectangular block with dark bands at mid-height and at roof level.

Pilotage

2.320

1 Pilotage is compulsory and is carried out during daylight hours only. The pilot boards the vessel at the anchorage (32°49′·3N 22°39′·0E) from a tug. Vessel is secured stern-to on two dolphins using a Mediterranean moor with up to 10 shackles of cable on each anchor and two tugs assisting. The pilot remains on board and one tug remains on standby nearby throughout cargo operations. There is a least depth (2000) of approximately 12 m at the dolphins.

Principal marks

2.321

1 **Landmarks**:

Four chimneys (elevation 47 m) (close SW).

Three large silver-coloured oil storage tanks (close W).

2 Desalination plant (to the SE).

A battery and a small dark-coloured cylindrical tower (2 miles SW), on the highest ground in the vicinity, which show up well against the yellow ground.

Berth

2.322

1 An oil unloading jetty (32°47′·3N 22°35′·4E) extends about 550 m NE from the coast in the vicinity of the oil tanks.

Close NW of the jetty there is a small cove with a pebble beach and bottom where small vessels may obtain shelter from NW winds.

Darnah

Chart 3401, plan of Darnah

General information

2.323

1 **Position.** Darnah, sometimes known as Derna, (32°46′N 22°39′E) is an important commercial centre situated at the mouth of Wādī Darnah, which reaches the sea in a remarkable ravine breaking the coastal range of hills.

Within the town there is a Roman Catholic church and eight mosques, the largest of which has 42 domes.

2 **Function.** Darnah is a small commercial harbour with reasonable equipment for handling bulk, container, general and RoRo vessels.

Principal imports include grain, livestock, animal feedstuffs and general cargo; exports include wool, cement and fish.

3 **Approach and entry.** The port is approached through an Approach Reporting Point and entered between breakwater heads. For details of Approach Reporting Points see 1.41, 2.4, and *Admiralty List of Radio Signals Volume 6 (3).*

Traffic. In 2007 there were 12 ship calls with a total of 32 773 dwt.

Port Authority. Socialist Ports Co., Darnah, Libya.

Limiting conditions

2.324

1 **Controlling depths.** The entrance was dredged to 10 m and the harbour dredged to 9 m (1984).

Density of water. Dock density 1·025 g/cm^3.

Maximum size of vessel: 150 m LOA, draught 8·2 m and 10 000 dwt.

Arrival information

2.325

1 **Anchorage.** The designated anchorage is within 5 cable radius of 32°47′N 22°42′E, as shown on the chart (see also 1.43).

The water in the bay is extremely clear, the bottom being visible to a depth of 15 m.

2 **Pilotage** is compulsory. Vessels are not permitted to enter harbour between 2100 and 0600 local time. For details see *Admiralty List of Radio Signals Volume 6 (3).*

Tugs are available.

Harbour

2.326

1 **General layout.** The harbour is enclosed by N and S breakwaters, the heads of which form an E facing entrance. It is fully quayed on three sides but is subject to constant silting caused by large quantities of weed brought in by the current.

Climate information: see 1.184 and 1.190.

Directions

2.327

1 **Landmarks** (with positions from N Breakwater Head Light (32°45′·9N 22°39′·8E)):

Redoubts on either side of Wādī Darnah (5 cables NW); a tall circular reservoir stands close to the W redoubt.

2 Caserma Salsa (6 cables SW), a large barracks standing on high ground.

Radio mast (red lights) (1¾ miles S).

Major light:

Darnah Light (32°44′·5N 22°40′·5E) (2.317).

2.328

1 **Approach and entry.** From the Approach Reporting Point (2.323), shown on the chart, the track leads S for about 11 miles to the anchorage (2.325) or 12¼ miles to the fairway light buoy (safe water) at the end of the approach channel, about 1 mile E from the N breakwater head. Thence a buoyed channel leads W to the harbour entrance.

2 **Useful marks:**

Light on head of S Breakwater (32°45′·8N 22°39′·7E).

Berths

2.329

1 Berths for handling general cargoes, containers and grain are indicated on the plan. There is a total of about 940 m of berthing space available. In 1984 it was reported that Berths No 2 and 3 had depths alongside of 9 to 10 m, the remainder a depth of 7·5 m.

Port services

2.330

1 **Facilities:** hospital.

Supplies: provisions; fresh water.

Minor harbour and bay

Sūsah

2.331

1 **Description.** Sūsah (32°54′N 21°58′E), a small town, stands between two small elevations, on each side of which is a battery. A group of columns, the remains of the ancient city, lies E of the town.

2 By day the town, surrounded by green vegetation, stands out very clearly against the high rocky coastline; a square fort of red stone is situated prominently in the background, about 60 m higher than the town.

The principal exports are skins, tallow, wool, charcoal and firewood.

3 **Directions**

Landmarks: Sūsah Lighthouse (white concrete tower, 7 m in height) (32°54′N 21°58′E) is clearly visible at a distance of 6 miles.

A flagstaff stands on a building 280 m WSW of the light-structure.

A minaret and a belfry, 100 m SSE and 250 m SW, respectively, of the light-structure.

4 **Approach and entry.** Sūsah should be approached with the lighthouse bearing less than 159°, which leads clear of dangers. The left edge of Scoglio Sharkea may be used for cross bearings. Dangers which should be taken account of are as follows (with positions from Sūsah Lighthouse):

La Seignelay Shoal (750 m N) has a least depth of 4·9 m over it; a shoal with a depth of 3·4 m, and a 4·3 m rocky patch, lie 400 m and 1050 m, respectively, E of the shoal.

5 Scoglio Hammàm and Scoglio Sharkea, both above-water rocks, lie together (750 m NE).

Foul ground extends offshore both E and W of the town.

An above-water rock (2 miles ENE), and a rock with a depth of 0·9 m over it close E, 2½ cables offshore, both usually marked by breakers.

2.332

1 **Anchorage.** HMS *Corunna* (2400 tons) obtained anchorage in 1963 in a depth of 26 m, rocky bottom, but it was reported that with winds of more than force 3–4, from W through N to E, the use of this anchorage would be unwise; at such times the sea breaks strongly along the very broken coast.

Closer inshore, anchorage may be obtained with Sūsah Light bearing less than 159°, good holding ground, sand and rock, in depths of from 10 to 18 m, but this berth is equally exposed.

2 **Harbour.** A small rocky promontory extends N from the middle of the town; on the NE side are numerous concrete blocks, probably the remains of an old jetty, which extend 15 m seaward. The shore is fronted by a small wharf extending in a NE-SW direction, connected to the town by a broken-surfaced road. This wharf, roughly constructed of concrete blocks, is only 0·5 m above HW, and is probably awash in rough weather. Depths alongside are about 1·5 m at the SW end, decreasing to about 0·9 m abreast an iron gantry, and to 0·3 m at the NE end of the wharf. Boats should approach the wharf in a fairly wide sweep, so as to go alongside heading NE.

3 Landing can also be effected on the sandy beach NW of the lighthouse, but the beach shelves gradually, preventing a dry landing.

The wharf and beach are only usable in moderate winds.

Marsá al Hilāl

2.333

1 **Description.** Marsá al Hilāl (32°55′N 22°11′E), an open bay, lies S of Ra's al Hilāl; on the NW and W sides the land maintains a uniform height of about 30 m, but at the S end of the bay Khashm Raḩab rises to 360 m, with a rounded summit. The shores of the bay are indented by two small coves, in which there are large caves visible from seaward; an old Roman jetty, awash, is situated 1¼ miles S of the light-structure.

2 **Anchorage.** Good anchorage is obtainable, well sheltered from winds between NNW, through W, to SE, in depths from 11 to 18 m, with good holding ground of sand and weed. Small vessels may obtain good shelter from N winds close to the shore.

3 **Landing place.** A concrete pier 6 m wide, equipped with bollards, extends ½ cable SE from a beach composed of rock and pebbles at the head of the bay. There are depths of 5·2 to 7·0 m alongside the pier; farther inshore the depths shoal rapidly to about 0·6 m at the inshore end.

Fresh provisions are obtainable.

RA'S AT TĪN TO ŢUBRUQ INCLUDING KHALĪJ AL BUMBAH

General information

Chart 3401

Route

2.334

1 From a position NNE of Ra's at Tīn (32°38′N 23°07′E) the track leads SE, across the entrance of Khalīj al Bumbah (Gulf of Bomba), for about 52 miles, to a position NE of Ţubruq (32°04′N 24°00′E).

Description

2.335

1 Khalīj al Bumbah is a wide gulf lying between Ra's at Tīn and Ra's al Maḩaţţah, 40 miles SE. It contains several partially sheltered bays.

Topography

2.336

1 Between Ra's at Tīn and Bumbah Point, 14 miles S, the coast is low and sandy, with several off-lying rocks and islets.

The coast E of Minqār 'Ayn al Ghazālah (32°13′N 23°19′E) is low; Ra's Amam, 7½ miles E, has two prominent sandhills close E of it, covered with low scrub which becomes sparser farther E.

2 Shoals extend up to 1 mile offshore for 8 miles E of the mouth of Wādī as Suwaynīyāt (32°11′N 23°37′E). A watch tower stands 3 miles E of Wādī as Suwaynīyāt, 5 cables inland.

Ra's al Karrāth (32°10′N 23°47′E) has a white tower standing on a hill 47 m high 1 mile SW. The reddish-coloured ruins of Zāwiyat al Muraşşaş, and the ruins of 'Akramah, 5½ miles WSW and 9 miles SSW, respectively, of Ra's al Karrāth may be seen from offshore.

3 From Ra's al Karrāth and Marsá al 'Awdah, 8 miles SE, the coast is steep-to, low and sandy. Marsá as Sahl, 3½ miles SE of Ra's al Karrāth, is the most noticeable of the numerous coves which indent this stretch, and may be identified from W by three large white patches on the coast.

4 A remarkable cave, 2½ miles E of Marsá as Sahl, has a circular mouth rising to a height of 30 m above the water.

From Marsá al 'Awdah (32°07′N 23°56′E) to Minqār al Markab, 4½ miles ESE, the coast is low but rises gradually inland to a height of about 40 m. A long white sand dune, S of Minqār al Markab, is conspicuous in contrast to the reddish grey of the higher land to the W.

Currents

2.337

1 In Khalīj al Bumbah currents are usually variable, but with a prolonged NW wind, mainly during the summer, a branch of the E-going current may be expected to run S past Ra's at Tīn into the gulf at rates of up to ½ kn.

Directions

(continued from 2.318)

Principal marks

2.338

1 **Landmarks:**

Ra's at Tīn Lighthouse (black metal framework tower, 7 m in height) (32°37′·8N 23°07′·0E).

Fort Perrone (32°06′·1N 23°56′·2E), the walls of which are prominent. A shoal extends 4 cables offshore from the fort and a 2·8 m patch lies 5 cables offshore 3 miles farther ESE.

2 Ţubruq Lighthouse (metal framework tower on black and white chequered building) (32°05′·3N 23°59′·4E).

War memorial (32°03′·4N 23°58′·6E).

Major light:

Ţubruq Light — as above.

Ra's at Tīn to Ţubruq

2.339

1 From a position NE of Ra's at Tīn (32°38′N 23°07′E) the track leads SE, passing (with positions from Jazīrat al 'Ulbah (32°14′N 23°17′E)):

NE of Jazīrat Umm al Qarāmī (15 miles NW), two above-water rocks lying close together, with a 2·9 m patch between them and the shore. A conspicuous white house stands near the coast on the mainland, 2 miles SW. Thence:

2 NE of Jazīrat Barda'ah (9 miles NNW), a high rocky islet and the most prominent object in the gulf, thence:

NE of a dangerous wreck (24 miles E).

The track then leads to a position NE of Ţubruq (32°04′N 24°00′E).

3 **Useful marks:**

Sīdī Muḩammad Marabout (32°07′·6N 23°44′·8E), has a white dome visible only on a SW bearing.

Sīdī Bū Ghufayfah Marabout (32°06′·0N 23°54′·2E), white with a red dome.

(Directions continue at 2.370)

Anchorages

Marsá Umm al Qarāmī

2.340

1 Marsá Umm al Qarāmī (32°34′N 23°07′E) is a bay in the NW part of Khalīj al Bumbah. Anchorage may be obtained, as shown on the chart, sheltered from W and NW winds, 3½ miles S of Ra's at Tīn, in a depth of about 15 m, sand. The current in Marsá Umm al Qarāmī is SW-going.

Local knowledge is required.

Menelao Bay

2.341

1 **Description.** Menelao Bay is entered between Bumbah Point (32°24′N 23°08′E) and Ra's al Milḩ, 4½ miles S, and is open to the E. The current in the bay is W-going.

Bumbah Point may be identified by a group of ruined houses on it, visible at a considerable distance. Jazīrat Mişrātah, 1¾ miles NNE, and Al Jazīrah al Wāţi'ah, 1½ miles E, are both low islets; the current runs NE between Bumbah Point and Jazīrat Mişrātah.

2 **Anchorage** may be obtained, as shown on the chart, 1½ miles S of Bumbah Point in a depth of about 11 m, sheltered from N winds.

Jazīrat al 'Ulbah

2.342

1 **Description.** Jazīrat al 'Ulbah (32°14′N 23°17′E), a low island, has several ruins on it. A shoal, with depth of less than 5 m over it, extends 1¼ miles NW from the island. The channel between Jazīrat al 'Ulbah and Minqār 'Ayn al Ghazālah, 2 miles SE, is encumbered with rocks and shoals.

2 **Anchorage**, sheltered from E winds, is obtainable by small vessels about 1 mile WNW of the island, as shown on the chart.

ŢUBRUQ

General information

Charts 3657, 3401

Position

2.343

1 Ţubruq (Tòbruch) (32°04′N 24°00′E), formerly known as Tobruk, lies in a natural inlet on the NE coast of Libya, about 64 miles WNW of the border with Egypt.

Function

2.344

1 The inlet contains a small commercial harbour, fronting the town of Ţubruq, which handles mainly general cargo, and an oil terminal at Marsá al Ḩarīqah (Marsá el Hariga) on the S side. In 1988 the population of Ţubruq region was about 110 900.

Approach and entry

2.345

1 The port is approached through the Approach Reporting Point, shown on the chart, and entered between Punta Tòbruch and the E entrance point of Marsá Umm esc-Sciausc, an inlet 1¼ miles SSE. Leading lights and leading beacons aid entry.

For details of Approach Reporting Points see 1.41, 2.4, and *Admiralty List of Radio Signals Volume 6 (3)*.

Traffic

2.346

1 In 2007 there were 69 ship calls with a total of 3 381 067 dwt.

Port Authority

2.347

1 Socialist Ports Co., Ţubruq, Libya.

Limiting conditions

Density of water

2.348

1 Density of water in the dock is 1·025 g/cm^3.

Maximum size of vessel handled

2.349

1 335 m LOA, 18·3 m draught, Marsá al Ḩarīqah (2.362).

Local weather and sea state

2.350

1 The inlet is spacious and well sheltered from all winds except from E, which may raise a fairly heavy sea, the effect of which lessens towards the head of the harbour. A considerable sea is also experienced on the S side of the harbour during strong N and NE winds.

Arrival information

Outer anchorage

2.351

1 Anchorage may be obtained in an area, partially shown on the chart, between the parallels of 32°03′·7N and 32°05′·5N and the meridians of 24°02′·0E and 24°03′·0E. The anchorage has depths of about 14·6 to 23·8 m (48 ft to 13 fm), sand and weed.

Inner anchorage

2.352

1 The bottom of Ţubruq Bay is sandy with patches of weed, and anchors are liable to drag. Much of the harbour is strewn with obstructions, the positions of which can be seen on the chart. The anchorage area W of a line joining Punta Tòbruch and Minqār al Ḩarīqah (Mengar el Hariga), 1 mile SW, is clear of obstructions, but debris projecting up to 0·6 m from the bottom may still exist in places.

2 The best anchorage for large vessels is about 9 cables WSW of Punta Tòbruch, as shown on the chart, in a depth of about 15 m, sand and weed, fairly good holding ground, but with strong E winds a heavy swell is experienced. Small vessels anchor nearer the head of the harbour.

Pilotage

2.353

1 Pilotage is compulsory with 72 hours notice being required. The pilot boards SE of Punta Tòbruch Light (32°04′·4N 24°00′·6E).

For details seeand *Admiralty List of Radio Signals Volume 6 (3).*

Tugs

2.354

1 Tugs are available.

Restricted area

2.355

1 An area surrounding the oil terminal, shown on the chart, extending 2 cables offshore for a distance of 1¼ miles, is restricted; no craft is allowed within it without the permission of the oil company.

Harbour

General layout

2.356

1 The commercial harbour lies on the N side of the bay and comprises two piers that extend S and WSW from the shore, to enclose the harbour area.

The oil terminal lies on the S shore of the bay. It comprises two offshore jetties, connected to the shore by walkways. The larger, E jetty has two **T**-shaped piers. The W jetty has a short berthing face with breasting dolphins.

Dangers

2.357

1 The entire harbour area contains numerous charted wrecks, obstructions and other dangers, most of which are relics of World War II.

Directions for entering harbour

Principal marks

2.358

1 **Landmarks:**

Ţubruq Lighthouse (32°05′·3N 23°59′·4E) (2.338).

Punta Tòbruch Light (white pyramid, black diagonal stripes, 5 m in height) (32°04′·4N 24°00′·6E).

German War Memorial (yellow square building with round towers at each corner) (32°03′·4N 23°58′·6E), visible at a distance of 12 miles.

Four oil tanks (large, grey, 17 m in height) (5 cables SE of the German War Memorial).

Deep-draught vessels

2.359

1 From the Approach Reporting Point (2.345) the track leads 4 miles SE to a position about 4 miles NE of Punta Tòbruch Light. Thence the pilot boarding point is approached on the following leading line:

Marsá Umm esc-Sciausc Leading Lights.

Front light (white diamond on metal framework tower) (32°03′·3N 24°00′·9E).

Rear light (similar structure) (314 m from front light).

2 The alignment (224¾°) of these lights leads SW for about 4 miles, passing (with positions from Punta Tòbruch Light (32°04′·4N 24°00′·6E)):

SE of a shoal with a depth of 8·2 m (27 ft) over it (1½ miles NE), thence:

Clear of a depth of 16·8 m (55 ft) (2 miles ENE), thence:

3 SE of a line of shoal patches (1 mile NE), with a least depth of 9·1 m (30 ft) over them. These patches are the outer shoals of an area, with depths of less than 11 m (36 ft), extending up to 8½ cables from the shore between Minqār al Markab (Mengàr el-Mèrcheb) (8 cables N) and Punta Tòbruch.

4 This alignment has a least depth of 19·8 m (65 ft) along it; deep-draught vessels should remain on the line until in the vicinity of a light-buoy (white spherical). Thence the track leads WNW towards the berths; deep-draught vessels should pass SSW of a second light buoy (white spherical) (5 cables S).

Lesser draught vessels

2.360

1 From the Approach Reporting Point (2.343) the track leads SE for about 3½ miles to the alignment (224½°) of following leading beacons:

Front beacon (black diamond, white stripe on pole) (32°03′·5N 24°00′·2E).

Rear beacon (similar mark and pole) (310 m from front beacon).

2 This alignment leads in depths of not less than 12·8 m (42 ft) to the Fairway Light Buoy, passing the dangers noted above for deep-draught vessels. A buoy (starboard hand) is moored 4 cables SW of Punta Tòbruch.

Caution. The leading beacons may be difficult to distinguish; a small stone hut painted black and white in chequers, but not conspicuous, stands at an elevation of 82 m, 7 cables SW of the front beacon, in line with which it bears 225°.

Berths

Commercial harbour

2.361

1 There are nine berths with depths from 5 to 9·5 m.

Marsá al Ḩarīqah Oil Terminal

2.362

1 Marsá al Ḩarīqah (Marsá el Hariga) Oil Terminal lies on the S side of Ţubruq Bay and contains the following berths (with positions from Punta Tòbruch Light (32°04′·4N 24°00′·6E)):

East jetty (8 cables SSW). Length 800 m with two **T**-shaped berths, each 30 m long with depths of about 18 m alongside; lights are exhibited from the E berth, Berth No 1, and from the E end of the jetty head.

2 **West jetty** (1¼ miles SW). Length 200 m, with a berthing face about 40 m long in the centre, with depths of not less than 12 m alongside, fitted with breasting dolphins. Lights are exhibited from each end of the jetty and from the berth. Vessels up to 35 000 dwt, length 190 m and draught 9·1 m, can be accommodated.

Port services

Repairs

2.363

1 Limited facilities only; small patent slip.

Other facilities

2.364

1 Hospital; dirty ballast accepted.

Supplies

2.365

1 Limited quantities of fuel available; no provisions or fresh water.

Communications

2.366

1 El-Adem Airport, 26 km S.

ŢUBRUQ TO RA'S AL MURAYSAH

General information

Chart 3401

Route

2.367

1 From a position NE of Ţubruq (32°04′N 24°00′E) the track leads E, for about 54 miles, to a position NE of Ra's al Muraysah (31°55′N 25°02′E).

Topography

2.368

1 The coast E of Ţubruq is rugged and intersected by numerous small streams. As far as Marsá Bayād (32°03′N 24°02′E) the coast is moderately low, but farther E the tableland, about 90 m high, slopes steeply to the sea.

A remarkable point, 3¾ miles E of Marsá Bayād, consists of square white rocks. Jazīrat az Zaytūn, close to this point, is a slender strip of low, dark, inconspicuous rocks.

2 Wādī Bū Lilla (32°00′N 24°12′E) reaches the sea 1 mile SE of Sheik Rocks; the coast E becomes lower for a few miles, and thence high and rugged. Wādī al Kibāsh, 7 miles E of Wādī Bū Lilla, flows through a prominent narrow gully.

Wādī as Sahl (31°59′N 24°33′E) can be identified by numerous palm trees. The coast for 6 miles E is fringed with rocks and shoals.

3 Wādī at Ţarfāqī (32°00′N 24°37′E) consists of a dense grove of palm trees. Minqār Ghurāb, 1¾ miles NE, is a sand dune 21 m high, rising steeply from the sea with several dark patches of scrub on its slopes. The coast E of Minqār Ghurāb consists of low white sandhills. The coast E of Minqār Bū Shaykhah continues sandy, but of darker colour.

Currents

2.369

1 Between Ţubruq (32°04′N 24°00′E) and Ra's al Muraysah (31°55′N 25°03′E) dangerous onshore sets in excess of 1 kn may be experienced with prolonged NW winds.

Directions

(continued from 2.339)

Principal marks

2.370

1 **Landmarks:**

Beacon (black and white diagonal stripes, 3-sided, on tripod, 12 m in height) (32°00′·8N 24°00′·2E).

Ra's 'Azzāz Lighthouse (metal framework tower, 11 m in height) (31°58′·2N 24°58′·8E).

2 **Major light:**

Ţubruq Light (32°05′·3N 23°59′·4E) (2.338).

Ţubruq to Ra's al Muraysah

2.371

1 From a position NE of Ţubruq (32°04′N 24°00′E) the track leads E, passing (with positions from Ra's al Kibāsh (32°00′N 24°21′E)):

N of Secca Ahal (12½ miles W), thence:

N of Sheik Rocks (9 miles W), which lie 1 mile offshore, with foul ground between them and the coast, where there is a prominent cleft, thence:

N of Ra's al Kibāsh (32°00′N 24°21′E). This point, with a rock awash 5 cables offshore, is low and difficult to distinguish; the coast E of the point falls less steeply to the sea. Thence:

2 N of Secca Bū al 'Ilfrīt (3½ miles E), rocks awash, thence:

N of Jazīrat al Ḩimārah (7 miles E), a low rocky islet surrounded by rocks awash; shoal water extends 5 cables offshore in this vicinity. Thence:

N of Secca as Sahl (10½ miles E), and:

N of Secche Amied (12 miles E), thence:

3 N of an isolated shoal patch (16 miles E), with a depth of 5·7 m over it, which lies 1 mile NW of Minqār Bū Shaykhah from which foul ground extends 5 cables NNE. A stranded wreck lies close by. Thence:

N of Ra's Wannah (20 miles E), which has a small cairn on its summit. Collinetta di Rās Uénna, on the E slope of which are two ruined buildings, rises ¾ cable S of the point. Thence:

2.372

1 N of a shoal (22 miles E), with a depth of 4·6 m over it, that extends from the coast 1½ miles E of Ra's Wannah, thence:

N of Ra's al 'Awrā (27 miles E), the W entrance point of Marsá al 'Awrā, which is surmounted by a large cairn. Between Ra's al 'Awrā and Ra's 'Azzāz, 5½ miles E, submerged rocks lie up to 6 cables offshore. Thence:

2 N of a shoal (31 miles E), with a depth of 6 m over it, which lies 1½ miles NE of Ra's Bū Ḩuiqūmah. A stranded wreck lies between the point and the shoal. Thence:

N of Ra's 'Azzāz (32½ miles E), which may be identified by a group of palm trees standing behind the sand dunes SE of it; a submerged reef extends 1 mile E. Thence:

3 N of a patch (34 miles E), with a depth of 4 m over it, which lies between Ra's al Manāstīr and Ra's Bū Wushaykah.

The track then leads to a position NE of Ra's al Muraysah (35½ miles E).

4 **Useful mark:**

Sīdī Hāshim Marabout (31°57′N 24°34′E).

(Directions continue for coastal passage at 3.12)

Anchorage

Marsá Lukk

2.373

1 Marsá Lukk (32°01′·3N 24°46′·1E) affords anchorage in depths of about 12 m, sand and weed, good holding ground, 6½ cables E of Jazīrat Lukk, a small low black rock. Ridotta Lukk, a prominent white structure surrounded by stone huts, stands close SW of the bay; a house with a turret stands at the head of the bay.

Local knowledge is required.

NOTES

Chapter 3 - Ra's Al Muraysah to Tel Rafah

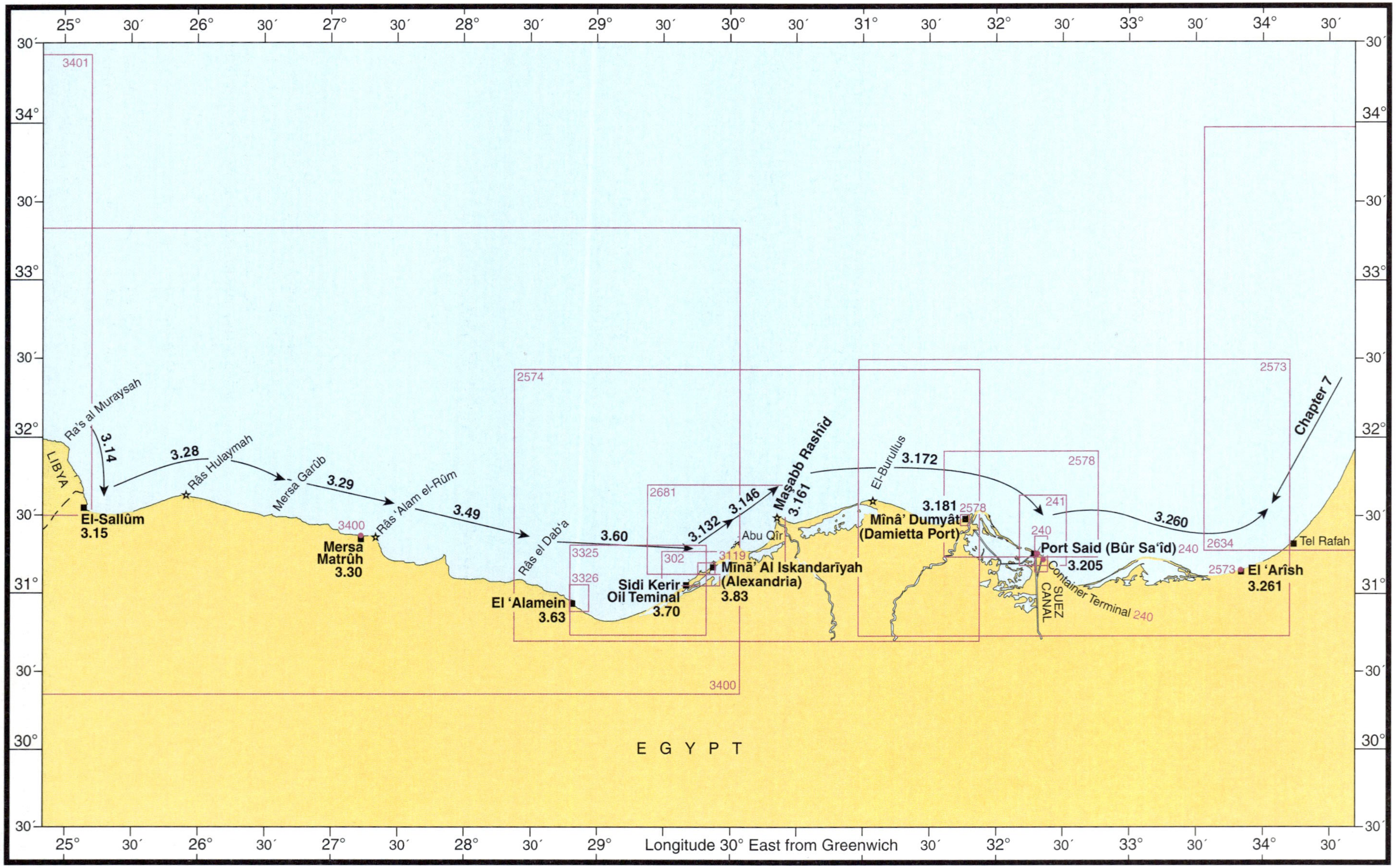

CHAPTER 3

COASTS OF LIBYA AND EGYPT — RA'S AL MURAYSAH TO TEL RAFAH

GENERAL INFORMATION

Chart 183

Scope of the chapter

3.1

1 The area covered by this chapter comprises the coastal waters of Libya and Egypt from Ra's al Muraysah (31°55′N 25°02′E) to Tel Rafah (31°19′N 34°13′E), about 475 miles to the E.

The description includes the principal ports of Mīnā' Al Iskandarīyah (Alexandria) (3.83), Mînâ' Dumyâṭ (Damietta Port) (3.181) and Port Said (Bûr Sa'îd) (3.205), and the oil terminals situated at Mersa el Hamra (El 'Alamein) (3.63) and Sidi Kerir (3.70).

2 The chapter is divided into the following sections:

Ra's al Muraysah to Mīnā' Al Iskandarīyah (3.6).
Mīnā' Al Iskandarīyah to Ṭâbiyet El-Burg (3.78).
Ṭâbiyet El-Burg to Tel Rafah (3.138).

Traffic regulations

3.2

1 **Prohibited areas.** Areas extending as much as 25 miles from the Egyptian coast may be prohibited for navigation. Vessels bound for Egyptian ports or navigating off the coast are advised to obtain the latest information from their agents.

2 **Offshore routes.** Vessels navigating to and from Egyptian ports are advised by the Egyptian authorities to keep 12 miles offshore by day and 24 miles offshore at night.

3 **Coastal routes.** Vessels coasting between El-Sallûm (3.15), Mersa Maṭrûḥ (3.30), Mīnā' Al Iskandarīyah (3.83), Port Said (3.205) and El 'Arîsh (3.261) should use the recommended routes shown on the large scale charts.

Arrival information

3.3

1 Vessels bound for Egyptian ports are required to comply with the following:

1. Mariners should send an ETA at least 24 hours in advance stating the vessel's last port of call, position, course and speed.
2. Port Authorities should be contacted for entry instructions when within 24 miles of the port of arrival.

Currents

3.4

1 The general E-going current near the coast of Egypt is reinforced by water from NW, particularly in summer when NW winds prevail over the SE Mediterranean, and runs with a high degree of constancy at a mean rate of about ¾ kn between Maṣabb Rashîd (Rosetta Mouth) and Port Said.

2 The current E of Port Said remains fairly constant, but near El 'Arîsh its mean rate decreases to less than ½ kn.

Rescue

3.5

1 For information on rescue see 1.64 and *Admiralty List of Radio Signals Volume 5.*

RA'S AL MURAYSAH TO MĪNĀ' AL ISKANDARĪYAH

GENERAL INFORMATION

Chart 3400

Area covered

3.6

1 The area covered by this section comprises:

Ra's Al Muraysah to El-Sallûm (3.8).
El-Sallûm to Râs 'Alam El-Rûm (3.24).
Râs 'Alam El-Rûm to Râs El Dab'a (3.43).
Râs El Dab'a to Mīnā' Al Iskandarīyah (3.53).

Inadequately surveyed areas

3.7

1 With the exception of Sidi Kerir and El 'Alamein oil terminals, the area off the coast of Egypt, W of longitude 29°38′E to the Libyan border has not been adequately surveyed.

2 Mariners are warned that uncharted dangers may exist, especially within the 50 m contour, and the position of charted dangers may be in error.

RA'S AL MURAYSAH TO EL-SALLÛM

General information

Chart 3400

Route

3.8

1 From a position NE of Ra's al Muraysah (31°55′N 25°02′E) the route leads SSE, for about 23 miles into Khalîg As Sallûm, to a position in the Approach Sector for El-Sallûm, about 6 miles E of Marsá ar Ramlah (31°41′N 25°08′E).

Topography

3.9

1 The coastline between Ra's al Muraysah and Sîdi Barrâni, 48 miles SE, is indented by Khalîg As Sallûm. The W shore of the gulf is moderately high with cliffs, the coast S of Ra's al Muraysah being precipitous, broken by many gullies, and steep-to; the S and SE sides of the gulf, however, are low, sandy and backed by a ridge of white sandhills.

Currents

3.10

1 A branch of the main E-going current is thought to form a clockwise circulation in Khalîg As Sallûm, with a mean rate of ¼ to ½ kn.

International boundary

3.11

1 The boundary between Libya and Egypt reaches the coast about 17 miles SSE of Ra's al Muraysah.

Directions

(continued from 2.372)

Landmark

3.12

1 Ridotta er-Ràmla (31°41′N 25°08′E), an old redoubt, standing W of the head of Marsá ar Ramlah.

Other aid to navigation

3.13

1 **Racon:**

El-Sallûm (31°34′N 25°10′E).

For details see *Admiralty List of Radio Signals Volume 2.*

Ra's al Muraysah to El Sallûm

3.14

1 From a position NE of Ra's al Muraysah (31°55′N 25°02′E) the track leads SSE, passing (with positions from Ra's al Muraysah):

ENE of Marsá al Muraysah (1½ miles S) (3.22), an anchorage. There is a stranded wreck on the shore W of this anchorage. Thence:

ENE of Mīnā' Bardīyah (10 miles SSE) (3.23), a small harbour from which Minqār Rā'ī Rūhah Light (metal framework tower on a black and white concrete base) is exhibited, thence:

2 ENE of Marsá al Murayghah (13½ miles SSE), a cove which affords shelter to small vessels except during E winds; local knowledge is required. There is a depth of 3 m about ¼ cable from the head of the cove, where there is a beach.

The track then leads to a position about 6 miles E of Marsá ar Ramlah (15 miles SSE). This cove, with a depth of 10 m about ¾ cable from the sandy beach at its head, is similar to Marsá al Murayghah.

(Directions continue for the coastal route at 3.27 and for El-Sallûm at 3.18)

El-Sallûm

General information

3.15

1 **Position.** El-Sallûm (31°34′N 25°10′E), the ancient Roman port of Baranis, is situated on the NW side of the Bay of Sallûm, which lies at the head of Khalîg As Sallûm.

Topography. Observatory Point, 1 mile SW of Beacon Point, projecting into the bay and forming part of the harbour of El-Sallûm, is the S extremity of a plateau 23 m high, on which stand coastguard and other buildings.

2 The W and SW sides of Bay of Sallûm are low and sandy; two small houses, situated near the coast 1 mile S of Observatory Point, are prominent. Yorke Patches, 3 cables S of Observatory Point, consist of several rocks, with depths of 5·5 m over them.

In the vicinity of El-Sallûm the water is exceptionally clear, the bottom being visible at a depth of 31 m in smooth water.

3 **Approach and entry.** The port is approached from the NE within the limits of the Approach Sector, as shown on the chart. The bay, in which the port lies, is then entered between Beacon Point (31°34′N 25°11′E) and Rocky Point, 2 miles S.

Arrival information

3.16

1 **Anchorage.** There is a designated anchorage area at the S end of the Approach Sector, as shown on the chart, 2½ miles NE of Beacon Point. The holding ground is fair with sand and weed.

Small vessels may obtain good anchorage 1 cable SE of Observatory Point, in a depth of 8·5 m, sand and weed.

2 **Regulation.** In 1974 the Egyptian authorities stated that El-Sallûm was not open for navigation until further notice.

Harbour

3.17

1 **General layout.** The harbour is situated in the vicinity of Observatory Point, in the NW corner of the Bay of Sallûm.

Climate information: see 1.184 and 1.191.

Directions

(continued from 3.14)

3.18

1 **Landmarks:**

Beacon Point, which is surmounted by a beacon (stone obelisk, 9 m in height); within it is a small plateau 29 m high. A cone-shaped pagoda about 6 m in height stands W of the beacon, on the high ground of the point.

2 Fort Sallûm, 1¼ miles W of Beacon Point, is a conspicuous old white fort, with a barracks close N, standing on the edge of the plateau at an elevation of 180 m. These buildings are especially prominent when approaching El-Sallûm from E.

Other aid to navigation:

Racon: El-Sallûm (31°34′N 25°10′E).

For details see *Admiralty List of Radio Signals Volume 2.*

3.19

1 **Approach.** Vessels approaching El-Sallûm should do so within the approach sector and proceed to the waiting anchorage, both of which are shown on the chart.

Entry. From a position E of Marsá ar Ramlah (31°41′N 25°08′E) the track leads 7 miles SSW, passing (with positions from Beacon Point (31°34′N 25°11′E)):

ESE of an obstruction (5 miles N), over which the depth is unknown.

2 The track then leads to a position in the waiting anchorage, ESE of El Hashafa, 2½ miles NNW of Beacon Point. El Hashafa consists of two small islets lying 1 cable offshore, the higher of which has an elevation of 20 m.

Caution. A wreck, with a depth of 11 m over it, lies on the S edge of the waiting anchorage, about 1 mile NE of Beacon Point.

3 **Useful mark:**

El-Sallûm Light (white metal mast, black top, 10 m in height) (31°33′·7N 25°09′·9E), exhibited from the head of the pier at Observatory Point.

Berths

3.20

1 **Pier.** A stone pier, with depths from 4·6 to 6·1 m alongside, and with two red warping buoys near its head, extends SW from Observatory Point, but it is only suitable for small vessels in fair weather. A distilling plant stands at

the root of the pier. A mooring buoy lies 1½ cables ESE of Observatory Point.

2 **Jetties.** A small wooden jetty, with a depth of 1·2 m at its head, and a stone jetty, are situated 2 cables NW and 4 cables SW, respectively, of Observatory Point.

Bay. The bay NW of Observatory Point is well sheltered, with depths of 3·0 to 4·6 m. On its NE side a rubble breakwater 152 m long affords protection for lighters in depths of 1·2 to 2·1 m.

Port services

3.21

1 **Supplies:** small quantities available.

Anchorage

Marsá al Muraysah

3.22

1 Marsá al Muraysah (31°54′·5N 25°03′·6E) affords good anchorage, sheltered from W winds.

Local knowledge is required.

Minor harbour

Mīnā' Bardīyah

3.23

1 **Description.** Mīnā' Bardīyah (31°45′N 25°06′E) is a natural harbour entered NW of Minqār Rā'ī Rūhah, with an elevation of 95 m; a light (3.14) is exhibited from this point.

A prominent tower stands on the cliffs on the N side of the entrance, 5 cables NW of the light. The village, largely in ruins, is situated close SW and consists of some white houses and a prominent minaret; these provide a useful landmark for Mīnā' Bardīyah, which is not easily identified from seaward.

2 **Outer anchorage.** Anchorage outside the harbour entrance is obtainable with the tower bearing 255°, distant 5 cables, in depths of 42 m, sand.

Harbour. The harbour has two shallow bays at its head, the of which the E is foul. The shores are high and rocky, and shelter is afforded except from NE winds.

3 The best anchorage is in a depth of about 5 m in the W bay; the bottom is mostly sand. Light land and sea breezes are experienced, the latter setting up a slight swell; at night the land breeze may cause a vessel at anchor to lie across the swell, and it is advisable to lay out a line from the stern to a masonry pier, on the NW side of the bay, which in 1956 was in ruins. Ships boats can use the pier, but there are obstructions alongside.

EL-SALLÛM TO RÂS 'ALAM EL-RÛM

General information

Chart 3400

Route

3.24

1 From a position about 9 miles E of Marsá ar Ramlah (31°41′N 25°08′E) the coastal route follows the recommended track, shown on the chart, ENE for 32 miles and then ESE for 76 miles, to a position in the Approach Sector for Mersa Maṭrûḥ, about 9½ miles N of Râs 'Alam el-Rûm (31°22′N 27°21′E).

Topography

3.25

1 **El-Sallûm to Sîdi Barrâni.** Haggag el Aqaba, the Great Libyan Plateau, lies with its NE edge extending SE from near El-Sallûm, gradually receding from the coast. Near the coast the plateau varies from 183 to 195 m in elevation, and is intersected by numerous short water courses. The summit is very flat, the soil consisting of sand and stones, and it is sparsely covered with very low scrub, and with occasional patches of rudimentary cultivation.

Between Haggag el Aqaba and the coast, there is a plain, considerably cultivated, which varies in width from a few hundred metres in the W part to 20 miles in the E part, as the plateau recedes from the sea.

2 The coastline is low and sandy, with occasional rocky points, and is bordered by rocks in many places. The villages are mostly situated where breaks in the coastline form safe harbours for vessels of a suitable size.

Between El-Sallûm (31°34′N 25°10′E) and Râs el Seiyâda, 16 miles ESE, the coast is fronted by a salt marsh; the sandhills behind it rise to a greatest elevation of 31 m. Thence from Râs el Seiyâda to Sîdi Barrâni, 24 miles ENE, the coast is backed by hills rising to an elevation of 64 m from 2 to 3 miles inland.

3 **Sîdi Barrâni to Râs 'Alam el-Rûm.** The coast between Sîdi Barrâni (31°37′N 25°55′E) and Râs Abu Lâho, 57 miles ESE, is low and backed by small sandhills. The coastal hills rise to an elevation of over 100 m further inland.

From Râs Abu Lâho to Mersa Maṭrûḥ, 9 miles ESE, the coast at first rises in cliffs, being bordered by rocks, but changes to sand dunes in the vicinity of Mersa Maṭrûḥ. Thence from Mersa Maṭrûḥ to Râs 'Alam el-Rûm, 5½ miles E, the coast is rocky and fronted by off-lying rocks; close inland is a chain of salt lagoons.

Currents

3.26

1 Between Sîdi Barrâni (31°37′N 25°55′E) and Râs 'Alam el-Rûm, 76 miles ESE, during summer when the prevailing wind is between NW and N, onshore sets of about ½ kn are frequently experienced.

Directions

(continued from 3.14)

Aids to navigation

3.27

1 **Racons:**

El-Sallûm (31°34′N 25°10′E).

Sîdi Barrâni (31°37′N 25°55′E).

Râs 'Alam el-Rûm (31°22′N 27°21′E).

For details see *Admiralty List of Radio Signals Volume 2.*

El-Sallûm to Mersa Garûb

3.28

1 From a position about 9 miles E of Marsá ar Ramlah (31°41′N 25°08′E) the track leads ENE, passing (with positions from Sîdi Barrâni Light (31°37′N 25°55′E)):

NNW of Râs el Seiyâda (24 miles WSW), a low rocky point. Between El-Sallûm and Râs el Seiyâda depths of less than 10 m extend 2 miles offshore in places; a rock 2 m high lies off Râs el Seiyâda. Thence:

2 To a position N of Râs Hulaymah (1 mile W). Sîdi Barrâni, close by Râs Hulaymah, is situated on land which rises gradually from the coast. A light (white metal mast, red top, 10 m in height) is

exhibited from Sîdi Barrâni; close E stands a prominent beacon (black post, spherical cage topmark, 6 m in height). The coastguard station is also prominent. For details on anchoring off Sîdi Barrâni see 3.40.

3 The track then leads ESE, passing:

NNE of Mersa el Tarfâya (10 miles ESE). An area of foul ground, with a least depth of 9·1 m over it, extends NE of this small bay. Between Sîdi Barrâni and Mersa el Tarfâya, rocky reefs and areas of foul ground, which are steep-to, extend offshore; in places there are depths of 20 m, less than 1 mile outside these reefs. Thence:

4 NNE of Taifa Rock (16 miles E), 2¼ miles offshore, which is steep-to, with submerged rocks around it. In 1945 it was reported that the depths E of the rock were very irregular, varying from 9 to 37 m within a short distance of the rock. A shoal, with a depth of 7·3 m over it, and which has not been examined, was reported in 1938 to lie 2½ miles NW of Taifa Rock. Thence:

5 NNE of a dangerous wreck (28 miles ESE) lying about 2 miles offshore.

The track then leads to a position NNE of Mersa Garûb (34 miles ESE); foul ground lies to the W of this bay.

Mersa Garûb to Râs ʻAlam el-Rûm

3.29

1 From the position NNE of Mersa Garûb (31°30′N 26°34′E) the track continues ESE, passing (with positions from the light at Râs ʻAlam el-Rûm (31°22′N 27°21′E)):

NNE of Gezìrat Ishaila (37 miles WNW), an islet about 18 m high, from which reefs extend 1¾ miles WSW. About 1¼ miles ESE of the islet is a detached reef, and patches of reef extend for about 10 miles E, parallel to the coast. There is an anchorage (3.41) in the vicinity of Gezìrat Ishaila. Thence:

2 NNE of Râs Abu Lâho (19 miles WNW), which is moderately high with cliffs; a range of hills 183 m high extends about 8 miles S from it. A rocky bay, the shores of which are high, lies between Râs Abu Lâho and Râs Umm el Rakham, 3½ miles SE. Thence:

NNE of Râs Umm el Rakham (14½ miles WNW), on the E side of which there is a bay with an anchorage (3.42).

3 The track then leads to a position in the Approach Sector for Mersa Maṭrûḥ (3.30), about 9½ miles N of Râs ʻAlam el-Rûm (31°22′N 27°21′E). A light (white metal mast, red band, 10 m in height) is exhibited from the point. Râs ʻAlam el Rûm is the termination of a spur, 41 m high, from the apex of two ranges of hills which run W and S from the point.

(Directions for the coastal route continue at 3.47)

(Directions for Mersa Maṭrûḥ are given at 3.34)

Mersa Maṭrûḥ

Chart 3400, plan of Mersa Maṭrûh

General information

3.30

1 **Position.** Mersa Maṭrûḥ (31°22′N 27°14′E) is situated on the N coast of Egypt, 135 miles W of Mīnā’ Al Iskandarīyah.

Function. The old harbour at the E end of the inlet is a small commercial port, whilst in the lagoon to the W is a new harbour facility, reported (2007) to be in use as a naval base, but being converted for commercial use.

2 **Historical note.** Mersa Maṭrûḥ was known in ancient times as Paraetonium. After founding Alexandria, the new conquerer of Egypt and recently anointed pharaoh, Alexander the Great, stopped here during his dangerous expedition to the major oasis at Siwa, the home to the world renowned Oracle of the god Amun.

3 **Topography.** Mersa Maṭrûḥ is an inlet completely sheltered from seaward by reefs. The W shore of the inlet, S of the entrance, is sandy and liable to inundation; the S shore consists of a range of sandhills from 6 to 9 m high, with scrub and some palm trees. Rocks lie up to 1 cable off the S shore in places. The town of Maṭrûḥ is situated on the S shore.

4 Point Labeit (31°22′·2N 27°13′·6E), the W entrance point of Mersa Maṭrûḥ, is 2 m high. Pinnacle Rock, 11 m high and conspicuous, and Square Rock, 6 m high, lie 2½ cables WNW of Point Labeit.

Maṭrûḥ Point, 7 cables E of Point Labeit, is the E entrance point to Mersa Maṭrûḥ, and the W extremity of a rocky spit 7 cables long which rises to a height of 21 m at its E end.

5 A lagoon extends W for 2½ miles from Point Labeit, close within the coast, with depths of 5·3 to 12·8 m. It appears to have been extensively used by the Romans as a harbour; there are numerous ruins, and in places the remains of aqueducts, wharves and piers are still visible. The ruins of Old Maṭrûḥ, the ancient town, are situated in an oasis at the W end of the lagoon.

6 **Approach and entry.** Vessels approaching Maṭrûḥ should do so within the Approach Sector, indicated on chart 3400. Thence the inlet is entered between Point Labeit, to the W, and the W extremity of Maṭrûḥ Reef, extending 5½ cables W from Maṭrûḥ Point, to the E. From the entrance a narrow and winding channel leads to the old harbour at Maṭrûḥ.

Limiting conditions

3.31

1 **Controlling depths.** There are least charted depths of 8·4 m in the harbour entrance, 5·3 m in the channel leading to the old harbour on the E side of Mersa Maṭrûḥ, and 8·5 m in the channel leading to the new harbour in the lagoon to the W of Mersa Maṭrûḥ. However, it was reported (1993) that this channel had been dredged to a depth of 9 m.

2 **Deepest and longest berth.** At the new harbour (3.38).

Abnormal water levels. The water backs up in Mersa Maṭrûḥ at the approach of strong winds from NW, and during N winds the water level in the harbour may rise about 0·9 m above normal.

3 **Maximum size of vessel handled.** The maximum permissable draught is 8 m. The old harbour can accommodate vessels at the stone quay (3.38) up to 3000 tons.

Arrival information

3.32

1 **Outer anchorage.** A waiting anchorage of approximately 1½ miles radius is positioned about 3 miles N of Point Labeit. The anchorage is exposed and the holding is reported to be poor.

Harbour

3.33

1 **General layout.** The old harbour for Maṭrûḥ is situated on the E side of Mersa Maṭrûḥ. Harbour Point (31°21′·7N

27°14′·7E), the SE entrance point of the harbour, lies 4 cables SE of Maṭrûḥ Point, and is sandy and remarkably steep-to; in recent years it has extended N. A rubble breakwater extends 2½ cables SW from the N side of the harbour, and gives additional protection from W; its extremity forms the NW entrance point of the harbour.

2 The E and S shores of the harbour are flat and sandy, and liable to inundation; a submerged obstruction lies ½ cable SE of Harbour Point, close offshore, and two ruined jetties are situated 1¼ cables SE of the point. Drama Point lies 1½ cables SE of Harbour Point; a wreck, with a depth of 0·6 m over it, lies close NE of Drama Point, and there are stranded wrecks on the N and E shores of the harbour. Depths in the harbour are from 6·7 to 12·4 m on the W side but decrease rapidly to the E.

3 The new harbour lies at the E end of the lagoon which opens to the W of Mersa Maṭrûḥ. It is entered by a channel about 5 cables long running WSW from a position 1 cable S of Point Labeit. The channel is marked by buoys and beacons and is about 1 cable wide at its narrowest point. The harbour consists of a turning area, minimum depth 9 m, off a single quay on the S shore of the lagoon.

Directions for entering harbour

3.34

1 **Landmarks.** The following objects are conspicuous on approaching Mersa Maṭrûḥ:

Lido Hotel, a red building 6½ cables S of Point Labeit (31°22′·2N 27°13′·6E).

Minaret of Sidi Awam Mosque, 35 m high, 1½ cables SE of Lido Hotel.

Bank building, 6 cables S of Maṭrûḥ Point (31°22′·0N 27°14′·5E).

2 Minaret 1½ cables SSE of the bank.

Four radio masts, about 21 m high, 3½ cables S of the bank.

Water-tower 2½ miles SW of Maṭrûḥ Point.

Television mast with an elevation of 100 m stands about 1 mile ESE of Maṭrûḥ Point.

3 On nearer approach, the following objects become prominent:

The two entrance leading beacons (3.35).

Port office flagstaff (24 m high), 3½ cables E of the bank building.

Rest house, with a flagstaff, on the skyline 6 cables S of the bank.

3.35

1 **Caution.** An appreciable set may be experienced across the entrance in either direction. In addition, a W wind tends to blow across the entrance during the summer months, and an E wind in the winter. It is at times necessary to close the harbour in heavy seas due to the dangerous entrance.

2 From a position in the waiting anchorage (3.32) the track leads S, passing W of a dangerous wreck, 9½ cables NE of Point Labeit, to the entrance leading line. This leading line should be gained as soon as the beacons can be distinguished, so as to steady the vessel on the correct course before reaching the entrance, which is only ½ cable wide.

3 **Entrance leading beacons:**

Front beacon (black and white bands) (31°21′·6N 27°13′·4E).

Rear beacon (similar) (1¾ cables from front beacon).

The alignment (210°) of these beacons leads SSW, passing (with positions from Point Labeit):

WNW of Nury Rock (2 cables E), a dangerous rock, thence:

ESE of a light-beacon (starboard hand) (green cylindrical GRP tower) (¾ cable E), marking the edge of the reefs extending 1 cable E of Labeit Point, and:

4 WNW of a light-beacon (port hand) (red cylindrical GRP tower) (1½ cables ESE), marking the W extremity of Maṭrûḥ Reef. The reef extends 5½ cables W from Maṭrûḥ Point, and has on it a number of above-water rocks; White Rock, 2 cables W of Maṭrûḥ Point, is 3 m high and conspicuous.

Thence to a position about 1¼ cables SE of Point Labeit.

3.36

1 **Old harbour.** The track continues SSW for about 1½ cables and then leads SSE, E and NE, through a channel, to the old harbour, passing W and S of the large shoal area S of Maṭrûḥ Reef. The reef is encumbered with rocks over which there are depths of 0·6 to 0·9 m; the most important are Senussi Rocks, Askeri Rocks and Jaafar Rocks, on which the sea breaks heavily even with moderate winds. The channel is marked by buoys (lateral) and by leading beacons, in succession as follows:

2 Leading beacons (poles, rectangle topmarks) (31°21′·4N 27°13′·8E), ¾ cable E of Sidi Awam Mosque, in line bear 169°, thence:

Leading beacons (poles, diamond topmarks) (31°21′·4N 27°14′·1E) in line bearing 129°, thence:

Leading beacons (poles, triangle topmarks) (31°21′·6N 27°14′·6E) in line bearing 090°, thence:

Leading beacons (31°21′·9N 27°14′·9E), in line bearing 051°, lead into the old harbour.

3.37

1 **New harbour.** From a position about 1¼ cables SE of Point Labeit the track continues WSW passing (with positions from Point Labeit):

SSE of a stranded wreck (1 cable SW), thence:

NNW of a stranded wreck (3 cables SW).

The track then leads through a channel marked by buoys and beacons into the new harbour.

Berths

3.38

1 **Old harbour** (31°21′·8N 27°14′·8E):

Anchorage. The best place for anchoring is about 1½ cables N of Drama Point, in a depth of about 7 m, fair holding ground of mud over sand, heading W with a stern anchor out. In light to moderate winds a vessel can anchor in the deeper water N of Harbour Point.

2 **Berths.** A stone quay about 80 m long, with adepth of 6 m alongside, is situated at Drama Point.

A 90 m berth, constructed in 1971, with a depth of 2·4 m to receive lighters. Two wooden scaffold structures suitable only for launches.

3 **New harbour** (31°21′·7N 27°12′·7E):

Berths. A quay, about 1000 m long, extends along the S shore of the harbour. Charted depths alongside are from 10·5 m to 10·9 m.

Port services

3.39

1 **Supplies:** a few fresh provisions may be obtained; marine diesel is available in limited quantities.

Communications. Maṭrûḥ is connected to the Egyptian railway system; there is an airport situated close S of the town.

Anchorages

Sîdi Barrâni

3.40

1 **Anchorage** may be obtained off Sîdi Barrâni (31°37′N 25°55′E), 2 cables NE of the light-structure (3.28), in a depth of 16 m, but it is entirely exposed.

2 **Landing place.** A small cove, 2 cables E of the light-structure, provides fair shelter from N swell and can be used as a boat landing. A reef, awash, extending 1 cable W of the E entrance point is the only danger in the approach; the cove is 37 m in width and fringed with rocks. A small pier, with sheer legs and a jib, is situated on the W side of the cove.

3 **Caution.** In 1945 it was reported that in the approach to Sîdi Barrâni from N, soundings between the charted 100 m line and the shore did not agree with those shown on the chart.

Gezîrat Ishaila

3.41

1 Anchorage may be obtained, in case of emergency, about 3 cables S of Gezîrat Ishaila (31°31′N 26°38′E) (3.29), in depths of 8·5 to 9·1 m, sand, but caution is necessary as this vicinity has been only cursorily surveyed.

Mersa Umm el Rakham

3.42

1 Mersa Umm el Rakham, situated on the E side of Râs Umm el Rakham (31°24′N 27°04′E), is a bay with low shores. From the point a broken line of rocky reefs extends E for 4½ miles, the outer 3 miles forming Umm el Rakham Reef which is partly above water.

2 Anchorage, sheltered from N and W winds, may be obtained 4 cables SE of the highest part of Umm el Rakham Reef, in depths of about 16 m, sand. The anchorage should be approached with caution.

RÂS ‘ALAM EL-RÛM TO RÂS EL DAB‘A

General information

Chart 3400

Route

3.43

1 From a position about 9½ miles N of Râs ‘Alam el-Rûm (31°22′N 27°21′E) the coastal route follows the recommended track, as shown on the chart, for about 60 miles ESE, to a position NNE of Râs el Dab‘a (31°05′N 28°26′E).

Topography

3.44

1 Between Râs ‘Alam el Rûm (3.29) and Râs el Ḫekma, 27 miles ESE, the coast is indented by Khalîg Abû Ḫashâ’ifa, which contains several sandy bays, and is backed by hills which rise to an elevation of 163 m, 18 miles SE of Râs ‘Alam el Rûm. Râs el Ḫekma is bordered by black rocks which show up well against white sandhills.

2 Thence the coastline is indented by Khalîg el Ḫekma, entered between Râs el Ḫekma and Râs Abu Girâb, 18 miles SE. A line of remarkable black cliffs extends from 4 to 8 miles W of Râs Abu Girâb and a cliff, 26 m high and 1½ miles long, is situated 6 miles to the E.

Prohibited area

3.45

1 At Râs el Ḫekma there is an Entry Prohibited area, as shown on the chart, the limits of which are defined by a circle, radius 5 miles, centred on position 31°13′·5N 27°52′·0E.

Currents

3.46

1 Between Râs ‘Alam el-Rûm (31°22′N 27°21′E) and Râs el Ḫekma, 27 miles ESE, during summer when the prevailing wind is between NW and N, onshore sets of about ½ kn are frequently experienced.

Directions

(continued from 3.29)

Landmark

3.47

1 Coastguard watch tower at Râs el Dab‘a (31°05′N 28°26′E).

Other aid to navigation

3.48

1 **Racon:**

Râs ‘Alam el-Rûm (31°22′N 27°21′E).

For details see *Admiralty List of Radio Signals Volume 2.*

Râs ‘Alam el-Rûm to Râs el Dab‘a

3.49

1 From a position about 9½ miles N of Râs ‘Alam el-Rûm (31°22′N 27°21′E) the track leads ESE, passing (with positions from Râs el Ḫekma (31°15′N 27°51′E)):

NNE of Khalîg Abû Ḫashâ’ifa (19 miles W), which is entered between Râs ‘Alam el Rûm and Râs Ḫawâla, 14 miles SE. The W side of this gulf is encumbered by Medina Reefs which extend from 2 to 8 miles SSE of Râs ‘Alam el Rûm, and from 2 to 3 miles offshore. Râs Ḫawâla is fringed with submerged rocks; Mersa Ḫawâla lies on the E side of the point. Thence:

2 NNE of Mersa Abu Ḫashafa (11¾ miles WSW) (3.51) and Mersa Bâghûsh (10½ miles WSW) (3.52), thence:

NNE of Râs el Ḫekma, the N extremity of which appears as an island from a distance of about 10 miles on some bearings owing to a remarkable gap in the land a short distance within the point. A mooring buoy is charted 3½ miles SE of Râs el Ḫekma. Thence:

3 NNE of Khalîg el Ḫekma (8 miles SE), a gulf, also known as Khalîg el Kanâyis. The gulf is fringed with dangerous rocks and reefs including El Homfis Rocks, 6¾ miles SSE of Râs el Ḫekma. El Homfis Rocks consist of two above-water rocks, the larger of which is 3 m high, and a rock awash, ½ cable SE, on which the sea breaks. There are depths of 7·3 and 11 m inside these rocks, which lie 1¼ miles offshore. Thence:

4 NNE of Gharqân Reef (12 miles SE), which extends 2 miles ENE from Râs el Gharqân; the E end of the reef is 1 mile offshore, and there are depths of 5·5 to 9·1 m between the reef and the mainland. Hâshafat el Qûṭṭ is an islet 7 m high, lying in the middle of Gharqân Reef. Thence:

NNE of Râs Abu Girâb (18 miles SE); hills rise to an elevation of 67 m close W of Râs Abu Girâb. Thence:

NNE of Abu Samra Reef (22½ miles SE), which has depths of less than 2 m over it, and is nearly connected to the mainland SW by a spit with a depth of 5·5 m over it.

5 The track then leads to a position NNE of Râs el Dab‘a (31°05′N 28°26′E); a reef extends for a distance of 3½ miles W from the point 5 cables offshore.

Useful marks:

Beacon (elevation 91 m) (31°11′N 27°51′E).

Beacon (elevation 102 m) (31°08′N 27°51′E).

Beacon (31°06′N 27°54′E).

(Directions continue at 3.58)

Minor harbours

Mersa el Fâllih

3.50

1 **General information.** Mersa el Fâllih (31°21′N 27°21′E) is a cove which can be identified by conspicuous salt stacks close N of it.

A rocky shoal, with depths of less than 2 m over it, lies off the entrance to Mersa el Fâllih; its N end is marked by a beacon from which a light is occasionally exhibited. A second beacon stands 100 m W, within the cove, where there are depths of 0·9 to 1·8 m.

2 **Anchorage.** A beacon, which, in line with Râs ‘Alam el Rûm Light (3.29), bears 318°, stands on the coast 3 cables NNE of the cove; a pair of beacons, in line bearing 270°, stand close S of the cove. A mooring buoy is situated at the junction of these transits; anchorage, within a radius of 2 cables of the buoy, is obtainable in depths of 7 to 15 m, sand and rock.

3 **Berth.** A jetty extends 75 m SSW from the N entrance point of the cove; lights are occasionally exhibited from the NE corner and the head of the jetty.

Local knowledge is required.

Mersa Abu Ḫashafa

3.51

1 **General information.** Mersa Abu Ḫashafa (31°12′N 27°39′E), on the E side of Râs Abu Ḫashafa, has an anchorage within it. Râs Abu Ḫashafa is a bluff, white headland which is not conspicuous; there is a small cairn on its extremity.

Rocky shoals extend up to 1¾ cables seaward on the N and NE sides of the point. Abu Ḫashafa Island, 3 cables SE of the point, is surrounded by a reef; and a spit, with a least depth of 1·8 m over it, extends 3½ cables ESE.

2 **Anchorage.** The recommended place to anchor is 2½ cables S of the E end of Abu Hashafa Island, in a depth of 11 m, sand with patches of rock. This berth is sheltered from NW and W winds, but the holding ground is not good.

Local knowledge is required.

Mersa Bâghûsh

3.52

1 **Description.** Mersa Bâghûsh (31°11′N 27°40′E) is a minor harbour suitable for small vessels. Hashafet el Nagith, the E point of the harbour, is a large black rock which shows clearly against the sandhills behind it, and is connected to the mainland by a narrow neck. The harbour, lying within a line of rocks extending W from Hashafet el Nagith, is entered by three narrow passages through the rocks, in the E one of which is a depth of 5·5 m; there are depths in the harbour of 1·8 to 5·5 m.

Local knowledge is required.

RÂS EL DAB‘A TO MĪNĀ’ AL ISKANDARĪYAH

General information

Charts 2681, 3325, 2574

Route

3.53

1 From a position NNE of Râs el Dab‘a (31°05′N 28°26′E) the coastal route follows the recommended track, as shown on the chart, for about 66 miles ESE to a position in the waiting area for Mīnā’ Al Iskandarīyah, 4 miles NNW of Ţābiyat al ‘Abbasīyah (31°09′N 29°47′E).

This route passes N of Arabs Gulf, known to the Egyptians as Khalîg el ‘Arab, which lies between Râs el Dab‘a and Mīnā’ Al Iskandarīyah.

Topography

3.54

1 Between Râs el Dab‘a and Râs el Shaqîq, 22 miles ESE, the coast is fringed by rocky reefs. Thence the coast between Râs el Shaqîq (30°57′N 28°50′E) and El ‘Amayid, 20 miles ESE, is bordered by rocks and shoals. Tell Alam el-Milh, 12½ miles SE of Râs el Shaqîq, is a hill 24 m high, standing on the edge of a salt marsh, 5 cables inland. Gebel Khashm el ‘Eish, 101 m high, is the highest of a range of hills 5 miles S of El ‘Amayid.

2 The coast between El ‘Amayid (30°50′N 29°12′E) and Burg Abu Sîr, 18 miles ENE, consists of a sandy beach, with low hills close inland, fronted for nearly the whole of its extent by numerous reefs and foul ground.

3 Burg Abu Sîr (Abu Sîr on chart 3325) (30°57′N 29°31′E), about 37 m high, rises 7 cables inland, and is surmounted by Taposiris, an ancient Egyptian walled town. Arab’s Tower, standing on a hill close NE of Burg Abu Sîr, is the prominent remains of a Roman lighthouse, the top of which is 56 m high. Kôm el Nugûs, 1 mile NE of Burg Abu Sîr, is a prominent bare hill 49 m high, the highest land in the vicinity. A range of hills 15 miles long, lying parallel to the coast SE of Burg Abu Sîr, and 6 miles inland, rises to an elevation of about 84 m.

4 The coast between Burg Abu Sîr and Ţābiyat al ‘Abbasīyah, 18½ miles NE, is low and sandy, and fronted at a distance of 5 cables to 1½ miles offshore by a line of reefs, with depths of less than 10 m, extending from the E end of Abu Sîr Reef to the coast at Ţābiyat al ‘Abbasīyah. A rocky islet 4 m high, with a rock 2 m high close NE, lies on this line of reefs, 5 miles SW of Ţābiyat al ‘Abbasīyah.

5 A line of barren hills, about 30 m high, lies 1½ miles inland between Burg Abu Sîr and a position 4 miles E of Ţābiyat al ‘Abbasīyah; several old square towers, 6 m in height, are situated on the summit of this line of hills.

Currents

3.55

1 A branch of the main E-going current curves S into Arabs Gulf at a mean rate of about ½ kn. In summer the rate increases to 1 kn or more at times, and near the coast the current may be W-going.

Prohibited area

3.56

1 At Abu Sîr there is an Entry Prohibited area, as shown on the chart, the limits of which are defined by a circle, radius 5 miles, centred on position 30°54′N 29°32′E.

Caution

3.57

1 If navigating within Khalîg el 'Arab frequent soundings should be taken owing to the indraught of the coastal currents (3.55).

Directions

(continued from 3.49)

Principal marks

3.58

1 **Landmarks:**

Radio mast (red lights) (30°56′·0N 28°49′·6E) at El 'Alamein Oil Terminal.

Oil tanks, close E of above radio mast.

Major lights:

Râs el Shaqîq Light (white daymark on framework tower) (30°57′·3N 28°49′·7E).

2 Al 'Ajami Light (31°08′·9N 29°47′·2E) (3.109).

Great Pass Beacon Light (31°10′·0N 29°48′·5E) (3.109).

Ad Dukhaylah Rear Leading Light (31°08′·0N 29°48′·7E) (3.109).

Râs-el-Tîn Light (31°11′·8N 29°51′·7E) (3.109).

Other aids to navigation

3.59

1 **Racons:**

Râs el Shaqîq Light (30°57′·3N 28°49′·7E).

Al 'Ajami Light (31°08′·9N 29°47′·2E).

Râs-el-Tîn Light (31°11′·8N 29°51′·7E).

For details see *Admiralty List of Radio Signals Volume 2.*

Râs el Dab'a to Mīnā' Al Iskandarīyah

3.60

1 From a position NNE of (31°05′N 28°26′E) the track leads ESE, passing (with positions from Râs el Shaqîq Light (30°57′·3N 28°49′·7E)):

NNE of a reef (19¼ miles WNW) extending 1 mile offshore with depths of 5 m or less over it, thence:

2 NNE of Sha'b Tannûm (13 miles WNW), which is nearly awash. The reef extends 1½ miles from Râs Abu el Gurûf and is almost steep-to on its N side; the 200 m depth contour lies only 1½ miles N of it. Reefs also extend 1 mile seaward from a point on the coast 6 miles ESE of Râs Abu el Gurûf. Thence:

3 NNE Râs Gibeiṣa (4 miles WNW), fringed by rocks which extend 7½ cables N, thence:

NNE of Râs el Shaqîq; Sha'b Gibeiṣa, with a depth of 2 m or less over it, lies 3½ miles ESE of the point, 1 mile offshore. Thence:

NNE of El 'Alamein Oil Terminal (close by) (3.63), thence:

4 NNE of Sha'b el Shaqîq (4½ miles SE), a rocky shoal, thence:

NNE of Sha'b el Shammâma (10 miles SE), a group of banks with a least depth of 1·3 m over them, lying up to 3 miles offshore from El 'Alamein.

5 NNE of a breakwater (12 miles SE) extending 5 cables NE from the shore on the W side of the entrance to an extensive lagoon. Entry is prohibited to an area on either side of the entry channel, as shown on the chart.

3.61

1 The track then continues ESE, passing (with positions from Ţābiyat al 'Abbasīyah (31°09′N 29°47′E)):

NNE of Sha'b Medîna (29 miles SW), with dangerous underwater rocks and a rock awash on it, lying 5 miles offshore. Two mooring buoys lie 3½ miles N of the reef. Thence:

2 NNE of Victorieuse Rock (21½ miles SW), nearly awash, lying 4½ miles offshore. Mooring buoys are situated 1½ miles SSW and 2 miles E of the rock. Thence:

3 NNE of Abu Sîr Reef (16 miles SW), which extends 6 miles ENE from a position 4 miles NW of Burg Abu Sîr (3.54), with depths of less than 10 m over it; a dangerous underwater rock lies 1¼ miles within its W end, and a dangerous underwater rock, the position of which is doubtful, with a depth of less than 2 m over it, lies 2¾ miles within the E end. Thence:

4 NNE of Sidi Kerir Oil Terminal (9 miles WSW) (3.70).

The track then leads to a position in the waiting area for Mīnā' Al Iskandarīyah, about 4 miles NNW of Ţābiyat al 'Abbasīyah (31°09′N 29°47′E). There is a small tanker terminal (3.77) 2½ miles W of Ţābiyat al 'Abbasīyah, and foul ground extends 1¼ miles SW from the point.

3.62

1 **Useful marks:**

A small mosque at Sîdi 'Abd el-Raḥman (30°58′N 28°44′E), 1¾ miles SW of Râs Gibeiṣa (3.60), is prominent.

Monument (Italian war memorial) (30°54·3′N 28°50·4′E).

2 Monument (German war memorial) (30°53·4′N 28°52·5′E).

(Directions continue for Mīnā' Al Iskandarīyah *at 3.109, and for the coastal route at 3.130)*

El 'Alamein Oil Terminal

Chart 3326

General information

3.63

1 **Position.** El 'Alamein Oil Terminal (30°56′N 28°50′E) is situated in Mersa el Hamra, a small bay between Râs el Shaqîq and Sha'b el Shaqîq, 5 miles SE.

Function. The terminal is for the use of tankers loading crude oil.

2 **Port limits.** The limits of the terminal, which extend 4 miles offshore, are shown on the chart.

Port Authority. Western Desert Petroleum Co., PO Box 2130, Cairo, Egypt.

Limiting conditions

3.64

1 **Density of water:** 1·025 g/cm^3.

Maximum size of vessel handled: 100 000 dwt; draught 16 m.

Arrival information

3.65

1 **Notice of ETA:** 72, 48, 24 and 12 hours.

Waiting anchorage. Vessels awaiting a berth should anchor about 2 miles E of the SBM (see Caution below) in a depth of about 23 m; the holding is reported to be good. Anchoring is prohibited SW of the SBM, as shown on the chart.

2 **Caution.** A dangerous wreck (position approximate) lies 1½ miles Eof the SBM; and a second wreck, with a depth of 24·5 m over it, lies 1½ miles NW.

Pilots. Pilotage is compulsory and available during daylight hours only. The boarding place is about 2 miles

NE of the SBM. The pilot vessel, a converted fishing boat, is white with a yellow funnel.

3 For details see *Admiralty List of Radio Signals Volume 6 (3)*.

Tugs. Mooring boats are available. Tugs are not available.

Harbour

3.66

1 **General layout.** The terminal lies in an open roadstead and is equipped with one SBM.

Directions

3.67

1 From seaward to the pilot boarding position NE of the terminal the chart is sufficient guide.

Landmarks:

Radio mast (30°56′·0N 28°49′·6E) (3.58).

Oil tanks situated close E of above radio mast.

Monument (Italian war memorial) (30°54′·3N 28°50′·4E).

2 Monument (German war memorial) (30°53′·4N 28°52′·5E).

Major light:

Râs el Shaqîq Light (30°57′·3N 28°49′·7E) (3.58).

Other aid to navigation:

Racon: Râs el Shaqîq Light (30°57′·3N 28°49′·7E).

For details see *Admiralty List of Radio Signals Volume 2.*

Berth

3.68

1 The loading berth, an SBM marked by a light, is moored 2½ miles NE of Râs el Shaqîq at the seaward ends of two submarine oil pipelines.

Berthing is normally carried out during daylight hours only. Vessels arriving after dark should keep 50 miles offshore.

Port services

3.69

1 **Repairs.** Small repairs can be undertaken; divers are available.

Communications. The nearest airport is at Mīnā' Al Iskandarīyah, about 100 km E.

Sidi Kerir Oil Terminal

Charts 302, 3325

General information

3.70

1 **Position and function.** Sidi Kerir Oil Terminal (31°03′N 29°40′E), the N terminal of the SUMED pipeline (1.89), is situated 8 miles SW of Ţābiyat al 'Abbasīyah. The SUMED assigned area is shown on the chart.

2 **Traffic.** In 2007 there were 705 ship calls with a total of 112 612 691 dwt.

Port Authority. Arab Petroleum Pipelines Co., 431 Al-Geish, Loran, Alexandria, Egypt.

Arrival information

3.71

1 **Notice of ETA.** Upon sailing from previous port, thence 72, 48 and 24 hours before arrival.

Prohibited area. Within the assigned area navigation is prohibited within about 1 mile of the shore, as shown on the charts.

2 **Waiting anchorage.** The anchorage for tankers waiting for a berth lies adjacent to the NNW limit of the assigned area in depths from 40 to 50 m, as shown on the charts.

Caution. A dangerous wreck lies in position 31°08′·7N 29°41′·1E, 2 miles ESE of the SE corner of the waiting area.

3 **Pilots.** Pilotage is compulsory. The pilot, who acts as mooring master, prefers to board by helicopter during daylight hours, but will board from a pilot vessel at any time. The pilot boards about 2 miles N of SBM No 1, as shown on the chart.

For details see *Admiralty List of Radio Signals Volume 6 (3).*

Tugs are available.

Harbour

3.72

1 **General layout.** The terminal, in an open roadstead, comprises six SBMs, marked by lights, lying from 2½ to 4½ miles offshore at the seaward ends of submarine oil pipelines.

Flow. The current generally sets E at a rate up to 0·5 kn. The tidal streams set SW and NE, parallel to the coast, at a rate of 0·5 kn at the surface.

2 **Local weather.** The prevailing winds from April to September are from NNW but become rather more variable in direction from October to March. Visibility is usually excellent with few sand storms and infrequent fog. Sub-zero temperatures are unknown and there are very few rain squalls.

Directions

3.73

1 From seaward to the pilot boarding position N of Sidi Kerir the chart is sufficient guide.

Landmarks:

A tank farm at the terminal shows up well on radar at a distance of 20 miles.

2 Radio mast (red lights) (31°02′·9N 29°40′·2E), close SW of the tank farm.

Other aid to navigation:

Racon: Al 'Ajami Light (31°08′·9N 29°47′·2E).

For details see *Admiralty List of Radio Signals Volume 2.*

Berths

3.74

1 **Berths** are as follows:

Three SBMs suitable for tankers of up to 150 000 dwt and 16·4 m draught. Depth at the berth is 18·3 m.

Three SBMs suitable for tankers of up to 500 000 dwt and 22·9 m draught. Depth at the berth is 25·9 m.

Port services

3.75

1 **Facilities:** oily waste reception.

Supplies: fuel and fresh water not available.

Anchorage

Chart 3325

3.76

1 During offshore winds good anchorage may be obtained 2½ miles N of El 'Amayid Lighthouse (ruins) (30°50′N 29°12′E), in a depth of about 12 m.

Caution. This anchorage lies within an inadequately surveyed area (3.7).

Ţābiyat al ‘Abbasīyah

Chart 302

3.77

1 A mooring area (31°08′·5N 29°45′·0E), for tankers up to 50 000 tons and 13·7 m draught, is established about 2½ miles W of Ţābiyat al ‘Abbasīyah. Vessels proceeding to the area must embark a pilot off Mīnā’ Al Iskandarīyah; see note on chart.

2 A Single Point Mooring, 8 cables WSW of the mooring area, lies at the seaward end of a submarine pipeline extending 1¾ miles NW from the shore. A light is exhibited from the buoy.

MĪNĀ’ AL ISKANDARĪYAH TO ŢÂBIYET EL-BURG

GENERAL INFORMATION

Charts 3119, 2681, 2574

Area covered

3.78

1 The area covered by this section includes Mīnā’ Al Iskandarīyah, the largest port in Egypt and the principal port in the E Mediterranean, and the coastal waters from Mīnā’ Al Iskandarīyah to Ţâbiyet El-Burg. The section is arranged as follows:

Mīnā’ Al Iskandarīyah including Ad Dukhaylah (3.83).

Mīnā’ Al Iskandarīyah to Ţâbiyet El-Burg (3.125).

Topography

3.79

1 The coast in the vicinity of Mīnā’ Al Iskandarīyah is generally low and featureless.

From Ţābiyat al ‘Abbasīyah (31°09′N 29°47′E) (3.61) a breakwater, intersected by an area of reclaimed land containing Al ‘Ajami Light, Jazīrat al Murābiţ and Jazīrat al Akrāsh, extends NE and ENE for 1¼ miles.

2 Jazīrat al Murābiţ is surmounted by an old fort with a conspicuous tower 15 m high and has been detected on radar at a distance of 30 miles. Ţâbiyet El-Burg (31°20′N 30°04′E), 18 miles NE, has been mistaken for the fort on Jazīrat al Murābiţ which is somewhat similar. However, whereas Gezîret Disûqî (31°21′N 30°06′E) (3.141) appears like a saddle-backed hill and the land SW of Ţâbiyet El-Burg is moderately high, the coast recedes S from Jazīrat al Murābiţ and the land SW is low and sandy.

3 The line of hills (3.54) lying about 1½ miles inland of Ţābiyat al ‘Abbasīyah continues NE as a narrow rocky ridge which terminates between Ad Dukhaylah and Al Maks. The ridge has been much quarried near Ad Dukhaylah and presents an irregular outline.

4 Buḩeiret Maryût, the lake behind the town of Mīnā’ Al Iskandarīyah and separated from the sea by a flat strip of land less than 1 mile wide, is connected to the sea by Khandag Bâb el ‘Arab which flows into Ghubbet Bâb el ‘Arab. In August the level of the sea is 4 m above that of the lake, which dries over a large area.

5 The town of Mīnā’ Al Iskandarīyah stands on flat, low-lying ground on and within a peninsula projecting 1 mile NNW from the line of the coast. Ţâbiyet el Atta, at the N end of the peninsula, is reported to have been detected on radar at a distance of 30 miles. From Ra’s at Tīn, at the W end of the peninsula, Outer Breakwater extends SW and SSW for about 2 miles; the top of the breakwater is about 3 m above the lowest level of the sea.

Depths

3.80

1 Depths decrease gradually towards the shore. Except to enter one of the passes leading to Mīnā’ Al Iskandarīyah or Ad Dukhaylah, vessels should keep in depths of more than 37 m.

Currents

3.81

1 A NE-going current may be experienced when approaching from offshore.

2 Strong winds from the NW quadrant generate a NE-going current which follows the shore from Gezîret el Marâbiţ. The current generally sets NE across El Bûghâz el Kebír at a rate of about 1 kn, and a considerable cross-current has been experienced in El Bûghâz. Across the entrance to Mīnā’ Al Iskandarīyah Harbour the current sets N.

Caution

3.82

1 Aids to navigation in the approaches to Mīnā’ Al Iskandarīyah are reported unreliable. Buoys are liable to be changed or removed without warning.

MĪNĀ’ AL ISKANDARĪYAH INCLUDING AD DUKHAYLAH

General information

Charts 3119, 302

Position

3.83

1 Mīnā’ Al Iskandarīyah lies between Ţābiyat al ‘Abbasīyah (31°09′N 29°47′E) and El Mînâ’ el Sharqîya (7 miles NE). Formerly known as Alexandria, it is the principal harbour in Egypt.

Function

3.84

1 Mīnā’ Al Iskandarīyah, which in 1998 had an estimated population of 3 485 000, comprises Mīnā’ Al Iskandarīyah Harbour (3.104), Ad Dukhaylah (3.105) and Al Maks (3.105). It is a major commercial and industrial port with 30% of Egypt’s industry located in the area. The port handles 75% of Egypt’s trade and has modern facilities for handling vessels and cargoes of all types.

2 The principal exports are agricultural products, cotton, onions, garlics, rice, groundnuts, citrons, fruits, vegetables, molasses, oil products, industrial products and cotton yarn.

The chief imports are agricultural products, tea, grain, coal, coffee, timber, tobacco, industrial products, machinery and motor vehicles.

History

3.85

1 The ancient city of Alexandria, founded in 332 BC by Alexander the Great from whom it took its name, was so magnificent that the Romans ranked it next to their own capital. Pompey's Pillar still stands, and several ruins of the epoch remain. The ancient harbour is now known as El Mînâ' el Sharqîya.

2 In 1517 the city was taken by the Turks and reduced to ruins. By 1778 the population was only about 6000, but under Mohammed Ali (1805–49) (1.84) the city recovered.

Until 1882, when it was bombarded by the British fleet, the city was very strongly fortified. In addition to several forts within the city walls, a chain of forts, redoubts and round towers crowns the surrounding heights and extends W for several miles along the coast.

Port limits

3.86

1 The outer limit of the port is a line drawn NNE from Ţābiyat al 'Abbasīyah (31°09′N 29°47′E) to a position about 2 cables seaward of Al Būghāz (Boghaz Pass) thence ENE to Ra's at Tīn.

Approach and entry

3.87

1 Approach to, or departure from the harbour must be made through the Approach Sector, shown on the charts, centred on 31°16′N 29°37′E. Two waiting areas (3.99) are located at the SE end.

2 Mīnā' Al Iskandarīyah Harbour is then entered by passing through Al Būghāz al Akbar (3.113), or Al Būghāz (3.115), and thence between the heads of Outer Breakwater and Quarantine Breakwater. Ad Dukhaylah Harbour is entered through Ad Dukhaylah Pass (3.112).

Traffic

3.88

1 **Mīnā' Al Iskandarīyah.** In 2007 there were 4149 ship calls with a total of 53 474 134 dwt.

Ad Dukhaylah. In 2007 there were 704 ship calls with a total of 20 868 928 dwt.

Port Authority

3.89

1 Mīnā' Al Iskandarīyah Authority, 106 El Horreya Avenue, Mīnā' Al Iskandarīyah, Egypt.

The Harbour Master's office is situated in the Port Control Tower (31°11′·3N 29°52′·2E) (3.109) at the NW end of Coal Quay.

Limiting conditions

Controlling depths and maximum draughts

3.90

1 The inner approaches, between Ţābiyat al 'Abbasīyah and Ra's at Tīn, are encumbered by a line of reefs and shallow water, about 1 mile in width, between the 10 m depth contours. The depths in the passes leading through the reefs and shallows are as follows (positioned from Great Pass (31°10′·0N 29°48′·5E)):

2 Ad Dukhaylah Pass (5 cables NNW), for the use of vessels approaching Ad Dukhaylah Harbour, is 200 m wide. In 2008 the least depth on the centreline was 20 m.

Maximum allowable draught is 18 m, and maximum breadth from 20 to 50 m.

3 Al Būghāz al Akbar (Great Pass) (5 cables NW), the principal pass for vessels approaching Mīnā' Al Iskandarīyah Harbour. It is 200 m wide, with a sandstone bottom. In 2008 the least depth on the centreline was 14·2 m.

Maximum allowable draught is 12 m, and maximum breadth is 50 m.

4 Al Būghāz (Boghaz Pass) (1 mile NNE), which is 100 m wide. In 2008 the least depth on the centreline was 8·5 m. The depth is affected by the wind to the extent of 0·9 m; with smooth water in summer the depth is more than usual, but in winter, when the sea is generally somewhat heavy, the depth is less.

5 Maximum allowable draught is 7·5 m and maximum breadth is 25 m.

Corvette Pass ($2\frac{1}{4}$ miles NE), which has a least charted depth of 5·5 m on the leading line.

Deepest and longest berths

3.91

1 **Mīnā' Al Iskandarīyah Harbour:**

Container terminal (3.117).

Ad Dukhaylah Harbour:

Deepest berth; Mineral Jetty (3.119).

Longest berth; General Cargo Pier (3.119).

Tidal levels

3.92

1 Mean spring range about 0·2 m; mean neap range about 0·0 m. For further information see *Admiralty Tide Tables Volume 2*.

Abnormal water levels

3.93

1 Strong W winds raise the sea level 0·5 m above that of ordinary HW, and nearly 0·9 m above the low level caused by strong E winds. The MSL in August, September and October is 0·2 m higher than in February, March and April.

An automatic tide gauge is situated near the SE end of Quarantine Breakwater.

Density of water

3.94

1 1·030 g/cm^3.

Maximum size of vessel handled

3.95

1 The maximum size of vessel handled is approximately 140 000 dwt.

Arrival information

Vessel Traffic Service

3.96

1 A Vessel Traffic Service with full radar surveillance is maintained for the regulation of shipping.

Signal stations

3.97

1 Signal stations in the port are as follows (positioned from Ra's at Tīn Light (31°11′·7N 29°51′·7E)):

Marşad Kawm an Nadrah (Fort Napoleon) ($1\frac{1}{2}$ miles E), a group of dwellings on top of a hill, with a conspicuous tower 60 m high.

2 Qamarīyah Signal Station (conspicuous white circular tower and flagstaff) (1¾ miles S), standing on Qamarīyah Hill.

Notice of ETA

3.98

1 ETA should be sent 24 hours in advance. Vessels should establish communication with Mīnā' Al Iskandarīyah radio when approaching the waiting area and before anchoring.

Waiting areas

3.99

1 Two waiting areas (31°14′N 29°44′E) are established in the approach sector between 5 and 10 miles from Al Maks High Light. Depths are from 35 to 55 m, good holding ground, but the area is very exposed and it is sometimes untenable in winter. The N side of the waiting area is reserved for Ad Dukhaylah, and the S side for Mīnā' Al Iskandarīyah.

2 Radio contact has to be made before anchoring; see 3.98.

In Mīnā' Al Iskandarīyah Harbour two designated waiting areas are established on the SE and NW sides of Outer Harbour, both have six anchorage areas contained within them. The NW anchorage areas have radii of 140 m, and the SW ones 140 to 187·5 m.

Prohibited anchorages and areas

3.100

1 **Anchoring prohibited:**

In the entrance channel (3.104) for Mīnā' Al Iskandarīyah Harbour.

In an area 2 cables wide extending 1 mile WNW close N of Great Pass Low Light (31°09′·3N 29°50′·8E), as shown on the chart.

Within about 1 cable of a wreck, with a depth of 23·5 m over it, lying 3¾ miles W of Ra's at Tīn Light (31°11′·8N 29°51′·7E). The wreck is marked by a buoy (port hand).

2 **Anchoring and fishing prohibited:**

Within an area (31°14′N 29°49′E) extending 5 miles NW from Mīnā' Al Iskandarīyah Harbour. Vessels may pass through this area, keeping strictly to the recommended track shown on the charts.

In an area surrounding a gas pipeline leading from the shore (31°08′·2N 29°49′·5E) to the LPG Terminal 1¾ miles SW of the harbour entrance. For further information on pipelines see 1.26.

3 **Prohibited areas:**

Within an area radius 1¾ miles centred on 31°12′·0N 29°51′·8E to the NW of the harbour.

In Mīnā' Al Iskandarīyah Harbour (3.104) prohibited areas front the naval base in Outer Harbour, and the NW side of Inner Harbour, as shown on the chart.

Pilotage and tugs

3.101

1 **Pilotage,** which is available 24 hours, is compulsory for all vessels over 300 gt. The pilotage service provides sea and harbour pilots. The sea pilots take vessels from sea to the harbour entrance; the harbour pilots from the harbour entrance to the assigned berth.

2 The boarding place for sea pilots in moderate winds is about 2 cables N of the light buoy (safe water) (31°11′·7N 29°47′·2E). The pilot boat has a blue hull and white upperworks.

For details see *Admiralty List of Radio Signals Volume 6 (3)*.

Tugs are available and compulsory for vessels over 82 m in length.

Traffic regulations

3.102

1 The following regulations apply to Al Būghāz al Akbar and Al Būghāz.

General:

Only one power-driven vessel at a time is permitted to use a particular pass.

power-driven vessels leaving the port have priority over those entering.

Vessels not intending to enter harbour should not approach the passes except in unavoidable circumstances.

2 Before entering a pass from seaward, power-driven vessels must, between sunrise and sunset, display the flags **PZH** of *International Code of Signals*, signifying wait and sound their whistles or sirens. After sunset a blue light should be exhibited, and whistles or sirens sounded, by all power-driven vessels approaching from seaward.

3 If an out-going power-driven vessel is in a pass at the time an in-coming power-driven vessel arrives at the seaward end, the out-going vessel will display **PZH** in *International Code of Signals*, or exhibit a blue light at night, and sound her whistle or siren; the in-coming vessel should then wait outside until the pass is clear.

4 **By day:**

Out-going power-driven vessels must not approach No 8 Light Buoy, if using Al Būghāz al Akbar, or Al Qiṭṭ, if using Al Būghāz, within 5 cables, in the event of a power-driven vessel entering the pass they require to use from seaward, until the in-coming vessel is inside and clear of the pass. Vessels must not lie with the leading marks in line, so as to obscure them from a vessel entering.

5 Should both passes be signalled as in use, the out-going power-driven vessel must stop off Qamarīyah Signal Station (3.97) until the Signal Station indicates that all is clear.

When two vessels are proceeding out of the same pass, the second vessel must not bring the leading marks in line, so as to obscure them from the leading vessel, until the first vessel is outside and clear.

6 If two power-driven vessels are likely to pass one another in the narrows between the breakwaters at the entrance of Mīnā' Al Iskandarīyah Harbour, the out-going vessel is to give way and stop until the in-coming one has entered.

7 **At night:**

Only Al Būghāz al Akbar is used at night. and an out-going power-driven vessel must stop off Qamarîya Signal Station when a signal shows that the pass is being used by an in-coming power-driven vessel, until the signal station indicates that the pass is clear.

8 It is not permissible to enter or leave certain general cargo, coal, grain and petroleum berths from sunset to sunrise.

Sailing vessels crossing the paths of power-driven vessels in the passes do so at their own risk.

Sailing vessels must not anchor in the harbour entrance between the breakwaters.

9 The following regulations apply to Ad Dukhaylah Pass.

General:

The pass is used both day and night.

It is not permissible to enter or leave the petroleum berths and the largest mineral berth from sunset to sunrise, and to berth in wind speeds of more than 15 kns.

Regulations

3.103

1 The following regulations apply to Mīnā' Al Iskandarīyah Harbour:

General. In 1976 vessels were allowed to enter and leave Mīnā' Al Iskandarīyah by day or night, subject to regulations issued from time to time in Egyptian Notices to Mariners. In 1987 it was reported that tankers were not permitted to enter at night.

2 **Signal flags.** All in-coming vessels are to display the quarantine flag and their number before rounding Outer Breakwater, and are to keep the former flying until pratique is obtained, and the latter until they arrive in Inner Harbour, or for a reasonable time after anchoring in Outer Harbour.

Speed limits. No vessel is to proceed at a greater speed than 10 kn when in Outer Harbour, nor greater than 5 kn when rounding Coal Quay and in Inner Harbour.

3 **Anchoring on arrival.** Vessels arriving must wait at anchor in the quarantine anchorage in Outer Harbour for pratique, customs and police formalities, after which they will be authorized to proceed to their berths, having embarked the harbour pilot who is supplied on application to the Harbour Master. Inner Harbour should not be entered until a berth has been assigned.

Warships. When a warship has obtained permission to enter Inner Harbour, a representative of the Port Authority will indicate the buoy to be used.

4 **Declaration of arrival** must be made at the port office in Arsenal Basin within 24 hours of arrival. The boarding office will be open every day from 0800 to 1430, except on Sundays, single day holidays, and the first day of longer holidays. During the remaining days of the longer holidays the boarding service will be maintained. Vessels arriving after 1900 will not receive clearance until the following morning but, if cargo working can be commenced immediately, communication with the shore may be granted on arrival.

5 **Fire on board.** A vessel arriving with fire on board will not be permitted to enter Inner Harbour, but will be taken to such anchorage as the Harbour Master may direct.

Dangerous cargoes. When a vessel has powder or other explosives on board, a red flag by day and a red light at night are to be displayed before entering Outer Harbour. Vessels with explosives or petroleum on board are to anchor in Outer Harbour, and are not allowed in Inner Harbour.

6 **Responsibility.** Shipping companies and owners, conjointly with the captains of the vessels, will be held responsible for the observance of the above regulations, and for any collision or damage which may result from the infringement of them.

7 **Berthing applications.** Application for a berth alongside a quay, or for permission to secure to a buoy, must be made to the superintendent of the quay at the quay office on PL Form No 180 (supplied gratis to shipping agents and captains on request). Berthing applications should be presented at least 24 hours before the vessel's arrival, and departure applications at least 2 hours before departure. Berthing at, and departure from, Petroleum Harbour is prohibited between sunset and sunrise. Applications for berths in Arsenal and Careening Basins, and on the E side of Inner Harbour N of Tur'at al Maḩmūdīyah must be approved by the Customs Administration before being sent to the quay office. If a particular berth is required, the vessel first entering the harbour will have the prior claim, and should that vessel be placed in quarantine the next in order of entering will take precedence of others. No vessel will be forced to take any particular berth if it is not desired by the agent or captain.

Harbour

General layout

3.104

1 **Description.** The port of Mīnā' Al Iskandarīyah is divided into three main commercial berthing areas, Mīnā' Al Iskandarīyah Harbour, Ad Dukhaylah and Al Maks. El Mînâ' el Sharqîya (3·139), NE of Iskandarîya Harbour, is used mainly by small vessels.

2 **Mīnā' Al Iskandarīyah Harbour** (31°11′N 29°52′E). This is a large artificial harbour fronting the W side of Mīnā' Al Iskandarīyah. It is protected from NW by Outer Breakwater (3.79) and from SW by Quarantine Breakwater. It is divided into Outer and Inner Harbours, as shown on the chart. The harbour accommodates passenger vessels and most types of cargo vessels. A naval base is situated on the NW side of the harbour.

3 From the head of Outer Breakwater an entrance channel 200 m in width leads through Outer Harbour to a turning area in Inner Harbour about 2 miles NE. The principal berthing areas for cargo and passenger vessels are situated on the SE sides of Outer and Inner Harbours.

4 Outer Harbour has depths from 8·4 to 15·7 m, except on its W side where depths from 0·6 to 7·3 m extend up to 4 cables E of Outer Breakwater. Harbour Bank, the E part of this shoal area, has numerous stranded wrecks on it.

Inner Harbour has depths from 4·6 to 14·4 m, except for a bank with depths from 0·8 to 8·1 m extending 3½ cables from its N shore.

3.105

1 **Ad Dukhaylah (El Dikheila)** (31°09′N 29°48′E), a new artificial harbour, is situated about 3 miles SW of Mīnā' Al Iskandarīyah Harbour. It is protected from N by the area of reclaimed land and breakwater (3.79) extending 1¼ miles ENE from Ţābiyat al 'Abbasīyah.

2 The harbour serves a steelworks situated nearby. In addition there are berths for bulk, petroleum, coal, general cargo, container and RoRo traffic. Further development and expansion of the port and facilities are in progress (1997).

Al Maks. The area to the W of Al Maks (31°09′N 29°50′E), a village situated between Ad Dukhaylah and Mīnā' Al Iskandarīyah, contains a tanker mooring area and a LPG terminal.

3 **Development.** Container terminals are being developed at Mīnā' Al Iskandarīyah Harbour and Ad Dukhaylah, with an alongside depth of 12 m and a quay length of 380 m

and 560 m respectively. The first phase is due for completion in 2007.

Traffic signals

3.106

1 The traffic signals (diagram 3.106) are displayed from Qamarīyah Signal Station (3.97).

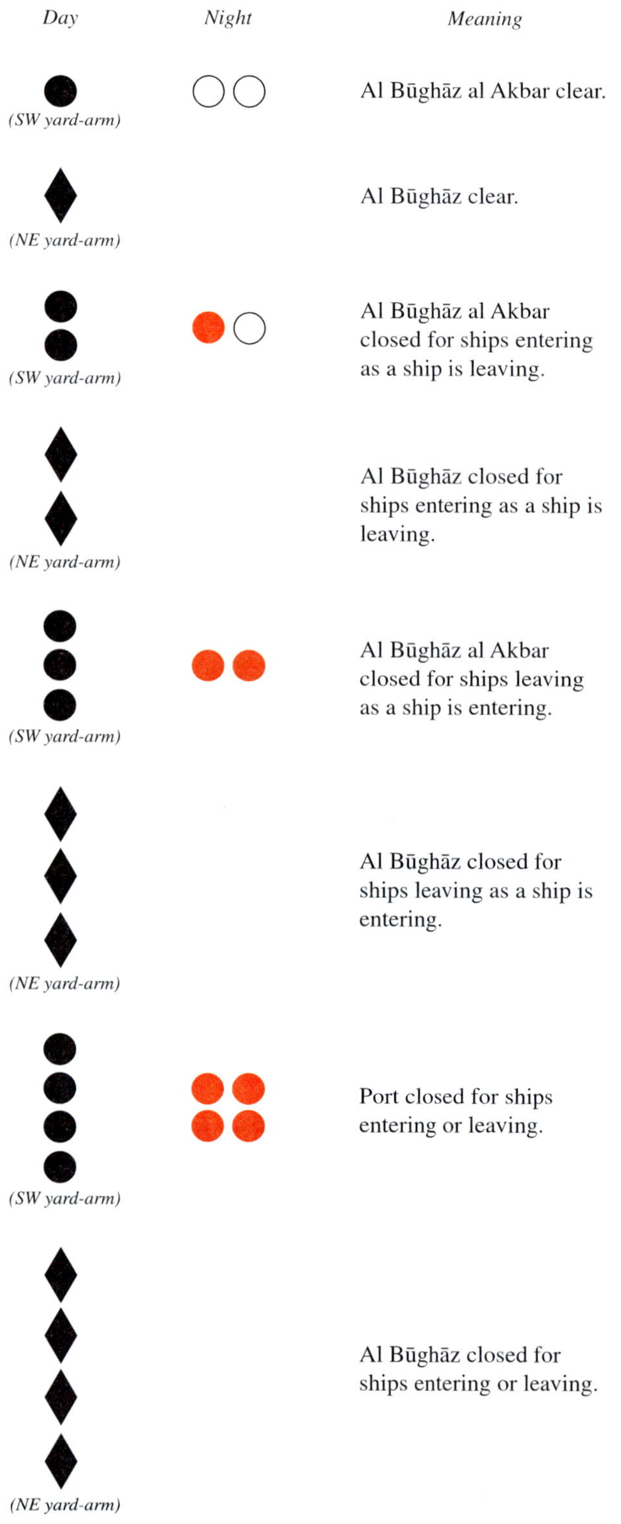

Mīnā' Al Iskandarīyah - traffic signals (3.106)

Note. A vessel is deemed to be in:

Al Būghāz al Akbar when between Great Pass Beacon (3.113) and No 8 Light Buoy, 1¼ miles ESE.

2 Al Būghāz when between the beacon (post) (31°10′·6N 29°49′·5E), situated 1½ cables ENE of Outer Shoal, and Al Qiṭṭ, 4 cables SE.

Dredging operations

3.107

1 The following regulations apply while dredging operations are in progress in a pass:

The dredger displays a square red flag while working. When the flag is dipped the pass is clear.

Out-going vessels must not proceed from the breakwater, where they should sound their whistles, to the entrance of the pass until the dredger has signalled that the pass is clear.

2 In-coming vessels must, on nearing the pass, sound their whistles and remain outside the pass until the dredger has signalled that the pass is clear.

Vessels must pass the dredger at slow speed. A black ball at the yard-arm denotes the side on which the vessel is to pass.

3 The dredger, when working at night, carries three lights: one at the bow, one at the stern and one on the bridge. When not working at night she carries two white lights at the masthead. When the dredger is working at night leaving the pass free, she will carry a white light at the masthead and two white lights above the bulwarks on the side a vessel is to pass.

Climate information

3.108

1 See 1.184 and 1.192.

Directions

(continued from 3.62)

Principal marks

3.109

1 **Landmarks:**

Ra's at Tīn Lighthouse (white round tower, black bands, 55 m in height) (31°11′·7N 29°51′·7E), usually the first object to be sighted by vessels approaching from NW. Two radio masts (red lights, 27 m in height) stand 2 and 3 cables, respectively, NE of the lighthouse.

2 Dome (47 m in height) (31°12′·0N 29°52′·1E) of Sarây Ra's at Tīn.

El Anfûshi Minaret (75 m in height) (31°12′·3N 29°52′·9E) (chart 302).

Dome (51 m in height) (31°12′·6N 29°55′·1E) (chart 302) of Saint Mark's College.

3 Port control tower (56 m in height) (31°11′·3N 29°52′·2E).

Stagni Tower (52 m in height) (31°10′·2N 29°52′·2E).

Silo (61 m in height) (31°09′·8N 29°51′·4E), a large building which has been sighted at 20 miles.

Ra's at Tīn Lighthouse (3.109)
(Original dated 1998)

(Photograph - Crown Copyright)

Disused port control tower (42 m in height) (31°09′·7N 29°51′·2E).

4 Al Maks High Lighthouse (white round tower, black top with ball and spike) (31°09′·1N 29°51′·2E).

Ţābiyat al Shafākhānah (31°09′·0N 29°50′·7E), a fort.

Tower (90 m in height, position approximate) (31°08′·7N 29°50′·3E).

Chimneys (cement works) (31°08′·5N 29°50′·3E).

5 **Major lights:**

Al ʻAjami Light (white stone tower, black stripes, 14 m in height) (31°08′·9N 29°47′·2E).

Ad Dukhaylah Rear Leading Light (yellow concrete tower, red bands) (31°08′·0N 29°48′·7E).

Al Maks High Lighthouse (3.109)
(Original dated 1998)

(Photograph - Crown Copyright)

Great Pass Light (white round concrete tower with red and green bands), (31°10′·0N 29°48′·5E).

Ra's at Tīn Light — as above.

Great Pass Light (3.109)
(Original dated 1997)

(Photograph - Crown Copyright)

Other aids to navigation

3.110

1 **Racons:**

Al ʻAjami Light (31°08′·9N 29°47′·2E).

Great Pass Light (31°10′·0N 29°48′·5E).

Ra's at Tīn Light (31°11′·7N 29°51′·7E).

For details see *Admiralty List of Radio Signals Volume 2.*

Approaches

3.111

1 From a position in the waiting area for Mīnā' Al Iskandarīyah, about 4 miles NNW of Ţābiyat al ʻAbbasīyah (31°08′·7N 29°46′·9E) (3.61) the track leads ESE and SE, for about 3 miles, passing (with positions from Great Pass Light (31°10′·0N 29°48′·5E)):

2 Close to the pilot boarding position (3.101) and a light buoy (safe water) which is close SSW of a wreck (2 miles NNW) within a prohibited anchorage area (3.100). And:

NE of two dangerous wrecks (2½ miles W).

The track then leads to a position close NW of the entrance to Al Būghāz al Akbar and Ad Dukhaylah Passes.

(Directions for Mīnā' Al Iskandarīyah Harbour continue at 3.113)

Ad Dukhaylah Harbour

3.112

1 **Caution.** For controlling depth see 3.90.

From a position close NW of the entrance to Ad Dukhaylah (El Dikheila) Pass, the track leads SE for a short distance onto the following leading line:

Ad Dukhaylah Pass Front Light (white round metal beacon, black bands) (31°08′·4N 29°48′·6E), exhibited from the head of Mineral Jetty.

Ad Dukhaylah Pass Rear Light (650 m SSE) (3.109), exhibited from the root of Mineral Jetty.

2 The alignment (173°) of these lights leads S through the centre of Ad Dukhaylah Pass, a dredged channel, the sides of which are marked by light buoys (lateral), passing (positioned from Great Pass Light (31°10′·0N 29°48′·5E)):

W of Great Pass Light (3.109), thence:

W of a bank on which lie Hydrographer Shoal (3½ cables SE) (3.113), Requin Shoal (4½ cables SE) and Seuil Shoal (5½ cables SE), thence:

3 E of Al Madjul (3 cables SW), a small patch, thence:

W of a dangerous wreck (6 cables S), thence:

E of the head of Ad Dukhaylah Breakwater (7 cables SSW), from which a light (metal beacon on concrete base) is exhibited.

4 The track then leads to a position W of D8 Light Buoy (port hand) (1 mile S), from where the berths in Dukhaylah Harbour can be directly accessed.

Useful marks:

Beacon (conspicuous, orange framework) (31°09′·5N 29°47′·7E).

Jâmi ‘Abu Nâgi (conspicuous minaret, 32 m in height) (31°08′·0N 29°49′·0E).

Al Būghāz al Akbar (Great Pass)

(continued from 3.111)

3.113

1 **Caution.** For controlling depth see 3.90.

Leading lights:

Great Pass Low Light (white round tower, red stripes, 20 m in height) (31°09′·3N 29°50′·8E).

Great Pass Low Light (3.113)
(Original dated 1997)

(Photograph - Crown Copyright)

Al Maks High Light (4 cables ESE) (3.109).

From a position close NW of the entrance to the pass the alignment (113°) of these lights, which should be maintained as accurately as possible, leads ESE through the centre of the dredged channel, marked by light buoys (lateral), passing (with positions from Great Pass Beacon (31°10′·0N 29°48′·5E)):

2 NNE of a dangerous wreck (7 cables WNW),thence:

NNE of Great Pass, from which a light (3.109) is exhibited, and:

SSW of several wrecks (2½ cables NE), lying on the NW corner of a large area of shoal water. No 4 Light Buoy (port hand) marks the SW side of these wrecks. Thence:

3 NNE of Hydrographer Shoal Light Beacon (black metal tower, white bands, 9 m in height) (3½ cables ESE); a dangerous wreck lies on the S part of the shoal. Thence:

NNE of a wreck (5 cables SE), with a depth of 5·8 m over it, lying to the E of Requin Shoal, and:

4 SSW of North Shoal Light Beacon (red square metal tower, white bands, 7 m in height) (6 cables E). There are several dangerous submerged wrecks lying close S of this beacon. Thence:

SSW of a dangerous wreck (9 cables ESE), thence:

NNE of a dangerous wreck (1 mile SE), to a position NNE of SB1 Buoy (starboard hand) (1¼ miles SE).

5 **Clearing marks.** Two pairs of beacons, each pair in line bearing 113°, mark the SW and NE sides of the pass, respectively (positioned from Great Pass Low Light).

SW marks:

Front beacon (post, black cone topmark) (½ cable WSW).

Rear beacon (mast, black cone topmark) (4½ cables SE).

NE marks:

Front beacon (post, red can topmark) (½ cable ENE).

Rear beacon (mast, red can topmark) (3½ cables ESE).

Mīnā’ Al Iskandarīyah Harbour

3.114

1 From the position NNE of SB1 Buoy (starboard hand) (31°09′·5N 29°49′·8E), at the SE end of Al Būghāz al Akbar, the track leads E and NE, passing (with positions from head of Outer Breakwater (31°09′·9N 29°50′·8E)):

N of a dangerous wreck (5 cables SSW), thence:

NW of a lighthouse (disused) (5 cables S), thence:

2 SE of the head of Outer Breakwater, from which a light (red metal framework tower, white stripes) is exhibited. Thence:

NW of the head of Quarantine Breakwater (2½ cables E), from which a light (green metal framework tower, white stripe) is exhibited.

3 Thence into Outer Harbour, through which a recommended channel, as shown on the chart, leads to Inner Harbour.

Useful marks (positioned from head of Outer Breakwater):

Great Pass Low Light (6½ cables S) (3.113).

Disused port control tower (4½ cables SE) (3.109), standing near the root of Quarantine Breakwater.

Alternative channel

Al Būghāz (Boghaz Pass or The Pass)

3.115

1 **Caution.** Al Būghāz cannot be used at night, and it is impracticable for deep-draught vessels when there is a heavy sea or swell; for controlling depth see 3.90. In 1987 the pass was prohibited for navigation until further notice.

Leading marks:

Lighthouse (disused) (31°09′·4N 29°50′·8E).

Al Maks High Lighthouse (4½ cables SE) (3.109).

2 From a position in the vicinity of 31°11′·3N 29°48′·6E the alignment (134°) of these lighthouses, which should be gained well to seaward of the entrance to the pass and maintained as accurately as possible, leads SE through the centre of the channel, passing (with positions from the disused front lighthouse):

3 NE of Outer Shoal (1¾ miles NW), which is unmarked, and:

SW of a metal post (1¾ miles NW) which marks a 5·6 m patch, thence:

NE of Al Far (1½ miles WNW), a shoal marked by a beacon, and:

4 SW of Al Qiţţ (1¼ miles NW), a shoal with wrecks on it. There is a least depth of 1·8 m over the shoal; a beacon (post, position approximate) stands N of the shoal. Thence:

Close SW of a light buoy (port hand) (7 cables NW), to a position about 3½ cables SW of the head of Outer Breakwater.

5 **Clearing marks.** Two pairs of beacons, each pair in line bearing 134°, mark the SW and NE sides of the pass, respectively (positioned from Boghaz Low Lighthouse).

SW marks:

Front beacon (pole, black diamond topmark) (1 cable SSE).

6 Rear beacon (mast, black cone topmark) (5 cables SE).

NE marks:

Front beacon (pole, red can topmark) (1 cable SE).

Rear beacon (mast, red can topmark) (3½ cables SE).

(Directions for entering Mīnā' Al Iskandarīyah Harbour are given at 3.114)

Side channel

Corvette Pass

3.116

1 **Caution.** Corvette Pass, lying mainly within a prohibited area (3.105), is suitable only for small vessels; local knowledge is required. For controlling depth see 3.90.

Leading beacons:

Front beacon (pole, two framework diamond topmarks, elevation 27 m) (31°09′·0N 29°50′·4E).

Rear beacon (pole, two framework ball topmarks, elevation 35 m) (3 cables S).

2 From a position about 1 mile W of Ra's at Tīn Lighthouse (31°11′·7N 29°51′·7E) (3.109), the alignment (181½°) of these beacons leads S through the centre of the channel, passing (with positions from head of Outer Breakwater (31°09′·9N 29°50′·8E)):

3 W of Al Ikhwan (1 mile N), a rocky shoal. A shoal, with a depth of 4·3 m over it and marked by a buoy, lies close E of the leading line in this vicinity. And:

E of Al Hūt (1 mile NNW), a rocky shoal marked at its N end by a beacon (black, 5 m in height), thence:

4 E of a buoy (conical) (6 cables NNW), thence:

Between two buoys (conical) (5 cables NNW), thence:

W of a dangerous wreck (2 cables NW), thence:

E of a light buoy (port hand) (4¼ cables W), to a position about 3½ cables SW of the head of Outer Breakwater.

(Directions for entering Mīnā' Al Iskandarīyah Harbour are given at 3.114)

Basins and berths

Mīnā' Al Iskandarīyah

3.117

1 **General information.** Berths are numbered in sequence from No 1 at the head of the harbour. Depths alongside berths are shown on the chart.

Inner Harbour (positioned from port control tower (31°11′·3N 29°52′·2E)):

2 **Arsenal Basin** (7 cables NNE), containing Arsenal Quay, has a charted depth of 7·6 m in the fairway, but there are depths of less than 5 m around the sides of the basin. Small vessels must not exceed a speed of 4 kn. The basin contains several jetties on its N side, and Nos 1 to 12 Berths. The berths are used by Ports and Lighthouses Administration, police, immigration and customs vessels, and offshore oil rig vessels. A stranded wreck was reported (2005) alongside berth number 12. Careening Basin, in the SE corner of Arsenal Basin, can be used only by boats. Old Customs Quay, on the E side of the basin, is 330 m long and the usual landing place. At No 6 Berth are the disinfecting station and the quarantine and passport offices.

3 **Passenger Quay** (6 cables NE) contains Nos 14 to 24 Berths. No 18 Berth can accommodate two RoRo vessels.

Central Quay (5¾ cables ENE) extends S from the root of Passenger Quay. Used to accommodate general cargo vessels.

Al Maḩmūdīyah Quay (4½ cables E) contains Nos 33 to 43 Berths; dry bulk.

4 **Military Quay** (3½ cables ESE) contains Nos 45 to 47 Berths.

Container terminal (2 cables ENE), constructed by extending Coal Quay, contains Nos 49 to 54 Berths. The terminal has an area of 163 000 sqm and is equipped with three gantry cranes. RoRo facilities are also available.

3.118

1 **Outer Harbour** (positioned from port control tower (31°11′·3N 29°52′·2E)):

Coal Basin (1 cable SSE) contains Nos 60 to 64 Berths.

Nitrate Quay (4½ cables SE), extending SW from the root of Coal Quay, contains Nos 65 to 68 Berths.

2 **Container Terminal** (1¼ miles SSW) consist of three berths Nos 71 to 73.

Mīnā al Qamarīyah (1½ miles SSW), protected from NW by a mole, is connected to River Nile by a barge canal entered from its S corner. Numerous barges and lighters are berthed in the basin. Berth No 85 on the SW side is used to handle grain.

3 **Petroleum Harbour** (1¾ miles SSW) has general depths from 11 to 16 m. There are five berths for tankers, the deepest of which can accommodate tankers of up to 213 m in length and 10 m draught. Quarantine Quay and Livestock Quay are situated in the SW corner of the harbour.

Ad Dukhaylah

3.119

1 The harbour contains the following berthing areas (positioned from Al 'Ajami Light (31°08′·9N 29°47′·2E)):

Mineral Jetty (1¼ miles SE). Used by vessels discharging iron ore and coal. It is quayed for

600 m on the W side with depths alongside from 16 to 20 m. A light (metal beacon, 5 m in height) is exhibited from a dolphin at the head of the jetty. Vessels up to 165 000 dwt can be accommodated; maximum draught 17·2 m.

2 **Petroleum Jetty** (11 cables SE). A petroleum and coal berth 288 m in length, able to accommodate vessels of 12 m maximum draught.

General Cargo Pier (7½ cables SE), with a total quay length of 780 m, on its NW and SE sides; depths alongside 12 to 15 m. The NE extremity of the pier is marked by lights.

3 **Container Terminal** (4½ cables SE), with a total quay length, on its NW and SE sides, of 740 m; 12 to 14maximum draught 11·5 to 13 m. The NE extremity of the terminal is marked by lights.

Al Maks

3.120

1 **LPG Terminal.** A platform (31°08′·9N 29°49′·1E) for the use of tankers discharging LPG to a chemical works is situated at the seaward end of a submarine pipeline extending 6½ cables NNW from the shore. Lights are exhibited from the platform, and the heads of the jetty.

2 **Tanker mooring area** for butane tankers up to 3000 dwt and 7·3 m draught is established about 5 cables ENE of the LPG Terminal.

Port services

Repairs

3.121

1 Mīnā' Al Iskandarīyah shipyard (31°10′·4N 29°52′·0E) can undertake large hull and machinery repairs. There are two dry docks and a floating dock with the following dimensions:

1st drydock: length 260 m; breadth 39·6 m; depth 9·5 m; handles vessels up to 85 000 dwt.

2nd drydock: length 162 m; breadth 19·5 m; lifting capacity 5000 tonnes.

2 Floating dock: length 152 m; breadth 23 m; lifting capacity 6000 tonnes.

There is also a shiplift on the NW side of Outer Harbour, with a lifting capacity of 600 tonnes on two ways, able to handle small vessels up to 1500 dwt.

Other facilities

3.122

1 Hospitals; Sailors' Home, near the entrance to El Mahmûdîya Qanât; floating cranes, up to 200 tons capacity; Ship Sanitation Control and Exemption Certificates are issued; oily waste and garbage disposal; fumigation.

Supplies

3.123

1 Fuel, by barge; fresh water at most alongside berths, and by barge to vessels at anchor; fresh provisions.

Harbour regulations

3.124

1 **Police.** The port police office is situated at the landing stage in Careening Basin (3.117). The port police launches fly a green pendant with the word "Police" in white letters.

Vessels requiring assistance from the port police should display flags **ST** of the International Code.

2 Any vessel ordered by the port police to have no communication with the shore will display flags **TP** of the International Code by day, and a red light at night.

Fire. Vessels requiring the fire brigade or fire float should use the following signals:

Day: flags **DQ** of the International Code.

3 Night: a gun or explosive signal, fired at intervals of one minute, or continuous sounding with any fog signal apparatus.

Vessels leaving which require a pilot should apply to the port offices and display the pilot flag.

MĪNĀ' AL ISKANDARĪYAH TO ṬÂBIYET EL-BURG

General information

Charts 302, 2681

Route

3.125

1 From a position about 4 miles NNW of Ṭābiyat al 'Abbasīyah (31°09′N 29°47′E), the coastal route follows the recommended track, as shown on the chart, for about 17 miles NE, to a position 5 miles NW of Ṭâbiyet El-Burg (31°20′N 30°04′E).

Topography

3.126

1 From Ra's at Tīn (31°12′N 29°52′E) to Ṭâbiyet El Atta, 1¼ miles NE, the coast is bounded by a seawall. The coastline is then indented by the harbour of El Mînâ' el Sharqîya (3.133).

2 The coast between the site of Ṭâbiyet El Silsila (31°13′N 29°54′E), on the E side of El Mînâ' el Sharqîya, and Ṭâbiyet El-Burg, 11 miles NE, is sandy with numerous cliffs. It is fringed with rocks and shoal water which in places extends 1½ miles offshore. A seawall extends from El Mînâ' el Sharqîya to El Muntaza Harbour, 7½ miles NE.

3 El Ibrâhîmîya and El Raml, suburbs of Mīnā' Al Iskandarīyah, extend along the coast from El Mînâ' el Sharqîya for 4½ miles.

Depths

3.127

1 Depths off the coast between El Muntaza Harbour (31°17′N 30°01′E) and Gezîret Disûqî, 6 miles NE, are very irregular; vessels are recommended to keep in depths of more than 20 m.

Prohibited anchorage

3.128

1 Anchoring is prohibited within an area, shown on the chart, extending 10 miles off the coast between the site of Ṭâbiyet El Silsila (31°13′N 29°54′E) and Ṭâbiyet El-Burg, 11 miles NE, owing to the presence of submarine cables (see 1.26).

2 Within the W part of this area lies a restricted area (31°16′·0N 29°52′·4E) in which both anchoring and the carriage of explosives are prohibited. The limits of the restricted area are shown on the chart.

For information on submarine cables see 1.26.

Prohibited area

3.129

1 Navigation is prohibited up to 3 miles of the coast, in the vicinity of El Muntaza Palace (31°17′·3N 30°01′·0E), between Ṭâbiyet El-Burg and El Raml, 7½ miles SW, as shown on the chart.

Directions
(continued from 3.62)

Principal marks
3.130

1 **Landmarks:**

Ra's at Tīn Lighthouse (31°11′·7N 29°51′·7E) (3.109).

Dome (31°12′·0N 29°52′·1E) of Sarāy Ra's at Tīn (3.109).

El Anfûshi Minaret (31°12′·3N 29°52′·9E) (3.109).

Dome (31°12′·6N 29°55′·1E) (3.109) of Saint Mark's College.

2 Radio mast (obstruction lights, 103 m in height) (31°14′·7N 29°58′·7E), standing 5 cables SSE of Qasr el-Safâ (3.132).

Minaret at Sîdi Bishr (44 m in height) (31°15′·6N 29°59′·1E), is conspicuous.

3 El Muntaza Palace (31°17′·3N 30°01′·0E), on the S side of El Muntaza Harbour (3.137), is a large red conspicuous building with a tower 37 m high; a water tower 3 cables S of the palace is prominent.

Ṭâbiyet el-Raml (31°18′·5N 30°04′·1E) (3.144).

4 **Major lights:**

Al 'Ajami Light (31°08′·9N 29°47′·2E) (3.109).

Great Pass Light (31°10′·0N 29°48′·5E) (3.109).

Ra's at Tīn Light — as above.

Other aids to navigation
3.131

1 **Racons:**

Al 'Ajami Light (31°08′·9N 29°47′·2E).

Râs-el-Tîn Light (31°11′·7N 29°51′·7E).

For details see *Admiralty List of Radio Signals Volume 2.*

Mīnā' Al Iskandarīyah to Ṭâbiyet El-Burg
3.132

1 From a position in the waiting area for Mīnā' Al Iskandarīyah, about 4 miles NNW of Ţābiyat al 'Abbasīyah (31°09′N 29°47′E) (3.61) the track leads NE, passing (with positions from Ṭâbiyet Qâitbâi (31°13′N 29°53′E)):

NW of the entrances (4½ miles SW) to the passes leading to Ad Dukhaylah and Mīnā' Al Iskandarīyah, thence:

NW of a dangerous rock (2¼ miles W), thence:

2 NW of El Anfûshi Bay (8 cables SW), entered between Sarāy Ra's at Tīn and Ṭâbiyet el Atta. The bay is encumbered with foul ground and is fronted by reefs lying from 2 to 4 cables off the coast; El-Esed, a dangerous rock, lies at the W end of the reefs and a stranded wreck lies on the reefs 2½ cables W of Ṭâbiyet el Atta. The bay is only used by fishing vessels. Thence:

3 NW of Ṭâbiyet Qâitbâi (3.134), from which a light is exhibited, and which forms the NW side of El Mînâ' el Sharqîya (3.133), thence:

NW of Bittern Shoal (9 cables N), thence:

NW of Ibn Asîl (9 miles NE), a dangerous rocky patch, with a depth of less than 2 m over it, on which the sea breaks heavily, thence:

4 NW of El Ukhtein (11 miles NE), a patch formed by submerged ruins over which the sea constantly breaks; shoals, with depths of 4·6 m and 6·4 m over them, lie close together 5 cables SW of El Ukhtein.

5 The track then leads to a position NW of Ṭâbiyet El-Burg (11¾ miles NE) (3.79), which is conspicuous.

Useful marks:

Qasr el-Safâ (31°15′·2N 29°58′·5E), standing on a high seawall, is a prominent building with a pointed cupola (42 m in height).

An islet (31°15′·8N 29°58′·7E), 2 m high, surmounted by a beacon (black and white chequered metal framework, 5 m in height).

(Directions continue at 3.144)

El Mînâ' el Sharqîya

Chart 302

General information
3.133

1 **Position.** El Mînâ' el Sharqîya is contained between Ṭâbiyet Qâitbâi (31°13′N 29°53′E) and the site of Ṭâbiyet El Silsila, 1 mile E.

2 **Function.** In ancient times, when the harbour was in use, ships were guided there by fires on the top of the Pharos, a white marble tower which stood in the position of Ṭâbiyet Qâitbâi, and Cleopatra's Needle stood near the S shore. The harbour, much encumbered by dangers, is now little frequented, and although vessels occasionally shelter there, strong N winds cause a heavy swell, and the holding ground of rock, sand and weed is poor.

Harbour
3.134

1 **General layout.** The harbour is circular, being protected from N by a breakwater extending 2½ cables E from Ṭâbiyet Qâitbâi and by El Silsila Breakwater, which is detached, extending from a point 1 cable W of the site of Ṭâbiyet El Silsila, for 4 cables W to the harbour entrance.

2 Ṭâbiyet Qâitbâi, on the site of the famous ancient Pharos, is square and surmounted by a light-structure. Ṭâbiyet El Silsila stood at the end of a low, rocky point 3 cables in length, which has since been artificially built up.

Directions
3.135

1 **Principal marks:** see 3.130.

From seaward the track leads S, passing (with positions from Ṭâbiyet Qâitbâi (31°13′N 29°53′E)):

Clear of Bittern Shoal (9 cables N), thence:

W of El Hassan (1 mile ENE), a dangerous rock with a depth of 3·8 m over it; steep-to on its seaward side. El Nassar, an extensive rocky bank with several very shallow heads, over which the sea usually breaks, lies 2½ cables SW of El Hassan. Thence:

2 E of Diamond Rock (1 cable NW), awash, and Yarf el Wasat (3 cables E), with a depth of 4·9 m over it, lying close N of the W breakwater, thence:

Between the heads of the breakwaters (3½ cables E) into the harbour. A light (green metal mast, 10 m in height) is exhibited from the head of the W breakwater, and a light (red concrete tower, 6 m in height) is exhibited from the W end of El Silsila Breakwater.

3 **Caution.** Amongst the dangers which encumber the inside of the harbour are (with positions from Ṭâbiyet Qâitbâi):

El Ganem, a rock with 2·7 m over it (1½ cables SSE).

A patch (3 cables SE), with a depth of 1·7 m over it, next to a mooring buoy.

A patch (5½ cables SSE), with a depth of 1·9 m over it.

4 El Fullil (6½ cables SSE), a rock with 0·9 m over it. There are also three dangerous below-water rocks lying 1½ cables, 2 cables and 4¼ cables ENE of El Fullil.

El Jemel (1 mile SE), a rock with a depth of less than 2 m over it.

Useful mark:

Light exhibited from Ṭâbiyet Qâitbâi.

Anchor berths

3.136

1 Anchorage may be obtained, as shown on the chart, about 2 cables SSE of the light-structure on the head of the W breakwater, in a depth of about 9 m; there are several mooring buoys in this vicinity.

Small vessels anchor under the lee of Ṭâbiyet Qâitbâi and secure their sterns to the breakwater.

Minor harbours

Chart 2681

El Muntaza

3.137

1 El Muntaza Harbour (31°17′N 30°01′E) is a small artificial harbour, with depths from 2·7 to 4·9 m in it, formed by a breakwater extending S from Gezîret Halâwa, a peninsula. The SE end of Gezîret Halâwa consists of a narrow sandbank which does not cover at high water, and a bridge also connects Gezîret Halâwa to the mainland. El Muntaza Palace (3.130) stands on the S side of El Muntaza Harbour.

Caution. See 3.129.

ṬÂBIYET EL-BURG TO TEL RAFAH

GENERAL INFORMATION

Charts 2573, 2574, 2634

Area covered

3.138

1 The area covered by this section comprises:

Ṭâbiyet El-Burg to Râs Umm El-Nabâyil (3.140).
Râs Umm El-Nabâyil to Port Said (3.164).
Port Said (3.205).
Port Said to Tel Rafah (3.251).

Nahr El Nîl (River Nile) delta

3.139

1 A few miles N of El Qâhira (1.82), Nahr El Nîl (River Nile) divides into two main streams which enter the Mediterranean through Maṣabb Rashîd (Rosetta Mouth) (31°28′N 30°22′E) and Maṣabb Dumyâṭ (Damietta Mouth) (31°32′N 31°51′E), respectively; the area enclosed between the two branches is the present delta of Nahr El Nîl. Considerable erosion of the delta coast has taken place in recent years, especially in the vicinity of Maṣabb Rashîd and Maṣabb Dumyâṭ, and near Cape Burullus (31°35′N 30°59′E).

2 The annual rising of Nahr El Nîl commences at Aswân about mid-June and continues for about two months, the greatest rate of flow being attained towards the end of August. From the end of September the flow rate gradually decreases, the fall being spread over a rather longer period than the rising of the river.

Aswân High Dam controls the flow of water downstream throughout the year. There is also a concrete barrage, with a lock, 8 miles SSE of Rashîd (Rosetta), and an earth dam 4 miles SW of Dumyât (Damietta).

ṬÂBIYET EL-BURG TO RÂS UMM EL-NABÂYIL

General information

Chart 2681

Route

3.140

1 From a position 5 miles NW of Ṭâbiyet El-Burg (31°20′N 30°04′E) the coastal route follows the recommended track, as shown on the chart, for about 22 miles NE, to a position about 11 miles NNW of Râs Umm El-Nabâyil (31°29′N 30°22′E).

Topography

3.141

1 The main feature of this part of the coast is Khalîg Abu Qîr (Abu Qîr Bay), which lies between Ṭâbiyet El-Burg (31°20′N 30°04′E) and the W entrance point of Maṣabb Rashîd (Rosetta Mouth), 17 miles NE. A number of forts stand on the shores of the bay, which are very low and sandy; coastguard stations are established at some of the forts, as shown on the chart.

The SW side of Khalîg Abu Qîr is encumbered by Gezîret Disûqî (31°21′N 30°06′E), historically known as Nelson Island. The island is 9 m high, and fringed for the greater part by foul ground. Many reefs, shoals and patches of foul ground, on which the sea breaks, lie between Gezîret Disûqî and Ṭâbiyet El-Burg.

2 A seawall extends along the coast between Ṭâbiyet Raml and El Ma'dîya Port, 5 miles SE. Forts Nos 1, 3 and 4 stand behind this wall; Fort No 1 is in ruins, the remainder are each 11 m high.

Ṭâbiyet El Ma'dîya, 10 m high, Ṭâbiyet el-Labbânî, 5 m high, Ṭâbiyet el-Kalakh, 8 m high, and Ṭâbiyet el-Gazâyir, 7 m high, stand on the coast between El Ma'dîya Port and Idku, 8 miles ENE.

Idku (31°18′N 30°18′E), a village situated on a sandhill, 24 m high, on the N bank of Buḥeiret Idku, contains a minaret 37 m high. Sandhills from 15 to 30 m high extend NE as far as Nahr El Nîl (River Nile) (3.139).

3 Ṭâbiyet el-Sheikh, on the shore abreast Idku, is 12 m high, surmounted by some black huts. Between Ṭâbiyet el-Sheikh and Maṣabb Rashîd, 10 miles NNE, stand Ṭâbiyet el-Nawa, 8 m high, Ṭâbiyet el-'Alâyim, 8 m high, Ṭâbiyet el-Farash, 5 m high, and Ṭâbiyet el-'Abd, 11 m high, all of which have the appearance of sand mounds except for Ṭâbiyet el-'Abd, which is surmounted by some black huts.

Marine exploitation

3.142

1 There are three gas-producing fields in the vicinity of Khalîg Abu Qîr; Abu Qîr Bay Gas Field, West Abu Qîr Gas Field and North Abu Qîr Gas Field. These consist of lighted platforms and wellheads, connected to each other, and the shore, by gas pipelines. Drilling rigs may be

encountered in the area; they exhibit numerous lights and all vessels should keep well clear of them.

2 For information on safety zones and pipelines see 1.7 and 1.8.

Submarine cable

3.143

1 A submarine cable is laid across Khalîg Abu Qîr from a position 4 miles NW of Ţâbiyet El-Burg (31°20′N 30°04′E) to a position 8 miles NNW of Râs Umm El-Nabâyil (31°29′N 30°22′E).

For information on submarine cables see 1.26.

Directions

(continued from 3.132)

Principal marks

3.144

1 **Landmark:**

Water tank on columns on Ţâbiyet el-Raml (38 m in height) (31°18′·5N 30°04′·1E).

Major light:

Rosetta Light (white daymark on framework tower, white dwelling) (31°26′·6N 30°25′·9E).

Other aids to navigation

3.145

1 **Racons:**

Gezîret Disûqî (31°21′·5N 30°06′·4E).

North Abu Qîr Gas Field Platform NAQ P–1D (31°35′·0N 30°07′·7E).

Rosetta Lighthouse (31°26′·6N 30°25′·9E).

For details see *Admiralty List of Radio Signals Volume 2.*

Ţâbiyet El-Burg to Râs Umm El-Nabâyil

3.146

1 From a position 5 miles NW of Ţâbiyet El-Burg (31°20′N 30°04′E) the track leads NE, passing (with positions from Gezîret Disûqî Light (31°21′·5N 30°06′·4E)):

NW of Dahl Sultân (1¾ miles NW), an isolated shoal, and:

NW of Gezîret Disûqî (3.141), from the summit of which a light (white metal mast, red top, 10 m in height) is exhibited, thence:

2 NW of West A/Q Platform (5¾ miles N), from where a light is exhibited, and:

SE of two mooring buoys (11½ miles NNW), thence:

SE of El-Dahl el-Akhdar (12¼ miles N), an isolated shoal; there is a dangerous wreck 2 miles SSE of El-Dahl el-Akhdar. Thence:

3 SE of NAF 1/NAF 2 Platform (13¼ miles N) and NAQ P–1D Platform, thence:

SE of a wreck (12 miles NNE), lying 3 cables NW of the recommended route, with a depth of 19 m over it, thence:

4 SE of a wellhead (13½ miles NNE), thence:

NW of another wellhead (31°35′·2N 30°14′·3E); dangerous wrecks lie 1 mile SE and 3¾ miles SE, respectively, of this wellhead.

The track then leads to a position 11 miles NNW of Râs Umm El-Nabâyil (31°29′N 30°22′E).

(Directions continue at 3.170)

Abu Qîr

General information

3.147

1 **Position.** Abu Qîr (31°19′N 30°04′E) is situated on the E side of the W entrance point of Khalîg Abu Qîr.

Function. Abu Qîr is mainly a military port, however it is also an expanding commercial port which consists of a converted bulk carrier for the import and storage of grain. Phosphate and fertiliser are also handled as well as an offshore berth for the export of ammonia.

2 **Port Authority.** Mīnā' Al Iskandarīyah Authority, 106 El Horreya Avenue, Mīnā' Al Iskandarīyah, Egypt.

Port operator. Abu Qîr Fertilizer and Chemical Industries Co., Tabiah-Khat Rashid, Mīnā' Al Iskandarīyah, Egypt.

Limiting conditions

3.148

1 **Controlling depth.** The national chart gives a depth of 9 m on the leading line (2005).

Maximum size of vessel handled:

Abu Qîr Port: 210 m LOA, 8 m draught.

Ammonia berth: 150 m LOA, 22 m beam, 7·5 m draught, 15 000 dwt.

Arrival information

3.149

1 **Anchorages.** There is a designated waiting area for Abu Qîr port, radius 5 cables, 1½ miles NW of Gezîret Disûqî.

There is an anchorage for small vessels, as shown on the chart, close S of Gezîret Disûqî (31°21′·5N 30°06′·4E) (3.141). Vessels may anchor, in charted depths of 6 to 7 m, with the E extremity of Gezîret Disûqî bearing about 353°, distance 6½ cables.

2 **Pilotage** is compulsory for the Ammonia Berth and is available 0800 to 1800 local time; the pilot boards in the waiting area centered on 31°21′N 30°09′E. Vessels should not pass the arrival light buoy without contacting the pilot service.

Directions

3.150

1 **Abu Qîr port.** From a position about 1½ miles NNW of Gezîret Disûqî (Nelson Island) (31°21′·5N 30°06′·4E) the track leads S for 1½ miles, passing (with positions from Gezîret Disûqî Light):

E of a shoal (1 mile NW), with a depth of 8 m over it, lying 7 cables E of Dahl Sultân, and:

W of Culloden Reef (6 cables NE), thence:

Close W of Gezîret Disûqî.

2 **Leading lights:**

Front light (white triangle, apex up, black bands on red and white metal tower, 15 m in height) (31°18′·6N 30°04′·9E).

Rear light (white triangle, apex down, black bands on red and white metal tower, 18 m in height) (175 m SSW of front light).

3 The alignment (195°) of these lights then leads 1½ miles SSW along a recommended track, marked by light buoys, passing:

ESE of a dangerous wreck (with 1·5 m over it) (1¾ miles WSW), and:

WNW of the foul ground (6 cables SW), extending 8 cables SSW from Gezîret Disûqî, thence:

4 Close ESE of a dangerous rock (1¾ miles SW), close N of the harbour breakwater, and:

WNW of a patch (1¼ miles S) of foul ground, on which the sea breaks in rough seas.

The recommended track then turns SW, passing NW of an isolated structure 180 m in length (2 miles SSW), then close ESE of the head of the harbour breakwater (2 miles SW), from which a light is exhibited, thence into the harbour.

5 **Ammonia Berth.** From a position about 4 miles NW of Gezîret Disûqî (31°21′·5N 30°06′·4E) the track leads E for about 4 miles, passing (with positions from Gezîret Disûqî Light):

N of Dahl Sultân (1¾ miles NW), an isolated shoal, thence:

S of the wellhead (3½ miles N), lying 2 miles S of West A/Q Platform, to a position close NE of the arrival light buoy (2½ miles NNE).

6 Thence follow the recommended track SSE, as shown on the chart, passing:

WSW of a wellhead (4¼ miles NE), lying 1¼ miles WSW of Q,A/Q P–2 Platform, thence:

ENE of a dangerous wreck (1¾ miles NE) lying on the E extremity of Culloden Reef. This reef, with a least depth of 4·0 m over it, is separated from Gezîret Disûqî by rocks and shoals. Patches of foul ground on which the sea breaks lie on the S side of the reef. Thence proceed to the waiting area or continue towards the Ammonia Berth.

7 **Caution.** A dangerous wreck lies close ESE of the turning buoy at the Ammonia Berth.

(Directions for El Ma'dîya Port *continue at 3.153)*

Berths

3.151

1 **Abu Qîr port.** There are eight quays with a total length of 3000 m with depths alongside of 5·0 to 10 m. The berths handle general and bulk cargoes.

Ammonia Berth (31°19′·4N 30°09′·6E). Consists of four mooring buoys; the berth can be used by two vessels during daylight hours only. Depth alongside 10 m.

El Ma'dîya Port

General information

3.152

1 **Position and function.** El Ma'dîya Port (31°16′·2N 30°09′·2E) is situated on the S side of Khalîg Abu Qîr. It consists of a small harbour enclosed by two breakwaters, entrance open ENE, on the S shore of Khalîg Abu Qîr.

Pilotage is compulsory and the pilot boards in the waiting area centred on 31°20′·0N 30°08′·7E.

2 For details see *Admiralty List of Radio Signals Volume 6 (3).*

Prohibited anchorage area. On the S side of Khalîg Abu Qîr anchoring is prohibited within an area, shown on the chart, encompassing pipelines laid from the shore to the Ammonia Berth (31°19′·4N 30°09′·6E).

Directions

(continued from 3.150)

3.153

1 Vessels heading for the harbour at El Ma'dîya Port follow the directions given for Abu Qîr Ammonia Berth, and pass W of the berth onto the following leading line:

Front light (yellow triangle, apex down, on orange framework tower, black band, 15 m in height) (31°16′·3N 30°09′·1E).

2 Rear light (yellow triangle, apex up, on orange framework tower, black band, 24 m in height) (375 m S of front light).

The alignment (177½°) of these lights leads S through a channel, 100 m wide, marked by spar buoys, and thence between the breakwaters into the harbour. Lights are exhibited from the heads of the breakwaters.

3.154

1 **Useful marks:**

Chimneys (31°16′·6N 30°05′·2E).
Towers (31°16′·2N 30°05′·9E).
Water tower (31°16′·3N 30°08′·2E).
Tower (31°15′·9N 30°09′·2E).
Gas flare tower (31°16′·0N 30°09′·5E).

Berths

3.155

1 **Harbour.** The harbour is quayed on all sides, and depths within the harbour are from 4·7 to 6·5 m.

Fishing Ports. Old Ma'dîya Fishing Port is situated 1¼ miles E of El Ma'dîya Port, with a new fishing harbour, New Ma'dîya Fishing Port, immediately E. Both harbours are protected by breakwaters extending N and exhibit lights at their heads.

Idku LNG Port

General information

3.156

1 **Position and function.** Idku LNG Port (31°21′N 30°19′E) is situated on the E side of Khalîg Abu Qîr. It consists of a loading jetty for the export of LNG, and a small harbour.

2 **Port limits.** Idku LNG Port consists of the waters enclosed within a line drawn NW from a position on the shore, 5 cables S of the jetty, for a distance of 4 miles; thence NNE for 1¼ miles, returning to the shore 7½ cables N of the jetty. Fishing is prohibited within the port limits.

3 **Traffic.** In 2007 there were 10 ship calls with a total of 766 079 dwt.

Port operator. Egyptian Operating Company for Natural Gas Liquefication Projects S.A.E., 2 Port Said Street, Maadi, Cairo, Egypt.

Limiting conditions

3.157

1 Vessels of up to 117 000 tonnes displacement with length 300 m and draught 11·7 m can be accommodated.

Arrival information

3.158

1 **Notice of ETA:** 72, 48, 24 and 6 hours.

Waiting anchorage. There is a designated waiting anchorage, centered on 31°27′·6N 30°13′·6E, 2½ miles NW of the landfall buoy.

Pilots. Pilotage is compulsory.

Directions

3.159

1 From a position about 4½ miles NW of Gezîret Disûqî (31°21′·5N 30°06′·4E) (3.147) the track leads E for about 9 miles towards the pilot station, passing (with positions from Gezîret Disûqî Light) (3.152):

S of West A/Q Platform (6 miles N), and:

N of the wellhead (3½ miles N), lying 2 miles S of West A/Q Platform, thence:

2 Clear of a dangerous wreck (position approximate) (5½ miles NE), thence:

N of Q, A/Q P-2 Platform (5½ miles NE), thence:

N of A/Q P-1 Platform (7½ miles ENE), to a position 1½ miles NW of the landfall buoy (8 miles ENE).

The track then leads SE, clear of two wellheads close by the landfall buoy, thence:

3 **Leading lights:**

Front light (red triangle, apex up, on red tower) (31°22′·2N 30°18′·4E).

Rear light (red rectangle on red tower) (200 m SE of front light).

The alignment (135°) of these lights leads SE through a buoyed channel (dredged to 14 m), 230 m wide and 2·2 miles long, to the turning basin.

Berth

3.160

1 **LNG Berth** (31°22′·1N 30°17′·7E). Consists of a single berth situated at the end of a trestle style jetty, which is 10m wide and 1·3 miles in length extending NW from the shore. A detached breakwater (lit at its N and S ends), about 250 m to the NW, protects the berth from the prevailing NW winds. A turning basin, reportedly dredged to 13·5 m, connects the dredged channel to the berth.

2 Vessels normally berth port side to and the depth of water alongside is reportedly dredged to 13 m. A mooring buoy is located approximately midway along the detached breakwater, on the shoreward side.

Maṣabb Rashîd

Charts 2681, 2574

General information

3.161

1 **Description.** Maṣabb Rashîd (Rosetta Mouth) (31°28′N 30°22′E), from 2½ to 5 cables in width, is nearly barred by extensive sandbanks which extend 1¼ miles seaward. These banks vary their formation and position in accordance with the state of the river and the prevailing wind conditions. At times the banks extend right around the mouth of the river into Khalîg Abu Qîr.

In the summer a large sardine fishing fleet is usually to be found near and W of Maṣabb Rashîd.

2 **Topography.** El Bûghâz Fort West and El Bûghâz Fort East stand on the W and E sides of the river 1 mile above the mouth and are disused. The coastguard barracks, 5 cables S, has a bright red roof and is prominent.

Thick palm groves line the river banks, their NW limit being clearly defined, and thence villages extend along the banks almost as far as Rashîd.

3 Burg Migheizil Minaret, 19 m high, stands on the E bank, 1¾ miles inside the river entrance; Ṭâbiyet el-Qâitbâi, now disused, stands on the opposite bank.

Limiting conditions

3.162

1 **Controlling depths.** The very narrow channel which lies between the sandbanks has a depth of about 2 m, but its position continually alters; local craft are brought into the river by a pilot who sounds out the channel shortly before their arrival.

Inside the bar, the depths increase rapidly to between 3·7 and 6·1 m, and these depths are maintained for many miles.

Harbour

3.163

1 **Description.** Rashîd (Rosetta) (31°24′N 30°25′E), which has a population of about 25 000, stands on the W bank of the river, 5½ miles above its mouth. It contains two minarets, 40 m and 36 m high.

Communications: Rashîd is connected to the Egyptian state railway system.

RÂS UMM EL-NABÂYIL TO PORT SAID

General information

Charts 2574, 2573

Route

3.164

1 From a position about 11 miles NNW of Râs Umm El-Nabâyil (31°29′N 30°22′E) the coastal route follows the recommended track, shown on the chart, for about 40 miles ENE, thence 46 miles E to a position N of the precautionary area in the NW approaches to Port Said.

Topography

3.165

1 From Râs Umm El-Nabâyil (31°29′N 30°22′E), the NE entrance point of Maṣabb Rashîd, to Cape Burullus, 33 miles ENE, the coast is low and sandy. Thence from Cape Burullus to Maṣabb Dumyâṭ (Damietta Mouth), 40 miles E, the coast consists of low sandhills.

El ‘Aiyâsh Fort No 6 and El Qar‘a Fort No 5 stand near the coast 10 and 19 miles, respectively, ESE of El-Burullus Light (31°35′·9N 31°04′·9E); both are in ruins, appearing like sand mounds. Coastguard stations are situated near the forts.

2 Ashtum Gamasa Fort No 4 (31°26′N 31°33′E), situated at the mouth of Bahr Basandila, is a ruin 8 m high which appears like a flat-topped brown mound; coastguard buildings are situated within its walls.

Forts Nos 3, 2 and 1 stand between 7 and 12 miles ENE of Fort No 4; all are in ruins and appear like sand mounds. At Fort No 3 the buildings of a coastguard station show over the top of the mound.

Nature of seabed

3.166

1 Between Maṣabb Rashîd and Maṣabb Dumyâṭ the bottom close off the coast is mostly dark, heavy sand, quite different from that found W of Khalîg Abu Qîr, which is light in colour and formed of coral and shells.

Currents

3.167

1 The current is uncertain, but generally E-going at ½ to 1 kn. It is greatly influenced both in rate and direction by strong winds and sets into the bays.

Within about ½ cable of the shore there is a strong W-going current, and consequently great care should be taken when landing.

See also 3.4.

Marine exploitation

3.168

1 Numerous unmarked wellheads, some projecting as much as 6 m above the seabed exist mainly between the 200 m depth contour and the coast.

Considerable activity associated with exploration for oil or gas may also be encountered in the area covered by this sub-section. Drilling rigs carry numerous lights and all vessels should keep well clear of them.

2 **Caution.** There are several oil and gas production platforms situated off the coast between Cape Burullus (31°35′N 30°59′E) and Port Said, about 65 miles ESE,

which are not charted. For remarks on safety zones and submarine pipelines see 1.7 and 1.8.

Prohibited areas

3.169

1 Fishing is prohibited in an area extending up to 12 miles offshore, as shown on the chart, N of Maṣabb Dumyâṭ (31°32′N 31°51′E).

Directions

(continued from 3.146)

Principal marks

3.170

1 **Landmarks:**

Kôm el-Mastarôh (31°29′·3N 30°41′·4E), 23 m high, and Kôm el-Magsaba (31°30′·4N 30°44′·4E), 15 m high, lying 17 and 20 miles, respectively, E of Maṣabb Rashîd, are good landmarks when near the coast.

Water tower (31°35′·2N 30°59′E) at Cape Burullus.

Silo (31°28′·2N 31°46′·0E) at Mînâ' Dumyâṭ (Dumyâṭ Port); reported to provide a good radar response.

2 **Major lights:**

Rosetta Light (31°26′·6N 30°25′·9E) (3.144).

El-Burullus Light (white daymark on framework tower, white dwelling) (31°35′·9N 31°04′·9E). A large hotel and a number of houses are situated in the vicinity of the light-structure.

3 Maṣabb Dumyâṭ (Damietta) Light (white daymark on framework tower, white dwelling) (31°31′·4N 31°50′·9E), exhibited from the E side of the river mouth. The light-structure is visible before the land is sighted.

Port Said Light (31°16′·4N 32°17′·6E) (3.236).

Other aids to navigation

3.171

1 **Racons:**

Rosetta Lighthouse (31°26′·6N 30°25′·9E).

Gas production platform (31°45′·8N 30°34′·3E), NE of Rosetta.

Gas production platform (31°50′·8N 30°38′·1E), NE of Rosetta.

2 El-Burullus (31°35′·9N 31°04′·9E).

Maṣabb Dumyâṭ (Damietta) (31°31′·4N 31°50′·9E).

Port Said (31°16′·4N 32°17′·6E).

For details see *Admiralty List of Radio Signals Volume 2.*

Râs Umm El-Nabâyil to Port Said

3.172

1 From a position about 11 miles NNW of (31°29′N 30°22′E) the recommended track leads ENE, passing (with positions from El-Burullus Light (31°35′·9N 31°04′·9E)):

NNW of two dangerous wrecks (25 and 29¼ miles W), and:

NNW of the coast (20 miles WSW) separating Buḥeiret el Burullus (Lake Burullus) from the sea; stranded wrecks lie along the shore. Thence:

2 SSE of Rosetta 2 Platform (28 miles WNW), the S of a group of gas production platforms (lit). Thence:

NNW of Cape Burullus (31°35′N 30°59′E), the E entrance point of a small outlet from Buḥeiret el Burullus; this outlet is navigable by light-draught fishing vessels. There is a dangerous wreck about 1 mile NNW of the entrance to the outlet, and shoals, with depths of 7·8, 9·6 and 9·1 m over them, lie 3¼ miles NW of the cape.

3 Thence from a position N of El-Burullus Light the track leads E, passing:

Clear of a wellhead (12 miles NE) and between Baltim E and Baltim S Gasfields. A third platform is located approximately 9½ miles NW of Baltim E. Thence:

N of a reported (1993) 13·4 m sounding (22 miles E). Thence:

4 N of Damietta Banks (29 miles E), which consist of three narrow banks of sand and mud lying between 3 and 8½ miles offshore. The least depth on each bank occurs at or near its E end, that on the outer bank being 6·7 m, on the middle bank 3·0 m, and on the inner bank 5·2 m. Thence:

N of the TSS (31°45′N 31°42′E) in the NW approaches to Mînâ' Dumyâṭ, thence:

5 N of Maṣabb Dumyâṭ (31°32′N 31°51′E) (3.187), thence:

N of a dangerous wreck (position approximate) (31°45′N 31°52′E), to the vicinity of 31°46′N 31°56′E.

(Directions for Port Said are given at 3.236)

(Directions for the coastal route continue at 3.258)

Maṣabb Dumyâṭ

General information

3.173

1 **Position.** Maṣabb Dumyâṭ (Damietta Mouth) (31°32′N 31°51′E) is entered between Râs el Barr, the termination of a low sandspit which forms the W bank of the river, and Kawa Burun, a low point 1 mile NE.

Topography. Fort Esh-Sharqiya and Fort El-Sheikh Yusef are situated 2 cables SSW and 6 cables SW, respectively, of Maṣabb Dumyâṭ Light; both are in ruins, and appear like flat-topped sand mounds.

2 Fort 'Ezbet el Burg, 1 mile SSW of Maṣabb Dumyâṭ Light (3.170), has prominent yellow walls and is considerably larger than Fort Esh-Sharqiya; it is the headquarters of the local coastguard. Two minarets stand close S of this fort. Another fort, with a minaret close SSE, stands SSW of Fort 'Ezbet el Burg.

Several palm groves, visible from seaward, are situated on the E bank between Fort 'Ezbet el Burg and Dumyâṭ, 5 miles SSW.

Limiting conditions

3.174

1 **Depths.** A sandbank, partly awash, fills the entrance except for two very narrow channels. One channel, with a greatest depth over a shifting bar of 2·4 m, lies 5 cables NE of Râs el Barr; the other, with a shifting bar having a greatest depth of 1·2 m, lies close off Kawa Burun. After heavy gales these channels are liable to alter both in position and depth, so the passage should not be attempted even in boats without the aid of the local pilot. A heavy surf usually breaks on the sandbank, and landing is frequently impossible for several days in succession. In 1975 it was reported that considerable silting had occurred in Maṣabb Dumyâṭ, and that depths at the entrance were less than 2 m.

Arrival information

3.175

1 **Anchorage.** Small vessels often anchor NW of the bar in a depth of about 7 m. During W winds they sometimes shelter under Kawa Burun.

Pilotage. A local pilot boards vessels outside the bar if weather permits. At other times he waits in the channel and indicates the passage.

Directions

3.176

1 **Landmarks:**

Silo (31°28′·2N 31°46′·0E), at Mînâ' Dumyâṭ.

Water tower (23 m in height) (31°31′·2N 31°50′·7E), standing close S of Fort Esh-Sharqiya.

Minaret (26 m in height) (31°31′·0N 31°50′·2E), standing 2½ cables SSW of Fort El-Sheikh Yusef.

2 Tower (67 m in height), standing on the E bank of Nahr El Nîl (River Nile) (3.139).

Major light:

Maṣabb Dumyâṭ (Damietta) Light (3.170).

3.177

1 **Caution** is necessary in approaching Maṣabb Dumyâṭ as depths of less than 10 m extend 3½ miles NNE of Kawa Burun, and there is an occasional indraught; constant sounding is therefore necessary. The coast around the river mouth was reported (1979) to give a good radar picture at a range of 9 to 10 miles.

2 **Useful marks:**

Light (green concrete tower, 10 m in height), 4 cables NW of Maṣabb Dumyâṭ Light, exhibited from the W side of the entrance.

El Girbi Light (white pyramidal tower, black bands, concrete base, 4 m in height), in the river abreast Fort 'Ezbet el Burg.

Dumyâṭ

3.178

1 **Description.** Dumyâṭ (Damietta) (31°25′N 31°49′E) (3·183), a town with a population of about 97 000, stands surrounded by trees on the E bank of Nahr El Nîl (River Nile) (3.139), up to 6½ miles from Maṣabb Dumyâṭ.

The town contains several high minarets and chimneys, and two water towers, the N about 30 m high, the S about 49 m high. All these objects appear above the trees and are visible from seaward.

Berths. There are two quays and four wooden piers; commercial shipping is handled at Mînâ' Dumyâṭ (3.181).

Canal and lake entrance

Chart 2573

Qanât el Manzala

3.179

1 Qanât el Manzala (Manzala Canal) connects Shatt Gheit el-Nasara, 1 mile E of Dumyâṭ (31°25′N 31°49′E), El Maṭarîya (31°11′N 32°02′E) and Port Said (31°16′N 32°19′E), passing through Buḥeiret El Manzala. From a position 5 miles SE of Dumyâṭ a branch connects with Nahr El Nîl (River Nile) (3.139) 2 miles SW of the town. The canal, which is 22 m wide with depths from 1·2 to 1·5 m, is maintained by dredging and is marked by iron and wood piles. It can be used by vessels up to 35 m long, 7 m beam and a maximum draught of 1·2 m.

2 A regular ferry service runs in conjunction with the railway service between Dumyâṭ and El Manṣûra (31°03′N 31°23′E).

Chart 241

El-Gamîl

3.180

1 **Description.** El-Gamîl entrance (31°17′N 32°13′E) to Buḥeiret el Manzala is ½ cable wide, with a depth of 0·9 m on the bar.

Tidal streams have been observed in the entrance channel. The in-going stream flows along the coast from W and enters Buḥeiret el Manzala obliquely; the out-going stream issues at a great rate after HW, and carries with it quantities of mud.

2 **Prohibited area.** Entry is prohibited into an area in the vicinity of El-Gamîl entrance, as shown on the chart.

Useful marks:

Three beacons (rectangular), Nos 3, 2 and 1, stand prominently on the coast 3 cables, 2½ miles and 3½ miles, respectively, ESE of El-Gamîl entrance.

Towers standing 1 mile and 1½ miles ESE of El-Gamîl entrance.

MÎNÂ' DUMYÂṬ

General information

Chart 2578

Position

3.181

1 **Position.** Mînâ' Dumyâṭ (Damietta Port) (31°29′N 31°45′E) is situated about 5 miles SW of Maṣabb Dumyâṭ (Damietta Mouth).

Function

3.182

1 The port, which opened for traffic in 1986, is intended to serve the Nile delta region, importing cement, grain and general cargo, and exporting agricultural products, fertilisers and furniture. It is also a container transhipment port and LPG/LNG terminal. The latter has an area of 3 200 000 m^2 with the capacity to produce 4 800 000 tonnes of liquefied gas annually.

Approach and entry

3.183

1 The harbour is approached through a buoyed channel, 300 m in width, extending NNE from the harbour for about 6 miles, and entered between two breakwaters.

Traffic

3.184

1 In 2007 there were 1781 ship calls with a total of 31 276 421 dwt.

Port authority

3.185

1 Damietta Port Authority, PO Box 13, Damietta, Egypt.

Limiting conditions

Controlling depths

3.186

1 The approach channel has a maintained depth of 15·0 m, and the turning basin in the harbour was dredged to a depth of 14·5 m in 1986.

Density of water

3.187

1 1·030 g/cm^3.

Maximum size of vessel handled

3.188

1 RoRo ships, container ships and bulk carriers up to 250 m long, draught 13 m; general cargo ships, draught 11·0 m; gas tankers up to 140 500 m^3, 300 m LOA, 12 m draught.

Limiting berthing conditions at the LNG terminal

3.189

1 20 kn of wind; 1 m wave height; 1 mile visibility.

Arrival information

Vessel traffic service

3.190

1 A VTS Scheme with full radar surveillance is maintained for the regulation of shipping. For details see *Admiralty List of Radio Signals Volume 6 (3)*.

Notice of ETA

3.191

1 Vessels should send ETA to the Port Authority 7 days and 24 hours in advance.

Waiting areas

3.192

1 An area (31°37′N 31°45′E), marked by five light buoys, lies 8 miles N of the harbour entrance. Depths are from 16 to 20 m and approach from NW is advised. An area for gas tankers is established, centred on ~~31°42′·2N 31°38′·1E,~~ with a radius of 1 mile.

46/10 ~~31°40·0N 31°54·4E~~
03/11 31°42·2N 31°38·1E

Pilotage

3.193

1 Pilotage is compulsory. When approaching the waiting area vessels should call the pilot station on VHF radio stating their draught, length and cargo. The pilot boards in position 31°35′·8N 31°46′·8E, in the S part of the waiting area.

For details see *Admiralty List of Radio Signals Volume 6 (3).*

Tugs

3.194

1 Tugs are available and compulsory for vessels over 2000 gt.

Traffic regulations

3.195

1 **TSS** have been established in the NW and NE approaches to Mînâ' Dumyâț, as shown on the chart. These TSS are IMO-adopted and Rule 10 of *International Regulations for Preventing Collisions at Sea (1972)* applies.

Harbour

General layout

3.196

1 The harbour entrance is protected by breakwaters projecting from the shore; West Breakwater is 1400 m long and East Breakwater is 560 m long. Inside the harbour there is a turning basin off which lie the berthing areas.

Opposite the root of the West Breakwater a barge canal leads ESE, for 2½ miles, connecting the harbour with Nahr El Nîl (River Nile) (3.139).

2 **Development.** A transhipment container terminal is being built (2008), which will be capable of handling up to 4 million teu. The terminal is expected to be operational by late 2009 and will include a quay 2360 m long.

Directions

Principal marks

3.197

1 **Landmarks:**

Silo (31°28′·2N 31°46′·0E), standing 1½ miles SSE of the harbour entrance.

Port Authority building (31°28′·3N 31°45′·6E), standing 1 mile S of the harbour entrance.

2 **Major light:**

Maṣabb Dumyâț (Damietta) Light (3.170).

Approach from NW

3.198

1 From the vicinity of 31°46′N 31°40′E, the track leads SE through the TSS to a precautionary area centred 7½ miles NNW of Maṣab Dumyâț Light (31°31′·4N 31°50′·9E). A light buoy (safe water) is located 4 cables S of the precautionary area.

2 Thence the track leads SSW to the following leading line:

Mînâ' Dumyâț Front Light.

Mînâ' Dumyâț Rear Light (metal tower, 20 m in height) (31°28′N 31°45′E).

3 The alignment (191½°) leads through the approach channel marked by numbered pairs of light buoys (lateral). The harbour is entered between the heads of the breakwaters, from each of which a light (metal tower, 10 m in height) is exhibited.

Approach from NE

3.199

1 From the vicinity of 31°46′N 32°01′E, the track leads SW through the precautionary area in the NW approaches to Port Said, thence through the TSS to the Mînâ' Dumyâț precautionary area, noting a light buoy to the S of the area (3.197), thence to the Mînâ' Dumyâț leading line.

Berths

3.200

1 The harbour contains five main berthing areas as follows:

Container berths Nos 1 to 4; total length 1050 m; depth alongside 14·5 m; No 1 Berth has a RoRo ramp at its NW end.

General cargo wharf berths Nos 5 to 8; total length 800 m; depth alongside 12·0 m; No 8 Berth has a RoRo ramp at its SE end.

2 Bulk cargo wharf berths Nos 9 to 12; total length 900 m; depth alongside 12·0 m.

Grain wharf berths Nos 13 and 14; total length 600 m; depth alongside 14·5 m.

Multi purpose berths 15 and 16; total length 590 m; depth alongside 14·5 m.

3 LPG and LNG terminals located on the NW and W side of the basin respectively. Depth alongside the LNG terminal, 14 m; vessels normally berth port side alongside.

Port services

Repairs

3.201

1 Minor repairs only.

Other facilities

3.202

1 Hospitals at Râs el Barr, 6 km, and at Dumyâṭ, 8 km; oily waste disposal; Ship Sanitation Control and Exemption Certificates issued; containers for garbage disposal.

Supplies

3.203

1 Fuel; fresh water available by barge; provisions. Provisions are available at the LNG terminal.

Communications

3.204

1 Airport at Port Said (Bûr Sa'id), 60 km; international airport at Cairo, 180 km.

PORT SAID

General information

Charts 241, 240

Position

3.205

1 Port Said (Bûr Sa'îd) (31°16′N 32°19′E) is situated at the N end of Suez Canal (1.88).

Function

3.206

1 Port Said is the second port of Egypt. It has facilities for handling general cargo, container and RoRo traffic, grain carriers and tankers. It is also a port of call for passenger ships. Most Mediterranean languages are spoken, and English is understood by most officials.

The principal exports are raw cotton, rice and petroleum. The chief imports are agricultural products, chemicals, mining and quarrying machinery, metal products, and transportation equipment.

2 The town of Port Said, situated on the W side of the harbour, was created in 1859 to serve the needs of the Suez Canal, which was then being cut; it has a population of about 492 000.

Port Fouad (Bûr Fu'âd), on the E side of the harbour, contains a free trade zone and the residences of the Canal Authority's employees, workshops and shipyards.

Topography

3.207

1 The coast near Port Said is unusually low, and it is not visible from more than about 3 miles offshore.

Between Maṣabb Dumyâṭ and Port Said, 27 miles SE, lies the Bight of Dîba. The shore of the bight is a strip of very low sand, about 2 cables wide in places, separating Buḥeirat el Manzala (Lake Manzala) from the sea.

2 Fort El-Dîba (31°21′N 32°04′E) stands in ruins at the ancient Mendesian mouth of River Nile, now closed. A second fort, 5 cables SSW of Fort El-Dîba, which appears as a flat-topped sand mound, is used as a coastguard station.

Approach and entry

3.208

1 **Approach.** Port Said is approached from seaward through either the NW or NE TSS. Thence vessels required to wait before entering the harbour, or the canal, proceed to the South Anchorage, or one of the North Anchorages, depending on draught.

2 **Entry.** Dredged approach channels lead to the respective entrances to Port Said Harbour and Port Said By-pass. The channels are marked by light buoys which give a good radar response. Because of dredging or other operations the light buoys may be temporarily removed, displaced or changed.

3 **Port Said Harbour Approach Channel**. From South Anchorage Port Said Harbour is entered via Port Said Harbour Approach Channel, which leads from Fairway Light Buoy (31°21′N 32°21′E) to the harbour entrance, about 5 miles SSW. It is used by vessels entering and leaving Port Said Harbour, and by vessels entering Suez Canal West Branch. From the harbour entrance the fairway then passes through the basins and between mooring buoys to the N end of Suez Canal West Branch, 3 miles SSW.

4 **Port Said By-pass Approach Channel**. This channel extends from Hm 195 Light Buoy (31°25′N 32°24′E) to the entrance to Port Said By-pass, 10½ miles SSW. It is used by deep-draught vessels entering Suez Canal from the North Anchorages, and by all vessels leaving the canal.

Suez Canal, known to the Egyptians as Qanât el Suweis, is described in full in *Red Sea and Gulf of Aden Pilot.*

Traffic

3.209

1 In 2007 there were 11 012 ship calls with a total of 582 820 060 dwt.

Port Authority

3.210

1 Port Said Port Authority, Mostafa Kamel & Azmy Street, Railway Square, Port Said, Egypt.

Limiting conditions

Controlling depths

3.211

1 Port Said Harbour approach has a maintained centreline depth of 16·5 m, and a least maintained depth in the harbour of 14·8 m. The approach channel leading to Port Said By-pass has a least maintained centreline depth of 22·5 m; and the Suez Canal Container Terminal has a dredged depth of 16·5 m.

The maximum permitted draught for vessels is determined by the Suez Canal Authority.

Deepest and longest berth

3.212

1 Container Terminal in Abbas Hilmi Basin (3.246).

Tidal levels

3.213

1 Mean spring range about 0·3 m; mean neap range 0·1 m. For further information see *Admiralty Tide Tables Volume 2.*

Abnormal water levels

3.214

1 At Port Said the MSL varies with the seasons, the lowest level occurring in February and the highest in July. The mean difference, however, does not exceed 0·2 m. During a period of six years the difference between the highest and lowest levels observed was 1·4 m.

In summer, strong N winds can raise the level by 0·3 m, and occasionally by as much as 0·6 m.

Density of water

3.215

1 Density of water in the harbour is 1·030 g/cm^3.

Local weather

3.216

1 Entering Port Said Harbour during a W gale is very dangerous and should be avoided, especially at night.

Arrival information

Notice of ETA

3.217

1 The Suez Canal Authority require 5 days advance notice to book a vessel for transit through the canal. The following information should also be sent at least 48 and 24 hours in advance to Suez Canal Authority, Ismailia, (SUQ), directly or through a vessel's agent, or diplomatic representative in the case of a warship:

Type of vessel, nationality and name (with former name, if any).

2 Suez Canal gross tonnage (SCGT), dwt, draught and beam.

Whether vessel intends to transit the canal or stop in the harbours, including the duration of stay in harbour, if appropriate.

ETA off Port Said.

Whether carrying dangerous cargo, stating quantity, class, and where stowed.

Waiting anchorages

3.218

1 **General information.** Anchorage areas for vessels waiting to enter Port Said Harbour or Suez Canal are established in Port Said Roads. If practicable, vessels should avoid arriving between 0100 and 0500 when convoys leave the anchorages to enter Suez Canal. Anchorages are as follows:

North Anchorage (Zone One) (31°28′N 32°19′E) is for the use of deep-draught vessels with draughts exceeding 12·8 m waiting to enter Suez Canal.

2 **North Anchorage (Zone Two)** (31°24′N 32°18′E) is for the use of deep-draught vessels waiting to enter Suez Canal. Vessels authorized to use this anchorage are large container ships, VLCCs in ballast or partially loaded, and vessels drawing between 11·9 m and 12·8 m. The anchor berths, each with a radius of 750 m, are designated V1 to V8, as shown on the chart.

3 **South Anchorage** (31°22′N 32°19′E) is for the use of vessels drawing up to 11·9 m waiting to enter Port Said Harbour or Suez Canal through Port Said Harbour. The anchor berths, each with a radius of 500 m, are designated C1 to C15, as shown on the chart. The bottom is mud, good holding ground.

Prohibited anchorage area

3.219

1 Anchoring is prohibited between the E limits of the anchorage areas and the approach channels, as indicated on the chart.

Anchoring and fishing are also prohibited in the Bight of Dîba, to the W of the anchorage areas; the limits are shown on the chart.

Gas pipelines and platforms

3.220

1 Submarine gas pipelines are laid from a position on the shore, 3 and 6¾ miles WNW of El-Gamîl entrance (31°17′N 32°13′E). The pipelines and their associated platforms extend up to 40 miles NNW, thence for a farther 40 miles E. Lights are exhibited from the platforms.

For information on pipelines see 1.8.

Cargo transhipment areas

3.221

1 There are designated cargo transhipment areas, shown on the chart, situated E and NE of the entrance to Port Said By-pass Approach Fairway as follows:

North area (31°26′·5N 32°27′·5E). For vessels with draught exceeding 18·3 m.

South area (31°24′·5N 32°26′·5E). For vessels with draught less than 18·3 m.

Pilotage

3.222

1 **Pilotage** is compulsory for all vessels entering, leaving, moving, changing berth, or manoeuvring within canal waters or Port Said Harbour.

When advised that the pilot vessel is approaching, a vessel must make ready to embark the pilot and to enter the approach channel without delay. If at anchor, cable should be shortened in and a lee made for the pilot vessel to come alongside in safety.

2 A charge will be made when a pilot is called out too soon, or when he is kept on board beyond the time required for pilotage proper.

Boarding places are as follows:

For entering Port Said Harbour, E of Fairway Light Buoy (31°21′N 32°21′E).

3 For entering Port Said By-pass the pilot boards in the North Anchorages (3.218).

If rough seas prevents pilots from boarding at the usual places, the Port Authority may authorize vessels to follow the pilot vessel and embark pilots as follows:

For Port Said Harbour, in the lee of West Breakwater (31°18′N 32°21′E).

For Port Said By-pass, at Hm 00 (31°15′N 32°21′E).

4 When considering whether it is safe to follow the pilot vessel, or whether to remain at sea or to anchor, masters should bear in mind that the pilot may not be aware of the vessel's draught.

Vessels are not permitted to enter without a pilot when conditions prohibit the pilot vessel from leaving the harbour.

5 **Pilot vessels** have the word 'Pilote' on each bow, and a black funnel with a white band. By day they fly Flag G and at night they exhibit a white light over a red light.

For details see *Admiralty List of Radio Signals Volume 6 (3)*.

Pilot signals

3.223

1 The pilot signals (diagram 3.223) are in use.

*Signals must be clearly visible to the signal station at the Canal Authority's Offices (3.231) and must be displayed 30 minutes before sailing time if shifting berth or proceeding to sea, and 2 hours in advance if entering the canal.

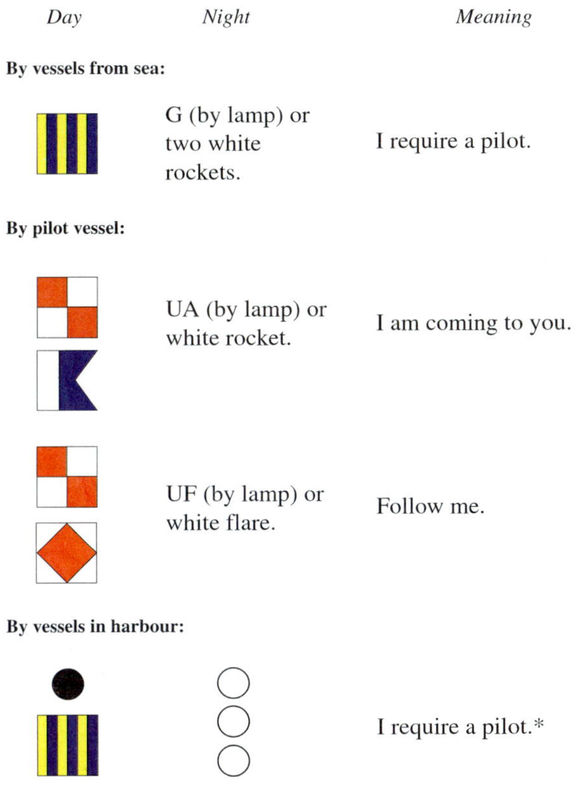

Port Said (Bûr Sa'îd) - pilot signals (3.223)

Tugs

3.224

1 Tugs are available and assist vessels berthing in Port Said Harbour.

Traffic regulations

3.225

1 **General.** Regulations for navigation in Port Said Harbour and Suez Canal are contained in *Rules of Navigation* issued by Suez Canal Authority. Extracts from the rules are given in *Red Sea and Gulf of Aden Pilot*, and pilots carry a copy of the rules for the use of masters.

2 **TSS** have been established in the NW and NE approaches to Port Said, as shown on the chart. These TSS are IMO-adopted and Rule 10 of *International Regulations for Preventing Collisions at Sea (1972)* applies.

3 **Vessel Traffic Service** with full radar surveillance is maintained for the regulation of shipping. For details see *Admiralty List of Radio Signals Volume 6 (3)*.

Time of entry and departure. Vessels are permitted to enter Port Said Harbour by day or night, subject to regulations issued from time to time in Egyptian Notices to Mariners.

Quarantine

3.226

1 The Health Officer boards vessels on arrival. The quarantine station is situated on the E bank close S of Husein Basin. There is also a floating quarantine station in Abbas Hilmi Basin.

2 Vessels in quarantine are permitted to pass through Suez Canal subject to no communication with the shore. A vessel arriving from Suways (Suez) in quarantine, the period of which has expired before arrival at Port Said, will be permitted to berth only in Outer Harbour Basin unless a written statement from the Quarantine Authority confirming expiry of the quarantine period is received by the vessel's agent.

Notice of medical requirements

3.227

1 Medical requirements should be sent to agents at least 24 hours before arrival.

Harbour

General layout

3.228

1 **Entrance.** The entrance to Port Said Harbour is protected by West and East Breakwaters.

West Breakwater extends 2 miles NE from the shore on the W side of the entrance. A submerged prolongation extends a further 1¼ miles NE from its head, marked on its SE side by a line of small white buoys, 1 cable apart, which are difficult to identify.

East Breakwater extends NNE for about 6 cables from reclaimed land on the E side of the harbour.

2 **Basins.** The principal parts of the harbour are as follows:

Outer Harbour, which extends from the harbour entrance to Ismâîl Basin, 1¼ miles SW, and includes North Basin and Outer Harbour Basin. Blocks Basin, at the SE corner of Outer Harbour Basin, contains two floating docks. General Workshop Basin, close SW, contains the Canal Authority workshops and shipyard.

3 Ismâîl Basin, the inner harbour; Commercial Basin, Arsenal Basin and Shirîf Basin, are situated on the NW side of Ismâîl Basin.

Abbas Hilmi Basin, between Ismâîl Basin and Husein Basin, which is quayed on its NW side.

4 Husein Basin, which is the area between Abbas Hilmi Basin and the entrance to Suez Canal West Branch. Berths for the use of tankers front oil depots on the W side of the basin. Salt Basin serves a salt works on the E bank. Work is in progress (2008) on a 400 m extension to the main container quay, which will be completed within the next two years. The quay will offer a deeper draught of 16 m alongside.

5 Suez Canal Container Terminal, which opened in 2004, is situated at the N end of the Suez Canal E of Port Said By-pass. The port has a separate entrance from seaward, protected by breakwaters, and from its S side a connecting channel leads SW to join the Port Said By-pass. The port currently consists of a container terminal, with quay length of 1200 m and a depth alongside and in the turning area of 16·5 m. Works are in progress to

the N (2004) and S (2008) of the quay. Current handling capacity (2008) is around 2·2 million teu.

6 **Developments.** The first of four additional 300 m long berths is due to be operational in early 2010 and phase two should be completed by 2011. At this point the terminal will have 2400 m of quay with an alongside depth of 17·5 m.

Dredging operations

3.229

1 For several months of the year hopper dredgers work underway in the approach channels. The dredgers dump soil in spoil grounds about 2 miles ESE of Port Said By-pass Approach Channel as shown on the chart.

2 **Dredger signals.** In addition to the signals prescribed by *International Regulations for Preventing Collisions at Sea*, dredgers working underway exhibit the signals in diagram 3.229.1.

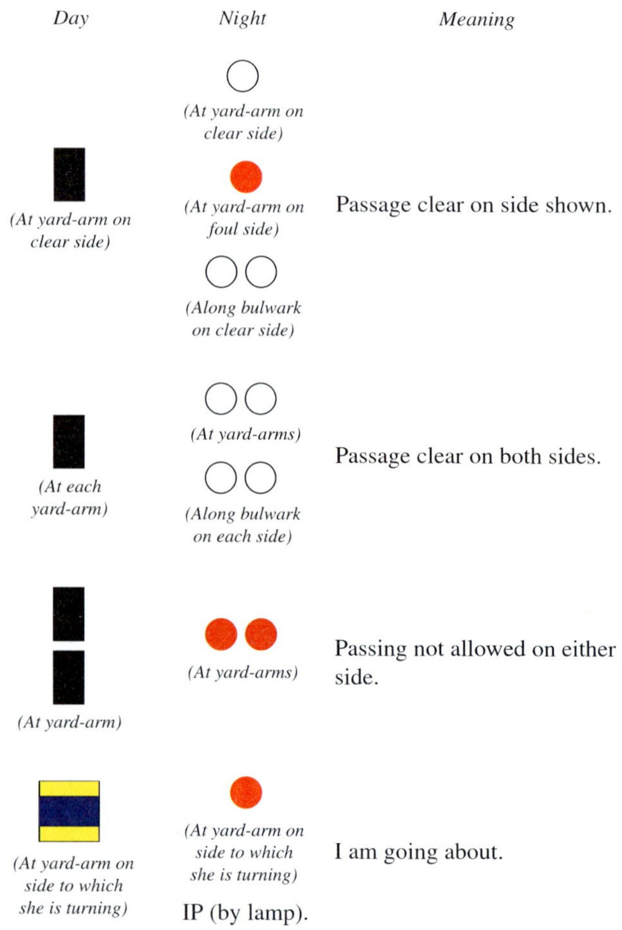

Port Said (Bûr Sa‘îd) - dredger (underway) signals (3.229.1)

Stationary dredgers, floating cranes and certain other craft working for Suez Canal Authority show the signals in diagram 3.229.2.

Submarine cables and pipelines

3.230

1 In Port Said Harbour submarine cables and pipelines cross the fairway at the N end of Ismâîl Basin and S of Salt Basin. Anchoring is prohibited in the vicinity, as shown on the chart.

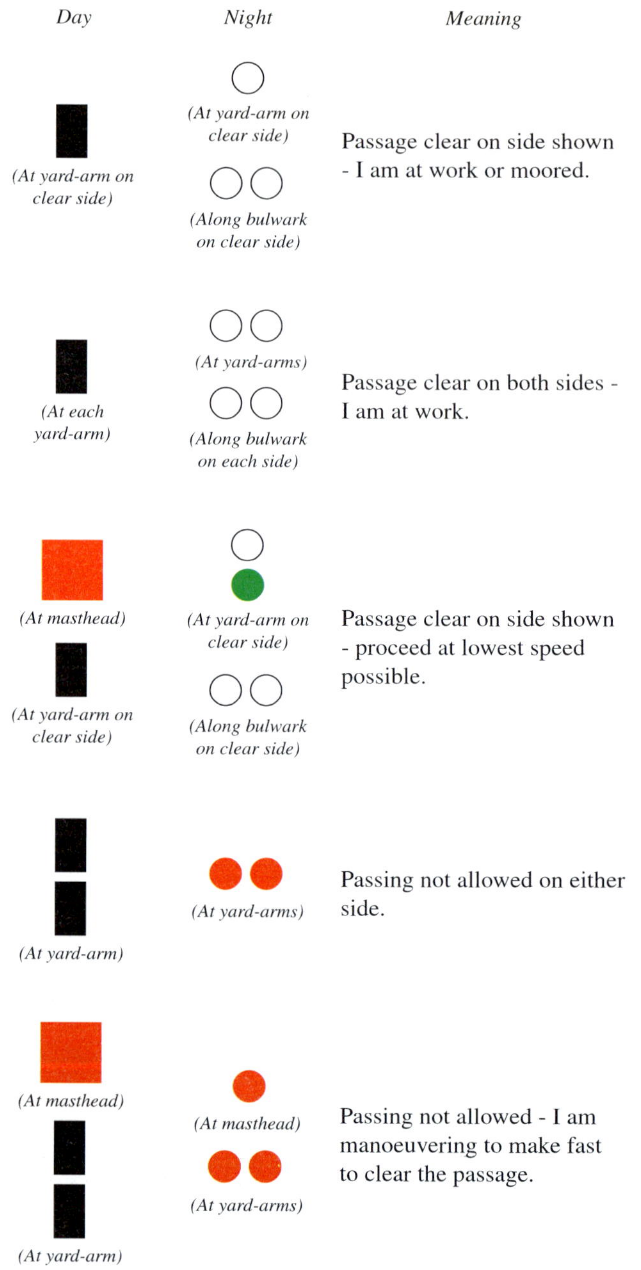

Port Said (Bûr Sa‘îd) - dredger (stationary) signals (3.229.2)

For information on pipelines see 1.8 and for submarine cables see 1.26.

Signal stations

3.231

1 Signal stations are situated as follows:

Suez Canal Authority’s Offices signal station (31°15′·4N 32°18′·5E) standing on the W side of Port Said Harbour.

SCA Signal Tower (31°13′·5N 32°20′·5E) standing on the W side of Port Said By-pass.

Dangerous cargo signals

3.232

1 When entering Port Said Harbour or Port Said By-pass vessels carrying dangerous cargo must display the appropriate signal(s) (diagram 3.232).

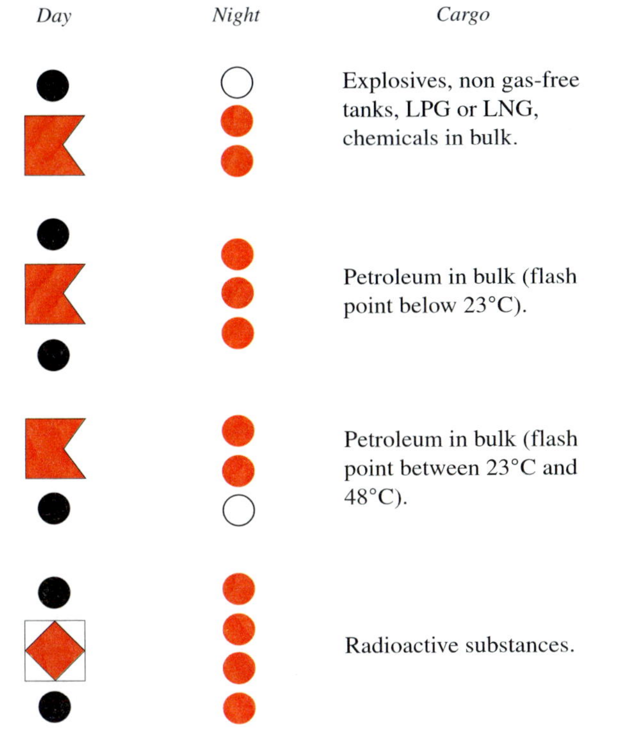

Port Said (Bûr Saʻîd) - dangerous cargo signals (3.232)

Manoeuvring signals

3.233

1 The signals (diagram 3.233) are shown by vessels manoeuvring in Port Said Harbour. A vessel showing one of the signals must not be passed or overtaken. When the manoeuvre has been completed the signal must be hauled down or extinguished.

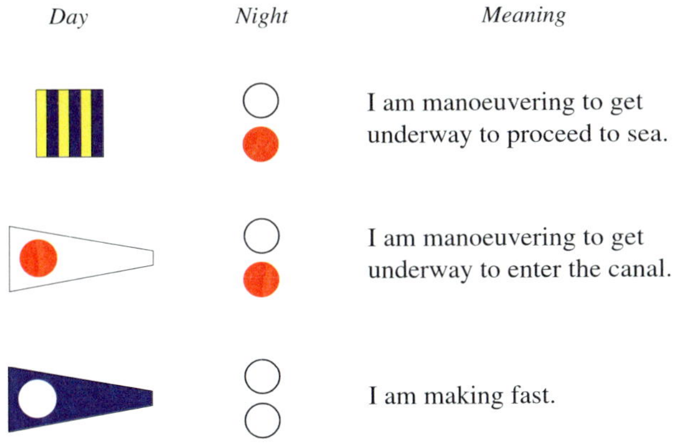

Port Said (Bûr Saʻîd) - manoeuvring signals (3.233)

Traffic signals

3.234

1 Signals to regulate the movement of vessels entering and leaving Port Said Harbour, and to indicate berths allocated, are shown at the signal station at Suez Canal Authority's Offices. Detail of the day and night signals are given in *Rules of Navigation* (3.225).

Natural conditions

3.235

1 **Currents.** In the approaches to Port Said the current is variable and much affected by the wind. With prolonged winds from NW or N, especially in summer, it is SSE-going at rates from ½ to 1½ kn.

In 1996 it was reported that a sudden and severe set had been experienced in the vicinity of light buoys Hm 60 and Hm 80, in the Port Said By-pass Approach Channel.

Climate information: see 1.184 and 1.193.

Directions for entering

Principal marks

3.236

1 **Landmarks** (positioned from Port Said High Lighthouse (31°15′·9N 32°18′·8E)):

Two minarets (3½ cables N).

Port Said High Lighthouse (disused) (conspicuous white octagonal stone tower, black stripes, 59 m in height).

Radio tower (red and white) (4 cables W).

Radio tower (red light) (1¼ miles WSW).

2 Dome (conspicuous, green-tiled, 37 m in height) (4¾ cables SSW), the central and highest dome of Suez Canal Authority's Offices.

Mosque and two minarets (6½ cables SSE).

Radio mast (red obstruction lights) (1½ miles SE).

SCA Signal Tower (grey metal tower, black band, lantern at mid-level, 40 m in height) (2¾ miles SE).

3 **Major lights:**

El Bahar Tower Light (white framework tower, redbands, 42 m in height) (31°18′·1N 32°21′·6E) (ruins 2007).

Port Said Light (white daymark on framework tower) (31°16′·4N 32°17′·6E).

Other aids to navigation

3.237

1 **Racons:**

Port Said (31°16′·4N 32°17′·6E).

El Bahar Tower (31°18′·1N 32°21′·6E)

For details see *Admiralty List of Radio Signals Volume 2.*

From sea to Port Said Roads

3.238

1 **Caution.** Owing to the uncertainty of the current, and the low-lying coast in the vicinity, Port Said should be approached with caution.

Approach from NW. From the vicinity of 31°46′N 31°56′E, the track leads SE, passing through a precautionary area and thence through the SE-bound lane of the TSS, passing:

2 NE of Barr el-Dahra (31°30′N 31°57′E), a narrow strip of land separating Buḥeiret El Manzala from the sea, and:

NE of the Bight of Dîba (3.207).

Approach from NE. From the vicinity of 31°47′N 32°36′E, the track leads S then SW within the TSS to the vicinity of 31°35′N 32°21′E.

Thence from the end of either TSS vessels should proceed to the appropriate waiting anchorage (3.218).

North Anchorage (Zone One) to Port Said By-pass

3.239

1 From the anchorage (31°28′N 32°19′E), the track leads initially ESE for about 4½ miles, passing NE of a wreck (31°25′N 32°23′E), with a depth of 10·5 m over it, marked by a light buoy (isolated danger), to a position N of Hm 215 Light Buoys (lateral) (31°26′N 32°24′E), marking the N end of Port Said By-pass Approach Channel.

2 The track then leads SSW for 11¾ miles through a channel, marked by pairs of numbered light buoys (lateral), to Port Said By-pass (31°14′·8N 32°21′E), passing:

ESE of the junction (31°19′·5N 32°22′·3E) with Port Said Harbour Approach Channel, thence:

ESE of El Bahar Tower Light (31°18′·1N 32°21′·6E) (3.236).

3 The entrance to Port Said By-pass is protected by W and E breakwaters extending NNE from the shore for 8 cables and 1¼ miles respectively. A light (metal tower, white band) is exhibited from the head of each breakwater.

North Anchorage (Zone Two) to Port Said By-pass

3.240

1 From the anchorage (31°24′N 32°18′E), the track leads initially ESE for about 3 miles, to join the Port Said By-pass Approach Channel close W of Hm 150 Light Buoy (lateral). The track then leads SSW for 8 miles through a channel, marked by pairs of numbered light buoys (lateral), to Port Said By-pass (31°14′·8N 32°21′E), passing:

2 ESE of the junction (31°19′·5N 32°22′·3E) with Port Said Harbour Approach Channel, thence:

ESE of El Bahar Tower Light (31°18′·1N 32°21′·6E) (3.236).

South Anchorage to Port Said Harbour

3.241

1 From the South Anchorage the track leads initially ESE for a short distance to a position close NNE of Fairway Light Buoy (N cardinal) (31°21′N 32°21′E). The track then leads SSE for 2¼ miles passing:

ENE of Nos 8, 7, and 6 Light Buoys (starboard hand), and:

The track then leads to a position close NW of Hm 83 Light Buoy (N cardinal) at the beginning of the Port Said leading line.

2 **Port Said Leading Lights:**

Front light (triangle on grey metal framework tower, 40 m in height) (31°15′·0N 32°18′·2E).

Rear light (round shape on grey metal framework tower, 54 m in height) (5½ cables SW of front light).

The alignment (217¾°) of these lights leads SW, for 3½ miles, through Port Said Harbour Approach Channel, marked by pairs of numbered light buoys (lateral), passing (with positions from El Bahar Tower Light (31°18′·1N 32°21′·6E)):

3 NW of El Bahar Tower Light (3.236), and:

SE of the prolongation (6 cables NW) of the West Breakwater (3.228), thence:

SE of West Breakwater (1 mile WSW), thence:

NW of the head (2¼ miles SW) of East Breakwater, from where a light (metal framework tower) is exhibited, into the harbour.

It has been reported (2008) that the leading lights were difficult to distinguish from the shore lights and the lights of ships moored on the W side of the harbour.

4 **Caution.** During strong W winds a very strong current flows across the outer part of the channel, and care is necessary to avoid being set on to the bank on the SE side of the channel. In these conditions, if entering without a pilot, mariners are advised to gain the alignment of the leading lights well to seaward of Hm 83 Light Buoy, passing at a speed of about 10 kn, and thence pass close SE of the starboard hand light buoys. When in the lee of West Breakwater, speed may be reduced and the pilot embarked.

Directions for leaving

Port Said Harbour to sea

3.242

1 From the harbour entrance (31°16′·6N 32°19′·8E), with the alignment (217¾°) of the leading lights (3.241), astern, the approach channel should be followed to the vicinity of Hm 83 Light Buoy, 3½ miles NE, where the pilot is disembarked.

2 From this position vessels are required to continue N to the vicinity of 31°30′N 32°22′E, as shown on the chart.

Thence vessels should adjust course as required to join the outbound lane of the appropriate TSS.

Port Said By-pass to sea

3.243

1 From the entrance to Port Said By-pass (31°14′·8N 32°21′E) the fairway of the approach channel should be followed to Hm 80 Light Buoys, 5 miles NNE, where the pilot is disembarked.

2 From this position vessels are required to keep in the approach channel as far as Hm 195 Light Buoys, 6 miles farther NNE, thence continue N to the vicinity of 31°30′N 32°24′E, as shown on the chart.

Thence vessels should adjust course as required to join the outbound lane of the appropriate TSS.

Caution. See 3.235.

Basins and berths

General information

3.244

1 Berths are allocated by the Port Authority.

Moorings

3.245

1 Mooring berths are numbered from the harbour entrance as shown on the plan.

Outer Harbour Basin:

Isolated berths, alongside root of West Breakwater: berths 1I, 2I and 3I; maximum length of vessel 266 m at 3I.

2 North Basin, W of the head of East Breakwater: berths 1A and 2A; maximum length of vessel 252 m at 2A.

Outer Harbour Basin, E side: berths 3A to 8A; no limit to length.

Outer Harbour Basin, W side: berths 1R to 4R; maximum length of vessel 297 m at 4R.

Outer Harbour Basin, SW end: berths 1B to 3B; maximum length of vessel 222 m at 3B.

3 **Ismâîl Basin** (explosives berths):

East side: berths 5B to 7B; maximum length of vessel 182 m at 7B.

West side: berth 6R; length 232 m.

Husein Basin (oil berth):

West side: berth 4E; maximum length of vessel 172 m.

Berths

3.246

1 **Shirîf Basin:** berths for commercial vessels on the SW quay; length 510 m; maximum draught alongside 8·2 m.

Abbas Hilmi Basin:

Container berth: length 345 m; dredged depth of 13·6 m alongside.

RoRo berth at N end of container berth: length 40 m; depth alongside 8·2 m.

Multi-purpose berth (S of container berth): length 250 m; maximum draught 13·6 m.

2 **Fishing harbour.** The fishing harbour, situated at the root of West Breakwater, has depths from 2·1 to 4·3 m and is divided into four basins.

Commercial Basin and Arsenal Basin. These basins, which open from the NW side of Ismâîl Basin, are mostly used by vessels belonging to Suez Canal Authority.

3 **General Workshop Basin.** This basin on the SW side of Central Mole, with charted depths from 2·4 to 6·4 m, is used by Suez Canal Authority for berthing and repairing its floating plant. It is bordered by the authority's workshops, and contains a small floating dock and slipways.

4 **Other basins.** Several small shallow basins, and slipways, are situated on the NW side of Port Fouad. Lateral Basin and Port Fouad Basin front the NW and SW sides of Port Fouad respectively.

Port services

Repairs

3.247

1 Facilities exist for all kinds of repairs to vessels up to 50 000 dwt. There are three floating docks, the largest having a lifting capacity of 25 000 tonnes; length 230 m; breadth 35 m; maximum 50 000 dwt. There are also several slipways and a building yard.

Other facilities

3.248

1 Floating cranes, owned by Suez Canal Authority; lighters and launches; Ship Sanitation Control and Exemption Certificates are issued; hospitals; garbage disposal.

Supplies

3.249

1 Fuel at the fuel berths, by tanker to vessels in the anchorages, or by self-propelled barge to vessels in harbour; fresh water from barge; provisions.

Communications

3.250

1 Cairo International Airport, about 200 km distant.

PORT SAID TO TEL RAFAH

General information

Charts 2573, 2634

Route

3.251

1 From a position in the vicinity of 31°46′N 31°56′E the coastal route follows the recommended track, shown on the chart, for 47 miles E, thence 47 miles ESE to a position 20 miles NNW of El ‘Arîsh. Here the recommended route for El ‘Arîsh traffic leads SSE to a position about 3½ miles NNW of the port whilst the coastal route continues ESE for a further 20 miles to a position NW of Tel Rafah (31°19′N 34°13′E).

Topography

3.252

1 The coast between Port Said (31°16′N 32°19′E) and El ‘Arîsh, 78 miles E, is almost entirely extremely low lying, with many shoals extending up to about 16 miles offshore.

From the vicinity of 31°03′N 32°40′E the coast as far as Kathîb el Qals, 23 miles ENE, consists of a narrow strip of sand separating Sabkhet El-Bardawîl, an extensive salt lake, from the sea. Kathîb el Qals (31°13′N 33°05′E), ancient Casius Mons, is a small but remarkable range of sandhills 58 m high. The coastal strip of sand here is 1 mile wide.

2 The coast between Kathîb el Qals and Rās el-Abid, 18 miles ESE, is a continuation of the narrow and very low strip of sand separating Sabkhet El-Bardawîl from the sea.

Between Rās el-Abid and El ‘Arîsh, 20 miles farther E, the coast is low and sandy. A palm grove is situated 5 miles W, and a conspicuous sandhill 137 m high 8 miles SSW, respectively, of El ‘Arîsh.

3 Between El ‘Arîsh and Tel Rafah, 24 miles ENE, the coast consists of almost bare sandhills from 45 to 60 m high. Close inland there are numerous scattered palm trees and bushes; the mountain ranges inland are visible behind the sandhills. Depths off this stretch of coast are less regular than farther NE.

The coast NE of Tel Rafah is described in Chapter 7.

International boundary

3.253

1 The international boundary between Egypt and Israel in the vicinity of Tel Rafah (31°19′N 34°13′E) has not been finalized.

Marine exploitation

3.254

1 Considerable activity associated with exploration for oil and gas may be encountered in the area covered by this sub-section. Drilling rigs carry numerous lights and all vessels should keep well clear of them.

2 **Caution.** There are several oil and gas production platforms, and pipelines, situated in the approaches to Port Said, which are not charted. For remarks on safety zones and submarine pipelines see 1.7 and 1.8.

Currents

3.255

1 See 3.4.

Offshore dangers

3.256

1 Owing to lack of modern hydrographic data, depths and the positions of shoals within 10 miles of the coast between 32°30′E and 33°30′E must be considered approximate.

Depths of 4·4 and 4·7 m lie 13½ miles NNW of Kathîb el Qals (31°13′N 33°05′E), and depths from 8·8 to 10·0 m lie within 3½ miles WNW of these depths.

2 Numerous and extensive shoals with depths from 3·7 to 11·0 m are charted within a radius of 11 miles of Kathîb el Qals; reports received in 1925 and 1944 indicate that in these areas there is less water than is charted. An obstruction was reported in 1914 to lie 3 miles NNW of Kathîb el Qals.

The coast in the vicinity of Kathîb el Qals should be approached with caution.

Caution

3.257

1 Along this part of the Egyptian coast proceed with the greatest caution, particularly in autumn and winter when N to W winds sometimes blow hard.

During fog, sounding is essential; in general, keep in depths of more than 20 m, but between the meridians of 33°00′E and 33°20′E, where the 20 m depth contour lies close to shoal water, keep in depths of more than 40 m.

Directions
(continued from 3.172)

Principal marks
3.258

1 **Landmarks:**

For landmarks in the vicinity of Port Said see 3.236.

Minaret (31°07′·5N 33°47′·8E) at El 'Arîsh.

El-Thamila (30°54′·3N 33°44′·5E), a hill with an elevation of 363 m.

2 **Major lights:**

El Bahar Tower Light (31°18′·1N 32°21′·6E) (3.236).

Port Said Light (31°16′·3N 32°17′·6E) (3.236).

El 'Arîsh Light (white concrete tower with black bands) (31°08′·7N 33°48′·9E).

Other aids to navigation
3.259

1 **Racons:**

Port Said (31°16′·3N 32°17′·6E).

El Bahar Tower (31°18′·1N 32°21′·6E).

El 'Arîsh (31°08′·7N 33°48′·9E).

For details see *Admiralty List of Radio Signals Volume 2.*

Port Said to Tel Rafah
3.260

1 From a position in the vicinity of 31°46′N 31°56′E, the track follows the recommended route leading E, passing (with positions from El Bahar Tower Light (31°18′·1N 32°21′·6E)):

N of the precautionary area in the NW approaches to Port Said (33 miles NW), thence:

S of the Temsah Gasfield (32 miles NNW), see 3.254, thence:

N of the Wakar Gasfield (25 miles NNW), thence:

2 N of the NE TSS (30 miles NE) and Khalîg el Tîna (17 miles ESE), lying between Port Said and Kathîb el Qals (3.252), 40 miles E; the gulf is shallow, with depths of less than 10 m within 7 miles of its head. A gas pipeline extends from the head of Khalîg el Tîna to the TAO production terminal, 33 miles N. The platform is lit. Further gas pipelines and platforms are located between positions 13 miles W and 15 miles SE of TAO platform.

3 Thence the track leads ESE, passing:

NNE of a shoal (31°31′N 32°55′E) which was reported in 1956 to have a depth of 24 m over it, thence:

NNE of a shoal (31°25′N 32°58′E), with a depth of 4·7 m over it, lying on the edge of shoal water extending NNW of Kathîb el Qals.

4 The track then leads to a position about 20 miles NNW of El 'Arîsh (31°09′N 33°49′E) (3.261) where the recommended route leads SSE to El 'Arîsh and the coastal route continues ESE to a position NW of Tel Rafah (31°19′N 34°13′E), passing:

NNE of two mooring buoys (31°20′N 34°11′E).

Useful mark:

A square ruined fort (31°09′N 32°28′E), 10½ miles SE of Port Said, 9 m high, is identifiable.

(Directions continue, in the reverse direction, for the coast of Israel at 7.313)

El 'Arîsh

Chart 2573 plan of El 'Arîsh Harbour

3.261

1 **General information.** El 'Arîsh (31°09′N 33°49′E) is a small port. The town is situated 1 mile from the coast on low ground on the banks of Wâdi el 'Arîsh, amidst palm trees and sand dunes. Numerous buildings are visible from seaward, and the minaret (3.258) of a mosque is conspicuous.

2 **Limiting conditions:**

Times of arrival and departure. Vessels are not permitted to approach the port until 0600 local time, and must leave one hour before sunset.

Maximum size of vessel handled. Vessels up to 5000 tons can use the port.

Climate information: see 1.184 and 1.194.

3 **Arrival information:**

Waiting anchorage. There is a designated area, radius 1 mile, 2 miles N of the harbour entrance, for vessels awaiting a berth.

Submarine pipeline. A submarine natural gas pipeline extends approximately 98 km NE from a position 13 miles ENE of El 'Arîsh to Ashqelon, Israel (7.312).

Pilots and tugs. Pilotage is compulsory; tugs are available.

4 **Directions.** From seaward the track leads SW on the alignment (213°) of a pair of leading lights (31°08′·7N 33°48′·6E), through a channel, 2 miles long, 100 m wide, with a least charted depth of 7 m, and thence between the heads of two breakwaters into the harbour.

Lights (towers) are exhibited from the heads of the breakwaters.

5 **Berth.** Quay 200 m long; depth alongside of 6·5 m; used for the export of coal from a mine at El Maghara.

Communications. El 'Arîsh is connected to the Egyptian state railway system.

3.262

1 A good landing place in fair weather exists 10 miles ENE of El 'Arîsh (31°09′N 33°49′E), where a small natural harbour is formed by a slight bend in the coast and a few off-lying rocks.

Caution. A dangerous wreck lies 2½ miles N of the landing place, as shown on the chart.

NOTES

Chapter 4 - South Coast of Kríti, south-east coasts of Kásos, Kárpathos and Ródos

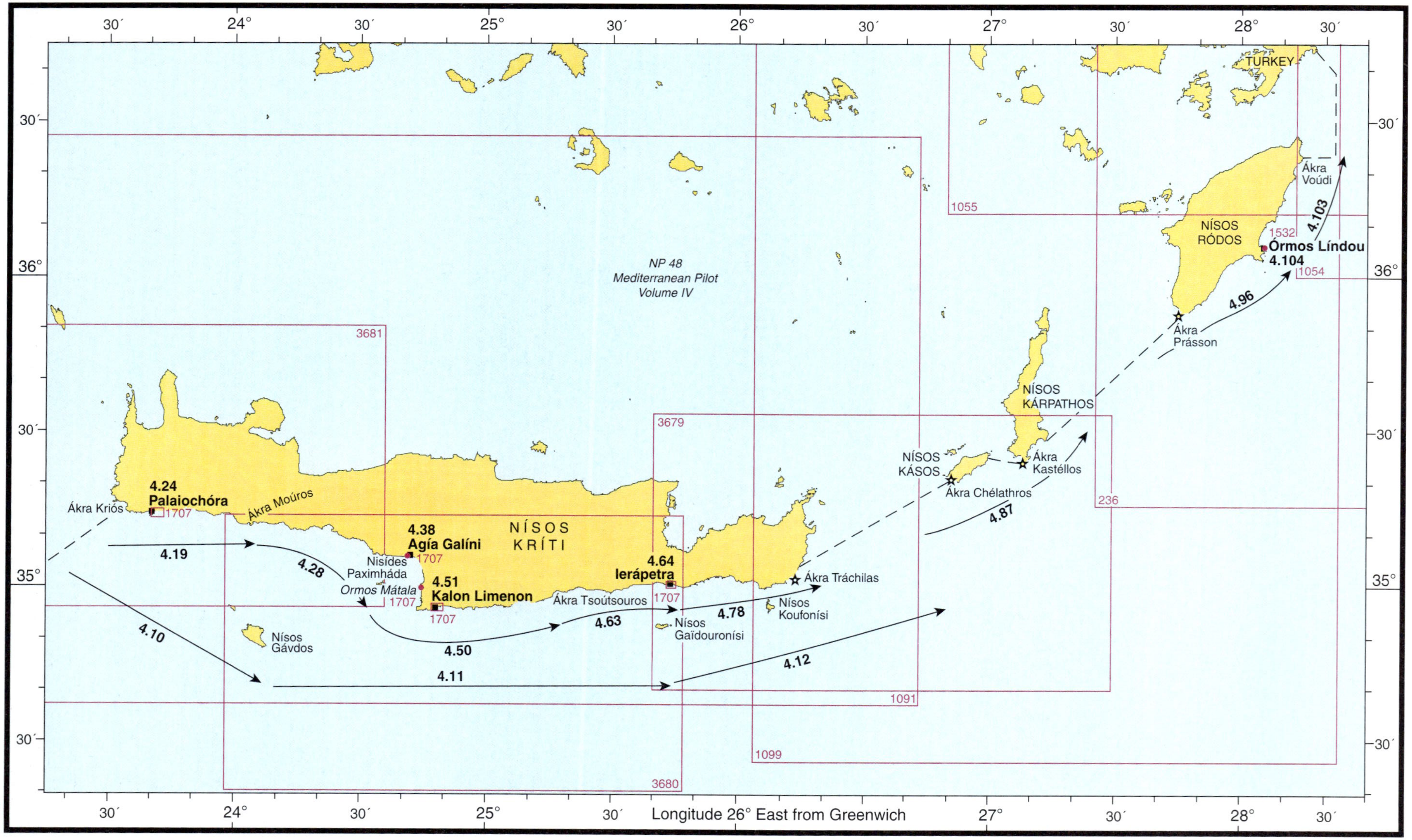

CHAPTER 4

SOUTH COASTS OF GREEK ISLANDS FROM NÍSOS KRÍTI TO NÍSOS RÓDOS — ÁKRA KRIÓS TO ÁKRA VOÚDHI

GENERAL INFORMATION

Chart 183

Scope of the chapter

4.1

1 The area covered by this chapter extends from the vicinity of 35°05′N 23°20′E, off the SW of Nísos Kríti, to that of 36°20′N 28°23′E, in the SE approach to Rhodes Channel, 260 miles ENE.

The chapter comprises the following sections:

South coast of Nísos Kríti (4.3).

Passage SE of Nísos Kásos and Nísos Kárpathos (4.85).

Passage SE of Nísos Ródos (4.91).

2 Stenó Kásou (35°20′N 26°36′E), Stenó Karpáthou (35°55′N 27°30′E) and Rhodes Channel (36°31′N 28°06′E), channels leading into the Aegean Sea from E, are described in *Mediterranean Pilot Volume IV.*

Rescue

4.2

1 For information on rescue see 1.67 and *Admiralty List of Radio Signals Volume 5.*

SOUTH COAST OF NÍSOS KRÍTI

GENERAL INFORMATION

Chart 1091

Area covered

4.3

1 The area covered by this section comprises:

Offshore passage S of Nísos Kríti (4.8).

Coastal route from Ákra Kriós to Ákra Moúros (4.16).

Coastal route from Ákra Moúros to Kólpos Messará (4.25).

2 Kólpos Messará (4.34).

Coastal route from Kólpos Messará to Ákra Tsoútsouros (4.46).

Coastal route from Ákra Tsoútsouros to Ierápetra (4.59).

Coastal passage from Ierápetra to Ákra Tráchilas passing through Stenó Koufonísou (4.73).

Topography

4.4

1 Between Ákra Kriós (35°14′N 23°35′E) and Ákra Tráchilas (35°02′N 26°14′E), about 130 miles E, the S coast of Nísos Kríti is mostly high and precipitous and is backed by an almost continuous range of mountains. The only significant break in the mountains is the isthmus of Ierápetra which extends from the vicinity of Ierápetra (35°00′N 25°44′E) to the head of Kólpos Mirambéllou (7 miles NNE).

The principal groups of mountains are:

2 Levká Óri (35°18′N 24°02′E), meaning White Mountains, which rise sheer from the S coast to elevations of more than 2000 m and dominate the W end of the island. The mountains appear as a broad mass of crests with a serrated outline, bare white rock in summer and snow-covered in winter. Páchnes, the summit, is 2454 m high, but Sóros Griás, 2322 m high and situated 2 miles NE of Páchnes, is more easily distinguished owing to its conical form.

3 Ídi Óros (35°14′N 24°46′E), ancient Mount Ida and also known as Óros Psiloríti, which culminates in three lofty peaks near the middle of the island. Tímios Stavrós, the W peak, has an elevation of 2456 m and is the highest point in Kríti. From SW and S the summit of Ídi Óros appears broad-shaped. Clouds covering the summit portend NW winds in summer and rain in winter.

4 Díkti Óros (35°06′N 25°28′E), also known as Óri Lasithíou, which lies W of the isthmus of Ierápetra. Afféndis Kristós, the highest peak, has an elevation of 2141 m.

Mountains of the Sitía region (35°05′N 25°53′E), consisting of Óros Thriptis and Óros Ornón, which lie E of the isthmus of Ierápetra. Aféndis Kavoúsi, the highest of these mountains, has an elevation of 1476 m.

Radar response

4.5

1 The high and precipitous S coast of Nísos Kríti, and the outlying islands, give a good radar response.

Natural conditions

4.6

1 **Wind and sea.** During the winter, S winds create very rough sea conditions along the entire S coast of Nísos Kríti.

With N winds, strong squalls blow down from the mountains. The squalls often begin suddenly, and close offshore they may be violent.

2 **Currents.** Near the S coast of Nísos Kríti, currents appear to be very weak and variable in direction. However little information is available.

It was reported that in August 1982, during a light WSW wind, the following currents were experienced:

About 6 miles N of Nisída Gavdopoúla (34°56′N 24°00′E), NE-going at a rate of 3½ kn.

About 11 miles NE of Nísos Gávdos (34°50′N 24°04′E), SSE-going at a rate of nearly 3½ kn.

Coastal and offshore shelter

4.7

1 There are no entirely secure ports or anchorages on the S coast of Nísos Kríti. Several bays afford temporary

anchorage during the summer months, or with N winds, but the room available for anchoring is generally limited and the depths increase very rapidly to seaward.

2 The best harbours are:

Galíni (35°06′N 24°41′E) (4.38).

Órmos Kalon Limenon (Kaloí Liménes) (34°56′N 24°48′E) (4.51).

Offshore, the best shelter from N winds is found in the lee of Díkti Óros between Órmos Keratókambos (35°00′N 25°23′E) and Ierápetra, 18 miles E.

OFFSHORE PASSAGE SOUTH OF NÍSOS KRÍTI

General information

Chart 1091

Route

4.8

1 The offshore passage S of Nísos Kríti leads from the vicinity of 35°05′N 23°20′E to that of 35°00′N 26°45′E, about 168 miles E, passing S of the outlying islands.

Directions

Principal marks

4.9

1 **Landmarks:**

Radomes (white) (35°19′N 23°37′E).

Levká Óri (35°18′N 24°02′E) (4.4).

Nísos Gávdos (34°50′N 24°04′E) (4.10).

Ídi Óros (35°14′N 24°46′E) (4.4).

Óros Kófinas (34°58′N 25°05′E) (4.49).

Nísos Gaïdouronísi (34°52′N 25°42′E) (4.11).

Nísos Koufonísi (34°56′N 26°09′E) (4.12).

Charts 1091, 3681, 3680

Ákra Kriós to Nísos Gávdos

4.10

1 From the vicinity of 35′05′N 23°20′E, the track leads SE, passing:

SW of Nisída Gavdopoúla (34°56′N 24°00′E), an islet 113 m high lying 16 miles S of Nísos Kríti. Nisída Gavdopoúla Light (metal framework tower, 4 m in height) is exhibited from the NW extremity of the islet. Thence:

2 SW of Nísos Gávdos (34°50′N 24°04′E), ancient Clauda, a small island. The SW side of the island consists of high cliffs rising to a peak 368 m high (345 m high on chart 3680). The N part of the island, terminating in Ákra Lakonísi, is low and shelving. Ákra Tripití, the termination of the high cliffs at the S point of the island, is remarkable for three natural arches. Nísos Gávdos Light (white metal framework tower, 6 m in height) is exhibited from Ákra Tripití.

The track then leads to a position S of Nísos Gávdos.

Chart 3680

Nísos Gávdos to Nísos Gaïdouronísi

4.11

1 From a position S of Nísos Gávdos (34°50′N 24°04′E) the track leads E, passing:

S of Ákra Lítinos (34°55′N 24°44′E) (Ákra Líthinon on chart 3680) (4.50), thence:

S of Megalonísi (4.50), 3¼ miles E of Ákra Lítinos.

2 The track then leads to a position S of Nísos Gaïdouronísi (34°52′N 25°42′E), a small uninhabited island, generally low and with a small summit 27 m high at its NE end. Although a light (4.63) is exhibited from the N side of the island it is obscured to the S. Mikronísi, a conical islet 16 m high, lies 5 cables E of the island. About 2½ miles SSE of Mikronísi, near the edge of the coastal bank, a depth of 16 m was reported in 1955.

Chart 3679

Nísos Gaïdouronísi to Stenó Kásou

4.12

1 From a position S of Nísos Gaïdouronísi the track then leads ENE, passing:

SSE of Nísos Koufonísi (34°56′N 26°09′E), a small island 64 m high, remarkable for its high white cliffs which are unlike any others in the locality. Koufonísi Light (metal framework, 5 m in height) is exhibited from near the summit of the island. Nísos Koufonísi is surrounded by rocks, islets and reefs, and close approach to it is extremely dangerous. Thence:

2 SSE of Nisídes Kaválloi (35°02′N 26°14′E) (4.78), lying about 5 cables S of Ákra Tráchilas. A light (4.78) is exhibited from Nisídes Kaválloi.

The track then leads to the vicinity of 35°00′N 26°45′E, at the S end of Stenó Kásou.

(Directions for the coastal route SE of Nísos Kásos and Nísos Kárpathos are given at 4.87)

(Directions for the passage through Stenó Kásou are given in Mediterranean Pilot Volume IV)

Passage between Nísos Gávdos and Nisída Gavdopoúla

Chart 3680

4.13

1 If passing between Nísos Gávdos (34°50′N 24°04′E) (4.10) and Nisída Gavdopoúla, 4 miles NW, it should be noted that a dangerous rock lies 7 cables N of Gaïdouronísi, the N of two rocky islets situated on a reef extending about 1¼ miles from Ákra Lakonísi.

Anchorages

Nísos Gávdos

4.14

1 **Local knowledge** is required.

Anchorage. Nísos Gávdos (34°50′N 24°04′E) (4.10) affords temporary anchorage in suitable conditions as follows:

Off Órmos Korés, on the E side of the island, in depths from 20 to 40 m, firm sand and mud. The bay is free from dangers except for a partly submerged wreck in the S part.

Off the SE side of the island, E of Ákra Tripití, in a depth of 25 m.

2 **Landing places.** In suitable conditions landing can be effected in Órmos Korés, close S of Ákra Boúta where there is a small pier. A track leads to the village of Kastríous in the centre of the island. In summer it is possible to land near a cluster of houses on the NW coast, between Ákra Padouráki and Ákra Lakonísi, 1½ miles NE.

Communications. There is an occasional ferry service to Palaiochóra (4.24).

Charts 3679, 3680

Nísos Gaïdouronísi

4.15

1 Nísos Gaïdouronísi (34°52′N 25°42′E) (4.11) provides shelter from both N and S winds. Depending on the wind,

temporary anchorage may be obtained on the coastal bank either S or N of the island.

With S winds the best berth is in a depth of 15 m, about 6 cables NNW of Mikronísi (4.11), with the summit of the islet bearing 158° and the NE extremity of Nísos Gaïdouronísi bearing 221°; the bottom is fine sand and with sufficient cable out the holding is good.

2 In a SE or S gale it is advisable to anchor off the N side of Nísos Gaïdouronísi, not less than 5 cables offshore, in depths from 18 to 22 m, clean white sand. It is necessary to be prepared to weigh anchor as soon as the wind veers to W or NW, when shelter may be obtained off the S side of the island.

COASTAL ROUTE FROM ÁKRA KRIÓS TO ÁKRA MOÚROS

General information

Chart 3681

Route

4.16

1 From the vicinity of 35°05′N 23°20′E, SW of Ákra Kriós, the coastal route leads E, for about 37 miles, to a position 6½ miles S of Ákra Moúros (35°12′N 24°04′E).

Topography

4.17

1 Between Ákra Flomés (35°14′N 23°46′E) and Ákra Moúros, 15 miles E, lofty ridges descend abruptly to the coast from the bold and bare peaks of Levká Óri (4.4). The middle and lower slopes are covered in places with forests of stunted fir and cypress trees.

Directions

Principal marks

4.18

1 **Landmarks:**

Radar domes (two conspicuous white domes) (35°19′N 23°37′E).

Church (35°15′N 23°48′E), at the village of Soúyia.

Tower (conspicuous ruin) (35°14′N 23°58′E), standing close W of the mouth of Farángi Samarias, a remarkable gorge which extends inland from the head of Órmos Ágios Roúmelis.

Ákra Kriós to Ákra Moúros

4.19

1 From the vicinity of 35°05′N 23°20′E the track leads E, passing (with positions from Ákra Flomés (35°14′N 23°46′E)):

S of Ákra Kriós (8½ miles W), a bold headland. The cape is said to resemble a ram's forehead, but it is only 127 m high and not remarkable. Thence:

S of Ákra Tráchalo (6¼ miles W), a small promontory fringed by rocks and reefs, and with a sandy cove close W, thence:

2 S of Nisída Schistó (4½ miles W), an islet 12 m high lying close off the SW extremity of Chersónisos Sélino Kastélli, a low flat peninsula with steep cliff-like sides. Nisída Schistó Light (white pyramid with gallery, 5 m in height) is exhibited from the N side of the islet. A ruined Venetian fort stands on Chersónisos Sélino Kastélli. Thence:

S of Ákra Dialiskári (2 miles WNW), thence:

3 S of Ákra Flomés (35°14′N 23°46′E), a high precipitous headland, thence:

S of Ákra Mávro Moúri (1 mile E), a precipitous headland with a prominent cave at its base, thence:

S of Ákra Kalotrivídis (7¾ miles E), thence:

N of Nisída Gavdopoúla (34°56′N 24°00′E) (4.10).

The track then leads to a position about 6½ miles S of Ákra Moúros (15¼ miles ESE), the extremity of a small peninsula.

4.20

1 **Useful marks:**

Elafónisos Light (35°16′N 23°32′E) (see *Mediterranean Pilot Volume IV*).

Ákra Tripití (35°14′N 23°52′E), a high headland on which a chapel stands at an elevation of 406 m.

(Directions continue for the coastal route at 4.28)

Anchorages

Órmos Krioú Chalíkia

4.21

1 Órmos Krioú Chalíkia (35°14′N 23°36′E), a small bay close E of Ákra Kriós (4.19), affords temporary shelter during N winds although violent gusts and squalls are frequent. A dark rock lies 1¼ cables off the W entrance point. The NE shore of the bay is sandy.

Órmos Soúyias

4.22

1 Vessels may anchor in Órmos Soúyias (35°15′N 23°49′E), but it affords no shelter from N winds which blow with considerable strength in the vicinity and make it almost impossible for vessels to remain at anchor in the bay.

A light is exhibited in the NW part of the bay, close S of the church (4.18).

Órmos Foinikiás

4.23

1 Órmos Foinikiás (35°12′N 24°04′E), though seldom used, is a better anchorage than Órmos Loutró (4.29) during strong N winds. A good berth is about 2 cables offshore in the E part of the bay, in a depth of 13 m, sand, as shown on the chart.

Minor harbour

Chart 1707, plan of Agkyrovólia Palaiochóras

Palaiochóra

4.24

1 **Description.** Palaiochóra (35°14′N 23°41′E), formerly known as Sélino Kastélli, is a village situated on the E side of a low isthmus connecting Chersónisos Sélino Kastélli to the mainland.

2 **Water levels.** N winds cause the sea level to fall by up to 0·3 m, while S winds raise the sea level by up to 0·3 m.

Current. A W current of up to 3 kn has been observed, which changes direction according to the prevailing winds.

3 **Harbour.** A harbour, 250 m by 350 m, lies to the SW of the village; the entrance is 40 m wide and faces E.

Useful marks (positioned from Nisída Schistó Light (35°13′·4N 23°40′·3E)):

Panayía church (conspicuous white building with red dome) (7 cables NE).

Spire (conspicuous) (1 mile NE), standing in a cemetery.

4 **Anchorages.** Bays on each side of Chersónisos Sélino Kastélli, afford temporary anchorage during strong N winds but the shelter is not as good as that in Órmos Vrouleá (35°15′N 23°33′E) (see *Mediterranean Pilot Volume IV*). Caution is necessary as sudden violent gusts are frequent,

and squalls of exceptional force can blow up. The bays are exposed to the full force of S gales which occur in winter.

5 The W bay is the better anchorage and is recommended if taking temporary shelter from a N gale. Changes in wind directions must be guarded against.

The E bay is preferable in summer as it is sheltered from W winds. A good berth for small vessels during N winds is in a depth of 15 m, sand, about 1¼ miles ENE of Panayía church, abreast a rocky point, as shown on the plan.

6 **Directions.** Approach the harbour from E and keep close to the S breakwater to avoid underwater rocks lying close to the N breakwater. Depths in the entrance 2·8 m.

Berths. A quay, 50 m long, with depths alongside of 1·1 to 2·3 m, is located ½ cable NE of Panayía church; the E part of the quay ends in a jetty 18 m long and 8 m wide. A quay extends 1½ cables NNE from the root of the jetty.

7 Palaiochóra harbour is quayed on all sides; two jetties, one **T**-shaped, extend from the N shore. Depths in the harbour 2·1 to 3·8 m.

Supplies: fuel by tanker; fresh water and provisions.

Communications: occasional ferry service to Nísos Gávdos (34°50′N 24°04′E) (4.10) and Nisída Elafónisos (35°16′N 23°32′E) (see *Mediterranean Pilot Volume IV*), as well as Soúyia (4.18), Ágia Roumeli (35°14′N 23°58·E) and Chóra Sfakion (4.30); bus to Chaniá.

COASTAL ROUTE FROM ÁKRA MOÚROS TO KÓLPOS MESSARÁ

General information

Chart 3680

Route

4.25

1 From a position about 6½ miles S of Ákra Moúros (35°12′N 24°04′E) the coastal route leads E for about 16 miles, thence SE for about 10 miles, to a position SW of Nisídes Paximádia (35°00′N 24°35′E), situated in the approaches to Kólpos Messará.

Topography

4.26

1 The mountains backing the coast between Ákra Moúros (35°12′N 24°04′E) and Ákra Mélissa, 25 miles ESE, are lower and less precipitous than Levká Óri (4.4) to the W.

Several steep-sided valleys extend inland from the heads of bays.

Local winds

4.27

1 During strong N winds violent squalls blow down the valleys to the coast.

Directions

(continued from 4.20)

4.28

1 From a position about 6½ miles S of Ákra Moúros the track leads E and SE, passing (with positions given from Ákra Ágios Kiriakís (35°12′N 24°09′E)):

S of Ákra Ágios Kiriakís, a steeply sloping projection, thence:

2 S of Ákra Frangokástello (4½ miles E), a low projection which derives its name from a Venetian fort built on it in 1371; the ruins of the fort are prominent. Katonísi, close S of Ákra Frangokástello, is 1 m high and the largest of a group of above-water rocks lying on a reef which extends 4 cables SE of the cape. Thence:

S of Ákra Stavrós (10½ miles E), a rocky headland 402 m high. Thence:

3 To a position S of Ákra Kakómouri (12½ miles E), a rocky projection 207 m high.

The track then leads SE, passing:

SW of Ákra Mélissa (35°06′N 24°34′E), the W entrance point of Kólpos Messará (4.34).

Thence the track leads to a position SW of Nisídes Paximádia (35°00′N 24°35′E), two rocky islets; the W islet is 252 m high, the E is 166 m high. There is deep water all round the islets, but the narrow channel between them is encumbered with rocks.

4 **Useful marks:**

Chóra Sfakíon (35°12′N 24°08′E) (4.30).

Monastery (35°13′·1N 24°12′·1E) (not charted), standing 3 miles ENE of Ákra Ágios Kiriakís at an elevation of about 500 m.

Church (conspicuous) (35°11′N 24°25′E).

Monastery (white buildings) (35°09′N 24°27′E).

Church (conspicuous pale red building) (35°09′N 24°29′E).

(Directions for Kólpos Messará are given at 4.37)

(Directions for the coastal route continue at 4.49)

Anchorages and harbours

Órmos Loutró

4.29

1 **Description.** Órmos Loutró (35°12′N 24°05′E), lying close S of the highest part of Levká Óri (4.4), is considered to be one of the most sheltered anchorages off the S coast of Nísos Kríti. The full force of S winds is not felt in the bay, and the swell which enters is not heavy. The most dangerous winds in winter are N gales, which blow down from the mountains in fierce squalls. Violent wind eddies may be experienced in the entrance to the bay which lies between Nisída Loutró (35°11′·8N 24°05′·0E) and Ákra Stavrós (not named on chart 3680), 7½ cables farther ENE.

The village of Loutró is situated behind a narrow strip of shingle beach at the NW corner of the bay.

2 **Useful mark:**

Nisída Loutró Light (metal framework, 4 m in height) (35°11′·8N 24°05′·0E), exhibited from the NE end of Nisída Loutró, a small islet 11 m high lying close off the W entrance point of Órmos Loutró.

3 **Anchorage.** The bottom is mostly sand, with sand and gravel in parts. It is inadvisable to anchor in the middle of the bay, where the depths are greater than 35 m, owing to the violent wind eddies liable to be experienced there. The W corner of the bay provides the best shelter, but local knowledge is necessary. Small vessels may anchor N of Nisída Loutró in depths from 27 to 37 m, or closer inshore in about 18 m.

Órmos Sfakíon

4.30

1 **Description.** Órmos Sfakíon (35°12′N 24°08′E) is entered between Ákra Ágios Kiriakís (4.28) and a point 1 mile WNW. Apart from a small sandy beach at the head of the bay, the shores are fringed by dangerous rocks. Chóra Sfakíon, the white buildings of which are visible from a considerable distance, is situated at the head of the bay. The village has a population of about 400 and is a popular holiday resort during the summer; a harbour fronts the village.

2 **Useful marks:**

Chóra Sfakíon Light (metal framework tower with gallery, red band) (35°12′·1N 24°08′·1E), exhibited from the head of the mole.

3 **Anchorage.** Temporary anchorage in a depth of 24 m, sand and weed, may be obtained 2 cables S of Vráchoi Trís Volákous, three above-water rocks lying 1 cable SW of the promontory fronting Chóra Sfakíon.

4 **Chóra Sfakíon.** A small semicircular harbour, protected from the SW by an angled mole, fronts the village; a light is exhibited from the head of the mole. From a position 130 m SE of the head of the mole is a jetty 12 m long and 10 m wide, a ramp is located on the jetty. Depths within the harbour are less than 3 m.

5 **Cautions.** Above and below-water rocks are located near the shore of the harbour. Submarine cables run from the E shore of the harbour close by the head of the mole in a W direction. Anchoring and fishing are prohibited on either side of the cables.

Mávri Limnióna

4.31

1 **Description.** Mávri Limnióna (35°11′·9N 24°08′·3E) is located 1½ cables SE of Chóra Sfakíon. The harbour is semicircular in shape and a mole extends 1 cable NW from the SW corner of the bay; the head of the mole forms an entrance 80 m wide from the N shore. A jetty is under construction (2007) near the N extremity of the harbour.

Ákra Frangokástello

4.32

1 Temporary anchorage may be obtained in the vicinity of Ákra Frangokástello (35°11′N 24°14′E) (4.28) as follows:

In a bay W of the point.

In a bay E of the point.

Local knowledge is necessary.

2 **Harbour.** The small harbour of Frangokástellos is located near the W part of the bay. It is protected to the SW by a mole extending 115 m SE from Ákra Frangokástello; a short distance E of the root of the mole is a ramp.

Órmos Pláka

4.33

1 Órmos Pláka (35°11′N 24°23′E), entered between Ákra Stavrós (4.28) and Ákra Kakómouri, affords temporary anchorage. The bay is not a good anchorage as it is open S, and N winds blow down from the mountains with exceptional strength. The E side of the bay is sandy with depths of 10 m about 4 cables offshore.

KÓLPOS MESSARÁ

General information

Chart 3680

Description

4.34

1 Kólpos Messará (35°03′N 24°43′E) is a gulf, entered between Ákra Mélissa and Ákra Lítinos (Ákra Líthinon on chart 3680), 14 miles SE. The small port of Agía Galíni (35°06′N 24°41′E) (4.38) is situated on the N side of the gulf. There are no known dangers other than those charted close to the shore.

Topography

4.35

1 The coast on the N side of Kólpos Messará, from Ákra Mélissa to Ákra Kakóskalo, 8 miles E, is for the most part high and precipitous with Ídi Óros (4.4) lying about 8 miles inland from the head of the gulf. A valley, through which Plótis Potámos flows to the sea, extends N from the vicinity of Agía Galíni.

2 From Ákra Kakóskalo the coast is low and sandy for 5 miles S and is backed by an extensive plain through which Gero-Potámos flows to the sea. Numerous glass houses sometimes give the locality the appearance of a large lake.

3 From the vicinity of Órmos Mátala (35°00′N 24°45′E) to Ákra Lítinos, 4½ miles S, the coast consists of low white cliffs backed by Asteroúsia Óros (4.47) extending E.

Natural conditions

4.36

1 **Squalls.** The squalls (4.6) which blow down from the mountains during N winds are exceptionally strong in Kólpos Messará.

Sea conditions. Winds from W, or the sea breeze, often raise a heavy sea in the gulf.

2 **Weather portents:**

A fleecy bank of white clouds enveloping Tímios Stavrós (35°14′N 24°46′E) (4.4), and some of the neighbouring peaks, portends and accompanies N gales.

Cloud on the W part of Vouvála (35°07′N 24°38′E), a mountain 947 m high, portends SW winds.

Cloud above Ákra Lítinos (34°56′N 24°44′E) portends S winds.

Directions

4.37

1 Kólpos Messará may be approached from W, passing between Ákra Mélissa (35°06′N 24°34′E) and Nisídes Paximádia (4.28), 5¾ miles S, or from the S, passing W of Ákra Lítinos (34°56′N 24°44′E) and thence E of Nisídes Paximádia.

The chart is sufficient guide for navigation within the gulf.

2 **Useful mark:**

Ákra Lítinos Light (34°55′N 24°44′E) (4.50).

Agía Galíni

Chart 1707, plan of Agía Galíni

General information

4.38

1 **Description.** Agía Galíni (35°06′N 24°41′E) is a small port with an open anchorage and an artificial harbour. The harbour is protected from all winds, and during the summer it affords the best shelter for small vessels on the S coast of Nísos Kríti. The village stands on rising ground behind the harbour and is a holiday resort.

2 **Function.** The harbour was built in 1953 to serve the fertile Pediás Messará, but most of the produce of the region is now conveyed to Iráklion (1.90) by road and the harbour is little used commercially.

3 **Water levels.** N winds cause the sea level to fall by up to 0·4–0·5 m, while SSW winds raise the sea level by up to 0·7 m.

Current. A current of between 1 to 1·5 kn has been observed; the direction depends on the prevailing winds.

Arrival information

4.39

1 **Anchorage.** Good anchorage may be obtained outside the harbour as follows:

In a depth of 10 m, with the head of the mole bearing 349°, distance 200 m.

See caution at 4.43.

Harbour

4.40

1 The harbour is formed by a high mole projecting ESE from the shore for 140 m, thence NE for 170 m; a light (framework tower, red band, with gallery, 6 m in height) is exhibited from the head of the mole. From the root of the mole a broad quay extends NE for 95 m with a ramp at its NE extremity.

Berths

4.41

1 Mole (ESE arm, 140 m length): depths alongside vary from 2·1 to 4·2 m.

Broad quay: depths alongside vary from 2·1 to 2·7 m.

Ramp: charted depth alongside 3 m.

Port services

4.42

1 **Facilities:** customs, post office, rural surgery and pharmacies.

Supplies: fresh water; fuel is available from a tank by the quay as well as from vehicles; provisions in limited quantities.

Anchorages

Chart 3680

Caution

4.43

1 Vessels at anchor in Kólpos Messará should put to sea without delay on warning of a N gale. Shelter from N gales may be obtained in Órmos Kalon Limenon (34°56′N 24°48′E) (4.51). Boats unable to reach Órmos Kalon Limenon may obtain shelter in the lee of Nisídes Paximádia (35°00′N 24°35′E) (4.28).

East side of Kólpos Messará

4.44

1 **Description.** The E side of Kólpos Messará, off the sandy beach extending S from Ákra Kakóskalo (35°05′N 24°44′E), affords the best anchorage in the gulf. Depths decrease gradually from 30 m at 1 mile offshore to 10 m at 5 cables offshore; the bottom is firm sand. The wreckage of an aircraft, with a depth of 4 m over it, is charted about 3 cables offshore abreast the mouth of Gero-Potámos.

2 **Useful marks:**

A light (metal framework tower with gallery, red band) (35°04′·8N 24°44′·2E) exhibited from the head of the W mole at Kókkinos Pírgos.

A light (metal framework tower with gallery, green band) (35°04′·9N 24°44′·3E) exhibited from the head of the E mole at Kókkinos Pírgos.

3 **Landing place.** A fishing shelter, suitable for use in favourable weather, is situated at Kókkinos Pírgos, formerly a small port, close E of Ákra Kakóskalo. The shelter is protected by two moles; its entrance faces S and is about 70 m wide.

4 **Town.** Timbákion is situated 1¾ miles ESE of Ákra Kakóskalo on the road from Agía Galíni (4.38).

Caution. A fish farm marked by 4 light buoys (special) is located 1¼ miles SW of Kókkinos Pírgos Light.

Charts 1707 plan of Órmos Mátala, 3680

Órmos Mátala

4.45

1 **Description.** Órmos Mátala (35°00′N 24°45′E) is a small natural harbour which may be identified by white cliffs on the N side of the entrance. The cliffs on the N side of the bay are 45 m high and those on the S side are 13 m high. The head of the bay is sandy.

2 **Historical note.** Mátala was a port from early Roman until Byzantine times. Numerous cave-dwellings are cut in the cliffs on each side of the bay, but some are now as much as 4·5 m below sea level owing to the subsidence of this part of the coast.

3 **Anchorage.** Órmos Mátala affords good temporary anchorage, but is exposed to the sea breeze and is subject to squalls during strong N winds; see caution at 4.43. Recommended berths are:

In a depth of 25 m, fine sand, with the N entrance point bearing 100°, distance 4 cables.

4 In a depth of 17 m, fine sand, suitable for small vessels, with the N entrance point bearing 080°, distance 2 cables.

In depths of less than 5 m, sand, off the sandy beach at the head of the bay taking care to avoid a rocky area lying about 40 m off the beach.

5 **Landing place.** A natural landing place with depths alongside of nearly 1·8 m, and with steps cut in the rock, is situated on the S side of the bay.

Supplies: provisions in limited quantities at Mátala, a village on the SE side of the bay.

COASTAL ROUTE FROM KÓLPOS MESSARÁ TO ÁKRA TSOÚTSOUROS

General information

Chart 3680

Route

4.46

1 From a position SW of Nisídes Paximádia (35°00′N 24°35′E), situated in the approaches to Kólpos Messará, the coastal route leads SE for 9 miles to a position about 4 miles SW of Ákra Lítinos (34°55′N 24°44′E) (Ákra Líthinon on chart 3680), thence E for 30 miles to a position about 5 miles S of Ákra Tsoútsouros (34°58′N 25°16′E).

Topography

4.47

1 Asteroúsia Óros, a mountain range, lies parallel to the coast between Ákra Lítinos (34°55′N 24°44′E) and Ákra Tsoútsouros, 27 miles E.

Local winds

4.48

1 Off the coast between Ákra Lítinos and Ákra Tsoútsouros the N winds of summer are not steady and gust more violently than in the lee of Díkti Óros (4.4) to the E.

Directions

(continued from 4.28)

Principal mark

4.49

1 **Landmark:**

Óros Kófinas (34°58′N 25°05′E), the summit of Asteroúsia Óros, which is 1231 m high and terminates in a remarkable pointed crag.

Kólpos Messará to Ákra Tsoútsouros

4.50

1 From a position SW of Nisídes Paximádia (35°00′N 24°35′E) the track leads SE and E, passing (with positions from Ákra Lítinos (34°55′N 24°44′E)):

SW and S of Ákra Lítinos (Ákra Líthinon on Chart 3680), a bold cliff-faced headland forming the W termination of Asteroúsia Óros. Ákra Lítinos Light (metal framework, 3 m in height) is exhibited from the point. Thence:

2 S of Nisída Papadóplaka (2¾ miles E), a small islet lying 2½ cables offshore, thence:

S of Megalonísi (3¼ miles E), an islet 59 m high. Megalonísi Light (white pyramid with gallery, 6 m in height) is exhibited from the summit of the islet. Thence:

S of Ákra Kefála (9¼ miles E), a prominent headland which from certain directions has the appearance of a crouching lion, thence:

3 S of Ákra Tráfoulas (11¼ miles E), the E entrance point of Órmos Léndas (4.58), thence:

S of Ákra Martélos (34°56′N 25°06′E), a high headland, thence:

S of Ákra Alikapóritha (34°57′N 25°11′E), which forms the SE side of Órmos Vála.

The track then leads to a position about 5 miles S of Ákra Tsoútsouros (34°58′N 25°16′E).

4 **Useful marks:**

Nisída Ágios Pávlos (34°56′N 24°48′E) (4.55).

Church (conspicuous) (34°56′N 24°54′E).

Church (conspicuous) (34°56′N 24°56′E).

Monastery (34°56′N 25°05′E), standing among pine woods and fronted by two large rocks.

Church (conspicuous) (34°57′N 25°08′E).

(Directions for the coastal route continue at 4.62)

Órmos Kalon Limenon (Kaloí Liménes)

Chart 1707, plan of Órmos Kalon Limenon

General information

4.51

1 **Position.** Órmos Kalon Limenon (34°56′N 24°48′E), situated midway along the S coast of Nísos Kríti, is entered between Ákra Ágios Pávlos and Nisída Tráfos, 1¼ miles ENE.

Function. The harbour is used for bunkering ships from storage tanks, managed by SEKA SA, Piraeus, situated on Nisída Ágios Pávlos. There is a small settlement on the N side of the harbour.

2 **History.** Órmos Kalon Limenon is the 'fair havens' from which Saint Paul sailed prior to being shipwrecked on Malta in AD 59. The ancient town of Lasaía stood near the NE entrance point of the bay; the remains of a mole lie between Nisída Tráfos and a sandy promontory close N.

3 **Port Authority.** Kalon Limenon Port Authority, GR–700 09 Kalon Limenon, Iráklion, Kríti, Greece.

Limiting conditions

4.52

1 **Maximum size of vessel handled.** The bunkering station accommodates ships drawing up to 13·5 m; there is no restriction on vessel's length.

Arrival information

4.53

1 **Notice of ETA:** 48 hours.

Outer anchorage. Recommended berths:

In a depth of 62 m, sand, with Nisída Tráfos bearing 000°, distance 5 cables; suitable for large vessels.

In depths from 11 to 30 m, sand, between Nisída Ágios Pávlos and Mavronísi, 3 cables NNE.

2 **Prohibited anchorage.** Owing to the presence of submarine cables and pipelines, anchoring is prohibited between Nisída Ágios Pávlos and the coast NW, as shown on the chart.

For information on pipelines see 1.8 and for submarine cables see 1.26.

3 **Pilotage** is compulsory for vessels berthing at the oil fuel station; a pilot is available at all times. The boarding place is about 1 mile SE of Nisída Ágios Pávlos.

For details see *Admiralty List of Radio Signals Volume 6 (3).*

Tug is available.

Harbour

4.54

1 Órmos Kalon Limenon is a large bay, encumbered on its N and E sides by islets and dangerous rocks. The W corner of the bay forms a natural harbour protected by Nisída Ágios Pávlos, on the N side of which are situated bunkering berths.

2 The W part of Órmos Kalon Limenon affords good shelter from winds between SW and N; during N winds, when violent gusts and squalls may be experienced elsewhere on the coast, there is often only a moderate and steady breeze in this part of the bay.

Directions

4.55

1 The main approach to Órmos Kalon Limenon should be made from the SE, the chart being sufficient guide.

For smaller vessels, approaching from the W, it is possible to pass either S or N of Nisída Papadóplaka (34°55′N 24°47′E) (4.50); a bank with a depth over it of 7 m extends about 1 cable W of the islet, and an 11 m patch lies ¾ cable N. It is usual to pass S of Megalonísi (4.50), as a shoal, with a depth of 4·7 m over it, lies in the middle of the fairway N of the island.

2 **Useful marks** (positioned from Megalonísi Light (34°55′N 24°48′E)):

Ágios Pávlos church (3 cables N).

Nisída Ágios Pávlos (3½ cables NE), an islet 28 m high. Several conspicuous white oil storage tanks stand on the islet and give it the appearance of a fort when viewed from a distance.

3 Settlement (white buildings) (5½ cables NNE).

Mavronísi (8 cables NE), a steep-sided black rock 11 m high.

Cliff (triangular-shaped) (1¼ miles NE), situated close E of a valley.
Nisída Tráfos, an islet 22 m high, 4 cables E of the cliff.

Berths

4.56

1 **Berths.** Three **T**-headed piers project about 50 m from the N side of Nisída Ágios Pávlos. Ships usually berth port side to. Depending on the berth, the offshore anchor may be let go to facilitate departure.

Mooring. A mooring buoy for the use of harbour craft lies about 1½ cables NW of Nisída Ágios Pávlos.

Port services

4.57

1 **Facilities:** fuel barges; customs; medical.

Supplies: fresh water; fuel oil, all grades; provisions and stores, subject to 48 hours notice.

Communications: air services from Iráklion airport, 80 km NE.

Anchorage

Chart 3680

Órmos Léndas

4.58

1 Órmos Léndas (Léntas) (34°56′N 24°56′E) affords only temporary shelter. The anchorage, in the outer part of a small cove at the NW corner of the bay, has a depth of 5 m and is sheltered from W although the sea can be rather disturbed.

2 The small village of Léndas is situated at the head of the cove near the conspicuous church. A fisherman's refuge is located at the NE head of the bay. Lights mark the entrance. Nearby are the ruins of Lebina, the principal port of Gortyna, the Minoan city which was situated on Pediás Messará, 8 miles NNE.

Local knowledge is required.

COASTAL ROUTE FROM ÁKRA TSOÚTSOUROS TO IERÁPETRA

General information

Chart 3680

Route

4.59

1 From a position about 5 miles S of Ákra Tsoútsouros (34°58′N 25°16′E) the coastal route leads ENE, for 24 miles, to a position SSE of Ierápetra (35°00′N 25°44′E).

Topography

4.60

1 A gap in the mountains N of Órmos Tsoútsouros (34°59′N 25°17′E) forms the divide between Asteroúsia Óros (4.47), to the W, and Díkti Óros (4.4), which backs the coast as far as the isthmus of Ierápetra, about 20 miles E.

Local winds

4.61

1 During N winds it is usually calm for 5 or 6 miles offshore in the lee of Díkti Óros, with a steady breeze farther offshore.

Directions

(continued from 4.50)

Principal marks

4.62

1 **Landmarks:**

School (conspicuous) (35°00′N 25°35′E).
Nísos Gaïdouronísi (34°52′N 25°42′E) (4.11).

Ákra Tsoútsouros to Ierápetra

4.63

1 From a position about 5 miles S of Ákra Tsoútsouros (34°58′N 25°16′E) the track leads ENE, passing (with positions from Ákra Theófilos (34°59′N 25°30′E)):

SSE of Ákra Peristeriónas (4¼ miles W); a rock awash lies close S of the point. Thence:
SSE of Árvis monastery (2½ miles W), a small harbour and fisherman's refuge are situated nearby. Thence:
SSE of Ákra Theófilos, a salient point. Ákra Theófilos Light (white round hut with metal framework, 5 m in height) is exhibited from the point. Thence:

2 SSE of Ýfalos Kalóyeroi (7 miles E), a reef which dries in places, lying about 6 cables offshore abreast the termination of olive groves which extend from Ierápetra, 4½ miles E. The position of the reef is not easily identified and it should be given a wide berth. Thence:

3 SSE of Ákra Kalamáki (8¼ miles E). The village of Gra-Liyia lies 1½ miles NE of the point and a small harbour, protected by two S moles, is being constructed (2004). Thence:
NNW of Nísos Gaïdouronísi (11 miles SE) (4.11). Gaïdouronísi Light (white round hut with metal framework, 5 m in height) is exhibited from the N side of the W part of the island.

4 The track then leads to a position SSE of Ákra Ierápetra (35°00′N 25°44′E), a low promontory surmounted by a small Venetian fort and fronted by a boat harbour. A light (white six-sided hut with column and gallery, red band) is exhibited from the SE head of the mole forming the boat harbour.

(Directions continue for the coastal route at 4.77)

Ierápetra

Chart 1707 plan of Ierápetra

General information

4.64

1 **Position.** Ierápetra (35°00′N 25°44′E), situated towards the E end of the S coast of Nísos Kríti, is a small port comprising an outer anchorage and an artificial boat harbour.

2 **Function.** The town, situated close N of Ákra Ierápetra (4.63), is the largest on the S coast of Nísos Kríti. Tomatoes, olive oil and soap are exported, but these are mainly conveyed by road to ports on the N coast of Nísos Kríti.

3 **Water levels.** N winds cause the sea level to fall by up to 0·2 m, while S winds raise the sea level by up to 0·2 m.

Current. The current runs parallel to the shore and changes direction according to the prevailing wind; the current can be strong under N winds.

4 **History.** Ancient Ierapytra, which was an important town during the Roman era, stood on the site of the present town. An artificial harbour formed by two moles fronted the E side of the town, but the stone blocks of the moles are now partly submerged and the harbour has largely silted up.

Anchorage

4.65

1 Órmos Ierápetras, entered between Ákra Ierápetra and a point about 1¾ miles E, affords some shelter during NW and N winds but it is open between E and S and swell often enters from this quarter.

2 Anchorage may be obtained in depths from 9 to 11 m, sand, avoiding a foul area, 6¼ cables ESE of the fort at the N entrance to the harbour.

The anchorage, 5 cables E of the fort, as shown on the chart, has a depth of about 8 m, sand and weed.

Harbour

4.66

1 An artificial boat harbour, about 290 m long and 150 m wide, fronts the SW side of Ákra Ierápetra. The harbour is protected from S by a curved mole. The entrance, open ENE and 30 m wide, lies close S of the fort. The maximum charted depth in the harbour is 2·8 m.

Directions

4.67

1 **Approach and entry.** The harbour is approached from S, passing between a shoal, with a least depth of 0·8 m, the SE end of which is marked by a buoy, and the head of a mole, from which a light (4.63) is exhibited.

Thence head WSW and enter the harbour, passing between the fort and the N side of the mole.

2 **Cautions.** During strong S winds there is a confused swell off the entrance which makes entry difficult.

A submarine effluent pipeline lies 8 cables WNW of the harbour. The pipeline extends 500 m SSW and a light buoy (special) marks the seaward limit. Anchoring and fishing are prohibited up to 500 m on either side of the pipeline.

3 **Useful marks** (with positions from the fort (35°00′·3N 25°44′·3E) (4.63)):

Minaret (conspicuous) (1½ cables NNW).

Factory chimney (conspicuous) (6 cables NE).

Port services

4.68

1 **Facilities:** customs; post office; hospital.

Supplies: fresh water; fuel by tanker; provisions.

Anchorages

Chart 3680

Órmos Tsoútsouros

4.69

1 **Description.** Órmos Tsoútsouros (34°59′N 25°17°E), entered between Ákra Tsoútsouros and a point 2 miles ENE, affords good shelter from winds between W and NW. The settlement of Tsoútsouros stands close E of the mouth of a stream which flows through a gorge to the head of the bay. A small harbour, quayed in its entirety, and consisting of a mole 274 m in length with a light at its head, fronts the village.

2 **Anchorage** may be obtained in depths from 10 to 20 m about 3 cables S of the mouth of the stream. During strong N winds the best shelter will be found off the E part of the settlement.

Órmos Keratókambos

4.70

1 **Description.** Órmos Keratókambos (35°00′N 25°22′E) indents the coast between the mouth of Potámos Anapódaris, one of the largest rivers in Kríti, and Ákra Peristeriónas, 4 miles E. The bay affords shelter only from N winds. With very strong winds communication with the shore is almost impossible and it is preferable to seek shelter in Órmos Tsoútsouros (4.69). A fisherman's refuge has been constructed in the bay.

2 **Anchorage.** Depths of 10 m or less exist within 3 cables of the shore which is clear of dangers apart from some charted rocks on the W and E sides. The best berth is near the head of the bay, about 5 cables offshore abreast the village of Kastrí (not charted).

Off Árvis monastery

4.71

1 **Description.** Árvis monastery (35°00′N 25°27′E) is situated 2½ miles WNW of Ákra Theófilos (4.63). West of the monastery the coast consists of low cliffs fringed by rocks; to the E it is sandy. A fisherman's refuge has been constructed close by.

2 **Anchorage.** Temporary anchorage may be obtained abreast the monastery where depths of 10 m extend 3 cables offshore. The anchorage may be used during strong N winds which do not gust in the locality.

Órmískos Psarí Foráda

4.72

1 Órmískos Psarí Foráda (34°59′N 25°30′E), a small bay between Ákra Sidonía and Ákra Theófilos, 8 cables E, affords temporary anchorage and landing.

COASTAL ROUTE FROM IERÁPETRA TO ÁKRA TRÁKHILAS, PASSING THROUGH STENÓ KOUFONÍSOU

General information

Chart 3679

Route

4.73

1 From a position SSE of Ákra Ierápetra (35°00′N 25°44′E) the coastal route leads E and then ENE, for about 28 miles, passing through Stenó Koufonísou, to a position ESE of Ákra Tráchilas (35°02′N 26°14′E).

Topography

4.74

1 Between the isthmus of Ierápetra (35°00′N 25°45′E) (4.4) and Ákra Goúdoura, about 17 miles E, the coast is low and sandy. Thence from Ákra Goúdoura to Ákra Tráchilas, a further 7 miles ENE, it becomes more hilly. The coastline is backed by the mountains of the Sitía region, some of which are more than 1000 m high.

Local winds

4.75

1 During N winds violent squalls are experienced off the coast between Ierápetra and Ákra Goúdoura, and in Stenó Koufonísou and its approaches. The squalls can be very dangerous for vessels under sail which should reduce sail and take all due precautions.

Exercise area

4.76

1 A firing range is located approximately between Ákra Katergo (35°00′N 25°49′E) and Ákra Goúdoura (4.78).

Directions

(continued from 4.63)

Principal marks

4.77

2 **Landmarks:**

Church (conspicuous small white building) (35°01′N 25°50′E).

Monastery (conspicuous building surrounded by high white wall) (35°01′N 26°03′E), situated on the E side of the mouth of a river.

Nísos Gaïdouronísi (34°52′N 25°42′E) (4.11).

Nísos Koufonísi (34°56′N 26°09′E) (4.12).

Ierápetra to Ákra Tráchilas

4.78

1 From a position SSE of Ákra Ierápetra (35°00′N 25°44′E) the track leads E, passing (with positions given from Nisída Fotiá (35°01′N 25°52′E)):

S of a drying rock (4 miles WSW), lying 2½ cables offshore, thence:

S of Nisída Fotiá, a small islet 9 m high, lying 3 cables offshore and surrounded by rocks, thence:

S of a dangerous rock (6½ miles E), lying 5 cables SE of Ákra Kaló Neró, thence:

S of Ákra Goúdoura (11 miles E), a steep headland, off the entrance to Stenó Koufonísou. The strait has a navigable width of about 1½ miles and depths of more than 200 m in mid channel.

2 The track then leads ENE, keeping 1 mile from the N side of the strait until the E extremity of Nísos Koufonísi bears 170°, passing (with positions from Ákra Goúdoura (35°00′N 26°06′E)):

SSE of Prasonísi (8 cables E), a small islet 4 m high, lying close offshore 5 cables SSE of an isolated hill 283 m high, thence:

3 NNW of a group of dangerous rocks (2½ miles SE) extending 5 cables N of Nisída Strongiló, the N of the islets surrounding Nísos Koufonísi. A stranded wreck lies near the N extremity of the rocks. Thence:

SSE of the harbour and fisherman's refuge in Órmos Atherinolakou (2½ miles E) (4.83).

SSE of Nisída Koúmeli (5¼ miles ENE), a small islet lying close off a point, thence:

4 SSE of Nisídes Kaválloi (35°02′N 26°14′E), three steep-to islets lying about 5 cables off Ákra Tráchilas; the S islet is 59 m high and the E is 47 m high. Nisídes Kaválloi Light (metal framework tower, 4 m in height) is exhibited from the S islet.; the light is obscured between the bearings of 063° and 069°, and between those of 225° and 252°.

Thence the track leads to a position ESE of Ákra Tráchilas (35°02′N 26°14′E).

(Directions for the E coast of Nísos Kríti are given in Mediterranean Pilot Volume IV)

(Directions for the coastal passage SE of Nísos Kásos and Nísos Kárpathos are given at 4.87)

Anchorages and harbour

Órmos Pezáki

4.79

1 Órmos Pezáki (35°00′·8N 25°50′·8E) is a small bay which serves as the landing place for the village of Koutsounára, 7 cables W. There is a depth of 11 m off the head of the bay, which is sandy.

Órmos Makrís Yialós

4.80

1 **Description.** Órmos Makrís Yialós (35°02′N 25°59′E), entered between Ákra Kaló Neró (4.78) and a point 2 miles WNW, is the best temporary anchorage between Ierápetra and Stenó Koufonísou. The bottom is sand and, except for rocks which front two small points near the head of the bay, the shores are sandy. The mouth of a stream lies 5 cables N of Ákra Kaló Neró.

2 **Harbour.** A small harbour is located close to the N shore in the NW extremity of the bay. The harbour is protected by a mole which runs 80 m NE; a light is exhibited from its head. A second mole is located to the NW of the first one. Works are in progress within the harbour (2004).

3 **Useful mark:**

A light (framework tower on hut, red band) (35°02′·3N 25°58′·5E) is exhibited from the W side of the bay.

Órmos Goúdouras

4.81

1 Órmos Goúdouras (35°00′N 26°04′E) is entered between Ákra Pláka and Ákra Goúdoura, 3½ miles ESE. The bottom is sand, and depths decrease to less than 20 m about 3 to 4 cables from the shore.

Caution

4.82

1 Anchoring in the lee of Nísos Koufonísi (34°56′N 26°09′E) (4.12) to shelter from S winds is not recommended due to the suddenness with which such winds veer to N in the locality.

Atherinolakos

4.83

1 **Description.** Órmos Atherinolakou (35°00′·5N 26°08′·7E) is a small bay 2½ miles E of Ákra Goúdoura. Depths vary from 12 to 16 m, and a harbour and refuge are located in the W part of the bay. The 11 m contour is marked by four light buoys (special), three of which are located in the N part of the bay and the fourth in the SW, close to the root of the harbour mole.

2 **Harbour.** Atherinolakos harbour is protected to the S by a dog-legged mole extending 360 m NE, a light (concrete column, 10 m in height) is located at its head. The entrance is open to the E. The S mole is quayed, with a ramp 50 m long at its root. Depths alongside the mole are 10·1 to 11·0 m, and 5·5 to 6·0 m at the ramp.

3 **Refuge.** A fisherman's refuge is located 400 m NW of the harbour mole. It is protected by an inner mole extending 35 m SE, and a dog-legged outer mole extending 130 m SW. The entrance which is 50 m wide opens SW. Depths in the fairway are approximately 3 m and a light (white metal column, green band, 3 m in height), is exhibited from the head of the outer mole.

Órmos Ámbelos

4.84

1 Órmos Ámbelos (35°02′N 26°13′E), lying between Ákra Tráchilas and a point 1 mile WSW, is entered from S by

passing W of Nisídes Kaválloi (4.78). Nisídes Kaválloi Light is obscured between the bearings of 103° and 181°.

2 The N part of the bay is sandy and there are depths of less than 10 m within 3 cables of the shore. The bay is not recommended as an anchorage during strong N winds owing to the violent squalls and gusts which blow down from the mountains. A peak 321 m high lies 5 cables NW of the head of the bay.

PASSAGE SOUTH-EAST OF NÍSOS KÁSOS AND NÍSOS KÁRPATHOS

General information

Charts 3679, 1099

Route

4.85

1 From a position about 7 miles SSE of Vrachónisis Pláti (35°22′N 26°49′E) the coastal route leads initially ENE, for about 17 miles, to the vicinity of Ákra Kastéllos (35°24′N 27°08′E), thence NE, for a further 14 miles, to a position E of Ákra Vólakas (35°28′N 27°14′E), at the SW end of Stenó Karpáthou.

Topography

4.86

1 **Nísos Kásos** (35°23′N 26°55′E) is of limestone formation and is generally mountainous. The highest peak, Korifí Príonas, elevation 601 m, lies in the NE part. The land slopes to the NW, where most of the villages are situated. The coastline consists mainly of high rocky cliffs, the S coast being inaccessible.

2 **Nísos Kárpathos** (35°35′N 27°09′E) is a long narrow island with a ridge of high mountains extending along its entire length. Korifí Kalolímni, the highest peak, rises to an elevation of 1215 m near the middle of the island. On all sides the coasts are steep and indented. Most of the inhabitants live in the S part of the island.

Directions

4.87

1 From a position about 7 miles SSE of Vrachónisis Pláti (35°22′N 26°49′E), from where a light (white round hut) is exhibited, the track leads initially ENE, passing (with positions from Vrachónisis Pláti):

SSE of Ákra Avláki (1½ miles SE), from which a light (metal framework on white round hut, 5 m in height) is exhibited, thence:

SSE of Ákra Chélathros (Klisouri) (3 miles ESE), the S point of Nísos Kásos, thence:

2 SSE of Ákra Troutzoúla (5 miles E), a salient point, thence:

SSE of Ákra Aktís (10 miles NE), a cape forming the NE point of Nísos Kásos, thence:

To a position SSE of Ákra Kastéllos (15½ miles ENE), the S point of Nísos Kárpathos. Ákra Kastéllos Light (white metal framework) is exhibited from the point.

3 The track then leads NE, passing (with positions from Ákra Kastéllos (35°24′N 27°08′E)):

SE of shoals, with depths over them from 3·6 to 5·5 m, fronting the coast between Ákra Kastéllos and Ákra Língi (2½ miles NE). A dangerous wreck (position approximate) lies on these shoals, which are covered by the red sector (225°–252°) of Ákra Kastéllos Light. Thence:

SE of Ákra Vólakas (6¾ miles NE), a cape forming the SE extremity of Chersónisos Voutheiá.

4 Thence the track leads to a position E of Ákra Vólakas, at the SW end of Stenó Karpáthou.

Useful mark:

Vrachónisis Strongilí Light (metal framework on white round hut, 5 m in height) (35°26′N 27°01′E).

(Directions for the passage between Nísos Kásos and Nísos Kárpathos, and for Stenó Karpáthou are given in Mediterranean Pilot Volume IV)

(Directions for the coastal route SE of Nísos Ródos are given at 4.95)

Anchorages

West of Ákra Avláki

4.88

1 A bay lying between Ákra Avláki (35°23′·5N 26°58′·4E), situated on the NE side of Nísos Kásos, and Skopélos Firá, 9 cables SW, a reef above water in places and extending 2½ cables offshore, affords good shelter during N winds. Anchorage may be obtained in a depth of about 15 m. The district is known locally as Ágios Mámmas.

Local knowledge is required.

Órmos Makrís Yialós

4.89

1 **Description.** Órmos Makrís Yialós (35°26′N 27°12′E) affords shelter from W or N winds, in moderate depths, about 3 cables offshore.

Warning. Vessels are prohibited from anchoring at a distance of less than 500 m from the fuel handling installation of the Air Force detatchment (35°25′·7N 27°09′·7E); apart from tankers serving the facility.

2 **Useful mark:**

Vrachónisis Moíra, a rocky islet lying 1¾ miles NNE of Ákra Língi (4.87). The islet is fringed by submerged rocks, and an above-water rock lies about 1 cable off its SW side.

Órmos Ámorfos

4.90

1 Órmos Ámorfos (35°28′·5N 27°13′·0E), entered between Ákra Vólakas and Ákra Skopí, about 2 miles WSW, affords shelter from W and N winds. Anchorage may be obtained, in moderate depths, about 3 cables offshore.

PASSAGE SOUTH-EAST OF NÍSOS RÓDOS

GENERAL INFORMATION

Charts 236, 1055

Area covered

4.91

1 The area covered by this section comprises:

Ákra Prásson to Ákra Líndos (4.93).

Ákra Líndos to Ákra Voúdi (4.100).

Topography

4.92

1 Nísos Ródos (36°10′N 27°55′E) is a mountainous island and the largest of Dodekánisoi (1.90). The mountains are heavily wooded, and there are areas of cultivation in the valleys and along the coast. Numerous streams, mostly dry in summer, flow through the level land towards the coast. Óros Atáviros (36°12′N 27°52′E), the summit of the island, is a reddish-brown mass rising to an elevation of 1216 m about 4 miles inland on the W side of the island. From the summit, the mountains decrease in elevation towards the NE end of the island where the town of Ródos, the capital of the island, is situated.

ÁKRA PRÁSSON TO ÁKRA LÍNDOS

General information

Chart 236

Route

4.93

1 From a position about 10 miles S of Ákra Prásson (35°53′N 27°45′E) the coastal route leads NE, for 28 miles, to a position about 5 miles SE of Ákra Líndos (36°03′N 28°05′E).

Topography

4.94

1 Between Ákra Viglí (35°55′N 27°51′E) and Ákra Mérminga, about 10 miles NE, the coast is generally low, rising in gentle slopes to hills inland.

Directions

Principal marks

4.95

1 **Landmark:**

Ákra Prásson Lighthouse (round tower and dwelling, 14 m in height) (35°53′N 27°45′E).

Major light:

Ákra Prásson Light — as above.

Ákra Prásson to Ákra Líndos

4.96

1 From a position about 10 miles S of Ákra Prásson (35°53′N 27°45′E) the track leads NE, passing (with positions from Ákra Prásson):

SE of Ákra Prásson, the extremity of a rocky peninsula forming the SW point of Nísos Ródos. The peninsula is connected to the coast by a low sandy isthmus and is often mistaken for an island. Ákra Prásson Light (4.95) is exhibited from the point. Thence:

2 SE of a shoal (3 miles ENE), with a depth of 4·6 m over it, lying 4 cables offshore. The line of bearing 268° of Ákra Prásson, open S of the point E of it, passes S of the shoal. Thence:

SE or NW of Vráchoi Chína (7½ miles E), two small steep-to rocks. The rocks are charted as 7 m high, but in 1964 it was reported that they were only between 2 and 4 m high. At night the rocks constitute a serious danger, and even by day they are difficult to see in low visibility. Thence:

3 SE of Ákra Viglí (5 miles ENE), a low point which can be identified by a short black tower standing near its extremity. The point is fronted by foul ground extending as much as 3 cables S. Thence:

SE of Ákra Ístros (6¼ miles NE), a whitish point near which lies a steep hill 50 m high. A dangerous wreck, the masts of which are visible, lies about 2½ cables SW of the point and is marked by a light buoy (isolated danger). Thence:

4 SE of a light (16¾ miles NE) marking the head of a jetty (4.99), thence:

SE or NW of Vráchos Paximáda (19 miles NE), a high steep-to rock. Vráchos Paximáda Light (metal column, white round hut, 6 m in height) is exhibited from the rock.

The track then leads to a position SE of Ákra Líndos (36°03′N 28°05′E), the SE extremity of a high flat promontory. A ruined tower stands on the point.

(Directions continue at 4.102)

Anchorages and landing places

Chart 236

Plimmíri

4.97

1 **Description.** Plimmíri (35°55′·8N 27°51′·5E), a village situated close NW of Ákra Ístros, is the landing place for Kattavía, 4½ miles WNW. The village can be identified by several small buildings surrounded by a white wall. A small pier, with a depth at its head of 3 m, fronts the village. The bottom is rock, and the shore in the vicinity is fringed with rocks extending about ½ cable offshore.

2 **Anchorage** may be obtained SSW of the head of the pier in a depth of 10 m, sand. Care is necessary to avoid the dangerous wreck lying 2½ cables SW of Ákra Ístros (4.96).

Between Ákra Ístros and Ákra Lachaniá

4.98

1 Anchorage in depths from 10 to 12 m can be obtained off the coast about midway between Ákra Ístros (35°56′N 27°52′E) (4.96) and Ákra Lachaniá, 2½ miles NE.

The village of Lachaniás, which may be identified by some windmills nearby, is situated 1½ miles W of Ákra Lachaniá.

Órmos Lárdos

4.99

1 **Description.** Órmos Lárdos (36°03′N 28°01′E) is a large bay indenting the coast between Ákra Líndos (4.96) and Ákra Mérminga, 5½ miles W. The bay is free from known dangers at more than 5 cables offshore, from which distance the depths decrease gradually, except for occasional rocks and shoals. A shoal fronting Ákra Yianoúri, a salient point 1¾ miles WNW of Ákra Líndos, is covered by the red sector (139°–184°) of Vráchos Paximáda Light (4.96). A light (36°04′·1N 28°00′·3E) is exhibited from the head of a 70 m jetty used by the Lárdos gypsum works.

2 **Anchorage.** In fair weather small vessels can anchor off a settlement situated near Ákra Yianoúri.

ÁKRA LÍNDOS TO ÁKRA VOÚDHI

General information

Charts 236, 1055

Route

4.100

1 From a position about 5 miles SE of Ákra Líndos (36°03′N 28°05′E) the coastal route leads NNE, for about 23 miles, to a position ESE of Ákra Voúdi (36°23′N 28°15′E).

Topography

4.101

1 The promontory between Ákra Líndos (36°03′N 28°05′E) and Ákra Ágios Aimilianós, 3 miles N, is a high plateau surmounted by a summit 459 m high; except for a few trees it is devoid of vegetation.

2 Between Ákra Ágios Aimilianós and Ákra Archányelos, about 5 miles NNE, the coast recedes to form a bight. Thence, to Ákra Váyia, about 4½ miles farther NNE, the coast is low, rocky and slightly indented.

Óros Zambíka, a mountain 305 m high, lies a short distance inland about 1½ miles SW of Ákra Váyia.

Directions

(continued from 4.96)

Principal marks

4.102

1 **Landmarks:**

Church (36°14′·2N 28°09′·0E).

Three conspicuous radio masts (red lights) (36°16′·0N 28°10′·0E).

Ákra Líndos to Ákra Voúdi

4.103

1 From a position about 5 miles SE of Ákra Líndos (36°03′N 28°05′E) the track leads NNE, passing (with positions given from Ákra Archányelos (36°11′N 28°08′E)):

ESE of Pénde Nisiá (7 miles SSW), a pair of above-water rocks fronting Ákra Zoumáni. The rocks are covered by the red sector (139°–184°) of Vráchos Paximáda Light (4.96). Detached rocky shoals, the shallowest with a depth of 5·9 m over it, lie as much as 1 mile SE of the outer rock in the white sector of the light. Thence:

2 ESE of Ákra Ágios Aimilianós (5 miles SSW), the NE point of the promontory, thence:

ESE of Ákra Archányelos, thence:

ESE of Vráchoi Exonísi (1 mile N), two islets lying within 3 cables of a point, thence:

ESE of Ákra Váyia (4½ miles NNE), thence:

ESE of Ákra Ladikó (9 miles NNE), which rises steeply to an elevation of 165 m. A white house stands on the summit, but it is not visible from N of the cape.

3 The track then leads to a position ESE of Ákra Voúdi (36°23′N 28°15′E), a low rocky point.

Useful marks:

Castle (36°05′·6N 28°05′·3E) (chart 1532, plan of Órmos Líndou (4.104).

Moní Eleoúsa (Eleousa Monastery) (36°20′·8N 28°10′·7E).

(Directions for Rhodes Channel are given in Mediterranean Pilot Volume IV)

Órmos Líndou

Chart 1532, plan of Órmos Líndou

General information

4.104

1 **Position.** Órmos Líndou (36°06′N 28°05′E) is a natural harbour situated midway along the SE coast of Nísos Ródos.

2 **Function.** The harbour, accessible to small vessels, affords good shelter from all but E and SE winds, although gusts are experienced during NW winds. The village of Líndos is situated on the N and W sides of a rocky hill rising from the S shore of the harbour. A conspicuous castle stands on the summit of the hill.

3 **Approach and entry.** The harbour is approached from SE and entered between the S entrance point and an islet, the S of two lying a short distance offshore on the N side of the approach, about 1½ cables NE.

Anchorage

4.105

1 Small vessels can anchor close within the entrance in depths from 5·6 to 14·6 m; the bottom is sand with some rock, providing good holding. The best anchorage is in the SW part of the harbour in depths from 5·8 to 8·2 m.

Numerous small mooring buoys are laid throughout the harbour.

Berths

4.106

1 A mole 60 m long projects NNW from the S shore of the harbour. Vessels of a suitable size berth stern to the W side of the mole.

Port services

4.107

1 **Facilities:** post office.

Supplies: limited amounts of water available; provisions.

Communications: bus service to the town of Ródos (4.92).

Anchorages

Chart 236

Órmos Víglika

4.108

1 **Description.** Órmos Víglika (36°08′N 28°08′E), is entered between Ákra Ágios Aimilianós and a bluff point 3½ miles N. Although open NE, it is reported to be a safe anchorage in winter as the wind seldom blows from that quarter and does not raise much sea.

2 **Anchorage.** The best anchorage, shown on the chart, well sheltered from SE, is in the SW corner of the bay in depths from 13 to 35 m, mud. Small vessels can anchor closer inshore.

Dangers to be avoided (positioned from Ákra Ágios Aimilianós):

Depth of 2 m (1 cable NW).

Group of above-water rocks lying close offshore (1¼ miles W).

3 **Useful marks** (positioned from Ákra Ágios Aimilianós):

Kálathos, a village (2¼ miles WNW).

Ruined castle (4 miles N), standing on the N entrance point of the bay.

White belfry, standing in the village of Málon (5¾ miles NNW) which is partly hidden by trees.

Órmos Malónas

4.109

1 **Description.** Órmos Malónas (36°10′N 28°09′E) indents the coast between Ákra Archányelos and the bluff point

2 miles WSW. A rocky patch with a depth over it of 4·8 m lies about 1¼ miles WSW of Ákra Archányelos.

2 **Caution.** Anchoring in the inlet at the head of the bay, 1½ miles W of Ákra Archányelos, should be avoided due to the probable existence of ammunition.

Chart 1055

Órmos Afándou

4.110

1 Órmos Afándou (36°17′N 28°12′E) lies between Ákra Váyia and Ákra Ladikó, about 4½ miles NNE. The shore of the bay consists mainly of a sandy beach, but for 1 mile SW of Ákra Ladikó it is steep and rocky. With the exception of a small patch, with a depth of 6·8 m over it, lying 5 cables offshore, about 1¼ miles N of Ákra Váyia, the bay is free from dangers.

Órmos Kalithión

4.111

1 Órmos Kalithión (36°21′N 28°13′E) is entered between a point 5 cables NNE of Ákra Ladikó and a point about 2¾ miles farther NNE.

The following dangers lie in the S part of the bay:

Rocky patch, with depths from 3·7 to 5·5 m over it, close NNE of the S entrance point.

2 Shoal, with a depth of 12·8 m over it, the charted position of which is approximate, lying in the middle of the bay about 1½ miles NNE of the S entrance point.

The N part of the bay is clear of dangers at more than 2½ cables offshore.

Cove south-west of Ákra Voúdi

4.112

1 A cove (36°23′·1N 28°14′·6E), in which are some mineral springs, lies about 5 cables SW of Ákra Voúdi. A landing quay for boats, with a depth of 1·5 m close off it, is situated on the S side of the cove.

NOTES

Chapter 5 - Marmaris to Ra's al Basīţ

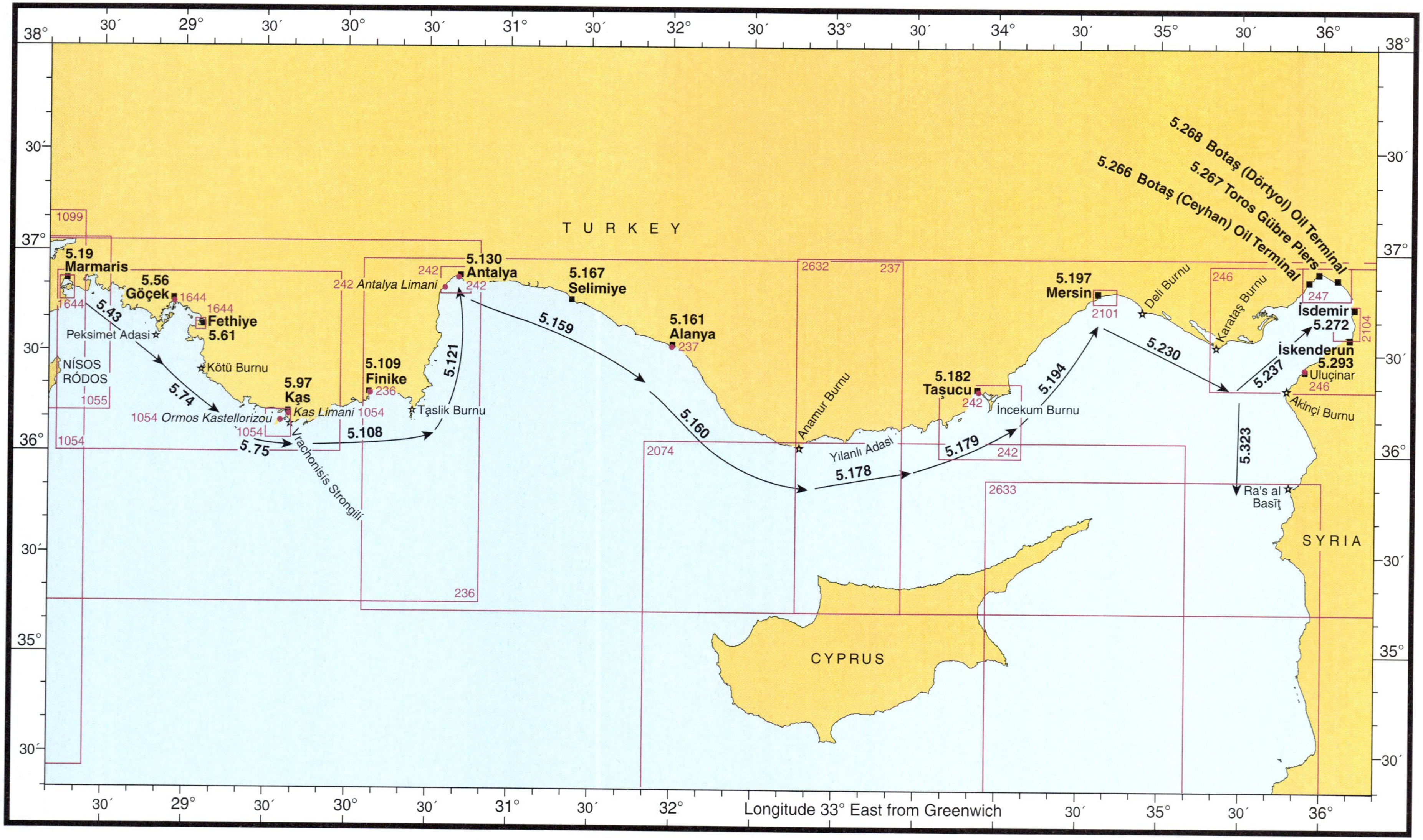

CHAPTER 5

SOUTH COAST OF TURKEY — KADIRGA BURNU TO ANTAKYA KÖRFEZİ

GENERAL INFORMATION

Chart 183

Scope of the chapter

5.1

1 The area covered by this chapter comprises the coastal waters of the S coast of Turkey from Kadırga Burnu (36°44′N 28°18′E) to the S part of Antakya Körfezi, 380 miles ESE. The description includes the principal ports of Marmaris (5.19), Karaağaç Limanı (5.29), Fethiye (5.61), Antalya (5.130), Mersin (5.197), İskenderun Limanı N terminals (5.246), İsdemir (5.272), and İskenderun (5.293).

2 The coast E of Taşlık Burnu (36°13′N 30°25′E) contains many open roadsteads which afford safe anchorage in summer. Yumurtalık Limanı (36°44′N 35°45′E) (5.238) affords shelter to large vessels. İskenderun Limanı (36°36′N 36°11′E) (5.293) is the safest anchorage between Yumurtalık Limanı and the coast of Israel.

3 The chapter is divided into the following sections:

Rhodes Channel to Antalya Körfezi (5.8).
Antalya Körfezi (5.115).
Antalya Körfezi to İskenderun Körfezi (5.172).
İskenderun Körfezi and Antakya Körfezi (5.231).

Topography

5.2

1 Toros Dağları dominates the hinterland, reaching elevations of over 3000 m in several places. On the S side of the range there is a steep scarp, which generally falls sharply to the coast, but leaves room for a few alluvial deltas and fertile plains in the vicinity of Antalya (36°53′N 30°42′E) and Mersin (36°48′N 34°38′E).

2 On parts of the coast the gravel beach has become a solid petrified mass, and caution is necessary in landing when there is any surf, as the appearance of the beach provides no warning.

Abnormal water levels

5.3

1 There is no tidal rise on the S coast of Turkey, but S and W winds raise the level of the sea sometimes as much as 0·6 m above the normal, and N and E winds lower it a similar amount.

Currents

5.4

1 The current on the S coast of Turkey, unless affected by gales, is generally W-going. The mean rate of ½ to ¾ kn is often considerably exceeded near the coast N of Cyprus, particularly with strong NE winds in winter.

2 To the W of Anamur Burnu (36°01′N 32°48′E), the S flank of the current loses water in a S direction between Cyprus and Kríti, this water rejoining the main E-going Mediterranean current off the N coast of Egypt. This process is enhanced in summer by the predominantly NW winds.

Fishing

5.5

1 Numerous marine farms have been established in the area covered by this chapter. They should be given a wide berth. Some of the marine farms are shown on the charts but only the ones that affect navigation are described in this chapter.

Diving

5.6

1 Diving restrictions apply in many areas along the Turkish coast (see 1.48).

Rescue

5.7

1 For information on rescue see 1.68 and *Admiralty List of Radio Signals Volume 5.*

RHODES CHANNEL TO ANTALYA KÖRFEZİ

GENERAL INFORMATION

Chart 236

Area covered

5.8

1 The area covered by this section comprises:

Marmaris Limanı (5.9).
Karaağaç Limanı (5.29).
Yılancık Adası to Fethiye Körfezi (5.41).
Fethiye Körfezi (5.49).
Fethiye Körfezi to Vrachonisís Strongilí (5.71).
Nísos Meyísti, Kaş Limanı and approaches (5.82).
Vrachonisís Strongilí to Taşlık Burnu (5.102).

MARMARİS LİMANI

General information

Charts 1054, 1644 plan of Marmaris

Description

5.9

1 Marmaris Limanı (36°50′N 28°16′E) is a landlocked harbour clear of dangers, bounded on the NW side by a plain through which run several streams; these streams nearly dry in summer.

2 The inner part of Marmaris Limanı is protected from the S by Yıldız Adası and Keçi Adası. Yıldız Adası is a peninsula connected to the E shore by an isthmus of shingle about 75 m wide; a hill, covered with pine trees,

Marmaris Limani from ESE (5.9)

(Original dated prior to 2000)

(Photograph - Peter Kleinoth)

rises in the middle of the peninsula to an elevation of 402 m and is crowned by the ruins of a fortress. Keçi Adası is an island with the ruins of a fortress standing on its W side.

Route

5.10

1 From a position about 4 miles ESE of Kadırga Burnu (36°44′N 28°18′E) the route leads NW, for about 7 miles, through the outer harbour to the inner harbour entrance. The inner harbour is entered between Sarımehmet Burnu (36°48′N 28°15′E), and Alkaya Burnu, 1½ miles E, the S extremity of Yıldız Adası. The entrance is divided into two channels by Keçi Adası.

2 The route then leads N, for a distance of 3½ miles, through Büyük Boğaz, the E and preferred channel, which lies between Yıldız Adası and Keçi Adası, and then across the inner harbour to Marmaris.

Depths

5.11

1 The shores of the inner harbour are steep-to, except on the NW side, where depths of less than 5 m extend 2 cables offshore in places. Bedir Adası, 2 cables N of the centre of Yıldız Adası, is steep-to, and the passage between it and the peninsula is clear of dangers in the fairway.

Harbour limits

5.12

1 Marmaris Limanı is divided into an inner and outer harbour, the limits of which are shown on the chart. The inner harbour is the sea area N of an E/W line drawn through Keçiada Light (36°47′·9N 28°15′·6E). The outer harbour is the sea area lying between a line drawn from Kadırga Burnu (36°44′N 28°18′E) to Turnalı Burnu, 6 miles NE, and the inner harbour limit.

Prohibited area

5.13

1 Anchoring and fishing are prohibited within an area, the limits of which are marked on the chart, centred on Keçiada Light (36°47′·9N 28°15′·6E).

Submarine cables

5.14

1 Several submarine cables are laid across the outer harbour of Marmaris Limanı, landing in Turunç Koyu (36°46′·5N 28°15′·0E) (5.26). Anchoring and fishing are prohibited in the vicinity of these cables in Turunç Koyu.

For information on submarine cables see 1.26.

Directions

Principal marks

5.15

1 **Landmarks:**

Kadırga Burnu (36°44′N 28°18′E), a moderately high cape backed by a picturesque mountain range rising to an elevation of 817 m, 3 miles WNW.

Yıldız Adası (36°48′N 28°17′E) (5.9), a peninsula.
Minaret (conspicuous), standing in the S part of the town of Marmaris (36°51′N 28°16′E).

Seaward to inner entrance

5.16

1 From a position about 4 miles ESE of Kadırga Burnu (36°44′N 28°18′E) the track leads initially NW, passing (with positions from Keçiada Light (36°47′·9N 28°15′·6E)):

SW of Turnalıkayası (6¾ miles ESE) (5.33), thence:

SW of Devetaşı (6 miles E), an above-water rock lying ¾ cable offshore; foul ground encircles it and extends NE to the coast. Thence:

2 NE of Kadırga Burnu (4½ miles SSE) (5.15), from where a light (white metal column on dwelling, 12 m in height) is exhibited, thence:

NE of Karaörün Burnu (3¼ miles SSE), which has some above-water rocks close E of it, thence:

NE of Kargataşı Adası (2 miles SSE), an islet steep-to except on its S side; the mainland 2½ cables W of the islet terminates in a high rocky point, with shoal water extending 2 cables offshore on its NW side. Thence:

3 SW of Alkaya Burnu (1½ miles ESE), the S point of Yıldız Adası, and:

NE of Turunç Koyu (1½ miles S) (5.26).

The track then leads to a position E of Sarımehmet Burnu (4 cables SSW). Between Turunç Koyu and Sarımehmet Burnu there are several small indentations separated by rocky points. The land behind Sarımehmet Burnu is high and picturesque.

Inner entrance to Marmaris

5.17

1 From the position E of Sarımehmet Burnu the track then leads generally N, passing (with positions from Keçiada Light (36°47′·9N 28°15′·6E)):

E of Keçiada Light (white metal column on dwelling, 12 m in height), exhibited from the S extremity of Adu Burnu, an islet lying close off the S end of Keçi Adası (5.9). Thence:

2 Through Büyük Boğaz (5 cables NE) (5.10) which separates Keçi Adası from Yıldız Adası; the shores of the channel are high and precipitous. Thence:

W of İnce Burnu (1 mile NNE), the NW point of Yıldız Adası, from which a light (white metal tower, 6 m in height) is exhibited, thence:

W of Bedir Adası (1½ miles NE) (5.11).

3 The track then continues NNE across the inner harbour of Marmaris Limanı to Marmaris (5.19).

Useful marks:

Pilav Tepe (red mound), 62 m high, close N of the town of Marmaris (36°51′N 28°16′E).

Hotel, 1¾ miles SW of Marmaris, which is prominent.

Side channel

Küçük Boğaz

5.18

1 Küçük Boğaz, passing W of Keçi Adası, is the alternative inner entrance to Marmaris Limanı. It is tortuous, being partially obstructed by Karga Adası, but otherwise the channel is deep and clear of dangers to within 1 cable of its shores.

Marmaris

Chart 1644 plan of Marmaris

General information

5.19

1 **Position.** Marmaris (36°51′N 28°16′E), a port of entry, is situated at the head of Marmaris Limanı on a rocky eminence, of which Town Point is the S extremity. The town lies in the centre of a very fertile though sparsely populated district; the mountains in the vicinity are covered with pine trees.

2 **Function.** The principal products are honey, turpentine and timber, but the town depends largely upon tourism for its livelihood. The population is about 4500.

Arrival information

5.20

1 **Notice of ETA:** 48, 24 and 12 hours in advance.

Pilotage. Foreign vessels of 150 gt or more entering or leaving the harbour, anchoring or berthing, must take a pilot. For details see *Admiralty List of Radio Signals Volume 6 (3).*

2 **Tugs** are available and compulsory for vessels over 2000 gt, and yachts over 500 gt.

Harbour

5.21

1 **General layout.** The port is situated in the N part of Marmaris Limani, the major part of which is to the E of Town Point.

Buoys. A mooring buoy is located 2 cables SSE of the head of the pier. Four buoys (spherical) are located close inshore, 2½ cables farther E.

2 **Traffic.** Care should be taken in Büyük Boğaz and Marmaris Limani due to large concentrations of small vessels, yachts and fishing boats. This is especially the case at night as their navigation lights are difficult to distinguish against the background light of the town.

Berths

5.22

1 **Town quays.** An L-shaped pier, the outer end of which is 91 m long, extends from the shore 1 cable NNW of Town Point, with depths alongside of about 8·7 m. Other quays, with depths of 4 to 5 m alongside, also face the SW and S side of Town Point.

2 **Town harbour.** Situated NE of Town Point, the town harbour is protected by a mole, with a depth of 2 to 4 m alongside. The quay in the harbour has depths of 2 to 2·8 m alongside.

Marmaris Ferry Quay from SSE (5.22)
(Original dated prior to 2005)

(Photograph - Marmaris Cruise Port)

3 **Ferry Quay.** Cruise liners and a ferry may berth on the S side of the mole protecting Marmaris Marina, 2 cables E of Town Point. The total length of the quay is 460 m. The longest berth is 305 m with a depth alongside of 12 m. The maximum size of vessel handled is 293·5 m.

Port services

5.23

1 **Repairs:** slipway for vessels up to 100 tons; there are also several boatyards with repair facilities around the inner harbour of Marmaris Limanı.

Other facilities: Ship Sanitation Control and Exemption Certificates are issued.

Supplies: fuel; fresh water from shore or barge; provisions.

Communications: there is an international airport S of Dalaman.

Anchorages

Chart 1054

Çaycağız Koyu

5.24

1 Çaycağız Koyu (36°44′N 28°18′E), formerly known as Kadırga Limanı, is entered between Kadırga Burnu (5.15) and a point 3½ cables NNW. Vessels may anchor in the NW or SW corners of the bay, in a depth of about 8 m. The anchorage is uncomfortable during E winds which often blow into the bay.

Kumlu Bükü

5.25

1 Kumlu Bükü (36°45′N 28°16′E), entered between a point 2½ cables WNW of Karaörün Burnu (5.16) and Asarcık Burnu, 1 mile NW, affords good anchorage in depths from 16 to 31 m, sand, sheltered from S through W to NW. During SE gales a heavy swell sets into the bay.

2 The ruins of Asarjik, ancient Samus, are situated on a cliff on Asarcık Burnu.

Chart 1644 plan of Marmaris

Turunç Koyu

5.26

1 Turunç Koyu (36°46′·5 N 28°15′·0 E), a small, well sheltered cove, has an anchorage on its S side, clear of the submarine cables (5.14), as shown on the chart. Anchor off the beach, in a depth of about 5 m; bottom sand and weed.

Yalancı Boğaz

5.27

1 **Description.** Yalancı Boğaz (36°49′N 28°19′E), on the E side of Yıldız Adası and S of the isthmus, has considerable depths; the lights of Marmaris can be seen at night from this vicinity, over the isthmus. Kütük Burnu forms the SW entrance point of Yalancı Boğaz.

2 **Caution.** A submarine outfall extends 4 cables SSE from the E extremity of the isthmus into Yalancı Boğaz, and 3 buoys (special) lie close W, midway along the outfall. A submarine cable extends 5 cables SE from the W extremity of the isthmus, then extends SE into Marmaris Limani. A buoy (spherical) lies close W of the cable, 4 cables from the head of the bay.

Marmaris Limanı inner harbour

5.28

1 Anchorages, which are shown on the chart in Marmaris Limanı inner harbour are as follows:

Secure anchorage is obtainable in the inner harbour of Marmaris Limanı in depths of from 13 to 37 m, good holding ground. Anchorage can also be obtained S of Yildiz Adasi.

2 Cove (36°48′·8N 28°16′·9E) on the N side of Yıldız Adası; depth 15 to 25 m; weedy bottom; not good holding ground.

A large marina is located in Yalancı Boğaz (36°49′N 28°18′E), on the E side of Yıldız Adası and N of the isthmus, light buoys (cardinal) mark the entrance.

Gölenye Limanı (36°48′·3N 28°14′·2E); depth 10 to 15 m.

KARAAĞAÇ LİMANI

General information

Chart 1054

Routes

5.29

1 Karaağaç Limanı, separated from Marmaris Limanı by a mountainous peninsula, is approached either from SW, passing WNW of Yılancık Adası (36°47′N 28°26′E), or from SE, passing NE of Yılancık Adası. Karaağaç Limanı is then entered through Aksaz Boğazı, passing E of Göllü Burnu (36°50′N 28°25′E).

Restricted area

5.30

1 A restricted area (36°47′N 28°27′E) in which anchoring, trawling, diving and landing are prohibited covers the approaches to Karaağaç Limanı, as shown on the chart.

Prohibited area

5.31

1 A prohibited area encompasses the waters of Karaağaç Limanı, N of a line drawn between Turnalı Burnu (36°47′N 28°24′E) and Gökyar Burnu, 3 miles NE, as shown on the chart.

Directions

Principal mark

5.32

1 **Landmark:**

Yılancık Adası (36°47′N 28°26′E), 95 m high, and steep-to. Yılancık Adası Light (white metal framework tower, 7 m in height) is exhibited from the summit of the island.

Approach from south-west

5.33

1 From a position about 4 miles ESE of Kadırga Burnu (36°44′N 28°18′E) the track leads NNE, passing (with positions from Yılancık Adası (36°47′N 28°26′E)):

WNW of Yılancık Bankı (1½ miles SSE), steep-to, with a least depth of 29 m over it, and:

2 ESE of Turnalıkayası (2 miles W), a dangerous rock, marked by a buoy (isolated danger), on which the sea usually breaks. The rock is covered by the red sector (086°–098°) of Yılancık Adası Light. A current, varying in direction, has been observed to flow over Turnalıkayası at rates from ½ to 1½ kn. Thence:

3 Between Yılancık Adası and Turnalı Burnu (2 miles NW). The coast N of Turnalı Burnu is bordered by

rocks and shoal water which extend 1 cable offshore in places.

The track then leads to a position W of Gökyar Burnu (2¾ miles NNE).

Approach from south-east

5.34

1 From a position about 2½ miles SW of Kızıl Burnu (36°47′N 28°32′E) the track leads NW, passing (with positions from Yılancık Adası (36°47′N 28°26′E)):

NE of Yılancık Bankı (1½ miles SSE), thence:

Between Yılancık Adası and Güdük Burnu (3¼ miles ENE). A rock awash lies off Güdük Burnu.

The track then leads to a position W of Gökyar Burnu (2¾ miles NNE).

Entry

5.35

1 From the position W of Gökyar Burnu (36°49′N 28°28′E) the track then leads N through Aksaz Boğaz, passing (with positions from Yılancık Adası (36°47′N 28°26′E)):

E of Deliklikaya Burnu (3½ miles N), from which a light (white metal framework tower, 6 m in height) is exhibited. High conical rocks and foul ground extend 1½ cables E of this point. Thence:

2 E of Göllü Burnu (4 miles N), and:

W of Buğluca (4 miles N), from which a light (white metal framework tower, 10 m in height) is exhibited. The light cannot be seen from seaward. The coastline on the E side of Aksaz Boğaz is fringed by foul ground which extends ½ cable offshore in places.

3 Thence into Karaağaç Limanı.

Useful mark:

Kargılı Burnu Light (white metal framework tower, 6 m in height) (36°52′N 28°26′E). The light is difficult to see from afar.

Anchorages and harbours

5.36

1 Secure anchorage is obtainable in depths of 18 to 46 m, good holding ground, within Karaağaç Limanı.

Aksaz Limanı

5.37

1 **Position and function.** Aksaz Limanı (36°51′N 28°24′E) is situated on the W side of Karaağaç Limanı. It serves as a Turkish naval base.

Caution. West Islet, on the W side of Aksaz Limanı, is surrounded by foul ground and shoal water. A light (white metal framework tower, 6 m in height) is exhibited from the islet.

2 **Anchorage.** Berths are available throughout Karaağaç Limanı.

Pilotage. Pilotage is available and is shared with Marmaris.

Tugs are available.

3 **Berths:**

Aksaz Repair Pier on the S side of Aksaz Limanı; NW-facing; length 462 m; least depth alongside 10·5 m. Four finger piers; a floating dock and slipway; lay up berth and a refuelling jetty complete the port.

4 Mooring buoys are laid in the W part of the bay.

Port services. Minor repairs; clinic; fuel; fresh water; provisions.

Kargılı Burnu - Main channel headmark (5.35)

(Original dated 2007)

(Photograph - Lt Bryan McCavour RN, HMS Northumberland)

Aksas Limanı Naval Base from E (5.37)
(Original dated 2007)

(Photograph - Lt Bryan McCavour RN, HMS Northumberland)

Yörük Bükü

5.38

1 Yörük Bükü (36°52′N 28°24′E), on the NW side of Karaağaç Limanı, is a well-sheltered bay.

Horoz Ada

5.39

1 Horoz Ada, 1¾ miles NE of Göllü Burnu, is 58 m high, and bordered by shallow water; there is foul ground between the islet and the mainland NNW.

In 1949 a vessel moored in the NE corner of the bay E of Horoz Ada, with stern lines to the shore. The anchor was dropped in a depth of 37 m and there was a depth of about 27 m at the stern, about 140 m from the shore. A full cargo of ore was embarked, using ship's gear, from lighters which loaded from a pier nearby.

2 Vessels must proceed to Marmaris (5.19) to enter and clear; the customs officials remain on board whilst the vessel is at Karaağaç Limanı. The Harbour Master at Karaağaç Limanı can act as pilot.

Dereağzı Limanı

5.40

1 Dereağzı Limanı lies between Gökyar Burnu (36°49′N 28°28′E) and İncecik Burnu, 1½ miles SE. The bay is open SW with a sandy beach at its head. A depth of 6 m lies 1 cable offshore 1 mile E of Gökyar Burnu.

YILANCIK ADASI TO FETHİYE KÖRFEZİ

General information

Chart 1054

Route

5.41

1 From a position about 4 miles ESE of Kadırga Burnu (36°44′N 28°18′E) the coastal route leads SE, for 25 miles, to a position about 7 miles SSW of Peksimet Adası (36°34′N 28°50′E).

Topography

5.42

1 The coastline between Yılancık Adası (36°47′N 28°26′E) and Peksimet Adası is rugged and steep-to, except for a low marshy area, to the E of Köyceğiz Limanı, through which Köyceğiz Çayı flows.

2 Eren Tepe, 539 m high, rises 2½ miles E of Akça Burun (36°39′N 28°48′E), and is the S summit of a mountain range extending N for several miles of which Hurmadağ, 2 miles N, is a prominent peak.

Directions

5.43

1 From a position about 4 miles ESE of Kadırga Burnu (36°44′N 28°18′E) the track leads SE, passing (with positions from Baba Adası Light (36°41′·6N 28°41′·7E)):

SW of Yılancık Bankı (12 miles WNW) (5.33), thence:

SW of Kızıl Burnu (9½ miles NW), the W entrance point of Köyceğiz Limanı (5.44), thence:

2 SW of Dişibilmez Burnu (3½ miles WNW), which rises steeply to an elevation of 382 m. A bay contained between Dişibilmez Burnu and Kara Burnu, 2 miles ESE, has considerable depths but affords no anchorage. Thence:

SW of Baba Adası, which has a large brick pyramid on its summit. Baba Adası Light (white metal framework pylon, 8 m in height) is exhibited from near the pyramid. Thence:

3 SW of Nar Adası (5 miles SE), an islet 23 m high and steep-to, standing 2 miles SW of Akça Burun.

The track then leads to a position about 7 miles SSW of Peksimet Adası (9¾ miles SE), 1¾ miles SW of Kurtoğlu Burnu (5.50). The islet is 18 m high and steep-to, but there are irregular depths between it and the cape. Peksimet Adası Light (metal framework tower, 8 m in height) is exhibited from the islet.

(Directions continue for Fethiye Körfezi at 5.51 and for the coastal route at 5.73)

Minor bays and anchorages

Köyceğiz Limanı

5.44

1 **Description.** Köyceğiz Limanı lies between Kızıl Burun (36°47′N 28°32′E) and Akiye Burnu, a point 2¾ miles ENE, and has considerable depths. It is open S, but Ekincik Limanı, at the head of the bay, affords safe anchorage to small vessels in most weathers.

2 **Useful marks:**

Karaçy Light (white metal framework tower, 7 m in height) is exhibited from a point 2¼ miles NNE of Kızıl Burun.

Delikada Light (36°48′N 28°36′E) (5.45).

Delikada and Köyceğiz Çayı

5.45

1 **Description.** Delikada (36°48′N 28°36′E) is an island close S of the E entrance point of Köyceğiz Limanı. Köyceğiz Çayı flows through marsh and swamp to disgorge close N of Delikada; the river mouth, 30 m wide, may be identified by some reddish coloured rock on its W entrance point. The bar at the river mouth rarely has more than 1 m over it, although there are depths of 3 to 8 m in the river itself.

2 The ruins of the ancient city of Caunos stand on the W bank of Köyceğiz Çayı, 2¼ miles inland, the walls and rock tombs being prominent from seaward.

Köyceğiz Gölü (36°53′N 28°37′E), a large brackish lake in which there are depths from 5·5 to 26 m, discharges to the sea through Köyceğiz Çayı. Yuvarlak Çay, the largest of several streams flowing into the lake, enters it on the SE side, and is of considerable size in winter. A small village stands on the NE shore of the lake.

3 **Local knowledge** is required for navigating Köyceğiz Çayı as the position and depths over the bar are constantly changing.

Anchorage. Good anchorage may be obtained, during the summer, near Delikada, off the mouth of the river, in depths of 5·5 to 16·5 m, sand and mud.

Useful mark:

Delikada Light (white metal tower, 6 m in height) is exhibited from the SW end of the island.

Bays north of Dişibilmez Burnu

5.46

1 Between Dişibilmez Burnu (36°42′N 28°38′E) and Delikada, 6½ miles N, the coast is indented by three bays, separated by Bozburun and Eşek Burnu, bold rocky points. In the N bay, contained between Delikada and Bozburun, 2¼ miles SSE, the depths shoal gradually but there is foul ground near its SE corner; a 25 m rocky shoal lies 1½ miles NW of Bozburun.

None of the bays are suitable for anchorage.

Dalaman Bükü

5.47

1 **Description.** Dalaman Bükü (36°42′N 28°45′E) lies between Kara Burnu and Akça Burun, 6½ miles SE, and is encumbered by Baba Adası (5.43) on its W side. Dalaman Nehri, a very rapid river, passes through an extensive plain and enters the sea 1½ miles ENE of Baba Adası. Shoal water extends 2 cables offshore in this vicinity, but elsewhere the shores of Dalaman Bükü, though low, are steep-to.

2 Along the coastline fronting the bay are a number of Hellenic and medieval ruins, hotels and apartment complexes.

Anchorage. Small vessels may obtain shelter between Baba Adası and the mainland, but S gales send in a heavy swell.

Gökgemile Koyu

5.48

1 Gökgemile Koyu (36°38′N 28°50′E), on the W side of Kapıdağı Yarımadası, is a small cove with depths suitable for anchoring.

FETHİYE KÖRFEZİ

General information

Chart 1054

Route

5.49

1 From a position about 7 miles SSW of Peksimet Adası (36°34′N 28°50′E) the route into Fethiye Körfezi, leads NE, for 13 miles, to a position about 3 miles SE of Kara Burnu (36°38′N 28°54′E), passing between Peksimet Adası and Dökükbaşı Burnu, 9 miles ESE.

Topography

5.50

1 Fethiye Körfezi (36°40′N 29°00′E) is entered between Kurtoğlu Burnu and Dökükbaşı Burnu, 8½ miles SE. The gulf is indented by many small bays and on its W side is encumbered by a string of islands, protecting Siralibük Limanı from the SE. Kurtoğlu Burnu is the S extremity of a rugged and bold peninsula, Kapıdağı Yarımadası, which rises to Baldiranlik Tepsi, 472 m high. The NW side of this peninsula is connected to the mainland by a narrow isthmus.

Directions

(continued from 5.43)

Principal marks

5.51

1 **Landmark:**

Television mast (36°38′·2N 29°05′·0E) standing on the summit of Oyuk Tepe.

Major light:

Kızıl Adası Light (white concrete tower dwelling, 13 m in height) (36°39′·3N 29°02′·5E) exhibited from the S point of the island.

Other aid to navigation

5.52

1 **Racon:** Kızıl Adası Lighthouse — as above.

Fethiye Körfezi

5.53

1 From a position about 7 miles SSW of Peksimet Adası (36°34′N 28°50′E) the track leads NE, passing (with positions from Peksimet Adası):

SE of Peksimet Adası (5.43), from which a light is exhibited, thence:

SE of Kurtoğlu Burnu (1¾ miles NE) (5.50), thence:

NW of Dökükbaşı Burnu (9 miles ESE), the SE entrance point of Fethiye Körfezi, and the W extremity of a peninsula. A light (white metal framework pylon, 8 m in height) is exhibited from the point. And:

2 SE of Kızılkuyruk Burnu (3 miles NE), thence:

NW of Boz Burnu (9¾ miles ENE); the coastline either side of Boz Burnu is bold and free from dangers.

The track then leads to a position about 3 miles SE of Kara Burnu.

(Directions continue for Göçek Limanı at 5.58 and for Fethiye Limanı at 5.64)

Side channels

Darboğaz

5.54

1 Darboğaz, suitable only for small vessels lies between Domuz Adası (36°40′N 28°54′E) and the NE extremity of Kapıdağı Yarımadası (5.50). It is 120 m wide, with depths of 16·5 m in mid-channel, and is clear of dangers. A rocky shoal, with a least depth of 12·4 m over it, lies 5 cables SE of this passage.

Passage east-north-east of Domuz Adası

5.55

1 This passage, lying between Domuz Adası (36°40′N 28°54′E) and Tersane Adası, close E, has a least depth of 44 m in its fairway and is 2 cables wide. At its N end, on the W side of the passage, there is an islet, with a rocky shoal between it and Domuz Adası, along with a patch, with a depth of 11 m over it, 2½ cables N.

Göçek Limanı

Charts 1054, 1644 plan of Göçek

General information

5.56

1 **Position.** Göçek Limanı (36°45′N 28°56′E), a well sheltered bay, is situated at the head of Fethiye Körfezi (5.50).

Function. The harbour is used for the export of locally mined chrome ore and is very popular with recreational craft, many of which are based there.

2 **Port limits.** The harbour limits are the sea area lying SW of a line drawn between Küçükkargi Burnu (36°42′·6N 29°00′·0E) and 36°33′·0N 28°51′·0E; W of a line drawn S from 36°33′·0N 28°51′·0E to the outer limit of territorial waters; E of a line drawn S from Kizil Burnu (36°47′·2N 28°32′·5E) to the outer limit of territorial waters.

3 **Traffic.** In 2007 there were six ship calls with a total of 27 451 dwt.

Port Authority. Fethiye Liman Baskanligi, Fethiye, Turkey.

Arrival information

5.57

1 **Anchorages:**

North side of Göçek Limanı in depths of 3 to 10 m, mud and weed.

West side of Göçek Limanı, NW of Iltur Club Marina, in depths of 5 to 12 m; good shelter.

Bay close S of Göçek town quay. Not the best anchorage as open to the prevailing wind.

Pilots. A local pilot may be obtainable.

Directions

(continued from 5.53)

5.58

1 From a position about 3 miles SE of Kara Burnu (36°38′N 28°54′E) the track leads N, passing (with positions from Göçek Adası Light (white metal framework tower, 6 m in height) (36°43′·7N 28°57′·0E)):

E of Tersane Adası (3¾ miles SSW), which rises to a cultivated plain with a greatest elevation of 231 m, thence:

2 W of İzkayası Siğlığı (3¾ miles SSE), consisting of two rocky patches, with a least depth of 4·6 m over them; the bank is steep-to. Thence:

W of Katrancık Adası (3¼ miles SE), which rises to an elevation of 104 m, and is rocky and barren; foul ground extends 2 cables from its SE end, with a 12 m patch 3 cables farther SE. Thence:

E of Yassıca Adaları (1½ miles SSW), consisting of several islands and rocks.

3 The track then leads to a position W of Doğan Burun (2¼ miles SE). Between Doğan Burun and the mouth of İnlice Çayı (5.69), 1¾ miles NW, the coast consists of high cliffs which are steep-to and rise to the hills 1 mile inland.

Thence the track leads NW into Göçek Limanı, passing between Göçek Adası and the shore to the E. At night keep within the white sector (314°–326°) of the light (white, metal framework tower, 6 m in height) exhibited from the S entrance point to Göçek Limanı, bearing about 320°.

Berths

5.59

1 **East side:**

Göçek town pier (36°45′·2N 28°56′·4E); consists of an angled pier; length 120 m; depths of 1 to 3 m alongside. Another pier lies close S.

Iltur Pier, close NW of Göçek town pier; depths of 2·5 to 4·0 m on the outside of the outer end, and 2·0 to 3·5 m on the inside.

2 **West side:**

Seka Quay, 6 cables W of town pier, consisting of two berths. No 1; length 200 m; depth alongside 12 m. No 2 berth; length 150 m; depth alongside 5 m. Vessels must use own gear for handling cargo.

Port services

5.60

1 **Facilities:** garbage disposal.

Supplies: fuel for small vessels; fresh water; provisions.

Communications. There is an international airport S of Dalaman, about 20 km by road.

Fethiye Limanı

Charts 1054, 1644 plan of Fethiye

General information

5.61

1 **Position.** Fethiye Limanı (36°38′N 29°06′E) is a natural harbour entered between Çamlı Burun (36°39′N 29°05′E) and Çalışır Burnu, 1½ miles ENE.

Function. The harbour is a loading point for locally-mined chrome and manganese ore, and also for agricultural produce and timber. The population is about 9000.

2 **Port limits.** Limanı is divided into an inner and outer harbour. The inner harbour is the sea area E and S of a line drawn from Paçarız Burnu (36°38′·5N 29°06′·1E) to the S extremity of Fethiye Adası, 3½ cables NNW, and a line drawn from the NE extremity of Fethiye Adası to the mainland, 2 cables E.

3 The outer harbour is the sea area lying S of a line drawn between 36°42′·6N 29°00′·0E and 36°33′·0N 28°51′·0E; E of a line drawn S from 36°33′·0N 28°51′·0E to the outer limit of territorial waters; W of a line drawn S

Fethiye Limani from WSW (5.61)

(Original dated prior to 2000)

(Photograph - Peter Kleinoth)

from 36°17′·6N 29°15′·8E to the outer limit of territorial waters, and the inner harbour limit.

4 **Traffic.** In 2007 there were 27 ship calls with a total of 166 677 dwt.

Port Authority. Harbour Master, Fethiye Liman Baskanligi, Fethiye, Turkey.

Arrival information

5.62

1 **Anchorage.** With position from Paçarız Burnu Light (36°38′·5N 29°06′·1E):

Paçarız Bükü (2 cables WSW). Anchorage may be obtained at the head of this bay in depths of 6 to 10 m; good shelter from the prevailing wind.

2 **Pilots.** Pilotage is not compulsory but can be arranged from İzmir if required.

Tugs. None available.

Harbour

5.63

1 Fethiye Limanı, almost entirely landlocked, affords complete shelter. The entrance to the harbour is encumbered by Fethiye Adası, which is 33 m high and covered with mediæval ruins and numerous villas. There are passages on either side; the SW passage is the wider and better of the two, but both are safe.

2 Fethiye (36°37′N 29°06′E) is situated on the S shore of Fethiye Limanı and is for the most part built on reclaimed land. A large marina, including a short pier, fronts the town; vessels up to 60 m LOA can be accommodated. A jetty for the export of chrome ore is situated on the N side of Fethiye Limanı at Çalışır Burnu (36°39′N 29°07′E).

3 The E shore of Fethiye Limanı is low and marshy and is fronted by a bank of mud, which dries in places. The W limit of the bank is marked by two light buoys (W cardinal); Kuzey Siğlik, 1¼ miles S of Çalışır Burnu, and Güney Siğlik, 4½ cables farther SSW.

4 The W shore is more steep to, with the main danger being a stranded wreck, marked by a buoy (isolated danger), lying 3 cables SSW of Aşıklar Burnu (36°38′N 29°06′E).

Directions

(continued from 5.53)

5.64

1 From a position about 3 miles SE of Kara Burnu (36°38′N 28°54′E) the track leads ENE, passing (with positions from Kızıl Adası Light (36°39′·3N 29°02′·5E)):

SSE of İzkayası Siğlığı (3 miles NW) (5.58), thence:

NNW of Şahin Burnu (1¾ miles S), the N extremity of a projection which rises to Belen Dağı, 528 m high, 1 mile S of the point, thence:

SSW of Kızıl Adası, from the S point of which is exhibited a light (5.51), thence:

N of Çamlı Burnu (36°39′N 29°05′E).

2 When Paçarız Burnu (36°38′·5N 29°06′·1E) bears 123° the track then leads SE, passing (with positions from Çamlı Burnu):

SW of Balık Kayası (1½ miles NNE), a group of dangerous rocks, 1 m or so above water and steep-to; a rocky shoal, with a depth of 5·5 m, lies

3 cables ESE of these rocks. Behind Balık Kayası the coast between Çalışır Burnu (36°39′N 29°07′E) and Uzun Burun, 4¼ miles NW, is low and marshy. Thence:

3 NE of Batıkkaya (4 cables E), from which a light (N cardinal on yellow concrete tower, black top, 5 m in height) is exhibited.

48/10 Thence through the SW entrance, passing: CLEAR OF DANGEROUS WRECK (8½ CABLES E) THENCE:

SW of the S end (1 mile E) of Fethiye Adası, from where a light (white metal column, 6 m in height) is exhibited, thence:

4 NE of Paçarız Burnu (1¼ miles ESE), from where a light (white six-sided concrete tower, green top, 8 m in height) is exhibited.

Thence shape course as convenient for Fethiye Limanı.

Berths

5.65

1 **Export jetty.** This jetty, situated on the SW extremity of Çalışır Burnu, with two hauling-off buoys, is used for loading chrome ore, and is connected by a light railway to the chrome mines situated in the mountains to the N. There are several mooring buoys in the vicinity of Çalışır Burnu.

2 **Fethiye.** The harbour side of the town forms a quay, the NW face of which has depths from 2·7 to 3·7 m alongside, increasing to 7·3 m a short distance offshore. Vessels berth stern to the quay. The N face of the quay has a depth of 0·9 m or less alongside.

3 A pier, situated at the W end of the town, is 1 cable long. The main berth for commercial vessels is on the E side of the pier; maximum draught 8 m. On the W side of the pier the maximum draught allowed is 9 m.

Port services

5.66

1 **Repairs:** facilities are available given one week's notice.

Other facilities: hospital in the town; Ship Sanitation Control and Exemption Certificates issued.

Supplies: fuel; fresh water is available but may be limited in the summer; provisions.

Communications. There is an international airport S of Dalaman, about 44 km distant by road.

Anchorages and harbours

5.67

1 Vessels may anchor, as shown on the chart, between Kızıl Adalar (36°40′N 29°03′E) and the mainland NE, in depths from 40 to 53 m, good holding ground and well sheltered from S.

2 Kızıl Adalar, consisting of Kızıl Adası and Deliklitaş Adaları, are a rocky group lying 1¼ miles off the NE shore of Fethiye Körfezi. A rock, marked by a buoy (W cardinal), on which the sea usually breaks lies 3 cables NW of Deliklitaş Adaları, the NW islets of the group. The bottom between the NW end of Kızıl Adalar and Katrancık Adası (5.58) and the mainland is rocky and uneven.

Küçük Kargı Koyu

5.68

1 Küçük Kargı Koyu, entered between Doğan Burun and a moderately high point 1 mile SE, is a small bay with a river flowing into its head; foul ground extends 1 cable from the W and S sides of the SE entrance point, which separates Küçük Kargı Koyu from a second small bay lying between it and Uzun Burun (36°42′N 29°02′E), 1 mile SE.

2 Rocks are reported to extend as much as ¾ cable from Uzun Burun and rocks awash lie about 4½ cables NNW of the point.

İnlice Çayı

5.69

1 İnlice Çayı (36°44′N 28°58′E) enters the sea in a small bay bounded on the W by a high, rugged cape. The river runs through a well cultivated valley, on the NW side of which, 2 miles within the river mouth, are the ruins of an ancient city, probably Dædala; numerous tombs, hewn out of the rock in the Lycian style, and the remains of immense walls, are to be seen.

Siralibük Limanı

5.70

1 **Description.** Siralibük Limanı (36°41′N 28°53′E) lies between the W shore of Fethiye Körfezi and a chain of islands between Domuz Adası and Göçek Adası, 4½ miles NNE. Mediæval remains are numerous in this locality.

2 The depths in Siralibük Limanı are too great to afford anchorage, except in several creeks where small vessels can shelter. The bottom NW of Tersane Adası is uneven, and shoals, with depths of 20·0, 18·3 and 15·0 m over them, are charted about 1¼ miles NW of the island. Two islets lie between Yassıca Adaları (5.58) and the mainland W; a light (isolated danger, 3 m in height) is exhibited from the N islet (36°42′·7N 28°55′·1E), and a group of above and below-water rocks extend 2½ cables N from it, marked by a buoy (N cardinal).

3 **Anchorages and berths:**

Tersane Adası (36°40′·6N 28°55′·0E). Good anchorage may be obtained in a small harbour on the NW side of Tersane Adası, where there is a small farm standing amongst extensive ruins.

Twenty Two Fathom Cove (36°38′·2N 28°52′·4E). This bay, on the S side of the entrance to Manastir Koyu, affords anchorage for vessels, in depths of 10 to 15 m, with a line ashore.

4 Manastir Koyu (36°38′·8N 28°51′·2E). Small vessels may anchor, with a line ashore, in Ruin Bay on the S side of Manastir Koyu; depth 10 to 12 m. There is also an anchorage in Wall Bay at the W end of Manastir Koyu; depth about 15 m.

Sarsala Koyu (36°39′·8N 28°51′·2E). There are a number of coves in this large bay in which vessels may anchor. Depths are from 8 to 15 m with a bottom of mostly sand, rocks and stones.

5 Deep Bay (36°40′·6N 28°51′·6E). There are a number of places within the bay in which vessels can anchor. On the SE side of the bay there is a narrow inlet with a catwalk along its E side, with depths of 2 to 3 m alongside.

Tomb Bay (36°41′·7N 28°52′·0E). Vessels may anchor at the head of the bay, in depths of 5 to 10 m, with a line ashore. On the S side of the bay, just inside the entrance, there is a quay, with depths of 2 to 3 m alongside.

6 Boynuz Bükü (36°42′·8N 28°54′·0E). A large bay situated on the coast opposite Yassıca Adaları (5.58). Anchorage may be obtained at the head of the bay in depths of 8 to 10 m, mud, providing good holding.

FETHİYE KÖRFEZİ TO VRACHONISÍS STRONGILÍ

General information

Chart 1054

Route

5.71

1 From a position about 7 miles SSW of Peksimet Adası (36°34′N 28°50′E) the coastal route leads SE, for 48 miles, to a position about 5 miles S of Vrachonisís Strongilí (36°07′N 29°38′E).

Chart 236

Submarine exercise area

5.72

1 Submarines exercise frequently in an area about 20 miles SSW of Dökükbaşı Burnu (36°33′N 29°01′E). A good lookout should be kept for them when passing through these waters. See *Annual Notice to Mariners No 8*.

Directions

(continued from 5.43)

Chart 1054

Principal marks

5.73

1 **Landmark:**

Television mast (red obstruction light) (36°15′N 29°21′E), standing on the W side of Yalı Limanı (5.80).

2 **Major light:**

Vrachonisís Strongilí Light (round tower and dwelling, 7 m in height) (36°07′N 29°38′E), exhibited from near the SW end of the island.

Peksimet Adası to Çatal Adaları

5.74

1 From a position about 7 miles SSW of Peksimet Adası (36°34′N 28°50′E), the track leads SE, passing (with positions from Kötü Burnu (36°23′N 29°06′E)):

SW of Dökükbaşı Burnu (10¼ miles NNW) (5.53), from where a light is exhibited, thence:

SW of Sümbeki Burnu (5 miles N). The coast, 5 miles N and S of Sümbeki Burnu, is lofty and bold, with several creeks in the S part which afford anchorage to small vessels with local knowledge. Thence:

2 SW of Kötü Burnu, which is one of the Seven Capes of Yediburunlar; Yedi Burun 1 mile N of Kötü Burun is the N-most cape of these seven. These are the extremities of spurs from a range of rugged mountains running parallel and close to the coast for 7 miles. A light (white metal framework tower, 6 m in height) is exhibited from Kötü Burnu. Thence:

3 SW of the other Capes of Yediburunlar, named from NW to SE, as Sancak Burnu (1 mile SE), İnkaklık Burnu (2½ miles SE), Yassıca Burnu (4 miles SE), Kılıç Burnu (5 miles SE) and İnce Burnu (6¼ miles SE). Thence:

4 SW of another İnce Burnu (13¼ miles SE); the ruins of Patara, an ancient city and port, lie close inland of İnce Burnu. Bishop Nicholas of Myra, the present-day Santa Claus, was born at Patara. Between İnce Burnu and İnce Burnu, 7 miles NW, the coast is fronted by a sandy beach with shoal water extending 7½ cables offshore; the mouth of Eşen Çayı cuts through this beach about midway along.

5 The track then leads to a position SW of Çatal Adaları (16 miles SE), from the SW extremity of which is exhibited a light (white metal framework tower, 6 m in height). Sıçan Adası lies close NE of Çatal Adaları.

Çatal Adaları to Vrachonisís Strongilí

5.75

1 The track then continues SE, passing (with positions from Çatal Adaları (36°13′N 29°21′E)):

SW of Sarıbelen Ada and Heybeli Ada (4½ miles E), thence:

SW of Öksüz Ada (5 miles SE), which is steep-to, thence:

2 SW of Nisída Ró (7¾ miles SE) (5.81), thence:

SW of the S extremity of Nísos Meyísti (12 miles SE) (5.83).

The track then leads to a position S of Vrachonisís Strongilí (36°07′N 29°38′E), where a light (5.73) is exhibited from the SW end.

3 This island, in the S entrance to Kólpos Kastellorízou, rises to an elevation of 197 m and is steep-to. A shoal area, with a least depth of 4 m over a rock, extends about 1½ cables SW from the island.

(Directions for the coastal route continue at 5.107)

Anchorages and harbours

5.76

1 Karacaören Bükü (36°32′·5N 29°03′·2E) is a small cove fronted by Karacaören Adaları, an islet lying 2½ miles E of Dökükbaşı Burnu (5.53). The islet is covered in ruins; rocky foul ground extends between the S extremity of the islet and the shore W. A light buoy (S cardinal) marks an islet between Karacaören Adaları and the shore.

2 There is reasonable sheltered anchorage at the head of the cove, in depths of 6 to 10 m, with a line to the shore. The bottom is thick weed over sand.

Gemiler Adası

5.77

1 Gemiler Adası (36°33′·2N 29°04′·2E) is an islet covered in ruins; good shelter may be obtained by small vessels in the channel, 1 cable wide, which separates Gemiler Adası from the mainland N.

Kalevezi Koyu

5.78

1 Kalevezi Koyu, entered 5 cables NE of Gemiler Adası is open S, with foul ground extending from its E shore. It contains several coves suitable for anchoring in, but only during light winds.

Keçiler, a town, lies 1 mile N of Kalevezi Koyu, and is situated on the S side of a well-cultivated, elevated plain which produces good wine and figs.

Ölüdeniz

5.79

1 Ölüdeniz (36°33′N 29°07′E), 5 cables N of Yoğan Burnu, is a beautiful landlocked bay.

To prevent pollution the harbour is closed to yachts; only caiques and rowing boats are permitted to enter.

Yalı Limanı

5.80

1 **Description.** Yalı Limanı is entered between Yalı Burnu (36°14′N 29°21′E) and İnce Burun, 2 miles ENE; a shoal, with a depth of 6·8 m over it, lies 2½ cables SSW of İnce Burun. Yalı Limanı affords indifferent anchorage owing to its considerable depths and exposure S, but none the less is popular with leisure craft. Its shores are steep-to but there are some rocks near the W shore.

2 **Harbour.** Kalkan, a village on the NE shore of the bay, is fronted by a small harbour protected from SW by a breakwater to which small vessels secure bow or stern-to. There are depths of 5·6 to 7 m within the harbour, and 1·4 to 3 m alongside. There is a light on either side of the SE facing entrance.

Supplies: fuel; fresh water; provisions.

Nisída Ró

5.81

1 Nisída Ró (36°09′N 29°30′E) has an inlet on the S side, suitable for the use of small vessels up to about 300 tons, with depths of 10 to 15 m, but it is affected by winds between E and SE. A bay on the W side of the island has similar depths, and is suitable for small vessels; on the N side of the island there is a small bay with a sandy beach.

NÍSOS MEYÍSTI, KAŞ LİMANI AND APPROACHES

General information

Charts 1054 and plan Approaches to Nísos Meyísti

Routes

5.82

1 Kólpos Kastellorízou (36°08′N 29°37′E), is the Greek name for the gulf between Nísos Meyísti (Kastellorízon) and the mainland NE. This subsection describes the following routes, which lead into the gulf from seaward:

Approach from W, passing N of Nisída Ró (36°09′N 29°30′E).

2 Approach from SW, passing W of Nísos Meyísti (36°09′N 29°35′E).

Approach from S or SE, passing E of Nísos Meyísti.

Topography

5.83

1 Kólpos Kastellorízou contains many islands and islets, the largest of which is Nísos Meyísti (Kastellorízon) (36°09′N 29°35′E), rising to an elevation of 273 m.

To the N, on the mainland between İnce Burun (36°14′N 29°25′E) and the root of Çukurbağ Yarımadası, 11 miles E, the coast is high and rugged.

National limits

5.84

1 Nísos Meyísti and the adjacent Greek islands are the E-most of Dodekánisos (1.90). The national limit between Greece and Turkey runs:

N of Nisída Ró (36°09′N 29°30′E), thence:

S of Gürmenli Kayaları, thence:

2 Between the N end of Nísos Meyísti and Çukurbağ Yarımadası, thence:

Between Vrachonisıs Psomí and Besmi Adası, thence:

Between Vrachonisís Strongilí and Başak Adası (36°08′N 29°39′E).

Currents

5.85

1 The W-going current off the coast of Turkey divides at Ulu Burun (36°08′N 29°41′E). One part continues W to pass S of Nísos Meyísti, while the other part flows through Kólpos Kastellorízou and Kas Channel at rates from ½ to 1½ kn.

2 Sometimes however, the entire current runs W. After passing S of Nísos Meyísti, a part of the current appears to flow N past the W side of the island, thence E through Kas Channel, thence S to rejoin the W-going current.

Directions

Principal marks

5.86

1 **Landmark:**

Radio mast (red obstruction lights) (36°10′N 29°39′E).

Major light:

Vrachonisís Strongilí Light (36°07′N 29°38′E) (5.73).

Approach from west

5.87

1 From a position W of Öksüz Ada (36°11′N 29°27′E) (5.75) the track leads E, passing (with positions from Ákra Ágios Stéfanos Light (36°10′N 29°35′E)):

S of Heybeli Ada (7¾ miles WNW), thence:

Either side of Öksüz Ada (7 miles W), noting a shoal depth of 25 m lying 1 mile NE of the islet, thence:

S of a dangerous rock (5½ miles NW), marked by a buoy (S cardinal). A patch, with a depth of 9·1 m over it, lies 8 cables NW of the rock. Thence:

2 N of Nisída Ró (4½ miles W), thence:

S of Gürmenli Adası (2¼ miles NW), an islet 30 m high, thence:

Either side of Gürmenli Kayaları (1½ miles W), a group of low and steep-to rocks, noting a shoal depth of 14 m.Thence:

3 N of the N end of Nísos Meyísti, from where Ákra Ágios Stéfanos Light (white metal framework, 5 m in height) is exhibited, and:

S of Ada Burnu (1¼ miles N), the SW extremity of Çukurbağ Yarımadası, thence:

4 Through Kas Channel, known to the Greeks as Stenó Vathi, which leads between Çukurbağ Yarımadası and Nísos Meyísti.

The track then leads to a position about 1 mile NW of Gata Burnu (2 miles E) off the entrance to Kaş Limanı (5.97).

5 **Clearing bearing.** The line of bearing 298° of Siçan Adası (36°13′·4N 29°22′·4E), open SW of Heybeli Ada, clears SW of the dangerous rock, 2 miles NE of Öksüz Ada.

Useful mark:

İnce Burnu Light (36°11′·0N 29°38′·5E) (5.98).

(Directions for Kaş Limanı continue at 5.98)

Approach from south-west

5.88

1 From a position S of Nisída Ró (36°09′N 29°30′E) the track leads NE, in the white sector of Ákra Ágios Stéfanos Light (060°-086°), passing with positions from the Light (36°10′N 29°35′E)):

NW of Ákra Zefírion (3 miles SSW), the S extremity of Nísos Meyísti, thence:

SE of Vrachonisís Savoúra (4 miles WSW), a small islet lying close off the SE coast of Nisída Ró, thence:

2 SE of Vrachonisís Tragónera (3½ miles W), an islet at the E end of Nisída Ró, thence:

NW of Ákra Limenári (1 mile SW), and:

SE of Gürmenli Kayaları (1½ miles W) (5.87).

The track then leads E through Kas Channel to a position about 1 mile NW of Gata Burnu (2 miles E) off the entrance to Kaş Limanı (5.97).

Useful mark:

İnce Burnu Light (36°11′·0N 29°38′·5E) (5.98).

(Directions for Kaş Limanı continue at 5.98)

Approach from south and south-east

5.89

1 From a position about 2 miles SW of Vrachonisís Strongilí Light (36°07′N 29°38′E) (5.73) the track leads N, passing (with positions from Vrachonisís Strongilí Light):

W of Vrachonisís Strongilí (5.75), thence:

E of Ákra Zefírion (3½ miles WNW), thence:

W of Başak Adası (1½ miles NE), lying close W of the island of Sarıada Adası. Vessels approaching Kólpos Kastellorízou from SE may pass between Başak Adası and Vrachonisís Strongilí. Thence:

2 E of Ákra Megálos Níftis (2½ miles NNW), the E extremity of Nísos Meyísti, thence:

W of Besmi Adası (2½ miles N), above water and surrounded by a reef, which lies 3 cables W of Kovan Adası. A patch of rocks with a depth of 1·8 m over them, lies 1 cable SSE. And:

E of Vráchoi Mávro Poíni (2½ miles NNW) and Vráchoi Mávro Poïnáki (2¾ miles NNW), above-water rocks surrounded by shoal water for a distance of ¼ cable, thence:

3 E of Ýfalos Koutsoumbás (2¾ miles NNW), a rock which dries, thence:

E of Vrachonisís Psomí (3 miles NNW), an islet with shoal water extending ¼ cable NE and SW, thence:

W of the islets (3 miles N) of Bayrak Adası and Heybeli Adası, thence:

E of Ákra Ágios Stéfanos (3½ miles NNW).

4 The track then leads to a position about 1 mile NW of Gata Burnu (3¾ miles N) off the entrance to Kaş Limanı (5.97). A restricted area where diving is prohibited is located S of Gata Burnu.

(Directions for Kaş Limanı continue at 5.98)

Liménas Kastellorízou

Chart 1054 plan of Órmos Kastellorízou

General information

5.90

1 **Position.** Liménas Kastellorízou (36°09′N 29°36′E) lies at the head of Órmos Kastellorízou, on the NE side of Nísos Meyísti. Meyísti is situated on the shores of the harbour, and is backed by steep hills.

2 **Approach and entry.** Liménas Kastellorízou can be approached from W, passing through Kas Channel, directions for which are given at 5.87, or from S, passing NNW of Vrachonisís Strongilí, directions for which are given at 5.89. The bay is entered between Ákra Megálos Níftis (36°09′N 29°36′E) and Ákra Ágios Stéfanos, 1 mile NNW.

Limiting conditions

5.91

1 **Depths.** There are depths of from 6·4 to 12·8 m in the central part of the harbour, which has a width of 1 cable, and is generally crowded with local craft.

Arrival information

5.92

1 **Outer anchorage.** A roadstead, with depths of from 11 to 17 m, sand and mud, situated 4½ cables NW of Ákra Megálos Níftis (36°08′·9N 29°36′·4E), is sheltered by Vrachonisís Psoradiá to the NW, Vrachonisís Polifádos to the N, and Vrachonisís Agrieliá and Vrachonisís Ágios Geórgios to the E. A rocky spit, with a least depth of 3·3 m over it, extends E from Vrachonisís Psoradiá leaving only a narrow channel, with a charted depth of 7·8 m, between its extremity and the coastal reef of Vrachonisís Polifádos; a narrow foul channel separates Vrachonisís Agrieliá and Vrachonisís Ágios Geórgios. The roadstead is entered between Vrachonisís Polifádos and Vrachonisís Agrieliá, where there is a width of ¾ cable between the charted 10 m contours.

2 Ormískos Mandráki (36°09′·1N 29°35′·8E), on the S side of the roadstead, provides sheltered anchorage in its outer part, except during N winds, in a depth of about 3·5 m with good holding ground; the inner part of the bay is shoal.

3 **Caution.** A NW-going current of nearly 2 kn has been observed running into the channels on each side of Vrachonisís Ágios Geórgios, and running out through the passage between Vrachonisís Psoradiá and Vrachonisís Polifádos. The conditions causing such a strong current are not known.

Harbour

5.93

1 **General layout.** The harbour, lying at the head of Órmos Kastellorízou, is enclosed by land on three sides, with a narrow entrance to the NNE. The main berthing area lies on the SE side of the harbour.

2 **Landmarks:**

A conspicuous pylon (36°09′·3N 29°35′·4E), 1¼ cables W of the light, stands near the W entrance point of the harbour.

Ruins of a castle (36°09′·2N 29°35′·6E) standing on the E side of the harbour. A windmill stands ½ cable S of the castle.

Directions

5.94

1 From a position about 3 cables SE of Ákra Ágios Stéfanos (36°09′·9N 29°36′·0E) the track leads SW into Liménas Kastellorízou, passing (with positions from Ákra Ágios Stéfanos):

NW of Vrachonisís Psomí (6½ cables SE) (6½ cables SE), thence:

2 NW of Vrachonisís Polifádos (6 cables S) and Vrachonisís Psoradiá (7 cables SSW), taking care to avoid a rocky shoal, with a least depth of 7·0 m over it, 1½ cables ENE of Vrachonisís Polifádos.

3 Thence enter the harbour, passing close NW of a shoal (7½ cables SW) with a depth of 8·2 m over it, nearly ¼ cable NNW of the light-structure (metal framework on white square hut, red band, 6 m in height) on the E entrance point.

Caution. A dangerous wreck lies close N of the quay (5.95).

Berths

5.95

1 There is a ferry quay 84 m long on the SE side of the harbour with depths alongside of 6·2 to 6·6 m. A slip for small craft is located on the N part of the quay, about 5 m from the shore.

Port services

5.96

1 **Repairs:** small boatyard in Ormískos Mandráki (36°09′·1N 29°35′·8E); minor repairs only. Slip at Liménas Kastellorízou.

Supplies: limited quantities of fuel and fresh water; fresh provisions may be obtained.

Kaş Limanı

Chart 1054 plan Approaches to Nísos Meyísti

General information

5.97

1 Kaş Limanı is a crescent-shaped bay, sheltered by the Greek island of Nísos Meyísti from SW, and by the narrow peninsula of Çukurbağ Yarımadası to the NW.

The bay is entered between Çondur Burnu (36°11′N 29°37′E) and İnce Burnu, 1½ miles ESE.

Directions

(continued from 5.87, 5.88 or 5.89)

5.98

1 From a position about 1 mile NW of Gata Burnu (36°10′·3N 29°37′·8E) the anchorages and the harbour at Kaş are directly accessible.

Useful marks:

İnce Burnu Light (white metal framework tower, 6 m in height) (36°11′·0N 29°38′·5E).

Kaş Light (white concrete tower, 7 m in height) (36°11′·9N 29°38′·6E), exhibited from the head of the harbour mole.

Anchorages

5.99

1 **Port Longos** (36°11′·6N 29°36′·7E), 2½ cables N of Çondur Burnu, affords anchorage to small vessels, in depths of 12 to 15 m; local knowledge is necessary. The bottom is sand with good holding.

Yarım Ada, an islet, lies in the S part of the anchorage.

2 **Kas** (36°12′·0N 29°38′·5E). There is an anchorage area, shown on the chart, close SW of the harbour mole; a buoy is moored in the N part of the anchorage.

Bayındır Limanı (36°10′·7N 29°38′·8E), a bay at the SE corner of Kaş Limanı, is easy to enter and affords good shelter, but the depths are considerable.

3 A rocky spit extends about ½ cable NE from İnce Burnu. A tongue of land, with a depth of 9·1 m close alongside rocks at its extremity, projects N from the head of the bay, like a pier.

Vessels either anchor, or moor with hawsers to the shore.

Chart 1054 plan Kaş Limanı

Harbour

5.100

1 **Description.** Kaş (36°12′·0N 29°38′·5E) is a village with a small harbour protected from the SW by a mole. The bottom of the harbour is reported to be very irregular and the holding ground poor.

Supplies: fresh water is available on the quay; fuel by tanker; provisions.

Anchorage

Chart 1054 plan Approaches to Nísos Meyísti

Bucak Denizi

5.101

1 **Description.** Bucak Denizi, also known as Port Vathi, lies between the mainland and Çukurbağ Yarımadası, which extends 2¾ miles WSW to Ada Burnu (36°11′N 29°35′E).

Kaş from SW (5.100)
(Original dated prior to 2000)

(Photograph - Peter Kleinoth)

The inlet has a least width of 2½ cables with a least depth of 8 m in the outer part, and 13 m in the inner part.

2 **Directions.** From a position about 1 mile NE of Gürmenli Adası (36°11′·2N 29°32′·9E) the inlet is entered by keeping within the white sector (065°–071°) of Kaş Mevkil Light (galvanised sheet iron tower, 10 m in height) (36°12′·5N 29°36′·9E), passing NNW of an above-water rock lying on the S side of the entrance; a shoal, with a least charted depth of 8·9 m over it, lies 2¼ cables WSW from this rock.

3 **Anchorage.** With local knowledge, sheltered anchorage may be obtained at the head of the inlet, in a depth of about 13 m.

Caution. At times winds from NNE blow with great force off the mountains.

VRACHONISÍS STRONGILÍ TO TAŞLIK BURNU

General information

Charts 236, 1054

Route

5.102

1 From a position about 5 miles S of Vrachonisís Strongilí (36°07′N 29°38′E) the coastal route leads ENE, for about 42 miles, to a position SE of Taşlik Burnu (36°13′N 30°25′E).

Topography

5.103

1 From Vrachonisís Strongilí to Taşdibi Burnu, 18 miles ENE, the coastline is indented by several inlets with islands lying off them. Thence a steep gravel beach extends 5 miles NE from Taşdibi Burnu; near its E end is a large brackish lake with a river flowing into its head. In the narrow entrance to the lake, between the end of the beach and Finike promontory, there is a depth of 0·9 m and depths of 2·7 m exist for some distance within the lake.

2 Finike promontory rises 4¾ miles NW to Şahin Tepe, which is 1499 m high; the mountains inland are snow-clad. Between Finike promontory and Karagöz Koyu, 12 miles E, on the W side of Taşlik Burnu, the N shore of Finike Körfezi is low and sandy.

Submarine exercise areas

5.104

1 Submarines exercise frequently in areas about 30 miles SSE of Ulu Burun (36°08′N 29°41′E), and 20 miles SSE of Taşlik Burnu (36°13′N 30°25′E), respectively. A good lookout should be kept for them when passing through these waters. See *Annual Notice to Mariners No 8*.

Firing practice area

5.105

1 There is a firing practice area in the vicinity of Taşlik Burnu, the limits of which are shown on the chart.

Current

5.106

1 The current off Taşlık Burnu is generally WSW-going at a mean rate of ¾ kn, but large variations in direction and rate have been observed.

Directions

(continued from 5.75)

Principal marks

5.107

1 **Landmarks:**

Radio mast (red obstruction lights) (36°10′N 29°39′E).

Ruined fort (36°12′N 29°52′E), surmounting a hill, 91 m high.

2 **Major lights:**

Vrachonisís Strongilí Light (36°07′N 29°38′E) (5.73).

Taşlık Burnu Light (white concrete tower and dwelling, 9 m in height) (36°13′N 30°25′E), exhibited 8 cables NNE of the cape.

Vrachonisís Strongilí to Taşlık Burnu

5.108

1 From a position about 5 miles S of Vrachonisís Strongilí (36°07′N 29°38′E), the track leads ENE, passing (with positions from Vrachonisís Strongilí):

SSE of Ulu Burun (3 miles NE). Between Ulu Burun (36°08′N 29°41′E) and the head of Asar Limanı or Hisar Limanı, 5 miles farther ENE, the coast is generally steep-to. Thence:

2 SSE of İç Ada (6 miles ENE) lying off the SW extremity of Sıçak Yarımadası. Akar Boğazı, the channel between İç Ada and Sıçak Yarımadası, is narrow but navigable; a strong eddy current has been observed running SE through it. Thence:

3 SSE of Sıçak Yarımadası (8 miles ENE), the peninsula which forms the SE side of Asar Limanı, thence:

SSE of Geyikova Adası (13 miles ENE), which rises to an elevation of 188 m. A light is exhibited from the W end of the island (5.110), and a light (white metal framework tower, 6 m in height) is exhibited from the E extremity of the island; Tek Adası lies 5 cables S of the latter point. Thence:

4 SSE of Taşdibi Burnu (18 miles ENE), the E extremity of a shallow, sandy bay; a ruined castle stands near the point. Thence:

SSE of Bunda Burnu (25 miles ENE), the S extremity of Finike promontory, thence:

SSE of Finike Körfezi (31 miles ENE), contained between Bunda Burnu and Taşlık Burnu. The harbour of Finike (5.109) is situated in the NW corner of the bay. Thence:

5 SSE of Şıldanlar Adaları (38 miles E), a group of four islets. The N islet is 137 m high; the largest islet, Devecitaşı Adası, 1½ miles S of the cape, is 156 m high. South Islet, 18 m high, lies 4 cables farther S, and Ateş Adası lies 1 mile SE of the largest islet. The passages between the islets, and between them and Taşlık Burnu, are navigable. The islets are all steep-to except Ateş Adası, from which a reef extends 1 cable E.

6 The track then leads to a position SE of Taşlık Burnu (36°13′N 30°25′E). It is steep-to, being the S extremity of

a promontory which rises to an elevation of 967 m, 4 miles NNE of the cape. Yardımcı Light (white metal framework tower, 5 m in height) is exhibited from the S extremity of the cape and Taşlık Burnu Light (5.107) is exhibited from a position 8 cables NNE of the cape.

(Directions continue at 5.120)

Finike

General information

5.109

1 **Position and function.** Finike (36°18′N 30°09′E), a small commercial harbour and marina, is situated on the NW side of Finike Körfezi near the mouths of two rivers. Chrome and magnesium ore, citrus fruit and timber are exported.

Useful mark:

Finike Light (metal framework tower, 30 m in height) is exhibited from the coast 1 mile S of the town.

2 **Anchorage**, which is shown on the chart, may be obtained 1 mile seaward of the town, in depths from 11 to 50 m. The anchorage is reported to be dangerous in winter, as it is exposed to strong gales from S.

Harbour. The small harbour is protected by two moles, from the heads of which lights (white concrete towers, 13 m in height) are exhibited. It accommodates vessels of less than 3000 gt.

3 **Berths.** There are two main quays arranged along the inside of the two moles, with smaller quays at the head of the harbour. The centre of the harbour is taken up by marina berths. Charted depths within the harbour vary from 2·7 to 5·6 m. Vessels up to 70 m LOA can be accommodated.

Repairs: minor mechanical repairs only.

Supplies: fuel; fresh water; provisions.

Anchorages

Geyikova Demiryeri

5.110

1 **Description.** Geyikova Demiryeri (36°11′N 29°52′E) lies between the central part of Geyikova Adası (5.108) and the mainland. It affords anchorage in depths of 7·3 to 42 m. The anchorage may be entered from either W or E. A light buoy (S cardinal) is moored close W of the anchorage area.

2 **Directions for the west entrance.** The W entrance, between Sıçak Yarımadası and Geyikova Adası, is divided by Kara Adası and Topak Adası into two channels, each 1¼ cables wide, with depths from 29 to 62 m in the fairway. The W channel is marked by the white sector (355°–358°) of a light (metal framework tower, 10 m in height), exhibited from the mainland 7½ cables N.

3 The E side of the E channel is marked by the light exhibited from the W extremity of Geyikova Adası. A rock with a depth of 1·2 m over it, on which the sea often breaks, lies 1 cable N of the W extremity of Geyikova Adası.

Directions for the east entrance. The E entrance, at the NE end of Geyikova Adası, is straight and clear of dangers beyond ½ cable from the shore on each side. There is generally a slight W-going current in the entrance.

4 **Other anchorages in the vicinity of Geyikova Demiryeri:**

Polemos Bükü (36°10′·0N 29°48′·2E), on the NE side of the isthmus which connects Sıçak Yarımadası to the mainland, affords anchorage to small vessels. The inlet, 1½ miles long, is free of dangers except

Finike from SE (5.109)

(Original dated prior to 2000)

(Photograph - Peter Kleinoth)

for several small islets on the N side. At the head of the inlet there are depths of 5 to 10 m, about 250 m from the shore, over a bottom of mud which provides good holding. Local knowledge is required.

5 Kaleüçağız Limanı (36°11′·8N 29°51′·0E), entered 5 cables W of the ruins of a fort (5.107), is landlocked with depths of from 3·7 to 9·1 m. Several islets and rocks encumber the entrance, which is divided by the N islet into two channels, in which there appear to be depths of 6·4 and 7·3 m, but neither has been closely examined. Kaleüçağız Köyü is situated on the N shore of the bay.

6 Kale Köy (36°11′·3N 29°51′·6E), situated on the NW side of Geyikova Demiryeri, is backed by a ruined fort (5.107) on a hill. Rocks, some above water, extend 1¾ cables offshore S of the fort and are marked by a light buoy (S cardinal). A small patch of submerged rocks lies close SW of an islet situated 6 cables ESE of the fort. Anchorage is most conveniently obtained 3 cables SE of the fort, with generally good holding ground.

7 Xera Cove (36°10′·4N 29°50′·8E), 2½ cables ENE of the W end of Geyikova Adası, affords restricted but sheltered anchorage for small vessels N of the ruins of a church. Vessels may anchor in depths of 4 to 10 m with a line ashore to the W side; the bottom is sandy with good holding.

8 Saint Stephanas Limanı (36°11′·1N 29°53′·4E), a small bay on the SE side of Geyikova Adası, with a rock awash and three islets off its entrance, affords anchorage to small vessels. The islets identify the entrance, which is difficult to pick out from a distance, and closer in, a cave on the E side of the entrance is conspicuous. Vessels may anchor at the head of the bay, in depths of 6 to 10 m, with a line ashore. The bottom is mud and weed providing good holding. Local knowledge is required.

Gökkaya Limanı

5.111

1 **Description.** Gökkaya Limanı (36°13′N 29°54′E) lies between the mainland and Aşırlı Ada. It is surrounded by precipitous rugged mountains covered with low bushes, and the N side of Aşırlı Ada attains an elevation of 82 m.

Directions. Kişneli Ada, 51 m high, is situated 400 m S of Aşırlı Ada, separated from the mainland by a channel about 80 m wide; an islet 22 m high lies close N, and Martinis Bank, above water, extends E from an unnamed islet 2 cables SW of Kişneli Ada.

2 The channel N of Aşırlı Ada has a least width of about 75 m, and a least depth of 7·8 m in the fairway. It leads directly to the anchorage, and is better than the channel S of Aşırlı Ada, which is narrower and intricate.

The S side of the N channel should be favoured, so as to avoid a patch of rocks extending ½ cable from the N shore abreast the middle of Aşırlı Ada.

3 **Caution.** A stranded wreck (mast, position approximate) lies close NE of the entrance to Gökkaya Limanı.

Anchorage. Light-draught vessels may obtain anchorage in Gökkaya Limanı, but the holding ground is not good, and vessels making a long stay should moor. For recreational craft the most popular area for anchoring is in the NW corner, in depths of 5 to 7 m, mud bottom with good holding, although anchorage may be obtained elsewhere.

Andraki

5.112

1 This is an open anchorage within a bay, 2 miles ENE of Gökkaya Limanı (5.111), but is not secure. Çalpan Burnu (36°14′N 29°57′E) forms the E entrance point of the bay, into the E side of which flows Andraki Nehri, which is very brackish in summer and has a bar, passable only by boats of light draught. There is a rough stone breakwater, in the NE corner of the bay, used by local boats.

Gök Limanı

5.113

1 Gök Limanı (36°16′N 30°08′E) lies between the E side of Finike promontory and a bold projection extending 1 mile S. There is a depth of 13 m at its head, but it is open to S winds. The entrance to the bay is obstructed by a shoal patch, with a depth of 9·5 m over it, which lies 5 cables SW of Güvercin Adası, 26 m high, off the E entrance point. The anchorage within Gök Limanı is not safe in the prevailing winds as a heavy swell rolls in.

2 There is a channel suitable for small vessels between Güvercin Adası and the E entrance point of Gök Limanı.

Karagöz Koyu

5.114

1 Karagöz Koyu (36°15′N 30°24′E) affords anchorage to vessels in its S part, sheltered except from W; near the NW entrance point of the bay are some white rocky cliffs resembling a castle. **Caution.** A fish farm is located in the NW part of the bay, close E of Akçaörgu Burnu.

Local knowledge is required.

ANTALYA KÖRFEZİ

GENERAL INFORMATION

Chart 237

Area covered

5.115

1 This section covers Antalya Körfezi, which lies between Taşlık Burnu (36°13′N 30°25′E) and Anamur Burnu (36°01′N 32°48′E), about 117 miles E. The section is arranged as follows:

Taşlık Burnu to Antalya (5.117).
Antalya (5.130).
Antalya to Anamur Burnu (5.154).

Submarine exercise areas

5.116

1 Submarines exercise frequently in areas about 20 miles NE, 40 miles E and 20 miles SSE of Taşlık Burnu (36°13′N 30°25′E), and 15 miles S of Anamur Burnu (36°01′N

32°48′E). A good lookout should be kept for them when passing through these waters. See *Annual Notice to Mariners No 8*.

TAŞLIK BURNU TO ANTALYA

General information

Charts 236, 237, 242

Route

5.117

1 From a position SE of Taşlik Burnu (36°13′N 30°25′E) the coastal route leads initially NNE, for about 21 miles, thence N for a further 20 miles to a position about 4 miles SW of Baba Burnu (36°51′N 30°45′E), in the approaches to Antalya.

Topography

5.118

1 The coast between Taşlık Burnu (36°13′N 30°25′E) and Çavuş Burnu, 10 miles NE, is mostly steep-to, but there are a few rocks lying close offshore.

From Çavuş Burnu the coast, for 8 miles N, is indented by a succession of small bays, and consists of black and crumbling rock, with reefs extending from 1 to 2 cables from every point. North of these points a sandy beach extends 2¼ miles NNE, and then to İnce Burnu, a further 1¾ miles NNE, the coast is indented by two small coves.

2 Between İnce Burnu and Koca Burnu, 4 miles NNE, the coast is formed by a gravel beach through which two rivers reach the sea. Two remarkable brown rocks, 100 m high, are situated inland 3 miles NNW of İnce Burnu.

The coast from Koca Burnu to Sıçan Adası, 12 miles N, has a high range of mountains running parallel to it, from 3 to 4 miles inland, spurs of which descend to the sea.

Submarine exercise areas

5.119

1 See 5.116.

Directions

(continued from 5.108)

Principal marks

5.120

1 **Landmark:**

Tahtalıdağı (36°32′N 30°26′E), a mountain with an elevation of 2366 m.

Major light:

Taşlık Burnu Light (36°13′N 30°25′E) (5.107).

Taşlık Burnu to Antalya

5.121

1 From a position SE of Taşlık Burnu (36°13′N 30°25′E) the track leads NNE, passing (with positions from Taşlık Burnu Light):

ESE of Suluada (3½ miles ENE), which is 165 m high, rugged and almost bare. A natural archway through the SE part of the island can be used by boats, but a strong W-going current runs through it. Thence:

2 ESE of Adrasan (Küçükçavus) Burnu (6 miles NE), the S entrance point of Çavuş Limanı (5.123). A light (white metal framework tower, 10 m in height) is exhibited from the point. Thence:

ESE of Çavuş Burnu (9 miles NE), which is separated from Pırasalı Ada, a barren island close E, by a channel with considerable depths, but in which the current is uncertain, thence:

3 E of Üçadalar (16 miles NNE), a group of three islets 23 m high. A reef extends 1½ cables NNE from the E islet, and a small patch of rocks lies the same distance E of a cove in this islet. A rock 3·9 m high is situated 3½ cables ESE of the E islet.

4 The track then leads N, passing (with positions from Koca Burnu Light (36°36′N 30°35′E)):

E of İnce Burnu (4 miles SSW), a salient feature, thence:

E of Koca Burnu, a bold cliff of white rock, rising to a hill 320 m high; foul ground extends 3 cables E and N of the cape. Koca Burnu Light (metal framework tower, 6 m in height) is exhibited from near the N extremity of the cape. Thence:

5 E of a reef (1¼ miles NW), from where a light (framework tower with concrete platform, 5 m in height) is exhibited. The reef lies 6 cables N of the entrance to Kemer Marina. Thence:

E of Azmak Burnu (6½ miles N), a patch with a depth of 8·3 m lies 7 cables ENE, thence:

6 E of Sıçan Adası (12½ miles N), which is 74 m high, and separated from the mainland by a narrow channel. The channel is much reduced in width by a shoal extending from the coast. Several marine farms extend from 1½ to 3 miles S of the islet. Thence:

7 E of a submarine pipeline extending 1¾ miles SSE from a position on the shore 1 mile NNE of Sıçan Adası. Several light buoys (special) mark the length of the pipeline and its end. Thence:

To a position SW of Baba Burnu (17 miles NNE), which is remarkable for its overhanging cliffs. Baba Burnu Light (white stone tower and dwelling, 6 m in height) is exhibited from the point.

(Directions for the coastal route continue at 5.158 and for Antalya at 5.146)

Anchorages

Suluada

5.122

1 Anchorage may be obtained between Suluada (36°14′N 30°29′E) and the mainland, in depth of 40 m, on a mostly rocky bottom. A small sandy beach on the SW side of the island allows landing in fair weather.

Caution. This anchorage is exposed to the prevailing wind and there is invariably some swell.

Çavuş Limanı

5.123

1 Çavuş Limanı (36°18′N 30°30′E) is open E, but it affords a little shelter to small vessels in a cove in its S part. It is popular with recreational craft.

Local knowledge is advisable.

Cineviz Limanı

5.124

1 Cineviz Limanı (36°22′N 30°30′E) is a bay on the N side of Cineviz Adası, a peninsula of white cliffs, 14 m high. There is also a cove on the S side of the isthmus which connects Cineviz Adası to the mainland. Cineviz Limanı has three above-water rocks in the middle of the entrance which are steep-to; at the head of the bay is a beach.

2 Anchorage is obtainable in a depth of about 16 m, good holding ground. Smaller vessels may anchor, in depths of 6

to 8 m, at the head of the bay; bottom sand and shingle but not everywhere good holding. Winds from N send in some swell, and heavy W squalls blow down from Musa Dağı, 987 m high, 1 mile SW.

Çıralı Limanı

5.125

1 Çıralı Limanı (36°24′N 30°29′E) is contained within points respectively 4 and 5¾ miles NNW of Çavuş Burnu. Çıralı, a village, stands on the SW shore of the bay, with the ruins of the ancient city of Olympus nearby. The anchorage within this bay is exposed and only really usable when winds are from S.

2 Yanar, on the side of a wooded hill near the N end of the bay, 1½ miles inland, is a volcano which emits a bright and constant flame.

Üçadalar

5.126

1 Üçadalar (36°28′N 30°33′E) (5.121) consists of a group of three islets. The E islet of the group has a cove. Anchorage may be obtained around the islets in depths of from 33 to 55 m.

Tekirova

5.127

1 Tekirova (36°31′N 30°33′E), ancient Phaselis, is a town in ruins situated on a peninsula, on either side of which are the remains of an artificial port.

The bay on the S side of the peninsula allows anchoring for recreational craft on its E and W sides, in depths of 5 to 6 m. The bottom is coarse sand with reasonable holding.

2 Vessels may also anchor in the bay on the N side of the peninsula, in depths of 4 to 6 m. The bottom is littered with large boulders and rocks.

Caution. In both the N and S anchorages and around the peninsula there are numerous above and below-water rocks, most of them the remains of ancient breakwaters.

Koca Burnu

5.128

1 At the S extremity of Koca Burnu (36°36′N 30°35′E) there is a creek in which small vessels can shelter, and in the middle of the cape there is a deep cave which could be entered by several boats. There is also a small bay on the N side of the cape into which a rivulet flows.

Kemer

5.129

1 There is a designated anchorage area close N of Kemer Marina (36°36′N 30°35′E). Its limits are defined by a line drawn joining the following positions:

36°37′·5N 30°34′·5E,
36°39′·5N 30°34′·5E,
36°39′·5N 30°35′·5E,
36°37′·5N 30°35′·5E.

ANTALYA

General information

Charts 237, 242, plan of Approaches to Antalya

Position

5.130

1 Antalya (36°53′N 30°42′E) is situated at the head of Antalya Körfezi. The town is built round its old harbour, on cliffs 30 m high, and is surrounded by an ancient ditch and a rampart with numerous towers.

Function

5.131

1 Antalya is a port of entry, importing fertilizers, industrial coke, caustic soda and machinery. Exports include barytes, cement, cotton, ferro-chromium, alumina, chrome ore, timber and citrus. It is also a major cruise port.

In 2007 the town had a population of about 800 000.

Topography

5.132

1 From 1 mile NNE of Sıçan Adası (36°48′N 30°35′E) to Antalya, 5½ miles NE, the coast is bordered by a steep gravel beach.

The country in the vicinity of Antalya is fertile, extensively cultivated and well-watered. Several streams fall from cliffs into the sea 7½ cables SE of the town.

Port limits

5.133

1 The port of Antalya Harbour Authority administers the area of sea N of a line:

Azmak Burnu (36°42′·2N 30°34′·5E) to 36°42′·2N 30°40′·0E.

Traffic

5.134

1 In 2007 there were 955 ship calls with a total of 5 607 742 dwt.

Port Authority

5.135

1 Ortadogu Antalya Liman Isletmeleri A.S., Buyuk Liman, 07070 Antalya, Turkey.

Limiting conditions

Deepest and longest berth

5.136

1 Alongside berth: TMO Quay, Antalya Limanı (5.149).

Tanker berth: tanker terminal (5.148), 2 miles NE of the commercial harbour.

Abnormal water levels

5.137

1 Tides are negligible, but S and SW winds may raise the sea level by 0·6 m, and NW and N winds may lower it by a similar amount.

Draught

5.138

1 The maximum permitted draught for entering the commercial harbour is 9·5 m.

Local weather

5.139

1 In summer moderate winds from between W and N prevail. In autumn and winter winds of force 5 or 6 from between ESE and S are experienced.

The appearance of low greyish clouds on the mountains W of Koca Burnu, 18 miles SSW, may indicate the approach of a Scirocco (1.173).

The commercial harbour is exposed to both N and S winds, and swell enters during S winds.

Arrival information

Notice of ETA

5.140

1 ETA should be sent 24 hours in advance. For further details see *Admiralty List of Radio Signals Volume 6 (3)*.

Anchorages

5.141

1 There are three designated anchorages, shown on the chart:

No 1 Anchorage (merchant ships and foreign warships) centred about 7 cables SE from Antalya Limanı breakwater head.

2 No 2 Anchorage (long term) centred about 1 mile SSW from Yat Limani (36°53′N 30°42′E). The holding is better in the N part of the anchorage.

No 3 Anchorage (explosives) centred about 2½ miles S from Antalya Limanı breakwater head, noting a marine farm close S.

3 **Caution.** A buoy marks the NW side of a wreck, with a depth of 16·4 m over it, lying 2¼ cables WSW of Yat Limanı, the entrance to the old harbour.

Off Baba Burnu. With strong onshore winds vessels should anchor off Baba Burnu (36°51′N 30°46′E) (5.121) to await favourable conditions for berthing. If a storm is forecast, vessels should put to sea.

Pilotage and tugs

5.142

1 **Pilotage** is compulsory for foreign vessels, and for Turkish vessels over 300 gt, berthing at the offshore tanker berths or entering the commercial harbour, Antalya Limanı (5.143). Foreign vessels over 100 gt entering Yat Limanı are requested to take a pilot.

The pilot boards 3 cables NE of the breakwater head of the commercial harbour, as shown on the chart.

2 For details see *Admiralty List of Radio Signals Volume 6 (3)*.

Tugs are available. If berthing at the offshore tanker berths, or entering the commercial harbour, vessels are required to employ one tug if over 500 gt or two tugs if over 4000 gt.

Harbour

General layout

5.143

1 Antalya Limanı (36°50′N 30°37′E), the commercial harbour, is situated at the head of Antalya Körfezi, on its W side, 5 miles SW of the town of Antalya. It is an artificial harbour protected by S and N breakwaters; a light is exhibited from the head of each breakwater. The S breakwater extends ESE from the shore for 2½ cables, forming Military Quay, thence NE for 4½ cables; the N breakwater extends from the shore SSE for 1½ cables, thence SW for 1½ cables. The harbour entrance, open NE, is about 1¼ cables wide. General depths within the harbour are from 4 to 10 m.

2 There are also two offshore tanker terminals, 5 cables SSW and 2 miles NE of the commercial harbour, respectively.

There are marinas at Setur Antalya, inside the commercial harbour, and at Yat Limanı, formed from the old harbour, at the town of Antalya.

Climate information

5.144

1 See 1.184 and 1.195.

Military Quay *Marina*

Antalya from SE (5.143)

(Original dated prior to 2000)

(Photograph - Peter Kleinoth)

Restricted area

5.145

1 A restricted area extending 1 cable NE and 2 cables SW, as shown on the chart, surrounds Military Quay situated in the S part of Antalya Limanı. Entry into this area is prohibited without the permission of the naval authorities.

Directions

(continued from 5.121)

Principal marks

5.146

1 **Landmarks:**

Casino tower (36°49′·3N 30°35′·0E).

Petrol offices (36°51′·9N 30°38′·3E); three prominent tanks nearby.

Concrete tower (prominent) standing 5 miles NNW of the town of Antalya.

Approach and entry

5.147

1 From a position about 4 miles SW of Baba Burnu (36°51′N 30°45′E) (5.121) the tanker terminals, Antalya Limanı and Yat Limanı can be directly accessed, the chart being sufficient guide.

Useful marks:

Lights (white towers, 10 m in height) exhibited from the heads of Antalya Limanı breakwaters (36°50′N 30°37′E).

Lights (white metal towers, 5 m in height) exhibited from the heads of Yat Limanı breakwaters (36°53′N 30°42′E).

Baba Burnu Light (36°51′N 30°45′E) (5.121).

Berths

Offshore tanker berths

5.148

1 **United Nations Terminal.** The terminal consists of four conventional buoy moorings (36°49′·5N 30°36′·6E), at the seaward ends of submarine pipelines extending about 3 to 5 cables offshore. The N berth is close SE of Antalya breakwater and from there the remaining berths lie in a SW direction for about 1 mile. Tankers up to 50 000 dwt and 12·0 m draught can be accommodated. Berthing is by day only.

2 **Terminal north-north-east of Antalya Limanı (Petrol Ofisi).** The terminal consists of two conventional buoy moorings, situated off the tank farm 2 miles NNE of the commercial harbour, at the seaward ends of submarine pipelines extending about 4 cables S and SSE from the shore.

Chart 242 plan Antalya Limanı

Antalya Limanı

5.149

1 With positions from the head of the N breakwater (36°50′·1N 30°36′·8E):

Mineral Quay (1 cable N): Berth 1; length 150 m; charted depth of 8·6 to 9·0 m alongside. General cargo and containers.

Motorboat Quay (1½ cables N): Berths 2 and 3; length 162 m; charted depth of 8 to 11 m alongside. General cargo.

2 RoRo Quay (2 cables N): Berth 4; length 35 m; charted depth of 8·4 m alongside.

General Cargo Quay (1½ cables NNW): Berths 5 and 6; length 290 m; charted depth 7·1 to 9·8 m alongside. General cargo and containers.

Aluminium Quay (1½ cables NW): Berth 7; length 170 m; charted depth of 9·5 m alongside. General cargo and containers.

3 Passenger Quay (2 cables W): Berth 8; length 170 m; charted depth of 9·8 m alongside.

TMO Quay (3 cables NW): Berths 9 and 10; length 340 m; charted depth of 8·9 to 10·2 m alongside. Passengers.

4 **Caution.** A depth of 8 m lies close NE of the E end of Berth 9.

SEKA Quay (4¼ cables NW): Berths 11 and 12; length 210 m; charted depth of 8·1 to 8·9 m alongside.

Military Quay (4 cables SSW): length about 270 m; charted depths of 2·8 to 5·5 m alongside.

Approaches to Antalya from ENE (5.147)

(Original dated 2002)

(Photograph - HMS Chatham Crown Copyright)

Port services

Repairs

5.150

1 Minor repairs can be effected.

Other facilities

5.151

1 Hospital in town; Ship Sanitation Control and Exemption Certificates; garbage and oily waste disposal.

Supplies

5.152

1 Fuel available by road tanker; fresh water; fresh provisions.

Communications

5.153

1 Internal air services from Antalya airport, 12 km ENE of the town.

ANTALYA TO ANAMUR BURNU

General information

Chart 237

Route

5.154

1 From a position about 4 miles SW of Baba Burnu (36°51′N 30°45′E) the coastal route leads generally SE, for about 118 miles, to a position S of Anamur Burnu (36°01′N 32°48′E).

Topography

5.155

1 The coast between Baba Burnu and Selimiye, 31 miles E, is low and sandy, with several rivers entering the sea along it. Sandhills, generally low, in some places bare and in others covered with bushes, stretch along the beach. A group of high sandhills stands about midway between Lara and Selimiye. Behind the coastal sandhills a broad irregular plain extends to the foot of the mountains. Along this stretch of coast depths of 9 m or less lie up to 1 mile offshore in places.

2 The coast between Selimiye and Kara Burnu, 16 miles ESE, is low and sandy. Several rapid rivers enter the sea through this stretch of coast, and rocks and shoal water extend offshore in places.

3 The coast between Kara Burnu and Kaleardı Burnu, 16½ miles ESE, at Alanya (36°32′N 32°00′E), is bordered by rocks and islets in places. Thence between Alanya and Anamur Burnu, 51 miles SE, the coast is mostly high and bold, with only a few indentations and no harbours.

Submarine exercise areas

5.156

1 See 5.116.

Regulations

5.157

1 Diving is prohibited in many coastal areas (see 1.48).

Directions

(continued from 5.121)

Principal marks

5.158

1 **Landmarks:**

Cebreis Dağı (36°31′N 32°13′E), 1649 m high.

Radio mast (position approximate), 3 miles ENE of Karataş Burnu (36°02′N 32°41′E).

2 **Major lights:**

Alanya Light (white stone tower and dwelling, 6 m in height) (36°32′N 32°00′E), exhibited from cliffs on the S side of the promontory extending S from Alanya.

Anamur Burnu Light (white stone tower and dwelling, 10 m in height) (36°01′N 32°48′E).

Antalya to Alanya

5.159

1 From a position about 4 miles SW of Baba Burnu (36°51′N 30°45′E) (5.121) the track leads SE, passing (with positions from Selimiye Light (36°46′N 31°23′E)):

SW of the remains of the artificial harbour of Lara (28¾ miles WNW), ancient Attalia. The town is in ruins with few remains. Thence:

SW of two submarine pipelines (28¼ miles WNW), which extend 3½ cables from the coast and are marked by buoys (special), thence:

2 SW of Aksu Çayı (23 miles WNW), thence:

SW of Köprü Çayı (11 miles NW). Both Aksu Çayı and Köprü Çayı are large rivers, with deep water inside their bars, but small boats can only enter with difficulty. Thence:

SW of the entrance to Acısu Dere (7½ miles NW). Rocky patches exist close offshore for 3 miles E of its mouth. Thence:

3 SW of Selimiye (5.167). A light is exhibited from the point projecting seaward from Selimiye, and patches with depths of 7·6 and 8·5 m over them lie about 1 and 2 miles W of the point respectively. Thence:

SW of the entrance to Manavgat Irmağı (5 miles ESE) (5.168). Submarine discharge pipes extend 1½ miles seaward from a point close E of the river mouth. Two superbuoys are moored, one on either side of the pipelines. Thence:

4 SW of Kara Burnu (15½ miles SE), a cliff covered with dark trees. An islet lies close off a point 5 cables NW of the cape, and there are several rocks in the vicinity. Thence:

SW of Fidan Burnu (21 miles SE), which projects 5 cables SW from the coastline. It is the supposed site of ancient Ptolemais, but the long pier which formed its harbour is now submerged. Patches of rock and irregular soundings, lie off the point.

5 The track then leads to a position SW of Kaleardı Burnu (32¾ miles SE) (5.161), from where a light is exhibited. A submarine discharge pipe extends 3 cables SSW from a point on the coast 3½ miles NW of Kaleardı Burnu.

Caution. Between Kara Burnu and Kaleardı Burnu, 16½ miles SE, the coast should be approached with caution as it is bordered by rocks and islets in places.

Alanya to Anamur Burnu

5.160

1 From a position SW of Kaleardı Burnu the track continues to lead SE, passing (with positions from Selinti Burnu Light (36°14′N 32°18′E)):

SW of Aydap (5 miles NNW), situated close NW of a promontory which extends 1 cable SW from the coast, and on which are the ruins of ancient Hamaxia. The cliffs of the promontory are 42 m high. The cove E of the promontory affords limited shelter. There is a marine farm 7 cables WSW of Aydap. Thence:

2 SW of Kale Burnu (2 miles NNW), the S entrance point of Halil Limanı (5.169). It has cliffs 176 m high on its S side. The ruins of Gazipaşa, ancient Trajanopolis, are situated near the mouth of Musa Çayı, a shallow river, and contain the mausoleum of the Emperor Trajan, a very large structure formerly surrounded by 110 columns. Thence:

3 SW of Selinti Burnu. A light (white metal framework pylon, 8 m in height) is exhibited from the point. Thence:

SW of Kesik Burnu (6¼ miles SE), thence:

SW of Yakacık Köyü (15½ miles SE), a small bay. Yakacık (36°06′N 32°35′E) is situated at the head of the bay. Thence:

4 SW of a dangerous wreck (position approximate) (19 miles SE), thence:

SW of Karataş Burnu (22 miles SE). There is an anchorage (5.170) in the bay E of this point.

The track then leads to a position S of Anamur Burnu (27½ miles SE). The point, where a light (5.158) is exhibited, has a W bluff 150 m high, bold and steep-to. The ruins of an old city cover the cape and vicinity.

5 **Useful mark:**

Two domes standing on a hill, 381 m high, 1 mile NNW of Anamur Burnu (36°01′N 32°48′E).

(Directions continue at 5.176)

Alanya

Chart 237 plan of Alanya

General information

5.161

1 **Position.** Alanya (36°32′N 32°00′E) stands on the E side of a promontory, 212 m high, which extends 1 mile S from the coastline.

Function. Alanya, with a population of about 12 000, consists of an old and a new town. The old town of Alanya stands on the promontory surrounded by a defensive wall; the houses are built in terraces, one above another, on its steep rocky slope. The modern part of Alanya, with many hotels, has spread out behind the sandy beaches on either side of the promontory.

2 Alanya mainly functions as a resort but bananas, oranges, pistachio nuts and beans are exported.

Topography. Kaleardı Burnu is the SW extremity of the above-mentioned promontory; there are dark reddish cliffs on either side of the cape, those to the N being 183 m high, and those to the E 152 m high. A high rocky ridge, on which stands a castle, extends 3 cables SW from the cape.

3 **Traffic.** In 2007 there were 109 ship calls with a total of 358 286 dwt.

Port Authority. ALIDAS Alanya Liman Isletmesi, Carsi Mah, Iskele Meydani, 07400 Alanya, Turkey.

Limiting conditions

5.162

1 **Maximum size of vessel handled:** 165 m LOA and 6·5 m draught for alongside berth.

Arrival information

5.163

1 **Port operations:** Continuous.

Notice of ETA: 24 hours.

Anchorages. Alanya Limanı, on the E side of the promontory, offers moderately good anchorage in several places. The anchorages must be used with caution, especially in winter, as the bottom is loose sand and a heavy surf rolls in during and after S winds. The anchorages, shown on the chart, are as follows:

2 Small vessels. Anchor in a depth of about 6 m, with Octagon Tower, 5 cables NNE of Alanya Light, bearing 250°, distant 6 cables.

General anchorage. Anchor in depths of 15 to 20 m, 5 to 6 cables SE of Octagon Tower.

Explosives anchorage. For vessels carrying explosives there is a designated anchorage about 2½ miles SE of Octagon Tower.

3 **Pilotage** is compulsory for vessels of 150 gt and greater. The pilot boards about 1 mile S from the jetty.

For further details see *Admiralty List of Radio Signals Volume 6 (3).*

Harbour

5.164

1 The harbour consists of a pile pier extending 1 cable ESE, thence 1¾ cables SE, from close E of Octagon Tower. A short mole extends NE from the root of the pier, behind which there is a basin. Lights (occasional) are exhibited from the head of the pier and the head of the mole.

Berths

5.165

1 The pile pier, length 300 m, is reported to have four berths with charted depths alongside of 6 to 8 m.

Port services

5.166

1 **Facilities:** small hospital in the town; Ship Sanitation Control and Exemption Certificates are issued; lighters for handling cargo from the anchorage; no cranes.

Supplies: small quantities of fresh provisions; fresh water on the pier.

Anchorages and harbours

Chart 237

Selimiye

5.167

1 **Description.** Selimiye (36°46′N 31°23′E), ancient Side, is situated on a point projecting SW from the coastline. Selimiye Light is exhibited from the point.

The harbours of this ancient town are now filled up, but numerous ruins, particularly an enormous theatre, remain well-preserved. A small village is situated among the ruins.

2 **Anchorage.** Small vessels may anchor on either side of the point; the N side affords the best shelter. On the N side anchor in depths of 3 to 6 m, hard sand. However this does not provide good holding and in the event of an increase in S winds it is best to seek shelter either at Kemer (5.129) or Antalya (5.130).

3 **Berths.** Limited berths are available to the E of the point, but rubble obstructions extend some distance underwater. **T**-shaped piers are located E and W of the point, with depths at their heads from 2 to 3 m.

Manavgat Irmağı

5.168

1 Manavgat Irmağı enters the sea 5½ miles ESE of Selimiye (36°46′N 31°23′E), with a depth of 0·9 m on the bar. The mouth of the river is not visible from seaward, as within the entrance it runs parallel with the coast, but muddy water discharged from the mouth extends several miles seaward. Close within the entrance the river is 1 cable wide, with a depth of 3·7 m, which increases to 6·4 m further upriver.

2 Manavgat Kalesi, a castle, stands on the right bank 4 miles within the entrance; here the river is ¼ cable wide,

with a depth of 4·0 m. The river reaches the coastal plain through a large and noticeable gap in the mountains.

Halil Limanı

5.169

1 Halil Limanı (36°15′·9N 32°16′·5E) contains an open anchorage on its N side, off the mouth of a river. Vessels may anchor in depths of 3 to 5 m, sand, but it is not suitable as an overnight anchorage.

Karataş

5.170

1 This is a small bay lying on the E side of Karataş Burnu (36°03′N 32°41′E). Anchorage may be obtained off the village at its head, in depths of 5 to 10 m, sand and rock.

Caution. There is a rocky patch just underwater in the middle of the bay and a rocky ledge runs around the edge of the bay extending 30 to 40 m offshore.

Anamur Burnu

5.171

1 Good anchorage is obtainable by vessels on the E side of Anamur Burnu (36°01′N 32°48′E) during fresh W sea breezes. The anchorage, which should only be used temporarily as it is exposed, has depths of 5 to 10 m with a sand and rock bottom.

Local knowledge is required.

2 A second anchorage, for larger vessels, can be obtained 5 miles NE of Anamur Burnu in depths of 31 to 40 m.

Climate information: There is a weather observing station at Anamur, 4 miles NNE of Anamur Burnu; for climatic table see 1.184 and 1.196.

ANTALYA KÖRFEZİ TO İSKENDERUN KÖRFEZİ

GENERAL INFORMATION

Charts 237, 2632

Area covered

5.172

1 The area covered by this section comprises:

Anamur Burnu to İncekum Burnu (5.173).

İncekum Burnu to Mersin (5.189).

Mersin (5.197)

Mersin to Karataş Burnu (5.226).

ANAMUR BURNU TO İNCEKUM BURNU

General information

Charts 237, 2632

Route

5.173

1 From a position S of Anamur Burnu (36°01′N 32°48′E) the coastal route leads 58 miles ENE to a position S of İncekum Burnu (36°14′N 33°57′E).

Topography

5.174

1 Between Anamur Burnu (36°01′N 32°48′E) and Iskele, 4½ miles NE, a village with a pier, the coast is bordered by a sandy beach. Anamur Çayı enters the sea close NE and Mabmuriye Kalesi (36°05′N 32°53′E), a large old castle, stands 1½ miles NE of the village.

2 From Mabmuriye Kalesi to Kızılliman Burnu, 9 miles E, the coast becomes higher, and is backed by high mountains which are visible from a great distance.

Thence the coast between Kızılliman Burnu and the W side of Taşucu Körfezi, 40 miles ENE, appears to be high and mostly steep-to, being indented by several bays.

Submarine exercise area

5.175

1 Submarines exercise frequently in an area 15 miles S of Anamur Burnu (36°01′N 32°48′E). A good lookout should be kept for them when passing through these waters. See *Annual Notice to Mariners No 8.*

Directions

(continued from 5.160)

Principal marks

5.176

1 **Major lights:**

Anamur Burnu Light (36°01′N 32°48′E) (5.158).

Ovacık Yarımadası Light (white metal column, 10 m in height) exhibited from Bölükada Burnu (36°08′N 33°41′E).

Other aid to navigation

5.177

1 **Racon:**

İncekum Burnu Light (36°14′N 33°57′E).

See *Admiralty List of Radio Signals Volume 2* for details.

Anamur Burnu to Yılanlı Adası

5.178

1 From a position S of Anamur Burnu (36°01′N 32°48′E) (5.160), the track leads ENE, passing (with positions from Anamur Burnu Light):

SSE of a submarine discharge pipe (1½ miles NE), marked by buoys, extending 1¼ miles S from the shore, thence:

SSE of Iskele Pier (4½ miles NE) and Mabmuriye Kalesi (6 miles NE) (5.174). Foul ground extends 5 cables offshore S of Mabmuriye Kalesi. Thence:

2 SSE of Bozyazı Ada (9½ miles NE), which lies close offshore. Softa Kalesi stands on a hill 201 m high, 2 miles NE of Bozyazı Ada. On the coast below the castle are the ruins of an ancient pier and town, probably Arsinoe. Thence:

SSE of Kızılliman Burnu (14 miles ENE), the extremity of a bold peninsula 193 m high. Between Bozyazı Ada and Kızılliman Burnu there are several small bays which might afford shelter to vessels; local knowledge is required. Thence:

3 SSE of Aksaz Adası (18 miles NE), a bare rock with shoal water on its SW side. In the bay behind Aksaz Adası rocks and shoal water extend up to 5 cables offshore. Thence:

SSE of Soğuksu Limanı (24¾ miles ENE) (5.185), several mooring buoys and a platform are located off the entrance, thence:

SSE of Aydıncık Limanı (26½ miles ENE) (5.186). Büyükada, an islet 35 m high, lies 1½ miles E of Aydıncık Limanı.

The track then leads to a position SSE of Yılanlı Adası (28½ miles ENE), a bare rock 29 m high.

Yılanlı Adası to İncekum Burnu

5.179

1 The track then continues ENE, passing (with positions from Ovacık Yarımadası Light (36°08′N 33°41′E)):

SSE of Sipahili Limanı (11 miles W), a bay which is entered between Sancak Burnu and a promontory 7 miles E. The bay contains islets and creeks which could be entered by small vessels but none of them affords shelter from SW winds. Local knowledge is required. Thence:

2 SSE of Beşparmak Adaları (7½ miles W), consisting of two islands separated from each other by a narrow rocky channel. Beşparmak Adası, the S and larger island is 104 m high. Thence:

SSE of Bölükada Burnu, from where Ovacık Yarımadası Light (5.176) is exhibited. It is the S extremity of Ovacık Yarımadası, a promontory 151 m high, connected to the mainland by a low narrow isthmus; on each side of the isthmus is a small bay, that on the W side being foul. Thence:

3 SSE of Dana Adası (5 miles NE), which rises to an elevation of 256 m near its SW extremity. A light (metal framework tower on concrete base, 4 m in height) is exhibited from the NE extremity of the island. A rock awash, and steep-to at a distance of less than 1 cable, lies WSW of the SW extremity of the island. Thence:

4 To a position S of İncekum Burnu (36°14′N 33°57′E), which is the extremity of a long, low projecting point of sand. An irregular shoal with depths of less than 10 m extends 3 miles SSW of the point. A light (platform on metal column, 12 m in height) is exhibited S of the point.

(Directions continue at 5.193)

Taşucu Körfezi

Chart 242 plans Approaches to Taşucu and Taşucu Limani

General information

5.180

1 **Description.** Taşucu Körfezi is a large bay, entered between İncekum Burnu (36°14′N 33°57′E) and a point on the coast 7 miles W.

Topography. The W shore of the bay is high and steep, with several small bays. The E shore of Taşucu Körfezi consists of low sandhills.

Currents. A current is reported to set SW across İncekum Burnu causing overfalls in places.

Directions

5.181

1 From a position about 6 miles E of Ovacık Yarımadası Light (5.176), exhibited from Bölükada Burnu (36°08′N 33°41′E), the track leads NNE, passing (with positions from Dana Adası Light (36°12′N 33°47′E)):

ESE of Dana Adası (5.179), from where a light is exhibited. The channel between the island and the mainland is known as Kargıcak Boğazı. Thence:

WNW of İncekum Burnu (8¼ miles ENE) (5.179), thence:

2 ESE of Ağalimanı Burnu (5½ miles NNE), the NE extremity of a peninsula on each side of which are bays which provide some shelter. A light (metal framework tower, 8 m in height) is exhibited from the point. Thence:

To a position close S of the harbour of Taşucu (5.182).

Taşucu

5.182

1 **Position and function.** Taşucu (36°19′N 33°53′E), at the head of Taşucu Körfezi, is the port for Silifke, 4 miles NNE.

Port Authority. SEKA-Taşucu Limanı, Seka Limanı, Taşucu, Silifke, Turkey.

Maximum size of vessel handled. Approximately 8000 dwt.

Anchorages. Close S of the harbour are two anchorages, the E being designated an explosives anchorage (see chart), sheltered from all winds except those between SE and SW: when these winds occur vessels should immediately proceed to sea.

2 **Harbour.** Taşucu Limanı comprises two artificial harbours fronting Taşucu. The E harbour, used by cargo vessels, has general depths from 5 to 11 m. The entrance faces WNW and lights (white metal framework towers, 4 m in height) are exhibited from the heads of the breakwaters.

The W harbour, used by ferries and yachts, has depths decreasing from 5 m in the entrance to shallows at its head. The entrance to this harbour faces ESE. Lights (white metal framework towers, 6 m in height) are exhibited from the heads of the breakwaters.

3 **Ağalar Limanı.** This small inlet on the NW side of Ağalimanı Burnu is a good harbour for small vessels. Liman Kalesi, a ruined castle at the N end of which is a prominent tower 11 m high, stands on the W side of the inlet, from where a jetty extends NE for about 500 m.

Climate information. There is a weather observing station at Silifke, 4 miles NNE of Taşucu; for climate information see 1.184 and 1.197.

4 **Berths:**

East harbour. There is a quay on the N side, about 320 m long, with depths alongside of 6 to 10 m.

West harbour. A jetty projects SSW from the W end of the S breakwater of the harbour. The jetty is about 140 m long with a depth of 8 m near its head. The W side of the harbour is quayed.

Facilities: harbour office; post office.

Supplies: fresh water; provisions can be obtained from Silifke.

Communications: ferry service to Kyrenia (6.200).

Anchorages and harbours

Chart 2632

Iskele

5.183

1 There is a designated anchorage area 5 miles NE of Anamur Burnu (36°01′N 32°48′E), off Iskele. Its limits are defined by a line joining the following positions:

36°01′·5N 32°52′·0E,
36°02′·5N 32°51′·0E,
36°03′·7N 32°55′·3E,
36°05′·0N 32°54′·5E.

Bozyazı Limanı

5.184

1 **Description.** Bozyazı Limanı (36°05′·8N 32°57′·7E) is a small harbour situated 2 miles W of Bozyazı Burnu. Its intended use is as a ferry port for a service to Kyrenia, in N Cyprus, but may also be used by recreational craft.

The harbour, with depths of about 5 m inside, is enclosed by two rubble breakwaters with the entrance between them facing NNE. Lights are exhibited from the heads of the breakwaters.

2 **Berths.** There are concrete quays inside the S breakwater and along the SW side of the harbour; total length about 400 m.

Facilities: freshwater; fuel; limited provisions from the village of Bozyazı 2½ km away.

Soğuksu Limanı

5.185

1 Soğuksu Limanı (36°08′N 33°18′E) is open to S and SE winds, but small vessels can obtain shelter in it. There is a small village 2½ cables N of the W entrance point.

The best anchorage is in the W side of the bay, N of the W entrance point, in depths of 5 to 7 m, clear of the marine farm. The bottom is sand and rock with good holding. In NE winds anchorage can be obtained off the river mouth, on the E side of the bay, but caution is needed owing to silting from the river.

Local knowledge is desirable.

Aydıncık Limanı

5.186

1 **Description.** Aydıncık Limanı (36°08′N 33°20′E) is a small but secure harbour with depths of 1·8 to 4·6 m inside. It is protected from SE by a breakwater about 200 m long and from NE by a short breakwater.

Aydıncık Light (white metal framework tower, 4 m in height) is exhibited from the S entrance point of the harbour. Nearby is a ruined fortress, and a few huts stand near the head of the harbour.

2 **Berths.** A quay fronts the NW side of the harbour; vessels moor stern- or bows-to the quay. Small vessels may also anchor on the W side of the harbour; the bottom is sand and mud.

Facilities: fresh water; fuel; provisions.

Ovacık Körfezi

5.187

1 **Description.** Ovacık Körfezi (36°10′N 33°37′E) is entered between Sulusalma Burnu and Ovacık Burnu, 5 miles ENE. Ovacık, a village with about 400 inhabitants, lies at the head of Ovacık Körfezi, near the ruins of Holmus, where there is a small pier.

2 **Anchorage**, exposed to winds from between SSE and WSW, may be obtained 7½ cables offshore, in a depth of 20 m with Sulusalma Burnu bearing 231°, and the SW extremity of Ovacık Burnu bearing 148°; this berth is used for loading grain from lighters.

3 **Useful marks:**

Two lights (concrete towers, 9 m in height) exhibited from the NE side of the bay.

Chart 242 plan Approaches to Taşucu

Ovacık Yarımadası

5.188

1 **Description.** The bay on the E side of Ovacık Yarımadası (36°09′N 33°41′E) affords good anchorage, being divided in two parts by Kösrelik Adası. A good berth is in the N part, with the NE point of the island bearing 162°, distant 2 cables, in a depth of about 33 m. Vessels may also anchor S of Kösrelik Adası, in depths of 4 to 5 m, mud and sand.

2 In 1973 a small wooden pier was reported to project from the shore W of Kösrelik Adası.

Caution. A reef, with a depth of less than 1·8 m over it, extends about 2 cables W from the W extremity of Kösrelik Adası.

İNCEKUM BURNU TO MERSİN

General information

Chart 2632

Route

5.189

1 From a position S of İncekum Burnu (36°14′N 33°57′E) the coastal route leads 50 miles NE, to a position about 11 miles WSW of Deli Burnu (36°43′N 34°54′E).

Topography

5.190

1 Between İncekum Burnu (36°14′N 33°57′E) and Susanoğlu, 12½ miles NNE, the coast consists of low sandhills, some of which are covered with shrubs. The line of sandhills is broken by Göksu Irmağı, which enters the sea 6 miles NE of İncekum Burnu.

2 Between Susanoğlu and Limonlu, 11½ miles NE, the coast is indented by numerous creeks and inlets, but there are no harbours or sheltered anchorages. The numerous ruins and towers, however, attest the ancient population and importance of this stretch of coast.

3 The coast NE of Limonlu rises gradually to a range of mountains from 5 to 8 miles inland, and several rivers discharge into the sea along this stretch of coast. The ruins of ancient Soli stand on a small projection 17 miles NE of Limonlu. Numerous vestiges of the city remain, including the masonry piers of the old port, which is now filled with sand.

Submarine exercise areas

5.191

1 Submarines exercise frequently in areas about 26 miles ENE, and 31 miles E, of İncekum Burnu (36°14′N 33°57′E). A good lookout should be kept for them in these waters. See *Annual Notice to Mariners No 8.*

Restricted area

5.192

1 Anchoring is prohibited in an area of 1½ miles radius, centred on position 36°35′·0N 34°19′·6E, owing to the presence of surface and underwater scientific instruments.

Directions

(continued from 5.179)

Principal mark

5.193

1 **Major light:**

Mersin Light (white stone tower and dwelling, 12 m in height) (36°47′N 34°37′E), exhibited from a point 5 cables SW of the inner harbour of Mersin. From S the light is difficult to distinguish from the lights of the town.

İncekum Burnu to Mersin

5.194

1 From a position S of İncekum Burnu (36°14′N 33°57′E) the track leads NE, passing (with positions from İncekum Burnu Light):

SE of the mouth of Göksu Irmağı (6¼ miles NE) which flows out with a strong current. Its muddy course is marked by a well defined line. Thence:

SE of Susanoğlu (12¾ miles NNE) (5.195), thence:

2 SE of Kizkalesı Ada (16½ miles NE), an islet on which stands a castle. The castle is conspicuous and nearly covers the islet; a tower 18 m high stands on its E side, and another tower, 15 m high, on its NW side. Körgös Kalesi, another castle, large, conspicuous and in ruins, stands 5 cables NNE of the islet on a point on the mainland from which a pier with a pedestal at its head extends 60 m SW. Thence:

3 SE of Ayaş (18½ miles NE), the site of the ancient island and important city of Eleusa, which is now a mere collection of huts. The coast in the vicinity presents a succession of ruins, amongst which the aqueduct, 6 miles long, extending from Eleusa to Lamas Dere, is remarkable. Thence:

SE of the mouth of Lamas Dere (24¼ miles NE). The mouth of the river is not visible until close offshore, as its outer reach runs parallel to the coast, and it enters the sea through a narrow opening hidden by sand dunes. Thence:

4 SE of the harbour of Odtü (25 miles NE) (5.196), also known as Limonlu, thence:

SE of the mouth of Alata Çayı (26½ miles NE). There is a landing stage in the mouth, and another one in the mouth of a river 5 miles farther NE.

The track then leads to a position about 11 miles WSW of Deli Burnu (36°43′N 34°54′E) (5.230), from which a light is exhibited.

(Directions continue for Mersin at 5.216 and for the coastal route at 5.229)

Anchorages and harbours

Susanoğlu

5.195

1 Susanoğlu (36°25′N 34°05′E), the port of Persentı, stands at the head of a bay which forms a small harbour, with rocks on its E side and a sandy beach on its W side. There are extensive ruins in the vicinity.

2 A quay extends 120 m SE, thence 80 m N, from the head of the bay. There is reported to be a depth of 1·8 m alongside. Good anchorage has been reported about 1 cable off the quay, or for larger vessels, 1 cable farther seaward.

Odtü

5.196

1 Odtü (36°34′N 34°15′E), also known as Limonlu, is a small artificial harbour protected by breakwaters. The harbour is used by the Turkish Marine Biology Institute.

There is a depth of about 4 m in the harbour entrance, but it is prone to silting. Inside the harbour there is a depth of about 5 m.

MERSİN

General information

Charts 2101, 2632

Position

5.197

1 Mersin (36°48′N 34°38′E) is a large port situated at the head of Mersin Körfezi.

Function

5.198

1 Mersin is a major commercial harbour serving the E Mediterranean region's industrial and agriculture exports together with a large amount of transit trade with the Middle East through its modern infrastructure and facilities. It is well-equipped to handle passenger, general cargo, container and RoRo vessels, bulk carriers and tankers. The inner harbour includes a military harbour, a fishing harbour and a yacht harbour.

The hinterland is well-cultivated. Cotton is grown, and there are important mining resources. The population is about 1 million.

Topography

5.199

1 Between Mersin and the village of Karaduvar, 3 miles E, the coast consists of low sandhills. Deliçayı, a broad stream, flows into the sea 1 mile E of Karaduvar.

Port limits

5.200

1 Mersin Harbour includes all the territorial waters between a line drawn S from position 36°27′·5N 34°08′·5E and a line drawn S from position 36°41′·5N 35°03′·0E.

Traffic

5.201

1 In 2007 there were 3176 ship calls with a total of 32 842 373 dwt.

Port Authority

5.202

1 Mersin International Port Management Inc., Yeni Mah. Ismet Inonu Bulvari No 78, Klas Plaza A Blok: 13 D: 25–26, 33050 Mersin, Turkey.

Limiting conditions

Controlling depths

5.203

1 There is a least charted depth of 13·2 m in the channel leading to Inner Harbour. A depth of 11·8 m, 2½ cables SE of the E breakwater head, lies close NE of the centre line. Inside Inner Harbour there is a least depth of 13·2 m 1½ cables W of the E breakwater head.

Deepest and longest berth

5.204

1 Tankers: ATAŞ Jetty (5.220).

Abnormal water levels

5.205

1 Winds from S and W may raise the sea level in the harbour by as much as 0·6 m. Winds from N and E may reduce the level by a similar amount.

Density of water

5.206

1 1·025 g/cm^3.

Arrival information

Notice of ETA

5.207

1 24 hours; for vessels carrying dangerous cargoes: 48 hours.

Anchorages

5.208

1 There are three designated anchorage areas in the open roadstead of the outer harbour, shown on the chart, centred as follows (with positions from Mersin Light (36°47′N 34°37′E):

General anchorage (4½ miles SE).

Explosives anchorage (7½ miles SE); a dangerous wreck lies in the NE corner.

2 Quarantine anchorage (10½ miles ESE).

In addition, for smaller vessels, anchorage may be obtained in a position 6¼ cables E of the head of South Breakwater, depth about 10 m, mud.

Prohibited anchorage area

5.209

1 Prohibited anchorage areas, as shown on the chart, are as follows:

Inshore of a line extending ENE from the head of East Breakwater for 2¼ miles thence NE to the coast. The area contains a spoil ground.

Within 2½ cables of the head of South Breakwater.

Pilotage

5.210

1 Pilotage is compulsory for Turkish vessels of 1000 gt or more and foreign vessels of 150 gt or more entering or leaving the harbour, anchoring and berthing.

The pilot boarding place is 1 mile SE of the Inner Harbour entrance, as shown on the chart.

For details see *Admiralty List of Radio Signals Volume 6 (3).*

Tugs

5.211

1 Tugs are available and their use is obligatory.

Regulations

5.212

1 **Permission to berth.** Vessels may only moor at or leave piers, jetties, installations, workplaces and buoys with the permission of the Harbour Master.

Naval Harbour. Entry is prohibited into the Naval Harbour situated at the head of Inner Harbour on its NE side, without the permission of the naval authorities.

Harbour

General layout

5.213

1 Mersin Limanı comprises an exposed Outer Harbour and an artificial Inner Harbour.

The Inner Harbour of Mersin Limanı is protected by South Breakwater and East Breakwater. The entrance, between the heads of the breakwaters, is about 245 m wide. From close within the harbour entrance a channel leads to the NE head of the harbour where there is a turning basin with a diameter of about 220 m.

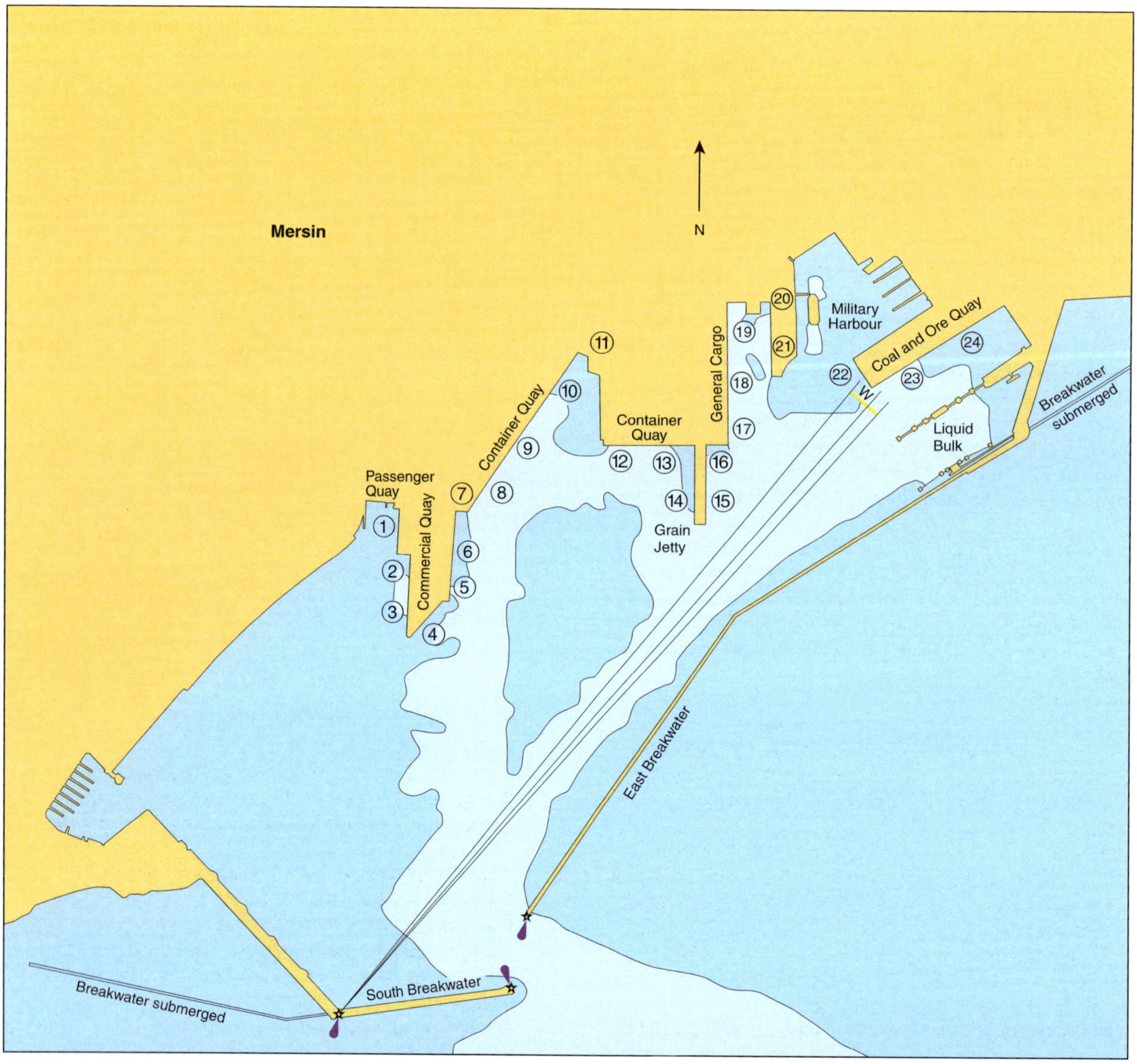

Mersin (5.213)

Mersin Harbour from SW (5.213)
(Original dated 1990)

(Photograph - Crown Copyright)

2 **Development.** Dredging of the container berths and turning area is now under way (2008), to accommodate vessels up to 7000 teu and with a maximum draught of 13·5 m.

Local weather

5.214

1 Winds are mostly from SW. In summer the weather is hot and humid and mosquitoes are troublesome.

Submarine pipelines

5.215

1 An underwater pipeline extends 5 cables SE from the elbow of South Breakwater.

Nine pipelines extend from the shore approximately two to seven miles E of the harbour, and terminate at buoys immediately N of the anchorage areas.

For further information on pipelines see 1.26.

Directions

(continued from 5.194)

Principal marks

5.216

1 **Landmarks** (positioned from head of Grain Jetty (36°48′N 34°39′E)):

New Mosque (minaret) (9½ cables W).

Hotel (red light) (1¼ miles WNW).

Silos (red light) (1¼ cables NNW).

Tower (grey cylindrical structure) on Çatal Hill (2 miles NE).

2 Chimney (36°49′N 34°44′E) (chart 2632).

Radio mast (105 m in height) (36°50′N 34°44′E) (chart 2632).

Major light:

Mersin Light (36°47′N 34°37′E) (5.193).

Entering harbour

5.217

1 From a position about 11 miles WSW of Deli Burnu (36°43′N 34°54′E) the track leads NNW, passing (with positions from the head of South Breakwater (36°47′·1N 34°38′·5E)):

Through the waiting anchorages (5.207), thence:

WSW of a lit mooring buoy (2¼ miles ESE), to a position about 1¼ miles SE of the head of South Breakwater.

2 From this position the track leads NW, passing:

Between two light buoys (lateral) (8 cables SE), thence:

NE of the head of South Breakwater; a light (white concrete tower, 5 m in height) is exhibited from its head. Thence:

3 SW of the head of East Breakwater (1½ cables N); a light (white concrete tower, 5 m in height) is exhibited from its head.

The track then leads to a position about 1½ cables WNW of the head of East Breakwater.

Inside harbour

5.218

1 **Direction light and leading lights:**

South Breakwater Direction Light (white metal tripod, 3 m in height) (36°47′·0N 34°38′·1E), exhibited from the SW elbow of South Breakwater. The light's white sector (219°–221½°) covers the fairway leading to the turning basin.

Sahilköy Front Light (metal framework tower, concrete base; 17 m in height) (36°48′·4N 34°39′·6E).

Sahilköy Rear Light (metal framework tower, concrete base; 20 m in height (189 m NE).

2 From the position 1½ cables WNW of the head of East Breakwater, with South Breakwater Direction Light bearing 220¼°, astern, the alignment (040½°) of Sahilköy Leading Lights, ahead, leads through the centre of the fairway, for 1 mile, passing (with positions given from head of Grain Jetty (36°48′N 34°39′E)):

SE of a light buoy (port hand) (7 cables SW), thence:

NW of a light buoy (starboard hand) (6½ cables SSW), thence:

3 SE of a light buoy (S cardinal) (6 cables SW), thence:

SE of a light buoy (isolated danger) (3 cables SW), thence:

NW of the NW elbow (2 cables SSE) of East Breakwater, thence:

SE of the head of Grain Jetty into the turning basin.

Berths

Moorings

5.219

1 **Outer Harbour.** A mooring buoy lies 2¼ miles ESE of the harbour entrance. There are nine tanker discharging berths from two to seven miles E from the harbour entrance.

Inner Harbour. Mooring buoys for the use of vessels awaiting an alongside berth are laid off the inner side of South Breakwater.

2 **Karaduvar Harbour.** A fishing harbour (36°48′N 34°42′E) fronts the village of Karaduvar, 1½ miles E of the commercial harbour of Mersin.

The harbour is protected by breakwaters and has depths from 2 to 6 m within it. Lights (towers, 4 m in height) are exhibited from the heads of the breakwaters.

Alongside berths

5.220

1 The principal berthing areas are situated on the N and E sides of Inner Harbour. There are 22 berths handling containers, dry bulk, general and liquid cargoes.

The largest berth is that of ATAŞ Jetty, length 600 m, depth alongside 14 m, in the NE corner, for the use of tankers. There is also a RoRo berth on the N side of the harbour, length 40 m, charted depth 9·8 m.

Caution. A wreck, visible above the surface, lies close W of the Grain Jetty.

Port services

Repairs

5.221

1 Minor repair facilities only.

Other facilities

5.222

1 Hospitals in the town; floating crane of 60 tonnes lifting capacity; Ship Sanitation Control and Exemption Certificates.

Supplies

5.223

1 Fuel oil; fresh water at the berths except for tankers which are supplied by barge; fresh provisions.

Communications

5.224

1 Internal air services from Adana airport, 75 km ENE.

Harbour regulation

5.225

1 Fishing and trawling are prohibited within 1 cable of the head of ATAŞ Jetty (5.220).

MERSİN TO KARATAŞ BURNU

General information

Chart 2632

Route

5.226

1 From a position about 11 miles WSW of Deli Burnu (36°14′N 33°57′E) the coastal route leads SE, for 45 miles, to a position 13 miles SE of Karataş Burnu (36°32′N 35°20′E), in the middle of the entrance to İskenderun Körfezi.

Topography

5.227

1 The coast between Karaduvar (36°48′N 34°42′E), close E of Mersin, and Kazanlı, 3 miles E, is low, and thence to the mouth of Tarsus Çayı, 5¼ miles SE, consists of sandhills. A hill, 366 m high, 7 miles NNE of Kazanlı, appears as an island from SW. From Tarsus Çayı the coastline then curves S to Deli Burnu, a point projecting SSW from the mainland.

2 Thence the coast between Deli Burnu and Karataş Burnu, 24 miles SE, consists of a beach rising to high sandhills, and becomes cliff fronted 5 cables N of Karataş Burnu. A sandy plain which extends some miles inland is largely mere desert, some parts of which are inundated with water, and others are sandhills with a few scattered bushes.

3 Akyatan Gölü, a salt lake 12 miles long, connects with the sea 1¼ miles NW of Karataş Burnu. The lake, in which there is a depth of about 1 m, contains turtle and fish; it is surrounded by barren sands, inhabited by large numbers of swans, pelicans and storks.

Submarine exercise areas

5.228

1 See 5.191.

Directions

(continued from 5.194)

Principal mark

5.229

1 **Major light:**

Karataş Burnu Light (white concrete tower and dwelling, 12 m in height) (36°32′N 35°20′E).

Mersin to Karataş Burnu

5.230

1 From a position 11 miles WSW of Deli Burnu (36°14′N 33°57′E) the track leads SE, passing (with positions from Deli Burnu):

SW of the mouth of Tarsus Çayı, which flows through Tarsus (36°55′N 34°55′E); it is ¼ cable wide at its mouth, where there is a depth of 3 m. Thence:

2 SW of Deli Burnu, from where a light (white metal framework pylon, 15 m in height) is exhibited. A spit extends 1 mile from Deli Burnu, which should not be approached into a depth of less than 22 m. Seyhan Nehri reaches the sea at Deli Burnu, through an entrance nearly ½ cable wide, where there is a depth of 3·6 m. Thence:

SW of the W mouth of Kurutma Kanalı (10½ miles SE), thence:

3 SW of Karataş Burnu (23½ miles SE), a fairly low white cliff on which stands a coastguard station with an elevation of 50 m, and from where a light is exhibited. The ruins of the ancient town and citadel of Megarsus stand prominently 5 cables NNE of the cape. A spit, with a depth of 4·3 m at its outer end, extends 2½ cables S of Karataş Burnu.

4 The track then leads to a position about 13 miles SE of Karataş Burnu, in the middle of the entrance to İskenderun Körfezi.

Useful mark:

Tower, with an elevation of 56 m, standing 2½ miles NE of Karataş Burnu (36°32′N 35°20′E).

(Directions continue for İskenderun Körfezi at 5.235 and for the coastal route S to Syria at 5.322)

İSKENDERUN KÖRFEZİ AND ANTAKYA KÖRFEZİ

GENERAL INFORMATION

Charts 2632, 246

Area covered

5.231

1 The area covered by this section comprises:

Karataş Burnu to the head of İskenderun Körfezi (5.232).

İskenderun Limanı N terminals (5.246).

İsdemir (5.272).

İskenderun (5.293).

Antakya Körfezi (5.318).

KARATAŞ BURNU TO THE HEAD OF İSKENDERUN KÖRFEZİ

General information

Charts 2632, 246, 247

Route

5.232

1 İskenderun Körfezi is entered between Karataş Burnu (36°32′N 35°20′E) and Akınçı Burnu, 25 miles SE. From a position 13 miles SE of Karataş Burnu, in the middle of the entrance to İskenderun Körfezi, the route leads 28 miles NE to the vicinity of 36°40′N 35°55′E.

Topography

5.233

1 The shores of İskenderun Körfezi vary considerably, but consist for the greater part of plains situated at the bases of mountains. Several mountain torrents and small streams flow into the gulf, the bottom of which is chiefly mud.

The NW shores of the gulf are backed by Cebeli Nur, a steep-sided range, which reaches an elevation of 788 m in a sharp peak, 7½ miles NE of Dede Dağı (36°49′N 35°33′E). Dede Dağı, a prominent crag 436 m high, stands at the SW end of Cebeli Nur, appearing wedge-shaped from S. Davud Dağı, 4½ miles E of Dede Dağı, has an elevation of 532 m, is flat-topped, and is surmounted by a television mast 140 m in height.

2 The NE shore of the gulf is backed by Nur Dağları and the Elma Dağ Range; the SE shore is backed by Kızıl Dağ. Bozdağ (36°49′N 36°23′E), 2240 m high, is the highest peak in steep and craggy Nur Dağları. Daz Tepe (36°34′N 36°16′E), 1795 m high, is one of numerous summits, with serrated sides, which form Elma Dağ Range.

Kızıl Dağ, a sharp rocky ridge with wooded slopes, extends NE at a nearly constant elevation from Ikiz Tepe (36°17′N 35°53′E) (chart 2632), a rugged peak 1725 m high.

Natural conditions

5.234

1 **Abnormal water levels.** Winds from S and W may sometimes raise the sea level by as much as 0·6 m, while N and E winds may lower it by a similar amount.

Tides in the gulf are negligible.

Directions

(continued from 5.230)

Principal marks

5.235

1 **Major lights:**

Karataş Burnu Light (36°32′N 35°20′E) (5.229).

Akınçı Burnu Light (white tower on building, 5 m in height) (36°19′N 35°47′E).

İskenderun Light (white concrete tower, 10 m in height) (36°32′N 36°03′E).

Other aid to navigation

5.236

1 **Racon:**

Devegeçeği Light (36°43′N 35°43′E) (5.237).

See *Admiralty List of Radio Signals Volume 2* for details.

Karataş Burnu to İskenderun Körfezi

5.237

1 From a position 13 miles SE of Karataş Burnu (36°32′N 35°20′E) the track leads NE, passing (with positions from Karataş Burnu):

SE of the harbour of Karataş (2½ miles NE) (5.243). A minaret with a white dome stands, at an elevation of 46 m, 4 cables WSW of Karataş. Thence:

2 SE of Kücük Adası (3¾ miles NE). Between Karataş Burnu and Kücük Adası the coast is mainly fringed with rocky ledges, and a coastal bank, with depths of less than 5 m over it, extends up to 8 cables offshore. The coast for 5 cables N of Kücük Adası is rocky. Thence:

3 SE of the mouth of Kurutma Kanalı (6 miles NE). The coast in the vicinity of the canal is bordered by low sand-dunes and is almost steep-to, affording good anchorage, sheltered from strong N winds, 1 mile offshore in depths of from 7 to 13 m, sand. Thence:

4 NW of Akınçı Burnu (36°19′N 35°47′E), the W termination of Kızıl Dağ, which rises to an elevation of 1698 m about 4 miles ESE of the cape; it is steep-to and has the appearance of a boar's snout from seaward. The mountains in the vicinity are densely wooded. A light (5.235) is exhibited from the cape. Thence:

5 SE of Hurma Boğazı (11 miles ENE), which is the mouth of Ceyhan Nehri, the principal stream flowing into İskenderun Körfezi. Agyatan Gölu, a salt water lagoon, connects with the sea 1 mile NW of Hurma Boğazı. Thence:

6 SE of Portakal Burnu (13¼ miles ENE), a rounded projection. The coast on either side of Portakal Burnu is bordered by sand dunes. Thence:

NW of Uluçınar (36°25′N 35°53′E) (5.244), thence:

SE of Devegeçeği (36°43′N 35°43′E) A light (white metal framework tower, 6 m in height) is exhibited from a position 1 mile WNW. A beacon is located 1¼ miles ESE of the light. Thence:

7 NW of İskenderun Light (5.235) (36°32′N 36°03′E). From the SW limit of İskenderun Harbour (36°36′N 36°09′E) to İskenderun Light the coast consists of rocks and shingle; behind it lies the flat, cultivated and in parts swampy plain of İskenderun. Thence to a point 4 miles farther SW the coast becomes steeper, rising abruptly to the foothills of Ada Tepe, 252 m high; these hills have low scrub and few trees and are partly cultivated. A similar cultivated plain extends from Ada Tepe, for 11 miles SW and S, to the foot of Kızıl Dağ (5.233).

8 Thence to the vicinity of 36°40′N 35°55′E, 10 miles NW of İskenderun Light. From here the harbours of İskenderun

Limanı N terminals (5.246), İsdemir (5.272) and İskenderun (5.293) can be directly accessed.

Useful mark:

Water tower, with an elevation of 56 m, standing 2½ miles NE of Karataş Burnu (36°32′N 35°20′E).

(Directions for İskenderun Körfezi N terminals continue at 5.264, for İsdemir at 5.285, and for İskenderun at 5.309)

Yumurtalık Limanı

Chart 246

General information

5.238

1 **Description.** Yumurtalık Limanı (36°44′N 35°45′E) is entered between Devegeçeği and a point 4½ miles NE. The bay affords shelter to large vessels and contains an offshore tanker berth.

Topography. The bay is very shallow at its head, and there are numerous lagoons on its S and W shore. On the SW side of the bay the coastline is continually changing. Farther inland to the W, the land consists of low, undulating, thickly wooded hills, while to the NW the hills rise to Dede Dağı (5.233) in remarkable pinnacles, and to Cebeli Nur.

2 On the N side of the bay between Yumurtalık (36°46′N 35°47′E) and the mouth of Bağırsak Dere, 2½ miles W, the shore is bordered by sandhills, and depths of less than 10 m extend up to 5 cables offshore. Thence between the mouth of Bağırsak Dere and Liman Burnu, 1 mile WSW, the shore consists of low clay hills, rising to cliffs 27 m high at the point. Depths of less than 5 m extend up to 3 cables offshore; drying rocks and foul ground extend up to 2 cables SE and SW of Liman Burnu, and a rock with a depth of 1·8 m over it lies 4 cables W of the point.

3 A dry uncultivated plain extends NW from Liman Burnu to the foot of Davud Dağı (5.233), 5 miles NW.

Caution. Numerous marine farms extend NNW from Devegeçeği. See also note on the chart.

Directions

5.239

1 If approaching from the S, pass at least 1 mile E of Devegeçeği (36°43′N 35°44′E), and keep Sultansüleyman Kalesi (36°46′N 35°47′E) bearing less than 014° until Liman Burnu (36°46′N 35°43′E) bears 317°, when it should be brought ahead.

If coming from the NE, bring Liman Burnu to bear at least 292° before entering the bay, which clears a shoal with a depth of 5·8 m over it, 1½ miles SW of Sultansüleyman Kalesi.

2 **Useful marks:**

A beacon (topmark triangle point up) standing about 1½ miles ESE of Devegeçeği Light (36°43′N 35°43′E).

Beacon standing on Liman Burnu (36°46′N 35°43′E).

Sultansüleyman Kalesi (ruined octagonal tower) standing 5 cables W of Yumurtalık (Adası) (36°46′N 35°47′E).

3 Yumurtalık Light (white metal framework tower, 10 m in height) (36°47′N 35°48′E) exhibited 7 cables NNE of the NE entrance point of Yumurtalık Limanı.

Anchorage

5.240

1 Yumurtalık Limanı affords anchorage in depths of from 7 to 18 m, mud, sheltered except from E and SE winds.

Large vessels may obtain anchorage, in a depth of 8·2 m, soft mud, 8 cables S of Limam Burnu, with Dede Dağı bearing 296°, on which bearing a small piece of tableland, in the first ridge of hills W of the bay, is a little open N of Dede Dağı.

2 Small vessels may obtain anchorage in depths from 4·6 to 5·5 m, soft mud, 1 mile WSW of Limam Burnu, with Sultansüleyman Kalesi just open S of the point. The holding ground in this part of the bay is considered to be generally good, but vessels sometimes drag their anchors.

Offshore tanker berth

5.241

1 A tanker mooring lies 1 mile SSE of the mouth of Bağırsak Dere, at the seaward end of a submarine pipeline. The mooring accommodates tankers up to 20 000 dwt and 10·3 m draught, which load crude oil from Iraq.

Anchoring is prohibited in the vicinity of the submarine pipeline, as shown on the chart.

2 **Development.** It has been reported (2006) that a loading jetty 2·5 km long with two berths for tankers up to 300 000 dwt, has been constructed close to the offshore tanker berth. The new terminal links Baku, Azerbaijan to Ceyhan, Turkey, via Tiblisi, Georgia and is known as the BTC pipeline, whose total length is 1760 km.

Yumurtalik

5.242

1 **Description.** Yumurtalık (36°46′N 35°47′E), a small harbour, is situated on the NE entrance point of Yumurtalık Limanı. It is fronted by an islet, 8 m high, on which stands Kız Kalesi, a massive building.

The harbour was originally built by the Genoese and served as an outlet for goods brought across land by caravan.

Caution. The point on which Yumurtalık stands is foul in all directions and a sandbank has built up on the inside of the breakwater of the harbour.

2 **Harbour.** The harbour is formed by ancient moles built of large stone blocks extending from each side of the islet towards the shore, and by a breakwater extending 2½ cables E of the point; a light (white metal framework tower, 6 m in height) is exhibited from the head of the breakwater. The mole N of the islet lies below water; the mole S of the islet is in pieces and in places below water.

The harbour has depths from 0·9 to 4·6 m in it, but is reported to be silting up considerably.

3 **Berths.** A quay about 100 m long, with a depth of 2 m in the approach and 2·4 m alongside, fronts the N side of the breakwater.

If there is no room alongside vessels may anchor between the islet and the harbour in depths of 3 to 4 m.

Supplies: freshwater; fuel; limited quantities of provisions.

Anchorages and harbours

Karataş

5.243

1 **Description.** Karataş (36°34′N 35°23′E) contains a custom house and a small artificial harbour. Lights (white concrete towers, 5 m in height) are exhibited from the heads of the breakwaters. Two islets front the harbour, a light being exhibited from the W islet, and rocky ledges

which dry extend 3 cables off the shore, 5 cables SW of the harbour.

2 **Port limits.** Karataş harbour limits includes all the territorial waters between a line drawn 12 miles S from position 36°41′·5N 35°03′·0E, on the coast near Tuz Gölü, and a line drawn 5 miles SE from Hurma Boğazi (5.237).

3 **Anchorages.** Vessels may obtain anchorage during summer in depths of 7 to 11 m, white sand, off the E of two islets each about 1 m high, which lie ENE of theserocky ledges.

Designated anchorages lie 4 miles SE and 7 miles ESE of the harbour. The latter anchorage is designated an explosives area.

Chart 246 plan of Uluçınar

Uluçınar

5.244

1 **Description.** Uluçınar (36°25′N 35°53′E) is a small resort village set in olive groves, standing on both sides of a shallow stream which flows into the S part of a bay 1¾ miles wide, entered SW of a low rocky point, near which stands a white mosque among trees. A rocky ledge, with a depth of 6·4 m over it, extends 1 mile SW from this point; good anchorage may be obtained in summer inshore of this ledge, in a depth of 8 m, sand. The ruins of the ancient walls of the town are still visible on the SW side of the bay.

2 **Berth.** There is a small jetty on the SW side of the bay. It lies within a restricted area into which entry is forbidden.

Caution. Depths close to the jetty are less than charted (2008).

Kişla Çayi

5.245

1 Kişla Çayi (36°21′N 35°49′E), 4 miles SW of Uluçınar, affords temporary anchorage offshore.

İSKENDERUN KÖRFEZİ — NORTHERN TERMINALS

General information

Chart 247

Position

5.246

1 The N terminals (36°52′N 36°02′E) are situated at the N head of İskenderun Körfezi and comprise: İsken Terminal, Botaş (Ceyhan) Oil Terminal, Toros Gübre Piers, Birleşik Petrol Terminal, Botaş (Dörtyol) Oil Terminal, Delta Oil Terminal and Aygaz LPG Terminal. A further three terminals are located SE of Botaş (Dörtyol) Oil Terminal, they are: BP Gas (2 pipelines), Milangas and Aytemiz Terminals.

Function

5.247

1 The N terminals in İskenderun Körfezi mainly serve as outlets for oil products and gas exported from Iraq by rail and pipeline. Toros Gübre Piers is a multi-purpose terminal with facilities for handling bulk carriers, tankers, container and RoRo vessels. At this terminal principal cargoes handled include grain, fertilisers, sulphur, coal, general cargo, edible oils and bulk liquid chemicals.

Topography

5.248

1 On the NW side of İskenderun Körfezi, the coast NE of Alakese Burnu (36°49′N 35°52′E), rises in undulating hills from 120 to 180 m high, interspersed with rocky and sandy bays. Alakese Burnu is a low promontory.

2 From a range of hills close W of Karagâh (36°56′N 36°01′E), situated at the head of İskenderun Körfezi, to Yakacık, 15 miles SE, the coast is bordered by an unbroken line of sand and shingle behind which lies the Plain of Issus. The plain is marshy near the sea. Several small streams flow out through the shingle, none of which can be entered by boats. The town of Dörtyol stands 4¾ miles N of Yakacık to the E of its oil terminals. It contains a minaret and a large school (white building with red roof). The railway station, distinguished by a water tower standing among trees, is situated 1½ miles WSW of the town.

Port limits

5.249

1 Ceyhan Harbour Limits encompass all of the waters enclosed within a line drawn SE from Hurma Boğazi (5.237) to 36°29′·6N 35°37′·4E; thence NE to a position on the shore at the mouth of Deli Çay (36°50′N 36°10′E).

Traffic

5.250

1 Botaş (Ceyhan) Oil Terminal:

In 2007 there were 103 ship calls with a total of 10 910 575 dwt.

Toros Gübre Piers:

In 2007 there were 239 ship calls with a total of 4 434 388 dwt.

Botaş (Dörtyol) Oil Terminal:

In 2007 there were 143 ship calls with a total of 3 631 933 dwt.

Port Authorities

5.251

1 Botaş (Ceyhan) Oil Terminal and Botaş (Dörtyol) Oil Terminal are operated by:

Botaş Bulge Mudurlugu.

Toros Gübre Piers operated by:

Toros Fertilizer and Chemical Industry Co Inc.

Delta Oil Terminal:

Delta Petroleum Products Trading Company, Yesil Terminali, 31650 Dörtyol, Turkey.

Limiting conditions

Depths

5.252

1 The depths shown on the plans of Botaş (Ceyhan) Oil Terminal and Toros Gübre Piers indicate general depths and should not be assumed to be accurate in detail.

Deepest and longest berth

5.253

1 Botaş (Ceyhan) Oil Terminal (5.266).

Maximum size of vessel handled

5.254

1 Botaş (Ceyhan) Oil Terminal; tankers up to 300 000 dwt and 22 m draught (5.266).

Toros Gübre Piers; bulk carriers up to 110 000 dwt (5.267).

Local weather

5.255

1 At Toros Gübre Piers wind and swell from SW render the berths unsafe.

Arrival information

Notice of ETA

5.256

1 Botaş (Ceyhan) and Botaş (Dörtyol) Oil Terminals; 72, 48, 24 and 4 hrs in advance. Aygaz Terminal: 7, 5, 3 days and 48 and 24 hours in advance.

Anchorages

5.257

1 A small anchorage area lies 1 mile W of İsken Terminal. There is a large anchorage area, about 3 miles SE of Botaş (Ceyhan) Oil Terminal, the holding ground is reported to be good. A third anchorage area lies 2½ miles WSW of Botaş (Dörtyol) Oil Terminal.

Before anchoring vessels should contact the Harbour Master for permission through the port radio.

Prohibited anchorage

5.258

1 Anchoring is prohibited within the port limits of Botaş (Ceyhan) except within the designated anchorage area.

Pilotage

5.259

1 **Pilotage** is compulsory; the terminal should be consulted for local regulations. The charted pilot boarding place is located in position 36°49′·5N 36°01′·5E, however for specific terminals the relevant port authority should be consulted. The pilot boat has a black hull and brown superstructure.

For details see *Admiralty List of Radio Signals Volume 6 (3).*

Tugs

5.260

1 Tugs are compulsory; the terminal should be consulted for local regulations. The tugs are equipped for fire fighting.

Movement restrictions

5.261

1 **Botaş (Ceyhan) and Botaş (Dörtyol) Oil Terminals;** berthing is carried out at all times of the day and night; vessels over 30 000 dwt during daytime only.

Toros Gübre Piers; berthing is carried out by day only, and is subject to weather conditions.

2 **Dörtyol and adjacent terminals;** berthing is by day only, but tankers may leave the terminals at any time of the day or night.

İsken Terminal; 24 hrs.

Harbour

General layout

5.262

1 **General information.** The N Terminals contain several cargo terminals situated along the shores of the head of İskenderun Körfezi; the main ones are as follows:

Botaş (Ceyhan) Oil Terminal (36°53′N 35°56′E), situated on the NW side of İskenderun Limanı. It exports crude oil transported by pipeline from Iraq. The BTC Jetty exports oil from the Sangachal Terminal in Baku, Azerbaijan.

2 Toros Gübre Piers (36°55′N 35°59′E), situated 3 miles NNE of Botaş (Ceyhan) Oil Terminal, are a multi-purpose terminal handling a wide variety of cargoes.

Botaş (Dörtyol) Oil Terminal (36°51′N 36°08′E), Delta Oil Terminal and Aygaz LPG Terminal, situated about 14 miles N of İskenderun, on the NE side of İskenderun Körfezi, export petroleum products transported from Iraq by rail.

3 **Development.** A pipeline under construction (2008), will link Samsun in the Black Sea to Botaş (Ceyhan) Oil Terminal.

Submarine pipeline

5.263

1 A submarine discharge pipe extends 5 cables S from a point on the shore 6¼ cables SW of the root of the W pier of Toros Gübre Piers.

Directions

(continued from 5.237)

5.264

1 From seaward to the pilot boarding position the chart is sufficient guide.

Berths

Chart 247

İsken Terminal

5.265

1 The terminal consists of a tanker loading berth composed of three lit mooring buoys in position 36°48′·3N 35°55′·5E.

An area into which entry is prohibited encloses a pipeline, Sugözü Thermal Power Station jetty and a platform. A light buoy (special) marks the seaward end of the pipeline, and lights are exhibited from the the head of the jetty and the platform.

2 An **L**-shaped jetty under construction (2006), extends ¾ mile SE from the shore, close NE of the terminal.

Botaş (Ceyhan) Oil Terminal

5.266

1 The terminal comprises a steel pile jetty extending from the shore for 5½ cables SE, thence 5½ cables S. Lights (masts) are exhibited from the head of the jetty, and 180 m inshore of the head, respectively.

2 Two loading platforms, known as Platform A and Platform B, on the outer part of the jetty provide four tanker berths, each with four loading arms, as follows:

Platform A, Berths 1 and 2; depth alongside 23 m; handles tankers up to 300 000 dwt.

Platform B, Berths 3 and 4; depth alongside 18 m; handles tankers up to 150 000 dwt.

BTC jetty is located 1 mile SW of the above.

A restricted area, shown on the chart, approximately 2½ miles square, surrounds both jetties. The area may be entered only by vessels using the terminal.

3 There is a boat harbour situated on the NE side of the root of the oil terminal jetty. It is formed by two small breakwaters. A light buoy is moored close NE of the entrance. There are depths of 4·0 to 5·5 m within the harbour.

4 The harbour is used by Botaş Oil Terminal tugs and workboats but if necessary the harbour master, after consultation with the harbour management, may permit berthing by other vessels of suitable size and draught.

Toros Gübre Piers

5.267

1 Toros Gübre Piers consist of Jetty No 1 and Jetty No 2; Jetty No 1 is the W-most pier:

2 Jetty No 1; length 1200 m consisting of a coastal and an outer platform; number of berths 3; maximum draught 11·2 m; maximum vessel size 40 000 dwt; a light (metal mast) is exhibited from the head of the jetty.

3 Jetty No 2; length 1600 m consisting of a coastal, central and main platform; number of berths 6; maximum draught 13·5 m; maximum vessel size 110 000 dwt; a light (dolphin) is exhibited from the head of the jetty.

4 There is a small boat harbour situated on the NE side of the root of Jetty No 1.

A third jetty and oil pipeline are located 7 cables SW of the boat harbour at Bayraktar; the jetty is being extended S.

Birleşik Petrol Terminal, Botaş (Dörtyol) Oil Terminal, Delta Oil Terminal and Aygaz LPG Terminal

5.268

1 **Birleşik Petrol Terminal.** Consists of a pipeline at the head of Ceyhan Limani midway between Toros Gübre Piers and Dörtyol Oil Terminal. The pipeline extends SSW from the shore for 1½ miles and a light buoy (special) is located at the seaward end.

Several terminals are located at Dörtyol, the main ones are described below.

Toros Gübre Piers from WSW (5.267)

(Original dated 2005)

(Photograph - Toros Gübre ve Kýmya End. Aþ)

2 **Botaş (Dörtyol) Oil Terminal.** The terminal consists of a **T**-headed pier projecting from the shore. A tower, with an oil storage tank close SE, stands near the root of the pier. Lights are exhibited from each end of the pierhead.

Tankers loading crude oil berth stern-to at the head of the pier which is 50 m long with a depth of 14 m alongside. A restricted area surounds the terminal, as shown on the chart.

3 **Delta Oil Terminal.** Consists of three buoy berths at the seaward end of submarine pipelines. Each berth has three mooring buoys, one ahead and two astern. Two berths handle vessels up to 40 000 dwt or LOA 240 m, draught 12·5 m, the third handles vessels up to 7 500 dwt or LOA 120 m, draught 7·5 m.

4 **Aygaz LPG Terminal.** Consists of two buoy berths at the seaward end of a submarine pipeline. The berth has three mooring buoys, one ahead and two astern. Handles LPG vessels up to 75 000 m^3 capacity, LOA 230 m, and draught 13·5 m.

Port services

Repairs

5.269

1 No facilities available.

Other facilities

5.270

1 Dirty ballast in limited quantities is accepted at Botaş Oil Terminal.

Supplies

5.271

1 Fuel available only at Toros Gübre Piers; fresh water at berths; provisions.

İSDEMIR

General information

Chart 2104

Position

5.272

1 İsdemir (36°44′N 36°11′E) is a port situated 7 miles N of İskenderun, on the NE side of İskenderun Körfezi.

Function

5.273

1 The port serves İskenderun Iron and Steel Works. Cargo handled: ore, pig iron, coal, general cargo, heavy lifts and petroleum products.

Port limits

5.274

1 İsdemir Harbour consists of the waters lying between the W main breakwater and the N secondary breakwater.

Port Authority

5.275

1 Directorate of İskenderun Iron and Steel Plants, 31319 İsdemir, Turkey.

Limiting conditions

Deepest and longest berth

5.276

1 North breakwater (5.286).

Maximum size of vessel handled

5.277

1 Vessels over 150 000 dwt and 16·4 m draft can be accommodated.

Regulation

5.278

1 Tankers, and vessels over 100 000 dwt, are not permitted to enter harbour during darkness.

Arrival information

Notice of ETA

5.279

1 24 hours; 72 hours if carrying dangerous cargoes.

Anchorage

5.280

1 Vessels awaiting a berth should anchor S of a line due W of the S breakwater, and at least 1 mile from the breakwater head.

Pilotage

5.281

1 Pilotage is compulsory and is available between 0800 and 2400 local time. The pilot boards between 5 cables and 1½ miles from the harbour entrance.

For details see *Admiralty List of Radio Signals Volume 6 (3)*.

Tugs

5.282

1 Tugs are available and compulsory for vessels over 500 gt.

Restricted area

5.283

1 A Naval Special Security Zone extends from a position about 1½ miles N of the harbour entrance to a position 1½ cables S of the root of the S breakwater. The area extends between 1 and 3 cables to seaward and encompasses the harbour entrance. Unauthorised entry to the area is prohibited.

Harbour

General layout

5.284

1 The Harbour is enclosed by two breakwaters from the heads of which lights (concrete towers) are exhibited. The harbour has charted depths of 6·0 to 18·5 m, with an entrance a little over 1 cable wide. The principal berthing area is on the N side of the harbour.

Outside the main harbour are the jetties of Ekinciler and Yazıcı, situated 2½ miles S of the Harbour.

Directions

(continued from 5.237)

5.285

1 From seaward to the pilot boarding position the chart is sufficient guide.

Berths

Harbour

5.286

1 The harbour contains two berths on the SE side of the N breakwater, and four berths on a broad mole projecting from the head of the harbour. A tanker berth is situated outside the harbour on the N breakwater, with depth alongside of 14 m.

2 The largest berth is the outer berth on the inside of the N breakwater; length 500 m; depth alongside 16 to 18 m. The inner berth is 240 m long with a depth alongside 11·5 to 12·0 m. The berths on the broad mole have depths alongside of from 8 m to 10 m. The tanker berth has depths alongside of 14 m; vessels moor stern-to with both anchors out.

Jetties

5.287

1 **Ekinciler Steel Factory Jetty** (36°41′·3N 36°11′·7E), with a platform at its outer end, is used for the handling of scrap, log and construction iron. Terminal operator: Ekinciler Demir Celik San. A.S. Liman Tesisleri Azganlik Köyu, Sarıseki Mevkii, 31200 İskenderun, Turkey. The jetty works 24 hours a day, all year round. The platform is 211 m long and 23 m wide; the jetty connecting it to the shore is 8 m wide. The jetty continues 51 m seaward, with a 9 m face at its head. A light is exhibited from the end of the jetty.

2 Depths alongside both sides of the platform increase to seaward from 13 to 19 m. Vessels up to 50 000 dwt can be accommodated on either side of the platform.

Anchorage: ahead of the jetty, the pilot station will provide the best location. Pilotage is compulsory and is based at İsdemir; tugs are available.

Services, see 5.289.

5.288

1 **Yazıcı Jetty** (36°41′·0N 36°12′·0E) extends 5½ cables from the shore, close S of Ekinciler Jetty. Cargo handled: scrap, log and construction iron. A light is exhibited from the head of the jetty. Terminal operator: Yazıci Demir Celik San. A.S. Liman Tesisleri Azganlik Köyu, Sarıseki Mevkii, 31200 İskenderun, Turkey.

2 Berths available: Nos 1 and 6, 200 m length; 24 m beam; 18·3 to 13·3 m depth; Nos 2 and 5, 200 m length; 24 m beam; 13·3 to 9 m depth; Nos 3 and 4, 300 m length; 13 m beam; 9 to 6 m depth. Depths decrease towards the shore. Vessels up to 50 000 dwt can be accommodated.

3 Anchorage: outside a 1 mile radius from the head of the jetty, the pilot station will provide the best location. Pilotage is based at İsdemir and is available 24 hours.

Services, see 5.289; oily waste disposal is not available.

Port services

Facilities

5.289

1 Oily waste and garbage reception.

Supplies

5.290

1 Fresh water; provisions in limited quantities.

Communications

5.291

1 Adana airport, about 120 km distant.

Anchorage

Yakacık

5.292

1 **Description.** Yakacık (36°45′N 36°12′E), situated amidst groves of trees 2 miles N of İsdemir, comprises a square tower on a point, a ruined castle, a domed mosque, a minaret and a walled village. The beach for 1 mile N of Yakacık is backed by low clay cliffs.

The ancient port of Yakacık is now partly inland and filled with sand and stones; the moles are still visible.

2 **Anchorage.** Good anchorage is obtainable in depths from 11 to 18 m, coral and sand, W of the point. The anchorage is not sheltered and only useful in light winds.

Caution. A conical buoy moored about 7½ cables WSW of Yakacık Tower marks the seaward end of a submarine pipeline extending from the N entrance point of Yakacık Çayı.

İSKENDERUN

General information

Chart 2104

Position

5.293

1 İskenderun (36°36′N 36°11′E) is situated at the head of İskenderun Limanı, a bay entered between Sahri Sakalieh Point (36°37′·8N 36°11′·9E) and Süleymaniye, a point 2·6 miles SW.

Function

5.294

1 İskenderun, in addition to its domestic traffic, serves as a transit port for countries of the Middle East. It is equipped with modern facilities for handling vessels of most types including RoRo, passenger and general cargo vessels, tankers and bulk carriers.

2 The principal exports are chrome ore, wood, cotton, grain and other agricultural products, and manufactured goods. The chief imports are manufactured goods, rice, sugar, coffee, salt, copper, iron and hardware.

3 The port has facilities for container and RoRo traffic, and there are facilities for the bulk handling of grain, coal and chrome ore. In 1997 the town had a population of 161 700.

Topography

5.295

1 The town of İskenderun contains Government offices which include a large house with a verandah and many arches, the law courts, and the post office (white building with clock tower). There are numerous oil tanks near the coast on the side of the bay.

2 To the N of the town of İskenderun lies Sarıseki (36°40′N 36°13′E), which is situated at the foot of a deep and very prominent chasm from which Derebani Dere flows through a swamp within the beach to the sea. A railway station (two white buildings with red roofs) stands close N of the mouth of the river.

3 Sarıseki Kalesi, a mediaeval fortress in ruins, stands 4 cables SE of the mouth of Derebani Dere on the N slope of low hills. Pillars of Jonas, 6 cables S of the river mouth, ancient Pylae Syriae, consist of the ruins of a limestone arch.

Port limits

5.296

1 İskenderun Harbour comprises of the sea area between the following positions: 35°55′·8N 35°55°·1E; 36°24′·4N 35°28′·2E and 36°49′·8N 36°10′·0E.

Traffic

5.297

1 In 2007 there were 1432 ship calls with a total of 14 086 838 dwt.

Port Authority

5.298

1 General Directorate of Turkish State Railways (TCDD) Liman Isletmesi Mudurlugu, Istasyon Caddesi, İskenderun, Turkey.

Limiting conditions

Deepest and longest berths

5.299

1 Deepest and longest berths are in Inner Harbour (5.311).

Maximum size of vessel handled

5.300

1 Vessels up to 185 m long and 10·2 m draught can berth alongside. Larger vessels must work cargo in the anchorage.

Local weather

5.301

1 In spring, gales occurring in İskenderun Körfezi do not seriously affect the port.

Gales from N or NE during the winter do not cause a heavy sea, but they raise a surf on the beach which prevents landing. A good sign of the approach of a N gale is a collection of fleecy clouds over the Plain of Issus (5.248), 15 miles N; the disappearance of these clouds indicates a cessation of the wind. The gales commence usually at sunrise or sunset, with a lull about noon and also just after sunset, when landing is often possible. Gales from N are sometimes followed by a SW swell.

2 Strong E gales, known as Raghiehs, occasionally occur in winter in the vicinity of İskenderun. They are usually of short duration and do not extend far offshore. An indication of their approach is given by the ragged appearance of the clouds on the summits of nearby mountains.

Yarık Kaya, a readily discernible chasm 3 miles SE of İskenderun, gives its name to a local katabatic wind which occasionally in winter blows from it with great violence. A SE squall in March 1960 rapidly increased to force 11, with frequent gusts to force 12.

Arrival information

Notice of ETA

5.302

1 24 hours; 48 hours if carrying dangerous cargoes.

Anchorages

5.303

1 **General anchorage;** a good anchor berth may be found 8 cables WSW of the W main breakwater light, in a depth of about 16 m, stiff mud, but the holding generally is not good. Winds from N are seldom so strong as to cause vessels with good anchors and cables to drag, but boatwork may be interrupted for a few hours.

2 **Explosives anchorage;** the anchorage for vessels carrying explosives is within a triangular area, as shown on the chart, 1 mile NW of the W main breakwater head.

Prohibited anchorage

5.304

1 Anchoring and fishing are prohibited in an area of 200 m radius based on a wreck, position approximate, close W of the explosives anchorage. Anchoring is prohibited within the harbour, close to the shore NE of the harbour and W of the fishing harbour, as shown on the chart.

Prohibited area

5.305

1 A maritime military security area is located 2¼ miles WSW from the harbour entrance, close N of İskenderun Airport. The area parallels the coast for 2 cables and extends ½ cable from the shore; entry is prohibited.

Pilotage

5.306

1 Pilotage is compulsory for Turkish vessels of 300 gt and above, and for all foreign vessels entering and leaving the main harbour or berthing at the buoys and jetty.

The pilot boards within a 2 mile radius of the harbour entrance. For details see *Admiralty List of Radio Signals Volume 6 (3)*.

Tugs

5.307

1 Tugs are available. Vessels of 500 gt and above berthing at or unberthing from jetties and piers must take one tug, vessels of 4000 grt and above require two tugs.

Harbour

General layout

5.308

1 İskenderun Harbour consists of the main harbour, three offshore tanker berths, NATO Jetty and Sarıseki Fertilizer Jetty. The main harbour is protected by W main breakwater which extends 7 cables NNE from the shore and by Deepwater Jetty, a concrete jetty 367 m long, which projects from the shore 4 cables SE of the head of the breakwater; a light (5.310) is exhibited from the head of the breakwater and another light (metal mast, 12 m in height) is exhibited from the head of Deepwater Jetty. A second jetty, 200 m long, projects from the shore about ½ cable S of Deepwater Jetty. The depth in the entrance to the Inner Harbour was 12 m in 1991.

2 There are two basins (5.312) at the head of the Inner Harbour. To the W of these basins outside the W main breakwater, there is a fishing harbour (5.314).

Three offshore tanker berths lie between 5 cables and 1 mile N of the main harbour entrance, and the NATO Jetty lies 3½ miles NNE.

3 **Developments.** A container terminal is planned (2007) for an area close N of the Deepwater Jetty.

Climate information: see 1.184 and 1.198.

Directions

(continued from 5.237)

Principal marks

5.309

1 **Landmarks** (positioned from the light (36°36′·2N 36°11′·2E) at the head of W main breakwater):

- Three chimneys (1 mile SSW);
- Three radio station towers (1 mile SE);
- Silo (red light at N end) (5½ cables SE).

Approach and entry

5.310

1 When approaching İskenderun from W, especially at night, the SW entrance point of the bay should be given a wide berth as the bottom rises steeply off it and the distance from the coast is very difficult to estimate owing to the high land beyond. Otherwise from seaward to the pilot boarding position the chart is sufficient guide.

2 **Useful mark:**

Light (white concrete tower, 10 m in height) exhibited from the head of the W main breakwater.

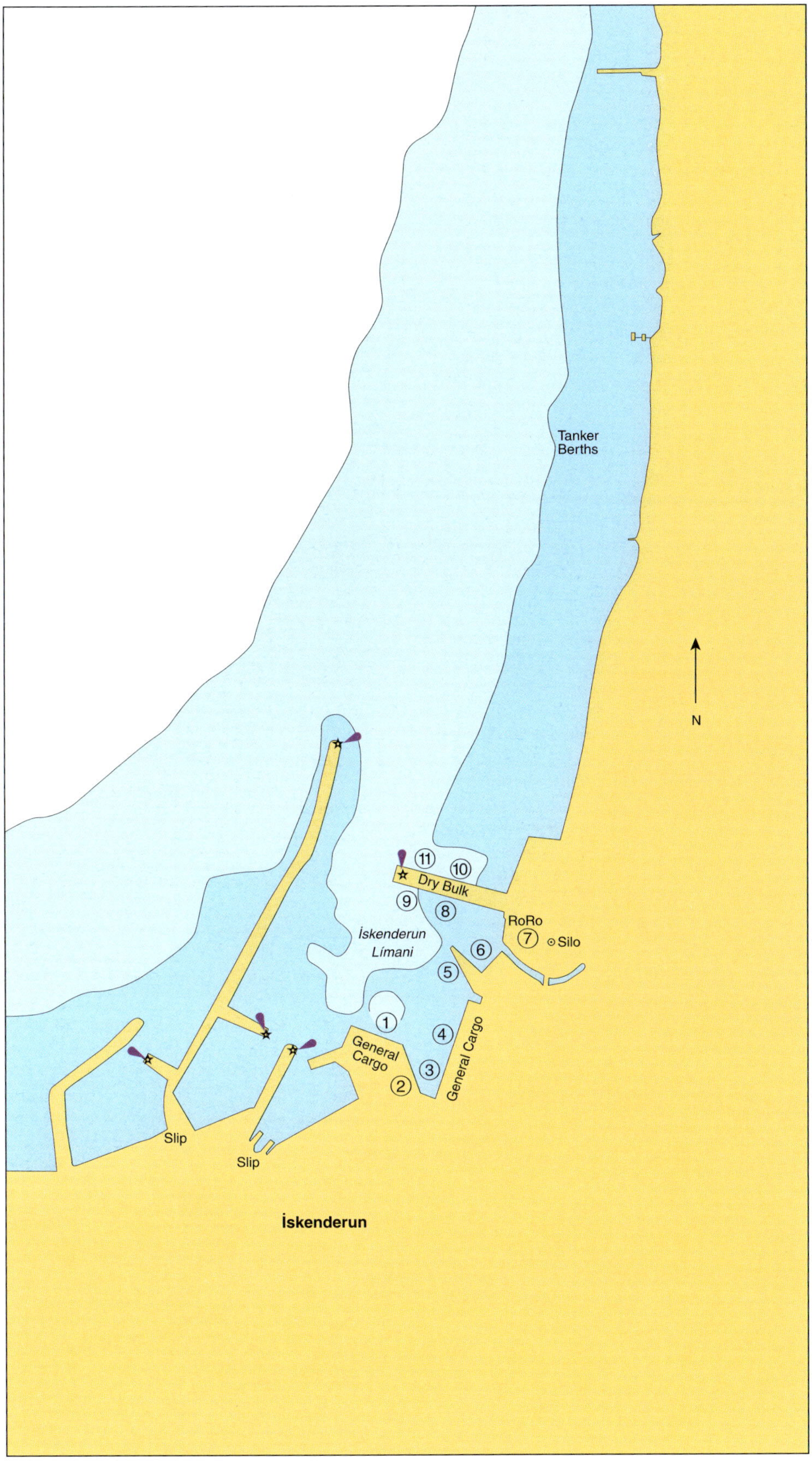

İskenderun (5.308)

Berths

Main harbour

5.311

1 Berths are numbered in sequence from No 1 at the S end of the harbour to No 10 at the outer end of the N side of Deepwater (Dry Bulk) Jetty (36°36′·0N 36°11′·4E). The berths handle general, containers and dry bulk cargoes.

2 The deepest berth is No 9, on the S side of Deepwater Jetty, with a depth alongside of 11 m. The longest berths are Nos 7 to 10, on Deepwater Jetty, with lengths of 180 m. There are RoRo berths at Nos 7 and 10, on either side of the root of Deepwater Jetty.

Basins at the head of the main harbour

5.312

1 At the head of the main harbour are two protected basins separated by a common mole projecting 2 cables NNE from the shore. A light (white concrete tower, 5 m in height) is exhibited from the head of the W mole and another light is exhibited from the head of the common mole.

2 The W basin is a Military Basin reserved for small military vessels. It has a depth of 4·0 m except at its head. The E basin is a quayed service harbour, with depths from 2·1 to 4·0 m in it. It is used by tugs, lighters and pontoons.

Offshore berths and jetties

5.313

1 **Tanker berths.** Three offshore tanker berths are situated between Sahri Sakalieh Point (36°37′·8N 36°11′·8E) and İskenderun Harbour, 1½ miles S. Mooring buoys lie at the seaward ends of submarine pipelines extending up to 4 cables offshore; tankers up to 35 000 dwt and 200 m LOA can be accommodated. Depths at the berths vary between 8 and 11·5 m. Cargo handled: refined products and chemicals. Anchoring is prohibited within 1 cable of the pipelines. Vessels berth during daylight hours. Numerous can and spar buoys also lie in this area up to 4 cables offshore.

2 **NATO Jetty** (36°39′·5N 36°12′·5E). This jetty projects 4 cables from the coast, 3 cables S of the mouth of Derebani Dere. Entry is prohibited to an area surrounding the jetty; the limits are shown on the chart. Permission is required from the naval authorities before berthing is allowed at this jetty.

3 **Sarıseki Fertilizer Jetty** (36°40′·0N 36°12′·5E) extends 4½ cables from the shore, 1 mile SSE of Yazıci Jetty. Cargo handled: fertilizer products, bulk cargo and liquid chemicals. A light is exhibited from the head of the jetty. Terminal operator: Gubretas Gubre Fabrikalari AS, 12 Eylul Caddesi, E-5 Karayolu Uzeri, Sarıseki Mevkii, İskenderun, Turkey. The jetty works 24 hours a day, all year round.

4 Berths available both sides of the jetty: Nos 6 and 5, 163 and 160 m long; 18 to 13 m depth; Nos 4 and 3, 104 m long; 10 to 8 m depth; Nos 2 and 1, 83 m long; 7 to 5 m depth. Depths decrease towards the shore. Vessels up to 55 000 dwt with maximum height above the surface of 10·8 m can be accommodated.

5 Anchorage: ahead of the jetty, the pilot station will provide the best location. Pilotage is compulsory and is based at İsdemir; tugs are available.

Services, see 5.289; oily waste disposal is not available.

Fishing harbour

5.314

1 The fishing harbour (36°35′·7N 36°10′·7E) is situated at the root of the W main breakwater, on its W side, and is protected from NW by its own breakwater. A light (white concrete tower, 5 m in height) is exhibited from the head of the NW breakwater and another light (concrete pillar, 6 m in height) is exhibited from the mole inside.

2 There are charted depths of 1·2 to 4·1 m inside the harbour. Fishing vessels of suitable draught, yachts and non-commercial vessels may berth here.

Port services

Repairs

5.315

1 There is a repair yard with modern facilities and a synchro-lift with a lifting capacity of 1500 tons. In the SW corner of Inner Harbour there is a repair yard for small vessels.

Other facilities

5.316

1 Hospital in the town; floating crane of 90 tonnes capacity; Ship Sanitation Control and Exemption Certificates; oily waste reception.

Supplies

5.317

1 Fuel oil at Deepwater Jetty, or by barge; fresh water at some berths, or by barge with capacity of 200 tons; provisions.

ANTAKYA KÖRFEZİ

General information

Chart 2632

Route

5.318

1 From a position about 13 miles SE of Karataş Burnu (36°32′N 35°20′E), in the middle of the entrance to İskenderun Körfezi, the coastal route leads S for about 30 miles across Antakya Körfezi, to a position W of Ra’s al Basīţ (35°51′N 35°48′E), in Syria.

Topography

5.319

1 From Akınçı Burnu (36°19′N 35°47′E) for 1½ miles S the coast is fringed with rocks and cliffs. Thence to İntiyas Kayası, 11½ miles SSE, where a fishermans’ shelter is located. The coast is bordered by long beaches with occasional cliffs and off-lying rocks, none of which is more than 3 cables offshore. The land is steep and densely wooded, rising to 1281 m at the summit of Koçcağiz Tepe (36°11′N 35°56′E). On the W slope of this range are numerous deep ravines, down which streams run during the greater part of the year.

2 From İntiyas Kayası a plain extends SE for 6 miles to the mouth of Asi Nehri. Thence from Asi Nehri to Ra’s al
3 Basīţ, 14¾ miles SSW, the coast becomes steeper with cliffs and in the vicinity of Ra’s al Basīţ is fringed with dangerous rocks.

International boundary

5.320

1 The boundary between Turkey and Syria reaches the coast at Kassab Bay (35°56′N 35°55′E).

Current

5.321

1 Near Ra’s al Basīţ the current is usually N-going at a mean rate of ½ kn.

Directions

(continued from 5.230)

Principal marks

5.322

1 **Landmark:**

Ra's al Basīţ (Rās el-Bassîte) (35°51′N 35°48′E) is a low lying point with a flat-topped limestone hill, about 50 m high, close E. Ra's al Basīţ Lighthouse (white tower, 12 m in height) stands on the W extremity of the hill.

Major light:

Akınçı Burnu Light (36°19′N 35°47′E) (5.235).

Antakya Körfezi

5.323

1 From a position about 13 miles SE of Karataş Burnu (36°32′N 35°20′E), the track leads S, passing (with positions from Akınçı Burnu Light (36°19′N 35°47′E)):

W of a cliff-faced point (1½ miles S), which has a rocky ledge extending 7½ cables SW from it with a rock awash at its outer end. In this vicinity keep at least 2 miles from the coast. Thence:

2 W of İntiyas Kayası (13 miles SSE), a white islet with several rocks lying off it. Rās el Mina, the point behind the islet, is well defined and prominent. The extensive ruins of the ancient city and port of Seleucia Pieria lie close SE of the point; they are white and visible from a considerable distance seaward. Thence:

3 W of the mouth of Asi Nehri (18½ miles SSE) (5.324). A white-domed tomb stands near the beach, on which landing is sometimes dangerous on account of the heavy surf, 2½ miles NNW of the river mouth. Samandağı, a village 1½ miles inland from the tomb, is marked by a clump of poplar trees. Thence:

4 W of Kassab Bay (24 miles SSE) in which there is an anchorage (5.325). Keldağ, 3 miles ENE of Kassab Bay, rises abruptly to an elevation of 1728 m and is conspicuous from S; the upper part is entirely bare, but the base and ridges which branch E are densely wooded. Thence:

5 W of Khalīj al Basīţ (27 miles S) in which there is another anchorage (5.326).

The track then leads to a position W of Ra's al Basīţ (35°51′N 35°48′E) (5.322), from where a light is exhibited.

(Directions continue at 7.10)

River and anchorages

Asi Nehri

5.324

1 **Description.** Asi Nehri (36°03′N 35°58′E) or Orontes River, rises in Jebel Liban, or Lebanon Range (7.124), and flows through Hatay (Antakya) to discharge near the middle of a long beach. On the bar the depths vary from 0·9 to 1·8 m but in summer it is difficult to enter even in a small boat; within the bar the depth is 2·7 m, and in winter this sluggish river is navigable for about 3 miles.

2 **Anchorage.** The usual anchorage is 5 cables off the bar, in a depth of 16 m, mud, but this berth is exposed to winds from NW through W to SW, and a heavy swell sets in and breaks on the bar.

Kassab Bay

5.325

1 Kassab Bay (35°56′N 35°55′E) affords anchorage 3½ cables offshore, with the ruins on the S side of the bay bearing 158°, and the S entrance point bearing 225°, in a depth of 35 m, sand; small vessels may anchor in depths of 13 to 18 m.

Khalīj al Basīţ

5.326

1 **Description.** Khalīj al Basīţ lies between Pigeon Islet (35°54′N 35°53′E) and Rās al Basīţ, 5 miles SW. Nabi Khudir, a conspicuous white mosque (not charted), stands on the summit of a cliff-faced point 2½ miles SSW of Pigeon Islet; several above-water rocks lie within 2 cables E of this point.

2 The ruins of ancient Posidium lie 4¼ miles SW of Pigeon Islet. An ancient mole extends a short distance E from the ruins, and ledge of rock projects 3 cables N.

Anchorage. The best anchorage in Khalīj al Basīţ is off Posidium with the head of the mole bearing 236° and the N extremity of Rās al Basīţ bearing 271°, in a depth of 15 m, sand and mud. The depths increase rapidly outside the anchorage, there being 55 m about 1¼ miles offshore.

Chapter 6 - Cyprus

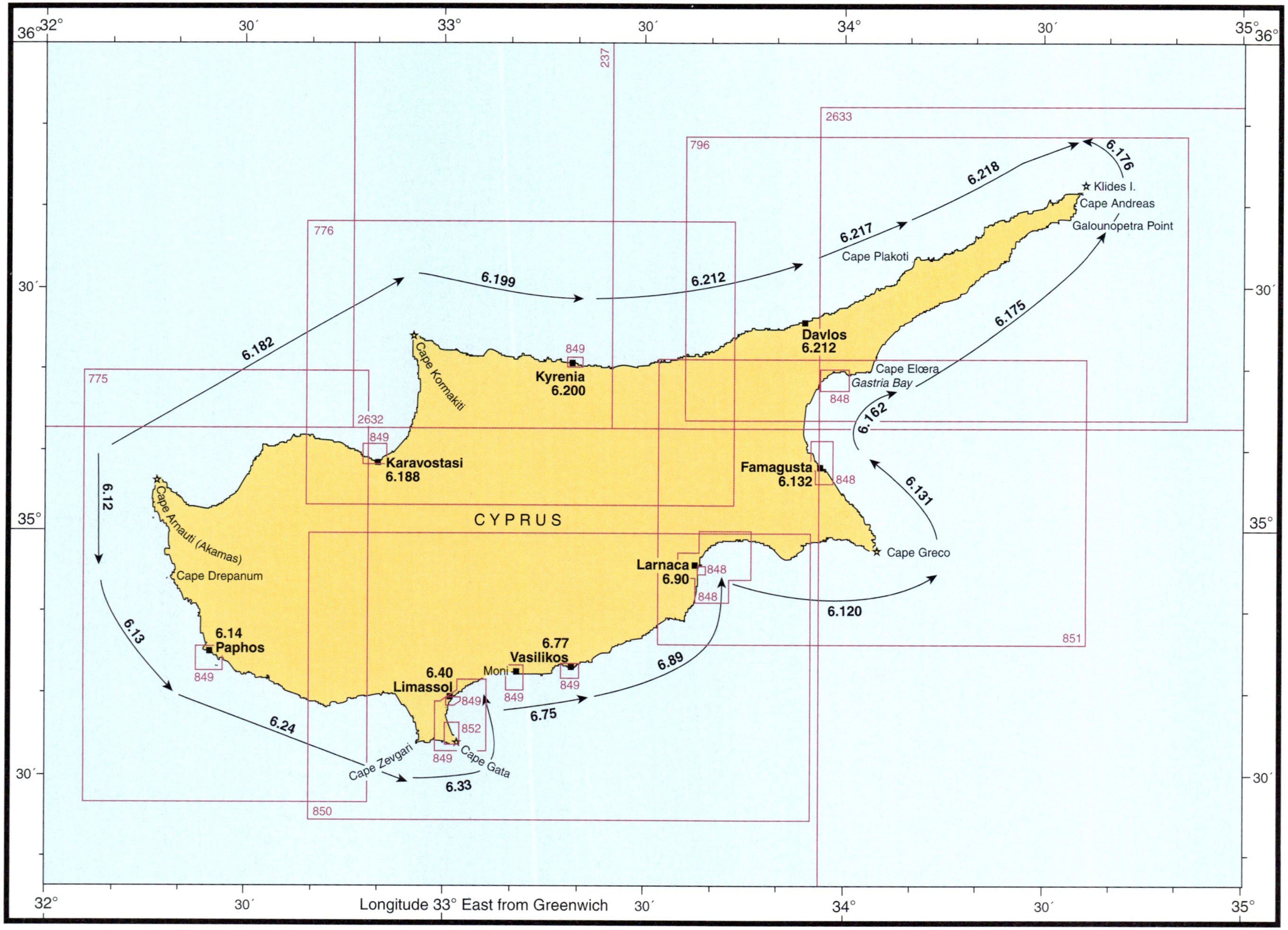

CHAPTER 6

CYPRUS

GENERAL INFORMATION

Chart 2074

Scope of the chapter

6.1

1 The area covered by this chapter comprises the coastal waters of Cyprus. The description includes the principal ports of Limassol (6.40), Larnaca (6.90), Famagusta (6.132) and Kyrenia (6.200).

Also described are other minor harbours around the coast, including Paphos (6.14) and Lachi (6.186), together with the open roadsteads of Karavostasi (6.188) and New Soli (6.188), on the N coast, which consist of loading jetties, anchorage berths and an offshore oil berth.

2 The chapter is divided into the following sections:

West and south-west coasts of Cyprus (6.7).
South coast of Cyprus (6.28).
East coast of Cyprus (6.127).
North coast of Cyprus (6.179).

Submarine exercise area

6.2

1 Submarines exercise frequently in an area centred 23 miles NNW of Cape Kormakiti (35°24′N 32°55′E). A good lookout should be kept for them when passing through these waters (see 1.6).

Dumping ground

6.3

1 An explosives dumping ground (34°23′N 34°08′E) lies 36 miles SE of Cape Kiti, as shown on the chart.

Rescue

6.4

1 For information on rescue see 1.69 and *Admiralty List of Radio Signals Volume 5.*

Currents

6.5

1 Generally, water flows around Cyprus in an anti-clockwise direction.

From Cape Arnauti (35°06′N 32°17′E) the current runs SE, becoming E-going from Paphos Point (34°45′N 32°24′E) to Cape Kiti (34°49′N 33°36′E). Variability is fairly low, and the mean rate of ½ to ¾ kn sometimes increases in spring and summer to 1½ kn with strong W winds.

2 Between Cape Kiti and Cape Andreas (35°41′N 34°35′E) the currents are very variable; the main stream is thought to run SE from Cape Kiti. Near the E coast a light N-going drift probably occurs, becoming NE-going near Boghaz (35°19′N 33°57′E). In winter, with E or NE gales, onshore sets may be experienced.

Along the N coast from Cape Andreas the current is mainly W-going at a mean rate of ¼ to ½ kn, but it is much affected by the wind; NE gales in winter will increase the rate to 1½ kn, whilst strong SW winds, in June and July particularly, may temporarily reverse the flow.

Orthography

6.6

1 Many places and geographical features in Cyprus, particularly in the N part of the island, have alternative Turkish names. The principal names are as follows:

Usual name	*Turkish name*
Akrotiri Bay (6.40)	Leymosun Körfezi
Andreas, Cape (6.176)	Zafer Burnu
Arnauti, Cape (6.12)	Arnaut Burnu
Boghaz (6.169)	Boğaz
Buffavento (6.211)	Bufaventu Tepe
Buffavento Castle (6.211)	Bufaventu Kalesi
Choti Island (6.212)	Dikelya
Chrysochou Bay (6.183)	Hrisofu Körfezi
Cyprus (1.108)	Kıbrıs
Dekelia (6.121)	Dikelya
Drepanum, Cape (6.12)	Drepona Burnu
Elœa, Cape (6.162)	Zeytin Burnu
Episkopi Bay (6.25)	Piskobu Körfezi
Famagusta (6.132)	Gazi Mağusa
Famagusta Bay (6.132)	Gazi Mağusa Körfezi
Galounopetra Point (6.175)	İyitaş Burnu
Gastria Bay (6.163)	Kalecik Limanı
Gata, Cape (6.33)	Dogan Burnu
Greco, Cape (6.120)	Poyraz Burnu
Kantara Castle (6.211)	Kantara Kalesi
Karavostasi (6.188)	Gemikonağı
Kiti, Cape (6.89)	Çite Burnu
Klides Islet (6.176)	Fener Adalar
Kokkino, Cape (6.182)	Kırmızi Burnu
Kormakiti, Cape (6.182)	Koruçam Burnu
Kornos, Mount (6.198)	Korno Tepe
Ktima (6.14)	Kasaba
Kyrenia (6.200)	Girni
Kyrenia Mountains (1.115)	Besparmak Dağalari
Larnaca (6.90)	Larnaka
Larnaca Bay (6.90)	Larnaka Körfezi
Lefka (6.188)	Lefke
Limassol (6.40)	Leymosun
Morphou (6.188)	Güzelyurt
Morphou Bay (6.188)	Güzelyurt Körfezi
Moulia Rocks (6.24)	Mulia Kayaları
Nicosia (1.108)	Lefkoşa
Paphos (6.14)	Baf

Usual name	*Turkish name*
Paphos Point (6.13)	Baf Burnu
Petounda Point (6.89)	Petunda Burnu
Phourni Rock (6.212)	Furni Kayası
Pyla, Cape (6.120)	Pile Burnu
Ronnas Bay (6.220)	Ronna Körfezi
Saint Hilarion Castle (6.198)	İlarionkalesi
Sina Oros (6.212)	Sinan Tepe
Stazousa Point (6.212)	Limanbaşı Burnu
Troodos, Mount (6.188)	Karlidağ
Trypa tou Vounou (6.200)	Karakulak Tepe
Vasilia (6.199)	Malazgirt
Vavilas Point (6.199)	Mutlu Burnu
Yeronisos (6.13)	Ágios Yeorgios Adası
Yialousa (6.217)	Maltepe
Zephyros Point (6.24)	Zefiro Burnu
Zevgari, Cape (6.24)	İkiz Burnu

WEST AND SOUTH-WEST COASTS OF CYPRUS

GENERAL INFORMATION

Charts 775, 850

Area covered

6.7

1 The area covered by this section comprises:

Cape Arnauti to Paphos (6.8).

Paphos to Cape Zevgari (6.21).

CAPE ARNAUTI TO PAPHOS

General information

Chart 775

Route

6.8

1 From a position about 6 miles NW of Cape Arnauti (Akamas) (35°06′N 32°17′E) the route leads initially 16 miles S to the vicinity of Cape Drepanum, then 14 miles SSE to a position about 5 miles SW of Paphos Point (34°45′N 32°24′E).

Topography

6.9

1 The coast between Cape Arnauti and Cape Yeranisou, 5 miles S, is high and precipitous, and fringed by ledges of sandstone rocks, nearly awash. Thence to Lara Point, a further 4 miles S, it continues high and precipitous, and forms a bay into which torrents from the adjacent hills flow in winter.

2 Between Lara Point and Cape Drepanum, 3 miles S, there are several sandy bays, and thence to Paphos Point the coast is bordered by below-water rocks which extend up to 2½ cables offshore in places.

Sea state

6.10

1 Except when calm, the sea breaks constantly on the reefs and ledges off the coast from Cape Arnauti (35°06′N 32°17′E) to Paphos Point, 22 miles SSE.

Directions

Principal marks

6.11

1 **Landmark:**

House, close S of Cape Arnauti (35°06′N 32°17′E).

Major lights:

Cape Arnauti Light (post, 3 m in height), exhibited from the peak 9 cables S of the cape.

Paphos Point Light (white round stone tower, 20 m in height) (34°45′N 32°24′E), exhibited from a position 4½ cables NE of the point.

Cape Arnauti to Cape Drepanum

6.12

1 From a position about 6 miles NW of Cape Arnauti (35°06′N 32°17′E) the track leads S, passing (with positions from Cape Arnauti):

W of Mazaki Islet (4 cables N), situated at the end of a ledge of below-water rocks; a ridge of foul ground extends 3 cables N from the islet. Thence:

2 W of Cape Arnauti, the NW extremity of Cyprus. It is a sharp, low headland, and the commencement of a mountain range of moderate height which extends SSE through the island. The cape rises to a double peak, 211 m high, 9 cables S; the W side is very steep, but the E side is thickly wooded, and slopes gradually to the beach. Thence:

3 W of Kannoudion Islet (4 miles S), thence:

W of Kionos Islet (5 miles S); Koppo Islet lies close offshore 4 cables farther NE. Shoal water extends 1½ miles offshore in the vicinity of these islets. Thence:

W of Cape Yeranisou (5¼ miles S), thence:

W of Lara Point (9¼ miles S), which is cliff-faced on its W side; boats occasionally shelter on its N and S sides. A small white house stands on the point.

4 The track then leads to a position W of Cape Drepanum (12¼ miles S), which is relatively low and flat in comparison with the coast N and has several rocks and submerged ledges off it. A white church with a red roof stands near the extremity of the cape and is conspicuous, particularly in the afternoon light. Ágios Geórgios fishing shelter is located approximately 2 cables NE of the point. A light is exhibited from the head of the breakwater.

Cape Drepanum to Paphos Point

6.13

1 From the position W of Cape Drepanum (34°54′N 32°19′E) the track leads SSE, passing (with positions from Cape Drepanum):

WSW of Yeronisos (3 cables SW), a flat-topped islet, thence:

WSW of Manijin Islet (1 mile SSE), thence:

WSW of two bays (3½ miles SE), the E of which is named Coral Bay. Peyia, a village, lies on the slopes 2 miles NE of these bays. Thence:

2 WSW of Orphourous Islet (7½ miles SSE), lying at the outer end of a rocky shoal which extends

4½ cables W from the shore. Several below-water rocks extend from the coast between the islet and Paphos Point. A conspicuous stranded wreck lies close N of the islet.

The track then leads to a position SW of Paphos Point (34°45′N 32°24′E), the extremity of a low peninsula.

(Directions for the coastal route continue at 6.23)

Paphos

Chart 849 plan of Paphos

General information

6.14

1 **Position**. Paphos (34°45′N 32°24′E), lies on the S side of a peninsula of which Paphos Point is the extremity. It has a population of about 40 900 (2000). Ktima, 1½ miles N of the harbour, is the capital of Paphos district.

2 **Function.** Paphos, no longer a commercial port, is a port of entry used by fishing vessels and recreational craft. The area is the centre of a large tourist trade.

Port Authority. Cyprus Ports Authority, 23 Crete Street, PO Box 22007, 1516 Nicosia, Cyprus.

Limiting conditions

6.15

1 **Controlling depth.** The channel leading into the harbour has a least charted depth of 3 m.

Maximum size of vessel handled: length 25 m, draught 2 m.

Arrival information

6.16

1 **Outer anchorage.** Off Paphos the anchorage is not good, being exposed to W and S winds; the holding ground of coarse sand and shell is poor. A suitable position, as shown on the chart, is with Paphos Point Light bearing 000°, distant 9 cables, in a depth of about 26 m. Gales from SE cause considerable swell.

Harbour

6.17

1 **General layout.** The harbour is protected by two moles; the NE mole is formed of rocky boulders, the SW is a solid curved breakwater extending SE from the shore.

Development. A marina is under construction (2007) and is expected to be completed by 2009.

Climate information: see 1.184 and 1.199.

Directions for entering harbour

6.18

1 **Landmarks** (positioned from Paphos Point Light (34°45′N 32°24′E)):

Minarets (1¼ miles NNE) (chart 775), in Ktima.

Belfry (white) (1 mile NE) (chart 775), in Ktima.

2 Fort (ruins, with an elevation of 14 m) (4 cables S).

Church dome (elevation of 30 m) (5 cables ESE).

Chimney (black) (7 cables ESE) (chart 775).

Chimney (elevation 100 m) (2½ miles E) (chart 775).

Major light:

Paphos Point Light (34°45′N 32°24′E) (6.11).

3 **Approaches.** The port should be approached with caution. From N, pass at least 1 mile W of Orphourous Islet (6.13) and Paphos Point, and then head in towards the anchorage or to the harbour entrance leading line.

Approaching from S, either steer for the W extremity of Paphos Point on a line of bearing of 338°, or steer along the alignment (009°) of the following marks:

Beacon (white) (34°45′·3N 32°24′·3E).

Paphos Point Light (3¾ cables N of beacon) (6.11).

This alignment also clears W of Moulia Rocks (34°43′N 32°26′E) (6.24).

4 Thence from a position about 6 cables SE of the harbour entrance, the track leads NW into the harbour, passing between two light buoys (lateral) moored off the heads of the harbour breakwaters.

Useful marks:

Light, exhibited from the head of the SW breakwater.

Moulia Rocks Light (34°43′N 32°26′E).

Berths

6.19

1 Iron pier at the head of the harbour; accommodates vessels up to 18 m in length and 2 m draught. There are depths of about 2·7 m over a small area off the pierhead, where vessels of light draught with local knowledge may take shelter, except in SE gales, which cause a considerable swell.

2 Iron jetty, close W of the pier; length 49 m; depth of 1·8 m at its end.

Pontoon berths 12 and 50 m long, close W of the jetty.

Port services

6.20

1 **Repairs:** minor repairs carried out.

Other facilities: custom house, with a flagstaff 14 m high, at the root of the pier; hospital at Ktima.

Supplies: fuel available from road tanker; fresh provisions; fresh water at the pier.

Communications. Paphos Airport is situated about 9 km SE of the harbour.

PAPHOS TO CAPE ZEVGARI

General information

Charts 775, 850

Route

6.21

1 From a position about 5 miles SW of Paphos Point (34°45′N 32°24′E), the coastal route leads SE for a distance of about 34 miles, to a position about 5 miles S of Cape Zevgari (34°34′N 32°56′E).

Topography

6.22

1 Between Paphos Point (34°45′N 32°24′E) and Cape Aspro, 16 miles ESE, the coast is low for 10 miles, after which it becomes cliff-faced, rising to the bold headland of the cape. The low section has beaches of sand and stones or shingle, which decrease in number after the cliffs are reached.

2 Rocks and submerged ledges are numerous off the coast but, apart from Moulia Rocks (6.24), they do not extend more than 2 cables offshore.

Inland, the hills are considerably broken up, forming no clearly defined summits, with the possible exception of a rounded hill, 410 m high, situated 7 miles ENE of Paphos Point.

For the topography of Episkopi Bay see 6.25.

Directions
(continued from 6.13)

Principal marks
6.23

1 **Landmark:**

Building (hospital) standing on Cape Zevgari (34°34′N 32°56′E).

Major lights:

Paphos Point Light (34°45′N 32°24′E) (6.11).
Cape Gata Light (34°34′N 33°01′E) (6.32).

Paphos to Cape Zevgari
6.24

1 From a position about 5 miles SW of Paphos Point (34°45′N 32°24′E) the track leads SE, passing (with positions from Cape Aspro (34°38′N 32°42′E)):

SW of Moulia Rocks (14¼ miles NW), which consists of two rocky shoals, with depths of less than 5 m over them. On the E shoal there are three dark-coloured above-water rocks, the highest being 2·7 m high from which a light is exhibited. On the W shoal there is a rock with less than 2 m over it, on which the sea breaks constantly. The channel between Moulia Rocks and the coast should only be used when calm by vessels having a maximum draught of 3·7 m; local knowledge is required. Thence:

2 SW of a marine farm (13½ miles NW), thence:

SW of a black rock (11 miles NW), 2·4 m high, lying ½ cable off the point S of Paphos Airport, thence:

SW of Zephyros Point (9¼ miles NW), which has a rock awash close S of it, thence:

SW of a marine farm (7 miles NW), marked by a light, lying 8 cables offshore, thence:

SW of Petra tou Romiou (4 miles NW), the legendary name of which was Venus Rocks; they lie close offshore and are conspicuous. Two of the rocks are 8 and 5 m high, and provide a useful navigational mark. Thence:

3 SW of Cape Aspro lying at the S point of the line of cliffs (6.22) which extend 1 mile E of the cape. These cliffs, divided into three main parts by two water courses, are light-coloured, sheer and magnificent, reaching a maximum elevation of 230 m 1 mile WNW of Cape Aspro; the land rises to an elevation of 276 m, 1 mile N of the cape. Depths of 5 m or less extend 4 cables ESE of Cape Aspro. Thence:

4 SW of Jubilee Shoal (3¼ miles ESE) (6.25).

The track then leads to a position S of Cape Zevgari (34°34′N 32°56′E), a toe, 2 cables wide, projecting 5 cables from the SW end of Akrotiri Peninsula, and sloping down to a height of 8 m at its extremity. Close NE the land rises to an elevation of 32 m. A conspicuous stranded wreck lies 2¼ miles N of Cape Zevgari; another stranded wreck, which covers, lies 1½ miles N of the cape. Three rocks, between 2 and 3 m high, lie close off the cape; shoal water and dangers extend 5 cables WSW and 4 cables S.

5 **Useful marks:**

Kouklia (34°42′N 32°34′E), a village, consisting of a group of white houses situated chiefly on the landward side of a low hill, on the summit of which is a large ruined building which at times casts a long shadow.

Three conspicuous domes (34°41′N 32°51′E).

(Directions for the coastal passage continue at 6.32)

Episkopi Bay

Chart 850

General information
6.25

1 **Topography.** Episkopi Bay lies between Cape Aspro (34°38′N 32°42′E) and Cape Zevgari, 12 miles SE. The N shore of the bay consists of a succession of small sandy bays, and towards its E end is backed by high white cliffs. The E shore is a low shingle beach to within 1½ miles of Cape Zevgari, whence it becomes cliff-faced and fronted by off-lying rocks.

2 Behind the NE shore of Episkopi Bay the village of Episkopi (34°40′N 32°54′E) stands on the slope of the hills which extend to the plain of Akrotiri Peninsula. In the village there is a minaret, with an elevation of 87 m; it is surrounded by tall cypress trees and difficult to distinguish. A white church with a red roof and an elevation of 89 m, 3 cables NW of the minaret, is more readily identified. Kouris Potamos, a broad river, flows close E of Episkopi.

3 Kolossi, 1½ miles E of Episkopi, consists of a village and a tower; the latter was built by the Knights Templar during their occupation of the island, and is not visible from seaward on all bearings.

Depths. Jubilee Shoal, 3½ miles ESE of Cape Aspro, has a least depth of 14·6 m over it; with this exception, the depths in Episkopi Bay are regular.

4 **Firing danger area.** Episkopi Bay is used for military exercises. There are two light buoys (special, DZ) moored in the bay, 5 cables WNW and 3¾ miles ESE respectively of Jubilee Shoal. A military target (orange) is situated 2½ miles ENE of Jubilee Shoal.

Anchorages
6.26

1 **General.** Anchorage, with good holding ground, mud and sand, may be obtained on the 20 m contour in any part of Episkopi Bay, but it is exposed to S and SW winds.

Pissouri Bay (34°38′N 32°44′E) is sandy. A large hotel stands on the shore. Anchorage for small vessels is obtainable, as shown on the chart, 1¼ miles E of Cape Aspro, in a depth of 10 m, mud and sand. This berth is partially sheltered by Cape Aspro from W winds.

2 **Evdimou Bay** (34°39′N 32°46′E) is also sandy. Anchorage, similar to that in Pissouri Bay, is obtainable, as shown on the chart, 3¼ miles E of Cape Aspro, in a depth of 10 m, sand.

Provisions and water are available in small quantities.

Anchorage

Chart 775

Moulia Rocks
6.27

1 Anchorage may be obtained, in summer, 3 cables E of Moulia Rocks (34°43′N 32°26′E) (6.24) in a depth of 13 m, sand and mud. This is the best anchorage off this coast; the holding ground is good and there is fair shelter from W winds.

SOUTH COAST OF CYPRUS

GENERAL INFORMATION

Chart 850

Area covered

6.28

1 The area covered by this section comprises:

Cape Zevgari to Limassol (6.29).
Limassol (6.40).
Limassol to Vasilikos (6.72).
Vasilikos to Larnaca (6.84).
Larnaca (6.90).
Larnaca to Cape Greco (6.116).

CAPE ZEVGARI TO LIMASSOL

General information

Charts 850, 849 plan of Approaches to Akrotiri Harbour and Limassol

Route

6.29

1 From a position about 5 miles S of Cape Zevgari (34°34′N 32°56′E) the route leads initially E, for about 9 miles, thence N, for a further 6 miles, into Akrotiri Bay and to a position SE of the entrance to Limassol Harbour (34°39′N 33°01′E).

Topography

6.30

1 Akrotiri Peninsula (34°35′N 32°58′E), with Cape Zevgari and Cape Gata projecting from its SW and SE extremities, respectively, extends 5 miles S from the general coastline, and is the S extremity of Cyprus. The highest part of the peninsula is at its S end, with an elevation of 64 m.

2 A large salt lake, with a depth of about 1·2 m, lies in the middle of the peninsula, the land on each side being very low. Akrotiri, a village, is situated at the SW corner of the lake; the church, white with a red roof, is visible from seaward on either side of the peninsula. The ruins of a monastery lie 1½ miles E of the church.

3 Between Cape Zevgari (34°34′N 32°56′E) and Cape Gata, 5 miles E, the coast of the peninsula is mainly cliff fronted and steep-to, with numerous indentations. Then for 2 miles NNW of Cape Gata the coast is rocky, fronted by rocky ledges, and backed by the slopes of high land at the S end of Akrotiri Peninsula. Farther N, as far as Limassol, the coast consists of shingle with a belt of coarse sand, containing about 5% of magnetic or black iron oxide. Landing in boats on the beach is, in most cases, hampered by isolated rocks and sandy ridges, with depths from 0·6 to 0·9 m over them, lying about 9 m offshore.

Restricted area

6.31

1 SBA 1, SBA 2 and SBA 3 light buoys (special), 3 cables E, 1½ miles NNW and 2 miles NNW of Cape Gata respectively, mark the seaward limits of a regulated area fronting the coast in the vicinity of Akrotiri Harbour.

Unauthorised landing on the coast within the Sovereign Base Area, see charts 849 and 850, is prohibited.

Directions

(continued from 6.24)

Principal marks

6.32

1 **Landmarks** (with positions from Cape Gata Lighthouse (34°34′N 33°01′E)):

Cape Gata Lighthouse (white stone tower), standing 6 cables WSW of Cape Gata. Three white patches may be seen before the lighthouse becomes not visible.

2 Radar scanner (1 mile WNW), the position of which is approximate, standing on a hill 62 m high.

Tower (1¼ miles WNW), the position of which is approximate.

Pylon (red and white) (2 miles NW).

Radar tower (red lights) (2 miles WNW).

3 Building (hospital) (4¼ miles W) standing on Cape Zevgari.

Radio masts (eight in two groups of four, red lights) (3½ miles NNW).

Major light:

Cape Gata Light — as above. An aero light (beacon) (2¼ miles NW) is exhibited from Akrotiri airfield, but is difficult to distinguish among other airfield lights.

Cape Zevgari to Limassol

6.33

1 From a position about 5 miles S of Cape Zevgari, the track leads initially E, passing (with positions from Cape Zevgari):

S of two light buoys (special, DZ) (1½ miles S and 2 miles SE), thence:

S of Vatha Rock (2 miles E), a rock 4 m high with below-water rocks around it, lying close offshore; many other below-water rocks lie close off this stretch of coast. Thence:

S of Cape Gata (5 miles E), a sheer cliff 52 m high. A remarkable cove is situated 1 mile W of the cape.

2 Thence round Cape Gata at a distance of not less than 1 mile, or keep in depths of more than 37 m. Cape Zevgari (6.24) should be kept bearing more than 278° until the water tower (6.59) in the central part of Limassol bears 354°, when course may be altered into Akrotiri Bay. The track then leads N, passing:

E of Cape Gata, thence:

E of Akrotiri Harbour (5 miles E) (6.34).

The track then leads to a position SE of the entrance to Limassol Harbour (34°40′N 33°02′E).

(Directions continue for Limassol Harbour at 6.59, and for the coastal route at 6.74)

Akrotiri Harbour

Chart 852

General information

6.34

1 **Position.** Akrotiri Harbour (34°34′N 33°02′E) is situated at the SE end of Akrotiri Peninsula, about 5 miles S of Limassol.

Function. The harbour serves the military base on Akrotiri Peninsula.

2 **Port limits.** Two buoys (special), 2½ cables NNE and 6 cables NNW of Cape Gata respectively, mark the seaward limits of the harbour, as shown on the chart. The area

within the harbour limits is restricted and fishing is prohibited.

Port Authority. Akrotiri Port Authority, The Commander, RAF Akrotiri, Sovereign Base Areas, Akrotiri, Cyprus.

Limiting conditions

6.35

1 **Tidal levels.** Mean spring range about 0·4 m; mean neap range about 0·1 m. For details see *Admiralty Tide Tables Volume 2.*

2 **Deepest and longest berth.** Offshore tanker berth (6.39).

Maximum size of vessel handled. Vessels up to 183 m in length, with a draught of 9·75 m, can use the tanker berth.

Arrival information

6.36

1 **Notice of ETA:** 24 hours.

Anchorage in depths from 20 to 25 m may be obtained within 4 cables of the outer dolphin of the RoRo Terminal.

2 **Pilotage** is compulsory for vessels proceeding to the offshore tanker berth and RoRo facilities. Vessels should obtain a pilot from Limassol. For details see *Admiralty List of Radio Signals Volume 6 (3).*

3 **Regulations.** Access is restricted; commercial traffic is not permitted without the written authority of the Station Commander of RAF Akrotiri.

Harbour

6.37

1 Akrotiri Harbour consists of a basin enclosed by a mole, open to the N. A light (framework tower) is exhibited from the head of the mole, and another light (framework tower) is exhibited from a point on the shore WSW of it. On the seaward side of the mole a short spur extends NE from the elbow, forming a RoRo berth.

Climate information: see 1.184 and 1.200.

Directions for entering harbour

6.38

1 From seaward to the berths and basin the chart is sufficient guide. To assist in berthing at the offshore tanker berth the approach to the buoy moored at the end of the pipeline is marked by the alignment (219¾°) of the following beacons:

Front beacon (white, diamond topmark, 2·5 m in height) (34°34′·5N 33°01′·7E).

2 Rear marks consisting of three beacons (orange, diamond topmarks, 2·5 m in height) (1¼ cables from front beacon).

The S side of the approach to the tanker berth is marked by the alignment (211¾°) of the following beacon and light:

Beacon (white, 2 m in height) (34°33′·9N 33°01′·5E).

Cape Gata Light (¾ cable SSW) (6.32).

3 **Caution.** An outfall extends seaward, for 4½ cables NNE, from a position on the shore 9 cables NNW of Cape Gata.

Useful mark:

Watch tower (34°34′·8N 33°01′·6E).

Berths

6.39

1 **Offshore tanker berth.** A submarine pipeline extends 4 cables ENE from a position on the shore, 5 cables N of the head of the harbour mole. Its seaward end is marked by a light buoy (special). Two buoys (spherical, orange) lie close WNW and SSE, respectively. The berth is surrounded by five mooring buoys (lighted). Vessels are berthed by day only.

2 **RoRo Terminal.** A berth with a least depth of 5·5 m, used by RoRo vessels, lies outside Akrotiri Harbour. The berth consists of a platform situated 50 m NE of the elbow of the harbour mole, to which it is connected by a bridge, and two berthing dolphins situated 35 and 115 m farther NE respectively; the dolphins are marked by lights. Vessels berth on the SE side of the dolphins and secure head or stern to the platform which is equipped with bollards. Ground moorings are laid NNE and ESE of the outer dolphin, to which they are attached by wire pendants.

Harbour basin. Within the basin there is a wharf 52 m long, with depths of up to 1·5 m alongside.

LIMASSOL

General information

Chart 849 plan Approaches to Akrotiri Harbour and Limassol, plan Limassol

Position

6.40

1 Limassol (Lemesos) (34°40′N 33°02′E) is situated on the S coast of Cyprus at the head of Akrotiri Bay, about 5½ miles N of Cape Gata (34°34′N 33°02′E).

Function

6.41

1 Limassol is a multipurpose port and the principal port of Cyprus with modern facilities for handling passenger, container, RoRo, general cargo vessels and bulk carriers. It also acts as a hub for transit container traffic.

Principal imports include grain, foodstuffs, machinery, vehicles, iron, timber and manufactured goods. Exports include citrus fruits, grapes, potatoes, wine, cement, scrap iron, various minerals, clothing and pharmaceutical products.

The town, second in importance after Nicosia, has a population of about 159 800 (2000).

Topography

6.42

1 Behind the town the land rises gradually in tree-covered, wedge-shaped hills. Troodos, the Government summer station and resort for visitors, is situated in the hills 17 miles NNW of the town and can be seen in the background (Chart 2074).

Traffic

6.43

1 In 2007 there were 3152 ship calls.with a total of 38 235 308 dwt.Total cargo handled in 2006 was about 4 million tonnes and the number of passenger movements was 600 000.

Port Authority

6.44

1 **Principal.** Cyprus Ports Authority, 23 Crete Street, PO Box 22007, 1516 Nicosia.

Local. Port Manager, Limassol New Port, PO Box 53331, 3302 Limassol.

Limiting conditions

Controlling depth

6.45

1 The entrance channel to Limassol Harbour is dredged to a depth of 15 m (1996) over a width of 150 m. The basin between the harbour entrance and the quays has also been dredged to 15 m over a width of 3 cables.

Deepest and longest berth

6.46

1 Container/RoRo berth (6.63).

Tidal levels

6.47

1 Mean spring range about 0·4 m; mean neap range about 0·2 m. For details see *Admiralty Tide Tables Volume 2.*

Density of water

6.48

1 1·026 g/cm^3.

Maximum size of vessel handled

6.49

1 Up to 13·5 m draught.

Arrival information

Vessel traffic service

6.50

1 A VTS is maintained for the regulation of shipping and operates 24 hours.

Vessels should contact the VTS when 12 miles from the port advising the following:

Vessels name, time and position, course and speed, draught, cargo and any defects or damage.

For details see *Admiralty List of Radio Signals Volume 6 (3).*

Notice of ETA

6.51

1 24 hours.

Outer anchorages

6.52

1 Anchorage may be obtained within the designated anchorage area centred 1 mile E of Limassol Lighter Basin, as shown on the chart, in depths of 10 to 70 m. The holding ground is good, and although the anchorage is open S and E, vessels with good anchors and cables do not normally drag during gales.

From October to April, when NE gales occur, it is usual to anchor in a depth of about 22 m.

2 During the summer the prevailing W winds sometimes reach gale force in the afternoon, making boat work uncomfortable. For this reason it is advisable for small vessels to anchor to the SW.

Weather prevents the working of cargo at the anchorage from October to March, for an average of 7 days per month.

Prohibited anchorage

6.53

1 Anchoring and fishing are prohibited within the approach channel, as shown on the chart.

Pilotage

6.54

1 Pilotage is compulsory and available 24 hours. The pilot boards 1 mile E of the head of Main Breakwater, as shown on the chart.

For details see *Admiralty List of Radio Signals Volume 6 (3).*

Tugs

6.55

1 Three tugs are available and meet vessels outside the harbour.

Notice of medical requirements

6.56

1 Notice of medical requirements should be sent at least 3 hours before arrival.

Marine farms

6.57

1 A marine farm, marked by four light buoys (cardinal), is positioned about 9 cables SE from the head of Main Breakwater. A second farm, closer inshore, is positioned about 2½ cables SE from the elbow of Main Breakwater.

Harbour

General layout

6.58

1 The port comprises Limassol Harbour, on the SW side of the town, and Limassol Lighter Basin 1½ miles NE, which fronts the town.

Limassol Harbour is an artificial harbour protected from S by Main Breakwater and from E by Lee Breakwater. The harbour is quayed on its E, N and W sides and partially quayed in West Basin.

2 Limassol Lighter Basin is protected by two breakwaters. The E breakwater extends 150 m SSE, thence 180 m SW, forming, respectively, East Quay and South Quay. The W breakwater extends 107 m S, leaving an entrance 46 m wide between the breakwater heads.

3 **Developments.** A new passenger terminal is planned for the E quay (2008). In 2008 work will commence to extend the container terminal by 520 m, and to complete the dredging of the berthing depth to 17 m.

Directions for entering harbour

(continued from 6.33)

Principal marks

6.59

4 **Landmarks** (positioned from Limassol Lighter Basin entrance (34°40′·1N 33°02′·5E)):

Grain silos (1¾ miles SW), standing near the W quay of Limassol Harbour.

Water tower (elevation 55 m) (6 cables NNW), situated in the central part of the town.

Cape Gata Lighthouse (6¼ miles S) (6.32).

Limassol Harbour

6.60

1 From a position about 3 miles SE of the entrance to Limassol Harbour the track leads NNW to the pilot station and thence to the beginning of the harbour entrance leading line:

Front light (orange diamond on metal framework tower) (34°38′·7N 33°00′·5E). The front light only becomes visible when nearly in line with the rear light.

Rear light (similar structure) (380 m from front light).

2 The alignment (248°) of these lights leads through the entrance channel, passing (with positions from the head (34°39′N 33°02′E) of Main Breakwater):

NNW of a wreck (4½ cables ENE), with a depth of 14 m over it and marked by a light buoy (isolated danger), thence:

SSE of a light buoy (starboard hand) (2 cables N) marking the N side of the channel, and:

3 NNW of the head of Main Breakwater, from which a light is exhibited, thence:

SSE of the head (4 cables W) of Lee Breakwater, from which a light (metal column, 9 m in height) is exhibited, into the harbour. There is a stranded wreck close to the head of this breakwater on the seaward side and two other stranded wrecks lie at its root.

4 **Caution.** It was reported (2001) that the leading lights may be obscured if large vessels are berthed on the S quay in West Basin.

Limassol Lighter Basin

6.61

1 Attention is drawn to the dangerous wreck (mast) lying 1¾ cables SSW of the entrance to the basin, otherwise from seaward to the basin the chart is sufficient guide.

Useful marks

6.62

1 Positioned from Limassol Lighter Basin entrance (34°40′·1N 33°02′·5E):

Lights (metal posts, 3 m in height) exhibited from the head of South Quay and the W breakwater at Limassol Lighter Basin.

Minaret (3 cables NW).

Minaret (3 cables NNE).

Berths

Limassol Harbour

6.63

1 Positioned from head (34°39′N 33°02′E) of Main Breakwater:

East Quay container berth (5½ cables NW): length 480 m; depth alongside 11 m.

North Quay (7 cables NW): length 290 m; depth alongside 11 m; used by passenger vessels.

2 West Quay (8 cables WNW): length 450 m; depths alongside of 11 to 13 m; used by grain carriers.

Container/RoRo Berth (8 cables W): length 320 m; depth alongside 14 m.

Container Berth (9 cables WSW) in West Basin: length 380 m; depths alongside 14 m.

Dolphin Berths (1 mile SW) Five berths in West Basin: length 1075 m; depths alongside 10·5 m.

3 Future developments include a further 2000 m of quay space in the W Basin by 2010, and the construction of an East Basin to E of Lee Breakwater. The port is to be dredged to a depth of 14·5 m.

Limassol Harbour from SW (6.63)

(Original dated 2002)

(Photograph - Cyprus Ports Authority)

Limassol Harbour from E (6.63)
(Original dated 2002)

(Photograph - Cyprus Ports Authority)

Limassol Lighter Basin

6.64

1 There are depths of 2·4 to 4·3 m within the basin, but a vessel up to 80 m in length and 4·3 m draught can berth alongside the SW end of South Quay, where there is a depth of 4·9 m.

Lighters berthed in the basin are unlit at night.

Piers

6.65

1 Limassol Pier, close NE of Limassol Lighter Basin, is an iron structure 115 m long, at the head of which there is a depth of about 4·6 m. Small vessels can lie alongside this pier, the outer 30 m of which has a width of 18 m.

An iron trestle pier 49 m long, with landing steps and a depth of 1 to 2 m alongside, projects from the quarantine station close W of the W breakwater of Limassol Lighter Basin.

A pier with a depth of 3·4 m at its head is situated 11 cables NE of Limassol Pier.

Landing places

6.66

1 There is a landing place at Limassol Pier, where there are steps on each side of the pierhead, and at the root of the pier on the NE side, where there is a depth of 1·5 m. During strong NE and SE gales it is impossible to land at the inshore steps, owing to the surf, but landing may then be possible at steps at the N end of Limassol Lighter Basin.

Port services

Repairs

6.67

1 Repairs of most kinds can be effected. A floating dock is moored in Limassol Harbour with the following dimensions:

> Length 62·9 m; maximum ship breadth 18·3 m; depth over keel blocks at MHWS 5·0 m; lift 1360 tons; maximum overall vessel length 74 m.

Other facilities

6.68

1 Hospital; compass adjustment; oily waste and garbage disposal; fumigation.

Supplies

6.69

1 **Supplies.** Fuel, by small tanker; fresh water, at the berths, or by barge at the anchorage; provisions.

Communications

6.70

1 International airports at Larnaca and Paphos, 70 km ENE and 63 km W respectively.

Cruises

6.71

1 Short cruises to Israel and Egypt.

LIMASSOL TO VASILIKOS

General information

Chart 850

Route

6.72

1 From a position about 3 miles SE of the entrance to Limassol Harbour (34°39′N 33°01′E) the coastal route leads ENE, for about 13 miles, to a position SSE of Vasilikos (34°43′N 33°19′E).

Topography

6.73

1 The coast between Limassol (34°39′N 33°01′E) and the mouth of Moni River, 8 miles ENE, is mainly shingle. Thence as far as Cape Dolos, 3½ miles E, it becomes rocky with detached rocks lying up to 1 cable offshore. The ruins of ancient Amathus, once famous for its metals, are situated on the coast 5¼ miles ENE of Limassol, but few traces of its harbour now remain except for a massive wall near the beach.

2 Light-coloured broken hills, sparsely wooded, form the background from 5 miles E of Limassol to Vasilikos. Vikla, a summit 163 m high, 1½ miles NW of Cape Dolos, is well defined, particularly from E.

Directions

(continued from 6.33)

Principal marks

6.74

1 **Landmarks:**

Admiralty House (34°41′·6N 33°05′·3E), 2½ miles NE of Limassol, is prominent, yellow with a red roof, and backed by dark green shrubs and trees; a flagstaff within the grounds is visible from seaward.

2 A large grey cement factory (34°42′·6N 33°11′·6E), with a tall chimney near its E end. At night it shows up well, illuminated by three closely-spaced clusters of lights.

Limassol to Vasilikos

6.75

1 From a position about 3 miles SE of the entrance to Limassol Harbour the track leads ENE, passing (with positions from Cape Dolos (34°42′N 33°16′E)):

SSE of a SPM (lit) (8¾ miles W) marking the seaward end of a water pipe, thence:

SSE of Moni (4½ miles W) where there is a marina and two offshore tanker berths (6.76), thence:

Clear of 2 tuna fish farms (1½ SSW and 1¾ miles S), marked by buoys, thence:

2 SSE of Cape Dolos; between Moni and Vasilikos Bay, E of Cape Dolos, there are several marine farms lying up to 1 mile offshore. Thence:

SSE of Vasilikos Bay (1 mile ENE), which lies between Cape Dolos and a point 2½ miles ENE.

The track then leads to a position SSE of Vasilikos (2¼ miles ENE).

3 **Useful marks:**

Radio mast (red lights) (34°44′N 33°08′E).

Moni power station chimneys (six) (34°43′N 33°11′E).

Chimney (red lights) at Vasilikos power station (34°43′·6N 33°17′·4E).

Radio mast (red lights) (34°47′N 33°18′E).

Radio masts (red lights), standing 3½ cables E of the village of Vasilikos.

(Directions continue at 6.88)

Moni

Chart 849 plan of Moni

6.76

1 **Position and function.** Two offshore tanker berths front the coast between St Raphael Limassol Marina (34°42′·6N 33°10′·0E) and the mouth of Moni River, 1½ miles E.

Port limits. From the coast to the limit of territorial waters between the meridians of 33°10′E and 33°13′E.

Traffic: In 2005 direct petroleum imports at Moni and Dekelia (6.121) were 720 000 tonnes.

2 **Port Authority.** Cyprus Ports Authority (6.77).

Operator. Moni Power Station, Electricity Authority of Cyprus.

Density of water: 1·026 g/cm^3.

Maximum size of vessel handled: *Seaway L*, LOA 213·3 m, 60 000 dwt.

3 **Pilotage** is compulsory and available during daylight hours only. Pilots are obtained from Limassol; advance notice is required.

Tugs are available from Limassol; prior notice is required.

Movement restriction. Berthing at night is not permitted. Weather permitting, unberthing can take place at anytime.

4 **Berths.** The W berth, which serves a power station, consists of mooring buoys at the seaward end of a pipeline extending 5 cables from the shore. The berth has a depth of 18 m and is suitable for tankers of up to 225 m in length and 12 m draught.

The E berth, which serves a cement factory, consists of two mooring buoys at the seaward end of a pipeline extending 2½ cables from the shore. The berth has a depth of 13·7 m and is suitable for tankers of up to 204 m in length and 10·7 m draught.

5 **Caution.** A marine farm is located 4 cables SE of the E berth.

Port services.

Repairs are not available.

Supplies. Fuel, by small tanker at the anchorage. Fresh water by barge, provisions.

Vasilikos

Chart 849 plan of Vasilikos

General information

6.77

1 **Position.** Vasilikos (34°43′N 33°19′E) is a small industrial harbour situated near the E entrance point of Vasilikos Bay, 15 miles ENE of Limassol.

Function. The principal function of the port is to service a large cement works close N of the harbour. It has facilities for handling bulk and liquid chemical products, together with a RoRo facility. An offshore SBM (6.80) is used by tankers supplying fuel to the power station 1 mile W of the harbour.

2 Exports include cement, clinker and gypsum. Imports include petroleum, coke and bulk liquid chemicals.

Port limits. Between lines of bearing of 162° drawn respectively from the mouth of the Maroni River (33°22′·1E) and from Cape Dolos to the limit of territorial waters (chart 850).

3 **Traffic.** In 2007 the port and facilities in Vasilikos Bay had 217 ship calls with a total of 1 627 861 dwt.

Port Authority. Cyprus Ports Authority, 23 Crete Street, PO Box 22007, CY 1516 Nicosia. The port is operated by the Vasilikos Cement Works Ltd.

Limiting conditions

6.78

1 **Controlling depth.** In 2006 the entrance channel and turning basin had a dredged depth of 10 m.

Deepest and longest berth: length 360 m; depth 9 m.

Density of water: 1·025 g/cm^3.

Maximum size of vessel handled. *Jeddah Cement II*, 41 094 dwt, LOA 184 m, beam 27·64 m.

Arrival information

6.79

1 **Notice of ETA:** 24 hours.

Outer anchorage: 9 cables S of breakwater in 30 m, noting a marine farm 3 cables farther SSE.

Pilotage is compulsory for all vessels. For details see *Admiralty List of Radio Signals Volume 6 (3)*.

2 **Tugs** can be obtained from Larnaca (6.90), subject to 12 hours notice.

Regulations. Berthing is by day only but unberthing is available 24 hours. Tankers, and other vessels carrying dangerous cargo, must obtain permission from the Port Manager before entry.

Harbour

6.80

1 The artificial harbour consists of a basin, enclosed W and S by a long curved breakwater and protected from E by a short breakwater, which together form the entrance, open E. A light is exhibited from the head of each breakwater. The mouth of Vasilo River lies at the root of the N breakwater.

A former disused offshore loading pylon lies close W of the S breakwater.

2 **Boat harbour.** A boat harbour, 5 cables W of the harbour, consists of a floating dry dock and boat shelter enclosed by two breakwaters. The entrance opens SSE and a light is exhibited from the head of the W breakwater.

Directions for entering harbour

6.81

1 From seaward to the harbour the chart is sufficient guide.

Useful mark:

Breakwater lights (6.80).

Berths

6.82

1 The artificial harbour contains a total quay length of 484 m. The main quay, on the N side, has a length of 360 m, and is used for bulk handling and discharge of oil for use in the factory. An overhead conveyor leads onto the berth. The W quay, 124 m, handles bulk and liquid chemical cargoes. There is a RoRo ramp, width 20 m, in the NW part of the harbour.

2 **SBM berth.** An SBM from which a light is exhibited (34°42′·4N 33°17′·9E) lies at the seaward end of a submarine pipeline extending 1¼ miles SSE from the shore in the vicinity of a power station. The SBM is equipped with two floating hoses, each of which is marked by 4 small flashing white lights. Anchoring and fishing are prohibited 200 m either side of the pipeline, and within 500 m radius of the SBM.

3 A light buoy (special) (chart 850) marks the seaward end of the power station cooling water intake, 4 cables inshore from the SBM.

Port services

6.83

1 **Repairs.** Minor repairs can be undertaken.

Other facilities: garbage removal; reception facilities for oily waste.

Supplies: fuel; stores; fresh water.

VASILIKOS TO LARNACA

General information

Chart 850

Route

6.84

1 From a position SSE of Vasilikos (34°43′N 33°19′E) the route leads initially ENE, for about 17 miles, to the vicinity of Cape Kiti (34°49′N 33°36′E); thence NNE, for a farther 9 miles, into Larnaca Bay in a position about 3 miles ESE of the entrance to the port of Larnaca (34°55′N 33°38′E).

Topography

6.85

1 Between Vasilikos (34°43′N 33°19′E) and Petounda Point, 10 miles ENE, hills much broken up and covered with trees approach the coast.

High Hill, 6 miles NE of Vasilikos, 284 m high, is well defined, more particularly from E. Mount Stavrovouni, 688 m high, 11½ miles NNE of Vasilikos, is isolated, surmounted by a monastery, and very conspicuous as soon as it is opened E of High Hill.

2 From Petounda Point to Cape Kiti, 6 miles ENE, the land near the coast is low-lying. Petounda Point, the hills already described, Zyyi and the windpump nearby, are the only identifiable objects between Cape Dolos and Cape Kiti.

3 The shore from Cape Kiti to Larnaca, 6 miles N, is cliff faced for 5 cables; thence a stone and shingle beach, backed by an extensive plain within which are large salt lakes. Rocks front the shore between Cape Kiti and Dades Point, 3½ miles NNE. Larnaca Airport is situated 1 mile NNW of Dades Point.

Depths

6.86

1 Between Zyyi, 1 mile ENE of Vasilikos, and Cape Kiti, 14 miles farther ENE, rocks extend about 2 cables offshore in places; the HW line is principally shingle except where there are cliffs. Depths are somewhat irregular under 22 m, the nature of the bottom changing from mud, in greater depths, to sand with rocky outcrops and patches of mud and weed.

Prohibited areas

6.87

1 **Dades Point.** Anchoring and trawling are prohibited in an area, shown on the charts, established within 5 cables of a submarine pipeline (intake for a desalination plant) extending 1 mile offshore from Dades Point (34°52′N 33°38′E). A light buoy (special) marks the E extremity and vessels are requested to give the area a wide berth.

2 **South of Larnaca.** Anchoring and trawling are prohibited in a cable landing area extending from 5 cables to 2½ miles S of Larnaca (34°55′N 33°38′E), up to 2¼ miles offshore, as shown on the charts.

Directions
(continued from 6.75)

Principal marks
6.88

1 **Landmark:**

Tower (square, 28 m in height), standing on high ground 1 mile N of Cape Kiti (34°49′N 33°36′E).

Vasilikos to Larnaca
6.89

1 **Caution.** When navigating between Vasilikos and Cape Kiti, keep in depths of 27 m or more.

From a position SSE of Vasilikos (34°43′N 33°19′E) the track leads ENE, passing (with positions from Cape Kiti Light (34°49′N 33°36′E)):

SSE of Pendaskino Point (10 miles WSW). A light buoy (ODAS, special) is moored 3¼ miles ESE of Pendaskino Point. Thence:

SSE of Petounda Point (5¾ miles WSW), which is cliff-faced with a height of 13 m. It is similar to Pendaskino Point. Thence:

2 SSE of Cape Kiti, which is formed of cliffs from 11 to 12 m high; the cliffs on the E side, although low, are white and very conspicuous, and are a good mark in low visibility. A light (white stone tower) is exhibited from the cape. Shoals lie up to 1 mile off Cape Kiti; for this reason give the cape a berth of at least 1½ miles, keeping in depths of 22 m or more.

3 The track then leads NNE, passing (with positions from Cape Kiti Light):

ESE of Cape Kiti; keep at least 1½ miles off the coast to the N of the cape. Thence:

ESE of Dades Point (3¼ miles NNE); a tower stands 7 cables SW of the point. Thence:

ESE of a dangerous wreck (5½ miles NNE), lying 1 mile ESE of Larnaca Fishing Harbour.

4 Thence to a position about 3 miles ESE of the entrance to the main harbour of Larnaca.

Caution. The shoal water off Dades Point lies within the white sector (270°–005°) of the light exhibited from the head of the main harbour South Breakwater.

Useful marks:

Two belfries, 20 and 25 m high, stand close together 1½ miles WNW of Cape Kiti. The village of Kiti, 2¼ miles NW of the cape, contains a third belfry 42 m high.

5 Hala Sultan Tekke (34°53′N 33°37′E), on the SW shore of the N salt lake, is a prominent mosque with a minaret 31 m high, and a dome.

(Directions for Larnaca continue at 6.108)
(Directions for the coastal route continue at 6.119)

LARNACA

General information

Chart 848

Position
6.90

1 Larnaca (34°55′N 33°38′E) is situated on the SE side of Cyprus, along the W shore of Larnaca Bay, which is entered between Cape Kiti (34°49′N 33°36′E) and Cape Pyla, 15 miles NE. The town extends for 1½ miles in a SE to NW direction, the part fronting the shore being about 1 mile in length.

Function
6.91

1 The second largest port in Cyprus, Larnaca is a modern commercial harbour with good facilities for handling a variety of ships including container, passenger, RoRo, bulk carriers and tankers at offshore berths.

Main exports; gypsum and potatoes. Main imports: grains and feedstuffs, iron, timber, chipboards, fertilizers, cars and petroleum products.

The town has a population of about 70 500 (2000).

Port limits
6.92

1 Port limits are contained within a bearing 089° to the high seas from Livadia church (34°57′N 33°38′E), and a bearing 089° from Hala Sultan Tekke Mosque (34°53′N 33°37′E).

Approach and entry
6.93

1 Larnaca main harbour is approached from E and entered through a channel dredged to 13 m (1991), over a width of 160 m. The channel leads into the harbour where there is a turning area dredged to 12 m.

Traffic
6.94

1 In 2005 there were 606 ship calls with a total net tonnage of 1·7 million tonnes, handling 855 000 tonnes of cargo, 4700 teu and 67 000 passengers.

Port Authority
6.95

1 **Principal:** Cyprus Ports Authority, 23 Crete Street, PO Box 22007, 1516 Nicosia.

Local: Larnaca Port Manager is the local authority.

Limiting conditions

Deepest and longest berth
6.96

1 Main harbour (6.110).

Maximum size of vessel handled
6.97

1 *Ever Goods* 270 m LOA; 53 000 dwt.

Arrival information

Notice of ETA
6.98

1 24 hours.

Anchorages
6.99

1 The anchorage off Larnaca is safe for well-found vessels throughout the year, although the holding ground is reported to be poor. During SE gales a short sea and a heavy swell run into the bay and render the anchorage uncomfortable.

2 Gales from NE and SW also cause swell, that from SW being the more troublesome. Gales from SE and S usually veer SW, and if vessels drag it is in a direction parallel to the shore. During summer the land and sea breezes are fairly regular; the sea breeze blows along the shore from S.

6.100

1 Cargo and passenger vessels should anchor S of a line drawn 090° from the head of the main harbour South Breakwater, between the prohibited anchorage areas shown on the chart.

Larnaca from S (6.106)
(Original dated 2002)

(Photograph - Cyprus Ports Authority)

Tankers awaiting a berth should anchor N of parallel 34°56′·2N.

Prohibited anchorage

6.101

1 Anchoring is prohibited in the approach to the main harbour, up to 1½ miles offshore, as shown on the charts.

For details of other prohibited anchorage areas S of the main harbour see 6.87.

Pilotage

6.102

1 Pilotage is not compulsory; however, special permission is required for not using a pilot. The service is available 0600-2400 hours. Pilots board in the roadstead, about 1 mile E from the harbour entrance.

For details see *Admiralty List of Radio Signals Volume 6 (3)*.

Tugs

6.103

1 Tugs are available.

Regulations

6.104

1 Tankers, gas carriers and vessels carrying dangerous cargoes are not permitted to enter port without special permission from the Port Manager; berthing at mooring buoys takes place only in daylight hours.

Berthing is carried out from 0600 hrs, vessels can depart at any time.

2 Cargo vessels can berth during the night provided that berth space is available and vessels commence cargo operations immediately.

Quarantine

6.105

1 Notice of medical requirements should be sent at least 3 hours before arrival.

Pratique is granted either before or after berthing as appropriate.

Harbour

General layout

6.106

1 The port of Larnaca is centred around an enclosed main harbour (34°55′·6N 33°38′·6E), with several buoyed offshore berths for oil and gas tankers to the N, and a yacht and fishing harbour to the S.

2 Larnaca main harbour, situated close N of the town, is an artificial harbour protected by S and N breakwaters. The inner parts of the breakwaters are quayed, and a pontoon projects from a mole at the NW corner of the harbour.

3 Larnaca marina (34°55′·0N 33°38′·5E), abreast the town, is protected from S and E by a curved breakwater. The marina entrance is open NNE. A landing place, consisting of a small iron jetty, 3 cables S of the marina, had a depth of 1·5 m alongside in 1960.

Larnaca fishing harbour, 1 mile S of the marina, is enclosed by two breakwaters. The harbour entrance is open N.

4 **Developments.** In 2008 the port awarded the first phase contract for a large development project, which aims to turn Larnaca into a leading cruiseship hub. A 1000 berth marina and superyacht facility is also planned. Construction work is scheduled to start at the end of 2009 and is expected to last around 10 years.

Climate information

6.107

1 See 1.184 and 1.201.

Directions

(continued from 6.89)

Principal marks

6.108

1 **Landmarks** (positions from the head of the main harbour South Breakwater):

Mount Stavrovouni (11 miles WSW) (6.85) (chart 850), which is conspicuous from any part of Larnaca Bay.

Jami Kebir Minaret (30 m high) (1 mile SSW); a yellow stone fort, used as a police station, stands close E of the minaret.

2 Government offices (yellow gables, grey roof) (7½ cables SW). The customs flagstaff (23 m high) stands close SE of the offices, and a radio mast stands close N.

Tannery (conspicuous long building, Greek lettering on roof) (5 cables WSW).

3 Santa Maria Church (white dome, 33 m high) (1 mile WSW).

Flares (1 mile NNW) of the oil refinery, visible at a considerable distance at night when lit.

Approach and entry

6.109

1 From a position about 3 miles ESE of the entrance to the main harbour of Larnaca the track leads initially NW to a position about 5 cables ENE of the harbour entrance. The line of bearing 242° leads WSW, passing (with positions given from the head of South Breakwater):

Close SSE of a light buoy (starboard hand) (3 cables NE), which marks the N side of the entrance to the approach channel, thence:

2 NNW of the head of South Breakwater, from where a light is exhibited, thence:

SSE of the head of North Breakwater, from where a light is exhibited, into the harbour.

Berths

Alongside berths

6.110

1 Berths are situated inside the main harbour (positions from the head of South Breakwater):

North Quay (2¾ cables NW); length 326 m, depth alongside 10 m.

Pontoon (3½ cables WNW): SW side, length 100 m, depth alongside 6·5 m; NE side, length 100 m, depth alongside 6·5 m.

South Quay (3 cables WSW); length 340 m, depth alongside 12 m; has a RoRo ramp at its W end.

Offshore tanker berths

6.111

1 A number of offshore berths for oil and gas tankers discharging to shore lie at the seaward ends of submarine pipelines extending about 5 cables offshore between 3½ cables and 1¾ miles NNE of the main harbour. The berths are as follows:

Cyprus Refinery Berth. Accommodates tankers up to 225 m long, 12·8 m draught and 40 000 dwt.

2 Petrolina Berth. Accommodates tankers up to 198 m in length, 12·2 m draught and 45 000 dwt.

LPG berths. There are three berths for LPG tankers, each of which can accept tankers of up to 110 m in length; the deepest berth has a depth of 13·5 m.

Port services

Repairs

6.112

1 Minor repairs can be effected.

Other facilities

6.113

1 Hospital in town; oily waste and garbage disposal.

Supplies

6.114

1 Fuel oil at berths and by barge in roads; fresh water; provisions.

Communications

6.115

1 There is an international airport at Larnaca, 8 km distant.

LARNACA TO CAPE GRECO

General information

Chart 851

Route

6.116

1 From a position about 3 miles ESE of the entrance to the port of Larnaca (34°55′N 33°38′E) the route leads E, for a distance of about 23 miles, to a position 5 miles SE of Cape Greco (34°57′N 34°05′E).

Topography

6.117

1 The shore between Larnaca (34°55′N 33°38′E) and Dekelia, 6 miles NE, is a sand and shingle beach, backed by a slight elevation on which stand several villages. Yerako Muti, a hill 208 m high, lies 5 miles N of Larnaca.

Aradippou, 3 miles NW of Larnaca, has a church with a belfry (78 m high) and Livadia, 2½ miles N of Larnaca, also contains a church with a belfry (36 m high).

2 Between Dekelia and Cape Pyla, 6½ miles ESE, the shore is rocky and backed by hills. Thence from Cape Pyla to Cape Greco, 11 miles E, the coast remains rocky, but there are one or two coves where boats can land.

Behind Cape Greco the land rises to Phanos, 175 m high, the summit of which is nearly flat with a scarp on the N and S sides. From Phano Hill the land slopes away W before rising again to Cape Pyla.

Depths

6.118

1 Depths increase rapidly offshore along the coast from Larnaca to Cape Greco; a remarkable indentation in the charted 200 m line approaches to within 1 mile of the shore, 3 miles W of Cape Pyla.

Directions

(continued from 6.89)

Principal marks

6.119

1 **Landmarks:**

Hospital (35°00′N 33°44′E) in Dekelia, standing at an elevation of 90 m. It is 120 m long and 29 m in height.

Four chimneys of Dekelia power station (34°59′N 33°45′E) standing prominently 3½ cables E of Quarantine Point; five other less prominent chimneys and a group of eight tanks stand 1 cable W of the four prominent chimneys.

2 Tower (4 m in height) in ruins, standing on Cape Pyla (34°56′N 33°51′E).

Dekelia power station from W (6.119)
(Original dated 2007)

An abrupt table cliff, 100 m high, which has the appearance of an old fortress, situated 1 mile WNW of Cape Greco (34°57′N 34°05′E).

Larnaca to Cape Greco

6.120

1 From a position about 3 miles ESE of the entrance to the port of Larnaca (34°55′N 33°38′E) the track leads E, passing (with positions from Cape Pyla (34°56′N 33°51′E)):

S of Dekelia (6 miles NW) (6.121), thence:

S of Cape Pyla, which is 95 m high. Seven light buoys (special, DZ) mark the outer limits of Pyla Firing Range; the outer buoys are moored 2¾ miles W, 2¼ miles SSW, and 2½ miles SE of the cape. Thence:

2 S of a marine farm (2¼ miles E), thence:

S of Makronisos (5 miles NE), a small point of land projecting 1 cable from the coast, thence:

S of a bay (7¾ miles ENE) lying on the SE side of the town of Agía (Ayia) Napa. Two submarine cables come ashore at the head of the bay. For information on submarine cables see 1.26.

3 The track then leads to a position 5 miles SE of Cape Greco. The cape is the SE extremity of Cyprus, and the termination of a small peninsula, connected to the mainland by a narrow isthmus, on the S side of which is a bay, 5 cables wide, with rocky shores, the bottom being sand with patches of weed. The cape is low and tapering, but there are depths of 18 m 1 cable offshore.

4 Cape Greco Light (white stone tower, 15 m in height) is exhibited from the cape. Three radio masts (red lights, 125 m in height) stand close NW of the light-structure.

Useful mark:

Radio mast (red lights) (35°00′N 34°02′E) position approximate, standing at Phanos.

(Directions continue at 6.130)

Dekelia

Chart 848 plan Approaches to Larnaca

General information

6.121

1 **Position and function.** Dekelia (34°59′N 33°44′E) is situated 6 miles NE of Larnaca. It forms an alternative anchorage and landing place to Larnaca during NE winds. It also contains an offshore berth for tankers supplying the power station at Dekelia.

2 **Traffic.** In 2005 direct petroleum imports at Moni (6.76) and Dekelia were 720 000 tonnes.

Port Authority. Cyprus Ports Authority, 23 Crete Street, PO Box 22007, 1516 Nicosia, Cyprus.

Arrival information

6.122

1 **Notice of ETA:** 24 hours.

Anchorage. Vessels may anchor, as shown on the chart, in a position 6 cables SSW of Quarantine Point (34°58′·8N 33°44′·3E), in depths of about 29 m, mud and weed with good holding ground.

2 **Pilotage** is compulsory for tankers berthing. Pilots are obtained from Larnaca (6.90). Vessels are not normally berthed at night, but may leave at any time.

Tugs. Available from Larnaca.

Harbour

6.123

1 **General layout.** The harbour consists of four coves, all open S; Quarantine Point separates the two E coves.

Landmarks:

Dekelia Beacon (stone, black and white bands; 6 m in height) (34°58′·8N 33°42′·8E) at an elevation of 11 m.

2 The garrison church, with a belfry prominent from seaward, stands 4 cables NNW of the point.

Hospital (35°00′N 33°44′E) (6.119).

Dekelia power station chimneys (34°59′N 33°45′E) (6.119).
Tower (34°58′·8N 33°43′·8E).

Directions

6.124

1 From seaward to the berths the chart is sufficient guide.

Berths

6.125

1 **Sovereign Base Area Berth.** A reinforced concrete jetty with a **Y**-shaped head extends nearly 1 cable from the shore 4½ cables W of Quarantine Point. This berth was for the exclusive use of the Sovereign Base Area, and is now disused and in an unsafe condition. The submerged remains of two dolphins are situated off the head of the jetty; depth over the inner dolphin is 2·1 m and over the outer dolphin 4·4 m.

2 Watson's Mole consists of a rubble breakwater extending 100 m E from the root of the jetty. A slipway, landing stage and pontoon are located on the N side, close to the root.

Fisherman's Cove, on the W side of Quarantine Point, contains a jetty of steel piles and concrete, with a depth of 2·1 m at its outer end. Boats should approach it on a NNE course, making the entrance to the cove midway between a point on the W side and a rocky islet 1 m high on the E side.

3 **Offshore berth.** An offshore berth for tankers supplying Dekelia power station fronts the coast about 7½ cables ESE of Quarantine Point. The berth, suitable for tankers up to 225 m in length and 12·5 m draught, is at the seaward end of a submarine pipeline extending SSE from the shore. Vessels secure bows S with two anchors laid out ahead, a head rope to a mooring buoy, and stern lines to two mooring buoys.

Port services

6.126

1 **Supplies.** Bunkering, stores, fresh water and provisions.

EAST COAST OF CYPRUS

GENERAL INFORMATION

Charts 851, 796

Area covered

6.127

1 The area covered by this section comprises:
Cape Greco to Famagusta (6.128).
Famagusta (6.132).
Famagusta to Cape Elœa (6.159).
Cape Elœa to Klides Islet (6.170).

CAPE GRECO TO FAMAGUSTA

Charts 851, 848 plan of Famagusta

Route

6.128

1 From a position 5 miles SE of Cape Greco (34°57′N 34°05′E) the route leads initially N, for about 7 miles, thence NW for a further 14 miles to the vicinity of 35°11′N 34°00′E, NE of the entrance to the harbour of Famagusta.

Depths

6.129

1 From a point about 2 miles NNW of Cape Greco to a position 7 miles NW the coast is bordered by rocky shoals which extend up to 6 cables offshore. Thence, for 2½ miles farther NW, the coast is bordered within depths of 10 m by a line of rocks and shoals lying up to 2½ cables offshore.

Directions

(continued from 6.120)

Principal marks

6.130

1 **Landmarks:**
Table cliff, 1 mile WNW of Cape Greco (34°57′N 34°05′E) (6.119).
Radio mast (red and white bands, red light, 51 m in height) (35°07′·2N 33°56′·2E).
Saint Nicholas Mosque (building 41 m high with minaret 50 m high) (35°07′·5N 33°56′·5E), standing in the centre of Famagusta.

2 **Major lights:**
South-east Bastion Light (stone tower, 11 m in height) (35°07′·4N 33°56′·8E), exhibited from near the S corner of Famagusta Inner Harbour.
Famagusta Light (white concrete tower, black stripes, 11 m in height) (35°08′·5N 33°55′·6E). The lighthouse is reported to be less conspicuous than the beacon 2 cables NE of it, and on W bearings from near the outer anchorage it is obscured over a small arc by a windmill.

Cape Greco to Famagusta

6.131

1 From a position 5 miles SE of Cape Greco (34°57′N 34°05′E) (6.120) the track leads initially N, passing E of Cape Greco to a position about 5 miles NE of the cape. The track then leads NW, passing (with positions from South-east Bastion Light (35°07′·4N 33°56′·8E)):
NE of Fig Tree Bay (8¼ miles SE), thence:
NE of a group of mooring buoys (4 miles SE), moored between 2 and 5 cables off the coast, thence:
NE of a stranded wreck (3½ miles SE), thence:

2 NE of a low sandstone point (5½ cables ESE). A chain of islets and reefs extends SSE, parallel with the coast, for 5 cables from this point; Pambouli, the largest of these islets, lies close off Glossa. Thence:
NE of Karavolos Patamothio (4 cables ESE), the S of a line of flat rocky islets extending 5 cables NNW from the same sandstone point. It has a large and prominent red-roofed house on it. Thence:
NE of Oxo Islet (3 cables ENE), 3 m high, thence:

3 NE of Messanisi or North Islet (3 cables NE), which is 0·3 m high, and is marked by a beacon (red, 4 m in height), thence:
NE of a line of shoals extending 1 mile NNW from the head (8 cables N) of Outer Breakwater. These shoals are covered by the red sector (216°–313°) of Famagusta Light (6.130). The area W of these shoals is sheltered from SE gales, and forms the approach to Famagusta Harbour.

4 The track then leads to the vicinity of 35°10′N 33°57′E, NE of the entrance to the harbour of Famagusta.

Useful mark:

Radio mast (red lights) (35°00′N 34°02′E) position approximate, standing at Phanos.

(Directions for Famagusta continue at 6.151)
(Directions for the coastal route continue at 6.161)

FAMAGUSTA

General information

Chart 848 plan of Famagusta

Position

6.132

1 Famagusta (35°07′N 33°56′E), on the E coast of Cyprus, is situated on the SW shore of Famagusta Bay, which is entered between Cape Greco (34°57′N 34°05′E) and Cape Elœa, 23 miles N.

Function

6.133

1 Famagusta is a medium-sized port, importing general cargo, oil and foodstuffs; exports include textiles and household goods, citrus fruits, potatoes and manufactured textiles.

The harbour contains a Freeport area.

History

6.134

1 Famagusta, ancient Ammochostus, as a port flourished under the Venetians, but after being captured by the Turks in 1571 it began to decay. In 1735 it was ruined by an earthquake.

2 In recent times Famagusta was the principal port of Cyprus, but since 1974 it has been declared closed to navigation by the Government of Cyprus as it lies within the area of the unrecognized Turkish Republic of Northern Cyprus (1.110), and its trade has diminished. The Turkish Republic of Northern Cyprus Ministry of Communications and Works states that the port is open to international shipping.

Town

6.135

1 The old town is enclosed by massive fortress walls, on the outer side of which is a ditch 24 m wide and 14 m deep. Openings have been made in the walls to facilitate communication between the town and the harbour.

Traffic

6.136

1 In 2007 there were 1087 ship calls with a total of 1 918 812 dwt.

Port Authority

6.137

1 Department of Ports, Ministry of Communications and Works, Famagusta, 10 Mersin, Turkey.

Limiting conditions

Controlling depth

6.138

1 The approach channel to Outer Harbour entrance has been dredged to a depth of 10·2 m over a width of 1 cable.

Deepest and longest berth

6.139

1 Outer Harbour, SW side (6.154).

Tidal levels

6.140

1 Mean spring range about 0·4 m; mean neap range about 0·1 m. For details see *Admiralty Tide Tables Volume 2.*

Density of water

6.141

1 Density of water in the dock is approximately 1·028 g/cm^3.

Maximum size of vessel handled

6.142

1 Vessels up to 220 m LOA and 9·15 m draught can be accommodated in the Outer Harbour. Vessels up to 131 m LOA and 6·7 m draught can enter the Inner Harbour.

Local weather

6.143

1 Strong ENE winds cause a heavy sea and sometimes a N-going current, with the result that vessels in the anchorage lie broadside on and roll considerably. Strong NW winds in winter raise a short choppy sea.

Strong ENE gales sometimes occur in October, December, January and March, when pressure is high. They may last three days, with a heavy sea.

2 During strong winds vessels may experience difficulty in entering and securing in Inner Harbour; strong E winds sometimes necessitate the closing of the harbour. In summer, vessels can usually enter without difficulty.

Arrival information

Notice of ETA

6.144

1 Notice of ETA should be sent to agents 24 hours in advance to arrange a pilot and berth.

Outer anchorage

6.145

1 Anchorage may be obtained in a depth of about 18 m, 1 mile NE of Famagusta Light (35°08′·5N 33°55′·6E), as shown on the chart.

If Famagusta Harbour is closed vessels may anchor off Boghaz (6.169).

Pilotage

6.146

1 Pilotage is compulsory for vessels over 300 grt. There is direct communication with the pilots by VHF during office hours.

Pilots board near Turning light buoy (35°09′·2N 33°56′·2E) or at the anchorage. For details see *Admiralty List of Radio Signals Volume 6 (3).*

Tugs

6.147

1 Tugs are available, and meet vessels at the entrance to Outer Harbour.

Regulations

6.148

1 Vessels are permitted to enter harbour between 0600 and sunset, or 2300 for passenger vessels. Vessels may leave harbour between 0600 and midnight.

Harbour

General layout

6.149

1 Famagusta Harbour comprises Outer Harbour and Inner Harbour. The Harbour Office is situated in the custom house (6.151).

Outer Harbour is protected from NE by Outer Breakwater which extends in an arc N and W from Messanisi. West Arm extends from the shore 3 cables WSW of the head of Outer Breakwater, forming the entrance, 1¼ cables wide, to Outer Harbour.

2 Inner Harbour is protected from NE by Karavolos Patamothio, Oxo Islet and Messanisi. Old Mole, which dries, extends W from Messanisi for 2¼ cables. The entrance to Inner Harbour, between the head of Old Mole and the quay on the SW side of Outer Harbour, is about 110 m wide. Within the entrance a basin, extending SE for 3 cables, has been dredged to a depth of 7·3 m; two dolphins are situated at the SE end of the basin.

Schooner Basin, at the SE end of Inner Harbour, is dredged to a depth of 2·7 m.

Traffic signals

6.150

1 The following traffic signals (diagram 6.150) are displayed on the flagstaff at the Harbour Office:

Day *Night* *Meaning*

Port closed; vessels may not enter or leave.

Famagusta - port entry signals (6.150)

2 While these signals are displayed, further signals as required will be made by International Code from the flagstaff, or by daylight flashing lamp.

Directions for entering harbour

(continued from 6.131)

Principal marks

6.151

1 **Landmarks** (positioned from Saint Nicholas Mosque (35°07′·5N 33°56′·5E)):

Saint Nicholas Mosque (6.130).

Hotel (white building) (8 cables ESE), prominent from S.

Radio mast (3½ cables SW) (6.130).

Custom house (white building with low square tower) (1½ cables E), and warehouses (red roofs) nearby, which are prominent on nearer approach.

2 Beacon (concrete structure, black and white bands, triangle topmark, 8 m height) (1½ miles NNW).

Hotel (red light) (35°12′·6N 33°53′·8E) (chart 851) standing near the coast 2½ miles N of Salamis, has been reported to be a useful mark when approaching Famagusta from SE.

Major lights:

South-east Bastion Light (3 cables ESE) (6.130).

Famagusta Light (1·3 miles NNW) (6.130).

Approach and entry

6.152

1 From the vicinity of 35°11′N 34°00′E the track initially leads W for a short distance to the beginning of the following leading line:

Beacon (35°08′·7N 33°55′·7E) (6.151).

Famagusta Light (6.130) (2 cables SW of front mark).

The alignment (216°) of these marks, and, by night, the E part of the white sector (178°–216°) of the light leads SW, passing (with positions from the beacon):

SE of a shoal (8 cables NNE), with a depth of 9·8 m over it, thence:

Close to Turning light buoy (W cardinal) (6 cables NE).

2 Thence, when SE Bastion Light (35°07′·4N 33°56′·8E) (6.130) is seen in the centre of the entrances to Outer and Inner Harbours, the track leads on the line of bearing 158½°, of the light, into Outer Harbour, passing:

Between the shoals (7 cables W) extending NNW from the head of Outer Breakwater and the mainland, thence:

WSW of the head (9 cables SE) of the Outer Breakwater from which a light (white metal framework tower, concrete base, 6 m in height) is exhibited, thence:

3 ENE of West Arm (9 cables SSE) from the head of which a light (white metal framework tower, concrete base, 6 m in height) is exhibited.

Caution. SE Bastion Light is usually partly obscured by fishing vessels' masts.

Useful mark:

Light (black metal column, 8 m in height) (35°07′·8N 33°56′·7E), exhibited from the head of Old Mole.

Berths

Anchorages

6.153

1 Anchorage may be obtained near the approach channel, inside the shoals, with Famagusta Lighthouse (35°08′·5N 33°55′·6E) bearing about 277°, distant 6½ cables, in a depth of about 12 m. The shoals give no protection to this berth in NE and E gales, and vessels should proceed to sea during a gale from this quarter.

2 Small vessels may anchor in the area sheltered by Outer Breakwater in depths of 5·5 to 7·3 m, or may enter Inner Harbour.

Alongside berths

6.154

1 **Outer Harbour.** On the SW side of Outer Harbour, there is 655 m of berthing space with a depth of 9·1 m alongside. Container, bulk and RoRo vessels may use these berths. General cargo and smaller vessels are usually handled in the Inner Harbour.

2 **Inner Harbour.** On the SW side of Inner Harbour a quay 540 m in length can accommodate vessels drawing up to 6·7 m; the heavy seas raised in the bay by strong NE winds are not felt to any marked extent by vessels berthed here. Mooring buoys are provided for hauling off vessels from the quay.

3 Schooner Jetty, extending 99 m E from the SE end of this quay, is constructed of iron, with depths from 3·7 to 5·5 m alongside. Small vessels, except when loading or discharging cargo, usually berth stern to this jetty with anchors out, or anchor in Schooner Basin, sometimes with

sterns secured to the mooring buoys. There is a lighter basin on the S side of Schooner Jetty.

Port services

Repairs

6.155

1 A shipyard is situated at the S end of Inner Harbour. The yard has three slips, one capable of taking coasters up to 75 m long and 2500 dwt, another capable of taking vessels of 60 m in length and the third for craft up to 20 m long and 200 dwt. Minor engine repairs can be carried out. Radar and radio repairs are undertaken. A floating dock, 25 m in length, is located on the S side of the West Arm in the Outer Harbour.

Other facilities

6.156

1 Hospital in the town; compass adjusting; RoRo facilities; oily waste and garbage reception.

Supplies

6.157

1 Fuel oil from road tankers; fresh water at the quays; provisions.

Communications

6.158

1 Ercan Airport is situated 9 km from Famagusta.

FAMAGUSTA TO CAPE ELŒA

Chart 851

Route

6.159

1 From the vicinity of 35°11′N 34°00′E, NE of the entrance to the harbour of Famagusta, the route leads NE for a distance of about 8 miles, to a position about 5 miles SE of Cape Elœa (35°20′N 34°04′E).

Topography

6.160

1 To the N of Famagusta the coastline is wooded. Salamis (35°10′N 33°55′E), once a port and now a shallow indentation, lies 3 miles NNW of Famagusta with the ruins of the town in amongst the trees. The church of Ágios Barnabas, standing on rising ground 1 mile SW of the ruins, is a large white building with twin domes.

2 The coast for 4 miles N of Salamis is low and densely wooded, with many modern buildings. Between a point 2½ miles NE of Spathariko (35°14′N 33°52′E) and Boghaz, 3¾ miles NNE, the coast is more open. Trikomo, 3 miles NNE of Spathariko, is a large village visible from SE and E through trees.

3 Between Gastria Bay (35°19′N 34°00′E) and Cape Elœa, 3 miles E, the coast is cliff fronted and thickly wooded with scrub and small trees.

Directions

(continued from 6.131)

Principal marks

6.161

1 **Landmark:**

Hotel (35°12′·6N 33°53′·8E) (6.151).

Oil tanks (35°19′·8N 33°59′·1E) standing on the NW side of Gastria Bay.

Silos (35 m in height) (35°19′·5N 34°00′·4E) standing on the E side of Gastria Bay.

2 Cape Elœa Lighthouse (white concrete tower, black bands, 11 m in height) (35°19′·7N 34°02′·9E).

Major light:

Famagusta Light (35°08′·5N 33°55′·6E) (6.130).

Famagusta to Cape Elœa

6.162

1 From the vicinity of 35°11′N 34°00′E the track leads NE, passing (with positions from Cape Elœa (35°20′N 34°04′E)):

SE of Boghaz (5½ miles WSW) (6.169), thence:

SE of Gastria Bay (3¼ miles W) (6.163).

2 The track then leads to a position about 5 miles SE of Cape Elœa. There are no off-lying dangers, but depths of less than 10 m extend 4 cables off the cape. A white house stands among low trees 7 cables N of the cape and a light (6.161) is exhibited from a position 7½ cables W of the cape.

3 **Useful marks:**

Radio mast (35°17′·7N 33°55′·0E).

Chimney (35°19′·1N 33°57′·7E) standing in a gypsum factory 5½ cables NE of Boghaz; a large white building stands 1½ cables W of the factory.

(Directions continue at 6.174)

Gastria Bay

Chart 848 plan of Gastria Bay

General information

6.163

1 **Position.** Gastria Bay (35°19′N 34°00′E), also known as Kalecik Limanı by Turkey, is situated on the E coast of Cyprus, on the N side of Famagusta Bay.

Function. The port imports petroleum products and cement clinker; cement is exported.

2 **Traffic.** In 2007 there were 116 port calls with a total of 460 293 dwt.

Port Authority. Department of Ports, Ministry of Communications and Works, Famagusta 10 Mersin Turkey.

Limiting conditions

6.164

1 **Density of water.** Approximately 1·030 g/cm^3.

Maximum size of vessel handled:

Tanker berths. No length restriction.

Cement jetty. Maximum LOA 100 m.

Arrival information

6.165

1 **Notice of ETA:** 24 hours.

Anchorage. Gastria Bay is reported to afford safe anchorage during NE winds, and in such conditions it is probably preferable to the anchorage off Boghaz (6.169).

Pilotage is not compulsory. Pilots are available from Famagusta.

Tugs are available from Famagusta.

Directions

6.166

1 From seaward to the oil berths and cement jetty the chart is sufficient guide.

Caution. Shoaling has been reported to have occurred in Gastria Bay.

Useful mark:

Castrouli (35°19′·4N 33°58′·8E), a small castle-shaped hill, 25 m high, covered with scrub, and surmounted by a small white cairn.

Berths

6.167

1 **Oil berths.** There are two offshore oil berths in Gastria Bay.

The W berth (35°19′·3N 33°59′·4E) comprises two mooring buoys laid at the seaward end of a submarine oil pipeline extending 410 m SSE from the shore about 5 cables E of Castrouli. The mooring buoys lie 160 m apart in a depth of about 9 m.

2 The E berth (35°19′·4N 33°59′·8E) comprises three mooring buoys laid at the seaward end of a submarine oil pipeline extending 400 m SSE from the shore about 8 cables E of Castrouli.

Cement jetty. A jetty (35°19′·1N 34°00′·2E) projects SW from the shore about 1¼ miles E of Castrouli. The jetty, which is reported to be 42 m long with a depth alongside of 6 m, is used by vessels of up to 100 m in length. Cement is loaded by conveyor belt. Two mooring buoys are laid 2 cables WSW of the jetty, close W of the end of an outfall extending 4 cables SSE from the shore.

Port services

6.168

1 **Repairs.** Minor repairs can be carried out.

Other facilities: hospital at Yeni Iskele; oily waste and garbage disposal.

Supplies. None available.

Communications. The nearest airport is Ercan Airport 50 km distant.

Anchorage

Boghaz

6.169

1 **Description.** Boghaz (35°19′N 33°57′E) is a small town standing at the end of a cultivated valley which extends 3 miles NE. A hotel fronts the town near the shore. Monarga, a small village, is situated 5 cables WNW. There is a gypsum factory 5½ cables NE of Boghaz.

2 **Anchorage.** The depths off Boghaz are irregular, the bottom being mainly of sand with rocky outcrops, though there is mud in places. Good anchorage may be obtained in depths of about 16 m with Castrouli cairn (6.166) bearing 032°, distant about 1¼ miles, as shown on the chart; protection from NE winds is reported to be good and ships are sent to anchor here when Famagusta Harbour is closed.

There are two mooring buoys close NE of the anchorage.

3 **Lighters.** A jetty at Boghaz has a short wooden extension at its NE end, with a depth of 1·8 m where lighters can load. A light is exhibited from the end of the jetty.

There is also a boat harbour, protected by moles to the S and NE, 1½ cables ENE of the gypsum factory.

CAPE ELŒA TO KLIDES ISLET

General information

Chart 796

Route

6.170

1 From a position about 5 miles SE of Cape Elœa (35°20′N 34°04′E) the route leads 31 miles NE, to a position 5 miles SE of Galounopetra Point (35°39′N 34°34′E), thence NNE for 8 miles to a position E of Klides Islet (35°42′N 34°36′E), and then NNW, for a further 7 miles, to a position about 5 miles N of Klides Islet.

Topography

6.171

1 From Cape Elœa to Koma tou Yialou, 7 miles NE, the coast is backed by low hills with the shore N of Palioura Point, 2 miles NNE of Cape Elœa, being fronted by sand dunes.

Between Koma tou Yialou and Melissakros Point, 16 miles NE, the coast is backed by low hills; cultivated fields can be seen in the valleys and on the tops of some of the flatter hills. The twin peaks of Mount Pamboulos (35°32′N 34°15′E) rise to elevations of 383 m and 357 m, the higher E summit being the most prominent in the area.

2 Between Melissakros Point (35°34′N 34°25′E) and Cape Andreas, 12 miles NE, there are numerous hills covered with scrub and small trees; those hills near the coast are steep-sided and rise to elevations of 30 to 143 m; those inland form part of the main ridge of Karpas Mountains (1.115) and rise to between 136 and 241 m. A few fields are visible between hills and on the tops of ridges.

Depths

6.172

1 Between Cape Elœa (35°20′N 34°04′E) and Cape Andreas the coast is steep-to with numerous submerged rocks close inshore, but with depths of 20 m and more at a distance of 4 to 5 cables offshore.

Currents

6.173

1 The strength and direction of the currents in the vicinity of Cape Andreas depend on the prevailing wind; close inshore the currents run along the coast.

Klides Islet should be rounded at a distance of at least 1 mile, as the current may attain a rate of 1½ kn and confused seas build up after strong winds; the strength and direction of the current may differ from one side of the islet to the other.

Directions

(continued from 6.162)

Other navigational aid

6.174

1 **Racon:**

Klides Islet Light (35°42′·5N 34°36′·3E).

Cape Elœa to Galounopetra Point

6.175

1 From a position about 5 miles SE of Cape Elœa (35°20′N 34°04′E) the track leads NE, passing (with positions from Cape Elœa):

- SE of Palioura Point (2 miles NNE); a stranded wreck lies 1½ cables N of the point. Thence:
- SE of a small fishing harbour backed by a hotel (6 miles NNE) situated near Koma tou Yialou (6.178). A marine farm lies about 1¾ miles E from the harbour. Thence:

2

- SE of Jila Islet (35°30′N 34°20′E), which lies 3 cables offshore with depths of 5 m and less extending 1½ cables S of it.

The track then continues NE, passing (with positions from Galounopetra Point (35°39′N 34°34′E)):

- SE of Melissakros Point (9 miles SW), thence:
- SE of Chelones Point (7½ miles SW), a small promontory, at the base of which is a white storehouse with a red roof; there is a jetty close SE of the storehouse. Thence:

3 SE of Chiomi Point (6¾ miles SW). Castle Rock, 2 miles N of Chiomi Point, is a prominent castellated outcrop of rock, 191 m high, near the top of the mountain ridge, with a somewhat similar summit, 241 m high, 2 miles SW. A tower stands close WSW of Castle Rock. Thence:

SE of Pachy Ammou Point (1½ miles WSW) which has prominent sand sweeps up the sides of the hills 5 cables W, and also between it and Galounopetra Point.

Thence to a position SE of Galounopetra, a rock 1·5 m high, lying 1½ cables S of Galounopetra Point.

Galounopetra Point to Klides Islet

6.176

1 From the position SE of Galounopetra Point (35°39′N 34°34′E) the track leads NNE, passing (with positions from Galounopetra Point):

ESE of Galounopetra Point, thence:

ESE of Cape Andreas (3½ miles NNE), the NE extremity of Cyprus, which has some ruins and tombs on it. The extremity of the cape is formed by a small but prominent table rock covered with grass, with an elevation of 35 m.

2 Thence to a position ESE of Klides Islet (4¼ miles NNE), lying 1 mile NE of Cape Andreas, with several rocks, above and below water, between them. A light (white metal tower, 10 m in height, racon) is exhibited from the NE end of the islet.

The track then leads NNW, passing (with positions from Klides Islet (35°42′N 34°36′E)):

ENE of Klides Islet, and:

WSW of off-lying banks with least depths of 73 m (8 miles NE) and 69 m (18 miles NE) (chart 2074) over them.

Thence to a position about 5 miles N of Klides Islet.

(Directions continue along the N coast of Cyprus, in reverse direction, at 6.218)

Anchorages and harbours

6.177

1 Anchorage is obtainable in depths of about 35 m, mud, about 5 cables offshore along the coast, between Melissakros Point and Cape Andreas, except off Galounopetra Point (6.175). The holding ground is good, but anchorage is recommended only during offshore winds or in good weather.

Koma tou Yialou

6.178

1 **Description.** Koma tou Yialou (35°26′N 34°08′E) is a small village containing two churches with belfries and a prominent long low school building with a red roof, all of which provide good landmarks.

Anchorage is obtainable with the breakwater bearing 320°, distant 6 cables, in a depth of 19 m, sand and weed, but is only suitable when winds are offshore or light.

NORTH COAST OF CYPRUS

GENERAL INFORMATION

Chart 2074

Area covered

6.179

1 The area covered by this section comprises:

Cape Arnauti to Cape Kormakiti (6.180).

Cape Kormakiti to Kyrenia (6.196).

Kyrenia to Davlos (6.208).

Davlos to Klides Islet (6.213).

CAPE ARNAUTI TO CAPE KORMAKITI

General information

Charts 775, 776

Route

6.180

1 From a position about 6 miles NW of Cape Arnauti (Akamas) (35°06′N 32°17′E) the route leads NE for about 40 miles to a position about 5 miles N of Cape Kormakiti (35°24′N 32°55′E).

Directions

Principal marks

6.181

1 **Landmarks:**

House, close S of Cape Arnauti (35°06′N 32°17′E).

Vouni Palace Hill (35°10′N 32°46′E), 2 miles SE of Cape Limniti, is conspicuous, 256 m high, and surmounted by the ruins of a Roman palace.

Sand scar (35°20′N 32°56′E) situated on the coast 4 miles S of Cape Kormakiti.

2 **Major lights:**

Cape Arnauti Light (6.11).

Cape Kormakiti Light (white metal framework tower, 22 m in height) (35°24′N 32°55′E), exhibited from the N extremity of the cape.

Cape Arnauti to Cape Kormakiti

6.182

1 From a position about 6 miles NW of Cape Arnauti (35°06′N 32°17′E) (6.12) the track leads NE, passing (with positions from Cape Arnauti):

NW of Mazaki Islet (4 cables N) (6.12), thence:

NW of Chrysochou Bay (5 miles E) (6.183), thence:

NW of Pomos Point (13¾ miles ENE), which is low and sandy, with several above-water rocks close N; shoal water extends 5 cables NW from the point. Thence:

NW of Stavromeni Point (17½ miles ENE), thence:

2 NW of Cape Kokkino (19½ miles ENE); between Pomos Point and Cape Kokkino the coast is rocky. Thence:

NW of Morphou Bay (27 miles ENE) (6.188), thence:

NW of Ormonde Bank (35¾ miles NE), with a depth of 19·8 m over it, lying 1¼ miles NW of Cape Kormakiti.

The track then leads to a position about 5 miles N of Cape Kormakiti (35¾ miles NE), the N extremity of a low point; Kormakiti Islet, 5·8 m high, lies close N. Shoal water and rocky ground extend 5 cables from the cape.

(Directions continue at 6.198)

Chrysochou Bay

Chart 775

General information

6.183

1 **Description.** Chrysochou Bay lies between Cape Arnauti (35°06′N 32°17′E) and Pomos Point, 14 miles ENE. Within the bay there are several anchorages of which the most important are off Lachi (6.186), and Mavroli (6.187).

2 **Topography.** Between Cape Arnauti and Lachi, 6½ miles SE, the shore is rocky and rugged. Between Lachi and a point 8½ miles NE there is a low sandy beach of which the last 2 miles are fringed by a ledge of submerged rocks; thence to Pomos Point, 3 miles farther NE, the shore is rugged and fronted by rocks above and below-water.

Directions

6.184

1 **Landmark:**

House, close S of Cape Arnauti (35°06′N 32°17′E).

Major light:

Cape Arnauti Light (6.11).

From north-west. From a position about 3 miles N of Cape Arnauti (35°06′N 32°17′E) (6.12) the track leads 7 miles SE to the head of the bay, passing (with positions from Cape Arnauti):

2 NE of a stranded wreck (5 cables SE), thence:

NE of Fontana Amorosa (1¼ miles SE), a small rocky bay and a good landing place for boats, thence:

NE of Kakoskaliou Islet (3 miles SE), lying 4 cables offshore. It has some rocks near it but affords no shelter.

3 **From north-north-east.** From a position about 3 miles NW of Pomos Point (35°10′N 32°33′E) (6.182) the track leads SSE to the head of the bay keeping well clear of any dangers; the chart is sufficient guide.

Useful mark:

Water tower (33 m in height), 2½ cables inland of the piers at Mavroli (35°03′N 32°27′E).

General anchorage

6.185

1 Vessels may obtain anchorage in summer between Kakoskaliou Islet (35°04′N 32°20′E) and Pomos Point, 12 miles NE, in moderate depths with good holding ground.

Lachi

6.186

1 **Position and function.** Lachi (Latsi) (35°02′N 32°24′E) is a small harbour on the NW coast of Cyprus, no longer in commercial use, now used by fishing and pleasure craft. The harbour is formed by two breakwaters and consists of two areas; the W basin is for the use of fishing vessels and E basin for pleasure craft. Between the heads of the breakwaters, from which lights are exhibited, lies the entrance, open E.

Anchorage. Vessels may obtain anchorage, as shown on the chart, 6 cables NNW of the head of the N breakwater, in depths of about 14 m, mud and rock, with good holding ground. The anchorage is exposed.

2 **Harbour and berths.** The W basin, with depths of 2·8 to 2·0 m, has a short jetty extending NNE on its S side, and quays in its N part on the inside of the N breakwater. A ramp is located in the SW corner. The E basin with depths of 3·2 m, has a 100 m quay on the S side of the main breakwater and two floating piers, 70 m long. Maximum size of vessel: 30 m LOA and 3·2 m draught can be accommodated.

3 **Facilities.** The nearest hospital is Paphos General Hospital, 40 km away.

Supplies: fuel; fresh water and provisions may be obtained.

Mavroli

6.187

1 **Description.** At Mavroli (35°03′N 32°27′E), 3 miles E of Lachi, there is a single pier 137 m in length, currently in disrepair. Formerly linked to a copper mine by a ropeway, the pier is closed to shipping, but repairs to the pier are in progress (2006).

Karavostasi, New Soli and approaches

Charts 775, 776, 849 plan of Karavostasi

General information

6.188

1 **Position.** Karavostasi (35°08′N 32°49′E) and New Soli (35°08′N 32°50′E) are situated at the head of Morphou Bay. The bay lies between Cape Kokkino (35°11′N 32°40′E) and Cape Kormakiti, 18 miles NE.

Function. Karavostasi, a port of entry, consists of a small group of houses near the shore, including a custom house with a flagstaff. The principal exports are carobs, olives, oranges and ore.

2 New Soli, 7 cables E of Karavostasi, is a village which has developed since the Cyprus Mines Corporation moved their pier and establishments here from Pendayia, 2 miles NE. The village contains a post office.

Topography. Between Cape Kokkino and Karavostasi and New Soli, on the S side of Morphou Bay, the shore is rocky. Between New Soli and a point 7 miles NE, the shore is low and of small stones; thence for 3 miles N it is sandy; for the last 6½ miles N to Cape Kormakiti the shore is rocky.

3 Lefka, 2 miles SSE of New Soli, is a village situated in a valley. Mount Troodos, 12½ miles S of New Soli, ancient Olympus, is 1951 m high and thickly covered with pine trees; near its summit are a military camp and an hotel (chart 2074).

Morphou (35°12′N 33°00′E) is the largest town in the district though it has no sea-borne trade. It stands on the S bank 4 miles from the mouth of River Serrachis, which becomes nearly lost by the time it reaches the coast 7 miles NE of New Soli.

4 **Port Authority.** Karavostasi Port Authority, c/o Port Headquarters, Famagusta (North Cyprus), Via Mersin 10 - Turkey.

Limiting conditions

6.189

1 **Density of water.** Approximately 1·025 g/cm^3.

Maximum size of vessel handled. Vessels with draughts up to 18 m can be accommodated.

Sea state. Gales from NW cause a heavy sea in the bay.

Arrival information

6.190

1 **Caution.** Lighter moorings, marked by small buoys, are laid 5 cables NNE of the village; do not anchor in this vicinity.

Anchorage. Good anchorage is obtainable in a depth of about 22 m, as shown on the chart, with the conspicuous chimney (6.191) bearing 145°, and Vouni Palace Hill (6.181) bearing 278°. At night, approach on the line of bearing, 140°, of Xeros Pier Light, and anchor when in a depth of about 22 m, at a distance of 7½ cables from the light. The holding ground is excellent, being of stiff mud and sand.

2 The shelter found at this anchorage from W winds is better than would be expected from the configuration of the land; even in NW gales it has been found that vessels can ride safely to their anchors. Owing to the hills to the S, the full force of the wind probably does not reach the S part of the bay and the backwash of the seas from the coast prevents a great strain coming on a vessel's cables. This does not apply in the E half of the bay, and it is for this reason that the Mines Corporation moved their pier from Pendayia to its present position at New Soli.

Pilotage is not compulsory; the company's pilot is available to assist in mooring.

Harbour

6.191

1 **General layout.** The harbour is an open roadstead with two jetties projecting from the shore NW of Karavostasi and E of New Soli.

Landmarks:

Vouni Palace Hill (6.181).

At New Soli (35°08′N 32°50′E) there are several large Corporation buildings, and a conspicuous chimney, standing close E and SE, respectively.

Sand scar (35°20′N 32°56′E) situated on the coast 4 miles S of Cape Kormakiti.

Directions for entering harbour

6.192

1 **From north-west.** From a position about 3 miles N of Cape Kokkino (35°12′N 32°40′E) the track leads 9 miles SE to the head of the bay, passing (with positions from Cape Kokkino):

NE of Cape Kokkino, thence:

NE of Petra tou Limniti (3½ miles ESE), a small islet lying close N of Cape Limniti; the cape is cliff-faced and fronted by boulders. Thence:

NE of Vouni Palace Hill (5½ miles ESE) (6.181); the coast hereabouts is cliff-faced and fronted by boulders.

2 **From north.** From a position about 5 miles NW of Cape Kormakiti (35°24′N 32°55′E) the track leads S for 17 miles, passing (with positions from Cape Kormakiti):

W of Ormonde Bank (1¼ miles NNW), thence:

W of Cape Kormakiti (6.182), thence:

W of a sand scar (4 miles S) on the coast.

The track then leads to the head of the bay clear of any dangers.

3 **Useful marks:**

Light exhibited from the head of Karavostasi ore jetty (35°09′N 32°49′E).

Light (grey metal tripod on building, 7 m in height) exhibited from close E of the root of Xeros Pier. (35°08′N 32°50′E).

Memorial (three inclined, tapering white columns) close W of the mouth of the River Lefkatis (35°08′·9N 32°50′·9E).

4 Mines Corporation hospital (35°09′N 32°52′E), a long, low, white building with a red roof, lying near the coast 2 miles NE of New Soli, with the remains of an old pier nearby. The building is hidden by trees from the anchorage.

Xeropotamos Monastery, 7 cables E of the hospital, a large building, now of little height, which can be seen through the trees.

A small watch tower standing on the coast on rising rocky ground, 7 miles NNW of Morphou.

Berths

6.193

1 **Karavostasi Ore Jetty:**

A jetty, 4 cables NW of the village, used for loading ore, extends 427 m NNE from the shore. Moorings for vessels using the jetty are laid off its head in a depth of about 18 m; ore is loaded by a conveyor belt at the rate of 1000 tons per hour. The conveyor was reported as derelict (2000).

2 **Xeros Pier**, close E of New Soli, is derelict. The wreck of a small tug lies on the foreshore close W of the root of the pier.

New Soli Oil Berth:

Consists of a pipeline extending 2¼ cables NNW from the coast close E of Xeros Pier, with mooring buoys at its seaward end.

Port services

6.194

1 **Facilities:** tank washing (slops) reception; garbage disposal.

Supplies: provisions available; fresh water can be supplied by the Mines Corporation lighter.

Anchorages

6.195

1 **Pyrgos Bay** (35°11′N 32°42′E), 1½ miles E of Cape Kokkino, is used by local craft as an anchorage, but at the first sign of a N gale they have to put to sea as the anchorage becomes dangerous.

Caution. One cylindrical and two spherical buoys are positioned close E of the bay.

2 **Loutros Bay** (35°11′N 32°45′E). Anchorage is obtainable in Loutros Bay in depths of 11 to 18 m, sand and weed; it is protected from W winds by Cape Limniti and an islet close N. The bay is used by local craft but they put to sea on the first indication of a N gale, when the anchorage becomes dangerous.

CAPE KORMAKITI TO KYRENIA

General information

Chart 776

Route

6.196

1 From a position about 5 miles N of Cape Kormakiti (35°24′N 32°55′E) the route leads ESE for 20 miles to a position about 5 miles N of Kyrenia (35°20′N 33°19′E).

Topography

6.197

1 From Cape Kormakiti the land rises to a small flat-topped hill 3 miles SE, from which steep and serrated ridges of hills and mountains run parallel to the N coast of the island, E to Cape Andreas (6.176).

Directions

(continued from 6.182)

Principal marks

6.198

1 **Landmarks:**

Mount Kornos (35°20′N 33°08′E), 946 m high, is well defined.

Cyprus Oil Industries factory (35°21′N 33°16′E), a large white building with a red roof, with a tall, square chimney.

Saint Hilarion Castle (35°19′N 33°17′E) with an elevation of 725 m.

2 Glykyotissa Church (Glykotissa) (small white building, rounded roof) (35°21′N 33°18′E), standing on the coast. A white house stands 1¼ cables WSW of the church.

Major lights:

Cape Kormakiti Light (35°24′N 32°55′E) (6.181).

Kyrenia Main Light (red and white framework tower on white building, 7 m in height) (35°20′N 33°20′E).

Cape Kormakiti to Kyrenia

6.199

1 From a position about 5 miles N of Cape Kormakiti (35°24′N 32°55′E) the track leads ESE, passing (with positions from Vavilas Point (35°22′N 33°07′E)):

NNE of Limanoudi Bay (7½ miles WNW), which is fringed with dangerous rocks, thence:

NNE of Georgios Bay (1½ miles W) in which there is an anchorage (6.207), thence:

2 NNE of Vavilas Point, (6.207) standing on the E side of Georgios Bay. The point projects 1 mile N from the general line of the coast; shoal water extends 5 cables NNW of the point. Vasilia, a village identifiable from seaward, is situated 1½ miles SSE of Vavilas Point. Thence:

NNE of two dangerous underwater rocks (8 cables E). Between Vavilas Point and Achirepietos Head, 4 miles E, the coast is almost entirely rocky, with below-water rocks close inshore, and depths of 11 m at 5 cables offshore. Thence:

3 NNE of Achirepietos Head (4 miles E) (6.207), which has an islet 3 m high 3½ cables ENE; shoal water extends from the coast to 1 cable N of the islet. A large white house, with a number of white buildings S of it, stands on the coast 6 cables SW of the point; a large monastery with a tower, and with a church close NE, stands on a low cliff 3 cables NE of this house. Lapithos and Karavas are villages situated 1½ miles SW and 1 mile S, respectively, of Achirepietos Head. Thence:

4 NNE of Trasha Island (7 miles ESE), 5 m high, lying close W of a point; the island is small and not discernible from a distance of more than 1 mile. The coast either side of Trasha Island, from Achirepietos Head to Kyrenia is rocky, with below-water rocks close inshore. Thence:

NNE of Snake Island (Yılan Adası) (8¾ miles ESE) lying 2 cables offshore; it is 14 m high, flat topped, and is steep-to.

The track then leads to a position about 5 miles N of Kyrenia (35°20′N 33°19′E).

5 **Useful marks:**

Two small houses, identifiable from seaward, standing 2½ cables SE of Cape Kormakiti (35°24′N 32°55′E).

The following villages, which are identifiable from seaward (positioned from Cape Kormakiti): Liveras (2 miles SE); Kormakiti (5¾ miles SE); Orga (6 miles ESE).

Monument (white inclined columns) on shore close S of Kalamoulia Island (35°21′N 33°14′E).

(Directions for the coastal route continue at 6.211)
(Directions for Kyrenia are given at 6.204)

Kyrenia

Chart 849 plan of Kyrenia

General information

6.200

1 **Position.** Kyrenia (35°20′N 33°19′E) is situated about midway along the N coast of Cyprus.

Function. It is the principal town and harbour on the N coast of Cyprus. Its main function is to service the tourist trade in the new harbour. The old harbour is now used only by pleasure craft and yachts.

2 **Topography.** Kyrenia, standing around its old harbour, is picturesquely situated with wooded slopes behind it rising abruptly to the mountain range, the summit of which is Trypa tou Vounou (936 m high), 3 miles S.

Traffic. Approximately 3100 vessels and 320 000 passengers annually.

Port Authority. Department of Ports, Ministry of Communications and Works, Famagusta, 10 Mersin, Turkey.

Limiting conditions

6.201

1 **Controlling depths:**

Old harbour. The least charted depth in the harbour entrance is 5 m, thence it shoals rapidly to 1 m, or less, in the inner harbour.

New harbour. The least charted depth in the harbour entrance is 6·8 m.

2 **Deepest and longest berth.** In the new harbour (6.205).

Tidal levels. Mean spring range about 0·4 m; mean neap range about 0·1 m. For details see *Admiralty Tide Tables Volume 2.*

Density of water. Approximately 1·025 g/cm^3.

Maximum size of vessel handled. Vessels up to 150 m length with a draught of 7·4 m.

Arrival information

6.202

1 **Outer anchorage.** The anchorage, as shown on the chart, lies 2½ cables NW of the head of the old harbour mole.

Two mooring buoys lie, respectively, 3 cables NNW and 3 cables NNE of the head of the old harbour mole, as shown on the chart.

2 **Pilotage** is available on request and is compulsory for vessels over 300 gt. For details see *Admiralty List of Radio Signals Volume 6 (3).*

Tugs. A tug is available.

Harbour

6.203

1 **General layout.** The port comprises an old harbour and a new harbour, the latter for the use of ferries and cruise ships.

Kyrenia old harbour (35°20′·5N 33°19′·3E) is an indentation of the coast protected from the N by a mole 2½ cables in length. On the S side of the harbour the ruins of an ancient mole extend from the shore near the NW corner of a fort, its outer end being marked by a beacon. The fort divides the harbour into an inner and outer part.

2 Kyrenia new harbour (35°20′·6N 33°20′·0E), situated 5 cables E of the old harbour, is an artificial harbour protected from the N by a breakwater extending from the shore for 400 m NE thence 600 m SE, and from the SE by

a breakwater 230 m in length. The entrance, between the heads of the breakwaters, is open SE.

Directions

6.204

1 **Landmarks:**

Chimney at Cyprus Oil Industries factory (35°21′N 33°16′E) (6.198) (chart 776).

Saint Hilarion Castle (35°19′N 33°17′E) (6.198) (chart 776).

Glykyotissa Church (35°21′N 33°18′E) (6.198) (chart 776), standing on the coast.

Greek Orthodox church (thin spire) (not charted) (35°20′·5N 33°19′·1E), standing on the W side of the old harbour.

2 Minaret (white) (not charted) (35°20′·5N 33°19′·2E), standing on the S side of the old harbour.

Fort (35°20′·5N 33°19′·3E), a massive Venetian building standing on the E side of the old harbour.

Abbey at Bellapais (ruins) (35°18′N 33°21′E) (chart 776); readily identifiable when the sun shines on it.

3 **Major light:**

Kyrenia Main Light (35°20′·4N 33°19′·8E) (6.198).

Approach and entry. From seaward to the harbours the chart is sufficient guide.

Useful marks:

Tower (tapering stone tower about 10 m in height) standing on the W knuckle of the old harbour mole (35°20′·6N 33°19′·2E).

4 Light (white metal framework tower, 8 m in height) exhibited from the head (35°20′·6N 33°19′·4E) of the old harbour mole.

Lights (white concrete towers, 8 m in height) exhibited from the heads of both breakwaters in the new harbour (35°20′·6N 33°20′·0E).

Berths

6.205

1 **Old harbour:**

Main jetty. There is a jetty near the custom house, on the W side of the harbour, used by vessels which anchor and secure astern.

Boat jetty. This jetty, in the SE corner of the harbour, has a depth of 1·2 m at its outer end. Landing steps at the jetty have a depth of less than 1·2 m alongside over a rocky bottom.

2 **New harbour.** Quays with a total length of 927 m provide eight berths with depths from 3 to 8 m alongside.

RoRo ramps are situated on each side of a jetty projecting from the NW quay.

Port services

6.206

1 **Repairs:** minor repairs carried out.

Other facilities. There is a hospital and post office in the town.

Supplies: fresh water; provisions; fuel available from road tankers.

Communications: ferry service to Taşucu (5.182); Ercan Airport, 37 km distant.

Anchorages and bays

Chart 776

6.207

1 **Georgios Bay** (35°22′N 33°05′E) affords anchorage, 6 cables offshore, in a depth of 22 m, mud; there is a prominent white house with a red roof on the SE coast of the bay.

Vavilas. The bay fronting the village of Vavilas, 4 cables SE of Vavilas Point (35°22′N 33°07′E), contains a small pier which in the past was used for shipping carobs.

2 **Achirepietos Head.** Anchorage may be obtained, as shown on the chart, off the W side of Achirepietos Head (35°21′N 33°12′E), 4 cables offshore, in a depth of 11 m, sand and mud.

KYRENIA TO DAVLOS

General information

Charts 776, 796

Route

6.208

1 From a position about 5 miles N of Kyrenia (35°20′N 33°19′E) the coastal route leads ENE for 27 miles to a position about 5 miles N of Davlos (35°25′N 33°54′E).

Topography

6.209

1 Between Kyrenia and Choti Island (35°21′N 33°33′E) the coast is generally rocky, with a few small sandy bays; small off-lying rocks are numerous, but there are depths of 11 m at 5 cables offshore.

Between Choti Island and Phourni Rock, 8 miles ENE, the coast is rocky, with below-water rocks lying close offshore. There are depths of 11 m at a distance of 4 cables from this stretch of coast.

2 Between Phourni Rock and Davlos, 10 miles ENE, the coast is mainly rocky with broken cliffs rising to an elevation of about 37 m in places. It is indented by numerous small coves having stony or sandy beaches some of which afford shelter and good landing for boats.

Tidal levels

6.210

1 At Davlos (35°25′N 33°54′E) the mean spring range is about 0·4 m; mean neap range about 0·1 m. For details see *Admiralty Tide Tables Volume 2.*

Directions

(continued from 6.199)

Principal marks

6.211

1 **Landmarks:**

Abbey at Bellapais (35°18′N 33°21′E) (6.203).

Buffavento Castle (35°17′N 33°25′E), 5½ miles SE of Kyrenia, stands on the summit of Buffavento, a mountain 955 m high.

2 Mount Pendadaktylos (35°17′N 33°28′E), 3 miles E of Buffavento Castle, a cluster of peaks of naked limestone like short fingers, rising to 741 m in height.

Zygo Vouno (35°19′N 33°38′E), a mountain 518 m high, standing 1 mile S of the village of Kaloyra.

Ágios Michalos Church (35°25′N 33°46′E).

3 Hotel (35°26′N 33°54′E); this is a small sandy-coloured building standing alone on the coast near Davlos.

Kantara (Kandara) Castle (35°24′N 33°55′E), 630 m high.

Major light

Kyrenia Main Light (35°20′N 33°20′E) (6.198).

Kyrenia to Davlos

6.212

1 From a position about 5 miles N of Kyrenia (35°20′N 33°19′E) the track leads ENE, passing (with positions from Stazousa Point (35°22′N 33°37′E)):

NNW of Choti Island (3 miles WSW), lying 2½ cables offshore. A large concrete warehouse stands on the coast 1 mile E of Choti Island. Thence:

NNW of Stazousa Point, which is steep-to. A rocky shoal, with a least depth of 1·5 m over it, lies close NW. Kaloyra, a village, lies 1¾ miles SE of the point. Thence:

2 NNW of Cyprium Bay Marina development (2¾ miles E), which is currently delayed (2008). Thence:

NNW of Phourni Rock (5 miles ENE), which lies 1 cable offshore and dries 0·3 m; a similar rock lies 1 mile SW. The sea breaks heavily on both these rocks except when calm.

3 NNW of Akanthou (7 miles ENE), a disused trading station with a ruined jetty. A storehouse and the church, which has one large and three small domes, are easily identifiable. Thence:

NNW of Ágios Therapon (11½ miles ENE), another disused trading station with a small jetty having a depth of 1·5 m at its head.

4 The track then leads to a position NNW of Davlos (35°25′N 33°54′E), which contains an easily identifiable church.

Useful marks:

Power station; chimney (red and white bands at top); tanks (35°20′N 33°28′E).

Radio mast (green light) standing on the summit of Sina Oros (35°23′N 33°53′E), 725 m high, 3¼ miles SE of Ágios Therapon.

(Directions continue at 6.216)

DAVLOS TO KLIDES ISLET

General information

Chart 796

Route

6.213

1 From a position about 5 miles N of Davlos (35°25′N 33°54′E) the coastal route leads NE for 40 miles to a position about 5 miles N of Klides Islet (35°42′N 34°36′E).

Topography

6.214

1 Between Davlos and Exarchos Bay, 31 miles ENE, the coast is mainly rocky, with broken cliffs rising to elevations of 37 and 46 m; there are numerous small coves with stony or sandy beaches, some of which are sheltered and afford good landing for boats.

2 Between Exarchos Bay and Cape Andreas, 5 miles ENE, the coast is generally rock bound and cliffy. Inland, the hills rise steeply at first, and then less steeply, to the summit ridge of Karpas Mountains (1.115).

Current

6.215

1 The current between Exarchos Bay (35°40′N 34°28′E) and Cape Andreas, 6 miles ENE, depends on the recent wind direction and strength.

Directions

(continued from 6.212)

Principal marks

6.216

1 **Landmarks:**

Ágios Photios (35°25′N 33°58′E), 496 m high.

Hotel, conspicuous (35°26′N 33°54′E) (6.211).

Lookout hut (35°28′N 34°02′E), standing at an elevation of 262 m.

Monastery (35°35′N 34°20′E), which looks like a white house and shows up against a heavily wooded background.

2 **Major light:**

Alici Burnu Light (white concrete tower, 3 m in height) (35°33′·7N 34°12′·6E).

Davlos to Cape Plakoti

6.217

1 From a position about 5 miles N of Davlos (35°25′N 33°54′E) the track leads NE, passing (with positions from Cape Plakoti (35°34′N 34°11′E)):

NW of Karavopetra (15 miles SW), a detached rock 1 m high, thence:

NW of Galounia Rocks (12½ miles SW) which are 5 m high; a landing suitable for boats exists 2 cables SSE of the rocks, near a disused trading station, being protected by Galounia Rocks and by a drying rock ledge lying parallel with the shore. Thence:

2 NW of Kalamoulia (10 miles SW), a rocky patch which dries 0·6 m. A rocky patch with a depth of 11·9 m over it lies midway between Galounia Rocks and Kalamoulia. Thence:

NW of a shoal (4¾ miles SW), with a depth of 9·1 m over it, lying 6 cables offshore.

3 The track then leads to a position NW of Cape Plakoti on the E side of which there is a jetty. The cape is a broad promontory projecting from the coast; a rocky patch with a depth of 13·4 m over it lies 1¼ miles WSW. Two churches situated in Yialousa, 1½ miles SE of Cape Plakoti, with white belfries, are easily identified.

Cape Plakoti to Klides Islet

6.218

1 From a position NW of Cape Plakoti (35°34′N 34°10′E) the track continues NE, passing (with positions from Lefko Island (35°39′N 34°25′E)):

NW of Yeni Erenkoy Fishing Harbour (not named) (11½ miles SW) and Alici Burnu Light (6.216). The monastery at Agía Trias, 1¼ miles S of the fishing harbour, has a belfry which shows up well when sunlit. Mount Pamboulos, 1 mile farther SE, is described at 6.171. Thence:

2 NW of Ágios Thyrsos (9¼ miles SW) (6.219), thence:

NW of a shoal (8 miles SW), with a depth of 6·7 m over it, thence:

NW of Ronnas Bay (4¾ miles SW) (6.220), thence:

NW of a rocky bluff (3½ miles SW), which shows up well from NE, thence:

NW of Ágios Philos (2½ miles SW) (6.221), a village on the coast, thence:

3 NW of Lefko Islet, which is the largest of several islets and rocky patches lying up to 5 cables from the coast between Ágios Philos and Exarchos Bay. A large rock, 1 mile E of Lefko Islet, 5 cables inland, resembles a small castle. Thence:

NW of Exarchos Bay (3 miles ENE) (6.222), thence:

NW of a bay (5 miles ENE) on the S side of which lies Mora Psaria (6.223) and on the E side Kordylia Nisha Islets (6.224), thence:

4 NW of Cape Andreas (8¾ miles ENE) (6.176), thence:

NW of Klides Islet (9¼ miles ENE) (6.176), to a position about 5 miles N of the islet.

Useful mark:

A large square rock (35°34′N 34°20′E) at an elevation of 219 m, which shows up well from seaward when sunlit.

(Directions for the E coast of Cyprus are given in reverse order at 6.176)

Anchorages and harbours

Ágios Thyrsos

6.219

1 Ágios Thyrsos (35°34′N 34°15′E), a village on the coast, consists of a group of white houses clustered round a small church with a spire. Anchorage may be obtained 3½ cables N of the church, in a depth of 18 m, sand and shell.

Ronnas Bay

6.220

1 Ronnas Bay (35°37′N 34°20′E) is entered 7½ miles ENE of Cape Plakoti; the W end of the bay is defined by a low rocky cape which provides some shelter from W winds. Landing is possible in the SW corner of the bay. A rocky ledge extends along the shore, and a rocky spit extends 2½ cables W from the N point of the bay, terminating in a depth of 5·5 m.

Ágios Philos

6.221

1 Ágios Philos (35°38′N 34°22′E) has a good boat landing well sheltered from E winds; winds from N, through W to SW raise a considerable surf and make landing dangerous. A shoal with a depth of 10·1 m over it lies 2 cables N. Anchorage is obtainable 5 cables WNW of Ágios Philos, in a depth of 29 m, sand and weed.

Exarchos Bay

6.222

1 **Description.** Exarchos Bay (35°40′N 34°28′E) is entered E of a low point which is not easy to identify; the cliffs which form the S shore of the bay, rising steeply to an elevation of 76 m, are easily discernible from seaward.

Anchorage may be obtained in the central part of Exarchos Bay in depths of 27 m, sand and shell bottom.

Mora Psaria

6.223

1 Mora Psaria (35°40′N 34°31′E), 1 mile E of Exarchos Bay, is sheltered from all winds except those between E, through N and NW, and provides a good boat landing place.

There is an anchorage 5 cables NE of Mora Psaria, where the depth is about 31 m.

Kordylia Nisha Islets

6.224

1 Kordylia Nisha Islets (35°41′N 34°32′E), 2¼ miles ENE of Exarchos Bay, give protection to a cove on the mainland which provides a good landing place except during N winds.

Chapter 7 - Ra's al Basīţ to Tel Rafah

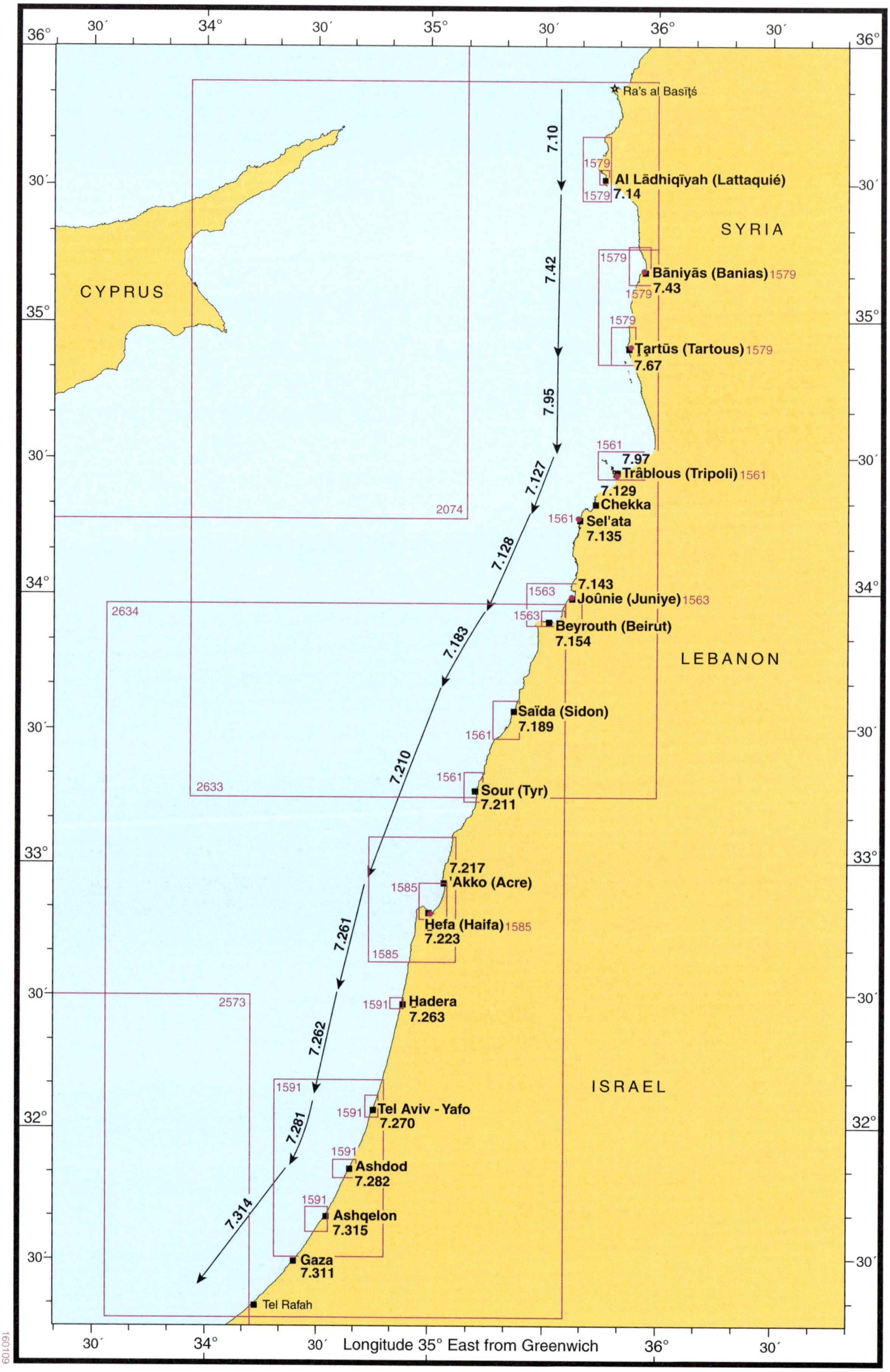

CHAPTER 7

COASTS OF SYRIA, LEBANON AND ISRAEL — ANTAKYA KÖRFEZİ TO TEL RAFAH

GENERAL INFORMATION

Chart 183

Scope of the chapter

7.1

1 This chapter describes the coastal waters of Syria, Lebanon and Israel from Ra's al Basīţ (Rās el-Bassîte) (35°51′N 35°48′E), on the S side of Antakya Körfezi, to Tel Rafah (31°19′N 34°13′E). The description includes the principal ports of Al Lādhiqīyah (Lattaquié) (7.14), Bāniyās (Banias) Oil Terminal (7.43), Ţarţūs (Tartous) (7.67), Trâblous (Tripoli) (7.97), Beyrouth (Beirut) (7.154), Zahrānī (Sidon) Oil Terminal (7.196), H̱efa (Haifa) (7.223), H̱adera (7.263), Ashdod (7.282) and Ashqelon Oil Terminal (7.315).

2 It is divided into the following sections:

Ra's al Basīţ to Trâblous (7.5).
Trâblous to H̱efa (7.122).
H̱efa to Tel Rafah (7.253).

Off-lying shoals

7.2

1 The extensive narrow ledges of rock which front the coast, and lie roughly parallel to its general direction, are a feature of the coasts of Lebanon and Israel. These ledges, which in places rise abruptly, appear to be of limestone formation, over which the depth varies from 5 to 18 m. In greater depths it is difficult to trace their extent, but it is possible that they are more or less continuous, though seldom sufficiently raised to afford any protection from the swell.

Rescue

7.3

1 For information on rescue see 1.70, 1.71, 1.72 and *Admiralty List of Radio Signals Volume 5*.

Currents

7.4

1 The main E-going current along the N coast of Africa turns N on the coast of Israel, maintaining a mean rate of ¼ to ½ kn. There is a fairly low degree of variability but onshore sets are common in summer.

2 The main stream flows near the coast as far as Tel Aviv-Yafo (32°03′N 34°45′E), but then runs temporarily NNW, a branch recurving in a clockwise direction so that the coasts of N Israel, and almost all of Lebanon, experience predominantly S or SE-going currents; the rate however is generally less than ¼ kn.

3 From Trâblous (34°26′N 35°51′E) to İskenderun Körfezi, 120 miles N, the N-going currents with a mean rate of ½ kn are again established.

RA'S AL BASĪŢ TO TRÂBLOUS

GENERAL INFORMATION

Chart 2633

Area covered

7.5

1 The area covered by this section comprises:

Ra's al Basīţ to Al Lādhiqīyah (7.8).
Al Lādhiqīyah (7.14).
Al Lādhiqīyah to Ţarţūs (7.38).
Ţarţūs Oil Terminal (7.53).
Ţarţūs (7.67).
Ţarţūs to Trâblous (7.91).
Trâblous (7.97).

Prohibited areas

7.6

1 Areas extending as much as 12 miles from the Syrian coast may be prohibited for navigation. Vessels bound for Syrian ports or navigating off the coast are advised to obtain the latest information from their agents. For further information see 1.49.

For requirements for vessels entering Lebanese territorial waters see 7.93.

Approach routes

7.7

1 Vessels bound for ports in Syria must use the Approach Routes, as shown on the charts, and call Syria Coast Radio Station when 50 miles off the Syrian coast. For other regulations see 1.49 and *Admiralty List of Radio Signals Volume 6 (3).*

RA'S AL BASĪŢ TO AL LĀDHIQĪYAH

General information

Chart 2633

Route

7.8

1 From a position W of Ra's al Basīţ (35°51′N 35°48′E) the coastal route leads S, for a distance of about 20 miles, to a position W of Al Lādhiqīyah (35°31′N 35°46′E).

Topography

7.9

1 Between Ra's al Basīţ (5.322) and Ra's Ibn Hāni (Rās Ibn Hâni), 17 miles S, the coast consists mostly of bold cliffs with a few sandy beaches, and is steep-to.

Directions

(continued from 5.323)

7.10

1 From a position W of Ra's al Basīţ (35°51′N 35°48′E) the track leads S, passing (with positions from Ra's al Basīţ):

W of a remarkable point (1 mile S), with a ruined watchtower on its summit, thence:
W of Sabagli (3 miles S), an open roadstead, thence:
W of Ra's al Fasurī (Rās el Fasori) (11 miles S), a conspicuous promontory from where Ra's al Fasurī

Light (white tower, black bands) is exhibited. Fasurī Islet lies close offshore in the bay on the N side of the point; a rocky shoal, with a depth of 5·5 m over it, lies 6 cables N of the islet. Thence:

2 W of Ra's Ibn Hāni (Rās Ibn Hâni) (17 miles S), the NW point of a low peninsula from where Ra's Ibn Hāni Light (white tower) is exhibited. From a distance S, the cape appears as a chain of rocky islets, with the light-structure well to seaward. Thence:

3 W of a shallow bay (18 miles S), almost entirely obstructed by a rocky reef, which is entered between a point 5 cables SSE of Rās Ibn Hāni and Ra's al Kunaydah (Rās el Kneda), 1 mile further SSE.

Caution. Stranded wrecks lie 2 cables N and 2½ cables W of Ra's al Kunaydah.

The track then leads to a position in the Approach Route W of Al Lādhiqīyah (35°31′N 35°46′E).

(Directions for the coastal route continue at 7.40)
(Directions for Al Lādhiqīyah are given at 7.28)

Minor harbours

Borj Islam Terminal

7.11

1 **Position.** Borj Islam Terminal (35°41′N 35°48′E) is situated on the NW coast of Syria, 10 miles N of Al Lādhiqīyah.

Function. The terminal handles LPG tankers up to 5000 tons.

Pilots. The pilot should be requested from Al Lādhiqīyah. The boarding point is off Ra's al Fasurī. A mooring launch is available.

2 **Directions.** Approach should be made by day as there are no night aids to navigation. A cement factory with a prominent chimney stands near the terminal and is a good mark. Vessels arriving at night should anchor off Al Lādhiqīyah (7.14).

Berth. Vessels berth close offshore with two anchors laid out ahead and with stern lines to the shore. The depth is 11 m at a distance of 40 m from the shore. There is a mooring buoy for transverse lines close W of the berth. The berth is exposed, particularly to W winds.

Chart 1579 plan of approaches to Al Lādhiqīyah

Mīnat al Bayḑā'

7.12

1 Mīnat al Bayḑā (Mīnat el-Beida on chart 2633) (35°37′N 35°46′E) is situated on the SW side of a small bay, with least depths of 7·3 m in the entrance decreasing gradually to the shore.

A breakwater extends about 460 m NNE from a position close inside the SW entrance point of the bay. Two quays provide about 475 m of berthing space, with depths of less than 5·5 m alongside. A basin, lined with concrete quays, lies on the S side of the bay.

A naval base lies close S of the root of the breakwater.

Anchorage

Mīnat al Quabbān

7.13

1 Mīnat al Quabbān (35°36′N 35°45′E) is the W of two sandy bays, encumbered with rocks and separated by a rocky point, on which stands a monument.

Anchorage may be obtained, as indicated on the plan, 4 cables NNW of the monument, in a depth of 14·6 m, sand. The anchorage is well-sheltered from strong SW summer breezes and landing is possible.

AL LĀDHIQĪYAH

General information

Chart 1579 plans of Approaches to Al Lādhiqīyah and Al Lādhiqīyah

Position

7.14

1 Al Lādhiqīyah (Lattaquié) (35°31′N 35°46′E), also known as Latakia or Lattakia, is situated on Ra's Ziyārah (Rās Ziaret), a promontory. From a distance of about 10 miles it appears as a flat island.

Function

7.15

1 Al Lādhiqīyah, the principal port of Syria, is a large commercial harbour with modern facilities to handle most types of vessel including container, RoRo, general cargo, bulk carriers and tankers.

Principal exports include bitumen, asphalt, cereals, cotton, fruits, eggs, vegetable oil, pottery and the famous Latakia tobacco which has been cultivated since the seventeenth century. Imports include manufactured goods, chemical products, vehicles, machinery, foodstuffs, and timber.

There is a population of about 345 000.

Approach and entry

7.16

1 Syrian regulations require ships to approach Al Lādhiqīyah through the designated Approach Route, the limits of which are shown on the chart, which leads E from a position about 12 miles W of the harbour entrance.

The harbour is entered by passing close N of the main breakwater on the alignment of leading lights.

Traffic

7.17

1 In 2007 the port had 1420 ship calls with a total of 16 363 107 dwt.

Port Authority

7.18

1 Latakia Port General Company, PO Box 220, Latakia, Syria.

Limiting conditions

Deepest and longest berth

7.19

1 General cargo quays (7.31).

Density of water

7.20

1 1·030 g/cm^3.

Maximum size of vessel handled

7.21

1 123 436 dwt, 261 m LOA; and *New Port* 240 m LOA, 13·3 m draught.

Local weather

7.22

1 From November to March heavy storms, sometimes lasting for two or three days and accompanied by heavy rains, may occur. The port may then be inaccessible, and cargo working in the anchorage will be halted.

Arrival information

Outer anchorage

7.23

1 The waiting anchorage area, the limits of which are shown on the chart, is centred about 8 cables SSW of the breakwater, with depths of about 18·5 m, sand and mud with good holding ground, but exposed in strong winds.

Prohibited anchorage

7.24

1 Navigation without a pilot, and anchoring, are prohibited E of a line extending NNW from the head of the breakwater.

Pilotage and tugs

7.25

1 **Pilotage** is compulsory for vessels over 1000 tons and available 0600 to 2200. Pilots board 1½ miles WSW of the breakwater head. Direct communication with the pilots can be made by VHF.

For details see *Admiralty List of Radio Signals Volume 6 (3).*

Tugs are available and compulsory.

Harbour

General layout

7.26

1 The artificial harbour, protected by a breakwater which extends NW for 1¾ cables from Ra's Ziyārah and then curves NNE for 5 cables and NNW for 9 cables, contains outer and inner harbours.

The main cargo area lies on the E side and the inner harbour consists of a basin in the SE part.

2 **Development.** A major development is currently in progress (2007), including extension of the main breakwater and deepening the entrance channel to 16 m. New quays for containers, general cargo and RoRo are being constructed close N of the existing berths.

Climate information

7.27

1 See 1.184 and 1.202.

Directions

(continued from 7.10)

Principal marks

7.28

1 **Landmarks** (positioned from Roman Catholic cathedral (35°30′·8N 35°46′·5E)):

Roman Catholic cathedral, with two prominent belfries, standing on the high slopes of the city.

Water tower (4¼ cables SW).

Silo (yellow and blue, 65 m in height) (6½ cables SW). The silo is visible from a long way off.

Tank (pumping station) (7 cables SW).

Tank farm (1¼ miles N), with a tower on the S and SE sides.

Approach

7.29

1 From the vicinity of 35°31′N 35°31′E at the beginning of the approach route to Al Lādhiqīyah, the track leads E, passing (with positions from the head of the main breakwater (35°32′N 35°45′E)):

N of a dangerous wreck (1¾ miles WSW), the position of which is approximate.

The track then leads to the pilot boarding position (1½ miles WSW).

2 **Useful marks:**

Stranded wreck lying about 1 cable SW of Ra's Ziyārah (35°29′·8N 35°46′·8E). Reported in 1983 to be conspicuous on radar.

El Burj Light (white tower 5 m in height) (35°30′·8N 35°46′·1E), 3 cables W of the Roman Catholic cathedral.

Entry

7.30

1 From the pilot boarding position the track leads initially NE, passing SE of a wreck with a depth of 12·8 m over it, to a position about 3½ cables NW of the head of the main breakwater (35°32′N 35°45′E).

Leading lights:

Front light (35°31′·8N 35°46′·1E).

Rear light (2¾ cables ESE of front light).

2 The alignment (115½°) of these lights then leads ESE, passing (with positions from the head of the main breakwater):

NNE of the head of the main breakwater, from which a light (green pylon) is exhibited, and:

SSW of a shoal (2¼ cables NNE), with a depth of 7·2 m over it. It is marked by a light buoy (port hand).

Once clear of the shoal leave the leading line and head SSE into the harbour.

Berths

Outer harbour

7.31

1 Positioned from Roman Catholic cathedral (35°30′·8N 35°46′·5E):

Silo Quay (7 cables SW), at the SW end of Main Quay, is 183 m long, with a depth of 7·5 m alongside; it is connected by an overhead transporter to the grain silo, situated close SE.

Main Quay (6 cables WSW) extends NNE for 4½ cables from the root of the breakwater, and provides 580 m of berths, with a depth alongside of 8·7 m.

2 **Passenger Quay** (4 cables W), the N face of Main Quay, is 180 m long, with a depth alongside of about 7·6 m.

General cargo quays (5 cables NW). These quays provide a total berthing length of about 4000 m; depths vary from 9·8 to 12·6 m alongside. Container and RoRo facilities are available.

3 One of the berths, 6½ cables NNW of the Roman Catholic cathedral, is obstructed by a stranded wreck.

Oil terminal (1¼ miles N). A tank farm, 8 cables E of the breakwater head, is connected by a submarine pipeline to a terminal consisting of three mooring buoys. Vessels up to 183 m long and 10·7 m draught can be accommodated.

Inner Harbour

7.32

1 Inner Harbour is entered between two quays, the width of the entrance being about 79 m. There are charted depths of 1·8 to 6·8 m in the harbour.

North, South and East Quays form their respective sides of Inner Harbour, and provide 855 m of berths, with depths alongside from 0·9 to 7·0 m.

2 South Basin, in which there is a disused slipway, is situated in the SW corner of Inner Harbour.

Vessels of up to 91 m in length, and drawing up to 5·2 m may safely enter Inner Harbour. Small sailing and fishing vessels secure either in South Basin or at North Quay.

Port services

Repairs

7.33

1 Engine and hull repairs undertaken.

Other facilities

7.34

1 Hospitals in the town; garbage disposal; oily waste reception using road tankers.

Supplies

7.35

1 Fuel of all kinds; fresh water of poor quality and scarce in summer, at the quays or by water barge.

Communications

7.36

1 Al Lādhiqīyah Airport, 20 km distant; Damascus International Airport, 340 km distant.

Minor harbour

7.37

1 **General information.** A fishing and yacht harbour is situated 6 cables NE of the main breakwater head. The harbour is protected by two moles, with its entrance open NW; lights are exhibited from the heads of the moles.

Caution. Two stranded wrecks lie 1½ cables W of the entrance.

AL LĀDHIQĪYAH TO ṬARṬŪS

General information

Chart 2633

Route

7.38

1 From a position W of Al Lādhiqīyah (35°31′N 35°46′E) the coastal route leads S, for a distance of 36 miles, to a position W of Ṭarṭūs.

Topography

7.39

1 The coast SE from Ra's Ziyārah (Rās Ziaret) (35°30′N 35°47′E) consists of rocky cliffs, with a sandy beach, for 1 mile, and thence, for 8 miles, of a continuous sandy beach. Although the depth off this part of the coast is moderate, anchorage is not recommended here, as it is open to S and SW winds.

From a point 8 miles SE of Ra's Ziyārah, for 9 miles S, as far as Ra's Baldat al Malik (Rās Beldet el Melik on chart 2633), the coast is bordered by a line of low cliffs, within which is an extensive and partly cultivated plain, gradually rising E towards a high range of hills which runs parallel to the coast.

2 Between Ra's Baldat al Malik (35°16′N 35°55′E) and Bāniyās, 4½ miles S, the coast is formed by a beach. Thence between Bāniyās and Ra's al Marj, 1½ miles SW, the coast is fringed with reefs, but there are no off-lying dangers.

The coast between Ra's al Burj (35°09′N 35°55′E) and Ṭarṭūs, 16 miles S, consists mostly of shingle beaches with off-lying rocks and shoal patches; vessels should not approach within 2 miles.

Directions

(continued from 7.10)

Principal marks

7.40

1 **Landmarks:**

Tell Soukas (35°18′N 35°55′E), a conical hill 40 m high.

Marqab Castle (35°09′·1N 35°57′·0E), 2 miles S of Bāniyās, a fortress surmounting a volcanic hill over 300 m high; a conspicuous dome is situated 8 cables NNE of the castle.

Tower (35°09′·2N 35°55′·7E).

2 **Major light:**

Ra's al Burj Light (white concrete tower, 11 m in height) (35°09′N 35°55′E), exhibited from the summit of Ḥarf aş Şalīb, 5 cables SSW of Ra's al Burj.

Other navigational aids

7.41

1 **Racons:**

'Arab al Mulk Light Buoy (35°16′·2N 35°54′·4E).

Marqab Light Buoy (35°12′·5N 35°54′·8E), moored 2 miles NW of Bāniyās.

For details see *Admiralty List of Radio Signals Volume 2.*

Al Lādhiqīyah to Ṭarṭūs

7.42

1 From a position in the Approach Route, W of Al Lādhiqīyah, the track leads S, passing (with positions from Ra's Ziyārah (Rās Ziaret on chart 2633) (35°30′N 35°49′E)):

W of Nahr el Kébîr (2 miles E), the largest river on the coasts of Syria, Lebanon and Israel, which enters the sea 1½ miles E of Ra's Ziyārah, thence:

W of Tartarus Şati (Tartarus Bank) (3½ miles SSW), a rocky bank with a least depth of 25 m over it, which is steep-to; there is a confused sea in its locality during SW gales. This bank, and other ledges on the coast, are frequented by sponge divers from the Aegean islands. Thence:

2 W of Tell Soukas (13 miles SSE) (7.40), thence:

W of two groups of rocks (14¾ miles SSE), awash, lying 7 and 12 cables NNW of Ra's Baldat al Malik, on a shore bank with depths of less than 5 m over them. 'Arab al Mulk Light Buoy (isolated danger) is moored close W of this bank. Thence:

W of Ra's Baldat al Malik (Rās Beldet el Melik) (16 miles SSE), a headland on the S side of the entrance to Nahr Sinn; Hurayşūn (Hareissoun), a village close within the point, contains some ruins. Thence:

3 W of Ra's al Marj (Rās el Marj) (21 miles SSE), on which stands a power station with two conspicuous chimneys (red and white bands, red lights). There is a small harbour on the S side of the point. The coastal waters S of Ra's al Marj have only been partially surveyed, and the coast should be approached with caution. Thence:

4 W of Ra's al Burj (Rās el Burj) (22 miles SSE), the extremity of the W spur of the hill surmounted by Marqab Castle. A remarkable fresh water spring exists in a depth of 33 m, a short distance offshore

with the middle of Marqab Castle in line with the black tower; fresh water rises to the surface with considerable force, giving the appearance of breakers, and the surface water is brackish. Thence:

5 W of Ra's al Ḩasan (Rās el Hassan) (31 miles SSE), which is rocky; Jazīrat an Naml (Ipsiri Islet), low and rocky, lies 7½ cables SW.

The track then leads to a position in the Approach Route, W of Ţarţūs (34°54′N 35°53′E).

(Directions for the coastal route continue at 7.94)
(Directions for Ţarţūs Oil Terminal are given at 7.64 and for Ţarţūs at 7.82)

Bāniyās Oil Terminal

Chart 1579, plans of Approaches to Bāniyās and Ţarţūs, and Bāniyās

General information

7.43

1 **Position.** Bāniyās, also known as Banias, Oil Terminal (35°14′N 35°57′E) is situated on the coast 3½ miles N of Bāniyās.

Function. The terminal is an outlet for crude oil transported by overland pipeline from Kirkuk, Iraq, and also handles other petroleum products. The pipeline is approximately 800 kms long and has a capacity of 300 000 barrels per day.

2 The Kirkuk-Banias pipeline was damaged in the Iraq war of 2003, but plans are in hand (2007) for its reconstruction.

Approach. Syrian regulations require ships to approach the oil terminal through the designated Approach Route, the limits of which are shown on the chart, which leads E from a position about 12 miles W of the offshore berths.

3 **Traffic.** In 2007 there were 335 ship calls with a total of 13 052 363 dwt.

Port Authority. Syrian Company for Oil Transport, PO Box 13, Banias (Tartous), Syria.

Limiting conditions

7.44

1 **Density of water:** 1·030 g/cm^3.

Maximum size of vessel handled. Tankers up to 130 000 dwt can be accommodated.

Arrival information

7.45

1 **Notice of ETA:** 72, 48, 24, 12 and 4 hours.

Anchorage. Vessels awaiting a berth may obtain anchorage, as shown on the chart, in depths from 14 to 18 m, S or SSW of No 6 Berth; the bottom is rock, coral and sand. Detached shoals with least depths of 10·3 and 2·1 m over them lie, respectively, 5 cables and 1 mile SE of No 6 Berth. Depths to seaward of the oil berths are too great for safe anchorage.

2 **Pilotage** is compulsory with berthing during daylight hours only. Pilot boards, as shown on the chart, in position 35°13′·5N 35°53′·8E, 1½ miles NNW of Marqab Light Buoy, and remains on board during cargo operations.

For details see *Admiralty List of Radio Signals* Volume 6 (3).

Tugs. There are no tugs, but small mooring boats are available to assist in berthing and unberthing.

Harbour

7.46

1 The terminal, in an open roadstead, consists of six submarine oil pipelines extending from the coast between the S entrance point of Mīnat Hurayşūn and the mouth of Nahr Hurayşūn (1¾ miles SSE). The pipelines are connected to a tank farm standing close inland between Nahr Hurayşūn and Nahr Jawbar, 9 cables SSE.

Directions

7.47

1 From seaward the track leads E through the Approach Route to the oil terminal; the chart is sufficient guide.

Berths

7.48

1 Six oil berths, numbered 2 to 7 from N, lie at the respective ends of submarine pipelines. Each berth consists of four or five mooring buoys to which vessels secure heading SW with both bower anchors down; the holding ground is reported to be good.

2 The maximum size of vessel permitted at each berth is as follows:

Berth No	*Length (m)*	*Draught (m)*
2	282 (loading) 274 (discharging)	15·8 (summer) 15·2 (winter)
3	282 (loading) 274 (discharging)	16·1 (summer) 15·5 (winter)
4	228	12·8
5	256 (summer) 248 (winter)	13·1 (summer) 12·5 (winter)
6	213 (summer) 198 (winter)	10·3 (summer) 9·7 (winter)
7	213	7·3 (LPG) 8·5 (Jet Fuel, summer) 7·9 (Jet Fuel, winter)

3 There is a boat harbour (35°13′·4N 35°56′·8E) at the S end of the terminal. It is protected by two moles; a light (black pylon) is exhibited from the head of each mole. The entrance, open N, is 61 m wide. Within the harbour a quay extends 100 m N from the inner part of the S mole. A radio tower (red and white bands) stands nearly 1 cable ESE of the root of the S mole.

Port services

7.49

1 **Supplies:** diesel in drums; fresh water by barge; provisions.

Communications. Al Lādhiqīyah Airport, 35 km distant. The nearest international airports are Damascus International Airport, 300 km distant, and Beyrouth (Lebanon), 181 km distant.

Anchorages and harbours

Chart 2633

Jeble

7.50

1 **Position.** Jeble (35°22′N 35°55′E) is a town lying close to the coast, built from the ruins of the ancient city and surrounded by gardens.

Landmark:

Sultan Ibrahim Mosque (35°22′N 35°55′E), on the N outskirts of the town, with three domes and a minaret, is prominent.

Anchorage. Anchorage may be obtained 3 cables offshore by small vessels, but it is open to W and SW winds. Local knowledge is necessary.

2 **Harbour.** Jeble contains a small circular harbour, which can accommodate a few small vessels in fair weather. The harbour must be approached from NW because of off-lying rocks. The entrance, with a depth of about 7·3 m, is narrow, and marked on each side by a light (black pylon).

Berths. There are two quays within the harbour. Depths inside the harbour vary from 5·2 to 6·1 m.

Chart 1579, plan of Bāniyās

7.51

Mīnat Hurayşūn

1 Mīnat Hurayşūn (Hareissoun Bay), a small bay, is situated close N of Bāniyās Oil Terminal (35°13′N 35°57′E) (7.43). It is entered between the S extremity of Ra's Baldat al Malik and a foul rocky point 5 cables SSE. An islet, 2 m high and surrounded by a reef, lies close SW of the S entrance point.

Chart 1579, plan of Bāniyās

Bāniyās

7.52

1 **Position.** Bāniyās (35°11′·1N 35°56′·5E), lies between the mouths of Nahr Ja'm and Nahr Bāniyās.

Function. A port of call for small coasting vessels.

Anchorage. There is an anchorage, as shown on the chart, 1½ miles NW of the harbour, close to Marqab Light Buoy.

Harbour. A small artificial harbour fronts the town.

2 **Directions.** Bāniyās is approached from seaward through the Approach Route, shown on the chart. Thence from the pilot station (35°13′·5N 35°53′·8E) the track leads SE, passing (with positions from Bāniyās Harbour):

SW of Bāniyās Oil Terminal (2½ miles N), thence:

NE of Marqab Light Buoy (2 miles NW), thence:

NE of two mooring buoys (1¼ miles WNW).

3 The track then continues SE to the harbour entrance. In the approach to Bāniyās depths are very irregular, with several rocky shoals, and the coast in the vicinity should be given a berth of at least 1 mile.

Landmarks:

Marqab Castle (35°09′·1N 35°57′E) (7.40), 2 miles S of Bāniyās.

Minaret (35°10′·9N 35°56′·7E) on the NW side of the town.

4 **Other navigational aid:**

Racon: Marqab Light Buoy (35°12′·5N 35°54′·8E).

ŢARŢŪS OIL TERMINAL

General information

Chart 1579, plans of Ţarţūs and approaches

Position

7.53

1 Ţarţūs, also known as Tartous, Oil Terminal (34°58′N 35°53′E), fronts an oil refinery, about 4 miles N of Ţarţūs.

Function

7.54

1 The terminal exports crude oil.

Approach

7.55

1 Syrian regulations require ships to approach the oil terminal through the designated Approach Route, the limits of which are shown on the chart, which leads E from a position about 12 miles W of the harbour of Ţarţūs.

Port Authority

7.56

1 Ţarţūs Port Authority, BP 86, Ţarţūs, Syria. Operating company: Syrian Crude Oil Transportation Company, PO Box 52, Ţarţūs, Syria.

Limiting conditions

Maximum size of vessel handled

7.57

1 Tankers up to 100 000 dwt, maximum length 280 m and 20·5 m draught.

Arrival information

Port operations

7.58

1 The terminal should be contacted at least two hours before arrival at the anchorage for berthing instructions.

For details see *Admiralty List of Radio Signals Volume 6 (3).*

Notice of ETA

7.59

1 72 and 24 hours.

Prohibited anchorage

7.60

1 Anchoring is prohibited in the approaches to the berths, from 3½ miles SW of the terminal, as shown on the chart.

Pilotage

7.61

1 Pilotage is compulsory and available during daylight hours only. Pilot boards about 1½ miles W of the entrance (34°54′·6N 35°51′·2E) to the cargo harbour and remains on board throughout the operation.

For details see *Admiralty List of Radio Signals Volume 6 (3).*

Tugs

7.62

1 Tugs are compulsory for mooring/unmooring.

Regulations

7.63

1 Berthing is carried out in daylight only.

Directions for entering harbour

7.64

1 From the vicinity of 34°55′N 35°38′E at the beginning of the approach route to Ţarţūs, the track leads E to a position about 4 miles SW of the oil terminal. Thence approach to the berths, about 3 miles NE, should be made keeping clear of two dangerous wrecks, shown on the chart, 3 miles SW and 1 mile SW of the oil terminal respectively.

2 **Useful marks** (positioned from Ra's al Ḩasan (34°59′·1N 35°52′·7E)):

Refinery chimneys (red lights) (1¼ miles SE).

A conspicuous stranded wreck (3¼ miles S).

Lights (7.84) exhibited from the head of Ţarţūs breakwaters.

Light (7.96) exhibited from Jazīrat Arwād (Île de Rouâd) (34°51′N 35°51′E).

Berths

7.65

1 The terminal consists of two buoyed berths as follows:

Berth No 1, the N berth, with a depth of 23 m.

Berth No 2, the S berth, with a depth of 22 m.

Port services

7.66

1 For port services see Ţarţūs (7.87).

ŢARŢŪS

General information

Chart 1579, plan of Ţarţūs

Position

7.67

1 Ţarţūs, also known as Tartous, (34°54′N 35°53′E) lies on the SW coast of Syria, about 22 miles N of the border with Lebanon.

The port comprises an artificial harbour fronting the ancient port of Al Mīnā', 5 cables N of the town.

Function

7.68

1 Ţarţūs is a major commercial harbour with facilities for handling various cargoes including containers, bulk minerals and grain, general and RoRo traffic. It is also a naval base and tourist centre.

The port is used for Iraqi imports to aid reconstruction in Iraq.

There is a population of about 93 000 (2007).

Approach and entry

7.69

1 Syrian regulations require ships to approach Ţarţūs through the designated Approach Route, the limits of which are shown on the chart, which leads E from a position about 12 miles W of the harbour entrance.

The harbour is entered through a buoyed channel, passing between the breakwater heads.

Traffic

7.70

1 In 2007 there were 2122 ship calls with a total of 20 594 116 dwt.

Port Authority

7.71

1 Tartous Port General Company, PO Box 86, Tartous, Syria.

Limiting conditions

Controlling depth

7.72

1 **Controlling depth.** There is a least charted depth of 10 m in the entrance channel to the harbour. Within the entrance there is a turning basin, 2½ cables in diameter, dredged to a depth of 12·8 m.

Caution. Depths in the entrance channel and in the dredged areas within the harbour come from unconfirmed sources.

Deepest and longest berth

7.73

1 Berths 4 and 7 (7.86).

Density of water

7.74

1 1·030 g/cm^3.

Maximum size of vessel handled

7.75

1 Vessels up to 65 000 tonnes, with a draught of 14·9 m, have been handled.

Arrival information

Notice of ETA

7.76

1 72 and 24 hours.

Anchorage

7.77

1 Vessels waiting to enter harbour can obtain anchorage, as shown on the chart, 3 to 7 cables W of the head of the W breakwater, in depths from 14 to 20 m, coral, good holding ground.

Pilotage

7.78

1 Pilotage is compulsory and available during daylight hours. Pilot boards 1½ miles W of the W breakwater head, as shown on the chart. For details see *Admiralty List of Radio Signals Volume 6 (3).*

Tugs

7.79

1 Tugs are available.

Harbour

General layout

7.80

1 Ţarţūs Harbour is protected by W and N breakwaters extending 1 mile from the shore. Inside the harbour three broad moles project WSW from the shore to form four basins in which are arranged the berths.

Developments. Two new quays: one of 260 m length, 11 m depth, in the commercial and tourist complex; and one of 470 m length, 13 m depth in the container terminal. Construction of new grain silos. Syrian railways are completing (2008) a direct rail link to the Iraqi border.

Local weather

7.81

1 Winds from E slightly predominate from November to February. Strong winds are comparatively frequent from December to April, occurring on about 20% of days from January to March.

SW gales, and the accompanying swell, make some berths in the harbour most uncomfortable.

Directions

Principal marks

7.82

1 **Landmarks** (positioned from the head of the W breakwater (34°54′·6N 35°51′·3E)):

Silos (7 cables ESE), standing near the head of Mole A.

Two minarets 1 cable apart (1½ miles SE), standing in the N part of Ţarţūs.

Observatory (1¼ miles ESE).

Approach

7.83

1 From the vicinity of 34°55′N 35°39′E at the beginning of the approach route to Ţarţūs, the track leads E to the pilot boarding position. The chart is sufficient guide.

Entry

7.84

1 From the pilot boarding position the track leads 1¼ miles ENE to a position about 5 cables NW of the head of W breakwater. **Caution.** A dangerous wreck (position doubtful) lies 5 cables NNW of the W breakwater.

2 The track then leads SE through the buoyed entrance channel, and between the breakwater heads. A light (black metal framework tower) is exhibited from the head of the E breakwater.

Useful mark. Light exhibited from Jazīrat Arwād (Île de Rouâd) (34°51′N 35°51′E) (7.96).

Berths

Moorings

7.85

1 There are numerous moorings on the inside of the W breakwater. Vessels berth with both anchors down and stern lines to the breakwater, bows out.

Alongside

7.86

1 The harbour consists of four basins separated by Moles A, B and C, with about 9000 m of berthing space. These basins contain berths numbered in sequence from No 1 in Basin 4, at the N end of the harbour, to No 22 in Basin 1 at the S end, with depths alongside varying from 4 to 13 m.

2 The deepest and longest berths are No's 4 and 7 in Basin 3, with a charted depth of 13 m alongside. There are RoRo facilities on the S side of Mole B and also at Mole C. The Phosphate Quay, berths 18 and 19, at the S end of the harbour, specialises in the handling of phosphate.

For caution on depths see 7.72.

Port services

Facilities

7.87

1 Ţarţūs National Hospital; garbage disposal.

Other facilities

7.88

1 Ship Sanitation Control Exemption Certificates are issued.

Supplies

7.89

1 Fuel oil; fresh water.

Communications

7.90

1 Al Lādhiqīyah Airport, 65 km distant. The nearest international airports are Damascus International Airport, 250 km distant, and Beyrouth (Lebanon), 131 km distant.

ŢARŢŪS TO TRÂBLOUS

General information

Chart 2633

Route

7.91

1 From a position W of Ţarţūs (34°54′N 35°53′E), the coastal route leads S, for a distance of about 28 miles, to a position WNW of Jazīrat Ramkin (Ramkin Islet) (34°30′N 35°46′E), near Trâblous (Tripoli) (34°26′N 35°51′E).

Topography

7.92

1 From Ţarţūs (34°54′N 35°53′E) the coast for 21 miles SSE consists of a shingle beach, bordered by shallow water, with off-lying rocky patches.

At Marathus (34°50′N 35°55′E), a ruined ancient city, the hills recede inland, leaving between them and the sea a large cultivated plain studded with tumuli, on most of which are villages. Nahr al Kabīr (not charted) is the largest of five rivers which intersect this plain, winding W through the opening in the mountains N of Qornet el Aaroûba (34°27′N 36°15′E) (chart 183), 2215 m high, the N peak of Lebanon Range (7.124).

2 S of the mouth of En Nahr el Barid (7.95), 23½ miles SSE of Ţarţūs, the high land once more approaches the coast.

Regulations

7.93

1 All vessels entering Lebanese territorial waters should obtain permission to enter 24 hours in advance, through the agent.

For further details see 1.51 and *Admiralty List of Radio Signals Volume 6 (3).*

Directions

(continued from 7.42)

Principal marks

7.94

1 **Landmark:**

Factory building (34°32′N 35°59′E).

Major light:

Jazīrat Ramkin Light (white tower, 5 m in height), exhibited from Jazīrat Ramkin (34°30′N 35°46′E).

Ţarţūs to Trâblous

7.95

1 From a position in the Approach Route W of Ţarţūs the track leads S, passing (with positions from Jazīrat Arwād (34°51′N 35°51′E)):

W of Jazīrat Arwād (Île de Rouâd) (7.96), an island from which a light is exhibited. A line of islets and rocky shoals extends SSE for 9 miles from the island. During W gales the sea breaks heavily over these islets and rocky shoals. Thence:

2 W of a bank (1 mile SSE), with a depth of 4·3 m over it, thence:

W of Al 'Abbās (El Abbas) (2¼ miles SSE), an islet 4 m high; a rock which dries 0·3 m and a rock awash lie close together 5 cables S of the islet. Thence:

W of Abū al Fāris (El Faris) (4 miles SSE); two islets, each of which is 2 m high, lie close together 6 cables SSE of Abū al Fāris. Thence:

3 W of a shoal tongue (8 miles SSE), with a depth of 3·7 m over it, which is the continuation of the line

of reefs extending SSE from Jazīrat Arwād. Thence:

W of Ash Shaykh Jābir (Sheikh Jaber) (13¾ miles SSE), a tomb standing on the N side of the entrance to Nahr al Kabīr (7.92). The international boundary between Syria and Lebanon reaches the coast in this vicinity. Thence:

4 W of Qal'at Hakmun, (21¼ miles SSE) which consists of two mounds, covered with ruins, lying at the mouth of En Nahr el Barid.

The track then leads to a position WNW of Jazīrat Ramkin (34°30′N 35°46′E), the outermost of a chain of islets and low rocks extending 3¾ miles NW from Al Mīnā' (El Mina), a low promontory.

Al Ballān (El Bellan), 6 cables NW of Al Mīnā', is 6 m high and the highest of the islets.

5 **Useful mark:**

Pillar (large cylindrical block on a square pedestal) (34°50′N 35°55′E) surmounted by a cone-shaped stone 5 m in height, at an elevation of 32 m. Marathus (7.92) lies close N.

(Directions for the coastal route continue at 7.126)
(Directions for Trâblous are given at 7.112)

Minor harbour and anchorage

Chart 1579, plan of Ţarţūs

Jazīrat Arwād

7.96

1 **Description.** Jazīrat Arwād (Île de Rouâd on chart 2633) (34°51′N 35°51′E), is situated 2½ miles SSW of Ţarţūs.

The island is 24 m high and affords, on the E side, the best shelter along the coast for vessels of moderate draught. On the W side of the island are the remains of a stone wall and off the NW side lies Ilot Ishtār.

2 **Harbour.** On the E side of the island there is a harbour enclosed by two ancient moles constructed of huge stones and extended in more recent times. The NE mole curves in towards the island from its N end in a generally SE direction for 3 cables and the SE mole extends NE for about a cable with a short elbow to the NW. The entrance so formed is marked on each mole head by lights (black pylons). The harbour is divided by a quay extending about ½ cable from the island such that the entrance gives direct access to the S, or fishing, part of the harbour.

3 **Anchorage.** Anchorage may be obtained 3 cables NE of the harbour entrance, in depths from 9 to 11 m, sand and mud, as shown on the chart. Winds from SW send in a heavy swell.

Directions. Leading marks:

Beacon C (white) (34°51′·6N 35°53′·5E).

Beacon B (white) (6 cables from front beacon).

From a position about 2 miles WNW of Jazīrat Arwād the alignment (095°) of these beacons leads E, passing (with positions from Jazīrat Arwād Light):

N of Banc Charner (3 cables N), a rocky patch, thence:

4 S of a rocky patch (7 cables NNE), with a depth of 4·5 m over it, and:

N of a wreck (3 cables NE), with a depth of 3 m over it, marked by a buoy liable to drag.

The track then leaves the leading line to lead for a short distance SE to the anchorage.

5 **Useful marks:**

A large dismantled fort, with a minaret at its NE angle, crowning the middle of the island, with smaller forts at each corner.

Jazīrat Arwād Light (white tower on fortress, 4 m in height) exhibited from the main fort.

TRÂBLOUS

General information

Chart 1561 plan of Trâblous

Position

7.97

1 Trâblous, also known as Tripoli, (34°26′N 35°51′E) lies on the NW coast of Lebanon close to the Syrian border, and is situated on both banks of Nahr Abū' Alī, 1 mile from its mouth.

The harbour lies about 1 mile NW of the city at Al Mīna'.

Function

7.98

1 It is a medium sized commercial harbour with an offshore oil terminal situated NE. Its principal function was as an outlet for oil, transported from Iraq by overland pipeline, but this trade has declined in recent years.

Principal exports include oil, petroleum products, citrus fruits and olive oil. Imports include grain, manufactured goods, iron, timber and coal.

There is a population of about 160 000 (1998).

Approach and entry

7.99

1 United Nations Interim Force In Lebanon (UNIFIL) Maritime Task Force (MTF) is monitoring merchant traffic sailing towards Lebanese ports or transiting Lebanese Territorial Waters. For Lebanese regulations see 1.51 and *Admiralty List of Radio Signals Volume 6 (3).*

2 Trâblous is approached through a fairway passing seaward of Jazīrat Ramkin (34°30′N 35°46′E) and is entered through a dredged channel between a detached breakwater to the NW and a mole extending NNW from the shore.

Traffic

7.100

1 In 2007 there were 443 ship calls with a total of 2 931 763 dwt.

Port Authority

7.101

1 Trâblous Port Authority, Service d'Exploitation du Port, Trâblous, Lebanon.

Limiting conditions

Controlling depth

7.102

1 The entrance channel to the harbour has a minimum dredged depth of 11·7 m (2001). Within the harbour the maximum dredged depth is 9·7 m (2001).

Density of water

7.103

1 1·030 g/cm^3.

Maximum size of vessel handled

7.104

1 The harbour can accommodate vessels up to 150 m in length. Larger vessels have to anchor in the roadstead and work cargo with lighters. The maximum size of vessel handled at the oil terminal is 250 000 dwt.

Arrival information

Notice of ETA

7.105

1 For the dry cargo port, Masters should keep their agent advised of their ETA. For the oil terminal, ETA 72, 48 and 24 hours in advance is required, with confirmation 2 hours before arrival at Trâblous Roads.

Outer anchorages

7.106

1 Trâblous roadstead is divided into N and S anchorage areas by a line drawn from Ra's al Ladūs (34°28′·1N 35°53′·9E) to Jazīrat Ramkin, 7 miles WNW. The N area is used by tankers waiting to berth at the oil terminal.

In the S area, anchorage may be obtained about 9 cables NNW of the head of Jetée du Large (7.110) in depths of about 13 m, sand, as shown on the chart.

2 Anchorage may also be obtained about 1 mile SW of Al Mīna' in depths of about 18 m, sand, as shown on the chart.

Anchoring and passage are prohibited within an area extending 2 miles from the coast in the vicinity of the oil terminal, as shown on the chart. The NW limit of the area is marked by light buoys (special).

Pilotage

7.107

1 Pilotage is compulsory and available 24 hours for the tanker terminal and the dry cargo harbour. Pilot boards for tanker terminal, 2 miles NE of the NE end (34°28′·1N 35°49′·5E) of the detached breakwater, and for the dry cargo harbour 1½ miles N of the same breakwater head, as shown on the chart.

For details see *Admiralty List of Radio Signals Volume* 6 (3).

Tugs

7.108

1 Tugs are available in the dry cargo port. There are no tugs at the oil terminal, but a mooring barge is available for the connection of hoses.

Harbour regulation

7.109

1 Fishing is prohibited at all times.

Harbour

General layout

7.110

1 The harbour is protected from N by a detached breakwater and from E by the main, or East jetty, which is a broad expanse also serving as an extensive cargo handling area. The breakwater extends ENE and NE from Al Baqar, an islet lying close N of Al Mīna'. The jetty extends 5 cables NNW from Tower of Lions (7.112) and has a narrow spur extending a further 1½ cables off its NE end. Works were in progress (2006) on the NE side of the jetty.

2 **Developments.** Works are in progress (2007) to extend the detached breakwater 1000 m seaward, and to construct a secondary breakwater to the E. The works are marked by light buoys.

Local weather

7.111

1 Winds from between SW and NW predominate throughout the year, but to a lesser extent in winter than in summer. Near gale force 7 is reached on 3% of occasions between January and May, and rarely during other months.

Directions

Principal marks

7.112

1 **Landmarks** (positioned from the signal station (34°27′·8N 35°53′·0E), a yellow building with flagstaff):

Ra's al Ladūs (7 cables ENE), a rocky bluff 40 m high.

Building (1 mile SE).

Radio mast (red lights) (3 cables SW).

Flare (orange) (5 cables SW), visible from a considerable distance. A chimney stands close N.

Tower of Lions (2¾ miles WSW), a tower 21 m high, from which a light is occasionally exhibited.

2 Château de Raymond (2¾ miles SW), a large castle falling into ruins, standing on a hill 60 m high, in the S part of Trâblous.

Silo (3 miles W), standing near the NW corner of the main jetty.

Radio tower (red lights, 75 m in height) (3 miles WSW).

Major light:

Jazīrat Ramkin Light (34°30′N 35°46′E) (7.94).

Approach

7.113

1 From a position about 8 miles WNW of Jazīrat Ramkin (34°30′N 35°46′E) (7.95), the track leads E, passing N of Jazīrat Ramkin, to a position about 1 mile N of Jazīrat an Nakhl (34°29′·7N 35°46′·4E). The track then leads SE to the pilot boarding position, passing (with positions from the E head of the breakwater (34°27′·9N 35°49′·5E)):

NE of Jazīrat an Nakhl (3 miles NW) and Jazīrat Sanānī (2¾ miles NW), thence:

2 Clear of a dangerous wreck (2¼ miles NNW), the position of which is approximate. The masts of the wreck are visible.

The track then leads to the pilot station (1½ miles N). For vessels bound for the oil terminal the track leads a further 2¼ miles E to the oil terminal pilot boarding position, and thence as required to the berths.

Entry

7.114

1 From the pilot boarding position, the track leads SE to the entrance channel, passing (with positions from the E head of the breakwater (34°27′·9N 35°49′·5E)):

Clear of a wreck (1¼ miles N), with a depth of 6·7 m over it, thence:

ENE of a line of islets situated on a bank extending 1½ miles NNW of Al Baqar (9 cables SW), and:

WSW of two moored vessels (1¼ miles NE and 8 cables ENE) to a position off the entrance to the harbour.

2 The track then leads SW through a channel, 1 cable wide, marked at its outer end by a buoy (starboard hand) and dredged to a minimum depth of 11·7 m (2001), passing:

NW of a buoy (port hand) (4 cables ENE), thence:

Between the heads of the breakwater and the main jetty (3 cables S), into the harbour. Lights (pylons, 6 m in height) are exhibited from the heads of both jetties.

3 An area dredged to a depth of 9·7 m lies inside the entrance, as shown on the plan. The remainder of the harbour has depths of 5 m and less.

A dangerous wreck lies close inside the W end of the breakwater and another lies close NW of the head of the harbour.

Side channel

7.115

1 Sanānī Channel (34°29′N 35°47′E), a narrow unmarked passage 1½ miles SE of Jazīrat Ramkin, leads between Jazīrat Sanānī and the NW extremity of a shoal area, with a line of islets on it, extending 1¾ miles NW from Al Mina.

Local knowledge is required.

Berths

Harbour

7.116

1 **Main (East) jetty.** The quay is 600 m long, 100 m wide, with a maximum depth of 9·7 m alongside. It is low and unfendered.

Detached breakwater. In fair weather vessels may lie about 9 m off the inner side of the breakwater, with stern hawsers to bollards and with both anchors down; the bottom is mud.

2 **Fishing harbour.** The fishing harbour is at Al Mīna' in the SW part of Trâblous Harbour. It is enclosed by two arms with a NE-facing entrance.

Landing places. Sheikh Affan Jetty, 6¼ cables WNW of Tower of Lions near the post office, is constructed of concrete piles with depths from 1·5 to 4·0 m alongside.

During strong NE winds there is good landing for boats on a sandy beach S of an ancient wall on the SW side of Al Mīna' promontory.

Oil terminal

7.117

1 **Main berths.** The terminal contains four numbered berths, which consist of mooring buoys at the seaward ends of submarine oil pipelines extending up to 1½ miles from the shore, as shown on the plan; Nos 1 to 3 are marked by lights.

Vessels berth using two anchors with stern lines to the buoys lying head to wind and sea. The maximum permitted draughts allow for an underkeel clearance of 1·9 m; during the summer months a reduced clearance of 1·2 m may be permitted at No 2 Berth. Details off the berths are as follow:

2 Berth No 1: maximum draught 17·0 m; maximum 140 000 dwt.

Berth No 2: maximum draught 18·3 m; maximum 250 000 dwt.

Berth No 3: maximum draught 14·3 m; maximum 87 000 dwt.

Berth No 4: maximum draught 9·8 m; maximum 25 000 dwt. A vessel is moored at the end of this berth and there are two other vessels moored 5 cables S.

3 **Other berths.** Two submarine oil pipelines extend NNE from the shore, 6 cables E of Digue Est (7.110), as shown on the chart, with moored vessels at their ends.

Port services

Repairs

7.118

1 Shipyard with slipway, capacity 1000 dwt.

Other facilities

7.119

1 Hospital.

Supplies

7.120

1 Fuel oil; fresh water; provisions.

Communications

7.121

1 Beyrouth International Airport, 100 km from Trâblous.

TRÂBLOUS TO ḪEFA

GENERAL INFORMATION

Chart 2633

Area covered

7.122

1 The area covered by this section comprises:

Trâblous to Beyrouth (7.123).
Beyrouth (7.154).
Beyrouth to Az Zahrānī (7.179).
Az Zahrānī to Ḫefa (7.204).
Ḫefa (7.223).

TRÂBLOUS TO BEYROUTH

General information

Chart 2633

Route

7.123

1 From a position WNW of Jazīrat Ramkin (34°30′N 35°46′E), near Trâblous (34°26′N 35°51′E), the coastal route leads SSW, for a distance of about 39 miles, to a position WNW of Râs Beyrouth (Rās Beirut) (33°54′N 35°28′E).

Chart 183

Topography

7.124

1 The coast for 2¾ miles S of Al Mīna' (El Mina) (34°27′N 35°48′E) is mostly a sandy beach, partly bordered by rocks, thence for 1½ miles SW it is rocky.

Jebel Liban, or Lebanon Range, extends 70 miles SSW from Qornet el Aaroûba (34°27′N 36°15′E) (7.92). The elevations decrease at first, S of this peak, but 6 miles SW increase to a high bluff shoulder; 4½ miles farther SW lies Qornet es Saouda, 3088 m, the highest peak in the range.

2 Jebel Qrâssia (34°16′N 36°06′E) rises to 3044 m. The Cedars of Lebanon are a group of trees standing at an elevation of 2042 m on the W slope of the range, 2½ miles WSW of Jebel Qrâssia, and are visible from seaward in the vicinity of the coast 20 miles W.

Between Rās Sel'ata (34°16′N 35°39′E) and Rās Maâmelteïn, 15 miles S, the coast has a barren aspect and consists of rocky points, the ends of the high rugged spurs of Lebanon Range, interspersed with small sandy bays.

Regulations

7.125

1 For regulations concerning entry to Lebanese territorial waters see 7.93.

Directions
(continued from 7.95)

Chart 2633
Principal marks
7.126
1 **Landmarks:**
Monastery standing on Mar Ya'qub (34°23′N 35°49′E), 226 m high.
Jebel Sannîne (33°57′N 35°53′E), 2628 m high, visible up to 50 miles.
Statue standing on a monastery (white) (33°57′·4N 35°36′·1E), near the N bank of Nahr el Kalb, 1 cable inland.
2 **Major lights:**
Jazīrat Ramkin Light (34°30′N 35°46′E) (7.94).
Râs Beyrouth Light (grey tower, black bands, 27 m in height) (33°54′·0N 35°28′·2E).

Trâblous to Rās Aamchîte
7.127
1 From a position about 8 miles WNW of Jazīrat Ramkin (34°30′N 35°46′E) the track leads SSW, passing (with positions from Jazīrat Ramkin);
WNW of Al Mīna' (El Mina) (4 miles S) (7.95), thence:
WNW of Kalmoun Light (white pylon, black bands) (7 miles S), thence:
WNW of En Rās Natur (7 miles SSW), on which there is a large square building, thence:
2 WNW of Enfe Light (white pylon with black bands), which is exhibited from a point close N of the village of Enfe. Burj Enfe, a ruin, stands on a rocky islet close off the village. Thence:
WNW of Rās esh Shiq'a (12 miles SSW). A prominent hillock 233 m high, stands above the point. Thence:
3 WNW of Rās Sel'ata or Rā's Kubba (15 miles SSW), which is steep-to and surmounted by a tower. Thence:
WNW of Rās Burbara (19½ miles SSW).
The track then leads to a position WNW of Rās Aamchîte (34°09′N 35°38′E). Terouel Light (white metal with black bands) is exhibited from the point.

Rās Aamchîte to Beyrouth
7.128
1 From a position WNW of Rās Aamchîte (34°09′N 35°38′E) the track continues SSW, passing (with positions from Rās Aamchîte):
WNW of Jebaïl (2¼ miles SSE), a village, from where a light is exhibited. A high square tower stands in the centre of the village. There is a landing place in a small cove N of the village. Another light (pylon) is exhibited from a position 1 mile S of the village. Thence:
2 WNW of Nahr Ibrâhim (5½ miles S), a river, which is spanned 2½ cables inland by a bridge carrying the Trâblous-Beyrouth road, thence:
WNW of Râs el Maâmelteïn (Rās Ma'ameltein) (7½ miles S). Tabarja Light (white tower, black bands) is exhibited from a position 3½ cables N. Thence:
WNW of Râs et Taïr (10 miles S), low and shingly, which forms the S entrance point to Baie de Joûnié (Juniye Bay) (7.143), thence:
3 WNW of Rās el Kalb (Rās el Kelb) (11¾ miles S). Nahr el Kalb (Nahr el Kelb) enters the sea 2½ cables NE of the point. It is the largest river on this coast with the exception of Nahr Abu' Ali (7.97); there is very little water on the bar during the summer.
The track then leads to a position WNW of Râs Beyrouth (33°54′N 35°28′E).
(Directions continue for the coastal route at 7.182, and for Beyrouth at 7.170)

Chekka

Chart 2633
General information
7.129
1 **Position.** Chekka (34°20′N 35°43′E), an open roadstead, is situated in Il Huri Bay, close W of Chekka el Atiqâ, a village, 10 miles SW of Trâblous.
Function. The harbour serves a large cement works. Principal imports are phosphates, machinery parts and firebricks; exports are cement and chemicals.
2 **Traffic.** 355 000 tonnes of cargo handled annually.
Port Authority. Trâblous Port Authority, Service d'Exploitation du Port, Trâblous, Lebanon.

Limiting conditions
7.130
1 **Maximum size of vessel handled:** Maximum winter draught 8 m; maximum summer draught 8·2 m.

Arrival information
7.131
1 **Notice of ETA:** 7, 3, 2 and 1 day before arrival.
Anchorage. May be obtained in the S part of Il Huri Bay, 1¼ miles WSW of Chekka, in a depth of 16 m, sand, sheltered from strong SW summer breezes, as shown on the chart.
Pilot is available. Berthing and sailing during daylight hours only.
Tugs are not available.

Directions
7.132
1 **Useful marks:**
The cement works usually emit a dense cloud of white smoke, which is a good mark by day, visible for many miles; the light from the works can usually be seen at night.
Chekka Light (white pylon, black bands) is exhibited 7½ cables W of the village.

Berths
7.133
1 Chekka contains two berths as follows:
Quay No 1: length 40 m; depth alongside 9·1 m; maximum draught 8·5 m; handles vessels up to 15 000 dwt.
Quay No 2: length 45 m; depth alongside 9·1 m; maximum draught 8·2 m; handles vessels up to 15 000 dwt.
Tankers drawing up to 6·1 m berth stern-to.
2 **Caution.** The quays are exposed to SW winds. In the event of swell, vessels must leave the berths and anchor in the bay.

Port services
7.134
1 **Supplies.** Fresh water, provisions and medical facilities are available.

Sel'ata

Chart 1561 plan of Sel'ata

General information

7.135

1 **Position.** Sel'ata (34°17′N 35°39′E) is situated about 24 miles NNE of Beyrouth.

Function. Import of agricultural goods for processing and distribution, and export of grain. Lebanon Chemicals Company Wharf, ¾ mile farther S, handles chemical cargoes. The port is privately owned.

Limiting conditions

7.136

1 **Density of water.** 1·025 to 1·027 g/cm^3.

Maximum size of vessel handled:

Sel'ata. Vessels up to 150 m in length and 13 m draught. However vessels up to 200 m LOA have been accommodated.

Lebanon Chemical Company Wharf. Vessels up to 6000 dwt and 6·4 m draught.

Arrival information

7.137

1 **Notice of ETA:** 7, 3, 2 and 1 day before arrival.

Pilotage is available. For Sel'ata the pilot boards 5 cables N of the port. For Lebanon Chemical Company Wharf the boarding position is 1 mile SW of the pier. Details are given in *Admiralty List of Radio Signals Volume 6 (3)*.

Tugs are available.

Harbour

7.138

1 The harbour of Sel'ata is entered between the heads of the N and W breakwaters respectively, through a channel 14 m in depth.

Berths:

Sel'ata. One quay 150 m in length, which fronts the W breakwater.

2 Lebanon Chemical Company Plant Wharf. One pier 90 m long.

Developments. A total of eight quays are to be constructed capable of handling vessels up to 70 000 dwt (2006).

Port services

7.139

1 **Facilities.** Garbage disposal.

Supplies. Provisions and fresh water are available; fuel obtainable at Lebanon Chemical Company Plant Wharf.

Communications. Nearest airport, Beyrouth International, 67 km distant.

Amchit

Chart 2633

General information

7.140

1 **Position.** Amchit (34°09′N 35°37′E) is situated about 15 miles NNE of Beyrouth, close to Rās Aamchîte.

Port Authority. Beyrouth Port Authority, BP 1490, Port Office, Beyrouth, Lebanon.

Limiting conditions

7.141

1 **Maximum size of vessel handled:** 45 000 dwt, 200 m length, 14 to 15·9 m draught.

Harbour

7.142

1 **Function.** 3 CBM berths for oil and gas products.

Joûnié

Chart 1563 plan of Joûnié

General conditions

7.143

1 **Position.** Joûnié (Juniye) (33°59′N 35°38′E) is a small town situated 8 miles NE of Beyrouth, at the S entrance point to Baie de Joûnié (Juniye Bay).

Function. Handles mainly coastal vessels.

Traffic. Approximately 300 vessels are handled annually.

Port Authority. Joûnié Port Authority, Ministry of Defence, Sarba, Joûnié, Beyrouth, Lebanon.

Arrival information

7.144

1 **Notice of ETA:** 7, 3, 2 and 1 day before arrival.

Anchorage. Vessels may anchor in Baie de Joûnié 7 cables NE of Râs et Taïr, as shown on the chart, in depths of 13 to 15 m.

Pilotage is compulsory.

Tugs are not available.

Harbour

7.145

1 The harbour has facilities for yachts, coastal and fishing vessels. Lights mark the heads of the breakwaters and the entrances to the basins within the harbour. There are depths from 2·1 to 4·0 m alongside the berths.

Directions

7.146

1 **Landmarks:**

El Ghazîr and San Antonio Monasteries (34°01′·1N 35°40′·0E).

Statue of Notre Dame de Lebanon (white conical base) (33°58′·9N 35°39′·1E). A funicular railway, shown on the chart, runs from the coast to the vicinity of the statue.

2 Casino (34°00′·9N 35°38′·4E), standing on the N side of the bay.

Buildings (34°01′·0N 35°37′·5E), 1½ miles W of the casino.

7.147

1 **Approach and entry.** Joûnié is approached from W by entering Baie de Joûnié, between Rās Ma'ameltein (34°01′N 35°37′E) and Râs et Taïr, 1¾ miles farther S. The chart is sufficient guide.

Caution. There are considerable depths in the N and central parts of the bay, but shoal water with rocky ground extends 2½ cables from the SE and S shores.

Port services

7.148

1 **Repairs.** There are two slipways, one for vessels up to 40 tons and another for vessels up to 10 tons.

Other facilities. Hospitals.

Supplies. Fresh water; provisions.

Communications. Beyrouth International Airport, 30 km distant.

Terminal Zouq

Chart 1563

General information

7.149

1 **Position.** Terminal Zouq (33°58′N 35°36′E) is situated 6 miles NE of Beyrouth.

Function. The harbour is used by tankers serving a local power station and by LNG carriers.

Port operator. Zouk Power Station, Zouk Mkâyel, Sea Highway, Joûnié, Beyrouth. Lebanon.

The terminal is administered by Joûnié Port Authority.

Harbour

7.150

1 **Landmarks:**

Two conspicuous chimneys (red and white bands; red lights) (33°58′·2N 35°36′·2E).

Berths

7.151

1 There is an SBM, the position of which is approximate, 5 cables offshore, and there are mooring buoys in the bay close W of the chimneys.

Anchorages

Chart 2633

Batrun

7.152

1 Batrun (34°15′N 35°39′E), is a small village off which vessels occasionally anchor in a depth of 18 m, sand; the remains of the ancient port are still visible. Batrun Light (white pylon, black bands) is exhibited from Batrun; Fadous Light (similar structure) is exhibited 7½ cables S.

Chart 1563

Nahr el Kalb

7.153

1 Anchorage may be obtained, as shown on the chart, 5½ cables NW of the entrance to Nahr el Kalb (33°57′·5N 35°35′·8E) (7.128), in depths of 13 to 16 m, mud and sand.

BEYROUTH

General information

Chart 1563

Position

7.154

1 Beyrouth (Beirut) (33°54′N 35°31′E), the capital and principal port of Lebanon, is situated on the SW side of Jun el Khudr (Baie Saint Georges), about 1½ miles E of Râs Beyrouth (33°54′·0N 35°28′·2E).

Function

7.155

1 It is a major commercial and cultural centre. The port has facilities for handling most types of vessels including general cargo, container, bulk carriers and tankers.

Principal exports include cereals, fruit, vegetables, wool, cement, and other manufactured goods. Imports include industrial and manufactured goods, timber, iron and petroleum products.

There is a population of about 1·5 million.

Topography

7.156

1 Beyrouth is a large city with extensive suburbs, extending along the shores of Jun el Khudr. Its more ancient part, in which are the bazaars, is enclosed by an old wall.

The land S and W of Beyrouth rises in prominent hills of red sand, about 90 m high, which drifts with strong SW breezes in summer. The land E of the town rises rapidly, and 15 miles inland lie the high peaks of Lebanon Range (7.126).

2 Several streams flow into Jun el Khudr, including Nahr Beyrouth (Nahr Beirut), which is a small stream in summer.

Approach and entry

7.157

1 United Nations Interim Force In Lebanon (UNIFIL) Maritime Task Force (MTF) is monitoring merchant traffic sailing towards Lebanese ports or transiting Lebanese Territorial Waters. For Lebanese regulations see 1.51.

From seaward the harbour is approached through Jun el Khudr and entered between the head of the N breakwater and the W end of the detached breakwater.

Traffic

7.158

1 In 2007 the port had 2165 ship calls with a total of 34 896 374 dwt.

Port Authority

7.159

1 Beyrouth Port Authority, BP 1490, Port Office, Beyrouth, Lebanon.

Limiting conditions

Deepest and longest berth

7.160

1 No 16 (7.173).

Density of water

7.161

1 1·027 g/cm^3.

Maximum size of vessel handled

7.162

1 **Maximum size of vessel handled.** *Ypatianna*; 265 m in length, draught 12·9 m, 96 875 dwt.

Arrival information

Notice of ETA

7.163

1 Send ETA to agent 48 and 24 hours in advance; tankers 72, 48 and 24 hours.

Outer anchorages

7.164

1 **Temporary anchorage.** Vessels may obtain temporary anchorage as convenient N of the harbour breakwater; the greater part of the anchorage has a bottom of rock covered by sand or mud.

There is an anchorage area 7½ cables N of the root of the N breakwater, in a depth of about 66 m.

2 **Jun el Khudr anchorage.** A second anchorage area is in the vicinity of 33°54′·7N 35°34′·0E, on the SE side of Jun el Khudr, in a depth of 18 m, stiff mud.

Both anchorages are shown on the chart.

Prohibited anchorage

7.165

1 Anchoring is prohibited within 1¼ miles of the coast between Râs Minat el Hussein (33°54′·2N 35°29′·6E) and a point 5 cables E, as shown on the chart, owing to the existence of submarine cables. Anchoring is also prohibited off the entrance to the harbour.

Submarine cables

7.166

1 Two cables run generally NNW from the shore in the vicinity of the mouth of the Nahr el Maout. Four cables run WNW and W from the shore in the vicinity of Antélîas (33°55′N 35°35′E). One is marked by four buoys (special).

See also 7.165 and 1.26.

Pilotage and tugs

7.167

1 Pilotage is compulsory and available during daylight hours only. Pilot boards outside the breakwater, as shown on the chart.

For details see *Admiralty List of Radio Signals Volume 6 (3).*

Tugs are available.

Harbour

General layout

7.168

1 Beyrouth Harbour is protected from W through to N by a breakwater extending 1½ miles ENE from the shore at its W end. A detached angled breakwater, aligned approximately E/W in the entrance, provides protection for No 16 Berth.

The harbour has four basins along its S side.

2 There are charted depths of 11 to 16 m in the harbour. The offshore tanker berths lie E of the main harbour.

Natural conditions

7.169

1 **Currents.** A strong N-going current usually runs in the vicinity of Rās Beirut.

Climate information: see 1.184 and 1.203.

Directions

Principal marks

7.170

1 **Landmarks** (positioned from Râs Beyrouth Light (33°54′·0N 35°28′·2E)):

Radio mast (red and white lights, 46 m in height) (6 cables ENE), standing on Râs Mukerben.

Hotel (remarkable roof) (1¼ miles E), standing on Râs Minat el Hussein.

2 Armenian church (high conical tower) (1½ miles ESE). A palace stands close N.

Building Borj Rizk (2½ miles ESE), surmounted by a radio tower.

Silo (white) (2½ miles E), standing between No 2 and No 3 Basin.

Major light:

Râs Beyrouth Light (33°54′·0N 35°28′·2E) (7.126).

Approach

7.171

1 To the pilot boarding position NE of the N breakwater the chart is sufficient guide.

If approaching Beyrouth from S, Râs Beyrouth (33°54′N 35°28′E) should be rounded at a distance of at least 5 cables in order to clear a rocky ledge extending from Râs el Ghara, 4½ cables S.

Cautions. Mariners should obtain up-to-date local information concerning development works before navigating in Beyrouth harbour.

Entry

7.172

1 From the vicinity of the pilot boarding position the track leads SSE, S and thence SW into the harbour, passing (with positions from the N breakwater head):

E of a light buoy (starboard hand) (1 cable NE) marking the head of the breakwater, thence:

SE of N breakwater head, thence:

NW of a light buoy (port hand) (2 cables S) positioned off the W end of the detached breakwater.

2 For vessels bound for the berth at Coral Oil Depot (7.174) attention is drawn to the following:

A wreck with a depth of 2·5 m over it, marked by a buoy at each end, lies ¾ cable E of the berth, and a dangerous wreck lies 2 cables NW.

Le Mirmillon, a rock with a depth of 2·6 m over it, lying 1½ cables WNW of the berth, is the N-most of several rocks fronting the W entrance point of Nahr Beyrouth.

3 **Useful marks:**

Light (metal tower) (33°55′N 35°32′E) exhibited from the breakwater head.

Light (red metal tower) (33°54′·7N 35°32′·0) exhibited from the W head of the detached breakwater.

Light (metal tower) (33°54′·7N 35°32′·1) exhibited from the elbow head of the detached breakwater.

Light (green metal tower) (33°54′·7N 35°32′·3) exhibited from the E head of the detached breakwater.

Saint Francis Asylum (large crucifix) (33°54′·1N 35°35′·1E).

Berths

Alongside berths

7.173

1 The harbour is divided into four basins with a total of 16 berths. General, containers, and dry bulk cargoes are handled.

The deepest and longest berth is No 16: 600 m long; maximum draught 15·5 m. No 14 Berth in Basin No 4 also handles RoRo vessels.

Dora Oil Terminals

7.174

1 The following private oil terminals are situated outside the harbour in position (33°53′·8N 35°33′·3E). Their pipelines extend up to 7 cables offshore:

Medco. Discharge only. Gasoline and gas oil; bitumen; solvents and oils. Vessels up to 55 000 dwt; 200 m LOA and 10·5 m draught.

2 **MPC Miskaoui.** Discharge only. Gasoline and gas oil. Vessels up to 45 000 dwt; 200 m LOA and 11 m draught.

Coral Oil (33°54′·1N 35°32′·5E). Discharge only. Gasoline and gas oil; bitumen; solvents and oils. Vessels up to 35 000 dwt; 185 m LOA and 11 m draught. Vessels secure their sterns to three mooring buoys, with anchors out to the N.

3 **Wardieh.** Two CBM berths. Discharge only. Petroleum products. Berth No 1: vessels up to

Beyrouth Harbour from NE (7.168)

(Original dated 2001)

(Photograph - HMS Herald)

5000 dwt; 180 m LOA and 9·7 m draught; depth alongside 10 m. Berth No 2: vessels up to 40 000 dwt; 180 m LOA and 13 m draught; berth depth 14 m.

4 **Uniterminals.** Two CBM berths. Discharge only. Gasoline and gasoil; fuel oil; bitumen; solvents and oils. Berth No 1: vessels up to 4600 dwt; 100 m LOA and 5·4 m draught; berth depth 6 m; starboard anchor, port mooring buoy, two buoys aft. Berth No 2: vessels up to 60 000 dwt; 210 m LOA and 14 m draught; berth depth 16·5 m; two anchors forward, three mooring buoys aft.

5 **Gas Liban.** Discharge and load. Gas. Vessels up to 45 000 dwt; 8 m draught.

Vessels are berthed only during daylight hours at all the above-mentioned pipelines, but may leave at any time.

Port services

Repairs

7.175

1 Facilities for most types of repair; slipway, on W side of Basin No 1, with a breadth of 55 m and lifting capacity up to 1000 tons; divers.

Other facilities

7.176

1 Hospitals; compass adjustment; garbage disposal; no facilities for oily waste reception.

Sopplies

7.177

1 Fuel oil and marine diesel; fresh water at the quays or by water-boat; fresh provisions.

Communications

7.178

1 Beyrouth International Airport, 8 km distant.

BEYROUTH TO AZ ZAHRĀNĪ

General information

Charts 2633, 2634

Route

7.179

1 From a position WNW of Râs Beyrouth (Rās Beirut) (33°54′N 35°28′E) the coastal route leads SSW, for a distance of about 26 miles, to a position WNW of Az Zahrānī (33°30′N 35°21′E).

Topography

7.180

1 Between Râs Beyrouth and Rās Damur, 13 miles SSW, the coast consists of a sandy beach; inland, a rich, well cultivated plain with olive groves extends to the foot of hills which rise steeply. Numerous villages and monasteries are situated on the hillsides amidst vineyards and mulberry groves. From Rās Damur to Rās Jedra, 2½ miles S, the coast is bordered by a sandy beach; thence to Ra's aş Şakhrī (Cap Sahare), 2¾ miles farther S, it becomes more rocky and barren, with a few scattered villages on the ridges.

Traffic regulations

7.181

1 A prohibited area exists between Khaldi (33°47′N 35°29′E), 7 miles S of Rās Beyrouth, and Saïda (Sidon), 15 miles farther SSW. Vessels should not approach within 6½ miles of the coast.

Directions

(continued from 7.128)

Principal marks

7.182

1 **Landmarks:**

Five chimneys (33°40′N 35°25′E) at El Jiye.

Black chimney (33°29′·5N 35°20′·2E).

Major lights:

Râs Beyrouth Light (33°54′·0N 35°28′·2E) (7.126).

Beyrouth Airport (aero lights) (33°49′·5N 35°29′·4E) exhibited from control tower and hangar respectively.

Beyrouth to Az Zahrānī

7.183

1 From a position WNW of Râs Beyrouth (33°54′N 35°28′E) the track leads SSW, passing (with positions from Râs Beyrouth):

WNW of a outfall pipeline (4½ miles S), extending 3½ miles WSW from the shore in the vicinity of Beyrouth Airport (7.182). A radio mast stands 1½ miles farther S. Thence:

2 WNW of Nahr ed Damur (11½ miles S). Its mouth is obstructed by sandbanks and difficult to identify from seaward. Thence:

WNW of Rās Damur (13 miles SSW), thence:

WNW of El Jiye Port and Rās Jedra (15½ miles SSW)

WNW of Cap Sahare (Ra's aş Şakhrī on chart 1561) (18 miles SSW). Nahr Oula (Nahr al Awwālī on chart 1561) lies 1 mile S. Thence:

3 WNW of Az Zīrah (Ziri) (20 miles SSW), an island. Az Zīrah Light (white pylon, 4 m in height) is exhibited from the S extremity of the island. An islet lies close S, thence;

WNW of Saïda and Rās Abarou (Ra's 'Abrūh on chart 1561) (21 miles SSW).

The track then leads to a position WNW of Az Zahrānī (33°30′N 35°21′E).

4 **Useful mark:**

Nabi el Ouzaai (33°51′N 35°29′E), which has a prominent white minaret.

(Directions continue for the coastal route at 7.209, and for Zahrānī (Sidon) Terminal at 7.200)

El Jiye

Chart 2634

General information

7.184

1 **Position and function.** There is an oil terminal at El Jiye (33°40′N 35°25′E), 15 miles SSW of Beyrouth. The terminal supplies fuel oil to an electricity power plant, with a second berth for the discharge of gasoline.

Port Authority. Beyrouth Port Authority, BP 1490, Port Office, Beyrouth, Lebanon.

Port Operators. Electricite du Liban (EDL) and Cogico, El Jiye.

Limiting conditions

7.185

1 **Density of water:** 1·025 g/cm^3.

Maximum size of vessels handled: EDL berth: 80 000 dwt; berth depth 20 m. Cogico berth: vessels up to 200 m in length, 30 m beam, and with a draught of 10 m.

Arrival information

7.186

1 **Pilotage** is available.

Tugs. A small tug is available.

Berths

7.187

1 The terminal contains the following berths:

Two offshore tanker berths with conventional buoyed moorings at the ends of submarine pipelines.

A small quay for handling asphalt and jet fuel.

Port services

7.188

1 **Supplies:** fuel; provisions; fresh water available at quay.

Saïda

Chart 1561

General information

7.189

1 **Position.** Saïda (Sidon) (33°34′N 35°22′E) is situated 26 miles SSW of Beyrouth, on the NW slope of a rocky promontory. The town is almost encircled by a substantial wall. Château de la Mer, also known as Kalat al Bahr, an ancient ruined fortress, stands on a rock close off the N end of the town, to which it is connected by a bridge. Château de Saint Louis or Burj al Maisa, the old citadel said to have been built by Louis IX in 1253, stands in the SE part of the town, surmounted by a ruined tower, and forms a prominent landmark.

2 **Function.** The port handles general and bulk cargo, livestock and containers. It has a population of about 38 000.

Approach and entry. United Nations Interim Force In Lebanon (UNIFIL) Maritime Task Force (MTF) is monitoring merchant traffic sailing towards Lebanese ports or transiting Lebanese Territorial Waters. For Lebanese regulations see 1.51.

3 **Traffic.** In 2007 there were 71 ship calls with a total of 196 563 dwt.

Port Authority. Ministry of Public Works and Transport, Saïda, Lebanon.

Limiting conditions

7.190

1 **Maximum size of vessel handled.** Draught 5·5 m, LOA 120 m, 10 000 dwt.

Local weather and sea state. During the winter season, especially in the months of December, January and March, port operations may be disrupted by strong W winds and a heavy swell.

Arrival information

7.191

1 **Notice of ETA:** 7, 3, 2 and 1 day before arrival.

Anchorage. Vessels may obtain anchorage 6 cables N of the harbour, as shown on the chart, in depths of about 11 m.

Pilotage. Available.

Tugs. Normally not available.

Harbour

7.192

1 **General layout.** The port is formed by an outer breakwater, extending NE parallel to the shore, and by a short mole, extending NNW from the W side of the town.

The cargo berths are arranged along the outside of the outer breakwater. The harbour inside the breakwater and mole is now almost completely silted up.

Directions

7.193

1 **Landmark:**

Hotel standing near the coast, 1¼ miles NNE of Saïda.

North-west approach. From seaward the track leads initially to a position about 4 cables N of Az Zīrah (33°34′·4N 35°22′·1E), thence SE, passing (with positions from Az Zīrah Light (33°34′·3N 35°22′·1E)):

2 SW of Firefly Rock (7 cables NNE), with a least depth of 7·3 m over it, thence:

NE of the rocky spit (3 cables N) extending N from Az Zīrah, into the anchorage (7.191).

The track then leads S between Az Zīrah and the mainland to the harbour.

3 **West approach.** This is an alternative approach, depending on draught and size of vessel, which leads from seaward E, passing (with positions from Az Zīrah Light (33°34′·3N 35°22′·1E):

N of a dangerous wreck (1¼ miles SW), thence:

4 Between the islet (1 cable SSW) lying off the S side of Az Zīrah and the berths on the outside of the outer breakwater (3 cables S) of the harbour.

Useful mark:

Az Zīrah Light (33°34′·3N 35°22′·1E) (7.183).

Berths

7.194

1 There are two quays situated on the outside of the outer breakwater with a total of three berths. Length of berths and depths alongside not known.

Port services

7.195

1 **Facilities:** hospital; no facilities for oily waste disposal.

Supplies. Fresh water is available.

Zahrānī Terminal

Chart 1561

General information

7.196

1 **Position.** Zahrānī (Sidon) Terminal (33°30′N 35°20′E) is situated 4 miles SSW of Saïda, close NE of the mouth of Nahr az Zahrānī.

Function. The terminal was constructed for the export of crude oil transported by pipeline from Saudi Arabia.

In 2008 two berths were in use: Zahrānī Terminal, and to the N Zahrānī Power Plant Terminal.

2 **Traffic.** In 2007 there were 36 ship calls with a total of 1 505 316 dwt.

Port Authority. Trans-Arabian Pipeline Company, PO Box 11–1348, Beyrouth, Lebanon.

Limiting conditions

7.197

1 **Depths.** Zahrānī Terminal: berth depth 16·8 m; maximum draught 12·8 m. Zahrānī Power Plant Terminal: berth depth 21 to 22 m; maximum draught 13 m.

Maximum size of vessel handled. Zahrānī Terminal: Tankers with a maximum summer deadweight of 80 000 tonnes. Zahrānī Power Plant Terminal: tankers with a maximum summer deadweight of 60 000 tonnes.

Arrival information

7.198

1 **Port operations.** Loading takes place by day only.

Notice of ETA: 72, 24 and 12 hours in advance. The terminal should be contacted on VHF 4 hours before arrival to obtain weather and berthing information.

2 **Anchorage.** Vessels awaiting a berth can obtain good anchorage in depths from 29 to 37 m, sand, in the vicinity of 33°32′N 35°19′E. Vessels should not anchor N of this position as the depths are too great for good holding, nor within the prohibited anchorage area unless instructed to do so by the mooring master; see note on chart.

3 **Prohibited anchorage.** An area, shown on the chart, within which anchoring is prohibited extends from the mouth of Nahr az Zahrānī to Rās Abarou (Ra's 'Abrūh on chart 1561), a rocky point 4 miles NNE, enclosing the terminal. The NW and SW limits of the area are marked by buoys (white spar).

4 **Pilotage** is compulsory. A mooring master boards about 2 miles seaward of the waiting anchorage. Berthing during daytime only; unberthing is allowed at night.

For details see *Admiralty List of Radio Signals Volume 6 (3)*.

Tugs are not available.

Harbour

7.199

1 **General layout.** The terminal, in an open roadstead, has several submarine oil pipelines extending 1 mile offshore, at the end of which there are berths; of which only two are operational.

Directions

7.200

1 **Landmarks:**

Water tower (33°31′·0N 35°21′·4E).

Six radio towers (elevation 32 m) (33°30′·2N 35°20′·7E). Several lights (occasional) are exhibited from positions in the vicinity of the radio towers.

Black chimney (33°29′·5N 35°20′·2E).

2 **Approach.** Attention is drawn to the dangerous wreck, position approximate, charted 9 cables WNW of Ra's 'Abrūh (33°33′N 35°22′E), otherwise from seaward to the berths the chart is sufficient guide.

Useful mark:

Az Zīrah Light (33°34′·3N 35°22′·1E) (7.183).

Berths

7.201

1 The berths, at the seaward ends of the pipelines, are named EDL-SPM and SIDACO from S. Apart from the SPM, vssels berth bows W with both anchors down, and with stern lines to mooring buoys. A third berth ¾ mile N of SIDACO consists of seven mooring buoys.

2 An anchor beacon stands on the coast 1¼ cables NE of the inshore end of the pipeline at each berth; these beacons are floodlit at night when vessels are berthing of the jetty.

An **L**-shaped boat jetty (33°30′·4N 35°20′·5E) for the use of mooring launches projects from the coast at Az Zahrānī. There are depths from 4·3 to 4·9m alongside the outer part of the jetty.

Port services

7.202

1 **Facilities:** medical facilities are available in Saïda; no facilities for oily waste disposal.

Supplies: fuel oil is available to tankers at the berths; fresh water is not available; stores can be obtained with due notice.

2 **Harbour regulations.** As the berths are in an open roadstead, vessels must have engines and gear ready for immediate use with full power. Under no circumstances may engines be shut down for repair.

Shore leave is not permitted.

The oil company's booklet on port information and rules is available from vessels' agents.

Anchorage

Nahr al Awwālī

7.203

1 Anchorage may be obtained in a depth of about 16 m with the mouth of Nahr al Awwālī (33°35′·3N 35°23′·2E) (7.183) bearing about 100° distant 4½ cables.

AZ ZAHRĀNĪ TO ḪEFA

General information

Charts 2633, 2634, 1585

Route

7.204

1 From a position WNW of Az Zahrānī (33°30′N 35°21′E) the coastal route leads SSW, for a distance of about 43 miles, to a position WNW of Ḫefa (32°50′N 35°00′E).

Topography

7.205

1 Mount Hermon (33°25′N 35°51′E) (chart 183) or Jebel esh Sheikh is 2814 m high; its isolated cone, always snow-capped, is prominent when open S of Jebel er Rihan, 14 miles W.

2 Mishor 'Akko lies between Har Mushaqqa (33°06′N 35°08′E), which rises abruptly from its N end, and Har Karmel (Mount Carmel), 22 miles SSW. The plain is about 5 miles wide, studded with numerous villages and is fertile. Har Meron, 16½ miles ESE of Rosh HaNiqra, is 1199 m high, and the highest peak of a mountain range which rises gradually E of Mishor 'Akko.

Traffic regulations

7.206

1 For regulations concerning entry to Lebanese Territorial Waters see 7.93.

Vessels bound to and from Israeli ports are recommended by the Israeli authorities to use the routes shown on the chart.

For further information see 1.54 and *Admiralty List of Radio Signals Volume 6 (3)*.

Prohibited areas

7.207

1 Navigation is prohibited within the territorial waters of Lebanon between the parallels of 33°06′N and 33°15′N; see chart 2634.

Entry into Israeli waters and the following areas, without first obtaining permission, is prohibited (positioned from 'Akko Light (32°55′·2N 35°04′·0E)):

2 In Area No 69 B and Area No 69 C (a small uncharted strip immediately N of 69 B): from sunset to sunrise, within 6 miles of the coast between Rosh HaNiqra (10½ miles N) and a position 2 miles S.

In Area No 601: within 3¼ miles of the coast between Shave Ẕiyyon (3¾ miles N) and a position 2¼ miles S.

3 In Area No 603: within 5 cables of the coast from a position 1¾ miles SSE of 'Akko Light to a position 2¼ miles farther S.

Entry into Area No 69 A (not charted), a wedge-shaped area up to 12 miles from the coast at Rosh HaNiqra and N of Area No 69 C, is always prohibited.

Submarine cables

7.208

1 Submarine cables are laid along the entire coast of Israel. They mainly run parallel to the shore and in depths out to 100 m.

Directions

(continued from 7.183)

Principal marks

7.209

1 **Landmarks:**

Mount Hermon (33°25′N 35°51′E) (7.205).

Tower (33°16′·2N 35°11′·8E) at Sour.

Har Meron (33°00′N 35°25′E) (7.205).

Har Karmel (Mount Carmel) Lighthouse (white round tower and building, 20 m in height) (32°49′·7N 34°58′·1E). Carmelite Monastery of Saint Elias (red dome and belfry) stands close SE of the lighthouse.

2 **Major light:**

Har Karmel Light — as above.

Az Zahrānī to Ḫefa

7.210

1 From a position WNW of Az Zahrānī (33°30′N 35°20′E), the track leads SSW, passing (with positions from Sour (33°16′N 35°12′E));

WNW of Rās ech Chaq (12¼ miles NNE), thence:

WNW of Rās Sarafand (10½ miles NNE), a double-headed bluff cliff. Sarafand Light (white pylon, black bands) is exhibited from an islet which, with several rocks, extends 7½ cables W from the cape. Thence:

2 WNW of Rās Abu Sait (7 miles NNE). A reef, on which there are some above-water rocks, lies 1 mile S. Thence:

WNW of Nahr el Qasimiye (4½ miles NNE), the third largest river in Lebanon. Thence:

WNW of Sour (Tyr) (7.211); a light (white tower) is exhibited from the N side of the peninsula. Thence:

3 WNW of Râchîdîyé (2¼ miles S); nearby is a low mound on the summit of which is a remarkable square building. Rās el' Ain lies in the plain 5 cables S of Râchîdîyé. Thence:

WNW of Er Rās el Abyad (6¾ miles SSW), a bold white cliff on which are the ruins of an ancient temple, with several columns still standing. Tel Irmis, 1¾ miles SE of the cape, is a remarkable conical table-topped mountain 371 m high. Qal'at Shema, a castle, lies close ESE of the peak. Thence:

4 WNW of Rosh HaNiqra (11½ miles SSW), a prominent headland, 79 m high, with a round tower on its summit. The white face of the headland is conspicuous from W. The international boundary between Lebanon and Israel reaches the coast in the vicinity of Rosh HaNiqra. Thence:

WNW of an obstruction (16 miles SSW), thence:

5 WNW of Semeiriye Reefs (19 miles SSW), with a least depth of 4·9 m over them. Yussuf Reef, between Semeiriye Reefs and the coast, has a least depth of 4·9 m over it. The sea breaks on the shoalest parts of these reefs in rough winds. Thence:

WNW of 'Akko (22 miles SSW).

The track then leads to a position, in the approaches to Ḫefa, WNW of Rosh Hakarmel (32°50′N 34°58′E).

6 **Useful marks:**

Water tower (yellowish concrete, 46 m high) (33°01′N 35°06′E) at Nahariyya.

Water tower (32°59′N 35°05′E) at Shave Ẕiyyon.

Aqueduct (arched) (32°57′N 35°06′E).

Minaret (49 m high) (32°55′N 35°04′E).

(Directions for the coastal route continue at 7.260)

(Directions for Ḫefa are given at 7.242)

Sour

Chart 1561 plan of Sour

General information

7.211

1 **Position.** Sour (33°16′N 35°12′E), also known as Tyr, is situated 40 miles SSW of Beyrouth on a low, flat peninsula, once an island but now connected to the mainland by a sandy isthmus. The town is encircled by an old wall, fast crumbling away.

Function. The port consists of an open roadstead, on the N side of the peninsula, having three anchorage areas, with depths from 8 to 17 m. Cargo is worked into lighters. There is also a pier for RoRo traffic.

2 **Topography.** A line of islets, rocky shoals and shoal water extends about 1¼ miles NNE of the NW point of the peninsula. The highest is 1·3 m. The limit of the shoal water has a depth of 8·3 m. A line of rocky shoals extends about 1 mile S from Ra's Mīnat ar Rasās, the S point of the peninsula, on which are the remains of some ancient moles.

Traffic. In 2007 two ship calls with a total of 5760 dwt.

Port Authority. Ministry of Public Works and Transport, Sidon, Lebanon.

Arrival information

7.212

1 **Notice of ETA:** 7, 3, 2 and 1 day in advance.

Anchorages. Large vessels may anchor in depths from 15 to 17 m, sand and weed, with Marabout Ma'shuq bearing 152°, and the guard house on Ra's ad Din al Bahr bearing about 082°.

2 Vessels of moderate draught may anchor E of the islets and shoals lying N of Sour, in depths of about 8 m, gravel, as shown on the chart. This is considered the most secure anchorage on the coast.

Regulations. Navigation is prohibited within the coastal waters of Lebanon between the parallels of 33°06′N and 33°15′N.

Harbour

7.213

1 **Harbour.** On the NW side of Sour are the remains of moles which enclosed the ancient port. The harbour, now filled with sand, only affords shelter to the smallest coasting boats.

Directions

7.214

1 From seaward the track leads ENE with the summit of Mount Hermon (33°25′N 35°51′E) (chart 183) (7.205)

ahead bearing 079°. On nearing the anchorage, for large vessels, the alignment (082°) of the guard house on Ra's ad Dīn al Bahr (33°18′·5N 35°13′·4E) with the summit of Mount Hermon, continues to lead ENE, passing NNW of the shoals extending N from the town, to a position 1¼ miles WSW of Ra's ad Dīn al Bahr.

2 The track then leads SSE, for about 8 cables, with Marabout Ma'shūq (33°16′·1N 35°13′·4E) ahead bearing 152°, and thence SSW to the harbour, with a minaret (33°16′·3N 35°11′·8E) ahead bearing 202°.

Caution. A stranded wreck is situated close N of the harbour entrance.

3 **Clearing bearing.** If approaching from S the line of bearing, about 026°, of Rās Sarafand (33°26′N 35°16′E) (7.210) well open NW of the NW extremity of Sour peninsula, clears W of the dangers S of Sour peninsula. At night, do not approach the coast in depths of less than 33 m until Sour Light bears more than 028°.

4 **Useful marks** (positioned from Sour Light (33°16′·6N 35°11′·6E)):

- Sour Light (7.210).
- Tower (4 cables SSE).
- Marabout Ma'shuq (white building with an elevation of 40 m) (1½ miles ESE), standing on a rocky mound.
- Building (3 miles NNE).

Berths

7.215

1 A pier for RoRo traffic and a container park on the SE side of the harbour; there is a depth of 5·3 m at the pierhead.

Port services

7.216

1 **Supplies.** Fresh water is available.

'Akko

Chart 1585

General information

7.217

1 **Position.** 'Akko (32°55′N 35°04′E), formerly Acre, lies at the head of Mifraz 'Akko, on a small peninsula which forms the NE entrance point of Mifraz Hefa. 'Akko is of remarkable interest historically. The ancient fortifications and citadel are well-preserved and much has been achieved in the way of restoration and in clearing the debris consequent on the many sieges.

2 **Function.** The small harbour, close S of the town, is used by fishing boats and yachts. An offshore terminal, about 1 mile SSE, handles bulk chemical cargoes.

Arrival information

7.218

1 **Ship reporting system.** A ship reporting system is established for all vessels calling at Israeli ports and for all vessels within 25 miles of the coast. For details of information required see 1.54 and *Admiralty List of Radio Signals Volume 6 (3)*.

2 **Notice of ETA.** For vessels calling at the offshore berth ETA should be sent at least 12 hours in advance. For further details see *Admiralty List of Radio Signals Volume 6 (3)*.

Anchorages. For small vessels anchorage may be obtained about 2 cables SSW of Manara Rock, close E of the yacht harbour entrance, in depths of about 9 m.

Vessels bound for the chemical berth may obtain anchorage, as shown on the plan, about 1 mile S of 'Akko Light (32°55′·2N 35°04′·0E), close W of the berth, in depths of about 15 m.

3 **Pilots.** Pilotage is compulsory for all vessels calling at the offshore chemical berth. Pilots board at the Hefa pilot boarding position (7.237) and are available during daylight hours only.

For details see *Admiralty List of Radio Signals Volume 6 (3)*.

Restricted area. Approach to the pipeline, at the offshore chemical berth, is prohibited except for loading or discharge at its head. For details of a further prohibited area close S of the chemical berth see 7.207.

Harbour

7.219

1 **General layout.** On the SE side of 'Akko are the remains of the moles which formed the ancient port. The harbour consists of an angled mole, projecting about 1 cable E from the SE part of the town, with piers on its inner part, and another short mole on the N side forming an entrance open NE.

2 Within the moles is a basin which is sheltered in all weathers. There are depths of about 2 m in the entrance, and about 1·5 m in the middle of the basin.

Directions

7.220

1 From the pilot boarding position (32°50′·5N 35°01′·0E) off Hefa the track leads NNE, passing (with positions from 'Akko Light (32°55′·2N 35°04′·0E)):

- WNW of S.P.L. Berth (4½ miles SSW), and:
- ESE of a shoal (4½ miles SSW), with a depth of 13·5 m over it, marked by a light buoy (isolated danger), thence:
- WNW of Foxhound Reef (2½ miles SSW), a long narrow ledge of rocky formation with depths from 7·9 to 9·4 m over it, thence:
- 2 ESE of Talbot Reef (1½ miles SW), with depths from 7·6 to 9·1 m over it.

The track then leads to the anchorage off the chemical berth. Vessels proceeding to the harbour continue NNE passing ESE of 'Akko Ledge and then WNW of Manara Rock.

Small vessels may approach from W, the chart being sufficient guide.

Caution. Vernon Reefs, with a least depth of 5·8 m over them, extend N for 1 mile from a position 1 mile W of 'Akko.

3 **Useful marks** (positioned from 'Akko Light (32°55′·2N 35°04′·0E)):

- 'Akko Light (black and white chequered tower, 10 m in height), exhibited from the SW bastion of the old fortifications surrounding the town.
- Minaret (conspicuous, white with green top, 49 m high) (3 cables NNE).
- Light exhibited from breakwater (2 cables E).
- Light (tower in ruins) exhibited from Manara Rock (3 cables E).
- Clock tower (1½ cables ENE).

Offshore berth

7.221

1 The chemical berth consists of three mooring buoys situated at the seaward end of a pipeline, marked by a light buoy, which extends 5 cables W from a position on the coast 1¼ miles SE of 'Akko Light.

Port services

7.222

1 **Supplies.** Provisions are available.

H̱EFA

General information

Chart 1585

Position

7.223

1 H̱efa (Haifa) (32°49′N 35°00′E) extends for 2½ miles along the SW shore of Mifraz̲ H̱efa, and is spreading both along the coast and up the slopes of Har Karmel.

Function

7.224

1 H̱efa is the principal port of Israel and a centre of commerce. It has a large harbour, well equipped with modern facilities for handling all types of vessels including container, passenger, RoRo, bulk carriers and tankers. Principal exports include citrus fruits, chemicals, tyres, textiles and machinery. Imports include grain, raw materials, oil and petroleum products.

2 The port comprises H̱efa Harbour, Qishon Harbour and an oil terminal at Qiryat H̱ayyim. A free zone exists in Qishon Harbour. There is a population of about 270 800.

Topography

7.225

1 Mifraz̲ H̱efa (Haifa Bay) is entered between ‘Akko (32°55′N 35°04′E) and Rosh Hakarmel, 7½ miles SW. The E shore of the bay is backed by low sandhills, 5 to 12 m high. Tel Aféq, a hill 38 m high, lies 6½ miles ENE of H̱efa.

Har Karmel (Mount Carmel) is a table ridge rising abruptly within Rosh Hakarmel and extending SE for 12 miles; it attains an elevation of 546 m at 7½ miles from the cape.

2 Tel Shiqmona, 7 cables WSW of Rosh Hakarmel, is a remarkable hillock 15 m high. Rās el-Krum (chart 2634), 8 cables NE of Rosh Hakarmel, is the extremity of flat ground extending N from the base of Har Karmel.

Naẖal Qishon flows through ‘Emeq Yizre‘el, a plain E of Har Karmel, to enter the sea in the S part of Qishon Harbour.

Harbour limits

7.226

1 The outer limit of the harbour extends N for 3 miles, from a position 9 cables ENE of Rosh Hakarmel, thence E for 1¾ miles, S for 1½ miles and finally E to the coast, as shown on the chart.

Approach and entry

7.227

1 The recommended approaches to H̱efa are by the routes shown on the charts. For further details see 1.54 and *Admiralty List of Radio Signals Volume 6 (3)*.

The main harbour is entered via a two-way route and by passing S of Main Breakwater.

Traffic

7.228

1 In 2007 there were 2348 ship calls with a total of 33 838 016 dwt.

Port Authority

7.229

1 Israel Ports Development and Assets Company, H̱efa Port Company Ltd., PO Box 33539, H̱efa, Israel.

Limiting conditions

Deepest and longest berth

7.230

1 Deepest: Karmel Container Terminal; longest: East Container Terminal (7.245).

Density of water

7.231

1 1·025 g/cm^3.

Maximum size of vessel handled

7.232

1 Vessels up to 130 529 dwt, 272 m LOA and maximum draught 13·5 m, have been handled.

Arrival information

Ship reporting system

7.233

1 There is a ship reporting system for all vessels calling at Israeli ports and for all vessels within 25 miles of the coast.

For further details see 1.55 and *Admiralty List of Radio Signals Volume 6 (3)*.

Notice of ETA

7.234

1 An approximate ETA should be sent to the agent 7, 5 and 3 days before arrival with a definite ETA 48 and 24 hours before arrival.

Outer anchorage

7.235

1 Anchorage areas have been established, centred on the following positions:

Area A 32°50′·8N 34°59′·8E, six circular berths of 500 m diameter located SSW of the two-way route; vessels up to 140 m.

Area B 32°52′·0N 34°59′·9E, six circular berths of 750 m diameter located NNE of the two-way route; vessels up to 250 m.

2 Area C 32°53′·2N 35°01′·0E; chemical tankers and tankers up to 180 m.

Area D 32°54′·0N 35°00′·0E; vessels over 250 m.

Area G 32°52′·5N 34°59′·9E; vessels up to 250 m.

Area T 32°54′·9N 35°00′·3E; tankers over 180 m.

Prohibited anchorage

7.236

1 Anchoring and fishing are prohibited in the harbour approaches and in the vicinity of the oil terminal.

Pilotage and tugs

7.237

1 **Pilotage** is compulsory for all merchant vessels and is available 24 hours. Pilot boards 8 cables N of the head of Main Breakwater. The pilot boat is grey.

In addition, pilotage is compulsory for all vessels calling at the ‘Akko offshore chemical berth (7.217) and for oil tankers and vessels carrying, or having carried, petroleum, gas or chemical products, on transit between H̱efa and ‘Akko. Pilots for these vessels board off H̱efa and are available during daylight hours only.

2 Tankers bound for the oil terminal should contact H̱efa Port Control prior to arrival for details of pilot boarding position.

For details see *Admiralty List of Radio Signals Volume 6 (3)*.

Tugs are available.

Prohibited areas

7.238

1 There are several prohibited areas, as shown on the chart, in the approaches to Mifraẕ H̱efa. Permission must be obtained before entering these areas.

Harbours

General layout

7.239

1 **H̱efa Harbour**, sometimes referred to as Main Port, is protected from N by Main Breakwater which is 1½ miles long.

West Container Terminal is located opposite the root of the main breakwater.

East Container Terminal extends N from a position 9 cables SSW of the head of the main breakwater; the oil harbour is located on its W side. The channel leading to the W part of the harbour, between East Container Terminal and Main Breakwater, is 200 m wide with a depth of 14·4 m.

2 Karmel Container Terminal is parallel to, and 1½ cables E of, the E Container Terminal.

Naval Basin is situated in the NW corner of the harbour, on the inner side of Main Breakwater.

Qishon (Kishon) Harbour is situated at the mouth of Naẖal Qishon, its entrance protected by two breakwaters.

On the W side of the harbour there is a RoRo terminal and, close within the entrance, a yacht harbour and a cooling water basin.

On the E side of the harbour there is a basin which serves a shipyard and a chemicals terminal. A fishing basin is entered about 500 m S.

3 **Developments.** Works are in progress (2008) to the N of the root of Main Breakwater, the works are contained within a prohibited area.

Natural conditions

7.240

1 **Local weather and sea state.** In Mifraẕ H̱efa the sea breeze springs up at about 1000 and rapidly attains considerable force; between 1300 and 1400, at its strongest, it is sufficient to make boat work difficult. At about 1600 it dies away rapidly, and is usually calm by about 1800. In September, though the sea breeze generally decreases by nightfall, it seldom dies away before midnight. The land breeze springs up at about 2200, but blows only very gently until about 0600, when calm ensues until the sea breeze sets in again. Fog or mist may occur locally in the early morning.

The N part of the East Container Terminal (7.239) is reported to be exposed to the swell.

Climate information

7.241

1 See 1.184 and 1.204.

Directions

Principal marks

7.242

1 **Landmarks** (positioned from Har Karmel Lighthouse (32°49′·7N 34°58′·1E)):

Har Karmel Lighthouse (7.209).

Hospital (9 cables ENE). A college stands close NW of the hospital.

Grain silo (1¼ miles ESE).

Chimneys (red and white, red lights) (3 miles ESE) at a power station.

Cooling towers (80 m high) (4¾ miles ESE).

2 Bahai Tomb (golden cupola) (1¼ miles SE).

Dan Carmel Hotel (white) (1½ miles SE), standing on Har Karmel ridge above the level of early morning fog or mist.

Dan Panorama Hotel (1¾ miles SE).

University Tower (elevation 572 m, red lights) (4¾ miles SSE).

Major light:

Har Karmel Light — as above.

Approach and entry

7.243

1 From a position in the recommended approach route, about 10 miles WNW of H̱efa, the track leads ESE, passing (with positions from the head of Main Breakwater (32°49′·7N 35°01′·0E)):

NNE of Carmel Reefs (3¾ miles W), with a least depth of 3·8 m over them, on which the sea breaks. Obstructions are to be found close SW, 1½ miles SSW and 3 miles WSW of the S end of Carmel Reefs. A light buoy (special) is moored close W of Carmel Reefs. Thence:

2 NNE of Spartan Reef (2¾ miles WNW), with a least depth of 4·9 m over it, on which the sea breaks. A buoy (special) is moored close N of a wreck 5 cables SE of Spartan Reef; Thence:

NNE of a can buoy (non IALA), moored 8 cables NNE of Spartan Reef, thence into the ESE-bound lane of the two-way route:

NNE of a dangerous wreck marked by 4 light buoys (cardinal), thence:

3 SSW of a shoal, with a depth of 12·3 m over it, marked by a light buoy (spar, isolated danger). Vessels are advised to pass at least 3 cables from this buoy. Thence:

To the pilot boarding position.

4 From the pilot boarding position, 8 cables N of the head of Main Breakwater, the track leads SSE into the harbour, passing:

WSW of a wreck (7½ cables NE), with a depth of 10 m over it, marked by a light buoy (isolated danger), and clear of H̱efa 1 Light buoy (safe water) 4½ cables N, thence:

ENE of the head of Main Breakwater. A light (framework tower) is exhibited from the head of the breakwater, and a light buoy (green, non IALA) is moored close E.

5 **Approach from S.** Approach should be made through the recommended route, as shown on the chart. Thence from a position WNW of H̱efa, the directions previously given should be followed.

Useful marks:

Water tower (32°48′·0N 34°59′·0E).

Light (white concrete tower, 9 m in height) (32°49′·4N 35°00′·5E) exhibited from the head of Lee Breakwater.

Lights (grey metal framework towers) exhibited from the heads of the breakwaters at Qishon Harbour.

Berths

Dolphin berths

7.244

1 Five dolphins stand in a line close E of the naval basin, parallel to Main Breakwater. Vessels berth on both sides of the dolphins; berth length 296 m; depths 10·2 to 10·8 m.

Alongside berths

7.245

1 Positioned from the head of Main Breakwater (32°49′·7N 35°01′·0E):

Karmel Container Terminal (5 cables S); length of W side 700 m; charted depth 15·2 m.

East Container Terminal (9 cables SSE); length 960 m; maximum depth alongside 8·4 to 13·4 m.

Fuel Jetty (7 cables SW); berthing length 800 m; depth 10·2 m. Can accomadate two tankers simultaneously, one on either side.

Cargo Jetty (7½ cables SW), and other general and bulk cargo berths; total length 533 m; depths 5·1 to 9·6 m.

2 Passenger and general cargo berth (9 cables WSW); length 259 m; depth 10·3 m.

Automated Grain Terminal (9 cables W); length 23 m; depth 10·8 m.

West Container Terminal and RoRo ramp (1·1 miles W); length 520 m; depths of 3·9 to 14·1 m.

RoRo and Ferry Quay (finger jetty 1 cable N of West Container Terminal); berthing length 400 m; depth 7·5 m.

Qishon Harbour

7.246

1 Positioned from the head of E breakwater (32°49′·1N 35°01′·4E):

Gadot Terminal (2¼ cables SSE); length 260 m; depth 8·7 m.

Chemical Terminal (3½ cables ESE); length 260 m; depths 7·1 to 8·4 m.

West quay and RoRo berth (4¼ cables SSE); length 640 m; depths 7·5 to 9·8 m.

East Quishon Jetty (6¼ cables SSE); length 580 m; depths 9·7 to 11·1 m.

Shavit Marina and fishing harbour (7½ cables S); length approximately 1400 m (quays and pontoons); depths 2·8 to 3·5 m.

Oil terminal

7.247

1 **S.P.L. Berth.** The berth (32°51′N 35°02′E) consists of a submarine oil pipeline extending 1½ miles NW from the shore at Qiryat Ḫayyim, 1½ miles E of Main Breakwater head. Mooring buoys surround the seaward end of the pipeline and a light buoy (special) is moored 3½ cables NW, with another marker buoy 3 cables SSW. The berth is suitable for vessels with a draught up to 14·3 m.

Four disused submarine pipelines, shown on the chart, lie adjacent to this pipeline.

Port services

Repairs

7.248

1 The shipyard in Qishon Harbour, which builds ships of up to 25 000 dwt, can undertake hull, machinery, electrical and most other types of repair.

There are two floating docks; the largest has the following dimensions:

Length 227·5 m; breadth at entrance 37·0 m; lifting capacity 21 075 tonnes; maximum draught of vessel 8·0 m.

Caution. A wreck, marked by buoys and with a depth of 0·5 m over it, lies close SSE of the shipyard.

Other facilities

7.249

1 Hospitals in Ḫefa; 100-ton floating crane; oily waste reception and garbage disposal available.

Supplies

7.250

1 Fuel at berths or by barge; fresh water at most alongside berths or by water boat; fresh provisions.

Communications

7.251

1 The nearest international airport is Lod, 105 km distant.

Harbour regulations

7.252

1 A copy of the special harbour regulations should be obtained from the authorities on arrival.

ḪEFA TO TEL RAFAH

GENERAL INFORMATION

Chart 2634

Area covered

7.253

1 The area covered by this section comprises:

Ḫefa to Tel Aviv-Yafo (7.257).

Tel Aviv-Yafo to Ashdod (7.277).

Ashdod (7.282).

Ashdod to Tel Rafah (7.309).

Ship reporting system

7.254

1 There is a ship reporting system for all vessels calling at Israeli ports and for all vessels within 25 miles of the coast.

For further details see 1.55 and *Admiralty List of Radio Signals Volume 6 (3).*

Recommended approach routes

7.255

1 Vessels bound to and from Israeli ports are recommended by the Israeli authorities to use the routes shown on the chart.

For further information see 1.54 and *Admiralty List of Radio Signals Volume 6 (3).*

Submarine pipeline

7.256

1 A submerged gas pipeline is laid between 1½ and 2½ miles from the coast, from a position S of Dor (32°36′N 34°55′E) to Ashdod (31°49′N 34°39′E). The pipeline closes the shore at several locations; a 200 m restricted area exists either side of the pipeline.

ḨEFA TO TEL AVIV-YAFO

General information

Charts 1585, 1591, 2634

Route

7.257

1 From a position WNW of Rosh Hakarmel (32°50′N 34°58′E) the coastal route leads SSW, for a distance of 48 miles, to a position WNW of Tel Aviv-Yafo (32°05′N 34°46′E).

Topography

7.258

1 HaSharon, a plain, extends from a position 3 miles NE of Ḩorbat Qesari (32°30′N 34°54′E) to Yibna, 42 miles S, and to the foot of the mountains of Samaria, 8 to 10 miles inland; it consists of cultivated areas and pasture lands.

2 Between Ḩadera (32°28′N 34°53′E) and Tel Aviv-Yafo, 23 miles SSW, the foreshore is generally rocky; the coast consists of red cliffs broken by the mouths of the following streams (positioned from Ḩadera):

- Naḩal Ḩadera (5 cables SSW).
- Naḩal Alexander (4½ miles SSW).
- Naḩal Poleg (12½ miles SSW).

Prohibited areas

7.259

1 Navigation is prohibited, as shown on the chart, within the following areas:

- In an area, 14 miles N of Ḩadera (32°28′N 34°53′E), near ‘Atlit.
- Within an area 2 miles of the shore between about 13 and 15 miles SSW of Ḩadera, and also within about 5 cables of the shore off Tel Arshaf, 3 miles farther S.

2 For further details on requirements for vessels navigating in Israeli territorial waters see 1.54.

Directions

(continued from 7.210)

Principal marks

7.260

1 **Landmarks:**

- University Tower (32°46′N 35°01′E) (7.242).
- Three chimneys (red lights) (32°28′N 34°53′E).
- Tower (32°03′·3N 34°45′·1E) at Yafo.

Ḩefa to Ḩadera

7.261

1 From a position WNW of Rosh Hakarmel (32°50′N 34°58′E) the track leads SSW through the recommended fairway, passing (with positions from Rosh Hakarmel:

- WNW of Tel Shiqmona (1 mile SW) (7.225), on which stands the Oceanographic Institute. A wave recorder light buoy is moored 2 miles SSW of Tel Shiqmona. A charted obstruction lies 2½ miles WNW. Thence:

2
- WNW of Tiré Reefs (4½ miles SSW), on which the sea breaks. An area in which anchoring and fishing are prohibited, as shown on the chart, lies close W. Thence:
- WNW of ‘Atlit (9 miles SSW), which stands on a rocky promontory, having on its S side a small bay, open NW. ‘Atlit was the site of an ancient harbour. Thence:

3
- WNW of Sarafand and Kafr Lām (12 miles SSW), two villages which stand on a low rugged ridge 5 cables inland, thence:
- WNW of Dor (14 miles SSW), a village with a sandy beach, thence:
- WNW of Zikhron Ya’aqov (16 miles SSW), which contains two water towers, thence:
- WNW of Yonim Islet (17 miles SSW), lying close offshore. The islet is black and rocky. Thence:

4
- WNW of Ḩorbat Qesari (21 miles SSW). Once the capital and principal seaport of ancient Palestine, the port is now completely filled and nothing marks the site of the immense moles constructed by Herod. A minaret stands on the S side of the port.

5 The track then leads to a position WNW of Ḩadera (32°28′N 34°53′E).

Useful mark:

Square tower (ruins) (32°42′·4N 34°56′·1E), the top of which has an elevation of 33 m, NNW of ‘Atlit.

(Directions for Ḩadera are given at 7.267)

Ḩadera to Tel Aviv-Yafo

7.262

1 From a position WNW of Ḩadera (32°28′N 34°53′E), the track leads SSW, passing (with positions from Ḩadera);

- WNW of Mikhmoret Light (concrete building) (4 miles S). A marine farm lies 1¼ miles NW. Thence:
- WNW of Bet Yannay (6 miles S), thence:
- WNW of Netanya (7 miles S), a town in which there are three water towers, thence:

2
- WNW of Tel Arshaf (17 miles S), a conical hill within the cliffs. Ancient Apollonia, now only a mass of ruins, is situated on the hill. There is a loading place at Reshef, close S, in the vicinity of a minaret, shown on the chart. Thence:
- WNW of Herzliya Marina Light (32°10′·0N 34°47′·6E), exhibited from the breakwater head. Thence:
- WNW of an explosives dumping ground, shown on the chart, extending from 1¼ to 2¼ miles from the shore.

The track then leads to a position about 10 miles WNW of Tel Aviv-Yafo (32°05′N 34°46′E).

3 **Useful marks:**

- Water tower (32°13′·1N 34°49′·5E).
- Water tower (32°10′·4N 34°49′·0E).
- Water tower (32°10′·0N 34°50′·2E).

(Directions for the coastal route continue at 7.280)

Ḩadera

Chart 1591, plan of Ḩadera

General information

7.263

1 **Position.** Ḩadera (32°28′N 34°53′E) is situated midway between Ḩefa and Tel Aviv-Yafo.

Function. The terminal serves vessels supplying coal and oil to a power station on the coast.

Port limits. The harbour limit extends to about 4 miles offshore, as indicated on the chart.

Approach and entry. The Israeli authorities advise that vessels approaching the port should do so through the entrance to the approach channel, in position 32°28′·2N 33°56′·0E. The track then leads approximately 47 miles E to the port.

2 **Prohibited area.** A prohibited anchoring and fishing area of 2 cables width encloses a submarine gas pipeline which comes ashore at Naẖal Ḫadera. The pipeline continues S at a distance of approximately 1½ miles from the coast, coming ashore at Tel Aviv Power Station (7.272) and Ashdod (7.282).

Marine reserve lies from a position on the coast, from 1½ to 2¼ miles N of the root of the coal jetty. The area extends up to ¾ mile to seaward.

3 **Traffic.** In 2007 there were 55 ship calls with a total of 7 972 880 dwt.

Port Authority: Port Administration, PO Box 314, Ḫadera 38102, Israel.

Limiting conditions

7.264

1 **Density of water:** 1·025 g/cm^3.

Maximum size of vessel handled. The coal berth accommodates vessels up to 225 000 dwt with a maximum beam of 48 m and draft of 18 m. The tanker berth accommodates vessels up to 70 000 dwt.

Sea state. A heavy swell may be experienced during the winter months and vessels may be unable to berth.

Arrival information

7.265

1 **Ship reporting system.** For details see 1.54 and *Admiralty List of Radio Signals Volume 6 (3)*.

Anchorage. Two circular anchorage areas of diameter 5 cables, lie 1¼ to 2 miles NNW of the head of the coal jetty.

2 **Pilotage** is compulsory for vessels berthing at the terminal. The boarding place is 1¼ miles NNW of the head of the coal jetty.

For details see *Admiralty List of Radio Signals Volume 6 (3)*.

3 **Tugs** are available.

Regulations. Anchoring is prohibited within an area enclosing the whole terminal.

Fishing is prohibited within the harbour limits.

Harbour

7.266

1 **General layout.** The harbour consists of an open roadstead containing a coal jetty, and an oil berth consisting of a conventional buoy mooring. There is a small artificial boat harbour, enclosed by breakwaters with depths from 4 to 5 m situated at the root of the coal jetty. Nussani, a rock 0·3 m high, lies 2¾ cables NNE of the harbour entrance which is open N. A light is exhibited from the head of each breakwater.

Directions

7.267

1 **Landmarks:**

Three chimneys (7.260).

Coal jetty (32°28′·2N 34°52′E) extending 1 mile W from shore is reported conspicuous on radar.

Cranes on coal jetty.

2 **Approach and entry.** From seaward the approach is clear of any dangers, and depths of more than 20 m may be obtained to within 9 cables of the shore; the chart is sufficient guide.

Caution. A depth of 21·5 m is located 1½ miles NW of the head of the coal jetty.

3 **Useful mark:**

Light (32°28′·2N 34°51′·8E) exhibited from the head of the coal pier.

Berths

7.268

1 **Coal berth.** The coal pier consists of a 12 m wide trestle bridge carrying the conveyor equipment, extending 1700 m W from the shore.

It has a berthing jetty, 300 m long and 20 m wide, at its head, with a minimum depth of 20 m. The berth is fitted with breasting and berthing dolphins. A light buoy (cardinal) lies close SW of the head of the pier.

Vessels berth port side alongside the N side.

2 **Oil berth.** The oil berth, 5 cables N of the coal jetty, consists of four mooring buoys in a depth of about 18 m, at the seaward end of a submarine oil pipeline extending about 9 cables WNW from the shore. The berth is marked by two light buoys.

Port services

7.269

1 **Facilities:** regional hospital at Ḫadera or the Italian hospital at Ḫefa; garbage disposal; facilities for reception of oily waste.

Supplies: fuel by barge from Ḫefa; fresh water at coal berth; provisions.

Communications. The nearest international airport is Ben Gurion, 56 km distant.

Tel Aviv-Yafo

Charts 1591, 2634

General information

7.270

1 **Position.** Tel Aviv-Yafo (32°05′N 34°46′E), comprising Tel Aviv and Yafo (Jaffa) which have expanded to form a single town, extends SSW from the mouth of Naẖal Yarqon for about 6 miles.

Function. Tel Aviv-Yafo, with a population of about 360 400, is the commercial capital of Israel. Yafo was formerly the port for Jerusalem, 55 km SE.

2 Since the port of Ashdod (7.282) was opened (1965), the port of Tel Aviv-Yafo has been closed to commercial traffic. It is now a tourist area with yacht facilities.

Port limits. The harbour limits extend 1½ miles seaward from a position 2 cables S of Tel Aviv Port to a position close N of the power station harbour, and include the oil terminal.

3 The port limits for Tel Aviv Marina extend up to 2 cables offshore, and for Yafo harbour up to 3½ cables offshore.

Limiting conditions

7.271

1 **Sea state.** The anchorages off Tel Aviv and Yafo are very uncomfortable during W winds which send in a heavy swell, accompanied by a 1 to 1½ kn N-going current, causing vessels to roll heavily. Masters are advised to be prepared to get under way without delay and to remain at sea until the swell subsides.

Arrival information

7.272

1 **Ship reporting system.** For details see 1.54 and *Admiralty List of Radio Signals Volume 6 (3)*.

Anchoring and fishing are prohibited in a cable landing area extending 9 miles offshore, between a position 4½ cables S of Tel Aviv Port and a position 1½ miles farther S, as shown on the chart.

2 **Prohibited area.** A prohibited anchoring and fishing area of 2 cables width encloses a submarine gas pipeline which comes ashore at Tel Aviv Power Station. The pipeline continues N and S at a distance of approximately 1½ miles from the coast coming ashore at Naḫal Ḫadera (7.263) and Ashdod (7.282).

Harbour

7.273

1 **General layout.** Tel Aviv-Yafo, an open roadstead, consists of an offshore tanker berth, 1 mile NW of the mouth of Naḫal Yarqon (32°06′·2N 34°46′·6E), along with several minor harbours:

Tel Aviv Port, 3 cables SSW, is formed by two breakwaters with lights at their head. The entrance is open WNW.

2 Tel Aviv Marina, 1 mile SSW, is protected from W by a breakwater with a light at its head. The entrance is open N. A coastguard station is situated at the marina.

Yafo boat harbour, 3¼ miles SSW, is protected from the W by a breakwater, with a light at its head. The harbour is open N and contains a marina.

3 **Natural conditions:**

Climate information: see 1.184 and 1.205.

Currents. See 7.4.

Directions for tanker berth

7.274

1 **Landmarks** (positioned from spire (32°03′·0N 34°45′·0E)):

Spire of the Latin church in Yafo.

Tower (3¼ cables N) of the French convent.

Lighthouse (disused) (3 cables N).

Chimney (150 m in height) (3¾ miles NNE) of Tel Aviv power station, standing near the N entrance point of Naḫal Yarqon.

2 **Approach.** From seaward the approach is clear of dangers although attention is drawn to the vessel MV *Hatzvi* (32°07′·2N 34°41′·1E) moored offshore.

Useful mark:

A light (white metal column, 4 m in height) (32°06′·6N 34°46′·4E) is exhibited from the head of the breakwater fronting the power station.

Berth

7.275

1 **Tanker berth.** This offshore berth (32°06′·6N 34°45′·5E) consists of four mooring buoys, a light buoy and buoy, stationed at the seaward end of a submarine pipeline extending 8½ cables WNW from the coast.

Port services

7.276

1 **Repairs.** Minor repairs carried out at Tel Aviv Marina.

Other facilities: hospitals in Tel Aviv-Yafo; 50-ton travel hoist in Yafo boat harbour.

Supplies: fuel and fresh water for small vessels in Tel Aviv Marina and Yafo boat harbour.

TEL AVIV-YAFO TO ASHDOD

General information

Chart 1591

Route

7.277

1 From a position WNW of Tel Aviv-Yafo (32°05′N 34°46′E) the coastal route leads SSW through the recommended fairway, for a distance of 17 miles, to a position WNW of Ashdod (31°49′N 34°39′E).

Topography

7.278

1 The coast between Yafo (32°03′N 34°45′E) and Ashdod, 15 miles SSW, is for the most part featureless, consisting of bare undulating sandhills from 30 to 45 m high; a few scattered trees and bushes constitute the only vegetation.

Prohibited areas

7.279

1 Two firing practice areas, to which entry is prohibited and the limits of which are shown on the chart, are centred 7½ and 3½ miles N, respectively, from the head of Ashdod main breakwater (31°50′·2N 34°38′·2E).

A fish farm, to which entry is prohibited, is located 5¾ miles NW of Ashdod main breakwater. The area is marked by four light buoys (N, E, S and W cardinal).

Directions

(continued from 7.262)

Principal marks

7.280

1 **Landmarks:**

Tower (32°03′·3N 34°45′·1E), on church in Yafo.

Hotel (32°01′·8N 34°44′·5E).

Hotel (32°00′·7N 34°44′·2E).

Kefar HaNagid Aero Light (radio mast, 117 m in height, red lights) (31°53′·7N 34°45′·4E).

2 Radio mast (red lights) (31°49′·8N 34°39′·7E).

Ashdod Lighthouse (red and white chequered concrete water tower, 42 m in height) (31°48′·9N 34°38′·7E).

Major light:

Ashdod Light — as above.

Tel Aviv-Yafo to Ashdod

7.281

1 From a position WNW of Tel Aviv-Yafo (32°05′N 34°46′E) the track leads SSW, passing (with positions from the tower on the church in Yafo (32°03′·3N 34°45′·1E)):

WNW of I Adam (1¾ miles SSW), a rock 2 m high, which lies 1½ cables offshore. A marine farm, marked by a light buoy (special), has been established 7¼ miles W. Thence:

2 WNW of the mouth of Naḫal Soreq (7½ miles SSW). E Nabī Rūbīn, a white minaret, stands on the S bank of the river 1½ miles within its mouth. Thence:

WNW of a rocky bluff (8¼ miles SSW), 12 m high, which is situated 1 mile S of the mouth of Naḫal Soreq and is the only noticeable feature on the coast. Thence:

3 Clear of a wreck and obstruction (11½ miles SSW), thence:

The track then leads to a position WNW of Ashdod (31°50′N 34°38′E).

(Directions for the coastal route continue at 7.313)

(Directions for Ashdod are given at 7.299)

ASHDOD

General information

Charts 1591, 2634

Position

7.282

1 Ashdod (31°49′N 34°39′E) is situated 16 miles SSW of Tel Aviv-Yafo, at the mouth of Naẖal Lakhish.

Function

7.283

1 Ashdod is the largest port in Israel, handling about sixty percent of the country's cargo. The port can accommodate most types of vessel including passenger and cruise, general cargo/break-bulk, RoRo, container, bulk carriers, chemical carriers and tankers at the offshore oil berths.

Principal exports include citrus fruits, fertilisers, chemicals, oil and manufactured goods. Imports include coal, grain, general cargo and vehicles.

The town has a population of about 187 500.

Port limits

7.284

1 The port limits extend 2¼ miles from the coast, from a position close S of the root of the main breakwater, to a position 4½ miles farther N.

Approach and entry

7.285

1 Entry is from N using the TSS which leads between the breakwater heads.

Prohibited areas

7.286

1 A prohibited anchoring and fishing area of 2 cables width encloses two submarine gas pipelines which come ashore close N of the harbour entrance. The first pipeline continues N at a distance of approximately 1½ miles from the coast, coming ashore at Tel Aviv Power Station (7.272) and Naẖal H̱adera (7.263). The second pipeline extends approximately 20 miles WSW to Mari-B gas production platform (7.314).

Traffic

7.287

1 In 2007 there were 2288 ship calls with a total of 30 029 324 dwt.

Port Authority

7.288

1 Israel Ports Development and Assets Company, Ashdod Port Company, PO Box 9001, 77191 Ashdod, Israel.

Limiting conditions

Controlling depth

7.289

1 There is a least depth of 13·5 m in the approach channel to the harbour.

Deepest and longest berths

7.290

1 Eitan Terminal (7.301).

Maximum size of vessel handled

7.291

1 Bulk carriers up to 95 000 dwt are handled. It is reported that container ships up to 60 000 dwt and general cargo/break bulk vessels up to 30 000 dwt can be accommodated. Larger vessels up to 160 000 dwt can also enter the port but only with a partial load up to 95 000 tonnes. In 1989 the 120 000 dwt collier *MS Leon* entered the port with 85 000 tons of coal.

Arrival information

Ship reporting system

7.292

1 For details see 1.54 and *Admiralty List of Radio Signals Volume 6 (3)*.

Notice of ETA

7.293

1 12 hours.

Anchorage

7.294

1 Anchorage may be obtained in a central area about 2¼ miles WNW of Ashdod Light (31°48′·9N 34°38′·7E), in depths of about 34 m. The anchorage area extends up to 2 miles W, 3 miles SW and 2½ miles S from the head of the breakwater light. **Caution.** Two wrecks are located 2 and 2½ miles SW of the breakwater light. The anchorage is exposed to strong winds.

Prohibited areas

7.295

1 Anchoring and fishing are prohibited within the limits of the port.

Pilotage

7.296

1 Pilotage is compulsory and available 24 hours. Pilot boards about 1¼ miles WNW of the head of the main breakwater.

For details see *Admiralty List of Radio Signals Volume 6 (3)*.

Tugs

7.297

1 Tugs are available and meet vessels at the harbour entrance.

Harbour

General layout

7.298

1 **General information.** The harbour is protected from W by a double curved breakwater 3350 m long forming an entrance open N. The breakwater encloses an extensive basin with a series of moles extending from the shore in a WNW direction.

2 Ashdod Marina is situated about 1 mile S of Ashdod Port. The entrance which is open to the NW is marked by lights (31°48′N 34°38′E).

Development. A major development project is currently in progress (2008), including further extension of the main breakwater by 1000 m. This will allow the construction of another 2150 m of quay for container, bulk and general cargo.

Directions

Principal marks

7.299

1 **Landmarks** (positioned from Ashdod Light (31°48′·9N 34°38′·7E)):

Ashdod Lighthouse (7.280).
Radio mast (red lights) (1¼ miles NE).
Five chimneys (red lights) (1½ miles NNE).

Major light:

Ashdod Light (7.280).

Approach and entry

7.300

1 From the pilot boarding position the track continues E to the inbound lane of the TSS.

The inbound track leads 1 mile S, passing:

W of two litht buoys (port hand, spar), thence:

Clear of a wreck with a depth of 16 m over it, thence:

ESE of the head of the Main Breakwater from which a light is exhibited, thence:

Berths

Eitan Terminal

7.301

1 Eitan Terminal is located 1 mile N of Ashdod Light. It is a fully computerised container terminal which is located within the 1150 m main breakwater extension. The terminal consists of 1700 m of new quay with water depths up to 15·5 m. A light (column with gallery) is located in position 31°50′·2N 34°38′·6E.

Container and general cargo berths

7.302

1 Fifteen quays provide a total berthing length of 4060 m of which 3100 m are for general cargo, the remainder being divided between container traffic and bulk cargo. Quay No 1 on the N side of the harbour is the longest with a length of 770 m and alongside depth of 10 m. Quays 5, 9 and 12 are the deepest with depths of 13·9 m alongside.

There are facilities for RoRo vessels at Quays 1, 3, 5 and 7; four RoRo vessels can be accommodated, with a maximum ramp width of 24 m.

Mineral jetty

7.303

1 Situated in the S part of the harbour the mineral jetty consists of a 250 m long potash quay and an extension with berthing dolphins for the loading of phosphate.

The potash quay has a depth of 12 m alongside and handles vessels up to 45 000 dwt.

The phosphate loading berth has a depth alongside of 13·8 m and handles vessels up to 225 m in length, and 50 000 dwt.

Oil terminal

7.304

1 The oil terminal, 1¼ miles NNE of the harbour, is an outlet for crude oil carried by an overland pipeline from Eilat on the Red Sea. The terminal comprises two offshore conventional buoy mooring berths at the seaward ends of submarine oil pipelines projecting 6½ cables WNW and 9 cables NNW from the shore respectively.

2 Several marker light buoys and buoys are moored in the vicinity of the berths, as shown on the chart. A wreck, with a depth of 15 m over it, lies 5 cables SW of the S berth.

Port services

Repairs

7.305

1 Minor repairs can be undertaken.

Other facilities

7.306

1 Medical facilities; garbage disposal; no facilities for the reception of oily waste.

Supplies

7.307

1 Fuel oil and marine diesel; fresh water; provisions.

Communications

7.308

1 The nearest international airport is Ben Gurion, 40 km distant.

ASHDOD TO TEL RAFAH

General information

Charts 2634, 1591

Route

7.309

1 From a position WNW of Ashdod (31°49′N 34°39′E) the coastal route leads SW, for a distance of about 43 miles, to a position NW of Tel Rafah (31°19′N 34°13′E). The recommended route for vessels bound for Gaza (7.311) is shown on the chart.

Topography

7.310

1 Between Ashqelon (31°39′N 34°33′E) and Tel Rafah there is rather more vegetation, in the form of scattered trees and small copses, than is found N of Ashqelon, but, for the most part, undulating sandhills predominate.

Gaza

7.311

1 **Description.** Gaza (31°32′N 34°27′E) is the principal town of the Gaza Strip (Occupied Palestinian Territory). The Gaza Strip has an area of 365 sq km and in 1997 a census population of 1 022 027. The chief occupation of the inhabitants is agriculture, but there are also textiles, soap, olive-wood carvings and mother-of-pearl souvenir industries. Gaza International Airport, at the S edge of the district, opened in November 1998. Telecommunications development has been rapid, the number of fixed line telephone subscribers more than trebling between 1997 and 2000.

Prohibited areas

7.312

1 Navigation is prohibited within the following areas, shown on the chart:

Area No 608 (not charted) extending up to 1¼ miles offshore between 5 and 7 miles SSW of Ashdod Light (31°49′N 34°39′E). Entry into this area is always closed.

2 Area No1 608 A extending up to 3½ miles offshore, and is locate to seaward of Area No 608. Navigation is prohibited occassionally; a navigation warning is broadcast 7 days in advance.

Area No 610 extending up to 2½ miles from the coast off the port of Ashqelon (31°38′N 34°31′E) (7.315). Entry into this area is always closed.

3 Area No 609 and 609A extending up to 3 miles from the port of Ashqelon. Entry into Area 609 is always closed.

Area Nos 611 and 611A extending up to 12 miles from the port of Ashqelon. Permission to enter prohibited area 611 A should be obtained via the ship reporting system. Entry into Area 611 is always closed.

4 An area approximately 5 cables wide, where anchoring and trawling are prohibited, extends 7 miles WNW then 5 miles W, from a position

1¼ miles NE of the root of Ashqelon coal jetty. The area encloses a submarine natural gas pipeline, which extends approximately 98 km SW to a position 13 miles ENE of El ‘Arîsh, Egypt (3.261).

5 Anchoring is prohibited in an area which encloses SBM Nos 3 and 4; two buoys (special) mark the outer limits.

The areas are shown on the chart.

Prohibited area with a radius of 500 m centered on Mari-B platform (31°44′N 34°18′E). All vessels approaching within 5 miles shall initiate and maintain radio contact with the platform or with Ḩefa Radio.

6 Security Area K extending 20 miles NW from the coast at 31°35′N 34°29′E. Vessels may cross this area, keeping at least 3 miles offshore and parallel to the coast, only with prior permission from the Israeli Navy.

Maritime Zone L extends 20 miles to seaward from the Gaza Strip. In accordance with the agreements between Israel and the Palestinian Authority, entry by foreign vessels to this zone is prohibited.

7 Security Area M (not charted) extending 20 miles NW from the coast in the vicinity of Tel Rafah (31°20′N 34°13′E). The Israeli Authorities advise that entry is prohibited to the area.

For further details on requirements for vessels navigating in Israeli territorial waters see 1.54.

Directions

(continued from 7.281)

Principal marks

7.313

1 **Landmarks:**

Ashdod Lighthouse (31°48′·9N 34°38′·7E) (7.280).

En Nabī Husein Tomb (31°39′·8N 34°33′·6E), standing amongst trees on the summit of rising ground in the S part of Ashqelon.

Two chimneys (red and white lights) (31°38′·0N 34°31′·3E).

2 Ali el Muntar Tomb (31°29′·5N 34°28′·5E), a flat-topped hill 90 m high, surmounted by a tomb and some trees. It is conspicuous from seaward as it rises considerably higher than the surrounding foothills.

3 **Major lights:**

Ashdod Light (7.280).

Ashqelon Light (31°38′·2N 34°32′·5E).

Ashdod to Tel Rafah

7.314

1 From a position WNW of Ashdod (31°49′N 34°39′E) the track leads SW, passing (with positions from Ashqelon Light (31°38′·3N 34°32′·5E)):

Clear of three wrecks (11¼ miles N), thence:

NW of a dangerous wreck (5 miles N), thence:

NW of Ashqelon Oil Terminal (1½ miles WNW) (7.315), thence:

2 SE of Mari-B gas production platform (14 miles NW) (7.312), thence:

NW of Daribat el Bahr (8¼ miles SSW), the port of Gaza. The custom house (black and white building with flagstaff) stands close to a small landing pier with a depth of 1·5 m at its outer end. Thence:

3 NW of Naḩal Besor (13 miles SW), which enters the sea 4¾ miles SW of Daribat el Bahr, thence:

NW of Deir el Balah (16 miles SW), thence:

NW of Tel el Qatifa (19 miles SW); a rock almost awash lies 3½ cables off the coast. A buoy (spherical) is moored 7½ miles WSW of Tel el Qatifa. Thence:

NW of Tel Ridan (20 miles SW). A rocky ledge 0·3 m high lies 2 cables offshore. Thence:

4 NW of Khan Yunis (21½ miles SW) which lies 2½ miles inland near the crest of a gentle slope behind the sand hills. It is visible from seaward but the houses closely resemble the sandy foreground. Three buoys (spherical) are moored 3, 4 and 6 miles W of Khan Yunis, respectively.

The track then leads to a position NW of Tel Rafah (31°19′N 34°13′E).

(Directions continue, in the reverse direction, for the coast of Egypt at 3.258)

Ashqelon Oil Terminal

Chart 1591

General information

7.315

1 **Position.** Ashqelon Oil Terminal is situated about 2 miles SSW of the town of Ashqelon (31°40′N 34°33′E), 10 miles SSW of Ashdod.

Function. The terminal is the principal outlet for crude oil transported by overland pipeline from Eilat on the Red Sea.

2 **Topography.** Ashqelon, ancient Ascalon, was built in the form of a theatre, with two horns abutting on a line of bold cliffs which rises directly from the sea to an elevation of about 18 m. Little of the ancient city remains, except for huge ramparts on the S and SE sides which enclose a mass of ruins, groves of fruit trees, and gardens. El Jūra, a small modern village, lies close NE of the old town. The position of Ashqelon may be readily identified by the amount of cultivation in its vicinity, with groves of fruit trees covering a considerable area and extending to the coast, in contrast to arid wastes N and S of the town.

3 **Port limits.** The limits extend to 2½ miles offshore, as shown on the chart.

Approach. Ashqelon Oil Terminal is approached through the recommended route, as shown on the chart.

Traffic. In 2007 there were 154 tanker calls with a total of 13 560 096 dwt.

Port Operators. Ashqelon Terminal Eilat-Ashqelon Pipeline Company Ltd., PO Box 194, 78101 Ashqelon, Israel.

Limiting conditions

7.316

1 **Density of water.** 1·025–1·027 g/cm^3.

Maximum size of vessel handled. The maximum size of vessel handled is 280 000 dwt.

Arrival information

7.317

1 **Ship reporting system.** For details see 1.54 and *Admiralty List of Radio Signals Volume 6 (3)*.

Notice of ETA: 72, 48 and 24 hours.

Prohibited areas. See 7.312.

Pilotage is compulsory and provided from Ashdod. Pilot boards 3½ miles NW of Ashqelon Light in position 31°40′N 34°29′E.

2 For details see *Admiralty List of Radio Signals Volume 6 (3)*.

Tugs are available.

Harbour

7.318

1 **General layout.** The oil terminal, in an open roadstead, is comprised of four buoyed berths. A coal jetty extends 1¼ miles offshore from a position 5 cables S of the boat harbour.

A boat harbour for the use of oil terminal craft fronts the oil terminal. The harbour is protected by two breakwaters the heads of which are marked by lights.

Directions for entering harbour

7.319

1 **Landmarks** (positioned from Ashqelon Light (31°38′·2N 34°32′·5E)):

Tank farm (close NW).

En Nabī Husein Tomb (1¾ miles NE) (7.313).

Two chimneys (red and white lights) (1 mile WSW).

Major light:

Ashqelon Light (31°38′·2N 34°32′·5E).

2 **Approach.** From a position at the beginning of the recommended route, 45 miles WNW of Ashdod, the track leads ESE to a position about 10 miles WNW of Ashdod.

The track then leads 13 miles S through the recommended route to the pilot boarding positions off Ashqelon.

3 **Caution.** A wreck, position approximate, lies on the SE side of the bank 2½ miles NW from Ashqelon Light (7.318); 5 cables W from No 1 Berth, 8 cables NNW from No 2 Berth.

Berths

7.320

1 Positioned from Ashqelon Light (31°38′·2N 34°32′·5E):

No 1 Berth (2¼ miles NNW) is marked by two light buoys. Tankers up to 80 000 dwt, 250 m in length and 17·5 m draft moor in a depth of about 22 m, using both anchors with the stern secured to mooring buoys.

2 **No 2 Berth** (1¾ miles NW) marked by two light buoys. Vessels moor in a depth of about 19 m. Tankers up to 80 000 dwt, 250 m in length and 14·5 m draft can be accommodated.

No 3 Berth (2½ miles WNW), suitable for VLCC's, consists of a SPM, from which a light is exhibited, moored in a depth of 31 m. Oil hoses and mooring lines on the surface extend up to 300 m from the buoy.

3 **No 4 Berth** (2¾ miles W), suitable for VLCC's, consists of a SPM, from which a light is exhibited; vessels moor in a depth of 31 m.

Coal Berth (2½ miles W). The jetty is 24 m wide and approximately 284 m long and is marked by a light at the end. Vessels up to 200 000 dwt and 18 m draft can be accommodated. Minimum water depth alongside the berth is 22·5 m.

Port services

7.321

1 **Facilities:** modern well-equipped hospital; limited facilities for the reception of oily waste.

Supplies: fuel from Ashdod by barge; provisions from Ashdod; fresh water is available locally.

Communications. The nearest international airport is Ben Gurion, 70 km distant.

Distances table - Eastern Mediterranean

Note: For further information and notes on distances, see *Admiralty Distance Tables Atlantic Ocean* Part III Table IIIb.

	Adventure Bank (37°30′N 11°48′E)	Mīnā' Al Iskandarīyah (Alexandria)	Antalya	Ashdod	Banghāzī	Beyrouth (Beirut)	Famagusta	Fethiye	Ḩefa (Haifa)	Iskenderun	Al Lādhiqīyah (Lattaquié)	Limassol	Mersa Maţrūḩ	Mersin	Port Said (Bûr Sa'îd)	Ţarābulus (Tripoli)
Mīnā' Al Iskandarīyah (Alexandria)	967															
Antalya	961	340														
Ashdod	1178	257	358													
Banghāzī	514	533	621	768												
Beyrouth (Beirut)	1182	333	317	138	803											
Famagusta	1131	330	251	206	760	109										
Fethiye	847	330	138	407	534	373	325									
Ḩefa (Haifa)	1177	287	325	67	780	74	153	382								
Iskenderun	1196	454	274	303	852	174	141	374	243							
Al Lādhiqīyah (Lattaquié)	1174	395	253	228	825	97	92	353	167	79						
Limassol	1063	266	200	186	692	131	77	256	147	200	144					
Mersa Maţrūḩ	850	132	374	379	409	447	426	331	408	550	495	358				
Mersin	1137	419	215	295	793	176	114	315	238	78	91	175	492			
Port Said (Bûr Sa'îd)	1086	152	341	119	666	222	251	364	163	370	302	202	274	350		
Ţarābulus (Tripoli)	282	858	927	1093	355	1124	1078	819	1105	1158	1134	1010	734	1099	991	
Ţubruq (Tôbruch)	697	303	445	543	255	592	556	373	562	662	624	488	177	604	437	580

INDEX

Names without a paragraph number are for gazetteer purposes only

For transliteration of Greek orthography see 1.11

NOTES

PUBLICATIONS OF
UNITED KINGDOM HYDROGRAPHIC OFFICE

A complete list of Sailing Directions, Charts and other works published by United Kingdom Hydrographic Office, together with a list of Agents for their sale, is contained in the *Catalogue of Admiralty Charts and Publications*, published annually. The list of Admiralty Distributors is also on UKHO website (www.ukho.gov.uk), or it can be obtained from:

United Kingdom Hydrographic Office,
Admiralty Way,
Taunton, Somerset
TA1 2DN

Produced in the United Kingdom
by UKHO